THE MAN OF THE RENAISSANCE

THE MAN OF THE RENAISSANCE

FOUR LAWGIVERS:
Savonarola, Machiavelli, Castiglione, Aretino

by

RALPH ROEDER

with a new introduction by John R. Hale

TIME READING PROGRAM SPECIAL EDITION
TIME INCORPORATED • NEW YORK

EDITOR *Maitland A. Edey*
TEXT DIRECTOR *Jerry Korn*
ART DIRECTOR *Edward A. Hamilton*
CHIEF OF RESEARCH *Beatrice T. Dobie*

EDITOR, TIME READING PROGRAM *Max Gissen*
RESEARCHER *Joan Chambers*
DESIGNER *Albert Sherman*

PUBLISHER *Rhett Austell*
GENERAL MANAGER *Joseph C. Hazen Jr.*

TIME MAGAZINE
EDITOR *Roy Alexander*
MANAGING EDITOR *Otto Fuerbringer*
PUBLISHER *Bernhard M. Auer*

COVER *Copy of a 15th Century woodcut,*
Museo di Firenze Com' Era.
Photographed by N. R. Farbman

Copyright 1933, renewed 1961 by Ralph Roeder.
Reprinted by arrangement with The Viking Press, Inc.
Editors' Preface TIME Reading Program Introduction
and cover design © 1966 by Time Inc.
All rights reserved.
Printed in the United States of America.

TO MY WIFE

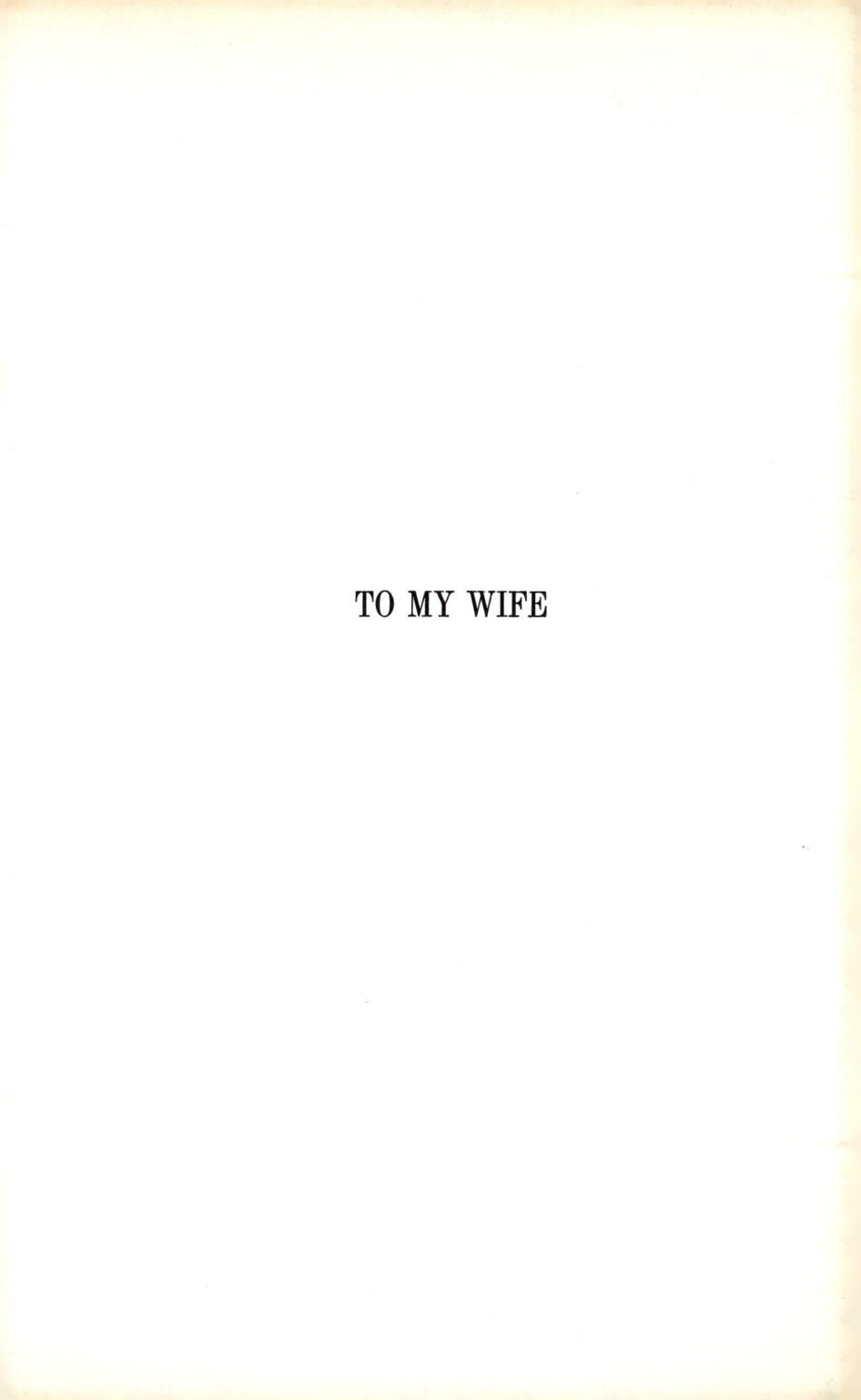

Contents

xi	EDITORS' PREFACE
xv	TIME READING PROGRAM INTRODUCTION
xxii	FOREWORD
1	SAVONAROLA
127	MACHIAVELLI
201	MACHIAVELLI AND CASTIGLIONE
297	CASTIGLIONE
457	ARETINO
503	BIBLIOGRAPHY
504	CHRONOLOGICAL TABLE
507	RELATIONSHIPS OF PRINCIPAL PERSONS
509	FAMILY TREE OF SENIOR BRANCH OF MEDICI

Illustrations

FACING PAGE	
34	SAVONAROLA
64	ALEXANDER VI
142	MACHIAVELLI
172	CAESAR BORGIA
216	JULIUS II
246	ISABELLA D'ESTE
254	FEDERICO GONZAGA
262	LEO X
292	GIULIANO DE' MEDICI
306	CASTIGLIONE
336	ELIZABETTA GONZAGA
350	BIBBIENA
382	FRANCESCOMARIA DELLA ROVERE
396	CLEMENT VII
426	GIOVANNI DELLE BANDE NERE
472	ARETINO

Ralph Roeder

Editors' Preface

The Man of the Renaissance is a history of a remarkable era told through the biographies of four famous Italians: Girolamo Savonarola, the fanatic monk who ruled Florence from 1494 until he was hanged for heresy and false prophecy in 1498; Niccolò Machiavelli, author of *The Prince*, a political treatise that is the one really lasting literary work of the Italian Renaissance; Count Baldassare Castiglione, whose etiquette book *The Courtier* reformed European manners; and Pietro Aretino, a satirist so abusive and clever that his comedies and letters earned him the title "The Scourge of Princes." Although all four men were contemporaries, they were remarkably different. Nevertheless, like a Hindu divinity with one body and four faces, the subjects of this book represent four dissimilar but definitive aspects of a single character—the Renaissance Man.

Like a skillful psychological novelist, Ralph Roeder is a master at depicting the slow process of accretion that leads to a grand passion and the equally small events that produce its dissolution. Human beings seldom wake up in the middle of the night and resolve that henceforth they will live entirely different lives; there are few recognition scenes in actual experience. More often, resolution grows stronger or weakens like a sickness that abates now only to worsen a moment later. In analyzing Savonarola, Mr. Roeder traces with a sure hand the fever chart of the monk's will. A physical coward, Savonarola quickly confessed on the rack that he was a false prophet who had deliberately duped the people of Florence by claiming divine powers. The moment he was released from torture, however, his moral heroism reasserted itself and he retracted his confession. Back and forth, back and forth, during 14 applications of torture, Savonarola alternated between his fears of momentary pain and his determination to defend his claims until the Pope's commissioners finally silenced his harrowing inner debate forever.

Similarly, Machiavelli fluctuated in his admiration for the ruthless tyrant Cesare Borgia. When Cesare was riding high as the victorious chief of the papal armies, Machiavelli dropped his habitual reserve and skepticism to write: "So spirited is this prince that there is nothing so great but seems small to him, and in the conquest of glory and states he never rests, nor admits either risk or fatigue; he appears before one knows where he comes from; he is loved by his soldiers and has recruited the best men in Italy; and all these things, added to his perpetual good fortune, make him victorious and formidable." But when Cesare's star fell, Machiavelli developed an overwhelming contempt for the fallen idol of his youth. Yet, as Mr. Roeder expertly reveals, this youthful admiration did not really vanish. Over the years it became sublimated into a veneration not for the blustering Cesare but for the *type* he had at first seemed to personify— the calm, calculating, utterly realistic ruler who obeys the principles of self-interest in his official decisions and practices Christian love and forbearance only among his intimates—in fact the ideal monarch delineated in *The Prince*.

Like his ideal ruler, Machiavelli made a clear division between his public and private life. The brand of cynical politics which he publicly avowed struck most of his readers as chillingly inhuman; in fact the English derived from both parts of Niccolò Machiavelli's name two epithets for the devil: "Old Nick" and "Match."

In total contrast to this evil reputation, Machiavelli was a sympathetic and eminently companionable friend, as Roeder reveals in one of the most entertaining sections of the book, the section that deals with the correspondence between the political theorist and his fellow diplomat Vettori. The two friends banter brilliantly about the multiple love affairs that plague and delight them and give each other playful advice. Which one of Machiavelli's critics could have guessed that this monster, soon after writing his infernal work, was more concerned about the affections of a Florentine widow whom he loved than the prospects of success for *The Prince*? "I have forsaken all thought of great and serious things," Machiavelli confessed to Vettori. "I find no pleasure now in reading of ancient or reasoning of modern life; everything is transformed into sweet themes, for which I thank Venus and all Cyprus. So that, if you care to write about your lady, write, and, as for other matters, you may discuss them with those who value and understand them more than I do, for I have found nothing but bitterness in them, and in this pleasure and profit."

Creative men often quickly outgrow their early work, yet have to live under its shadow for the rest of their productive years. Sergei Rachmaninoff hated playing his *Prelude in C Sharp Minor;* Marcel Duchamp's revolutionary painting, *Nude Descending a Staircase,* is more famous than he is; and Castiglione was bored by *The Courtier* as soon as he had completed it. After he married, Castiglione came to understand, according to Roeder, that "the life of the Courtier was a phantom existence, not only because he had outlived it, but because, as he now realized, it was a pose. All its aims—culture, ideals, friendship—were mere semblances of life, refined illusions of reality, eclipsed at last by a genuine experience. For

EDITORS' PREFACE

the first time, a profound and uncultivated feeling possessed him. . . . He was passionately in love with his wife."

Ralph Roeder's style is admirably suited to the explication of the tangled and conflicting emotions of his protagonists. Writers have two basic methods of showing the ambivalent feelings of their characters. One method, such as the one Henry James employed, keeps a running, up-to-minute account of all the contradictory ideas that pass through the subject's mind in quick succession. Although this approach can give an intimate, close-focus view of a sensibility, it can also become dull and effete. The broad outlines of the personality disappear under the excessive display of nuance, and the reader cannot see the forest for the trees. Mr. Roeder, like Marcel Proust or the Lawrence Durrell of *The Alexandria Quartet*, uses the other, more dramatic method. He takes one trait of a character at a time and renders it with bold, impressive strokes before he passes on to treat the opposite trait with equal depth. Thus he first establishes Pietro Aretino as a sarcastic, bitter gossip who would cut his mother's throat for profit. Only after this impression is firmly established through page after page of flowing narrative and apt quotations does Mr. Roeder make a sudden reversal and expose the loving, honorable, noble side of Aretino. Like a merchant who is ruthless on the exchange but tenderly solicitous at home, Aretino, as Roeder presents him, abandons his acerbic exterior the moment he is in the presence of Pierina Riccia, the 14-year-old girl he adores. This beguiling facet of Aretino's nature has seldom been explored; as the distinguished English historian John R. Hale points out in his Introduction to this special edition, "No one has written more sympathetically of Aretino . . . the prayer-writing pornographer."

Although *The Man of the Renaissance* abounds in such penetrating analyses of the dynamics that govern people and events, the book is never aridly abstract; every observation is grounded in vivid detail. When discussing the moral laxity of a Florentine convent, for instance, Mr. Roeder conveys the point by describing the frescoes on the convent walls: "Those cycles of martyrs, those fields of primrose faces, those parades of bland adolescents and lute-bellied virgins, perpetually circling the Celestial Throne — they were an insidious temptation to relax: their flesh was transfigured but it blushed; and their chaste hues—pious blues and maidenly carnations and mild gold—were a sedative, not a scourge, to the senses." In another place, Roeder epitomizes the corruption of the worst of the Renaissance popes, Alexander VI, by giving a hair-raising account of the decomposition of his corpse, a "huge carcass" that "seemed to exhale a lingering, fierce and foul vitality."

The author's capacity for making the past into a living present was immediately acclaimed by critics when the book was first published in 1933. "His book is as vital, as full-blooded, as dramatic as the age itself," wrote *The New York Times*. "One reads it with absorption, for a magnificent era in the life of man passes before one's eyes in a series of animated pictures." It was a Book-of-the-Month Club choice; encyclopedias later referred to it as an authoritative source; and TIME Magazine praised it as one of the best contemporary pieces of "graphic historical writing."

Unlike the florid characters he describes, Ralph Roeder is a reticent man who has lived most of his life outside of the public eye. He graduated from Harvard in 1911, but 20 years later he was unable to recall any of his classmates because he "never spoke to a living soul" while in school. During World War I he drove an ambulance for the Italian Army. After peace was declared, he worked as a stage manager in Paris and tried unsuccessfully to start an American newspaper in Rome. Back in Manhattan, he worked in a publishing house and began to write. In a recent explanation of the genesis of *The Man of the Renaissance*, Mr. Roeder has said, "What led me to the writing of the book was, obviously, my interest in the subject: more specifically, it was the result of a certain circumstantial commitment. After translating Prezzolini's *Machiavelli* for Brentano, the publisher invited me to do a study of Savonarola, which was my first book, and out of that came the conception of a study of the moral life of the Italian Renaissance, typified in four figures and four fundamental attitudes toward life. Three or four years went into the writing of the book. It was then that I contracted a very bad habit: the writing of very long books and the devotion of more and more time to their composition." *Catherine de' Medici* was the next product of the "very bad habit"; the most recent is a two-volume study of the Mexican President, Benito Juarez. Research for *Juarez and His Mexico* took Mr. Roeder to Mexico City, where he now lives, much honored by his adopted countrymen.

—THE EDITORS OF TIME

Introduction

> John R. Hale, one of Britain's leading Renaissance scholars, is chairman of the Department of History at the University of Warwick in England. He has also taught at Jesus College, Oxford, and at Cornell University. His books include *England and the Italian Renaissance, Machiavelli and Renaissance Italy, The Evolution of British Historiography* and *Renaissance* and *Age of Exploration,* two volumes in TIME-LIFE BOOKS' Great Ages of Man series.

This book is the vivid report of a raid carried out into the heart of one of history's most hotly debated territories: the Italian Renaissance.

For a century before Ralph Roeder wrote, historians had grappled with what had come to be known as the Renaissance Problem: How to achieve an explanation of this glittering and tumultuous period into which all of the contradictory and contrasting incidents could be fitted.

All the ordinary ingredients of a historical age were there: men raising families, earning a living, thinking about God, obeying or breaking the law, diverting themselves with mistresses or music. But in Italy, during the period in which Roeder was primarily interested, from 1494 to 1530, the ingredients were present in a formidably complicated mixture.

It was an age when family life was intense and loyal—and when bastardy was less of a slur than ever before or after. It was considered wrong to make money "breed" by asking interest on a loan or an investment, yet it was a time when great fortunes were made and lost, and capitalism came of age. Great churches were being built—the new St. Peter's in Rome among them—and religion permeated every aspect of life. Yet men were questioning the immortality of the soul and turning with admiration to the pagan ethic of Greece and Rome. Law was sophisticated and well served by men trained in the great universities; and statecraft—even before Machiavelli wrote *The Prince*—was carefully developed in theory and often wonderfully skillful in practice: yet crimes of violence made the streets unsafe at night, vendettas devastated whole countrysides, and assassinations and revolts played a large part in the political history of the peninsula. War, or the threat of war, was a condition of life in Italy during the time covered by the book. At the outset of the period, a French army was bulldozing its way through the mosaic of Italian states from the Alps to Naples and back. Toward the end, Rome itself was sacked by foreign troops—France, Spain and Germany sent in army after army. The Italian states, unable to combine in alliances firm enough to keep them out, even made war on one another.

Contradiction and contrast at their most brutal: this seemed the puzzling hallmark of the Renaissance. And the puzzle was made all the more dramatic and provoking by the coexistence of brutality and crime with art, literature and music, all of the utmost delicacy and refinement. For amid this marching and countermarching, Botticelli, Leonardo and Raphael painted, Bramante designed churches, Michelangelo sculptured, Ariosto wrote his romantic and evocative poem, *Orlando Furioso*.

This was perhaps the most dramatic aspect of the puzzle. On the one hand, political decline and humiliation (for the period opens with Italy free and ends with foreign domination), and on the other, the triumph of the arts. Defeats in war, governments overthrown, scandalous popes like Alexander Borgia on one side of the coin; on the other a roll call of names so illustrious for intellectual and artistic achievement that many have become household words: Leonardo, Raphael and Michelangelo, accompanied by Giorgione, Titian, Veronese, Fra Bartolommeo, Cellini, Andrea del Sarto, Pontormo, Sangallo, Machiavelli, Guicciardini, Castiglione, Vasari. This coincidence of conflict and creativity raised an issue which was eagerly debated by Roeder's predecessors: was an atmosphere of violence and instability necessary to raise the nervous temperature to a point at which creative inspiration can burn most fiercely?

Another controversy Roeder inherited concerned the modernity of the Renaissance. When did the Middle Ages stop? When did modern times begin? How great was the overlap? In the art of this period we see faces that remind us of our acquaintances, figures that could step down from a canvas or a frescoed wall and talk to us, statues that could walk, backgrounds that are like a photograph of a real town. Characters in plays like Machiavelli's *Mandragola* behave as we might behave—in our most cynical, not our most idealistic moments. Diplomats haggle as our own do, statesmen change front and take cover, in the modern manner, under protestations that they are acting for the "common good" and that "circumstances alter cases."

For the first time in history we are confronted with a scene in which we feel we could play a part, understanding the issues, recognizing the individuals. But how far were Renaissance men really different from medieval men, and how far do they simply *seem* different because of changes in artistic and literary conventions? And if they really were different from their medieval predecessors, were they therefore recognizably like us?

Was the Renaissance the beginning of modern times or an interim period during which modernity was conceived but not born? Or was it a period which has so strong a flavor of its own that it is irrelevant to see it either as the end of the Middle Ages or the beginning of modern times? Concentrating on one issue or the other, historians endlessly wrangled.

They wrangled too about the nature of Renaissance individualism. After reading the history of the Middle Ages, where personalities are all too often glimpsed rather than seen in the round, the protagonists of the Renaissance appear not only living, but larger than life. The lives of three individuals, chosen from innumerable eligibles, make the point. Cesare Borgia, the illegitimate son of Pope Alexander VI, seemed a monster to some of his contemporaries, a paragon of the shrewd political virtues to others. He was suspected of murdering his brother and committing incest with his sister. Machiavelli held up the way Cesare led some unreliable allies into a trap which killed them, and the way he put expediency before honor, as a model for any prince grappling with desperate circumstances.

Julius II, the pope who succeeded Alexander VI, combined deep personal piety with military zeal, conducting his own wars and nearly getting killed by a cannonball while in the front line one snowy winter. Julius' combination of learning and ferocity made him a legend in his lifetime; it is difficult not to feel that his intelligent ruthlessness goaded Michelangelo, his favorite painter and sculptor, into working to the very limits of his power on the ceiling of the Sistine Chapel and such statues as *Moses*. And no artist from previous centuries emerges with the swashbuckling three-dimensionality of Benvenuto Cellini, self-confessed lecher and murderer, immortal sculptor of the bronze Perseus and one of the most skillful goldsmiths who ever lived.

But again, how far is this impression of a novel manifestation of ebullient individualism due to a change in the sources of our knowledge? With the Renaissance came greater literacy, therefore more letters and diaries; prompted by classical models, authors wrote more biographies. Men became interested in being remembered for their actions as well as for their virtues; so princes hired writers to publicize them, and individuals, like Cellini, wrote autobiographies. And much of this evidence from which we re-create the lives of Renaissance men was multiplied and preserved by the novel craft of printing. How far were Renaissance men more individualistic than medieval men, and how far do they *appear* to be because we have more varied evidence about them?

The Man of the Renaissance was written in 1933, at a time when the full-blooded romantic view of the Renaissance as a period of great crimes and great achievements, great spiritual fervor and gross lust was being modified into a patient investigation of the quality of life for Renaissance Italians as a whole. Economic historians, social historians, intellectual historians agreed, as it were, to trace the quiet continuities rather than the rumbustious exceptions, to withdraw their eyes from bedroom and council-chamber keyholes and see the whole sweep of the late Middle Ages and the Renaissance from afar. A biographical approach gave way to a sociological, analytical one. The trumpeting procession of great men was stilled, and its place was taken by a faint archival hum.

With this approach Roeder had no patience. He was by instinct a biographer. *The Man of the Renaissance* was preceded by a biography of Savonarola (1930) and followed by one of Catherine de' Medici (1937). He had no interest in the masses save as a sounding board for the ideas of great men. He had no truck with archives, the only places where the lives of humble taxpayers and the day-to-day decisions of governments can be traced. He believed that great men symbolize the life of their age. Roeder, the Last Romantic of Renaissance historiography, adhered to a tradition as various as that of the great Swiss Jacob Burckhardt, the Englishman John Addington Symonds and the Russian novelist Dmitri Merezhkovski. He was also the last serious popularizer—for he wrote not for scholars but the general public—to believe that the part reveals the whole, the exception the norm, rather than vice versa.

He inherited the controversies I have mentioned, and he came down, with passion, on one side of each of them. To Roeder, the contrasts, defeats, failures of nerve and feverish excesses of the age were the preconditions for its greatest accomplishments. He saw the Renaissance as an age of individuals who, in wrestling to express themselves freely, help us to escape from the constraints of convention and tradition. He saw the heroes of *The Man of the Renaissance* as enduring types thrown into a specially sharp relief as they passed through the lurid illumination of the Renaissance. "Their lives," he wrote in his foreword, "embodied the adventures of the basic ideas that men live by; and they developed them with such transparent simplicity and extreme consistency that they live on for posterity as types. The ascetic virtue of Savonarola, the expedient virtue of Machiavelli, the convivial virtue of Castiglione, the animal virtue of Aretino—what are these but the final solutions of those who fear life, those who accept it, those who compromise with it, and those who succumb to it?"

This conviction gives the book its enduring quality. It has the lift, which so many cautious and scholarly books do not, of brilliant bias. This is Roeder's Renaissance. We read his book not to get The Whole Truth, which historians, even working as a team, can never give, but to experience an individual's record of his fascination with the past, as we experience Gibbon's Rome, or Michelet's France, or Parkman's American West. Historical literature has a place not only for what is currently held to be right, but for what was once passionately believed to be true.

We shall probably not see a book like this again, for the gap between the amateur and the professional historian has become too great. Historical novels will presumably continue to elicit the "oohs" and "aahs" granted to any skyrocket whose arc is predetermined to end in darkness. However, more thoughtful studies of the Italian Renaissance are likely to remain the preserve not of the serious nonacademic popularizer like Roeder, but of the professional scholar. Roeder occupied the middle ground with authority. He followed the best German life of Savonarola, and the best Italian biography of Machiavelli; his mastery of the difficult and highly idiomatic Italian of the Renaissance made him something of a pioneer in the translation of the private letters of Machiavelli and Aretino.

Roeder's interest in the Italian Renaissance had its limits; he kept within them, and his story gained in force and compression. The reader will find little about Naples or Genoa, historically important as they were, and not much about Milan. He will, on the other hand, find a rather disproportionate amount about Ferrara, for here Roeder was following one of the historians he most admired, the Italian Alessandro Luzio, who used the Gonzaga archives there to construct an incomparable picture of the courtly life of the time. He will find little about the arts. Roeder was, above all, a moralist. He was interested in action and thought, and the impact of events on men's philosophy of life. He did not include an artist among the four heroes with whom this book is concerned. He reacted to the written word, not to painting and sculpture, and he chose men who wrote copiously, and whose writings enshrine some of the supreme comments on their times—and, therefore, Roeder felt, on all times.

His choices are all men of the utmost fascination; Savonarola, Machiavelli and Castiglione, and, to a much lesser extent, Aretino, have all been subject to a great deal of reappraisal since Roeder wrote, but *The Man of the Renaissance* still remains a heady and beguiling introduction to them. Each man echoed some of the age's contradictions in his own person. Though the creative political role played by Savonarola is now not emphasized by scholars, there still remains something astounding about the part played by the saturnine friar's pulpit in skeptical, canny and pleasure-loving Florence. For three years his sermons held the imagination of

Florentines. He prophesied political disasters, and they came about; he was in touch with the men of destiny in Italy, and his sermons contained hot news from the crisis centers of the peninsula; he commented on the development of the new constitution to which Florence was adjusting itself after the flight of Piero de' Medici in 1494; he denounced slackness in churchmen to congregations who rejoiced in the scurrilous stories of Boccaccio about peccant nuns and monks; he flattered the poor by denouncing the abuses of the rich; and he charmed the intelligentsia by showing that he knew his Plato. And all this was in addition to the extraordinary power of his personality, his gift of moving men to a quickened sense of the spiritual, and his flattering suggestion that only in Florence was there a population fit to make their city a living witness to regenerate all humanity. Roeder does full justice to the variety of Savonarola's appeal, and to the fumbled tragedy that was his end.

He is excellent, too, in the way he shows how Machiavelli drew from the experience of his career as civil servant and diplomatist. By setting *The Prince* alongside the *Discourses,* later writers have decreased the contrast between Machiavelli the lover of Republican liberty and Machiavelli the preacher of circumspect tyranny; Roeder considers both aspects of the man, and his portrait is full of insight and sensitive understanding. So is that of Castiglione, the worried exponent of a "let's sweep our cosmic problems under the carpet and cultivate ourselves and one another" philosophy of life. And finally, no one has written more sympathetically of Aretino, the braggart-sage, the prayer-writing pornographer, whose pell-mell writings are a still hardly exploited guide to the high thoughts and the low actions of his day.

Historians no longer emphasize the break between the community-mindedness of the Middle Ages and the individualism of the Renaissance. It was a romantic view, tending to falsify both periods; Roeder, as we have seen, was its last and not least eloquent serious exponent. Writing in a heightened style that seems to owe a debt to the Baron Corvo of *Don Tarquinio* and *Chronicles of the House of Borgia,* he presents us with not only a memorable portrait of his dead heroes, but with a triumphant statement of a viewpoint that has fallen out of fashion. It is good to be reminded, so enjoyably and so usefully, what virtues fashion could command.

—JOHN R. HALE

Foreword

The four figures that follow illustrate four phases of the moral life of their age and, taken together, they compose the man of the Renaissance. The usual picture of that period is one of exuberant energy and positive achievement, and we are apt to forget that it was also one of mortal travail and misery. Its triumphs are preserved in art, its reverses in its spiritual story, and both were the result of the same cause—its supreme vitality. In the broadest sense the Renaissance might be described as one of those recurring crises in the annals of the race when a ferment of new life, like a rising sap, bursts the accepted codes of morality and men revert to Nature and the free play of instinct and experience in its conduct. But such revolutions are not accomplished without resistance or completed without reaction. In Italy the struggle was peculiarly acute because of the high civilization of the race, on the one hand, and its intense individualism, on the other. The Italian was a born individualist and the ferment of new life quickened his craving for unfettered self-expression; but he was also a civilized man who cherished humanity, and he was torn between the claims of Nature and human nature. Thus it was that in art his self-expression found full and free play, for there it was independent of consequences; but in life he could not emancipate himself from them and the result was spiritual turmoil and confusion. The force that created was the force that destroyed, and it was no coincidence perhaps that the artistic glories and the moral miseries of the age came to a climax together.

The Italian Renaissance culminated between the years 1494 and 1530; that span marked the apogee of its artistic development and the crisis of its religious, political, and social disintegration. No thinking man who lived through those four brief momentous decades was the same when they were over. In the lives of the four protagonists of the period it is possible to trace this development; they focus and foreshorten it, and they complement one another with a logical continuity. Together they loom like so many lawgivers, raised by the age to answer its perplexities. In the lawlessness of Nature the Renaissance man found the retribution of its freedom; he was at the mercy of chance; and the word which resounds down the age, the obscure power which dominated and haunted his life, was Fortune. The futility of destiny made faith a necessity; and the search for it produced the prophets who proposed and passed on the torch in turn from one to another. Seeking successively to master life by spirit, by intelligence, by refinement, and by instinct, they found, each according to the truth of his temperament, their vital principles in religion, in patriotism, in society, and in self-satisfaction; and between them they exhausted the alternatives. Their lives embodied the adventures of the basic ideas that men live by; and they developed them with such transparent simplicity and extreme consistency that they live on for posterity as types. The ascetic virtue of Savonarola, the expedient virtue of Machiavelli, the convivial virtue of Castiglione, the animal virtue of Aretino—what are these but the final solutions of those who fear life, those who accept it, those who compromise with it, and those who succumb to it? With the passage of time the ideas which they stated and lived with such force have become so familiar as to be commonplace; but they are commonplaces which the centuries cannot stale; if they are elementary, they are also fundamental. The lawgivers lie with their laws, but it was a man of the Renaissance who wrote: "Only the countenances of men change and the extrinsic colours, the same things always return, and nothing that we suffer but has happened to others before us." The obsolete is always reborn.

—RALPH ROEDER

PART ONE

Savonarola

1

If an arbitrary date were to be set at which to begin a moral history of the Renaissance, it might well be the 25th of April, 1475. On that day a young man entered the Convent of San Domenico in Bologna. He had fled from his home in Ferrara and he was exhausted by the long struggle which had preceded his flight. By what motives he was driven to it the Prior did not inquire. He may have noted in the raw-boned lad with the long sheep-like face certain eloquent features—the full passionate lips, the powerful nose, the glowing eyes, the thin skin which coloured as quickly as a girl's—and drawn his own conclusions; he may have felt under the manly manner an unweaned and almost feminine sensitiveness; but it was not this that moved his sympathy. It was his name. The name was one of considerable consequence. His father was a well-known physician; his grandfather had been an illustrious scholar, a professor of Medicine in the University of Ferrara, and Court doctor to the Este Dukes. The youth was an acquisition. Accordingly, while another candidate who entered the convent on the same day was promptly rechristened, he was admitted under his secular name of Girolamo Savonarola.

That the making of one more monk would prove of consequence to the moral development of the age was the last thing, however, which would have occurred to either the Prior or the novice. Yet it was the age which had forced the son of Niccolo Savonarola into the cloister. His first act, when the door was drawn and bolted behind him, was to write to his father explaining his motives for renouncing the world. In that hour of supreme decision he understood them with tragic lucidity, and he expounded them with all the logic he could muster.

"*Honorande pater mi,*" he began. "I know that you grieve greatly, particularly since I left you in secret, but I wish you to understand my mind and my purpose, so that you may be comforted and see that I have not acted as childishly as some may believe. In the first place, as a manly man and a despiser of perishable things, I expect you to be a partisan of truth rather than of feeling as womenkind are, and to judge by the dictates of reason whether or not I was bound to follow my purpose and flee the world." He had received a thorough education in logic and it was a time to think clearly. "*In primis:* the reason that moved me to enter religion is: first, the great misery of the world, the iniquities of men, the rapes, adulteries, larcenies, pride, idolatries, and cruel blasphemies which have brought the world so low that there is no longer anyone who does good; hence more than once a day I have sung this verse, weeping: *Heu fuge crudelas terras, fuge littus avarum!*[1] And this is why I could not suffer the great malice of the blind peoples of Italy, and the more so as I saw all virtues cast down and all vices raised up. This was the greatest suffering I could have in this world. Answer me then. Is it not great virtue in a man to flee the filth and iniquity of this wretched world and to live like a rational man and not like a beast among swine?" He appealed to him. "So, my very dear father, you have rather to thank Messer Iesu than to weep: He has given you a son and preserved him right well for twenty-three years, and not only this, but has deigned to make him His soldier. *Oimè,* do you not think it a great grace to have for your son a soldier of Christ Jesus?" He argued with him. "But to be brief: either you love me or you do not: I know you will not say you do not love me; if then you do, since I have two parts, body and soul, either you love the soul or the body more: you cannot say the body, because you would not love me, loving my vilest part: if then you love the soul, why not seek the good of the soul?" And yet . . . and yet . . . "Yet I know that the flesh must needs grieve somewhat, but it must be curbed by courage, especially in men like you who are wise and high-hearted. Do you not believe that it has been a great grief to me to leave you? Surely, I hope you believe me: never since the day

---

1 Ah, flee the lands of the unfeeling, the shores of the grasping flee!

I was born have I known greater grief or greater pain of mind, forsaking my own blood and going among strangers to sacrifice my body to Christ Jesus and to sell my will into the hands of those I have never known—but then, remembering that God calls me and that He did not disdain to serve among us worms, I should never have been so bold as to disobey His most sweet and holy call: Come unto me, all ye that labour and are heavy laden, and I will give you rest: take my burden upon you." And he concluded: "But, because I know that you will complain of my leaving you secretly and almost fleeing you, I will tell you this: so great was the pain and suffering I felt in my heart when I had to leave you that, if I had shown it, I truly believe my heart would have broken, and if I had thought of what I was doing I could not have done it: so do not wonder that I told you nothing. I left certain writings which will tell you more of me behind the books on the casement. I beg you, therefore, my dear father, to put an end to your complaints and to give me no more sorrow and pain than I have: not that I regret what I have done, for certainly I would not undo it, no, not though I thought to become greater than Caesar, but because I am still flesh like you and the senses are unruly to reason, so that I must struggle cruelly to keep the Demon from leaping on my back and downing me; and the more so when I feel your grief. Soon will they pass, these days when the wound is still fresh, and later I hope that you and I will be consoled in this world by grace and in the next by glory. No more remains to say but to beg you, as a man, to comfort my mother, whom I beseech, like you, to bless me; and I shall always pray fervently for your souls. Your son, Hieronymus Savonarola."

His father laid away the letter in an old book, on the fly-leaf of which he noted the dates of his son's birth and death to the world; and by way of obituary he added his laconic comment for posterity: "—and he left me, Niccolo Savonarola, his father, the enclosed exhortations and consolations for my comfort." He was baffled. All his hopes were invested in that boy; the family looked to him to continue its fortune; and now he had thrown everything away . . . why? Because of "the great misery of the world, the iniquities of men"? Niccolo Savonarola was too old to believe in so impersonal a motive; but he searched his memory in vain for a more secret grievance; and as no one understood him but his mother, he consulted her and they sent a final appeal to the fugitive, but the reply silenced them. The tenderness of the first letter had vanished and in its place was a note almost harsh. "Ye blind!" wrote the novice. "Why do you weep yet? Why do you lament? You hamper me, though you should rejoice and exult. What can I say if you grieve yet, save that you are my sworn enemies and foes to Virtue? If so, then I say to you: *Get ye behind me, all ye who work evil.*"

Harsh—he had a right to be. He could make his reason no plainer. "The great misery of the world, the iniquities of men . . . all virtues cast down, all vices raised up . . ." What motive could be more personal? In such a world life was unliveable: it meant intolerable thwarting, intolerable loneliness. Flight was his destiny: he had known it from birth. As long as he could remember he had always been haunted by the sense of life as something alien and distinct from himself. It had begun who knows when? perhaps with his first infant cry, when he emerged from the womb, when he was withdrawn from the long even sleep of nonentity, and he had always remembered what it was a wonder that anyone ever forgot—that first sense of life which recurred vaguely whenever he came out of sleep and resumed the harness of being—that sense which revived promptly under every disappointment and pain—that sense which he could not explain until he learned from his grandfather that life was an ordeal and that his soul, his *anima transmigratoria,* was merely migrating from one eternity to another. His sense of inner detachment had always been the most indelible of realities, and though, as he grew up, the habit of living spread over it like a thin film and dimmed it, the film was transparent. Surrounded by the affection of his family, immersed in congenial studies, he developed normally; nevertheless, to the pride of his elders, he displayed an aloofness and poise which surprised them. He felt no need of the company of other boys: they troubled his sense of identity which, like a reflection in water, wavered at the first questioning touch, and the Christian principles inculcated by his grandfather, which he practised without effort—for they were his own instincts—were not the habits of other lads of his age. He grew up a solitary.

When he was sixteen he was sent to the University. For the first time he mingled with his fellows, and he realized that all that he had been taught, that he believed and that he felt, was in conflict with the common conduct of men. "To be considered a man you must defile your mouth with the most filthy and brutal and tremendous blasphemies, and set on your neighbour to slay him, and sow seditions and brawls If you study philosophy and the good arts, you are considered a dreamer; if you live chastely and modestly, a fool; if you are pious, a hypocrite; if you believe in God, an imbecile; if you are charitable, effeminate." To be considered a man! That was the sting. He was approaching manhood, and his male pride was touched to the quick. In the promiscuous school of the world, he was initiated into the truth of Nature; from his fellow-students he learned that the only object of life was to live and its whole meaning the satisfaction of instinct and appetite; and he realized that the one virtue which men honoured in practice—whatever they might profess—was the animal virtue of sex—strength and lust. All the rest was sham and illusion. Virtue itself—supreme absurdity!—was a question of sex: there was a virtue of the male and a virtue of the female, and the code of Christ was proper only for women. Everything brutal was manly, everything humane effeminate, and to be considered a man he must choose between the habits of a world where, as he said bitterly, "all vices are lauded and all virtues derided," and his conscience.

He did not hesitate. In that crisis he could open his heart to no one without risking a sneer or a more galling womanish sympathy, but he communed with himself. The record accumulated and became a tract on *The Contempt of the World*. "There is no longer one man, no, not one who desires the good," he concluded. "We must learn from women and children, for they are the only ones who still preserve some shade of innocence. The good are oppressed, and the Italian people has become like the Egyptian which held the people of God in bondage." Then a righteous fury filled his pen, and his impotent revolt invoked Omnipotent Power. "But already famines and floods, sickness and other signs prefigure afflictions and foretell the Wrath of God. Open, open, O Lord, the waters of the Red Sea and submerge the impious in the waves of Your Wrath!"

The shock was too much for him, and the revulsion of feeling which ensued on it undermined his health. He left the University and returned to his home. Alone, in the bosom of his family, he recovered his calm; and time passed, time which changes all things, which could not touch him: time confirmed his bent and isolated him. Willingly and without a qualm he paid the price of consistency. His very recreations were solitary. If he was not in his study, he was in the nave of the neighbourhood church where the raw rumours of life reached him only as a vague echo, where the din of the street was dim and remote, and the stale sanctified air soothed him, and where he listened in the half-light to the drone of the flies flitting about the fonts, in which a tepid water lay stagnating. Or sometimes he went further. He loved the country and spent hours of communion with it in long lonely rambles along the slow-flowing Po. The wide, flat, treeless landscape had the featureless lineaments of eternity: and in its infinite spaces his being expanded in kindred immensity. Dilating on all sides to an ever-receding horizon, he followed it. The vast, low, alluvial plain, dozing under a moist sun, the murmuring river, roaming and grazing, a moving monotone of somnolent contentment, toward the sea, everything filled his mind with vague intimations of a "far country," a heavenly fatherland from which life had made him an exile and of which at birth he had a dim memory. He brought a book with him and pondered the words of Aquinas: "All being is perfect." Devoutly as he believed the Angelic Doctor, that problem was difficult until he stretched himself on the ground; and then, under the hot laden vines, what with the glare and the insinuating scent of the grape, he succumbed and understood and for an oblivious hour, at one with the satisfied earth, he dozed on the page where it was written that all being is perfect.

Such solitary proclivities disconcerted his parents. They sent him to Court; but after one visit he refused to return. The brilliant Court of Borso d'Este wooed him only to wound him. Among the naked athletes wrestling and racing under the eyes of preening women, or in the long formal allays of *Belriguardo,* loud with the rhythmic loquacity of voluble waters, where groups of lovers nestled, masking the insinuating hands that stole about waists and between knees, he had no place. It was a Court of Youth and he was just young enough to know how conservative was youth, how intolerant of deficiency or difference, and he returned to the pleasures of solitude—the long musing soliloquy of a lute or the self-communion of poetry.

About this time the house next door was rented by a Florentine exile, Roberto Strozzi. He was a member of an illustrious family and for a time the neighbours met on friendly terms, because they had nothing in common. But Strozzi was accompanied by an illegitimate daughter and a change came over the young Savonarola. He thawed, he expanded, he found his tongue and lost it unaccountably, his heavy face was transfigured, his self-sufficiency had vanished, and he did not miss it. Only a narrow alley lay between them, and in due time he came to the window and proposed marriage. She did not hesitate. Marriage between a Savonarola and a Strozzi? She had a lively sense of her birth and slammed the window.

He dismissed the incident and outgrew it; time passed, and all was the same, and the void within him reopened. "I began to reflect how we strive incessantly for unnecessary ends and neglect useful and necessary ones. And, considering how continually and violently we rush toward death, I determined to leave all else, to keep the end of man before my eyes, and to prepare for it with all my might. Through God's grace I began to despise all worldly things: an irresistible longing for my heavenly fatherland burned in my heart, and I resolved to serve my Lord Jesus Christ entirely." Life? What did it hold for him but perpetual thwarting? It was in the nature of things, and there could be no compromise. *Heu fuge!*—the line of Virgil welled up within him and he repeated it daily, as if he had composed it himself—*heu fuge crudelas terras, fuge littus avarum!* His emotion was still literary and he relieved it in a poem on *The Ruin of the World*:

> Seeing the world turned upside down
>   And every virtue spent
> And all customs of fair renown,

he brooded insatiably on the theme of all his thoughts. He saw "not a single man who blushes for his sins."

> Happy is he who lives by stealing
> And he that feeds on others' blood;
> Robbing widows and babes is good,
> Good to hear the poor appealing.
> Gentle the soul is and feeling
> That gains the most by force or fraud;
> He that despises Christ the Lord
> And seeks on others to trample,
> Him the world will honour.

For men like him the world had no use: the only place for a literal Christian was the cloister. And the craving for spiritual segregation, for freedom and peace, for that slow initiation into death which was the only solution of life, grew upon him, and what was a normal crisis of adolescence determined his vocation. Yet who would have had it otherwise? Those greensick and ingrowing feelings called him to the company of the prophets; his fear of life, his refusal to compromise with it, were a fundamental human experience; he was one man who could never harden himself, never sacrifice his integrity to the inexorable reality of nature; and it seemed as if he had been providentially preserved for that purpose.

But he was beset by scruples and doubts, and though he had made his decision it was long before he could nerve himself to act on it. "To forsake his own blood—to go among strangers—to sacrifice his body to Christ and sell his will into the hands of those he had never known!" His will, his free will; but what free will could he know in the world?

Then filial duty, filial affection, gave him pause. His father was in financial difficulties; his mother, with her sense of the intrinsic respectability of money, was worried; his sisters were without dowries: he was their mainstay: the whole future of the family rested on him. But his egoism proclaimed its rights. It hurried him on to an irrevocable step, though because it was irrevocable he shrank from it with covert dread. His mother divined what was coming. Finding him one day idly strumming his lute, she sat and listened, in the room humming with so many vibrations, to the monotonous twanging of a single chord. "Son," she said, "this is a sign of parting." He did not speak, nor did he trust himself to look at her; and she left him with downcast eyes, stubbornly plucking the aching note. The next day was a holiday; the family joined the crowds in the streets applauding the pageantry, the bonfires, the bells, and the hurly-burly; and when they returned he was gone. The phantoms of the past lay behind him and before him their realities.

2

Freedom and peace—"two things I loved above all, freedom and peace: to have freedom I would not take wife, and to find peace I fled the world and gained the port of religion." But was it really freedom and peace that he wanted? He entered the monastery, a virgin of twenty-three, and life was still strong in him. The lamentations of his parents exasperated it. It cost him a long struggle to mortify his affections; he fasted and flagellated himself strenuously, until at last his superiors were forced to moderate his austerities. But nothing could check him. Some instinct warned him, perhaps, that his genius was his power of feeling, and he lavished it incessantly on the worship of his Redeemer. He began to have visions, to fall into trances, and to pass through the strain, the revelation, and the ineffable exhaustion of mystic effusions. By the end of his novitiate he had already acquired a reputation for sanctity. Two monks from Vallombrosa, visiting the monastery, wished to pay their respects to the prodigy. They were somewhat disconcerted by their reception. The costly quality of their cloth caught his eye; they were forced to explain that it was not a luxury—the better the cloth the more durable it was—it really represented an economy. . . . He smiled an innocent smile. "What a pity," he sighed, "what a pity that San Benedetto and San Giovanni Gualberto did not know this secret. Who knows? Perhaps they too would have worn such cloth." The retort had a mild success at the refectory table, where it was repeated by the monks with smiles that showed their gums.

It was significant that he had to be urged, induced, and even forced to pursue the studies for which by training and ability he was eminently fitted. He had not entered religion, he said, "to exchange the Aristotle of the world for the Aristotle of the cloister." He submitted as a matter of discipline, but everything that reminded him of the past, that humoured his inclinations, and that tempted him to relax, he dreaded. In time, however, his natural aptitudes told. He studied with zeal and an easy conscience; and so congenial an activity won him freedom from the flesh and a measure of peace. He long remembered the four years he spent in the convent school as the happiest in his life. Freedom and peace—he had found them, and, if they were all he desired, his life might well have ended there. There was no reason why, like unnumbered others before and since who have sought the cloister, he should not sink into anonymity and oblivion. Why, in that living death which he desired as the nearest approximation to actual extinction, amid the tolling of bells, the telling of beads, the small tasks, the meditative lethargy of a studious and neutral routine, why should he not have passed away unknown? Steadfastly keeping his eyes on the end of man, why should he not have subsided into a death which had become familiar and easy, domestic and tame, and almost unreal? But it would have been too easy. A new phase of life was beginning, and it was woven of the same motives as the old.

In the cloister he was as alone as in the world. His ecstatic piety set him apart. He soon discovered that the convent was not what he had conceived it to be. It was not very different from the world—a sequestered microcosm, a small stagnant replica of the real world without. It was what its inmates made it, and it was all things to all men—a school for the studious, a haven for the heartsick, an asylum for the indigent, a nursery for the ambitious—all things, alas, but a congregation of mystic spirits akin to his own. The truth dawned on him slowly. The complacent mediocrity of his companions dismayed him; but the more he advanced in his chosen vocation, the higher he looked for inspiration, the grimmer the prospect became. The higher ranks of the hierarchy were filled with political priests and successful careerists, and it was inevitable that it should be so: the Church was a political institution; but it was also a spiritual one, and the confusion of its functions was profoundly demoralizing. The lives of the great ecclesiastics were indistinguishable from those of the laity: what was tolerable in a secular state was scandalous in a spiritual one; and the corruption of Rome—its simony, nepotism, and luxury—flowing down from the head through the members, infected the whole body. The entire edifice was rotten with a ramifying network of decay. He saw the issue with the absolute insight of innocent youth, and it affected him like a personal injury. The worldliness of the Church undermined the moral authority of a calling created to curb the brutality of the world; it violated his sanctuary, it defeated his flight; in the convent he found the world once more; and he could flee no further.

But who in the convent felt as he did? With the echo of each new scandal in Rome, his indignation rose. Yet who was he to protest? And in whom could he confide? He stifled his feelings; and when they grew too urgent he took up his pen. Within a year of his admission to the convent, he composed a sequel to *The Ruin of the World,* and lamented *The Ruin of the Church.* "Where are the saints and doctors of old? where the ancient candour, charity, and doctrine?" He appeals to the Bride of Christ, who takes him by the hand, leads him to a hovel, and replies: "When I beheld proud ambition penetrate into Rome and contaminate all things, then I retired to this place where I spend my life in mourning." He notes the bruises on her body and urges her to name her oppressor, to which she responds with a sigh:

> A false proud whore, the whore of Babylon.

And he takes flame:

> O God, Lady, that I might be the one
> To rend those mighty wings!

But the impulse is checked.

> Then she replied:
> It may not be. No tongue of man may chide
> Nor battle in my behalf. Mark my request.
> Weep and be silent: this seems to me best.

But he heaved under the heavy truth as under an incubus. On the walls the figure of St. Dominic, with his finger on his lips, enjoined silence and submission as the first rule of the Order. But to nurse such thoughts and smother them was to succumb to a worse sin—the sin of *akidia,* that essentially monastic sin of melancholy and sloth to which a virtuous nature was peculiarly prone. He could not be passive. In the convent he was trapped. He had fled the world only to find himself in an impasse; he was balked; and the logic of life forced him to turn, to advance, to grapple with the adversary. There was no eluding the world: it had followed him into his retreat, it had found him out; he could only fight it. It was both a moral necessity and a professional duty. The Order of St. Dominic was an order of militant preachers. Over the doorway the *Domini-cani* confronted the world: the hounds of the Lord with the torch in their teeth. They were missionaries. Whatever the figure of the Founder might enjoin within—silence, submission, discipline, study—these were but training toward their ultimate role. Sanctity was sterile; virtue was not an end in itself but an active principle for the diffusion of good. The coincidence of passion and duty inspired him, and an ardour of activity awoke in him as consuming as had once been his craving for extinction. Freedom and peace? Had he a right to them? They were self-indulgence, evasion.

The turning-point had come. Everything seemed to justify the highest expectations of his success as a preacher: he had the temperament, the learning and a power of feeling which amounted to genius, if he could communicate it. But his first efforts were unsuccessful. The public of Bologna, accustomed to the polished oratory of a university town, was critical. His delivery was feeble, he lacked self-confidence, he was lame. But his superiors encouraged him. These were minor defects, symptoms of inexperience, a mere matter of art, and art could be acquired. He studied with a professor in the University, but after a few lessons he convinced himself that eloquence could not be acquired by rote. Though his tutor assured him that "if he would add oratory to philosophy and theology he would win immortal encomiums," he forsook the study of Priscian and returned to his Bible. The business of developing his still small voice of conscience into a professional organ filled him with distaste. It smacked of insincerity; and the fact that an element of calculation was essential to conviction in art disgusted him. His deliberate effects, his studied tones, his rhetorical gestures confused him; he felt their hollowness too keenly to make them convincing to others: he began to lose heart, and his superiors, with the tact of experience, transferred him to the instruction of the novices.

At the end of his sixth year he was sent to Ferrara to begin his pastoral duties. A cutting comment sank in his memory. "The brothers," it was said, "must be in great need of workers." He took it to heart. "It was as if they had said: if they set so worthless a man as you to so great a task, they must indeed be hard pressed for workers." It was a painful homecoming, and to account for his failure in a profession for which he had sacrificed everything he was forced to resort to the old proverb: *Nemo profeta*—no man is a prophet in his own country. His parents, however, had to account to the neighbours, and when the clouds of war threatened Ferrara and forced the Dominican Convent to dispense with its superfluous members, he was relieved to be transferred to Florence. There at least he would be among strangers.

An incident which occurred on the way lent him some fleeting comfort. Travelling up the Po, he found himself among a boatload of soldiers whose gaming and blasphemies stung him into passionate protest: the words poured from him and he was amazed at his eloquence; and so were the soldiers who gathered about him, begging his forgiveness and his blessing. It was his first sensation of success but it was as fugitive as the banks slipping by. He had spoken at white-heat, but that compelling passion could not be commanded or calculated or counterfeited, or repeated. It was an impulse, and between the unpremeditated eloquence of a man-to-man argument and the studied flow of soul of the pulpit there was a gap which he could not cross and which shut him out from the Promised Land. The little elevation of the pulpit—by so narrow a margin was he missing his mission. Between him and his goal lay the contemptible impediment of art. The slow-flowing Po slipped by, receding toward the sea, and the powerful wake of waters seemed to solicit the traveller wooing him to drift back on the oblivious current. But the boat pushed on upstream, against the current, bearing him slowly toward new pastures . . . toward the Promised Land?

In Florence his failure was yet more dismal. He preached in San Lorenzo to a congregation which had dwindled by the end of Lent to twenty-five souls. Such friends as he found were his first critics. "Father," he was told, "there is no denying that your doctrine is true, useful, and necessary, but your manner of presenting it is lacking in grace, especially as we have the example of Fra Mariano before our eyes." Fra Mariano!—he was prepared for that comparison with the reigning virtuoso of the Florentine pulpits. The arch-type of the popular preacher, his name was on every tongue. The young monk from the provinces was unimpressed. "This florid speech and elegance must yield," he insisted, "to the simplicity of sound doctrine." But the results belied his conviction. The simplicity of sound doctrine, as he preached it, emptied the churches; the art of Fra Mariano filled them. Nor was that all. Mariano was no hypocrite, no caterer to frivolous taste: his doctrine was sound, his character unimpeachable. He practised the strictest austerity in his private life but he had the grace to conceal it: with grace everything could be accomplished in Florence. His amenity had won him the ear of Lorenzo de' Medici, who built him a church of his own. Nor did his conquests end there. The Humanists, who followed Lorenzo and set the intellectual fashions of Florence, were equally charmed. Even the sceptical Poliziano succumbed. Following the crowd, incredulous but curious, he visited one of his performances; and coming, as he admitted, to scoff, he remained, if not to pray, at least to applaud. To that delightful experience he devoted a glowing letter which was making the rounds of his friends and those of Fra Mariano. "I came very suspicious of and ill-disposed to his great fame. Hardly had I entered the church, however, when his habits, his face, and his figure changed my mind, and I immediately expected something impressive and grand. More than once, I confess, he seemed to me to greaten in the pulpit to more than human proportions. He speaks: I am all ears. I drink in his mellow voice, his apt words, his noble sentences. I discern the accents, I recognize the periods, I am dominated by the harmonious cadences. There is nothing confused, tame, or dull. He unfolds the argument, and I am convinced; introduces an apposite anecdote, and I am interested; modulates his voice, and I am charmed; is jocular, and I smile; presses me with serious truths, I yield to their force; appeals to the passions, and I weep; lifts his voice in wrath, and I tremble and wish myself away." Even more persuasive was his personal character. "There is nothing morose in his manner nor disagreeably austere; he does not disdain the charms of poetry and polite letters. He neither repels his hearers by undue severity nor misleads them by over-lenience. So many preachers fancy themselves the masters of life and death and abuse their powers and cavil at everything and weary us with perpetual admonitions. Mariano is moderation itself. A stern censor in the pulpit, he no sooner leaves it than he becomes civil and genial." In short, the ideal of Lorenzo the Magnificent. And such was the Florentine taste: a graceful austerity, an elegant asceticism, a liberal religion of enlightened common sense; and it was impressed on the newcomer that he must study that sophisticated public if he hoped to appeal to it. But what could such advice mean to the artless young preacher from the provinces? It was easy to be graceful when one did not feel deeply and to be accommodating when nothing was at stake. In the plausible manner of Fra Mariano he detected, without being able to expose, the lurking contamination of the world. It was not his business to flatter, it was his duty to cure. And yet . . . and yet . . . Fra Mariano, it was undeniable, was winning souls in the very citadel of religious indifference, among the advanced thinkers of the day, and accomplishing by grace what for the lack of it he was forced to forgo. The fact was irrefutable, and he determined to abandon the pulpit. The Promised Land lay before him—*ave atque vale.*

What else could he do? He was born to be baffled by the world. But the prospect of a long future of useless mediocrity was too bleak; in the extremity of his discouragement he recoiled from it. The struggle had only begun, and already he was shirking it. Had he a right to fail? Was his whole future to be defeated by . . . by what? Wherever he turned it haunted him. Everywhere in the subtle city, even in the cloisters of San Marco, in the conventual gardens crowded with antique sculpture, in the cells and corridors peopled with the bland visions of Fra Angelico, he was surrounded and troubled by the insidious challenge of art.

3

Recognizing his inexperience, his superiors sent him occasionally to neighbouring towns or to the little church of the Murate in a popular quarter, where his hearers were uncritical. In San Marco, meanwhile, he was assigned to the instruction of the novices. He was at ease in the intimacy of the classroom and his familiar homilies impressed his pupils. Often, in the morning, he would appear with tears in his eyes and expound the Scriptures with such a heartfelt fervour that he seemed, as one said, "not so much to have studied as meditated them." He had found his right field and, apparently, the limit of his development: to teach, to pass on the torch, to rear spiritual athletes for the arena he would never enter.

Among his pupils was a young monk in whom he took a peculiar interest. Fra Silvestro Maruffi had been afflicted since childhood with somnambulism, and his malady, which took strange forms, gave him a privileged position in the convent. His psyche was as mischievous as a monkey: he filled the dormitories with simian disasters. Whenever the brothers woke to find their faces smeared with sawdust from the spittoons, or the Prior missed his robes and traced them through the corridors, they knew what spirit had been walking. His malady, which he imputed to over-study, was regarded with sympathy, for he invariably awoke with sighs and groans and cries of *Jesus*. With time and bloodletting it was hoped that he would improve. In one respect he was thoroughly normal: he was an inveterate gossip and in his humble way he was an agent of the true and the good. As for his pranks, they were a source of innocent merriment and enlivened the monotony of convent life. Savonarola himself treated him with indulgence. One day, while he held his class in the garden, the sleepwalker slipped off into the arbour where he seized a stick and began to beat down the grapes; a friar followed and was furiously thwacked on the head—but who minded? The friar retreated, Fra Silvestro ate his fill, and, as Savonarola said, "the grapes being good did him no harm, and he awoke."

Soon his interest in this pupil grew. The moonstruck monk knew that he was a privileged character. His infirmity gave him a sickly sense of self-importance and he throve on it. In time he began to have visions of an edifying nature; he was even tempted to regard them as revelations. But Savonarola promptly scouted such presumptuous notions, and the youth obeyed and resisted temptation. He was perfectly sensible as soon as he secured a little attention. But he could not bear to be forgotten. In time, however, Savonarola himself was visited with visions. His vigils, his fasts, his mortifications, were incessant; his spirit became clairvoyant; and one day, in a nunnery, he heard a voice bidding him go forth and announce the coming scourge of God on a degenerate Church. Fra Silvestro was alarmed. If his own visions were delusions and he had resisted the temptation to believe them, he saw no reason why his master should be less sensible. Savonarola agreed, but gradually he began to concede the possibility that the revelations of his pupil might be authentic. Fra Silvestro was uncertain and jealous. Visions had hitherto been his monopoly. Mollified, sceptical, tempted, he believed and doubted, doubted and believed with mercurial volatility; and he exerted a peculiar power of suggestion on his master. Savonarola now found, whenever he was solicited by the unseen, the sleepwalker at his elbow in an attitude of vigilant suspicion. At one moment Fra Silvestro steadied him with his sanity, at another he seduced him with subconscious suggestion; he was alternately angel and ape; and he troubled his conscience with simian disasters.

Eventually, however, Savonarola was removed from the ambiguous influence of his pupil. Preaching in San Gimignano in 1486, he startled his hearers by predicting that the Church would be scourged and regenerated in the near future; the prophecy created a great impression; but he was careful to explain, on his return to Florence, that it was founded on natural reason and the interpretation of Scriptural texts. Then he was sent to Lombardy where, for the next four years, he lived the life of an itinerant preacher. He passed from town to town, footloose, free, unfettered, but not unmarked. Among the simple, wholesome people of the North, who spoke his own tongue, he began to make headway. He developed his own manner—a manner familiar and colloquial, strenuous and unstudied; he spoke to his congregations as he spoke to his novices, from the heart, with the intimacy of a man-to-man argument; he carried on—he whose life had been a monologue—a searching conversation with himself in the pulpit. And when these appeals did not suffice, he went further. Flagellating himself regularly, his visions recurred; he accepted them with caution; but at last, in Brescia, after a trance of five hours, he had a revelation whose reality he could no longer doubt, and he preached a sermon in which, invoking the twenty-four elders of the Apocalypse and foretelling the destruction of Brescia and the doom of Italy, he electrified and overpowered his hearers. Soaring on the wings of prophecy, his eloquence was supernal and irresistible.

His fame spread in the land; his self-confidence grew; yet he knew in what field he bore his best fruit. It was not in Florence; nor was it in Ferrara. When his mother urged him to return, "I have renounced this world and devoted myself to working the vineyard of the Lord in various cities," he replied, "to save not only my own soul but those of others as well. If the Lord has given me a talent, I must use it as He pleases; and since He has chosen me for this holy office, be content that I exercise it outside my own country, for here I bear far better fruit than in Ferrara. There it would befall me as it befell Christ when His countrymen said: Is not this man a smith and the son of a smith? But outside my own country this is not said to me: nay, when I propose to depart, men and women weep and cherish my words. I meant to write only a few lines but love has made my pen run on, and I have opened my heart to you more than I thought to do. Know, then, that I am more than ever resolved to expose my soul, my body, and all the learning God has given me for love of Him and the salvation of my neighbour; and since I cannot do this at home, I shall do it elsewhere. Exhort everyone to the good life. Today I leave for Genoa."

But it was not to be. He could not flicker out as a provincial preacher. In the fullness of time another call came. Seven years before, speaking on the corruption of the clergy at a Dominican Chapter, he had attracted the attention of an illustrious layman, Pico della Mirandola. Pico was a dilettante and he was profoundly moved by such burning conviction. It was the one quality he lacked. He had every other charm—youth, beauty, wealth, noble birth, a prodigious learning: he was a master of the *omnium scibile:* but he knew nothing with certitude. He envied the unknown monk who knew what he knew so thoroughly: he coveted his conviction even about such a commonplace as the corruption of the clergy. A fortnight he sang the praises of his discovery throughout Florence, then he forgot: his multifarious interests and activities claimed him. But in the meanwhile they had grown and almost ruined him. He conceived the idea of a universal intellectual congress in Florence and challenged the whole learned world to meet him in debate on any or all of nine hundred propositions embracing the entire field of human knowledge. Then Rome intervened: certain of his theological problems were declared unorthodox. Pico protested, and a scandal was only averted by the good offices of Lorenzo de' Medici. Disgusted by the censorship of free thought and more so by its hypocrisy, for the doctrinal rigour of Rome was indecent in view of the moral laxity that prevailed there, Pico no longer regarded the corruption of the clergy indifferently. The normal dubiety of his eye glowed with conviction, and memory opened and gave up a ghost: he recalled the Friar and hurried to San Marco. To his amazement he found that Savonarola had left Florence four years before. Pico hurried to Lorenzo de' Medici and begged his recall. Lorenzo listened. He knew nothing of the man, but the indignant dilettante was his dear friend, and San Marco was his own convent, founded by his grandfather. "With good will and good ink I am always ready to serve you," he said, and directed his secretary to write to the Lombard Dominicans.

The call had come. Savonarola was ready for it: he had matured, he was in full command of his powers, and he set forth to face the public of Fra Mariano once more. On the way, weak with mortification and fasting, he succumbed to sunstroke; but he was assisted by a passing Samaritan; and at the gates of Florence he was supported by a voice—

an inner voice diffused through the immensity of the heavens—bidding him advance and "remember to do what God bids you do." He abandoned himself to it. His footsteps were led. In San Marco he resumed his instruction of the novices, but new influences were at work. His lessons attracted a growing circle of laymen; the class moved into the garden, but the garden was too small to accommodate it; and after several weeks he was urged to ascend the pulpit. The invitation had come unsought, he had not lifted a finger to prompt it: it was a manifest summons. He spent the night in prayer and in the morning he announced, with certitude, that he would preach not only on the following Sunday but for eight years thereafter.

On August 1, 1489, an enormous congregation assembled in the Church of San Marco; the friars filled the choir and clung to the gratings to follow his ordeal. His professional life was at stake. It was his last chance in Florence: he was too old for another. All his past failures were congregated in that crowd which converted the church into a spiritual arena, and already in the sacristy he scented it waiting. It gripped him as he mounted the pulpit, step by step, toward his struggle. On all sides he was surrounded by the enemy of a lifetime, by a dense unfeeling mass of humanity, challenging him to master and move it. There could be no question of courting it; and the only alternative was to shock and violate, to rouse, to startle, and contradict it. He braced himself and began. With the voice of the whirlwind, he launched his prediction of the imminent scourging of the Church, and without waiting for its proven effect plunged into a furious improvisation that swept everything before it, attacking in rapid succession all the themes that kindled his indignation and his eloquence—the corruption of the clergy, the demoralization of the laity, the decay of the faith. The pent-up energies of years rose, the words poured from him like a rhetorical haemorrhage, anguish galvanized all his powers, and in a rush of invective, expostulation, threats, and appeals, he pressed and kneaded the multitude until the sluggish mass began to quicken and stir. Those who remembered him from San Lorenzo listened in amazement to a new man, whose voice was thrilling, whose gestures were sweeping, and who excited and troubled them with a new sensation. Under the rhetorical controversy, the ostensible subjects, and the impersonal words rose an inarticulate appeal which tugged at their nerves. The gaunt figure in the pulpit was like a castaway, crying, gesticulating for recognition and response, baring his heart, stripping his soul, spending his last breath to rejoin humanity; and when he had reached it, wrestling, appealing, forcing it to feel with him; and the multitude responded with a deepening silence, then with a tide of exclamations and sighs, and at last with a murmuring ovation. He had sprung the secret of the revivalist. As he descended, the public of Fra Mariano, rudely startled out of its habits but excited by his sensational novelty and still teeming with his hypnotic power, crowded about him. Sunday struck in his heart, his first day of rest in thirty-eight laborious years. An admiring throng followed him into the convent, and amid those flushed and enthusiastic faces he was no longer haunted by the insidious challenge of art.

4

Among the first to congratulate him was Fra Mariano. There could be no further doubt of his triumph; but it was a success fraught with danger, a sensational success which had to be sustained. Fra Silvestro, returning from San Gimignano, where he had been preaching on the momentous day, found the city humming with discussion of the new luminary and, in particular, of his prophetic lights. He was alarmed. He hurried to his master and reminded him that he had always been averse to such methods and had even written a tract against the preachers of novelties; nor did he hesitate to say—it was the privilege of their intimacy—that he thought him "mad and out of his senses." But Savonarola had outgrown him. To the doubting disciple he listened patiently, but only to assure him that he was "neither mad nor a dreamer"; he reminded him that his predictions were based on reason and that he would not venture to make them without great foundation; and he urged him to betake himself to prayer. Fra Silvestro, cowed but unconvinced, did so. Then, "whether it was my dreamy nature or a diabolical delusion," as he said later, "several times I seemed to be scolded by spirits for not believing him." Meanwhile he made a decisive discovery. The privileged place he had once enjoyed in his master's heart was now shared by another. Fra Domenico da Pescia, a robust countryman, had completely won the confidence of Savonarola by his blind trust and unquestioning devotion, and Fra Silvestro suffered the confused pangs of common sense and jealousy. He betook himself again to prayer, and this time he enjoyed an authentic revelation. He beheld their guardian angels linking their three hearts with a triple chain and dancing in the August sky; and he joined the believers; though, to be sure, as time went on, he was beset by recurring scruples and defended the prophet, as he admitted, "with the tongue and not with the heart."

For there was more than one danger in prophecy. It was associated with invalid women and vagabond friars, and it compromised the reputation of the new preacher. Among the educated classes Savonarola passed for "a simple soul." The hard-headed and fastidious Florentines were suspicious of extravagance; they respected their taste and intelligence. The Humanists, though they attended his sermons and were impressed, shrugged when they came out into the sun and dismissed him as a visionary spellbinder. This estimate, however, they were forced to revise when they met him. The man was difficult to reconcile with the forbidding prophet of the pulpit. His voice was even and low, his manner pleasant, he was open to discussion, and above all he was reasonable. He disclaimed all dogmatism and wished to be believed, he said, neither more nor less than another, wholly on the truth of his arguments. The most heated discussion brought only a faint flush to his face, and no one ever heard him raise his voice in anger. As the conversations progressed, they found him familiar with their philosophers—he had mastered Aristotle and made a digest of Plato—and both Poliziano and Marsilio Ficino, the President of the Platonic Academy, pronounced him a monk of remarkable culture. They had known few as enlightened even among the Cardinals and the *gran maestri*. He spoke their language, met them on their own ground, and was prepared to maintain the truths of Christianity "by reason alone, appealing to no authority, and proceeding as if no man in the world, however learned, were bound to believe in anything but natural reason." So much he conceded as a matter of courtesy, but with an evident mental reservation: for the argument invariably ended with a demonstration of the futility of reason without faith. "Your Aristotle," he said, "does not even succeed in proving the immortality of the soul; he remains uncertain about points so capital that I do not understand how you can waste so much labour on his pages." As for Plato, alas! "A simple old woman knows more of the true faith." He did not shatter their ideals: he shrugged. What seemed the prejudices of professional ignorance he pronounced with the coolness of one who had explored all their wisdom, and exhausted its vanity. The simple soul could be curiously disconcerting. "Some have so fettered themselves and surrendered their intelligence to the bondage of the ancients," he declared, "that they will say nothing contrary to their customs or that they have not said. The ancients have not said something, hence we must not say if. If the ancients have not done a beautiful deed, are we not to do it?" He succeeded, for a moment and even in their own eyes, in making the cult of antiquity seem a blind idolatry and superstitious fad; and he sowed doubt and self-searching among the scholars. Marsilio Ficino confessed that he had been more of a Platonist than a Christian; but he continued to burn his votive lamp to the divine Plato. He dreamed indeed of reconciling Plato and Christ: he could not decide between them. For his, in truth, was a generous idolatry. Like all his contemporaries, he had had a passion for the universal, for the unbroken continuity and undivided solidarity of human experience. The tomb had opened, disclosing a world which had gone before, and all that men had once suffered, thought, and believed could not be abolished because of the belated revelation of Christ. Antiquity was a part of the experience of the race and must be incorporated with its future; and whatever faith Ficino evolved—or, for that matter, any thinking man of the Renaissance —could only be one which embraced the whole of human experience. He respected the Friar; but as a prophet, in that age, he could only regard him as a reactionary.

There were other dangers and subtler ones than the suspicion of delusion and bigotry in the profession of a prophet. The contrast between the private and the pulpit manner of Savonarola was so marked as to present two distinct personalities and to raise the question which was the real one. Already his transformation was such that "those who had heard him before," said one observer, "called him the Miracle. The promptness of his speech, the lofty grandeur of his themes, the grace of his phrases, his clear and penetrating voice, his face not merely fervent but full of enthusiasm, and his beautiful gestures, pierced the hearts of his hearers so that they were not only wrapt in attention but transported beyond themselves." In his ordinary manner "it was not his way to recite, nor to shout, except when he warmed in the denunciation of vice"; but his ordinary manner no longer satisfied those who had known the excitement of his extraordinary moments, and he was under the constant compulsion to surpass himself. It was then that the warping and simplifying influence of the crowd came into play. When he treated the sermon as a logical exercise, the crowd cooled, and with the quick instinct of the orator he reverted to the rhapsodies which fired it. Then the great effusions followed—the long lamentations, the aching appeals, the dredging despairs, the quick hammering invectives, and the sudden cries of doom which loosened the floodtides of popular feeling. The effect was instantaneous. A contagious anxiety passed from the preacher to the crowd and from the crowd to the preacher, and the flock, stirring uneasily to the call of the pastor, undulated to his prompting and multiplied his marshalling will. When the fusion was complete, when his being flowed through the multitude, when he forced it to feel with him, when he was at one with the many, then and then only he lived; then, in that enlarged and intensified existence, he knew the solace of a vast fellow-feeling and an intoxicating illusion of personal power that touched the very quick of life; and that sensation, once known, he could no longer forgo. He craved it with a hungry and connubial ardour; he exerted all his powers to attain, maintain, and repeat it; but it could only be sustained, as the great sensations staled, by more and more potent ones. The necessity was inexorable; for there below, behind, about him was the pressure of an insatiable public, relentlessly urging him on. He became the creature of his own creation, and it almost seemed that in triumphing over the city of art he had succumbed to it. For, however sincere, spontaneous, and inspired his prophecies and his denunciations of sin, their repetition came to have a calculated effect: invariably he fell back on what stimulated him; and it became a question whether his eloquence was the result of his convictions or his convictions of his eloquence.

But there was only one way to prove his sincerity—to grow bolder. The normal life of a preacher in Florence was two Lenten seasons. At the end of that period his popularity had reached such proportions that San Marco could no longer accommodate his hearers, and he moved into the Duomo. His visions and prophecies attracted increasing criticism in the city because of the unwholesome agitation they aroused, and he was advised to desist. But "everything that diverted me from my first study distressed me," he said, in reviewing the struggle he went through at the time, "and as often as I thought of pursuing another way, I came to hate myself. I remember how, preaching in the Duomo in the year 1491, and having composed my sermon on these visions, I considered suppressing it and abstaining from them altogether in the future. God is my witness that I prayed all day and all night until dawn, and every other way, every other doctrine, was denied me. Toward dawn, being weary and downcast with the long vigil, I heard a voice saying:—Fool, do you not see that God bids you follow the same path?—And on that day I preached a terrible sermon."

No: he was not too bold; he was not bold enough. He was there for a purpose, and he could not be satisfied like Fra Mariano with a successful sermon: he had a mission to perform. There were crying abuses, which called for correction and a champion. Gradually his sermons began to harp on political and social issues. He inveighed against usury: "Because of avarice neither you nor your children lead a good life: you have found many ways of making money and many exchanges, which you call lawful but which are most unjust, and you have corrupted the offices and magistrates of the city. No one can persuade you that usury is sinful, you defend it at the peril of your souls. No one is ashamed of lending at usury, nay, those who do otherwise pass for fools. And so the words of Isaiah are verified in you:—Their sin, as in Sodom, was proclaimed and they heeded it not; and also the saying of Jeremiah:—Your brow is that of a whore, and you will not blush. You say: a good and glad life lies in gain, and Christ says: Blessed are the poor in spirit, for they shall inherit Heaven. You say: a blessed life lies in pleasures and sensuality; and Christ says: Blessed are they that weep, for they shall be comforted. You say: the good life is glory; and Christ says:—You shall be blessed when men persecute and revile you. Christ complains of you therefore, for, having toiled to reveal this life that all might be saved, He has a just grievance against you; and therefore He says through the mouth of the prophet:—I have worn myself out calling you, I have made my voice hoarse; for all day long I cry through the mouth of the preachers, and no one hears."

But indeed many heard. The practice of usury, intertwined as it was with the commercial life of the city and the structure of its great fortunes, was an inflammable issue: forty years before, Fra Bernardino da Feltre had been banished for agitating it. "Our affairs are going well because God aids us marvellously," he wrote to Fra Domenico, who was preaching in Pisa, "though we meet with opposition among the great of the city, and many fear we may meet the fate of Fra Bernardino, but I have faith in God. He gives me daily more strength and perseverance and I preach the regeneration of the Church, basing myself on Scripture alone. Take courage and return soon, and I will tell you the marvellous things of the Lord." He could afford to put a soft pedal now on his prophecies: these blows struck a chord more responsive. Amid opposition and excitement, discussion and danger, his pulse, and his eloquence, and his courage, and his perseverance, and his power. He felt his own reality at last, as never before, by the effect he produced; and it was no longer the ephemeral effect of rhetoric. After half a lifetime of meditation and passivity he disclosed a nature and a need for activity. "No man," he repeated, "knows more than he achieves."

His friends counselled caution, and by nature he was by no means reckless, but the line was narrow between the legitimate province of the preacher and the treacherous ground of the agitator, and whatever subject he broached in the pulpit seemed to carry him across it. Even that safe theme, the corruption of the clergy, led him into quicksands. "Fathers sacrifice to this false idol and urge their sons into ecclesiastical life, that they may enjoy benefices and prebendaries; and so you hear it said: *Happy the house that boasts a good clericality!* But I tell you: a time will come when you will say, *Woe to it,* and you will feel the edge of the sword. Take my advice: sooner let your sons follow the ordinary way than to undertake a religious life for profit. Nowadays there is no longer any grace or gift of the Holy Ghost that is not bought and sold. The poor, on the other hand, are oppressed by taxes, and when they pay intolerable sums, the rich cry: Give me the rest. Some, with an income of fifty, pay an impost of a hundred, while the rich pay little because their taxes are levied arbitrarily. When widows come weeping, they are told: Go to bed. When the poor complain, they are told: Pay, Pay!"

Now, the inequalities of the tax system lay at the root of the Medici government: they were no accidental corruption. It was by favouring his friends and fining his opponents that Lorenzo maintained his pacific political control of the city; and among those who denounced his influence as a tyranny the agitation of such abuses might go far. The authorities observed the development of the mystagogue into a demagogue with concern; and in due time the expected happened. He was invited to preach in the Palace. He accepted promptly, dreading nothing but the temptation to be discreet. "I am here in the waters of Tiberias," he said. "Before the Signori I do not feel master of myself as in church. I must be more measured and urbane, as Christ was in the house of the Pharisees. I shall say, therefore, that all the good and evil of a city depends on its head, whose responsibility is great even for small sins, for if he followed the right path the whole city would become holy. We must fish, therefore, in these waters with nets that let not even the little fish escape, and we must proceed without too many scruples and speak frankly and openly. Tyrants are incorrigible because they are proud, because they love flattery, because they will not restore ill-gotten gains. They give a free hand to bad officials; they yield to flattery; they do not heed the wretched; they do not condemn the rich; they expect the peasants and the poor to work for them *gratis,* or they allow their officials to oppress them; they corrupt the suffrage; they farm the taxes and burden the people more and more. It is your duty, therefore, to root out dissension, to do justice, and to demand honesty of everyone."

The sermon was a summary of all the charges levelled against Lorenzo by his enemies—favouritism, financial maladministration, manipulation of the ballot—all the normal corruptions in short by which, as a political boss, he controlled the machinery of a nominal Republic; and the Friar was prepared for the consequences. But they were not what he expected. Lorenzo was too shrewd to make a martyr of his critic. He had often been called a tyrant, and he smiled his sly, magnanimous smile at the name. His popularity was a sufficient refutation of the charge. If he was one, it was by necessity: because, as he wrote, "wealth without power is insecure." The Medici had merely anticipated their rivals in acquiring political power to protect their fortune, and they had used it wisely. They had identified their interests with those of the city, and both had prospered. Their tyranny rested, in the last analysis, on popular consent. Like his father and grandfather before him, Lorenzo occupied no official position in the state; the Republican façade remained intact; and what else mattered? Liberty? The Florentines were incapable of it. They craved it only when it was denied them and won it only to lose it. Lorenzo knew his countrymen, he knew their weakness for words. It was the word that mattered. Studiously respecting the appearance of liberty, he achieved the substance of it by an invisible dictatorship which substituted for the chronic factiousness of Florentine life order and stability. The result was a period of unprecedented peace and prosperity. Whatever corruption this paternalistic government cost was a small price to pay for its benefits. A few malcontents might murmur, but the public at large was satisfied. The Medici tyranny was an organic necessity; and in the face of such vital realities the protests of the Friar had the pathetic futility of doctrinaire ideals. Lorenzo, with cruel magnanimity, ignored them.

But the Friar could not be ignored indefinitely. Three months later he was elected Prior of San Marco. The convent was a Medici foundation, and it was customary for the new incumbent to pay a visit of courtesy to the head of the family which supported and endowed it; with this custom he refused to comply. "I recognize my election as coming from God alone, and to Him alone will I profess obedience," he declared. In vain his friends protested that it was unnecessary to antagonize Lorenzo and that a visit of ceremony was after all a small thing: no occasion was too small to mark his independence of the world. In vain they insisted that it was a matter, not of morals, but of manners: to him it was a question of principle. If he yielded, he would be taking the first step on that downward path at the end of which morals became as accommodating as manners and churches were built for Fra Mariano. Everything, in reality, was at stake. Lorenzo took a lighter view of the incident. "You see," he said, "a stranger comes into my house and will not even deign to visit me."

In a man as prominent as the Prior of San Marco so provocative an attitude was disturbing, however: he commanded a wide and impressionable audience for the dissemination of his ideas, and it was advisable that his ideas should be the right ones. They had never met, and Lorenzo was convinced that personal acquaintance would do much to dispel the man's prejudice. Lorenzo was right. The charm of his manner was disarming, it had won wars: who had ever resisted his tact, his humour, his shrewd sympathy? All he needed was a chance encounter. Accordingly, one morning he appeared in San Marco and strolled through the gardens. He did not ask for the Prior: he had his dignity to remember. But so had the Prior. The result was an extraordinary bout of tact, a long-drawn feint that was almost feminine in its punctilio. Lorenzo toiled through the cloister, nursed his game leg, and—too expert to startle his covey—inspected every vista with studied aimlessness and patient pertinacity. This manoeuvre was followed around every corner. The friars flew to the Prior, who was reading in his cell.—"The Magnifico is walking in the garden."—"Does he ask for me?"—"No."—"Then let him walk."—And walk Lorenzo did, warily, about and about the kennel, until at last, feeling the gout in his leg, with weary dignity he ambled away.

He was piqued. Though his advances were extremely guarded, he persisted. He attended Mass in San Marco on several occasions and sent liberal alms to the convent. But the Prior was intractable. When the alms were collected and a sum of gold was found in them, he sorted and sent the tainted moneys to a charitable order for distribution to the poor; and from the pulpit he declared that "the good dog does not cease barking in defence of his master when he is tossed a bone." Lorenzo's secretary varied the metaphor. *Vulpecula iste habet caudem depilatum*, he remarked in reporting the rebuff: "that fox has a skinned tail." And Lorenzo agreed.

Eager as Lorenzo was to ignore him, he found it more and more difficult to do so. Encouraged, so it seemed, by the licence accorded him, the Prior more than once inveighed against tyranny; nor did he hesitate to refer to what he called "this ghost of a Republic." Finally a deputation of five influential citizens called on him and urged him to moderate his tone, pointing out as patrons of San Marco the dangers which both he and the convent might incur, and dwelling on the impropriety of a cleric meddling in politics. "I know that you do not come of your own accord," he replied, "but that Lorenzo has sent you. Tell him to do penance for his sins, for the Lord fears no one and does not spare the princes of the world." When they hinted at the possibility of banishment, the prophetic flush mantled his face. "I do not fear your banishments," he retorted, "for this city of yours is like a grain in the ground. The new doctrine will triumph and the old one perish. Though I am a foreigner and Lorenzo a citizen, and the foremost in the city, I shall remain and he will pass away." And several days later, in the presence of witnesses, he took occasion to predict the death of three princes, the King of Naples, the Pope, and Lorenzo de' Medici.

Suffering as he did from gout, this was too pointed for the Magnifico to overlook. He sent for Fra Mariano, discussed this presumption of prophecy, and suggested that he preach a sermon on Acts i, 7: *It is not for you to know the times and the moments the Father hath fixed of His authority.* Fra Mariano, who had seen himself gradually eclipsed by the new favourite, accepted with alacrity, and on the appointed day a brilliant and partial public, which included Lorenzo, Poliziano, and Pico della Mirandola, assembled in his church of San Gallo. But alas, the years had irreparably ruined Fra Mariano. His moderation was no more. Instead of a sermon of consummate poise, proportion, and point, such as his patron had a right to expect from him, the incredulous congregation listened, at first with amazement and then with disgust, to a tirade of such breathless malice and feeble violence that even his sponsors were shocked. The fiasco not only gave a death-blow to his own reputation, it redounded to the credit of his rival. Realizing his mistake too late, he hurried to San Marco in an impulse of erratic panic, embraced the Prior, and invited him with effusive cordiality to celebrate Mass with him in San Gallo. The Prior accepted, but on the following Sunday he preached in his own church his own sermon on Acts i, 7.

Lorenzo made no further effort to curb him, and on his side Savonarola gave him no further cause for complaint. But it was a truce: peace there could never be between such incompatible natures. Their antagonism was fundamental, it seemed to attract and repel them magnetically, and there would have been something for ever lacking in the logic of their lives if they had not met in a final trial of strength. Lorenzo, said Poliziano, who was in his confidence, "kept a close watch over even the smallest actions of Savonarola in order to calumniate him and make him lose his credit, but he found him always holy and intact." Such incorruptible integrity intrigued him: it contradicted his whole experience of human nature. He assumed as an axiom that men were moved by self-interest, and the Friar was an exception, a moral anomaly, a man who was actuated apparently by no motive but a disinterested zeal for principle. Principle? He mistrusted it. Himself a thoroughly natural man, he was governed entirely by expediency. The practice of politics and the versatility of his interests had made him too familiar with the complexity of human affairs and the necessity of compromise to be capable of conviction: conviction was a vital limitation, principle was an impediment to the free play of instinct; and he lived by flair, by shrewdness, always alert to the prompting of life, improvising his conduct with every occasion, consistent to nothing but continual variety. He was an opportunist who had succeeded by adhering steadily to the possible, and the absolutes of the moralist were fatal to his scheme of things. The intractable spirit of Savonarola was an insistent provocation to his own. He admitted his honesty; but was he not honest himself? He followed Nature, for whom self-satisfaction was the only law and the principle of fertility. Disinterestedness—ah, that delicate vanity of the spirit!—that sterile virtue—that futile form of sentimentality—illusion—child's play. Self was the only sincerity; Nature blessed it; it was fruitful; while she laid her blight on human conceits that were irrelevant to her purpose. It was a maxim of his grandfather, Cosimo de' Medici, that "states are not ruled by paternosters"; but the Friar had challenged that truism and put the Decalogue into politics. With his growing popularity he had the power to lead and mislead opinion; and it was the weakness as well as the strength of Lorenzo's government that it rested so largely on personal popularity and public consent. An officious reformer, with no understanding of the complex political realities of which that government was the outcome, could create acute embarrassment by agitating its incidental abuses. It was easy to raise the inflammatory issue of liberty and tyranny, and to forget that liberty in Florence was synonymous with faction and unrest; or to exploit financial scandals and to overlook the millions which the Medici had spent out of their own pockets in behalf of the city. Compensation and conciliation lay at the root of Lorenzo's system: what he took with one hand he restored with the other; he worked like Nature without regard to the means but to the end, and the result was life and a working harmony of the whole. To pick flaws with the parts was a form of moral pedantry; and such simple-mindedness could be mischievous: it appealed to the crowd. Already there were disturbing rumours that the Magnifico was planning to assume official authority and to make himself Gonfalonier for life. Now that the Prior, whom he had vainly sought to ignore and to conciliate, was determined to trespass on politics, how much he could show him, how many mistakes he could spare him, if only they could meet! But how could they meet?

The Prior resisted all his advances. He too felt the significance of their spiritual antagonism. The issues which divided them admitted of no compromise. Lorenzo embodied in its most seductive form the tolerant, sceptical, enlightened spirit of the new age; he was surrounded by scholars who admired the Bible . . . as poetry; he wrote lewd and devotional verse with equal facility; his example encouraged the laxity of public morals and sanctioned that tepid spirit which Savonarola, in his efforts to revive a rigorous faith in Christianity, found more discouraging than determined opposition would have been. But what exasperated him above all in the Medici was his moral expediency. Moral expediency— it was a contradiction in terms. A morality of expediency, a morality as accommodating as manners, man-made, mutable, varying with circumstances and the accepted practices of the time, was the antithesis of the moral principle: it countenanced life instead of controlling it. In so convenient a system good and evil became interchangeable and meaningless, and ethical authority crumbled. But how could it be otherwise if the source of that authority was Nature? It was only by transcending Nature that conscience found its absolute principle. With Savonarola it was not a logical process, it was a crying need, a consuming passion of his being, that drove him into the arms of God in search of a superior power to dominate the lawlessness and brutality of life; and he could not rest until he had imposed that power on the world. He was possessed by the spirit of God. "Your word has become a fire burning the marrow of my bones," he cried in one of his sermons, and it was the burden of all of them. "I am fallen into derision and disgrace among men. But I invoke the Lord day and night, and I say to you: New times are at hand." But there before him, foiling, circumventing, soliciting, evading him—the personification of the world—loomed Lorenzo de' Medici. How indeed could they meet?

Within a few months their latent conflict came to a head. In April 1492, Lorenzo was a dying man. He had retired to his villa of Careggi, to decline in the country he loved, and to comply with the Nature which he had always obeyed. Over the walls of his sickroom ran the ribbon-like motto of his house: *Le Temps revient, Le Temps revient;* through the windows his eye rested on the pencilled foliage and the luminous horizons of spring. Spring, yes . . . Time returns . . . but what does it bring? It had brought him to the brink of the absolute: today was the seventh of April, tomorrow was the Day of Judgment. He sent for his son and heir, Piero, and laid down certain precepts of political conduct for his guidance. For his second son, Giovanni, the sixteen-year-old Cardinal who was in Rome, he had already written a letter of advice. As for the youngest, Giuliano, since he was not destined for public life, he might live as he pleased. The only immortality Lorenzo expected was his children; but with his usual prudence he prepared for whatever the hereafter might hold. He sent for a priest and insisted, when he came, on leaving his bed and meeting his Saviour on his knees. The exertion exhausted him and the last rites were administered. But he rallied and spent the next few hours chatting with his friends. Suddenly he asked for Savonarola. His strength was ebbing, the absolution he had received was perfunctory, he was anxious, and he insisted that "the one honest friar he knew" be called.

When the summons reached San Marco, Savonarola replied that anything he might say to Lorenzo would be unwelcome and useless; but upon the invitation being repeated he relented. Now that Lorenzo lay on the verge of the absolute, how much he could show him! Never, he admitted, had he known a man more gifted in the temporal sphere and he regretted that for his spiritual good he had not been called in sooner. Arriving in Careggi, he found the dying man anxiously waiting to open his soul to him. "God is good, God is good," the Prior repeated solicitously and consented to hear his confession on three conditions.

He named them. "First, a great and living faith in God's mercy"; to which the patient agreed promptly. "Second, that you restore, or direct your heirs to restore, all your ill-gotten gains." At that there was a pause: Lorenzo appeared puzzled; but finally he nodded. "Thirdly, that you restore the freedom of Florence." For a long moment the son of Piero and the grandson of Cosimo de' Medici stared at him incredulously, then he slowly rolled over and died.

5

Le Temps revient, Le Temps revient. . . . The meandering motto wound its timeless refrain about the walls of the death-chamber, which stood empty now and open to the whimpering winds of spring; and its murmur was not that of a dirge. The place which one Medici had vacated was immediately occupied by another. Of the three sons of Lorenzo, the one who resembled him least, however, was his heir. Playing with them as children on the floors of that very villa, the father had early discerned their destinies in their characters: Piero was *pazzo*, Giovanni *savio*, and Giuliano *buono*. The gentle Giuliano might be as easy-going as he pleased, he had no public responsibilities to face. Giovanni, the second, was a sagacious, circumspect, and adipose youth who could be trusted, now that he was a Cardinal, to advance the family fortunes in Rome and even perhaps to keep a watchful eye on the wayward impulses of his elder. For, by the accident of primogeniture, the political role for which Giovanni was so eminently fitted devolved upon Piero; and Piero was irresponsible. *Le Temps revient*, yes: but new times were at hand.

At twenty-two Piero was more immature than his younger brothers. From his father he had inherited only a powerful body. Now, a powerful body was a political asset. The rugged physique of the father, which gave him the look and the bearing of a manual toiler or a countryman, had fortified him in the popular regard; and so did his prodigious strength and his love of sport and the easy democratic familiarity which went with it. This much Piero appreciated. He displayed his own prowess and skill and animal spirits in snowball fights in the streets and in football matches in the Piazza; but what the people applauded in the father they criticized in the son. They were quick to sense the difference. What was spontaneous in one was condescending in the other. While Piero appeared to be courting popularity, at heart he was insolently indifferent to it. His attitude toward himself was that of a Roman baron. The maternal strain predominated in him, the overbearing blood of the Roman Orsini. He was but half a Florentine. High-handed and headstrong, neglecting the cardinal principle upon which the popularity and power of the Medici depended—that unassuming simplicity which Lorenzo, like his father and grandfather before him, had so assiduously cultivated—he behaved not as the first citizen of the Republic but as the hereditary prince of a despotism. Unconsciously he offended the people, and the Florentine populace with its sensitive instinct for propriety resented in a young man of such superior pretensions an indulgence in popular pastimes which was both unbecoming and patronizing, and which only served to remind them of his youth and irresponsibility. The same foreign and fatal deficiencies manifested themselves in his administration of the city. Impatient of advice, conscious of his inexperience, and determined not to admit it, he acted impulsively, blundered, grew stubborn, and, suddenly confused, reversed himself—with an unfortunate effect of caprice. These errors undermined public confidence, and with it the peculiar authority which the Medici had established in Florence. They would have been tolerated as those of a tyro, had not the tyro been Piero. What a contrast to his bland brother Giovanni, so modest, so fat, so slow, and so sure! In vain the boy-Cardinal cautioned his elder from afar: sixteen spoke to twenty-two. The athlete stood alone, aloof and vulnerable. Tall, strong, handsome, his pale face began to reveal an expression of moody reserve, from which it would have been a mistake to infer any real sensitiveness, and which soon became habitual. He was well-meaning but why, like his father, could he not be genial? He had been suckled at a dry udder. With a temperament so arbitrary and instable Piero seemed to present all the elements for the making of a tyrant. He quarrelled with his family and alienated many of the supporters of his House; Republican sentiment began to stir; and the malcontents found their way to San Marco.

The prolonged hostility of the Prior toward Lorenzo made him the natural focus about whom anti-Medicean sentiment rallied. At the same time the death bed scene had enhanced his prestige among the supporters of the Medici: the supreme attempt which Lorenzo had made to reconcile his critic seemed, in the eyes of the public, a recognition of his character and his influence. Among the people, too, he was popular by his consistent championing of their grievances. Even as a prophet he was gaining credit in many quarters. The death of Lorenzo, which fulfilled one prognostic, was followed, four months later, by that of the Pope, which realized another. Everything conspired to consolidate his influence; and the conduct of Piero promoted it.

The proclamation of the new Pope was greeted throughout Italy by a burst of predictions of the most contradictory character. In this as in other issues the North and the South could not agree. The King of Naples, who had some disputes pending with the Holy See, wept and declared that "a Pope had been created who would be the most pernicious in Italy." This opinion he based on the notorious scandals of his private life. The new Pontiff, as everyone knew, was an over-sexed old man who had led a lewd life from earliest youth. By various mothers he had five acknowledged children and, being the fondest of fathers, he made no secret of his consuming ambition for their aggrandizement. This ambition he was now in a position to gratify. By virtue of his vast wealth, after forty years of Pope-making during which he had garnered an unforgivable fortune, he had at last reached the papal throne, outstripping both his old foe Cardinal Giuliano della Rovere and his old friend Cardinal Ascanio Sforza; and there he now sat, the grossest of its incumbents, counting his family and the fleshpots, and not overfriendly to Naples. In the North opinion was different. Whatever his failings, he had the qualities of a political priest—shrewdness, energy, administrative ability, and an acute and comprehensive grasp of public affairs; and it was noted with relief that he began his reign by policing the Eternal City, where the death-rate had reached an average of fourteen murders a day and life was too lawless to be comfortable. He was too comfort-loving to neglect justice. A large bovine man of sanguine temperament, he weighed two hundred pounds' worth of stability and order. Milan, Venice, Genoa, Mantua, Siena, and Lucca expected "a glorious Pontiff." His name was Roderigo Borgia, and he assumed the title of Alexander VI.

The election of a new Pope introduced an element of uncertainty and the necessity of a delicate adjustment into the relations of the various states of the peninsula with each other and the Holy See. The most experienced diplomat in Italy since the passing of Lorenzo de' Medici was the Regent of Milan, Lodovico Sforza: upon him now devolved the focal and conciliatory role which Lorenzo had so long assumed and which had earned him the name of *the needle of the balance*. As a precaution against the future, he proposed that the allied states of Milan,

Florence, Naples, and Ferrara should present, in a united front, their joint congratulations to the new Pope. Eager to cut an independent figure, Piero de' Medici dissociated himself from this scheme and insisted on leading the Florentine delegation in person and alone. The Regent of Milan was a timid and suspicious man; he lent more gravity to his rebuff than it deserved and inferred from it designs of a political nature; and the cordial relations between Florence and Milan, which Lorenzo had promoted as an indispensable principle of the balance of power and the peace of Italy, were overcast by a fleeting cloud of mistrust. It was a small blunder but—no blunders were small in diplomacy—it augmented the lack of confidence which the young Medici inspired in Florence.

This gathering unrest was an insidious solicitation to the Prior of San Marco to assume a political role; but a political role was a snare he was careful to avoid. His concern was with something greater. His only interest in politics, and his only warrant for trespassing on secular affairs, was a moral one. He allowed nothing to divert him from it. The simoniacal election of the new Pope and his disreputable character had focused public attention once more on the demoralization of the Church; and it was there that his energy and his leadership were needed. He returned to his great theme of the degeneracy, the scourging, and the regeneration of the Church, and his visions and prophecies grew darker and more brilliant. In Advent he electrified his audience with the revelation of a vision which was subsequently reproduced in medals and engravings as the symbol of his doctrine—a clenched hand in a cloudy firmament clasping a sword, with the inscription, *Gladius Domini super terram cito et velociter.*[1] But what nothing could reproduce was the awful animation he gave to it in the pulpit—the evocation of a supernatural gloaming, of wandering voices proclaiming the Wrath of God in a lowering murk, of the spasms of lightning and cataracts of thunder and the sudden plunge of the sword as night and annihilation engulfed a world full of clamour and groans. No less successful was his spectral delineation of Rome eclipsed by a black Cross, rising like a tree of sorrow and shame from its rotten foundations and graven with the fatal characters: *Crux Irae Dei.* When his night-blooming voice divulged these visions in the cavernous vaults of the Duomo, the flagstones of the pavement were no colder than the congregation wrapt in a sepulchral trance; and when it shuffled out, blinking and chilly, into the sun, the

---

[1] The sword of the Lord, swift over the earth and sudden.

SAVONAROLA AS ST. PETER MARTYR, by Fra Bartolommeo
From the portrait in the Accademia di Belle Arti, Florence

taverns and wine-shops did a brisk business. And yet, terrible as those sermons were, their effect was fugitive. The world went on as before and, except among women, he made few converts. His power was still rhetorical.

It was a hollow triumph. The power of the Word would never beget reform without a practical example. It was necessary to begin at the bottom, to experiment with his ideas, and to re-create the world first in the convent; for the convent itself was tainted with the world and cried for reform. San Marco was less a sanctuary than a museum: its priceless collections of codices and antiques attracted a daily concourse of laymen, students, artists; the world seeped in, and its brackish ebb and flow bred an unwholesome atmosphere whose enervating effects were only too evident in the sloth and tepidity of the brethren. The whole environment was at fault. In those frescoed walls how was it possible to pursue the strenuous life of a spiritual athlete? Fra Angelico had transformed them into seraphic alcoves. Those theories of saints, those cycles of martyrs, those fields of primrose faces, those parades of bland adolescents and lute-bellied virgins, perpetually circling the Celestial Throne—they were an insidious temptation to relax: their flesh was transfigured but it blushed; and their chaste hues—pious blues and maidenly carnations and mild gold—were a sedative, not a scourge, to the senses. No: San Marco was tainted. His first impulse was to abandon it, to lead a general exodus into the country, to found a new house where the rule of the Founder might be observed in strict simplicity and uncompromising poverty. Money, to be sure, was required even for the construction of a poorhouse; but a campaign was started among the patrons of the convent, subscriptions were raised, land was purchased near Careggi, the ground was cleared, and plans were drawn for a suburban hermitage. Then the older brothers rebelled. Alarmed at the prospect of so radical a departure, they started a furtive opposition and persuaded the bankers to withdraw their support; and the scheme collapsed. But the Prior did not lose heart. It was too easy, no doubt, too easy to retreat and conduct his reform under ideal conditions; the true test lay in grappling with impediments and overcoming them. Human nature was the problem, not its environment. But first it was essential to have a free hand and undisputed authority in San Marco; and for this he needed the support of the Medici.

Some forty years before, the convent had been united for administrative purposes to the Lombard Congregation, and he had suffered more than once from the interference of his distant superiors. If, as he anticipated, resistance again developed, it would certainly work through those channels. Accordingly, after paving the way by two visits to Venice, where he secured the approval of the Dominican General, he sent Fra Domenico to Rome to petition the Pope for the autonomy of San Marco. The proposal, of course, met with prompt opposition from the Lombards, who were represented in Rome by the Papal Vice-Chancellor, Cardinal Ascanio Sforza. The brother of the Milanese Regent commanded the ear of Alexander: he had been responsible for his election and had succeeded to his vacated office. With such opposition Fra Domenico and his master were unable to cope, and the Prior accepted the assistance of the Medici when it was offered. Piero had his reasons for joining the struggle, and they were not so much pious as political and, above all, sporting. He was not unwilling to back Savonarola and to test and offset, if he could, the Milanese influence in Rome. He enlisted the aid of his brother the Cardinal, who was just learning the diplomatic ropes and for whom this was an excellent exercise. Giovanni was too young and too cautious to do much—his father had left him explicit instructions not to importune the See for unnecessary favours if he hoped to obtain real ones—but at least he secured the assistance of more seasoned diplomats. As the rival parties accumulated adherents, the contest, spreading and ramifying on all sides, developed into one of those complicated wire-pulling matches which exactly suited the tastes for intrigue and the professional abilities of the Roman Court. Nevertheless, the Milanese influence remained paramount. The Pope procrastinated. Fra Domenico laboured and prayed with unflagging zeal, but the outlook was black. "Be strong, do not doubt," his master wrote him, "and the victory will be yours: the Lord scatters the schemes of men and casts down the designs of princes." He offered up prayers incessantly; nor did he neglect self-help. When the Lombards spread a plausible rumour that there was a party in San Marco itself opposed to the separation, he summoned his flock and obtained their signatures to a unanimous appeal which he sent posthaste to Rome. His faith, his courage, his perseverance, were rewarded at last, though in an unforeseen manner. Suddenly the whole question was taken out of his hands. The Protector of the Order, Cardinal Caraffa of Naples, sympathized with his aims and had political reasons, as a Meridional, for opposing the Milanese influence. One evening, profiting by the exhaustion of the Pope after a trying conclave, he followed him into his private apartments, diverted his mind to agreeable subjects, and, at an opportune moment, produced a brief authorizing the separation of San Marco, which he invited him to sign. The Borgia was a lawyer bred: he smiled. But he shook his head. Cardinal Caraffa was a Southerner and respected his comfort. Feeling for his hand, he slipped off the seal-ring and smilingly stamped the fateful document. The Holy Father studied his hand, his plump, moist, eventide hand, undecided. At that moment a Lombard delegation was introduced with new and more pressing recommendations. "If you had come sooner," said His Holiness, "you would have been satisfied, but now what is done is done." And Fra Domenico, who was waiting without the door, hurried off, hugging the coveted brief.

The autonomy of San Marco, though a purely administrative question, was destined to have a far-reaching effect on Savonarola's career. For the moment, its results were happy. Henceforth he was responsible only to his Roman superiors, that is, to Cardinal Caraffa and the Pope; the General of the Order, moreover, confirmed his authority by naming him Provincial of Tuscany. The way was now clear for reform, and he attacked it with unhampered freedom and vigour. A great current of energy swept through the convent, rousing and airing its sloth and its mustiness. The malediction of St. Dominic—"Cursed be he who brings possessions into this Order!"—took on a terrible reality. The holdings of San Marco were sold and the monks were organized into two categories to make them self-supporting. The manual labourers supported the brain-workers by whatever trade they were skilled in—painting, sculpture, calligraphy, the illumination of manuscripts, and other crafts. The brain-workers were further subdivided and specialized, the mediocre confining themselves to cases of conscience and the exposition of Scripture, while preaching and the higher studies were reserved for the gifted. When these went forth to proselytize, they were accompanied by a lay-brother who maintained them by the work of his hands. "If they tell everyone the truth," said the Prior in explaining the purpose of this arrangement, "they will receive no alms, truth being commonly detested; and hence they will shrink from plainspeaking and be as muzzled dogs." Begging he discountenanced, but in the early days of the experiment the convent was reduced to such straits that collections had to be taken up from door to door. Poverty, the original rule of the Order, was rapidly realized; and the reformed Dominicans, once so conspicuous for the ample majesty of their flowing black and white robes, were now recognizable by their pinched hoods, abbreviated frocks, and ungainly figures. But the war on property went further: they could call nothing their own but their souls; books, clothes, cells, were periodically exchanged to remind those who still cherished them, by their constant circulation, of the transitory vanity of existence. The war on property was, in the last analysis, a war on personal identity, and for a time, in fact, a rudimentary form of monastic communism prevailed in San Marco.

This domestic revolution was not put through without resistance on the part of the older monks, who found themselves rudely disturbed in their comfortable slumbers; but their murmurs were overborne by the enthusiasm of the young. With the young behind him, nothing could stop the Prior—nothing but their own zeal. Outstripping his inspiration in their austerities, their fastings, and their fervour, many fell sick, and he was reluctantly forced to recognize the wisdom of his superiors, who had restrained his own early ardours, and to imitate it. He did so and bade farewell to his youth—youth with its unlimited aspirations, its uncompromising extremes, its magnificent recklessness. One concession led to another. The reform, in short, was mutual. He recognized the value of recreation. He had hoped, he had even determined, to abolish the ceremonial vainglories, the pageants and processions, to which his flock was addicted; now he restored them: through the cloisters the monks perambulated, chanting and contented, and sometimes they would circle, while the curious peered in from the street, about a boy, dressed up as the Virgin, whom they celebrated in singsong as their *mamma*. Occasionally there were outings in the country. A series of woodcuts popularized these pastoral pleasures, which reminded the Prior of his fast-vanishing youth. The long calm afternoons passed, amid the hum of cicadas, not without edification. While the flock settled on some suburban slope, overlooking the vista of Florence with its thickets of towers and the cupola of the Duomo swollen with prayer, the master expounded theological dilemmas and the mystery of Nature. But indeed there was no mystery, there was only the hum of the cicadas, the open book on his lap, the world at his feet, and the last word of Aquinas's philosophy in his hand, "All being is perfect." And whether he gazed toward Careggi with its abandoned hermitage or toward his flock or toward the roofs of the Medici, he was serenely unconscious of compromise.

There could be no compromise, only a pause. Though the older brethren complained that the results of the reform were not what they had been led to believe and regarded as mirific his high hopes that "an effusion of the Holy Spirit would come upon them, in such abundance that they would be amazed—that they would be a perfect Congregation —that men would come to them dumbfounded from every religion—

laymen of great credit and mind—and that it would be the most perfect of all religions"—yet a beginning had been made and the sequel soon belied them. Converts poured in from all classes and particularly from the well-born whom he favoured for their habits of breeding, ambition, and discipline. San Marco had always been an upper-class House and there was something strenuous and handsome in the new rule that appealed to the aristocratic temper. From Dante's day there still survived in Florentine life an ideal of plain living and high thinking and that fastidious austerity which distinguished its art. San Marco became too small to accommodate its recruits, and a tunnel had to be dug under the street to connect it with the new quarters in which the overflow was lodged. The reform began to spread throughout Tuscany. So heartening a response convinced the Prior that the embers had only to be stirred to revive and quicken the Faith; his energies and his confidence redoubled; and at this juncture he was suddenly swept by a great groundswell into a larger sphere of activity. The French invasion was at hand.

6

When Louis XI died, he left France a unified nation. This was the heritage he bequeathed to his son, Charles VIII. The visible symbol of this achievement was a standing army, the first in Europe, formidable in numbers, equipment, and discipline, and capable of every feat but one. Standing armies rarely stand. The nation was ripe for imperialism, and there was a classic reason for diverting its energies into foreign adventure: war abroad was the best, perhaps the only, guarantee of peace at home. Military glory, moreover, held a peculiar fascination for the young King. He was feeble-minded and misshapen. Stunted, spindle-shanked, rachitic, and rickety, the body was that of a gargoyle; and the mind which governed it was Gothic. Or was it the body which governed the mind? It seemed so. While the limbs limped, the spirit soared. His stature was puny, but he was every inch a king. Bred on books of piety and romance, he dreamed of emulating the exploits of Charlemagne and Saint Louis in a crusade against the Paynim. He was haunted by obsolete ideals of chivalry. The unattainable pricked him. It made him an Alpinist—by proxy. He forced his courtiers to conquer an inaccessible peak in his name. Otherwise he was, in the words of Commynes, "the kindest soul in the world." During his minority, these impulses had been curbed by his level-headed sister, but his favourites flattered them for their own ends and, when he graduated from her tutelage, they reasserted themselves. Having reached the age of reason, however, he was willing to satisfy his itch for the remote nearer home. Italy offered an outlet for it; and when he had finished with Italy he planned to push on to the Holy Land and Constantinople. The combination of a stunted body, a soaring imagination, a standing army, and an expanding nation was intoxicating; and delving into the archives he revived the Angevin claim to Naples.

The idea of an Italian invasion was by no means impractical. On the contrary, the political constitution of the peninsula invited it. It was a historic necessity. A shifting congeries of factious states, Italy was at the same stage of political development as France had been before the Valois centralized and consolidated it. In Italy there was no power capable of assuming this mission. Not only were these states inordinately jealous of their independence; by tradition they adhered to the medieval conception of a Universal Church and a Universal State, and, with the exception of the Republics of Florence and Venice, were nominal feudatories either of the Pope or the Emperor. The principle as well as the impulse of coalition was lacking, and the fact that the Papacy was itself one of these states was a constant obstacle to national union. Too weak to dominate, it was just strong enough to divide. When Rome attempted to assume national leadership, it became increasingly secular; and without achieving temporal success, it weakened its spiritual credit. But even had the impulse to unite been present, the means of opposing an effective military resistance to the foreigner were lacking. The warfare of the peninsula was waged by mercenaries. Passing from one employer to another, it was to their advantage, since the foe of today was the friend of tomorrow, to protract their campaigns, to do as little damage as possible, to harvest their pay, and to avoid decisive results. In short, they made war politely. Hence the Italian princes were primarily diplomats; but even their diplomacy suffered, resolving itself into a constant process of temporizing and ruse, procrastination and makeshifts, backed by a threat of force on which they could not rely. A final factor made Italy vulnerable: its culture, in which it surpassed the rest of Europe as much as it lagged behind it in political development. The rediscovery of antiquity had aroused an ardent sentiment of human solidarity; in the realm of the mind racial distinctions vanished; and the enthusiasm of the Humanists for learning and civilization filtered through all classes. It was, in fact, only after actual contact with the foreigner that national feeling developed, and from its only valid motive, the consciousness of a superior culture.

Now, no one appreciated these facts better than the prince who was responsible for bringing the French into Italy. In the ten years of his regency, Lodovico Sforza had made Milan one of the most powerful, prosperous, peaceful, and brilliant states in the peninsula, and he had accomplished this result by sheer diplomacy. The vast fertile Lombard plain—the granary of Italy—groaning with harvests and teeming with wealthy towns, lay open on all sides to invasion; it was a tempting prize to its neighbours; but he had mollified or outwitted them all. With France he had concluded an alliance; he had placed his niece on the imperial throne; Venice he had checked; the backbone of the peninsula he controlled through his alliance with Ferrara, Florence, and Naples; while, with the accession of Alexander VI to the Papacy, his brother, Cardinal Ascanio, assured his ascendancy in Rome. But he was a constant prey to apprehension. His power rested on a network of diplomatic engagements, unsupported by military strength. During a conflict with Venice, the Adriatic Republic had incited Louis of Orleans to press the claims which he inherited from his mother, Valentina Visconti, to the Milanese Duchy. The danger passed, but Lodovico was frightened into a blind loyalty to the French, and loyalty was a luxury which he allowed himself with none of his other allies. He was notorious for his perfidy. Unfortunately, he was not true to himself: the statesman in him was constantly betrayed by the man. The wariest of diplomats was an amiable, expansive, candid, and sanguine man, who took a childlike pride in his power and prestige, and in the tangible signs of it. Visitors whom he desired to impress were invariably ushered into the Sala del Tesoro; they rubbed their eyes, he rubbed his hands, they returned home blinded, he remained at home, blind. When the French alliance was signed in Milan, the envoys were shown as usual through that strange shrine where a fabulous fortune glittered, not only behind bars, on shelves, and in chests, but loosely, in reckless profusion, on the floor —mounds of gold so high "that a stag could not leap over them," silver candelabra as tall as a man, vases, salvers, gold plate, in serried rows, and the priceless collections of Sforza gems, each with its mysterious name: the *Marone*, the *Buratto*, the *Balasso*, the *Spigo*, the *Lupo*, the

Sempreviva della Moraglia.[1] They returned to France laden with gifts which they thought poor, and inflamed the cupidity of their countrymen with accounts of his treasure. Wealth, for Lodovico, was not merely power; its primary value was the consideration it excited; and after dazzling everyone else, he dazzled himself.

When the French invasion was first bruited, he made some attempts to discourage it; but gradually his attitude changed. His nephew, Gian Galeazzo Sforza, the heir to the Duchy, was approaching his majority. He was a congenital minor, happy with horses and dogs, and only too willing to leave the burdens of state to his uncle; but he had married a Neapolitan princess, Isabella of Aragon, who resented her subordinate position at the Milanese Court. When the Regent married, she trembled; when his son was christened with ducal honours, she complained to his father and grandfather in Naples. Her royal grandfather, having himself suggested to Lodovico some years before that he might do worse than occupy a throne he administered so well, was not perturbed; but her father, to whom she painted her wrongs in the most pathetic colours, was thoroughly exercised. Lodovico was warned to beware of suspicious characters coming from Naples. His resistance to the French invasion weakened.

It was a day when personalities played a preponderant part in politics. Apprehensive, and quick to resent even a fancied slight, Ludovico Sforza was both alarmed and annoyed by the attitude of the heir to the Neapolitan throne; and his annoyance, if anything, was greater than his alarm. He might yet have kept his head but for other developments. The little rift between Milan and Naples would never have been allowed to widen had Lorenzo de' Medici been living, for he had acted as the needle of the balance in the triple alliance. But he was dead, and Piero . . . was playing football. Moreover, Piero had annoyed the Regent on more than one occasion and, through his Roman relatives the Orsini, seemed to be leaning more and more toward Naples. And so now was the Pope, who was planning to marry his son Giuffredo to Sanchia of Aragon. Lodovico began to feel himself isolated in Italy. He took the final step and threw himself heart and soul into promoting the French invasion. When the old King of Naples warned him of the danger he was preparing for himself, "The time will come," he replied, "when all Italy will turn to me and pray to be delivered from the coming evils." The exchange of these civilities was interrupted only for a moment by the

---

[1] The *Chestnut*, the *Bombasine*, the *Balass Ruby*, the *Ear of Grain*, the *Wolf*, the *Ever-Quick Mulberry*.

death of the old King; his successor continued the conversation. "Tell Signor Lodovico," he said to the Milanese ambassador, "that he will be the first to rue the day when the French set foot in Italy."

From other quarters as well came warnings. The Pope addressed a bull to Charles VIII forbidding him at the peril of his soul to cross the Alps; and Cardinal Ascanio, seeing his influence at the Vatican waning, urged his brother to be careful. Lodovico had no secrets from the Cardinal. "There would be great difficulty in preventing the French from coming," he explained. "Moreover, I must admit that I consider their coming necessary, not that I desire it or seek the ruin of King Alfonso of Naples, to whom I am well disposed, as you soon will see, but I wish to *bring him down a peg,* so that the immoderate greatness to which we have raised him will not lead him to forget, as his father once forgot, that he must bear himself as an equal and not as a superior to his colleagues in Italy and, more particularly, toward us. To accomplish this, he must be occupied with his own affairs, if we are to prevent him from interfering with those of others. It is essential, therefore, that the French make a descent into Italy." He added, however: "That the results of their invasion may not exceed our requirements, and culminate in the complete ruin of the King of Naples, I have undertaken what you already know, namely, that the King of the Romans should cross the Alps at the same time. It will thus be possible to fix a limit to the progress of the French." There was something about Lodovico—something more than the supple grace of his corpulent body, the satisfied fullness of his jowls, the impenetrable lucidity of his level, lashless eyes—that was irresistibly suggestive of a sleek, overfed cat. The tame domestic prowler was now engaged, with feline self-confidence, in spiriting chestnuts from a fire which gave every promise of blazing up into a general conflagration. But what of that? There was always one barbarian to offset another; there was always his Tesoro; and there was a royal satisfaction in hiring crowned heads and upsetting the continent to snub the King of Naples.

But, above all, he was helpless. The Florentine ambassador joined the patriotic chorus, protesting in the name of Italy. "Italy?" said Lodovico—and the reply was historic—"You tell me of Italy; but I have never seen it. No one gives a thought to my affairs; I must provide for them myself in one way or another." As for his personal risk, he admitted it; but the greatest danger was "to be held of no account." Then, with ironic gravity, he consulted the Florentine. "Speak, speak," he said.

"What do our Florentine friends propose? Do not be angry: help me to think." The Florentine thought along the same lines as himself. "Attend to your own affairs," he wrote to Piero de' Medici. "Do you think Lodovico does not realize the danger to which he is exposing himself and others? Your advice will only make him more obstinate." From France the Florentine ambassador sent the same advice to the confused Medici. "The best thing is to cast anchor between Milan and Naples: let those that have bred the louse scratch it. . . . To prevent the invasion you would have to spend more money than Lodovico; the enterprise, therefore, will proceed. If the King conquers, all Italy will be overrun; if he loses, he will retaliate on our traders in France and above all on the Florentine." They were all of one mind, and no one could see Italy because of the Italians.

Then opposition developed from an unexpected quarter—in France itself. The invasion suddenly became unpopular. Its results were problematical, its expense was enormous, and before it had even started it had already cost heavy sacrifices. To secure the realm in his absence, the King concluded treaties, involving territorial concessions, with Spain and the Empire. He pledged the Crown jewels; he borrowed from Lodovico and a Genoese bank; but still he ran short of money. Struggling desperately to extricate himself from his difficulties, he grew obstinate; he had blundered too deep to retreat, the invasion alone could recoup his losses and restore his prestige; but the nearer it drew the more far-sighted he became; and when the preparations were at last completed, he frankly lost heart and hesitated. Then the Italians at his Court put their shoulders to the wheel. There were the Neapolitan exiles who assured him that Naples would rise to his support; there was that bitter enemy of the Pope, Cardinal Giuliano della Rovere, who urged him to carry his conquering banner to Rome; there was the Florentine Capponi, a disaffected supporter of the Medici, working for Piero's overthrow, who persuaded the King to expel the Florentine traders from France; and finally there was Lodovico with money, flattery, and encouragement. The situation had reversed itself: while the invaders recoiled, the invaded beckoned them on. In August 1494, the avalanche trembled and began to move. Charles borrowed his way through Savoy, disappeared into the Alps, and emerged, early in September, at Asti, where his ally met him and escorted him to the suburbs of Milan. The heat of the season and the sour wines impressed the French unpleasantly, but the King was in high spirits. He kissed the ladies, begged Lodovico's Duchess to dance for him, and bustled about on his weak legs with dispatch. Lodovico was less pleased. His guest obviously distrusted him and was publicly impolite: he was not an Italian. "The Most Christian King," he confided to a friend, "is young and foolish, with little presence of person and still less of mind. At Asti, when I treated important matters with him, his councillors spent their time eating and playing cards in his presence. He is haughty and ill-mannered and more than once, when we were together, he left me alone in the room, like a menial." The invasion had begun.

Swollen by the confluence of so many causes, it advanced like some complex, blundering, uncontrollable force, which absorbed its own authors, and which assumed more and more the featureless and irresistible likeness of Fate. Its full menace was still dimly felt; but the poets and prophets, the creatures of shaping imagination all compact, were the true seismographs of the situation, and their warning tremors sent a long vibration through the uneasy atmosphere and unsettled conditions of the peninsula. To Savonarola it was a providential disaster, and he laboured indefatigably to make it a successful calamity. "Men prosper or fail," said a Florentine statesman, "according as they move with the times." The times were now hurrying him forward with a relentless momentum with which he could barely keep pace. Two years before, in a series of sermons on the Flood, he had begun the construction of an allegorical Ark which he invited the faithful to enter: "Let everyone hasten to enter the Ark of the Lord. Noah invites everyone to enter, the door stands wide; but many will come when the Ark will be closed, and they will repent in vain." Elaborating with arid ingenuity the specifications of faith, these sermons had been admired at the time as oratory or as theology; but now they took on a new and literal reality. The formidable reputation of the French army, the futility of resistance, and a vague premonition of the complications lurking in the event, created a great undertow of popular feeling that reflected his own fatalism; and when he alluded to "a new Cyrus sent to castigate Italy for her sins," men swallowed hard. The French invasion floated him. In that hour of nameless anxiety and leaderless confusion, even a visionary and unearthly guidance was better than none, and the great *preacher for women* now addressed a congregation predominantly composed of men. He resumed his exposition of the Flood. He could not understand, he said, why it had taken him so long to construct the mystic Ark, unless a superior power had reserved him for the critical moment; and he hastened to complete it. At last, in September 1494, when the French reached Milan, he concluded amid scenes of panic excitement. The Duomo was thronged to the doors with a crowd which had been waiting from earliest morning; and as the prophet mounted the pulpit, spread his spectral arms, and launched through the reverberating vaults his diluvial cry, *Lo, I bring the waters upon the earth*, the abysmal alarm of the multitude stunned him himself. The crowd dispersed slowly and "everyone," said an eye-witness, "went his way through the city speechless with terror."

It was something to have created silence at last in a city so heedless and voluble. And now in that strained silence ominous sounds began to be heard, one here, one there, as the unrelieved nervousness of the populace sought an outlet.

The policy of the city toward the French remained undefined. Officially, it was neutral, but Piero de' Medici had neglected to reach, like his neighbours, a formal understanding with the King; and Florence lay directly on his line of march. Early in October Charles reached the frontier and set ahead for a safe-conduct through its territories. Such was the confusion of affairs in Florence that his envoys were put off with a vague answer and left, after five days, in anger. The King swore to sack Florence, crossed the border, exterminated the inhabitants of Fivizzano, and laid siege to the fortress of Pietrasanta. This foretaste of professional warfare shocked Piero de' Medici into action. Hurrying to the French camp, he offered not only the belated safe-conduct but the surrender of the fortresses, a large subsidy, and the occupation of Florence. Amazed at the facility with which he offered more than they had the temerity to ask, the French laughed at him behind his back and sent to Florence to learn whether he had the authority to negotiate. As he emerged from the King's tent, he met Lodovico Sforza returning from Milan, where the sudden death of his nephew and his own coronation had called him. Piero apologized for not welcoming him officially into Florentine territory: he had firmly intended to do so, he said, but he had missed him by taking the wrong road. "One of us certainly missed the right road," replied Lodovico dryly. "Perhaps," he continued, a little in the French fashion, "perhaps it is you who have taken the wrong one."

When the news reached Florence that the entire territory had been pledged to the French, the first sullen murmurs of revolt were heard in the streets. Little knots of malcontents roamed to and fro and gathered on the corners; there were demonstrations; but the popular unrest, lacking a leader, seethed without effect. Restless, aimless, the drifting agitators followed the crowds that swarmed into the Duomo where Savonarola held forth daily. A politician would have envied him that public, and a demagogue would have profited by it; it needed only a spark to fire it; but he had but one end in view and abstained from all political allusions. "Lo, the sword is come, the prophecies are verified, the scourging has begun. Lo, the Lord leads these armies. O Florence, the time of singing and dancing is over: now is the time to weep your sins with torrents of tears. Your sins, O Florence, your sins, O Rome, your sins, O Italy, are the cause of these afflictions. Repent, unite, give alms, and pray! O my people, I have been as a father to you: I have laboured all the time of my life to make you know the truth of faith and the good life, and I have had nothing but tribulations, insults, and scorn, for my pains. Give me good works, at least, for my reward. O my people, what have I ever desired but to see you united and saved? Repent: the Kingdom of Heaven is at hand." Day after day, he preached submission and concord indefatigably; it required all his energy to control the brewing storm he had raised; he struggled with the determination of despair, his strength gave way, he collapsed; but he succeeded. In that pregnant silence his voice prevailed.

The agitation, rising from the streets to the Duomo and from the Duomo to the Palace, found its orderly outlet there. At a council of prominent citizens, Piero Capponi voiced the general feeling: "Piero de' Medici is no longer capable of ruling; the Republic must provide for itself; it is time to be done with this government of children." He proposed that measures should be taken, that soldiers be recruited in the country and concealed in the cloisters, that an embassy be sent to the French King to treat for terms, and that, if it met Piero de' Medici, it should refuse to recognize him. The revolution had begun. A commission was immediately formed, and Capponi nominated its first member. "Do not neglect to send with the other ambassadors Father Girolamo Savonarola, for he has the love of the people." When the invitation was conveyed to the Prior, he begged time to consider. A new path was opening whose end he could not discern; for the first time his eloquence was facing the acid test of reality; but he could not conscientiously refuse a mission of mercy; and, after consulting his flock, he accepted. In his farewell sermon he reiterated his conciliatory appeals: "The Lord has heard your prayers. He has brought about a great revolution peaceably. He alone, when everyone else abandoned it, has come to the aid of the city. Wait, and you will see the disasters which will follow in others. Persevere, O people of Florence, in good works, persevere in peace. If you wish the Lord to persevere in mercy, be merciful to your brothers, your friends, your enemies; otherwise you will feel the scourges which are preparing for the rest of Italy. *Misericordiam volo*, saith the Lord. Woe to him who breaks His commandments!" Imperious, as on Sinai, he stood surveying, with upraised hand, the perennial spectre: now in reality the lawlessness and brutality of life were quelled by his word and his will; and descending with the firm tread of authority, he set forth for the French camp.

Meanwhile, Piero de' Medici, learning of these developments, sent his brother-in-law to raise recruits in the country, and posted back to Florence to make his peace with the populace. He found the city quiet, and its calm deceived him. He retired in good spirits, distributing wine and sweetmeats to the curious who gathered about his door. From a window he made a reassuring oration and scattered confetti; but the confetti fell like funereal flowers and lay soiling underfoot as the bystanders slowly dispersed. Toward evening of the following day—it was a Sunday and he had slept well—being apprised of the true state of affairs and the revolt of the Government, he sallied forth with his followers to force his way into the Communal Palace and proclaim a dictatorship; but the door was slammed in his face and he found himself surrounded by a silent crowd which jostled him about, flocking at his heels and flicking him with their bonnets. He wheeled and wheeled, irresolute, flushed, half-drew his sword, and suddenly made off, followed by a shower of stones and the hoots of a rabble of children. An hour later, he returned to the attack; but the temper of the city had rapidly changed. The streets leading to the Piazza were alive; from afar he heard, through a distant roar, the obsolete Republican cry, *Popolo e Libertà!* and, punctuating it, the sluggish pulse of the communal bell, booming in a lugubrious undertone through the November dusk. The past, the present, the future blurred in his brain. He was twenty-three and the centuries were echoing about him; he fell back. While he galloped away in search of reinforcements, his brother the Cardinal, who was then in Florence, ventured forth in pursuit of support. In the Corso a running mob overtook and hurried him into the Piazza where he was badly manhandled and only made his escape by stammering the popular cry, *Popolo e Libertà!* In a window of the Medici Palace the passersby caught a subsequent glimpse of him, kneeling with upraised hands and ears pink with prayer; he was not further molested, being regarded as "a good lad." A little later, he appeared in San Marco, deposited his valuables, borrowed a Dominican robe, and slipped off on the road to Rome. In the meantime, Piero was clattering through the popular quarters, scattering gold in a vain attempt to rally his followers; but he met only echoes and scurrying cats and squabbling beggars as he rode. Panic seized him; he made for the Porta San Gallo where his brother Giuliano and his brother-in-law Fabrizio Orsini were waiting with troops; a hurried confabulation ensued; then, bending to the necks of their horses, the whole troop vanished along the road to Bologna.

The revolution was over. In three hours the work of three generations of Medici had crumbled. It was, however, a final tribute to their popularity that the revolution was bloodless: an event unprecedented in Florentine annals. In large part this was due to the Friar's influence; but no less was it the work of the French. For the past fortnight the vanguard had been pouring into Florence, chalking up its quarters and submerging the city. This steady infiltration exercised a restraining influence on the crowd; and the result was doubly fortunate. During the tumult on that Sunday afternoon, the French were tempted to interfere and a few went so far as to raise the Medici cry, but they were warned not to meddle and they had the good sense to obey. Wandering through the narrow streets of Florence, they realized the dangers of fighting in those labyrinths of fortified alleys. Two days later, on a rumour of Piero's return, armed men sprang up on all sides and the French were informed that the city could raise 50,000 at the drop of a hat. Their behaviour was henceforth exemplary: they paid for their keep and not even the women were molested. The infant liberty of Florence, born under the very hoof of the invader, not only escaped the heel but delivered its parent.

But freedom had its price. That multiplying cry, *Popolo e Libertà!*, had already travelled far; it had drifted down the river and roused Pisa, which had lain for a hundred years under the Florentine yoke, and where Charles was now resting. Under cover of the French, Pisa revolted and appealed to the King to accept the title of Protector of its liberties. Liberty was a new word to him, he did not understand it; but the meaning dawned on him when a mob tore down the Florentine Marzocco and replaced it with a figure of himself with sword uplifted as its champion. He was by nature amiable and obliging; and he merely stared and dropped his jaw when his councillors protested that, as Pisa was Florentine territory and he had now been received there as a guest of the Republic, it was improper, from the point of view of the *droits des gens*, to promote the revolt of its subjects. The freedom of Pisa was, in fact, a heavy handicap to the freedom of Florence; for Pisa was its lungs on the sea, the necessary outlet for its maritime trade, and for years its future policy was determined by this untimely revolt. For the moment, it suffered the loss in grim silence; there were other and more pressing problems to negotiate. The Florentine fortresses had all been consigned to the French, and the King refused to discuss terms until he reached "the great city." He dismissed the commissioners with a curtness for which his unfamiliarity with the language was his only excuse and repeated in his French Italian that everything should be settled *dentro alla gran villa . . . dentro alla gran villa.*

Under these circumstances, the commissioners sent to treat with him could only attempt to predispose him favourably toward Florence; and they appealed to Savonarola. The Friar spoke French and he alone seemed to admire the King. Charles was more than a man to him: he was a godsend. He was the providential answer to all his prayers, the fulfilment of his prophecies, the realization of his lifelong dreams; he was that prodigy which the centuries in their slow revolutions sometimes evolve—a sovereign in whom Might and Right were for the nonce united. Or if he was not, it was for him to make him so. There was an affinity between them, and it was for him to reveal it. Magnifying him in imagination, the Friar transformed him into his own image and invested him with his own mission. The interview was, therefore, a monologue. When the tremendous moment came and the reality took shape in a gnome of a man reeking of perfume, the Friar raised an admonishing hand. "Most Christian King," he said in the low voice he reserved for his intimates, "you are an instrument in the hands of the Lord, who sends you to relieve the afflictions of Italy, as I have for years foretold, and to reform the Church, which lies prostrate in the dust. But if you are not just and merciful, if you fail to respect Florence, its women, its citizens, and its freedom, if you forget the mission God gives you, He will choose another to fulfil it, He will harden His hand and chastise you with terrible afflictions. These things I say to you from the Lord," he concluded respectfully. The King listened, dropped his jaw, and dismissed the Friar without committing himself: preserving in his impenetrability at least the first attribute of Fate.

A week after the revolution, Charles made his formal entrance into Florence, lance on thigh, in the traditional attitude of a conqueror. The crowds which had been waiting all day were deeply impressed by his legions, tramping by interminably with their swinging gait, their parti-coloured uniforms, their rigid discipline, and their great stature, for—

midable, unfamiliar, impersonal, irresistible, like those lumbering trains of mobile artillery which preceded and followed them; the spectacle overpowered them; and when, toward evening, in the autumnal dusk which multiplied their numbers, the King finally appeared at the gate which had been dismantled to admit him, expectation rose to a tremendous pitch. His progress was slow, halted by the addresses of municipal orators and the surging congestion in the dark thoroughfares; he was two hours in reaching the Duomo. There was time to inspect him. Mounted, he made a brave figure. In the November dusk, astride a black stallion, steadying his lance, and smiling vacantly through a slow drizzle of rain, he passed among the multitude like a figure on a float; but when he dismounted at the Duomo and stood, alone, as on a public stage, in front of the elaborate tabernacle and in the light of the flares, his puny figure was a revelation. The impressionable crowd took him to its heart with friendly huzzas, and he conquered Florence by his insignificance. Overnight the apprehension of years turned to carnival ribaldry; floats filled the streets, stalking giants paraded his passage, the obscene squeal of the bagpipes serenaded his sleep; and the prediction of Capponi was verified—"when once the Italians rub noses with the French, they will fear them less."

Then public opinion veered once more. When the celebrations subsided and he sat down to talk terms, his popularity capsized. He demanded not only a large indemnity and the occupation of Pisa and the fortresses until his return—the terms which Piero had offered and he had accepted—but the restoration of the Medici. A deadlock ensued; he had not yet fathomed the workings of that foreign word, Liberty. With every day the tension grew. There were clashes, at night, in blind alleys; there was talk of another Sicilian Vespers. Few ventured out after *Ave Maria*, and lights burned in the windows till midnight. "Everyone was so discouraged and intimidated," wrote a diarist, "that when we saw a man carrying stones or gravel, we went wild and struck out." The nervousness was mutual. For any reason or none, the city bolted its doors and the French fled to the bridges under a shower of stones. The King was apprehensive; when he appeared on the streets under heavy escort he shifted his direction continually and firmly refused to enter any building or enclosure. At this juncture, Savonarola again sought him out, urged him to remember his mission, not to tempt Providence, and to proceed to Rome. The Government also made a strong stand. In an interview which rapidly developed into an altercation, the King broke off the discussion, crying: "We will sound out our trumpets." Piero Capponi remained cool. "And we will sound out our bells," he replied; whereupon the King changed his tone. No more was said of the Medici, and his other terms were accepted. At a solemn Mass in the Duomo he accepted the title of Protector of Florentine liberties; and three days later he left the Medici Palace, which had been carefully looted to the cellar. Amid crowds of sullen spectators, the Flood oozed out of Florence, and the rooks flew southward.

7

When Savonarola first came to Florence, he was rejected as a foreigner; when he was accepted, it was still as a foreigner, alien in eloquence, in habits, in origin; and despite all his subsequent triumphs, a foreigner he had remained, the famous Fra Girolamo of Ferrara. But the invasion and the revolution naturalized him. The conspicuous patriotic part which he had played through that critical fortnight was publicly recognized, and the Government now invited him to collaborate in its reorganization. To collaborate—he could no more refuse such a call than he could decline his mission of mercy to the French King. It was a question of practical Christianity, and if his faith was not serviceable, what was its value? The Flood which had floated him had left, in subsiding, a vast and fallow field for him to cultivate. A new world was opening, a new Heaven and a new Earth, washed clean and impressionable, and in that virgin soil the first fruitful influence would have an incalculable consequence for good or evil. Yet the responsibility was overwhelming. He was fitted for it neither by training nor temperament; it meant the sacrifice of his cloistered freedom and peace, it meant a life of struggle and controversy, of personal peril even—for the politics of the period were a life-and-death matter—and a career of questionable propriety for a man of his cloth; it might jeopardize his spiritual authority, it was certain to be fraught with dangerous consequences. . . . But the obstacles only made his duty undeniable. And whatever hesitations he felt were finally dispelled by the form in which the appeal was made. He was urged to intervene as a mediator, to create confidence in the new Government and to lend the force of his eloquence to the fusion of the discordant elements in the city.

For the dangers of reconstruction were hardly less critical than those of revolution. At first it was hoped that the Republic, having sloughed off the Medici, would continue to function automatically; the machinery was intact; but it was soon seen to be rusty and warped by the manipulation of the Medici; it was in need of radical repair. In sixty years of despotism the old generation of practised politicians had died out, and the new were inexperienced and confused. To add to their difficulties, the Pisan revolt had been followed by that of Montepulciano and Arezzo; it was imperative to raise troops, to find money for the indemnity, to deal promptly and energetically with pressing problems on all sides; but the leaders of the revolution were lost in administrative disputes, and the popular unrest was reviving. The new constitution had been placed in the hands of experts—jurists and political theorists—where it gathered nothing but academic debates and legal complexities. Under pressure a charter was finally drafted, modelled on the Venetian constitution and modified to meet the democratic demands of Florence; but in working out its detail and adjusting its balance of powers, a deadlock ensued between the supporters of the Popular Party and the partisans of an oligarchical Republic. Meanwhile, as the people grew restless, the danger of an outbreak increased and with it a fear that the Medici would profit by it. Amid distress and disorder, inexperience, partisanship, and technical delays, it was felt that something yet more radical was needed —a leader whose disinterested influence could rally all classes and rise above them, a man whose passion for the common welfare could kindle that burning conviction and sweeping enthusiasm without which no movement can succeed, and who could be trusted to use that power prudently and without personal ambition, in a word, a political eunuch, a public-spirited foreigner; and at that moment the one man in Florence who met those requirements was Savonarola.

The suction of circumstances and the draught of his conscience both drew him into public life. He rose to it. In his first sermons he showed his prudence and his practical instinct, pleading for the revival of normal life and the relief of poverty and unemployment. "Give over pomps and vanities," he said, "sell your superfluities and relieve the poor. Citizens, collect alms in all the churches for the poor of the town and the country. Give them, this year at least, the subsidies of the University of Pisa; and if that will not suffice, let us seize the vessels and ornaments of the churches, and I shall be the first to contribute. But above all open the shops and give work to this people that stands idle in the streets." And he revealed his evangelical radicalism, building a political springsong on the Biblical canticle: *Sing a new hymn to the Lord:* "The Lord bids you renew everything and destroy the past; nothing must remain of our bad laws, our bad habits, our bad government. . . . This is a time when words must yield to facts, and vain ceremonies to true feelings. The Lord has said: I was anhungered, and ye gave me meat; I was naked, and ye clothed me. He did not say: Ye have built me a beautiful church or a fine convent. He desires only labours of love; love must renew all things." To feel truly: that was his whole principle and his whole genius, and his immense longing to express that power left him speechless, thrilling, a public lover. "O Florence," he cried, "I cannot tell you all that I feel in me. . . . If I could tell you, you would see a vessel new and sealed, full of fermenting must, that cannot issue forth!"

His programme was simple: it was the Decalogue. "O my people, you know that I have never wanted to intervene in matters of state: do you think I would do so now, if I did not see that it was necessary for the health of your souls? . . . Your reform must begin with the things of the spirit, which are above the material, of which they are the rule and the life; and your temporal good must serve your moral and religious welfare, on which it depends. And if you have heard say that *states are not ruled by paternosters*, remember that this is the rule of tyrants, of the enemies of God and the commonweal, the rule for oppressing and not for raising and liberating the city. If you desire a good government, you must restore it to God. Surely, I should not meddle in state matters, if this were not so. When, then, you have purged your souls, corrected your intentions, and condemned gaming, lechery, and blasphemy, turn to your government and make a first draft, leaving the details and corrections till later. And the first draft or model or substance should be this: that no man should receive any benefit except from the community, which alone must create the magistrates and approve the laws. The form best adapted to this city is that of a Grand Council, after the Venetian manner. I propose, therefore, that the people assemble under the sixteen Gonfalonieri and that each ward choose a form; of the sixteen thus obtained, the Gonfalonieri shall select four and submit them to the Signoria which, after solemn prayer, shall choose the best. And you may be sure that the form thus chosen by the people will come from God. I believe it will be the Venetian form, which you need not be ashamed to imitate, as they too had it from the Lord, from whom all good things come. You see that, ever since they have had their government in Venice, there have been no sects or dissension of any sort there; so that we must believe it is willed by God."

With the Friar to favour, the people to propose, the ward-leaders to select, the city fathers to elect, and God to ratify, the Venetian constitution was adopted, and the political ability of Savonarola was recognized with astonishment. "At this time," wrote the historian Nardi, "he was thought to know very little of active life and to reduce everything to morals and even more to true Christian philosophy. As for his doctrine, if it had been heeded, it would undoubtedly have disposed the minds of our citizens to receive every form of good and holy government. The things which he preached and supported over and over were, for the most part, finally enacted and accomplished, after much difficulty and opposition." Of all his difficulties the greatest was that of maintaining, however, the political neutrality which was his chief asset. The constitution was voted in the form he favoured, as a broad democratic charter; and from that moment, though he strove to preserve his non-partisan position, he was associated in the public mind with the Popular Party.

With each new problem the transformation of the recluse into an active political leader grew more marked: it was not so much a transformation as an emergence, the revelation of unsuspected aptitudes. He showed a surprising familiarity with both political theories and political conditions and, though he reasoned from general principles, he was not a doctrinaire. Of the three types of government, the monarchical, the oligarchical, and the democratic, the one to which he was drawn in theory was the first, because it reflected the constitution of the universe, of which God was the supreme ruler, and the strivings of Nature in all things for unity. A benevolent despotism was the best of all governments; but absolute power corrupts. "These principles," he concluded, "must be adapted to the nature of the people to which they are applied. Among the peoples of the North, where there is much force and little wit, and among those of the South, where on the contrary there is much wit and little force, the government of one man may sometimes be excellent. But in Italy, and above all in Florence, where force and intellect abound, where the minds are subtle and the spirits restless, the government of one man can only produce tyranny." The same disadvantages applied to an oligarchy, and hence "the only government which is suited to you is the civil and universal rule." These ideas were not original with himself—they were those of St. Thomas

Aquinas and the political theorists of the time—but they acquired a new meaning by the development he gave them. His political ideas derived from his religious principles, and freedom and self-determination were the indispensable prerequisites of the good life; and that idea was strictly original with himself. His moral fervour was his strength. Though he came from the convent, he brought to the world the qualities required of a leader in that crisis—the insight of detachment, the sense of fundamentals, the capacity for seeing and stating issues on broad simple lines, a selfless and unquestioned ardour for the common good, and his great genius for "feeling truly." How far honesty, conviction, common sense, and disinterestedness could carry him through the mazes of practical politics appeared as he passed from problem to problem with ever-increasing success.

The first reform which came before the new Government was that of the tax-system. When the demagogues and extremists of the Popular Party proposed the complete exemption from taxation of the *popolo minuto*, he intervened promptly. "Citizens," he said to a congregation four thousand strong, "I expect you to stand firm and love and help your Commune. The son is under such obligation to the father that he can never repay him. I say to you:—The Commune is your father, and everyone is bound to aid it.—And if you say: I have no profit in aiding it, remember that you cannot say so, for it protects your family, your children, and your goods. You should go to it and say:—Here are fifty florins, here are a hundred, a thousand. . . ." And his paternal influence was responsible for a fiscal reform which, abolishing all public loans and arbitrary levies, substituted, for the first time in Florence and in Italy, a regular and general ten per cent trade tax which endured until modern times.

This measure was followed by two others of no less consequence. The first was a general amnesty to the supporters of the late regime, a measure of pacification which he preached tirelessly, and to which the Government responded in solemn antiphony: "The Magnificent Signori and Gonfalonieri ordain a general peace and that all offences and penalties to which the supporters of the late Government are liable be remitted." The next was a judicial reform in which he struck his first snag. To correct the abuses of criminal and political justice, it was proposed to grant the accused a faculty of appeal to the Grand Council. On the necessity of some such measure all parties were agreed; but the crux of the question was whether the appeal should be lodged with the Upper or the Lower House of the Grand Council. Here the Oligarchical and the Popular Parties split and, to the amazement of the latter, Savonarola refused to support them. He perceived the danger of deciding such appeals in the Lower House with its large numbers and popular passions and favoured, in this case, the restricted jurisdiction of the Upper Chamber. He won no thanks from either side. The Oligarchical Party or, as they were nicknamed, the *Arrabbiati*, saw their opportunity. At their instigation a preacher attacked him with his own cry of *Liberty*; at the same time they swung over to the Populars and pushed through the bill in its rash form as an appeal to the Lower House. The stroke was doubly clever: it discredited him with his own party and left him the odium of whatever disorders the measure might breed for initiating it. Against such strategy he was powerless; and when he realized how astutely he had been outplayed, a note of violence and acrimony was heard for the first time in his sermons.

The developments of the next few months deepened his bitterness. His work had barely begun and already he found himself surrounded and circumvented by covert opposition with which he could not cope and which distorted his purposes and disfigured his credit. It was only waiting for his first mistake to attack him openly, and it soon found it. While the internal reform of the Republic was proceeding with brilliant success and rapidity, its external situation was disheartening. A desultory campaign was waged against Pisa, but the Government lacked the resources to pursue it effectively and what it could not accomplish by arms it attempted to achieve by diplomacy. Embassies were sent to the French King, who had now occupied Naples, reminding him of his pledge to restore Pisa when he had reached his objective; but his replies were evasive. Savonarola, however, guaranteed his good faith. In one of his sermons the Friar went so far as to say that he held Pisa in the hollow of his hand. The phrase was rash, and the Arrabbiati made capital of it, turning it into doggerel and reviving it on every new evasion of the King. But a far more serious consequence than his personal mortification grew out of this situation.

In March 1495—four months after the passage of the French through Florence—Charles was forced out of Naples by a revolt of the Barons. This was the moment for which Lodovico Sforza had been waiting. He was now ready to reverse himself, redeem the patriotic odium he had incurred, and emerge as the saviour of Italy; and to this end he had formed a League, embracing Venice, Rome, and Milan, the Emperor, and the King of Spain, for the purpose of cutting off the retreat of the French and crushing them when they returned north. Florence was invited to join it and complete the national confederation. Caught between two camps, it faced a crucial dilemma. The Arrabbiati favoured the League, but the Government was dominated by the Populars or, as they now became known, the *Frateschi*. The danger of the French, who were hurrying north, wasting the country, was immediate; that of antagonizing the Allies, remote; and Florence elected to remain neutral. The Arrabbiati denounced the Frateschi and focused the resentment of the League on Savonarola as their champion. As the French approached, it was learned that Piero de' Medici was in their camp. A panic ensued; the city rose; barricades were thrown up, the houses were provisioned and fortified; and preparations were made to resist another occupation at all costs. Savonarola was attacked on the street and was forced to accept the protection of an armed escort. There was only one way to retrieve the situation: he hurried to the French camp and persuaded the King to avoid Florence. On the all-important question of Pisa he obtained no satisfaction; but in the relief of an immediate danger averted, he was received on his return with a gratitude which amounted, among his followers, to veneration.

But the course of events was flowing with a terrible swiftness, and the remote peril soon made itself felt. The armies of the League, commanded by Francesco Gonzaga, the Marquis of Mantua, were awaiting the French at Fornovo on the confines of the Lombard plain. They had the advantage of numbers, freshness, and strategic position. Fornovo, in the valley of the Taro, commanded the Apennine pass through which the enemy, weary, depleted, ill-fed, and discouraged, was toiling. When the vanguard debouched, it was immediately raided by a body of Stradiots—the savage, head-hunting Albanian cavalry—who had been promised a gold coin and a kiss from the lips of their commander for every French head. The vanguard fell back, waiting for the main body with the King and the baggage-train to come up. When these arrived, they realized their desperate situation. Below them lay the long narrow valley of the Taro, where the road skirted the stream, a thin osier-lined stream, beyond which spread in a vast hemicycle the pavilions of the League. Confidence reigned in the Confederate camp: the breeze in the osiers was already the invisible footfall of victory and their sentinel ripple was as restless and alert as the lances lurking behind them. "*Illustrissima conjunx amatissima,*" the Marquis wrote to his wife, "the enemy is incredibly terrified," and he addressed his letter from the "victorious camp of the Very Holy and Serene League." He acted chivalrously, giving the enemy time to deploy and even entertaining the proposal which Charles sent to parley. While he did so, the French were quietly pushing along the road. When the advance column was almost within reach of the plain, he launched the attack. In the furious *mêlée* which followed, Charles, fighting vigorously, narrowly escaped capture, and the centre which he commanded would undoubtedly have been surrounded had not the Italian mercenaries stumbled into the baggage-train which they paused to plunder. Thanks to this respite night fell on an unsettled field. On the following morning Charles resumed negotiations; they were protracted during the day; another night passed; and when the Italians returned at daybreak, they found the French gone.

The issue of that battle was long after disputed in words. The French had made good their escape, but the Italians held the field and the booty, and the Venetians who had paid for the mercenaries celebrated the victory clamorously . . . "following their immemorial custom," said one commentator, "which ever was, is, and will be, to light bonfires and ring bells when they receive bad news and suffer reverses." A medal was coined in honour of Francesco Gonzaga with the inscription, *Ob Restitutem Italiae Libertatem*. When the clamour subsided, however, a more sober view of the victory prevailed. Charles had departed, swearing to return the following year to avenge his arms, seize Milan, and recover Naples. And now the real, the irreparable damage of the invasion was realized. Its facility and the immense booty which the French had garnered and lost made its repetition a foregone conclusion. On the field of Fornovo Italy had united, but it was the spasmodic contraction of a crisis; it was imperative to perpetuate the League; and in this purpose Venice, the Pope, and Lodovico Sforza drew together. The one state conspicuous by its absence and the importance of its central position in the peninsula was Florence; and concerted pressure was put upon it to join the patriotic confederacy.

The policy of Florence was determined by Pisa. The Government still hoped to recover it through the French, and Savonarola wrote to the King, warning him of a Divine Visitation, if he refused to keep faith. But the King was in France, counting his losses. Realizing the importance of Pisa, the Allies made it alternately a bait and a goad; they supplied it with subsidies and soldiers, reversed their strategy, and offered their assistance to Florence to subdue it; but their pressure and their persuasion met with nothing but rebuff and evasion from the Government. Florence would have nothing to do with the League, at least not as long as the Frateschi remained in power. Though Savonarola was not directly responsible for this policy, he was in sympathy with it. If he lacked the foresight of a statesman, it was because his vision was at once too wide and too narrow. Isolation was the best safeguard for his purpose—to re-create the Republic in the image of the City of God —and foreign commitments were certain to prove a distracting and dangerous influence at this critical period when its reform and reorganization had only begun. Detachment and hostility served to unite it; a lasting union, as he repeated incessantly, could only be a moral union, and to kindle and foster it he needed time and a small compact fold. Only then could the Republic achieve the mission he conceived for it. "You, my people," he promised the faithful, "will begin the reform of all Italy and spread your wings in the world, to bring the reform to all peoples. Remember that the Lord has given evident signs that He means to renew all things, and that you are the people chosen to commence this great enterprise, provided you observe the commandments of Him Who calls and invites you to return to the spiritual life." And why should not the Chosen People stand, as he stood, alone against the world?

But, though he was not responsible for the isolation of Florence, he bore the brunt of that policy. The Arrabbiati, more than ever determined to force Florence into the League, had another motive now for attempting to remove him. While their taunting song flew through the streets—

> In the pulpit you said, to feed
> Noble and people and patrician:
> "Pisa I hold in my hand."—Indeed?

> Ask pardon of all men, and mind:
> Feed Florence no longer on wind . . .

they communicated with Milan, and through Cardinal Sforza made representations to the Pope. The dangerous influence of the Friar was dwelt on; and particular stress was laid on the disturbing effects of his prophetic claims. Alexander, easy-going as he was, was known to take a serious view of stigmatics, hysterics, prophets, and all those who trespassed on the supernatural.

Meanwhile Savonarola had again returned to the reconstruction of the Republic. A bill was drafted under his dictation for the establishment of a *Monte di Pietà*, which undercut the Jews and put an end to "the pestiferous affliction and cankerous worm of usury, endured for sixty years in Florence, of the perfidious and God-hating Hebraic sect." But suddenly everything had to be laid aside in favour of a far more pressing measure: the abolition of the popular *parlamenti*. These assemblies of the people, summoned in the Piazza, in an emergency, to ratify by acclaim any innovation put before them, were an obsolete survival of the primitive life of Florence, and like all dead matter in a living organism, they were a source of disease and danger to the body politic. Nominally, they appealed to the popular will and flattered it with an appearance of freedom; but in practice they merely lent a show of legality to any violent change in the constitution or policies of the Government and, as such, were a supple instrument of tyranny. The Medici had employed them; and Piero, when he attempted to push into the Palace and proclaim a dictatorship, had proposed to summon a *parlamento*. Piero, it was now learned, was recruiting support among the Allies for an expedition to reinstate him in Florence. Savonarola, accordingly, summoned all his strength to suppress an institution, outworn and toxic, of which the enemies of the Republic could so easily take advantage, and which might at any moment undermine all that had been so laboriously accomplished. And then his strength failed him. The last six months, with their fever of unfamiliar activity, their taxing problems, their harassing enmities, their constant nervous strain, had told on a constitution already enfeebled by years of mortification; his gastritis broke out and the physicians insisted on rest. The word lashed him. Rest? At such a moment? With everything to do? He dared not rest; he could not afford to be sick. But to the advice of the physicians was now added an unanswerable argument—a Papal Brief, urging not only rest but a complete change of environment. "Beloved son," the Pope wrote, "greetings and Apostolic benedictions! We hear that among all who labour in the vineyards of the Lord, you toil with most zeal: for which we rejoice and give thanks to Almighty God. We hear likewise that you claim that your predictions of the future come not from you but from God; we desire, therefore, as it is our Pastoral duty, to converse with you, that being better informed through you of the will of God, we may fulfil it. We charge you, therefore, by virtue of holy obedience, to come to us with all speed, and we shall welcome you with love and charity." The muffling hand of Rome had fallen.

He met it adroitly, pitting his illness against his obedience, and doing what every public man in Italy did in a difficult moment. He temporized. In a reply as bland as the Brief, he dwelt on his grave sickness, which threatened his life and which obliged him to suspend study and preaching, and added: "Moreover, I am held to obey the benevolent intention rather than the literal word. The Lord having spared this city through me a great effusion of blood and converted it to good and holy laws, there are many enemies both within and without who, having hoped to reduce her to servitude and failed, desire my blood and have more than once attempted my life with poison and steel. I could not move without manifest danger, and even in the city I dare not walk in the street without an armed escort. Furthermore, this new reform which the Lord has been pleased to introduce through me into the city has as yet no firm roots and is in evident peril without constant support; my departure, therefore, in the opinion of all good and wise citizens, would be of grave detriment to the city, while it would be of little benefit in Rome. I cannot suppose that my superior desires the ruin of an entire city; I trust, therefore, that Your Holiness will kindly admit this delay, in order that we may bring to perfection this reform begun by the will of the Lord, for the advantage of which, I am certain, He has brought forth these impediments to my departure."

Having taken his illness as a pretext, he could deny it no longer; but, before it sealed his lips, he rallied all his energies to deal the *parlamenti* a death-blow. In the violence of his attack the strain which had told on his body betrayed itself at last in his spirit. Surrounded by unseen enemies and insidious forces, once more as in the days of obscurity, he felt himself isolated in the pulpit; and once more he summoned all his resources of eloquence, despair, and righteous wrath, to master his public. Beginning with terrible fulminations against unnatural vice—"Are ye wiser than God? I tell you, the Almighty wants justice: you must seize one of these and bring him here and say, this man merits death"—he swept on over the whole range of his reforms, riveting each with tremendous blows of breathless objurgation, and rising at last with Mosaic vehemence to blast the parliaments: "I have been thinking of these parliaments of yours, which are nothing but a means of destruction and must be abolished. Forward, my people! Are you not master now? You are. Forbid these parliaments then, unless you want to lose your government. Know that *parliament* means robbing the people of their rule. Remember, and teach it to your children. People! When you hear the bell ringing for parliament, rise and draw your sword and say:— What would you have? Cannot the Council accomplish everything? What law would you make? Can the Council not make it?—And I would have you make a provision that the Signoria swear, on entering office, to summon no parliament; and that anyone revealing an attempt to call a parliament, if he be of the Signori, receive a reward of 30,000 ducats, and all others, 1000. And if one of the Signori be guilty, let him pay with his head, and all others with exile and confiscation of their property. And make the Gonfalonieri swear, on entering office, that when they hear the bell ringing for parliament, they will run to the houses of the Signori and sack them; and each Gonfaloniere who sacks a house of the Signori shall have one fourth of his goods; the rest to go to his companions. *Idem*, that when the Signori want to call parliaments, as soon as they set foot on the platform, that they cease to be considered Signori, and every man may cut them to pieces without sin." Then he took leave of his public. "My people, when I am up here, I am always well; and if I were the same out of the pulpit as in it, I should never complain of my health. But when I come down, I must meet my scores, and it will be some time before I see you again, for I need time to heal. I shall preach again, if I live. I shall be gone a month, I think, unless your prayers call me back sooner. Meanwhile, Fra Domenico will preach; I shall return if I live. But the welfare of Florence will endure in any case. Though the wicked may labour, this seed will bear fruit. God wills it. I could name today the authors of your dangers, but I wish to harm no one, and you will know them when they are punished. I conclude now, I who have preached and laboured so much that I have cut off my life by many years and am short of breath.—Well, Friar, and what reward would you have?" he apostrophized himself with a last, long breath. "Martyrdom, I want martyrdom; I am ready to bear it; I beseech it of you, O Lord, every day, for love of this city."

The ecstasy faded, the fury subsided, the magistrates and the multitude rose, and he descended slowly, groping for his step, a small feeble figure, bowed with exhaustion and cramped with colic.

8

For a few weeks, in the confinement and calm of his sickbed, he found freedom and peace again. Day after day slipped by in blessed uneventfulness; and between him and the world a mist descended. In the ineffable relief, the ethereal apathy, of a light fever everything was obliterated. It was raining, and the only sound that reached him, as he lay on his pallet, was the long rush of the waters on the runnels of the eaves and the stones of the courtyard, washing away pain, washing away strife, washing away memory. The world became a place of silence and greyness and calm; and his being flowed, in a vague somnolence, with the waters. Slowly, as he lay there, his brain lapsed into mystic nonentity; light, very light, in the elation of fever, he hovered on the confines of death, hovered and yearned, buoyantly, toward the only release. Then, in the very void, vague shapes began to form and return like that motto he had known in the death-chamber of the Medici, furling and unfurling its immemorial murmur: *Le Temps revient, Le Temps revient*, and memory revived, and his identity was restored, and he felt and he thought. Another murmur moved in him, the sempiternal sound of his inner soliloquy, and as he recovered, that lonely habit again craved its outlet in the public colloquies he had developed with himself in the pulpit. He began to compose the sermons for his return, and they were saturated with the residue of sickness and solitude.

The pen travelled slowly over the paper. "A youth, leaving his home, embarked on a fishing vessel, and the captain brought him, fishing, into the high seas where the port was lost to sight; and the youth lamented loudly. O Florence! That youth, lamenting, stands here in the pulpit. I was led from my home to the port of religion, when I was three-and-twenty years of age, hoping to find freedom and peace, two things I loved above all. But there I looked upon the waters of the world, and began to win some few souls with my preaching; and finding my delight in it, the Lord set me on a vessel and brought me into the high seas where now I am, and I can see the port no longer. *Undique sunt angustiae*." The anguish of struggle surged up once more. "Before me, I see tribulations and tempests; behind me, I have lost the port and the wind drives me on. On the right are the elect, begging for help; on the left, the demons and the wicked, storming and harassing me; underfoot I see Hell, which I must fear as a man, for without the help of God I shall surely fall into it. O Lord! Lord! Where have you led me? To save some few souls I am come into an unquiet place, and I cannot return to my peace. Why have you made me a man of conflict and discord throughout the world? I was free, and now every man is my master. I see wars and discord coming upon me. O my friends, you at least, O chosen of God, for whom I suffer night and day, show me some mercy. Give me flowers, as the song says, *quia amore langueo*. The flowers are good deeds, and I ask nothing but that you please God and save your souls."

In the sensitiveness of convalescence, as in youth, once more he found himself "languishing for love," and more hopelessly than ever.

POPE ALEXANDER VI, by Pinturicchio
From the portrait in the Borgia Apartment in the Vatican

In six months he had undergone a profound transformation. The campaign which he began with such fervent appeals for conciliation, union, and charity had ended in bitterness, violence, and discord; and it had by no means ended yet. From the temper of Christ he had reverted to the temper of the Old Testament. But how could it be otherwise? A militant Christianity was incompatible with that divine serenity, that perfect comprehension, which action clouded and distorted, and which was possible only in the contemplative life of the cloister. It was his duty to fight and the world could only be fought with its own weapons, by force. The enemy turned not only his hand but his heart against him; and his cry welled up irresistibly: *Quia amore langueo.*

But he could not turn back. He was indispensable to the Republic. The change which had come over the city was as profound as in himself; but there was an underlying element which remained the same. The Republic still required, as in the days of the Medici, a controlling hand, unofficial and invisible, to make it function efficiently; and Lorenzo's ascendancy had, in fact, devolved upon him. It was almost as if the ghost of his old patient adversary were biding his time . . . but no! The spirit was different. Had he not proclaimed *a new head* to protect the liberties of Florence and cried, "This new head is Christ Jesus, He will be your King"? And had not the crowd cried *Viva Cristo?* Nevertheless, the virus of power had entered his veins and in its most insidious form, as an inalienable responsibility. Freedom and peace? Did he desire them indeed? Far gone were the days when he felt so alien to the world that he could only flee it; far gone the days when he was satisfied to dominate it with eloquence; he demanded tangible results now, permanent moral monuments to his being. The personal and passive mysticism of youth had developed into the public and dynamic mysticism of moving masses of men, of identifying himself with them and living, in a common cause, a common life. His very feelings in maturing were hardening and becoming impersonal. It is given to men to be disinterested but not selfless. The passion of moral reform, with its apparent altruism, seems to offer a curious anomaly in human nature; yet is not the desire to shape mankind to one's own ideals the quintessence of self-assertion? How various, subtle, and unconscious are the disguises the ego assumes, and how imperative its appetites! In fighting for his ideals Savonarola was fighting for himself; and if his ego had been less robust, his disinterestedness and his conscience would not have carried him far.

The month was over, his strength was reviving, and he prepared to return to the pulpit when another Brief arrived from Rome, directed to the hostile convent of Santa Croce, and denouncing him in the most extreme terms as "a lover of innovations and a disseminator of false doctrine." In conclusion, San Marco was formally reunited to the Lombard Congregation and the Prior was commanded to abstain from all preaching, public or private. He perceived at once that he had to reckon with powerful and persistent enemies in Rome. "I know the root of these snares," he wrote to a Dominican monk there. "I know that they come from perverse citizens who wish to re-establish tyranny in Florence, and who work hand in hand with certain princes in Italy.... Nevertheless, if I cannot save my conscience otherwise, I am determined to obey, so as not to sin even venially. For the moment, I am remaining quiet and making no precipitate decision, on the advice of the doctors." But prudence and patience and the physicians—he shook them all off, suddenly, as a new emergency recalled him to the pulpit. Piero de' Medici was about to take the field against Florence. "The life of man, O my brothers, is a continual strife upon earth," he reminded his flock, "and the greatest strife is that of the true Christian, since he must fight everything which opposes the spirit. God wills it to give us greater glory in the next world. You must not marvel if our innovations meet with so much opposition, I marvel that they do not meet with more. And because we must fight, we have returned to the field, to reorganize our scattered forces and prepare for a new war. Two things we propose to do: first, to fight, which we shall never cease to do till death; second, to conquer, for the cause of Christ is bound to triumph." However, "he that trusts in divine aid without helping himself," he added, "tempts the Lord."

The emergency passed. The Medici enterprise was abandoned for lack of funds; and at the same time to a letter of protest and appeal which he sent to the Pope the Holy Father replied with an indulgence which proved, if proof were yet necessary, that the inspiration of his previous Briefs had been purely political. "In other letters," Alexander wrote, "we have manifested our displeasure at these Florentine uprisings, of which your sermons have been a prime cause; since, instead of preaching against vice and recommending union, you have predicted the future, a thing which can only breed discord in any peaceful people, and far more in the Florentine, in whom lie so many seeds of ill humour and faction. For these reasons we summoned you to us, but now that, by your letters and the representations of many Cardinals, we feel that you are ready to obey the Roman Church, we rejoice greatly, in the conviction that you have erred rather through overweening simplicity than malice of spirit." No more was said of the Lombard Congregation, but he was categorically enjoined to abstain from preaching until further notice.

His martial spirit subsided, but only to find another outlet. The danger of the Medici had passed; there was no reason to risk further complications with Rome, which would only precipitate the Lombard question and destroy his autonomy; and the prohibition to preach proved, in fact, a pregnant impediment. Political reform was but the basis of moral reform, and he had been too occupied to devote his whole energy to the heart of his problem. Of what value was it to remodel institutions while men remained unchanged? He was free now—free, strong, influential, experienced, alive with power and will, capable at last of coping with the human animal. Among his own followers much had already been accomplished. They crowded the churches, they supported charities, they dressed their women soberly; shopkeepers spent their leisure hours reading the Bible; a number of merchants had voluntarily restored their illicit profits. The Government favoured these practices, which stimulated the *esprit de corps* of the Popular Party. Its decrees echoed not only the spirit but the very phraseology of the Friar. The political value of religious passion was recognized: the conviction, the coherence, the fervour, the capacity of sacrifice, the discipline which it bred, were powerful assets to the party and the Republic. The Arrabbiati, however, baited the new sect with merciless nicknames—*Piagnoni, Collitorti, Stropiccioni, Masticapaternostri*[1]—and reacted against the sanctimonious gloom which threatened to invade the city. They prepared to celebrate the Carnival of 1496 in the traditional manner. What that meant, everyone knew. It meant pandemonium. The abuses of Carnival had long been deplored, the magistrates had repeatedly attempted to suppress them, but in vain: the season was sacred to children, to whom nothing was sacred. The crowning nuisance was "the insane and brutal game of stones," which took a yearly toll of little lives. What others had failed to accomplish Savonarola now undertook with the reform of the children.

A sure instinct inspired him. The perversity of human nature could only be corrected by the most radical strategy, by seizing and shaping

---

[1] *Snivellers, Neck-twisters, Hypocrites, Prayer-munchers.*

the sons of Adam from childhood; but it was in childhood that instinct was strongest; and with singular prudence he attempted, not to eradicate, but to modify it. In this he followed the example of Lorenzo de' Medici, who had sought to civilize the Carnival by diverting the exuberance of the populace into festivals of pageantry and song. The Friar adopted both the principle and the artifices of his predecessor, adapting them to his own purpose. Fra Domenico, who acted as his factotum, enrolled the boys of the city in a military organization pledged to certain duties—to attend church regularly, to avoid public spectacles, such as races, fireworks, pageants, and acrobatic performances, to dress simply, to shun loose company, lewd poets, obscene books, dancing, fencing, and music schools, and to wear their hair short. Each squad elected its leader and four councillors to control him, and the functions of this moral police force were divided respectively among the Peace-Makers, who composed quarrels; the Correctors, who meted out punishments; the Almsmen, who collected charities; the Inquisitors, who spied out scandal; and the Street-Cleaners, who sanitated dark corners. The sense of responsibility appealed strongly to the self-importance of youth, and in their enthusiastic jealousy of their elders the boys cheerfully made the sacrifices required of them. The results of this campaign were evident at Carnival. Nothing had changed and everything was transformed. Still, as before, the boys barred the streets with long poles, begging pennies of the passers-by, but their collections were carried not to the taverns but to the altars which had been erected at the street-corners where swarms of children jingled their alms-basins. Still they danced about the bonfires in the Piazza; still they sang, but, instead of the *Canti Carnascialeschi*, hymns set to the same tunes; still they paraded, but with red crosses and olive boughs; and the game of stones was forgotten. During Lent their activities increased. They attacked the pastry-sellers, upsetting their stalls; they remonstrated with richly dressed women and, when remonstrance failed, stripped them of their veils and their vanities. The first of these incidents produced a vigorous but fruitless protest from the family of the victim. Behind the children was the Friar, and behind the Friar was the Government. Out of this reform grew a domestic crusade. With the zeal of converts and the ardour of minors, recognized and protected by public authority, they spied on and reported the sins of their parents and egged on the servants to do likewise; they patrolled the taverns and the streets and with such effect that at the cry, "Here come the boys of the Friar," dice disappeared and quiet games broke up in a flurry of heels. To protect them from reprisals, officers of the Government were deputed to accompany them.

On Palm Sunday a procession of five thousand children, robed in white, wreathed with olive, and carrying red crosses, followed by the magistrates, the heads of the Guilds, and an enormous crowd, and preceded by a tabernacle representing the entrance of Christ into Jerusalem, wound its way through the streets, amid a long din of recruiting clamour, crying, *Long live Christ our King!* In the Duomo the Friar preached to them; and they brought him, five thousand strong with their faith and their alms, the multitudinous vindication of his own youth.

9

A beginning had been made, but how much more remained to be done! All but everything. His hopes for the future lay in the young. "O Lord, from the mouths of these children will come your true praise. The philosophers praise by natural enlightenment, these by supernatural; the philosophers out of self-love, these from a pure heart; the philosophers with the tongue, these with deeds." But by his very success with them he knew how susceptible they were to influence; and the example of their parents was an influence which would eventually undermine his own, as they matured, unless he reclaimed their elders as completely. But there the fact which seemed to favour impeded him. In grafting religion upon politics, he perceived only too well that he was working at cross-purposes with the public. The Florentine people was essentially political; to partake of public life was the natural goal, the highest felicity, of its sons; and it was the political, not the religious reform to which they responded so passionately. For them the religious movement was a means to an end, as the political was with him; for the moment they met, but their aims were divergent and their fusion was, fundamentally, a basic confusion. The Florentine temperament—caustic, shrewd, cerebral—was not antagonistic to religion, it was indifferent to it, and the new classic culture had deepened its native scepticism. The religious revival, he realized, was a blaze in the wind, fanned by contrary currents, and too hysterical to be lasting. Converts who came to him, swept off their feet by his sermons and longing to renounce the world, were chagrined to find a cool and almost a discouraging reception, and were submitted to a long period of trial and self-searching to determine their fitness for the priesthood. The fatal facility of feeling of the Italian alarmed him; and there were hours when he seemed to be building on quicksand.

The heart of his problem loomed before him still, the perversity, brutality, and irresponsibility of man, a colossal, immovable, impregnable mass on which he had made but a superficial impression; the real struggle lay ahead; and he braced himself for it. The Government had appealed to Rome for a suspension of its prohibition in order to permit him to preach during Lent; and through the good offices of Cardinal Caraffa a tacit consent was given. Indeed the attitude of Rome seemed to be changing. A Dominican Bishop had examined his doctrine, approved it, and recommended to the Pope that he conciliate him, even, if necessary, going so far as to offer him the Purple. This suggestion was approved by Alexander; with his preference for easy solutions of unpleasant problems he acted on it promptly. When the offer was transmitted to San Marco, "Come to my next sermon," the Prior said to the emissary, "and you shall hear my reply to Rome."

Into those Lenten sermons he packed all his thunders, determined to strike while he could and to strike fearlessly at the venality of Rome. To the theme which had first introduced him to Florence he brought a redoubled fury. "The corruption of the clergy, the corruption of the Church, prevents the diffusion of the Spirit among the faithful," he repeated on every tone, on every occasion. Accordingly, he cast caution to the winds and lashed out with voluminous vehemence and a provocative rashness which seemed, at the moment when Rome was seeking to propitiate him, entirely uncalled for.

"What does it mean, Friar," he cross-examined himself, "what does it mean that you have been resting so long, and have not come to the camp to help your soldiers?—My sons, I have not been resting; on the contrary, I come from the camp and have been defending a stronghold which, if it had fallen, might have meant your ruin; but now, by the grace of God and thanks to your prayers, we have saved it.—Come, come, Friar, were you not afraid of death?—Surely not, my sons; if I were afraid, I would not come now when I am in greater danger than before.—Had you some scruples about preaching?—Not I.—Why then? We hear that a ban has come forbidding you to preach.—Have you read it? Who sent it? Suppose it to be so; do you not remember how I told you that, if it did come, it would have no value and would not profit the wicked and their lies?—What then? Friar, you are putting us off.—Listen to me patiently and I will tell you.

"I have been thinking: before I proceed, I must ponder my way and see if it be clear of all contamination. Seeing so much opposition in every quarter to a little man who is not worth threepence, I said in my heart: perhaps you have not pondered your step and your tongue has erred; and I examined every step carefully, one by one. I searched out my faith and in that field, certainly, I found the way clear, for I believe and have always believed all that the Holy Roman Church believes, and submit and have submitted to it. I have written to Rome that if I have preached or written anything heretical, I am ready to recant and correct myself in public. I am always ready to obey the Roman Church and I say that he who disobeys it will be damned." After this explicit declaration, however, he pointed out that "my superior cannot command me contrary to charity and the Gospel. I do not believe that the Pope would ever do so; but if he did I would say to him, You are no longer the Pastor, you are no longer the Roman Church, you err. I say: whenever one can clearly see that the commands of one's superiors are contrary to those of God and above all to the precepts of charity, no one is bound to obey, for it is written: It is more important to obey God than man." That this hazardous distinction would be manna to his critics he realized promptly, and before they could reinterpret his interpretation of duty, he anticipated them energetically:—"You there, you who write so many lies to Rome! What will you write now? I know well what you will write.—What, Friar?—You will write that one need not obey the Pope and that I do not mean to obey him. I have not said that. Write what I have said and you will find that it will do you no good." Imprudent? But how could he pause to be prudent? "When I saw many good men cooling and the wicked plucking up spirit, then I boldly determined to return here. But first I turned to the Lord, saying: I delighted in peace and quiet and you have drawn me forth, revealing your light to me; and I have done like the moth that singes its wings, coveting the light. I have burned, O Lord, the wings of contemplation I would be still and not speak, but I cannot; the Word of God is like a flame of fire in my heart, which must out or it will consume the marrow of my bones." And, launching more terribly than ever the annunciation of new cataclysms impending on Italy and above all on Rome, he appealed to the children: "In you are my hopes and the hopes of the Lord. You will rule well this city of Florence, because you have not contracted the habits of your fathers who cannot shed the customs of tyranny, and who do not know how great is the gift, which the Lord has made this people, of liberty. But you, old men, you spend your days in your shops and your clubs, spreading slander, and your letters bear many lies out of Florence. Hence many declare that I disturb Italy: this has been written to me in so many words. Where are my squadrons and my moneys to disturb Italy? I do not disturb, I foretell perturbations to come."

Protest as he might against misrepresentation, it was inevitable that, in the commotion of public opinion caused by utterances so inflammatory, his image should be reflected in forms ever more fluctuating and distorted. Throughout Italy and beyond the Alps a constant stream of letters carried the most conflicting accounts of his sermons to the four quarters of the compass. He mocked at excommunications, he treated the Pope worse than the Turk, and the princes of Italy worse than heretics, he was about to expose the sins of his persecutors, he was preparing new prophecies, he had become the tyrant of Florence, he would disperse the enemies of the Republic or confound them by a miracle—in such versions there was still, with all their exaggeration, a recognizable element of truth. Thought is always disfigured in passing through the mind of others; how much more so when it is incendiary and must filter through the overheated imagination of an unreasoning multitude seething with partisan passions! There was a tragic futility in his efforts to protect it by delicate distinctions. How could he hope to reconcile the mission of an agitator with the laborious scruples of caution and conscience? He was dismayed. Was that really himself—that blurred, extravagant image which the world held up to him as his own? He was still, he was more than ever, alone. But agitation was his only power and he accepted its consequences.

They were many and various. An outcrop of plots on his life, and a campaign of violent lampoons, were rigorously prosecuted by the Government. But his own defence was his sermons. They were published and circulated through Italy and Europe; they were even translated into Turkish and assiduously read by the Sultan. Responses came from all quarters; the issues he raised found an echo everywhere. The Duke of Ferrara became one of his most devoted adherents, the Duke of Milan one of his most pressing correspondents. "The Friar is now master of the people and can dictate its devotion to Your Lordship," wrote the Milanese ambassador to his master; and he was accordingly charged to approach Savonarola and induce him to support the League. The Friar replied that he was not "a proper instrument for that purpose." "The Florentines do not wish to enter the League, fearing that the Duke and the other powers might aim to destroy the popular government and set up a tyrant in Florence." When this reply was transmitted to Milan, there was an immediate repercussion in the Vatican. The Pope complained bitterly to the Florentine ambassador that the Republic was ruining Italy by refusing to join "the Holy League for the expulsion of the barbarians." He nodded his bovine head despondently and fell silent; then he began to deplore the influence of the Friar and the obstinacy with which he disregarded the ban. The ambassador was plainly surprised. He respectfully reminded His Holiness that he had consented to his preaching, whereupon the Holy Father sucked in his lip and changed the subject. "Well, well, we will not speak of Fra Girolamo now," he said. "A time may come when we can discuss him better. As for the rest, you give us nothing but words, you wish to keep a foot in both camps."

For six months this situation remained dormant. Meanwhile his moral reforms were making no headway. In the summer of 1496 a new French invasion was rumoured. To offset it, the League invited the Emperor Maximilian to descend into Italy, re-establish the Imperial authority, assume the Iron Crown, and become the arbiter of the dissensions of the peninsular powers. The danger of introducing new complications into Italy was minimized by the fact that Maximilian was short of money and men; he was hired, in fact, on the same footing as any other mercenary, at a fixed stipend, for three months. The contract was no sooner concluded than the League regretted it. The French, they learned, had abandoned the idea of another invasion. But it was too late, Maximilian had started, and some employment had to be found for him. He was re-engaged, therefore, to discipline Florence.

In October 1496, he entered Pisa, while a body of Papal troops led by the Pope's eldest son, the Duke of Gandia, created a diversion on the Florentine frontier, which forced the Republic to divide the scanty forces it still held in the field. With the aid of the Venetian fleet, Maximilian then proceeded to blockade Leghorn, the last remaining outlet of Florence on the sea. The effect in Florence was immediate and far-reaching. As the grip tightened on its vital artery, starving peasants flocked in from the country; the pest broke out; the hospitals were crowded; the poor passed away in the streets. The bread-lines in the Corn Market were so dense that cases of suffocation were a daily occurrence. Gloom and discouragement settled like a pall on the city. It was a pregnant atmosphere for the prophet, and when the authorities urged him to resume his sermons, he charged it with his quickening spirit. But his spirit was darkening. The Arrabbiati were openly proposing to change the Government, and one of his first efforts was to restrict the Grand Council. "Ungrateful people! God has given you this Grand Council, and you are seeking to ruin it," he cried, "by admitting the enemies of the country! That was not my intention. In the beginning, I allowed everyone to enter, because freedom was new and it was necessary to experiment; but I did not mean that the wicked should be included, as they now are." When, however, the measure came before the Grand Council, it was defeated; membership was enlarged and the legal age was lowered to pacify the Arrabbiati, with the result that they won an increased foothold in the Assembly.

He had other causes for discouragement. The atmosphere of Florence was unbreathable. "Do you see now," he thundered, swiftly garnering the harvest of affliction, "do you see now that, unless you change your life, you will suffer? O Florence, vice still flourishes; men game and blaspheme, and you bring calamities on yourself!" At moments the futility of the struggle overwhelmed him. The turbulent stream of life swept on, despite all his efforts to stem it. "It is as difficult to change its course as to change the course of the waters." And he upbraided his flock bitterly. "You have grown used to hearing me dinning, 'Do justice, do justice!' You will become like the crow on the belfry, which takes flight at the first sound of the bell; but when it grows accustomed to it, ring as you will, it sits on the bell and will not budge." Lip-service, lip-service, no change of heart! Religious processions were formed, the miraculous Madonna dell' Impruneta was brought to the city, and in the midst of these rites news came that a convoy of grain had slipped through the blockade; there was a wild outburst of thanksgiving; but he was unmoved. Discouraged by that fatal facility of feeling, "You must not yield so lightly to joy and despondency," he protested on the morrow. The mercurial spirit of the people, which had once made his triumph, was now his despair. Everything had been tried, persuasion, appeal, intimidation; nothing remained but to resort to the supreme argument—to force.

The crisis, with its need for public economy, and the depression, with its pervasive gloom, favoured him; and the Government wrote into the law-books a drastic series of moral reforms. Obsolete sumptuary laws were revived and enforced; women who appeared in public, extravagantly or immodestly dressed, were subject to flogging. Prostitutes were rounded up and expelled, to the sound of trumpets, from the city. Dowries were reduced. Taverns were closed, racing was suppressed, dancing was forbidden, even in the country where it was the only recreation. Gambling, blasphemy, and sodomy were penalized with the wrack, the pillory, and the pyre. Fasting was practised so assiduously that the butchers claimed a rebate on their taxes. The luxury trades went into bankruptcy, and on Sundays and Saints' Days, all shops with the exception of the apothecaries' were closed. The depression deepened until it touched bottom.

On All Saints' Day Savonarola preached on *The Art of Dying Well*. Death, he reminded his hearers, was the measure of life and the guide to its conduct. "Death is the solemn moment of our life; it is then that the devil delivers his supreme battle. It is as if he played chess with man all his days, waiting for the approach of death to checkmate him. To win that move is to win the battle of life. O my brothers, we live in the world only to learn how to die." In conclusion, he urged every man to keep at the head of his couch a graphic reminder of the grave, a true bill of mortality; and he drafted a series of images, which his artists hastened to realize, of the ubiquitous spectre, hovering autumnally with his restless flail and patient cry: *Ego sum*. He had touched bottom. Christianity has many phases, and he had reflected each in turn, but only to end, as he began, with its last word. It might ameliorate life, but at bottom it was its negation. Divulging at last the secret solution with which all his days he had been labouring, he raised and released his ultimate cry, the migratory call of death.

One thing more was needed—a public demonstration to impress indelibly on the simplest mind the import of the movement. The occasion came with the Carnival of 1497. It had been a fruitful year—fruitful of force, of recklessness, of fanaticism, of despotic urges—and its completion was celebrated by the Burning of the Vanities. Amid billowing clouds of smoke, the great pyramid of vainglories collected by his children—lewd pictures and books, lutes, cards, mirrors, and trinkets—crumbled on the Piazza, filling the nostrils of the godly with the acrid satisfaction of *Sic transit*...

10

The Imperial expedition melted away. But out of it grew a new series of difficulties with Rome. At the height of the blockade, while the Friar was labouring to reanimate the people, a new Brief came, uniting San Marco, not indeed with the Lombard Congregation, but with a new Tusco-Roman Congregation, under the patronage of Cardinal Caraffa. In this form it seemed to the Roman authorities that the Friar could not reasonably object to the yoke—it was light, and the reins were in the hands of friends—and a yoke had become necessary for his own good, to moderate the transports of a spirit constantly over-stimulated by popular pressure and visionary exaltation. But a yoke it was; and coming at that moment, it convinced Savonarola that it was merely one more political move to muzzle him. Instead of replying to it directly—that was useless—he published an appeal to the public, in which he exposed his grounds for rejecting it: the deplorable feuds existing between convents, the contamination which such a union would introduce among the reformed Dominicans; and concluded by imputing it to the machinations of his enemies and declaring: "When conscience shrinks from obeying the commands of one's superiors, one must first resist and protest humbly, which we have done; but if this does not suffice, then one must do like St. Paul, *qui coram omnibus restitit in faciem Petri.*"[1]

Nothing proved the need of the new Congregation and the wisdom of submitting his conduct to the sympathetic influence of those who could distinguish between the claims of conscience and discipline more clearly than this reply; and Cardinal Caraffa himself, shocked by the intractable attitude of his protégé, began to cool. There was talk of an excommunication, but the Vatican still deferred action. During Lent (1497), however, his sermons became more incendiary. Expounding the most complex and controversial problems involved in the Temporal Power, he rushed in boldly. "Riches," he insisted, in diagnosing the decay of the Church, "are what have ruined her.—Do you mean, Friar, that the Church should not hold temporal possessions?—That would be heresy and I do not say it." And he found himself hedging. "Let us say that the Church would be better off without riches, because there would be more union with God. Therefore I tell my monks: cling to

---

[1] "Who flung his heart and all else in the face of Peter."

poverty, for when riches come in, death enters the house." But he recovered the full sweep of conviction and invective when he enlarged on the pernicious influence of ecclesiastical wealth. "The earth," he cried, stigmatizing the clergy for its dereliction of duty, "is full of blood and they do not care; nay, they murder souls by their bad example. They have departed from God and their cult is to spend the whole night with whores and the day gossiping in sacristies; and the altar is the counter of the clergy. They say that God has no care for the world, that everything happens by chance, and they do not believe that Christ is present in the Sacrament.... Come here, wretched Church; I gave you, saith the Lord, fair vestments, and you have made idols of them. You have given my vessels to vainglory and my sacraments to simony; in your lechery you are a shameless whore; you are worse than a beast, you are an abominable monster. Once you blushed for your sins, but not now. The priests used to call their sons nephews; now they are not nephews, but sons, sons plain and simple! You have made a public place of the Church, you have built brothels everywhere.... And so, O whore of a Church, you have shown your foulness to the whole world, and your stench rises to Heaven. You have multiplied your fornications in Italy, in France, in Spain, everywhere. Lo, I put out my hand, saith the Lord, I am coming, you rascal, you slut! My sword shall be over your sons, your brothels, your whores, your palaces, and my judgment shall be manifest.... I tell you that we must burst this sepulchre, Christ wants to resuscitate His Church in spirit. We must all pray for this renovation. Write to France, to Germany, write everywhere and say: This Friar bids you go to the Lord and pray, for the Lord will come. Up, up, send out your couriers! Do you think that we only are good? that God has no servants elsewhere? Jesus Christ has many, and there are plenty in Spain, in France, in Germany, who stand listening and lamenting this infirmity.... They send and whisper in my ear and I say to them: Hide until you hear the word, *Lazarus, come forth*. I stand here because the Lord has placed me here and I wait. He will call me: then I shall send forth a great voice which will be heard in all Christendom, and it will make the body of the Church tremble, as that of Lazarus trembled at the voice of the Lord."

Then he took up the rumour of the forthcoming excommunication and tossed it to a climax of provocation. "Bring it in, the excommunication, bring it in on a spear, and open the gates to it! I will reply to it, and if I do not astound you, you may say what you will. I will make so many faces pale, both here and there, that you will find them enough; and I will send forth a voice that will move and make tremble the world. I know that there are those in Rome, who are toiling against me night and day. But, O Lord, this is what I desire, I crave only your Cross: make me to be persecuted. I ask you this grace, that you do not let me die in my bed, but that I may give my blood for you, as you gave yours for me. Meanwhile, my sons, do not doubt, for we shall surely have the help of the Lord."

These sermons attracted enormous audiences from all over the country, from neighbouring cities and from distant—the Duke of Ferrara came, incognito, expressly to hear them—and the multitudes, unable to find room in the Duomo, swarmed and settled like bees about the huge holy hive, drinking in the hum of that dynamic voice and relaying its megalomaniac echoes. Who could be deaf to it? Alexander alone seemed to be able to ignore it. Timid and shrewd, the ageing Borgia had too practised a touch to rouse an active hive; and the Friar was too deeply imbedded in the political life of Florence to be handled directly. But he worked, or at least he probed, in more devious ways. His eldest son Juan, Duke of Gandia, was about to be created Gonfalonier of the Church and needed practice in arms; and the Pope approached the Republic with a secret offer to restore Pisa to it in return for its adherence to the League. This time the Government was sufficiently curious to send an envoy extraordinary to Rome to discuss the question. The Pope was in one of his blunt moods and began the audience by lamenting the original sin of Italian politics—the French invasion. "God forgive the author of it," he sighed. "It is the cause of all the afflictions of Italy, and you should know it, since your state was dismembered by the loss of Pisa. It will be far worse if they return now. We are striving in every way, as the Lord God knows, to unite and make one body of Italy, and we count particularly on your perspicacity and foresight. With great difficulty we have persuaded the League to give you Pisa, provided you side with us and act as good Italians, leaving the French in France. But we must have better understandings and guarantees than words." Words, however, were all that the envoy was empowered to offer. He remarked, while the Pope paused to mop his brow, that the Florentines had always been and always would be *good Italians*, and that their faith might be trusted. At that the Holy Father lost patience. "Master Secretary," he snapped, "you are as fat as ourselves but, by your leave, you bring a lean commission, and if you have nothing else to say, you may retire." His temper was roused, his jocosity vanished, and, flushing, he blustered that Florence, if she would not join the League willingly, should do so by force and to her cost. The blood rushed to his head and he continued in querulous agitation, "We know that all this comes of your chatterbox and your faith in his prophecies, allowing him to insult and injure and threaten and abuse us, though we sit, *licet immeriti*, in this Holy See." With great difficulty the envoy appeased him and withdrew. The Duke of Gandia subsequently served his apprenticeship in an expedition against the Orsini. The Republic, learning that the Pope had in fact promised more than he could perform, since the Venetians were opposed to the restoration of Pisa, dropped the question.

But the problem of the Friar remained. "In every quarter in Rome," the ambassador reported, "the feeling against Savonarola is rising so high, that it is impossible to defend him." Alexander himself could no longer overlook him. Unable to link the two questions, the veteran lawyer was baffled. His advisers were clamouring for an excommunication, but he shrank from extreme measures. His instinct was for accommodation. He had gone far to conciliate him, too far perhaps, yielding to every protest, ignoring every outburst, stretching every point, but only to find his patience abused and his moderation misinterpreted. With each new concession the man became more provocative; his insubordination and inflammatory Lenten sermons had now reached a point which demanded disciplinary action. What exasperated him most was the necessity of acting contrary to his better judgment. Wary, easy-going, tolerant, he was unwilling to antagonize Florence or to aggravate the importance of the Friar by any suggestion of persecution. He understood him thoroughly; his errors were those, not of malice, but of overweening simplicity: he was "a chatterbox." When the Florentine ambassador dwelt on his great virtues, the Holy Father agreed courteously. "He must be a great saint," he said, meditatively pulling his ear. That was the difficulty. He appreciated sanctity—in its place. But that place was not the Vatican: no one expected the political clergy to practise the monastic virtues. With perfect sincerity he admired ideals which he did not share. There was his cult of the Virgin, for instance. He was devoted to her, as he was to all virgins. His genital energy gave him no qualms. The scandals of the past he had long since outlived, and they were scandals only because his family had pushed him as a child into the Church. What had he to blush for? Simony? Nepotism? He was ambitious, he adored his children, no tonsure could change that fact; he needed money and women, and he was no hypocrite. The Roman wits turned epigrams on his lubricity and his greed without ruffling his temper; he was fond of saying that anyone could write or speak as he pleased in Rome; he had a sage indifference to public opinion and a healthy contempt for personal abuse. But there were limits. He had his conscience too, and it was an administrative one. It was an unexpected feature of that gross, easy-going old man, that he could convert himself into an institution as easily as he dissociated himself from it. He was, in short, a politician. *Licet immeriti*, as he said, he sat in the Holy See; he performed its functions efficiently; and to be insulted and injured, threatened and abused, and publicly stigmatized for his paternity was, as all his advisers agreed, intolerable. An epigram was one thing, a sermon another. Honest the man might be, and ingenuous, but nothing was so mischievous as misguided virtue; and the fact remained that Savonarola was sowing scandals which others less disinterested than he—Cardinal della Rovere, for instance, who was working in France for the convocation of a General Council to remedy the disorders of the Church and to investigate the irregularities of his rival's election—might take advantage.

Amid these indecisions a possible solution presented itself. Piero de' Medici was raising another expedition—as when was he not?—to reinstate himself in Florence. But this was to be the final one. After wandering from Court to Court in Italy, the discredited pretender had drifted to Rome, where for a time he consoled himself in debauchery. But the Medici fortune was heavily entailed by debt, the palace in which Lorenzo had set up the Cardinal now was dismal and shabby, and shut up behind closed shutters the brothers jarred on each other. Lounging in bed until noon, Piero would call for the menu and, when he found it too frugal, fling out of the house to live on his friends. They dwindled rapidly. His temper became bitter and brutal. He treated his servants like dogs and his brother like a menial. When his partisans in Florence, profiting by the tension with Rome, proposed a new coup, his family, eager to be rid of him, made a heroic effort to finance it. Thirteen hundred men were recruited. Plans were carefully laid. His Florentine friends assured him that the city would rise and were already discussing its reorganization. With a Council of twenty-five or thirty leading citizens he would regain popular confidence—but they were promptly rebuffed. He gave them to understand that he needed no advice and proceeded to draw up, over his cups, vindictive lists of proscription. The discussion was dropped and the little group of exiles sat forlornly around the table, drinking to the restoration, while he worried his food —"in this matter of the mouth," said one of them, "he showed great diligence." At last, on April 27, 1497, he appeared before the walls with his troops. All day he waited, in a downpour of rain, for the city to rise; and, when night fell, overwhelmed by his inveterate sense of misfortune, he turned and rode back, a truant, to oblivion.

The Government immediately investigated the Medici plot. Though it worked quietly, excitement was intense. Profiting by the fury of factional feeling, the Arrabbiati, who had gained strength in the April elections, launched a new attack on Savonarola and the Popular Party. A demonstration was planned for Ascension Day (May 3). The authorities had decided to prevent further friction with Rome by suspending all preaching in Florence and closing the churches on the pretext of the plague and the approach of hot weather; but the Friar was scheduled to deliver a final sermon on Ascension Sunday, and trouble was so confidently expected that betting ran high on his appearance. The Compagnacci, a gang of young bloods who had taken the lead in flouting the Blue Laws, planned to blow up the pulpit, but, realizing that an act of terrorism would turn public opinion against them, they abandoned the scheme in favour of a mock outrage. In the early hours of Ascension morning, the Piagnoni found the pulpit draped with an ass-skin and smeared with ordure; and though, when the Friar appeared, everything had been removed, the nervousness of the crowd was such that it required little to convert it into a mob. Suddenly the explosion came. An alms-box fell, there was a wild rush for the doors, and the Friar was heard crying, "Ah, ah, the wicked will not hear!" His voice was drowned out in the din. Raising the crucifix and repeating, "Patience, patience, have faith in this and fear nothing," he attempted to rally his followers. Throughout the church their little red crosses travelled toward him, as they surged about the pulpit; the Compagnacci rushed them but were repulsed, and a half-hour later, amid cries of *Viva Cristo*, Savonarola was escorted to San Marco, where he concluded his sermon in the garden.

"The matter was of great moment," wrote the Milanese ambassador to his master, "and narrowly missed embroiling the whole city, and breeding serious trouble; but it passed without scandal." He likened the fury of faction in Florence to the days of the Guelfs and Ghibellines. A non-partisan commission was now formed by the Government to pacify the city; and Savonarola published a pastoral letter to his followers, in which he declared that he had decided "to imitate the example of Our Lord, who frequently yielded to the wrath of the Scribes and the Pharisees." "But," he continued, "that the work of the Lord may not crumble, and the wicked rejoice, we shall tell you by letter what we cannot by word. Do not be perturbed by these persecutions, but rejoice in them. Our prophecies will all be verified; first, our enemies slandered us; then, by crooked ways, they sought an excommunication; and, not having succeeded yet, they now attempt our life. So far no drop of blood has been shed, because the Lord, knowing our frailty, has not allowed us to be tempted beyond our strength; but little by little, as our tribulations increase, He will increase our faith, our virtue, and our spirit, for greater trials. He is preparing for us harsher persecutions, so that men, amazed by our constancy, may begin to believe that we are sustained by the certainty of a better life than this one, and commence to place their hopes in it."

The persecutions were not long in coming. In an Assembly summoned to discuss ways and means of pacifying the city, the Arrabbiati attempted to put through a bill banishing the Friar, as the root of Florentine dissensions. They were defeated, and they then wrote to Rome for their last hope—the excommunication. Feeling the storm gathering, Savonarola made a final effort to dispel it and wrote a conciliatory letter to Alexander. "Why is my Lord angered against his servant?" he began and, protesting the purity of his doctrine and his obedience to Rome, and lamenting that the Holy Father was so systematically misinformed, he rested his case on his published sermons. "If all human aid fails me," he concluded, "I shall place my hope in God, and make clear to the whole world the wickedness of those who may yet rue the enterprise they have undertaken."

The letter made an excellent impression on the Pope, but it came too late. The excommunication was already on its way. When the news leaked out, the Florentine ambassador attempted to trace its authors. He was informed by Cardinal Caraffa that it had been kept a close secret. All was conjecture. The Medici, at least—so the Cardinal assured him—had had nothing to do with it; for both Piero and his brother spoke well of the Friar; though it was true that the document had been drawn by their creature, Fra Mariano da Gennazzano. More than that he could not say, except that "finding the matter disposed, the medicine immediately took effect." As for appealing to the Pope, that was out of the question: he was engrossed in his family: the Duke of Gandia was taking the field, Cardinal Caesar Borgia was leaving as Legate to Naples, and the doting father could not be distracted. Perhaps, too, Cardinal Caraffa remembered the occasion on which he had obtained the Pope's signature to the document authorizing the separation of San Marco, and the words of the Holy Father to the Lombards: "If you had come sooner you would have been satisfied, but now what is done is done." At all events, he could only hope, he said, that the messenger who was now on his way to Florence "would have the wisdom not to arrive."

It was a slim hope. The messenger was a monk who was a political opponent of the Friar. Fearing to enter the city, however, he sent the Brief from Siena by other hands; and there were other delays. The Florentine clergy hesitated to accept it, as it was couched in the unusual form of a circular to the three major churches of Florence, and was unaccompanied by an Apostolic commissioner; and it was over a month after its dispatch when it was finally published. Then, on June 18, it was read with due solemnity from the designated pulpits, amid the tolling of bells, the guttering of tapers, and the unctuous attention of the assembled clergy. When the reading was over, the tapers were slowly extinguished, the booming of bells subsided, and for a long moment the faithful were plunged in silence and darkness.

11

For a long moment there was silence in Florence. Then the varied hum of the city resumed and through its blended din rose other sounds . . . catcalls and songs about San Marco, the twanging of lutes in dark alleys, the rattle of dice at the street-corners, the thunder of hooves at the races, the lamentations of the pious, the murmurs of psalms, the mutters of indignation and protest. San Marco was silent, but the familiar voice was not quite stifled. In little knots the Piagnoni forgathered on the streets to read and re-read his letter of protest against what he stigmatized as "this surreptitious excommunication." "This excommunication is invalid before God and man . . . pray and make ready for what is to come. . . . To submit to every sentence is asinine patience, foolish and hare-like fear. . . . Such sentences are nothing but violence, and natural right teaches us to repel force by force . . . enlighten the pusillanimous who believe the Supreme Pontiff to be almost a God with power over the heavens and earth. . . ." Muffled but not mute, smothered but inextinguishable, the murmur continued, irrepressibly heaving against the gag. And in the Palace the voice of authority took up its burden, dictating an official appeal to the Pope: "Blessed Father, the Papal Censures afflict us profoundly, both because of the respect which the Republic has always shown to the Supreme Keys, and because we see the wicked wrongfully accuse a most innocent man. We consider this man good, religious, and accomplished in all Christian things. For many years he has toiled for the welfare of this people, and it is impossible to find any fault in his life or his doctrine. We therefore urgently implore Your Holiness, in your paternal and divine charity, to judge this case personally, and to revoke these censures, not only as they affect Father Girolamo Savonarola, but also all those who may have incurred them. No greater favour could Your Holiness show this Republic, especially in these times of pestilence, when censures are of grave peril to our souls."

But Rome was hushed in a deeper silence, shocked by a tragedy in the Vatican whose first rumours reached Florence, by a singular coincidence, on the morrow of the excommunication, and which was immediately hailed by the Piagnoni as a Divine Visitation. The story leaked out slowly and the facts composed themselves cryptically. On the evening of June 14, the Duke of Gandia and his brother Cardinal Caesar supped with their mother, Vanozza, in her Roman vineyard. On their return the brothers, who were soon to leave for Naples together, parted, the Duke going to an assignation in the Ghetto. Cardinal Caesar, who was the last person to see him alive, could throw no light on his movements beyond the fact that "he wished to amuse himself." In the morning the Duke was missing, but no alarm was felt until evening when his horse was found running loose in the streets. Search was immediately instituted, and the body of one of his servants was found in an alley. The police force which the Pope had created on his accession was now on its professional mettle. Toward evening a boatman, whose barge was moored on the Tiber not far from the sewers, came forward with a story. In the early hours of the previous morning he had seen two men emerge from an alley and reconnoitre the bank where the refuse was dumped into the stream. The river and the street were deserted. They were followed by a horseman, masked and richly dressed, who was evidently a person of consequence, for he was accompanied by two footmen who helped him support a corpse on his saddle-bow. After a short pause, the body was heaved out; the horseman asked if it had fallen in midstream, to which the servants replied, *Si, Signore*. Lingering to scan the water, they saw the cloak floating and flung stones at it to sink it. Then, in the half-light they returned into the Ghetto. When the boatman was asked why he had not reported the crime immediately, he replied that in his time he had known a hundred such hugger-mugger murders, and no questions asked. The river was dragged, and the body of Juan Borgia was recovered.

Such were the facts; but it was the sequel which hushed Rome. On the morning when the disappearance of the Duke was first noticed, the Pope showed no alarm; he nodded, smiled knowingly, and worked as usual; but, as the day wore on, his eyes grew blank with dread, and when the body was recovered he collapsed. As it was borne through the Borgo to its burial, the crowd heard, or imagined it heard, intermittently from his rooms in the Vatican what it took to be the wails of the helpless old man—a long spasmodic cry rising and falling like the moans of a woman in labour, swelling incessantly and breaking over and over in a blood-curdling hiatus. For three days he lay without sleep or sustenance. The Cardinals plied his door and the lackeys tiptoed in and out, unnoticed. The first paroxysms were followed by stupor, but his clouded consciousness still heaved with long, convulsive spasms of memory. At first he saw nothing but the fact, the crushing fact which obliterated everything like an incubus, the fact of his first-born with his throat slit, his hands tied, his beard clotted with smut, and his blurred eyes gazing madly on eternity. The vision set his huge knees trembling. With fat hands he paddled on his pillow, and the yellow Tiber closed over his eyes. At intervals a low murmur muddied his lips, a haemorrhage of delirious words . . . "like smut, like smut" . . . The syllables swelled, pulsing from his bowels, irrepressible, monotonous . . . "like smut, like smut" . . . But at last the feverish litany subsided, he roamed the ceiling with clairvoyant eyes, and rose from his abysmal bed, rose from the river-bed, rose from the dead, and called for Vanozza. The woman who had borne him four children came and was closeted with him, and slowly she mothered him back to manhood. Meanwhile, the investigation of the crime continued without success. Indifferent to it, stunned, he sat in his chair, secretly pursuing his own; the gross mouth moved without sound, and the bald eyes grew big with the labouring revelations of the seer.

On June 19 he appeared in the Conclave. With his plethoric blood he was liable to fainting-spells, but he walked steadily, with his usual majesty, took his seat, and surveyed the hatted faces of the Cardinals. Their gloved hands lay in their scarlet laps, how unlike the small hands and ample laps of women! But he faced them calmly and read, in a low voice, his address to the Sacred and sexless College. "A greater sorrow than this could not be ours, for we loved him exceedingly, and now we can hold the Papacy nor any other matter of any concern. Had we seven Papacies, we would give them all to restore the Duke to life." The voice went on evenly. His life, he admitted, had been irregular but now "he knew neither flesh nor blood nor kindred nor affection. He cared no more for mortality; he would recognize this visitation as coming from the Lord. He would pay all heed to the religion of Christ, the honour of the Holy See, and the office of a virtuous Pope. He would seek nothing that was not holy, honest, and just, either from Princes or the Sacred College. . . . He would attend with all diligence to the reform of the Church and the order of the Temporal Power, that it might be maintained in peace and tranquillity, and give no further occasion for scandal." These resolutions were formally embodied in the creation of a commission of five Cardinals, under the presidency of Cardinal Caraffa, to study the problem of a radical reform of the Church: *reducatur ad pristinum statum.*

This chastened spirit manifested itself no less in the pursuit of the criminal. The mystery remained insoluble and the investigation was reduced to conjecture. But it was no less searching for that. Rumour uncovered what the law could not detect and, spreading like wildfire into every cranny of Rome, startled so many suspects from their lairs, disclosed so many corruptions, and threw the whole Papal Court into such commotion, that a general scandal threatened. The murderer was known to be a man of consequence, and the finger of suspicion pointed in turn to those closest the Papal throne. The number of motives and men appalled and bewildered the old man. The first was Cardinal Ascanio Sforza, who had quarrelled with the Duke for an affront, and who now fled to Grottoferrata. The Pope promptly recalled and publicly exonerated his Vice-Chancellor. Then the gossips fell on Giovanni Sforza, whose recent and reluctant divorce from Lucrezia Borgia on grounds of impotency had made him the laughing-stock of Italy. Him the Holy Father could not recall, as he had already fled Rome some months before in a mysterious panic; but he was careful to absolve his late son-in-law. Suspicion then flew to the Orsini, whose fiefs were in dispute with the Holy See and whom the Duke was to have attacked; but this clue the Pope likewise refused to pursue. Then rumour, so obstinately rebuffed, grew spiteful and crept nearer home. Giuffredo Borgia, his third son, was now named; an intrigue between his dissolute wife and the late Duke was supplied; but the old man, contracting yet further, quickly smothered that scandal. He no longer wished the Duke back; he only longed to forget. Sitting by the window, watching the river, the river he could never forget, he followed the tide of his own thoughts listlessly. But the world would not let him forget. A final and more vital blow was aimed at his bowels. This time it was Caesar, Cardinal Caesar who was restless in his ecclesiastical robes, who coveted his brother's baton as Commander-in-Chief of the armies of the Church, and who was the last person to see him alive; and this story, rapidly spreading, raised another: both brothers had scented each other in their sister's bed. Revolted, the old man recoiled; he quashed the whole investigation; and the scandal-mongers stood tongue-tied when Caesar returned from Naples and was embraced by his father without a word. He had reached the limits of suffering. Desperately as he quelled the inquest, he was haunted by a hideous insight and stupefied by a sense of supernatural retribution. The great body drooped in its chair; the bovine eyes brooded insatiably on their vision. They plumbed the Tiber, a murmuring sewer of scum, closing over his first-born; they closed, and under the bulging lids pursued their conclusions: there was but one. In his flesh he had sinned, in his flesh he was smitten. The collapse of the sensualist was a maudlin, a bottomless contrition. There were rumours of abdication; but they were quickly belied. Yet a change had come over him. The lax mouth, the veiled, weary, wistfully cynical eyes, betrayed, through the slackening flesh, the softening brain; and the reform of the Church began.

Even veteran diplomats were deceived. The Florentine ambassador wrote that, if the Commission fulfilled the hopes it inspired, the regeneration of the Church would indeed have been due, as the Friar predicted, to the sword. It was a large *if*; but at least the five Cardinals were men of excellent character, and a brave start was made. Cardinal Caraffa edited the articles of a constitution which was the object of careful consideration, mature reflection, and many erasures and emendations. The retinues of the members of the Sacred College were restricted, and women were forbidden the Apostolic Palace. The Commission would no doubt have gone further had it not gone so far: no change appeared in the domestic customs of the Court, and, though the Commission continued to sit, its results were abortive, and the constitution was never published. With one problem, however, it dealt firmly.

Among the letters of condolence which reached Alexander from all sides—even Cardinal della Rovere forgot his life-long feud and wrote very feelingly—was one from Savonarola. After assuring him of his sympathy and congratulating him on his Christian resolutions, in which he encouraged him to persevere, he passed to higher considerations. "Faith, Holy Father," he wrote, "Faith, so full of miracles and illustrious acts, confirmed by the blood of the martyrs, is our only tranquillity and the true consolation of the human heart. It transcends reason and the senses, it transports us from this world, exalts us to invisible things, and enlarges our souls." Rising in nostalgic reminder of their "heavenly fatherland," he took an optimistic view of the tragedy as a summons and urged Alexander to "respond to this happy call, that sorrow may suddenly be converted to joy. The Lord in His goodness overlooks all our sins. I announce things of which I am certain, and I suffer persecution for their sake. I urge Your Holiness to look favourably on this labour of faith, for which I am toiling continually, and to lend an ear no longer to the impious. The Lord will then give you the essence of joy instead of the spirit of sorrow; because the things I predict are all true, and no one who resists the Lord can ever find peace. These things, Blessed Father, I write, prompted by charity, and hoping that Your Holiness will be truly consoled by God; for before long the thunders of His Wrath will be heard, and blessed will they be who trust in Him. May the Lord of all mercy comfort Your Holiness in your tribulations."

The opportunity to moralize on the tragedy was tempting; and, if Alexander had resented the homily, he would only have been human; but he merely filed the letter and submitted the case of the Friar to the Commission. If it could do nothing else, it could at least reform reformers. The Cardinals gave the case careful and sympathetic consideration, but they would not be hurried. At this juncture—the July elections were approaching—the Florentine Government appealed for a fortnight's suspension of the ban to permit the Friar to preach. The Cardinals, however, were resolved to dissociate the issue from politics and to define it clearly. For this purpose time was required, to allow the heat of controversy to subside and the situation to resume its normal proportions; and so the summer passed. During this period of probation, a protracted campaign ensued between the partisans and opponents of the Friar to influence the Commission. "Knock, cry, make every possible effort, do not give over, spare yourself no fatigue until you succeed"— such were the instructions of the Florentine ambassador, peremptorily repeated in every dispatch; and he obeyed. Through the long, malarial Roman afternoons, he passed from palace to palace in the Borgo, from apartment to apartment in the Vatican, patiently pleading his client's cause. But he made little progress: he had nothing to offer. The Cardinal of Siena was ready to promise the repeal in return for a small accommodation—5000 ducats to settle a debt—but he received nothing. It was not merely that the Government was close or the Friar unbending. "I should repute it a far greater censure," the Friar replied, "to receive absolution at such a price." Allowance could be made for his principles; but it was not only toward corruption that he was uncompromising; he refused to discuss terms at all. Yet terms of some sort there must be, and those which the Commission eventually offered were reasonable. The ban, after rehearsing the history of the Congregational disputes, had explicitly stated that "Fra Girolamo is excommunicated because he has refused to obey our Apostolic admonitions and commands." The issue, it was true, was somewhat confused by a passage charging him with "sowing pernicious doctrine, to the scandal and distress of simple souls"; but this charge the Commission consented to waive, in an effort to strip the problem of all contentious questions and to define it clearly as one of discipline. Provided the Friar made an act of submission, either by coming to Rome or by accepting the Tusco-Roman Congregation, the Cardinals were prepared to recommend the repeal of the ban. Less the Holy See could not accept, and it was difficult to see how so reasonable an offer could be rejected.

But the Friar was governed by a logic deeper than reason. He was inflexible. All the absolutism of his nature, fostered by years of seclusion and inflamed by his struggle with the world, asserted itself at this critical moment. He insisted on defining the issue as a question of conscience. He could not or would not admit that no principle was involved, and that his position, on grounds of discipline, was indefensible. That misunderstanding was the turning-point of his career. Was it real or assumed? For the first time, in that life of undeviating honesty, the question arose. He had repeatedly asserted his submission to the Holy See and declared his readiness to accept public correction, if he erred; but the pride of a blameless man is a fierce and unreasoning thing, he was a public figure, he could not risk discredit, and in Rome his attitude was laid to obstinate self-will and political expediency. He seemed to expect the unconditional capitulation of Rome. Rather than believe him so ingenuous, the Cardinals imputed his conduct to motives that were disingenuous. But indeed he had travelled as far beyond calculation as reason. A terrible exaltation possessed him. Intoxicated with conviction, stimulated by struggle, and prepared for persecution, his inveterate habit of simplifying every problem, reducing it to the rudimentary black and white of right and wrong, and finding moral justification for his will, had at last developed into an obsession, which clouded his judgment and was perilously akin to mania. And the last restraints of caution now yielded to something yet more compelling—his fatalism. How could he defeat his destiny? Was it not martyrdom?

Yet—such was the strange confusion of his mind at this moment—while he did nothing to favour and everything to frustrate the negotiations with Rome, he continued to attribute their failure to the machinations of his enemies. "We have done our duty," he wrote to Ferrara, "and it seems that the Pope is well disposed, but that some powerful adversary stands in our way." The adversary was powerful, indeed, though his friends tried to exorcize it. "If Your Lordships cannot persuade his Paternity to consent to the union of the Congregations," the Florentine ambassador wrote to his Government, "or if the Signory will not give an undertaking that within two months Fra Girolamo will come to Rome, the absolution is not to be expected; but if the City will do this, neither the Pope nor the Cardinals are inclined to withhold it." But in vain; his efforts were unavailing; and the golden moment passed, unrecognized.

In August, the friends of Piero de' Medici, implicated in the plot to restore him during the previous spring, were brought to trial, condemned, and executed, after being denied the faculty of appeal to the Grand Council, which had been one of the boasted reforms of the Piagnoni. The victims were men of great family, they were personally popular, and the first blood shed by the Republic embittered not only their relatives but the populace and the neutral elements in the city. The Piagnoni grew unpopular. During the next few months the breach widened, and the Government, to recover its waning credit, urged Savonarola to reappear in the pulpit. He did not hesitate long. Everything urged him forward—six months of inactivity, the need of the Party, the appeals of the children, the crumbling of his work. The relaxation of public morals had proceeded apace ever since the excommunication, and to the protests of the pious a magistrate replied testily, expressing the general sentiment with a shrug: "We must cheer the people a little. Are we all to become monks?" Of the moral rigours of the preceding winter—the brief salutary winter of discontent—hardly a vestige remained. After six months of silence, he was all but forgotten.

Accordingly, he made a new effort to soften the Pope. "Holy Father," he wrote, "I kiss the feet of Your Holiness as a child, grieving at having incurred the displeasure of his father, desires and seeks every means of appeasing his anger, nor can any refusal make him despair of regaining his former favour, for it is written: Ask, and ye shall receive; knock, and it shall be opened to you. . . . To whom shall I turn if not, as one of his flock, to the Shepherd whose voice I love to hear, whose blessing I implore, whose saving presence I ardently desire? I would go at once and cast myself at his feet if I were safe on the way from malice and the plots of my enemies. As soon as I can do so safely I shall set out, and I wish that I might start immediately, in order to clear myself of every calumny. Meanwhile, I most humbly submit in all things, as I have ever done, to your authority, and if through any want of judgment or inadvertence on my part I have erred in anything, I humbly crave forgiveness, for you will find in me no wilful malice, at least." After composing this letter, he became sanguine. "He hopes," wrote the Ferrarese ambassador, after an interview with him, "that his affairs with the Pope will soon be settled: which, if it comes to pass, will turn to his great credit and commendation, and the more so as he has not yielded to the Pope's demands." The public, meanwhile, was warned of his return by a reissue of the famous medals bearing, on the face, the ram-like profile of the prophet, and, on the reverse, the fist clutching the sword. On Christmas Day he took the decisive step and celebrated Mass in San Marco. On the following Sunday the Signoria attended in a body and gave their official sanction to the occasion by kissing his hand at the altar.

The excitement on which the Party counted went off, however, like a damp fuse. The public was startled, but it was also shocked. The spectacle of the Signori doing homage to an excommunicated priest disconcerted even his own flock and caused one Piagnone to write that "it aroused much surprise among thoughtful men, both friends and foes." There was no conquering old habits. The awe of the immemorial ban, the hollow chill of the archangelic trump blasting the flight of fickle souls in the last eventide of the world, was stronger than reason. *Giusta vel ingiusta*, the word went, *temenda est*.[1] While the timid fell away, the fearless grew fanatical, and the Party, captured by the extremists, decided to force the issue. A month later he was announced to preach in the Duomo, benches were set up, and the Piagnoni patrolled the church to prevent a disturbance by the Arrabbiati. The Friar hesitated and cancelled the sermon, but his political friends insisted that he must preach before the March elections. The life of the Party was at stake. At this juncture the Ferrarese ambassador had an interview with the Friar at Fiesole. There, overlooking the city lying, like the kingdoms

---

[1] Just or unjust, it is to be feared.

of the world, radiant and tempting below, Savonarola discussed the situation calmly. His eyes, sunken and with what was now their settled expression of anxiety, took in the whole panorama, the present, the past, the future. He was determined, he said, to resume preaching in Lent, or perhaps sooner, if he were summoned by those "who had a right to command him." The drawn face, with the great beak of the nose and the firm generous mouth, was more than ever translucent with level sincerity; yet to a direct question he replied like a practised politician. "I asked him whether he were awaiting the orders of the Signory or those of the Pope. He replied that he would not consent to undertake this work at the bidding of the Signory, nor yet of the Pope, seeing what a life the latter continued to lead, and that he knew the Pope made no secret of his decision not to repeal the censure. He awaited the commands of one who was superior to the Pope and all his creatures. . . . I spoke of the murmurs in the city and of the scandal which might arise. He replied that, if he believed the excommunication to be valid, he would scrupulously observe it, nor would he preach, were he not more than certain no scandal would ensue."

What ensued, however, was something more dangerous than scandal. On February 11 (1498) he preached his sermon of re-entry. The congregation was small but the air was charged with excitement. Once more the intoxication of the crowd mounted to his nostrils, an irresistible afflatus. Beginning on a low thrilling note of enforced self-control, he examined the excommunication and repeated his familiar thesis that "God governs the world by secondary causes: the good prince and the good priest are merely instruments in His Hand to govern the people. When the instrument is abandoned by the Maker, then he is nothing but *a broken tool*. But how are we to know if the Prime Mover is present or no? See if his laws and commandments are contrary to charity and the good life, which are the root and principle of all wisdom; and when they are contrary, you may be sure that he is a broken tool and you are not bound to obey him." But repetition had staled it, the voice of reason was flat in the cold spaces of the vast, half-empty church, and from defence he veered to attack. "He therefore that commands us contrary to charity, which is the fullness of our law, *anathema sit!* Even if an angel were to say it, if the Virgin and all the saints were to say it, *anathema sit!* And if any Pope have ever pronounced the contrary, *anathema sit!* . . . O Lord, if ever I seek absolution from this censure, send me to Hell: I shall accuse myself of mortal sin!" But even his fulminations were familiar; after eight months his contact with the public was cold, the crowd had to be charged, roused, electrified again, and his tried resources no longer sufficed. "Brother," he went on, "I do not believe you: you have worked no miracles, that I should be bound to believe you against the Church.—What would you? It has not yet pleased the Lord to grant me a miracle.—But you said that the excommunication would be borne aloft on a lance.—I tell you, everything has not yet come to pass. But if you have eyes you must have seen that in Rome someone has lost his son, and how others here have lost their lives and gone to Hell, and you shall see their trials. As yet I have not been constrained to a miracle, but in His own time the Lord will extend His Hand, and already you have seen so many signs that there is no longer any need of a miracle. What greater miracle than the growth of our doctrine despite so much opposition? Citizens, women, we must give our lives for the truth. I turn to you, O Lord. You died for the truth, and I pray that you send me death in its defence, for the welfare of the elect and of this people."

The old fatality forced him on. In rousing the crowd he obeyed its promptings, and it was inevitable that, as he stimulated it with a *crescendo* of sensations, the lure of the supernatural should seize him at last. Rome had reminded the public that his prophetic claims were unsupported by miraculous powers; his critics had taken up the cry; to retreat now, or even to stand still, was to fail; eloquence was his one power and it demanded ever more dynamic climaxes, driving him blindly on beyond reason, beyond words, beyond sanity . . . to the very brink of the inane . . . to the brink of . . . He caught himself aghast, already half-hypnotized by the giddiness of the abyss. A miracle! Once more as in the days when Fra Silvestro challenged his prophetic claims, an occult power tugged at his sanity, straining, seducing, soliciting it. He drew back, but he hearkened. . . . Then the sober reality dawned on him in all its grim magnitude. His rhetorical power had mastered him; he had talked himself into an *impasse*. He hedged; he interpreted the rash words away. But they returned to plague him. What greater miracle than the growth of his doctrine? What need of other signs? But the expectation of a literal miracle had lodged in the minds of the populace, and the superstition he had exploited to further his doctrine now threatened to confound it. The pressure was there, inexorable, defying evasion and metaphors. On the last day of Carnival, he appeared in a pulpit outside of San Marco, blessed the multitude, and, holding up the Host, murmured: "O Lord, if I do not work with sincerity of soul, if my words do not come from You, strike me dead on the spot." The effect was tame. But in the afternoon friars and laymen, crowned with olive and clad in white, joined hands and circled the square and passed through the streets, singing: *Ecce quam bonum et quam jocundum habitare fratres in unum.*[1] He was satisfied. "I have made them mad," he said.

Mad? Maybe; but it was a madness that missed the sublime by a wide margin, and to miss was fatal. Miraculous mystifications served merely to excite the terrible sanity of popular ridicule. The caustic common sense of the Florentine rabble, which made short shrift of sham and extravagance, revived, and the quick Tuscan love of ribaldry. The spectacle of burghers and monks tripping fraternally, and the evangelical patter of their delirious sing-song

> Shout, shout, everyone, as I shout,
> Mad, mad, around and about . . .

with its specifics for salvation,

> Take three ounces at least of hope,
> Three of faith and six of love,
> Two of tears, mix and shove
> All in the furnace of fear;
> Boil three hours, strain it clear,
> Press it hard, and add so much
> Of sorrow, of meekness so much
> As madness needs to make it sweet . . .

were a godsend to the ungodly. When the Bonfire of Vanities was repeated that night, it was littered with refuse and dead cats.

The electoral returns were published on the same evening, and in the Signoria for March and April the Arrabbiati had won a majority. In the other departments of the Government, however, they were still outnumbered, and accordingly they were cautious. The temper, if not the position, of the two parties, was now strategically reversed. Realizing that the situation favoured them and that there was no need to precipitate it—that in fact the strength of the opposition lay in not opposing—the Arrabbiati became milder as the Piagnoni grew more foolhardy and, assuming a policy of compliance, they contented themselves with paying out rope to their colleagues.

This strategy was rewarded. In the reviving tension with Rome it was impossible to decide whether the Piagnoni were acting with method or madness. While they incited the Friar to preach, they continued to

---

[1] Lo, how good and joyous it is to live like brothers together.

press for the repeal of the ban. At first, indeed, in so addled a policy it was possible to suspect a strain of cunning. The French were again threatening an invasion and the Pope was again pressing Florence to join the League: the situation offered an opportunity to bargain. Even after the resumption of the sermons, Alexander continued to negotiate in behalf of the League, and his only allusion to the Friar was an injured complaint. "Well, well," he said to the Florentine ambassador, catching his breath quickly, "let your Fra Girolamo preach! I never should have thought you would use me so." But, as usual, the negotiations came to nothing, the French invasion was put off, and Alexander found himself confronting once more, with opaque eyes, the insoluble problem of the Friar.

It could not be minimized. The man was becoming a movement. During the long months of truce, a whole polemical literature had sprung up, assailing and defending the validity of the excommunication. Wherever men met, the subject was discussed, and overwrought advocates rushed into print to defend their conclusions: a question of discipline threatened to develop into one of dogma. That laymen should debate delicate theological problems perplexing even to the trained minds of seminarists and scholars; that they should support the dictates of independent judgment with Scripture; that they should discriminate between the Pope in his official and his human capacity; that they should cite the Fathers on the many glaring errors into which Popes and Councils had fallen—such embarrassing activities were in the highest degree unwholesome and dangerous and could only breed mischief and confusion in simple minds. The imprescriptible right of freedom of conscience, the authority of personal judgment—where might not such far-reaching issues lead? Thirty years later they led to the Reformation. And already there were signs of a latent unrest, an underground movement ramifying in every direction. Even from Germany the Friar boasted that he received letters of adherence, while in France Charles was submitting to the Sorbonne the question of his authority to summon a General Council for the reform of the Church. The alarmists in the Vatican began to stir. The insurrection of the Friar, supported by foreign sympathizers, abetted by official protection, and tolerated by public opinion, could no longer be subordinated to the secular interests of the Holy See. Religious disputes bored Alexander, but he drew himself up with a gesture and converted himself into an institution.

At his next audience the Florentine ambassador found a stormy session. In the presence of several Cardinals the Pope announced that, unless the sermons were suspended by Lent, he would pronounce an interdict on the city. The ambassador, before he could reply, was interrupted by the Cardinals, who read a batch of sonnets composed against the Pope in Florence, while the old man, nodding apostolically, underscored them with a rapid murmur: "So! I am to be turned into sonnets! Turned into sonnets!" Nor did he suffer his resolution to cool. Tossing the sonnets aside, he dismissed the ambassador and dictated a brief to the Republic, denouncing *the son of iniquity*, and demanding under pain of an interdict that he be sent to Rome where, if he repented, he would be "paternally received, for we desire not the death but the conversion of the sinner," or if this were impossible that, at least, he be "segregated from the people as a corrupt member and prevented from disseminating new scandal." Quick to wrath but easily appeased, he was satisfied that a threat would suffice, and the next day he had recovered his composure. Not even the Venetian ambassador could rouse him when he observed, in discussing the case, that the licence the Florentines allowed their Friar was a measure of their respect for His Holiness. Provided they honoured his brief, the Pope replied, the rest mattered little. One could not be thin-skinned and bear the name of Borgia. The Florentine ambassador now found him "very well disposed." The *son of iniquity* was for the moment forgotten. The Holy Father seemed to be his old sanguine self; only the eyes, the weary bovine eyes, were dull as he walked to the window and looked out over the river. For a fleeting second the regular healthy pulse of his body paused imperceptibly; then he roused himself and returned to business.

Meanwhile, the Papal Brief had been submitted to a Government Council in Florence. The phrase, *son of iniquity*, was particularly resented and the sense of the meeting was overwhelmingly in favour of resistance. In drawing up the reply, the compliant Signory of Arrabbiati faithfully reflected the sentiments of the Piagnoni, but it concluded the letter with the following passage: "We greatly regret that these matters have turned the heart of Your Holiness against us and deprived us of the hopes we entertained for the material welfare of our Republic; nevertheless, we shall remain faithful to the Church and the Catholic religion, declaring, however, that we care more for our Republic than for other considerations." The purpose of the letter, its malicious honesty and subtle indiscretion, was immediately decoded by the trained eye of the Milanese ambassador. "This letter," he promptly informed Lodovico Sforza in Milan, "has been written in the name of the Signoria only to force His Holiness to proceed further, so that those who say that he does not act of his own volition, but that the ban has been begged and bought in Florence, may be undeceived, and also so that the Signoria may more justifiably proceed against the Friar without incurring criticism from anyone."

This reply, which the Florentine ambassador lost no time in presenting, seriously alarmed Alexander. He handed it to the Bishop of Parma to read and listened with stolid attention and a deepening frown. "A wretched letter," he sighed, when the reading was over. Then the usual scene repeated itself—the slow flush, the choleric inflation, the sudden rush of querulous volubility. When he seemed to have waded to the end of his words, the ambassador attempted to put in with his usual formula, namely, that His Holiness was misinformed and the Friar calumniated; but its hollowness jarred on his own ears as much as on those of the Pope, who contradicted him hotly. He was not misinformed; he had read the sermons or enough of them at least to gather their tenor; he quoted the passage in which the Friar declared that he would go to Hell sooner than seek absolution; he caught up the book; he pointed to the words, *a broken tool*, and located the allusion to the death of the Duke of Gandia. Bending low over the obnoxious page, he breathed out his sense of the man who could reproach him with the loss of his son! Then he turned away, moodily sniffing his wrath, and the Florentine resumed his set speech, but only to be interrupted again; the old man, working himself up into a towering rage, repeated that neither Turk nor infidel would tolerate such conduct, that he did not censure his good doctrine or his good works but only his insubordination and his contempt of the Holy See; then, finally satisfied with his fury, he sighed and subsided. His gloom was profound, as he weighed his next step. Under Pope Sixtus IV, Florence had resisted and successfully ignored an interdict. He was at the end of his resources, and he brought the audience to an abrupt close, repeating that he would give the Republic one more chance to reconsider . . . one more . . . one more. . . On his way out, the ambassador was overtaken by the Bishop of Parma, who impressed on him that everything was lost; but, he added, if only the Friar could be induced to make *some show of submission*, the Pope would not refuse him permission to preach. The ambassador opened wide eyes. Was it possible—was the Bishop insinuating—that His Holiness would be satisfied with saving his face?

But the pressure was too strong. Alexander was goaded from all sides. All the irreconcilables in Rome were up in arms. The Florentine ambassador trembled for his life; his house was attacked; he wrote home, begging to be relieved of his post. It was impossible to mention the name of Savonarola in public—impossible, that is, except for one purpose. At this moment, like a ghost from the past, Fra Mariano da Gennazzano reappeared, riding the blast, voicing the anonymous fury of public opinion. He had prospered, he was General of his Order, he had his own church, but his heart still ached with his rival; and when it was proposed that he expose the fallacies of the Friar from his pulpit, he leapt to the suggestion with the same alacrity with which he had responded to a like invitation from Lorenzo de' Medici seven years before, and with the same results. Once more, before a brilliant and partial public, including the young Cardinal de' Medici, bland with his eyeglass like an umpire from the past, he abandoned himself to reckless scurrility. Time had taught him nothing. "The Cardinals and the congregation," said an eye-witness, "expected him to expose the alleged errors of Fra Girolamo and to refute them with sound and fundamental arguments, but these he could not supply, and so he helped himself out with vociferation." And it was vociferation of a violence which even in Rome, at that moment and in that age, disgusted his hearers. Crying "like one beside himself," he peppered the reprobate with abuse, and with an aim so blundering that it rebounded on himself and his sponsors. Mingling the lingo of the gutter with the malice of the sacristy, he attacked the personal character of the prophet and let fly at his pride and hypocrisy. The one he dismissed with a jibe at his medals—"medals are coined in his honour more often than Pope Alexander pisses"—and the other with a telling nudge: "He preaches poverty and wears a short robe but his pockets are lined with coin. I know, believe me, I know. It takes a friar to know a friar, we have more skins than an onion, if you would know the truth about one, ask another." His visions he dispelled with a hiccough: "Do you know when you see your visions? When you are full of good Trebbiano. You cannot deceive me." And his prophecies he did not even refute. "You call yourself a holy prophet, but when you burn, your boys will be the first to bring faggots to the fire." Befuddled with fustian and spite, he rose finally to the defence of the Holy See and surpassed himself: "O College! O Pontiff! Take measures against him! You know not his machinations, he will say things to darken the sun. But you make no provision against him: today anyone can frig you to your faces, and but for my reverence I would show you . . ." Whereupon, under the holy hood of the pulpit, he flashed the obscene gesture in their eyes. It was his testamentary act. The Cardinals and the congregation dispersed, "giving plain signs of their displeasure." The disgraced orator fell into a decline and died within the year. A paralysis seized him, but it spared the vital member: his tongue wagged to the end.

More composed but hardly less violent was the tone of the ultimatum which Alexander now dispatched to Florence. "Your conduct has profoundly incensed us. You have not only encouraged the disobedience of this Friar; but, by preventing all others from preaching, you have made him almost your oracle of Apollo. And we shall never relent, until reparation has been made to the dignity and honour of the Holy See, which this worm has been able, with your aid, to insult. Weigh your decision maturely; for only as you show yourselves ready to obey will we concede your requests for the material welfare of your Republic. In any event, reply with no more letters but with acts; for we are firmly resolved to tolerate your disobedience no longer; and we will place the interdict on your city, to last as long as you continue to favour this monstrous idol of yours." The Signoria was satisfied: the cue had been taken.

When the Council convened to consider this ultimatum, its temper had changed. The protests of the Florentine merchants in Rome, threatened not only with the ruin of their trade but with imprisonment and the confiscation of their property, found a loud and long echo in the debate, and the Piagnoni themselves realized that resistance was useless. The leader of the Party resigned himself with a protest. "To close San Marco," he said, "is a question which we have not even entertained. . . . This monastery is a school of goodness, and fifty years hence men will speak of it far more than they do now. As for the Friar, I urge you to honour and respect and prize him more than any man that has lived in the last two hundred years. These briefs do not proceed from the free will of the Pope but have been sued for by the enemies of the City. But we must go slowly, for, if we tighten this wheel, we shall gain nothing but trouble." The vote resulted in a split majority and the Signoria, unsatisfied, moved to carry the debate to the Popular Assembly. With the changed temper of the people toward the excesses of the Piagnoni, however, a popular referendum was a risk which the followers of the Friar were unwilling to face; they compromised and a transaction was concluded with the Arrabbiati by which, in return for the suspension of the sermons, the closure of San Marco would not be exacted.

When this decision was conveyed to the Friar, he received it calmly and asked for a night to consider his own decision. "You come from your masters?" he said to the emissary. "Very well, I must consult mine." It was a last futile gesture of independence; he knew that the end had come. His whole career had been founded on the confusion of political and religious passion; his political value was exhausted, his moral crusade was an embarrassment; and the Party, manoeuvring for political safety, had sacrificed him. It was inevitable. He had founded his life-work on a radical fallacy. His friends hoped that, when the storm blew over, he might resume; but he knew better. The eight years he had promised to preach were over; he would take leave on the morrow. He turned to his Bible and, searching for a text, pored over the tale of Jeremiah, the prophet who was cast away by the Lord when He no longer needed him, and stoned by men. The taper slowly aspired in the airless cell, and his shadow kept vigil beside him.

12

It was over. The great theocratic experiment had failed. It had been conducted under the most favourable conditions and carried to the most final conclusions; and the verdict was No. It had failed of its own inherent futility. Everything had been tried—appeal, intimidation, example, suasion, force—and what had been accomplished? He had demonstrated exhaustively the sterility of Christianity either as a system of statecraft or a way of practical life. The reform of the Republic was not religious, and the moral reform which he had grafted on it was already withering as soon as it was divorced from it and would be before long but a memory. By dint of adventitious circumstances he had succeeded for a moment, only to be ruined and cast aside—a broken tool. Henceforth he signed himself *servus Iesu Christi inutilis*. Nor was this all. "Good is by its very nature diffusive," Christ had revealed to him in a vision. "This is the sign by which the good shall be known: when a man imparts his goodness to others and makes them participate in it, then he is truly good and participates in my goodness. . . . Christian life consists in being compassionate and merciful. . . . In that lies the Christian religion, which is founded on love and charity." Had he not disfigured the true spirit of Christ by making it militant? Not only had the world not been regenerated, it had corrupted his creed; and

Christianity itself had been discredited by the fanatical confusion and extremes into which his experiment had fallen. How could it be otherwise? Christianity and life were incompatible. What had goodness to do with life or compassion with nature? The only true solution was the renunciation of the world and the real core of his creed was death. "Ye are dead, ye have naught to do with the world"—what could that mean to his generation? The Renaissance was swarming about him. In the cramped past, in the poverty and ignorance of the Middle Ages, it had been possible perhaps for so unworldly a faith to flourish; but with affluence and culture the world had outgrown the ascetic faith of its forefathers and rediscovered, in the Classic Revival, that of its ancestors, for whom the first and last law was the satisfaction of life. Life—imperfect, ruthless, lusty, lawless—was richly enough, and the only mastery of nature lay in its imitation. He had pitted himself against a reawakening world, and who of his contemporaries sincerely felt as he did? A handful, perhaps, a little breed of the elect . . . and his children. But they were growing up and nature would claim them. No. He had not quickened the conscience of the age, but he had clarified it; and whatever faith it was seeking, it was not literal Christianity.

As if to prove that the days of the prophet were over, the age was already raising a new one. Among those who followed the final sermons of the Friar in San Marco, in those March days preceding his suspension, was Niccolo Machiavelli. He rarely entered a church, but on this occasion he came as a student of politics to witness the last rally of one of the remarkable movements of his time. It was the crisis: the political and moral elements were parting; he was twenty-nine and about to enter public life, and his mind was forming. Dispassionate and independent, he was self-taught. What he knew he owed to observation and study, to his books, to the streets of Florence, and, above all, to the fact that he was born—it was a family trait—with open eyes. They were his genius. Black, small, deep-set and lynx-like, they penetrated sham and illusion with deadly accuracy; but they saw without seeing, their insight was cerebral, and they were without inner vision. Incapable of self-deception, he was equally incapable of faith. It was by looking about him that he had learned to live, and among the boys on the street he had early learned and easily accepted the fundamental fact that the only code of conduct men instinctively honour is the sexual morality of strength and lust. All the rest was illusion or sham. As he grew up, his favourite books confirmed and enlarged his vision. From the pages of Livy, Caesar, Cicero, Tacitus, and Suetonius, he drew his own ideal of virtue—the Roman ideal of civic virtue which made a religion of patriotism. Patriotism was his religion and the measure of his moral development. Growing up on the streets, his identity soon fused in that general Florentine family, whose traits he possessed to a marked degree —its love of liberty, its love of talk—perhaps the liberty it loved was the liberty to talk—its caustic wit, its scepticism, its materialism. When he read Roman history, it was with an eye on Florence. Steeped in the classic enthusiasm of his time, he was one of the first to outgrow the pedantic cult of antiquity of the scholars, and to turn to pagan thought for practical purposes. Delving into the tomb he sought, in the example of those Romans who were the ancestors of his own race and who had mastered the world, a modern inspiration. The secret of their success was their virtue . . . that virile *virtù*—courage, energy, skill, resourcefulness, strength—which was, like the *virtue* of an herb or a mineral, the inherent power of a man to function efficiently and fulfil his purpose. And since patriotism was his purpose, whatever impeded it—humanity or personal scruples—must be sacrificed with a robust conscience to the general welfare. Not that he was un-Christian. On the contrary, with his modesty, his honesty, his scrupulous personal integrity, his patient and self-effacing sense of duty, he was closer to the Christian than the pagan ideal of character. Far from possessing the virtues he admired, he admired what he lacked. He was not a man of action or efficiency, he was retiring, studious, self-respecting, and unresourceful; but he saw, with his unflinching eyes, that the world had no mercy on the weak and the unfit. His whole thought was coloured by a radical contradiction of his ideas and his conduct. At the root of his realistic view of life lay a romantic desire to escape, to transcend his limitations in the vicarious and glorified life of his country. He judged his countrymen, accordingly, with the same severity with which he judged himself; and he found them sadly degenerated from the antique stock. The Roman tradition had been broken by two calamities, the barbarian invasions and the effeminizing influence of Christianity; and they seemed to be repeated by the coincidence of the French invasion and the evangelical experiment of Savonarola. It was his favourite maxim that history repeated itself. But how little men learned! Humanity civilized itself slowly; while the head rose from primeval mire, the body remained earth-bound and primitive. The brute was indispensable to man. Italy had rediscovered civilization, but it was unable to protect it; its salvation lay in the Roman tradition, buried for five centuries in the tomb but still quick in the blood, and the first necessity was to revert to the antique stock. What he perceived so clearly, his countrymen realized vaguely and would not admit: they were muddle-headed. Half the evils of life were the result of loose thinking, of timidity, confusion, hypocrisy, of half-measures and inconsistency. The success of Savonarola proved it. By what spell had he hypnotized that normally sane Florentine people with his mixture of plain mystifications, obscure vaticinations, perfervid eloquence, and unworldly ideals? "As you say," said one of Machiavelli's friends, "Florence is founded under a planet such that men of this kind abound there and are willingly listened to." Precisely: there was a side of the Florentine nature which he lacked and which baffled him—its mysticism. Insensible to that obscure urge for passion and faith which inspired the Friar and his followers, he perceived that it challenged his convictions. It was a power, more potent than reason; it was a fact, and he never blinked facts. And so he came to San Marco to study its workings, and to estimate the man by his methods.

In the first days of March 1498, immediately after the election of the Arrabbiati to the Signoria, when the Friar had withdrawn from the Duomo to San Marco and was expounding his dispute with Rome and rallying his political support in Florence, the paths of Machiavelli and Savonarola crossed. The prophet whose life lay in his eyes watched the prophet whose life lay in his voice; and after the sermon he wrote his impressions to a friend in Rome. "Our Friar being now in his own house, you should have heard with what boldness he began his sermons and with what recklessness he followed them up. You would have been no little amazed; for, being profoundly unsure of himself, yet believing that the new Signoria would not harm him, and realizing that many citizens would be buried under his ruin, he began with great terrors, with reasons most compelling to those who did not dispute them, proving his own followers to be the salt of the earth and his enemies scoundrels, and touching every point which could weaken his opponents and strengthen his own party; of which, since I was present, I will briefly describe a few.

"The text of his first sermon in San Marco was this verse from Exodus: *Quanto magis premebant eos, tanto magis multiplicabantur et crescebant.*[1] And before coming to the exposition, he explained why he had retreated and said: *prudentia est recta ratio agibilium.*[2] Then he said that

---

[1] The more they are oppressed, the more will they grow and multiply.
[2] Prudence is the proper rule of conduct.

all men have, and have had, a different purpose. For Christians their purpose is Christ, for other men, both present and past, it is and has been different, according to their persuasions. We who are Christians, therefore, meaning to pursue our purpose which is Christ, must preserve His honour with the utmost prudence and respect for the time; and when the times require that we expose our lives, expose them; and when they require us to hide, we must hide, as we read of Christ and St. Paul; and thus we have done, for when it was right to face the storm we did so, as on Ascension Day, because the honour of God and the times demanded it; now the honour of God requires that we yield to wrath and we have yielded. After this speech, he sorted us into two bands, one fighting under God, which was himself and his followers, the other fighting under the Devil, which was his opponents; and having spoken of this at length, he began the exposition of the text from Exodus. . . . I report briefly, since the limits of a letter are too narrow for a long account. Then, to weaken his adversaries and to prepare a bridge to his next sermon, he said, as he always says, that our dissensions might produce a tyrant who would ruin our homes and waste our territory; and that this was not inconsistent with what he had previously stated, namely, that Florence would have a happy future and dominate Italy, because before long he would be driven out; and with this his sermon ended.

"The other day, still expounding Exodus and coming to the passage which says that Moses murdered an Egyptian, he told us that the Egyptian stood for the wicked and Moses for the preacher who murdered them by exposing their vices, and exclaimed: O man of Egypt, I have my knife out for you! And here he began to explode your books, O priests, and to abuse you in a manner that dogs would not have swallowed; then he added—and this was what he was leading up to— that he would give the Egyptian another great blow, and that there was someone in Florence who meant to make himself a tyrant and was holding councils and making plots for that purpose; and that to try to drive out the Friar, to excommunicate the Friar, to persecute the Friar, meant one thing and one thing only—to foster a tyrant; and he urged us to obey the laws. And he said so much that, after the sermon, men made public conjecture of one who is as likely to become a tyrant as you are to go to Heaven. But since then the Signoria has written in his favour to the Pope, and seeing that he no longer needs to fear his adversaries in Florence, whereas formerly he attempted to unite his own party in the hatred of their enemies and to frighten them with the prospect of a tyrant, now he changes his tune and, exhorting them all to union and making no more mention of tyrant or wickedness, seeks to incite them all against the Pope, and, turning them against him and his curbs, speaks of him as the most vicious man you can conceive; and thus, in my opinion, he follows the times and colours his lies accordingly."

An opportunist: judging the man by his methods, Machiavelli dismissed him as a time-serving and self-seeking demagogue, veering with every shift of the political wind; and twenty years later he still called him "artful." But to judge the man by his methods was the ingenuous error of a systematic cynic. The expedients of the spellbinder which he noted with such subacid sarcasm—the desperate shifts, the partisan appeals, the spectral terrors, the empty bugbears—these he detected quickly with his ferreting eyes; but through these makeshifts the unreasoning crowd sensed something more—the underlying and undeviating sincerity and consistency of the man. If anything was more transparent than his artfulness, it was his guilelessness; the Friar could only be understood by the simple, and Machiavelli was the dupe of his own shrewdness. He saw everything but his inspiration. Indifferent to his faith, he could only judge it by its effects. The fact had a profound bearing on his future. Reviewing those tragic days in San Marco much later, when he came to formulate his own gospel, he raised the question whether innovations succeed "by prayers or by force," and concluded: "All armed prophets have conquered, and all unarmed have been destroyed . . . as happened in our time to Fra Girolamo Savonarola, who was ruined with his new order of things as soon as the crowd ceased to believe in him." Such was his considered opinion of the power of faith. Had he not seen it?

13

But he had not yet seen all. The power of the Friar lay in the fugitive effect of his eloquence; he was officially silenced; his political support had failed; he was left to bear alone the brunt of his feud with Rome; and the Friar himself foresaw his fate. "The Master wields the hammer," he said in his last sermon, "and when He has employed it to His purpose, He does not replace it in the chest but casts it away.

So was it with Jeremiah; when He had used him as He would, He cast him aside to be stoned. So will it be with this hammer; when He has wielded it, He will cast it away." Never had he revealed himself more frankly. If he had not been led, he confessed, he might not have come so far. "In the beginning, when I embarked on this sea, I discerned something, but I was bidden not to fear and told that we should soon pass this first floodtide. If I had foreseen the end then, I might have fled, like Jonah in Tarsus." Now it was too late; he could only face the consequences; and, though the flesh was weak, he prayed that his faith might not fail. "The Lord is with me," he repeated in a final cry of assurance, desperately suggestive of reassurance. "O Lord, may I not say it? Surely I may say it. Therefore, I say boldly this morning: if I am deceived, Christ, you have deceived me! Holy Trinity, if I am deceived, you have deceived me! If I am deceived, Angels, you have deceived me! Saints in Paradise, Saints without number, if I am deceived, you have deceived me!"

The cry went up, like a rocket, in a void without echo. But was not the test of faith its self-sufficiency? He was cast back on himself to prove it. He was still led . . . led by defeat to a final manifestation of his power . . . challenged to prove his indomitable conviction and courage to the world . . . and to himself. Above all, to himself. His courage was not inborn; it had been forced by will and fostered by circumstances. It was the courage of necessity and excitement. In the pulpit he was fearless—"if I were always as I am here," he said, "I should never know fear"—but what was that courage which depended on the stimulation of the crowd? The test was to carry on the struggle alone; and no sooner had he descended from the pulpit than he took his first step. Too long had he been fighting facts with words; it was time to prove his faith by acts. He expected no quarter from Rome, and his haunting premonition of martyrdom hurried him on with the resolution of despair. A few of his close friends were now called to San Marco, sworn to secrecy, and entrusted with letters to the Courts of France, England, Germany, Spain, and Hungary. At the same time he wrote punctiliously to the Pope. "Holy Father," he explained, "I have always thought it the duty of a good Christian to defend the faith and correct morals, but in this labour I have encountered only trials and tribulations, not one man who would aid me. I had hoped in Your Holiness, but you have preferred to join my enemies and give fierce wolves leave to torment me cruelly. No heed has been paid to the reasons I gave, not to excuse my error, but to prove the truth of my doctrine, my innocence, and my obedience to the Church. I can no longer hope in Your Holiness; I must turn, therefore, to Him who elects the weak of this world to confound the strong lions of the wicked. He will aid me to sustain and prove against the whole world the sanctity of this work for which I suffer so much, and He will inflict the just penalty on those who persecute me and attempt to prevent it. For myself, I seek no earthly glory but await death with eagerness. I implore Your Holiness to delay no longer but to provide for your health."

A terrible letter, those who saw it called it; and terrible it was because the Friar made the mistake of being right once too often. Alexander was in a dangerous mood. The suspension of the sermons no longer satisfied him. Fra Domenico and others were preaching the subversive doctrines of their master; the movement was scotched, not crushed. The old politician was a prey to self-reproach. He rued his indulgence; he felt that, in waiving the surrender of Savonarola, he had acted weakly; and it was in this temper—baffled, irresolute, at odds with himself—that he read the warning letter of the Friar, with its veiled threat, its imperturbable assurance, its serene self-righteousness, and—most exasperating of all—its noble and melancholy tone of martyred injury. The dark Spanish blood of Roderigo Borgia began to burn. The hidalgo in him responded to the high moral courtesy and scrupulous loyalty with which that ominous letter warned him of some approaching attack; and he resented profoundly the impudence of such etiquette. The contents also perturbed him. He was completely in the dark; he had lost all his bearings. A few days later, however, he received a document addressed to the Florentine ambassador in France, which had been intercepted on the Milanese frontier by the agents of Lodovico Sforza. It was a secret communication written on behalf of the Friar, accompanied by a copy of his last letter to the Pope, and moving that the sovereigns of France, Spain, Germany, and Hungary should convoke a General Council for the reform of the Church. The Pope was incapable of it. "I testify, *in verbis Domini,* that this Alexander is no Pope, nor can be considered such, since, leaving aside his most execrable sin of simony, by which he bought the Papal throne and daily sells ecclesiastical benefices to the highest bidder and his other manifest vices, I affirm that he is no Christian and does not believe in God, which passes the limit of every infidelity." Such was the result of tolerance. It was incredible that the Friar had taken such a step on his own initiative alone; and Alexander cast about in confusion, counting and suspecting his influential friends in Rome, beginning with Cardinal Caraffa, and reckoning his own enemies up to that relentless one, Cardinal Giuliano della Rovere. The ruthlessness of terror rose in him. In the violent revulsion of a weak nature, he went blind with vindictiveness. He realized that with Savonarola there could be no half-measures; there would never be peace between them while they both breathed. But to forestall a schism in the Church he must risk a breach with the Republic; even in the blindness of bovine fury caution cramped his courage. The malignance of that dilemma fascinated him. Then something happened, swift, unlooked-for, catastrophic, which suddenly brought the solution of all his difficulties and the relief of all his fears.

14

The rise of the great Dominican had not passed uncontested by other Orders and his eclipse was followed by a prolonged clamour in rival convents. Immediately after his retirement a Franciscan friar, Fra Francesco da Puglia, took the pulpit, worrying his heels with furious charges of heresy, schism, and supernatural imposture. Savonarola had always ignored such manifestations of monastic jealousy. *"Filii matris mea pugnaverunt contra me,"*[1] was his only rebuke to a group of clerics who organized, in the first days of his political activity, a public protest against it; and he had gone his way unperturbed. But he was no longer in the pulpit, and his place had been taken by Fra Domenico. His old disciple seconded him ably according to his lights, turning his hand to every task, and rejoicing quite honestly in the name which the populace gave him of Brother Factotum. His abilities were primarily practical. Preaching in Prato the previous year, he had been challenged by this same Franciscan to an Ordeal by Fire; he had accepted unhesitatingly; whereupon the Franciscan promptly eclipsed himself and returned to Florence, but now he suddenly revived the challenge; and this time he was careful to direct it explicitly at Savonarola. It was no sooner published than Fra Domenico, feeling his master's honour to be at stake, and with a faith as unquestioning as his courage, accepted in his

[1] The sons of my mother fight against me.

stead. This he did on his own initiative, without consulting his master; and the dispute had arisen so swiftly that Savonarola, absorbed in his letters to the Princes, awoke to it too late to quench it.

Suddenly he was trapped. All about him he felt the earth giving out flames, wreathing his end with a mephitic leak. It was incredible, it was obsolete, an Ordeal by Fire had not been known for centuries, it belonged to the ages of barbarism and credulity. He rebuked Fra Domenico sternly. But he had kindled an ardour of faith in his eager disciple that equalled, that surpassed, his own; and his champion was determined to prove that faith by his fortitude. He was a simple soul; he refused to distinguish between moral and physical courage; besides, it was too late; the honour and prestige of their cause was at stake; he could not withdraw. Savonarola reluctantly yielded. There was only one alternative—to accept the challenge himself. But Fra Domenico would not hear of it. He insisted that his master reserve himself: his was a higher end; his work was not finished, the whole responsibility for the Council rested on him, and he could not jeopardize it. Savonarola listened with a parched heart and reluctantly agreed. His courage was unquestionable; he had proved it again and again in the pulpit; he was proving it now by his silence. To move, single-handed, the sovereigns of Christendom against Rome required courage of no mean order. And it required the rarest of courage to ignore the challenge and the interpretation which the vulgar would put on his reserve. And yet—his conscience cracked and the flame crept into his soul—he had a burning faith; but had he the faith to burn? The simple soul was right—the simple were always right—physical courage was the true test of the soul. How many times had he invoked martyrdom in the pulpit! And now . . . Now the hour had come, and something within him rose, something chill, profound, and mightier than himself, that seized him by the throat, equivocating desperately with his fate, protesting that his hour had not come—when it came, he would not fail. But who knows when his hour has come? Life has no finality. It is too elusive, too resourceful, too unpredictable. The hour strikes, unheard. The hour strikes, overtaking the hero, unawares. Fra Domenico was right, with his prompt, blind, unreasoning courage. But he had been born with it, a hardy peasant, without imagination enough to realize what he was facing. His master realized it and bore his agony already, redoubled by his own. How could he hold up his head again? How could he accept that sacrifice? He was ruined. His own disciple had robbed him of his palm of glory.

He no longer led, he followed. Whatever happened, he would never again be the same man. The moral ordeal had consumed his self-confidence.

Then the menace suddenly subsided. The Franciscan stubbornly refused to meet Fra Domenico, insisting that "the dispute was with Savonarola and with him he would enter the fire, though he believed he would burn, because he wished that disseminator of scandals and wicked doctrine to perish also; but with Fra Domenico he would have nothing to do." Thereupon the Franciscans proposed a new arrangement of two champions on either side. Savonarola profited by the lull to publish a defence of his position and to pour a smooth flow of reason on the dispute. "He had too great an undertaking in hand," he explained, "to lose himself in such wretched disputes." If his adversaries would bind themselves to settle the decision of his cause against the Church by the Ordeal, "he would not hesitate to enter the fire and was certain that he would issue from it unscathed. But if they expect the fire to prove the validity of the excommunication, let them reply to our reasons. Or is it a means of combating our prophecies? But we neither force nor urge anyone to believe us beyond his own inclination. We exhort men to live honestly and for that the fire of piety, the miracle of faith, is needed; all the rest matters nothing. . . . As for myself, I reserve myself for a greater task, in behalf of which I shall always be ready to lay down my life. A time will come when the Lord will disclose supernatural signs; for the present it is sufficient to point out that, by sending some of our friars, we expose ourselves also to the fury of the people in case the Lord should not bring them unscathed through the flame."

But the time for reason was past. The crowd which he had excited, only two months before, with miraculous promises, and which he had dominated so long with supernatural terrors, now was aflame with those passions which are the nemesis of the visionary, with that violent revulsion from the saint to the brute by which humanity recovers its mediocrity and its sanity. Its bloodlust was aroused, and all his enemies were exploiting it. The situation was brutal and could be met only in one way, by the one quality which the crowd respects—animal courage.

The Compagnacci, who were openly planning to repeat the disturbance they had missed on the occasion of the Ascension Day riot, were busily fanning the popular excitement and inciting the Franciscans. But the Franciscans were wavering and Fra Francesco da Puglia now withdrew. A substitute was induced to replace him, however, on an express understanding with the Compagnacci that the Ordeal would never take place. But that gang of young bloods was loose-mouthed, and the secret leaked out. Savonarola saw his opportunity. He could cope with false fire. In the hope of intimidating his enemies, he insisted on the most rigid guarantees and formidable preparations for the experiment; and the situation now turned to a sinister farce, a silent deadly game of bluff, in which each side sought to outface and outlast the other. But now from another quarter came a new gust of zeal. The example of Fra Domenico, with his uncompromising and uncalculating courage, had inspired not only the monks of San Marco but all the followers of the Friar with a like fervour; three hundred friars volunteered, and the laity stood up in church, men and women alike, offering themselves unflinchingly. Hysteria and histrionism, bravado and faith, were impenetrably confounded, and Savonarola was swept forward by the fanatical impulse of his followers. The stampede threatened to smother the fire or to end in a wholesale holocaust. And it threatened something else—a public commotion. The Government, which, under the instigation of the Arrabbiati, had reluctantly consented to tolerate and even to take charge of the experiment, now suffered qualms and summoned a Council to consider the wisdom of permitting it. Few took it seriously. One speaker suggested that a less cruel and no less trying ordeal for a friar would be a tub of cold water; or the water might even be lukewarm. This cynical jocularity reflected the general feeling. The question was regarded as "a preachers' squabble, to be settled in Rome, where they canonize saints, rather than in the Palace, where it is more proper to discuss money or war." The only protests it excited were remonstrances against its being discussed at all. "When I hear of such things," one indignant speaker went on record, "I do not know whether to wish myself alive or dead. If our ancestors who founded this city had ever dreamed that we should debate such matters and make ourselves the laughing-stock of the world, I believe they would never have consented to found anything at all." But what everyone took seriously was the dissension aroused by the Friar and the necessity of finally quelling it; and this sentiment dictated a decree, framed by the Signoria, which authorized the experiment but censured it and provided that, if either of the champions perished, his superior should be banished, and if both, that the penalty should apply to the Prior of San Marco alone.

Extraordinary precautions were taken on the morning of the Ordeal (April 7) for the protection of the city and the segregation of the spectators. The city gates were closed and guarded; the Palace, the Piazza, and all the issues to it were heavily policed: the spectators were searched for weapons as they struggled into the square, and women and children were excluded; but it was noticed that a corner had been allotted to the Compagnacci, and they were present to the number of several hundred men. It was a limpid April day, and long before dawn the irregular oblong and the neighbouring roofs were swarming with a crowd so dense that few could distinguish the pyre except as a space about which the swallows wheeled in fickle and inquisitive flight—the only moving things in that cramped multitude. But it was a long-suffering Italian throng that waited for its lethal holiday, eating and chatting, drinking and patient. The Ordeal was set for noon, and the crowd had been waiting seven daylight hours when the first contenders arrived. The Franciscans straggled in unobtrusively and their champion immediately slipped into the Palace to make his final arrangements with the Signori. They were followed by the Dominicans in solemn procession, bearing tapers, and chanting the psalm: *Exurgat Deus et dissipentur inimici eius.*[1] This was the first satisfactory spectacle of the day. The Loggia dei Lanzi had been divided into two sections, with an altar in each, and Savonarola was seen to enter the Dominican pen, carrying the Host, and after a brief prayer turn and face those acres of men without women. Near him a little red blur moving impatiently to and fro was identified as Fra Domenico in a scarlet chasuble. The long wait, the anticipation of hours and of years, was over; and a great silence settled over the crowd. But nothing happened. Noon struck with a prolonged clang from all the bells in the city and died away and the Palace remained closed. Neither the Signori nor the Franciscan champion appeared. For an hour, for two hours, the inexplicable delay continued. The Dominicans reflected the restlessness of the crowd and sent one of their number into the Palace. When he returned, there was a confabulation with the Franciscans and the crowd watched a dispute which they could only follow as a dumbshow but the sense of which, as it was transmitted to them, was that the Franciscans objected to the red chasuble of Fra Domenico. After some time Fra Domenico divested himself of it. There was a pause, the discussion was renewed, and the Dominican champion withdrew into the Palace, whence he presently emerged wearing another robe. But he emerged alone. The Franciscan remained invisible. The multitude soon became restive. Derisive cries and whistles broke out, multiplying rapidly, the Compagnacci pressed forward, and suddenly the Piazza was in an uproar. The crowd surged toward the Loggia, but

---

[1] God will arise and scatter His enemies.

the Government troops drove it back, and gradually the tumult subsided. Then the wait began again. The April sky darkened and began to shower but the multitude held its ground grimly through the sharp downpour and the rain passed as rapidly as it started. A stifling humidity rose from the pavement where the crowd was milling in puddles and dung, and as the interminable, enervating hours dragged on, a long murmur swelled and subsided and swelled, travelling back and forth in aimless and sullen gusts. Here and there some began to groan and others to mimic the chaffer in the Loggia. Fra Domenico was clutching his crucifix and bargaining for it with the Franciscans, to whom he surrendered it eventually, but only to exchange it for the Host, which he accepted from his master. Then the discussion flared up and grew audible enough to attract attention. Heated and long was the debate which ensued on the perplexing question whether or not the immaterial substance of the Sacrament could burn with the vessel which contained it; sacrilege was charged on all sides; Savonarola cited canonical authority, and his adversaries, finding him at last inclined to resist, redoubled their arguments. The debate spread to the crowd but on the more inflammable subject of who began it. At strategic points, voices rose, jeering the Dominicans and their prophet; evening was approaching and the multitudinous discussion was still in progress when the doors of the Palace opened and the Signori sent out orders to countermand the Ordeal.

Of all conclusions this was the most dangerous. The crowd was baffled, confused, and infuriated; the Franciscans dispersed rapidly, claiming the victory; and Savonarola and his two hundred monks, jostled and insulted by a sullen mob, only regained San Marco under the escort of their followers. Even the Piagnoni were disappointed and indignant; many complained that the Friar should himself have entered the fire; and his own monks, keyed up to an intense pitch of expectation and suddenly let down by this lame and impotent solution, were a prey now to disaffection and doubt. In the cheerless dusk of San Marco, transformed in a few hours by the spell of disenchantment into a place foreign and strange, Savonarola addressed a congregation of women who had remained there to pray; and, appealing from men to their mothers, he explained with the patient voice of a venerable child what had happened.

But what had happened? Several years later, Dolfo Spini, the leader of the Compagnacci, discussing the issue of that day in the shop of Sandro Botticelli where a little "Academy of idle hands" forgathered, boasted of the complete success of their scheme. "It had never been their intention," he said, "to send the friar of San Francesco into the fire, and they had so assured him; all they required was that he should make a play and prolong the affair until they could accomplish their purpose, which was to suppress the cause of the Friar and remove him from Florence." Their efforts to start a riot had been abortive; but the failure was more to their purpose than an outbreak would have been: the unsatisfied violence of the mob, with nothing accomplished, made everything possible. A storm was brewing and on the morrow it broke.

The next day was Palm Sunday. A Dominican was announced to preach in the Duomo; but at the door he was turned back by the Compagnacci, who entered the church, dismissed the congregation, and started on the run for San Marco. Through the calm Sabbath streets a familiar sound sent the prudent scurrying to cover—a sound which reminded them of that bloodless Sunday which marked the expulsion of the Medici—an echo now more ominous, for it was the regular rhythm of Florentine annals—the muffled sound of a dogged double-time mustering in a steady trot to the slaughter. It swept by and, when it had passed, cautious faces appeared at the windows; and through the hush that settled again drifted the distant din of "San Marco! To San Marco!" In the wake of that sound the curious inspected its first victims —a student who was breathing his life out over a book of psalms, and an aged oculist groping in the gutter for a place to die. In San Marco, vespers were over when a hail of stones flew through the doors, scattering the lingering worshippers with convulsive cries. In a moment the church emptied, and, when the monks had bolted the gates, there remained only some thirty citizens to defend them. But they were among the hardiest partisans of San Marco, and the monks themselves were by no means emasculated by monastic life. At the suggestion of Fra Silvestro, several had already prepared for such an emergency by laying in an arsenal—a dozen cuirasses, four or five crossbows, eighteen old halberds, and a barrel of powder and shot. Of these provisions Savonarola was ignorant and, when he arrived on the scene and found them being distributed, he protested, but without avail. His flock flew through the cloisters, crying *Viva Cristo.* The flame had come to San Marco and they were fired. In vain he repeated that Christ laid down his life without resistance, in vain until, unheeded, he heard himself. Then, seizing a crucifix, "This storm is for me, let me go," he cried, and made for the door. But his friends flung themselves on him and checked him. His friends? His hour was striking and the moment was passing, the reckless moment in which he had mastered himself, the supreme moment in which he despised life at last, finding it heroic and easy. But his friends would not have it. He had regained his authority, however, and forcing them to lay down their arms he led them in procession through the convent, chanting his spirit once more into its walls. While the walls were still reverberating to the double strain of that long evensong within and the pressure and din of the mob without, a summons from the mace-bearers of the Signoria suspended them both and a decree was read, commanding the defenders to lay down their arms and evacuate the convent, and pronouncing the exile of the Friar, who was given twelve hours to leave Florentine territory. A hurried consultation was held. The decree was regarded as a ruse of the mob, and it was resolved to ignore it; several of his partisans slipped out to fetch help, and the convent bell tolled the alarm.

Dusk was thickening, and the besiegers now redoubled their attacks. Fire was laid to the doors, and the rioters, scaling the rear walls of the cloister, penetrated into the infirmary, which they sacked, pushed through the sacristy, and forced the door into the choir. The monks, startled out of grace, rose in a cloud and, seizing tapers and crucifixes, fought like infuriated bats, and with such effect that they routed their assailants, hounded them through the cloister and, running to the roof, continued to pursue them with tiles. The assault subsided, and the defenders returned to the choir to make a hasty meal in the lull and to nurse and confess the wounded and dying. One of these expired still dancing in spirit and singing *Ecce quam bonum et jocundum habitare fratres in unum*! And indeed confidence reigned, the great bell continued to toll, and when a second summons to surrender came from the Signoria, it was rejected.

By now it was night. The doors were burning, a dense acrid smoke swept through the church, curling about the columns, swelling into a glowing canopy of billowing clouds, and inflating the vault; and in that sulphurous murk the ghostly flock rallied for a final stand. The windows were smashed and light travelled over the scene—a lurid light of dancing flames, darkness made visible to confound them. A young monk of German extraction and archangelic vigour leapt into the pulpit as the attack revived and, resting his crossbow on the lectern, lectured the night with lead. Amid the dull thud of bullets, the guttural shouts of the German, the hoarse murmur of prayers, the vague silhouettes moving like spectres in a mustering pandemonium, Savonarola was unheard.

Finally he rallied the few who would listen and led them to the Greek Library. There he took leave of them. A third summons had now come from the Signoria, demanding the immediate surrender of himself, Fra Silvestro, and Fra Domenico. Fra Silvestro had disappeared and Fra Domenico, suspecting a ruse of the mob, refused to surrender until the officers returned with a writ. There remained a few minutes more of freedom . . . freedom of will, freedom of speech; and Savonarola reaffirmed, standing there amid the silence of the past and the placid relics of lives that had already been lived, the truth of his doctrine. "What I have said I have had from God, and He is my witness in Heaven that I do not lie. I did not know that the City would turn against me so soon; but the Lord's will be done. My last word is this: faith, patience, and prayer are your arms. I leave you with anguish and sorrow, to place myself in the hands of our enemies. I do not know if they will take my life, but I am certain that if I die I can help you in Heaven more than I have been able to in life. Have courage, embrace the cross, and you will find the port of salvation." The mob was now invading the convent, the writ had not yet arrived, and his friends urged him to flee, while there was yet time. He hesitated. Suddenly a voice spoke, a voice that was not his own and that was still and small. Fra Malatesta Sacramoro, one of the monks whom the failure of the Ordeal had embittered, murmured: "Should not the shepherd lay down his life for the flock?" Savonarola looked at him and said nothing. Then he moved toward him deliberately and kissed him. Fra Malatesta presented him with the writ. The officers were at the door. His monks gathered about him, he embraced them one by one, and, as he passed out, he repeated that the work of God would go on and that his death would only speed it. A moment later they heard so appalling a clamour below that they concluded the crowd had killed him.

That would have been too simple. The crowd had been waiting three hours for this moment. It closed over him with a gluttonous surge, swept him under, disgorged him, bandied him about, and his guards, struggling to free him, were borne along, amid a bedlam of abuse. Lanterns were swung in his eyes, torches were thrust in his face with the cry: "Here is the true light." His hands, bound behind his back, were wrenched, his fingers twisted with a jeer: "Prophesy who struck you!" Caught up by the many-handed mothering mob, cramped in its convulsions, like an infant crushed in the womb, he was born, after forty-five years, to humanity. Not till he had lived could he die, not till he had known the full brutality of being. Pain was the only reality.

Lurching to and fro in that lunging, labouring, lynching mob, he was initiated into mankind and delivered at last of all his illusions: right and wrong, virtue and vice, were unmeaning words: there was only the shock and play of blind forces. Faith, patience, courage, spirit—all the poor fictions with which men mask the naked fact of their impotence —were left far behind in the Library where they belonged; they belonged to the half-life of the past, which another man had lived, not he. He was born now. Swept by a last rush into the Palace and left to the mercy of the law, he was sent sprawling with a kick and a cry to point it: "There is where he breeds Prophecy!"

Among those who were arrested that night was his brother Alberto Savonarola, who happened to be in Florence; but he was soon released and he returned to Ferrara to inform the family of what had actually befallen his famous brother, Girolamo.

15

The arrest of the Friar brought a vast relief to the Vatican. In the Borgia apartments, under the ultramarine vaults where Isis and Osiris and the Bull held their funereal parley, Alexander moved freely, dictating his correspondence with Florence: first, a Brief congratulating the Franciscans; then a second, which reiterated his satisfaction; then his benediction to the Signory, with a promise to reconsider their appeal for a ten per cent tax on ecclesiastical property; then his consent, after an audience with the Florentine ambassador, to the civil trial in Florence, stipulating, however, that two clerical authorities should sit with the magistrates and that, at its conclusion, the accused should be surrendered to his own representatives, either to be brought to Rome or to stand their ecclesiastical trial in Florence; and finally a plenary indulgence for the Octave of Easter. Isis and Osiris and the Bull pursued, overhead, their funereal parley.

Meanwhile in Florence preparations were rapidly improvised for the trial. The leading Piagnoni were arrested and questioned on the activities of the Friar; San Marco was searched for incriminating matter; and in the course of this search Fra Silvestro was unearthed and promptly surrendered to the authorities. The Government made some necessary adjustments in its machinery. In normal procedure the trial should have been conducted by the Eight—the Department of Criminal and Political Justice—which was still dominated by the Piagnoni. They were about to go out of office, however, and the Signori proceeded to a premature election of their successors. Then more cautious counsels prevailed, and an extraordinary commission of eighteen examiners was appointed to draw up the indictment and obtain evidence; and to this picked jury the trial was entrusted. Now that the machinery had been prepared, it was discovered that everything had been provided but the impeachment. On what grounds was the Friar to be tried? It was essential to give a legal colour to what, in fact, was a political prosecution, and it was impossible, on the face of it, to convict him of a statutory offence. His real offence was his influence; and in their determination to destroy it the jury resorted to charges which made the case a trial of character. They began by concentrating on his weak point—his prophetic claims. If he could be proved an impostor on one point, it would follow, by inference, that he was a charlatan on every other—so at least the legal mind worked.

Savonarola was brought from his cell and put to the torture. He succumbed immediately. All his life he had wandered among facts like a phantom, with only a dim memory and a dimmer premonition of pain to guide, or to lure, him toward reality; but he felt it now in the clutch of the wrack. Babbling deliriously, he complied to all the questions with which he was plied, but too incoherently to please his examiners. Something was still unbroken and he no sooner recovered than he repudiated his testimony and reaffirmed the truth of his doctrine. He was then permitted to write his own statement; but it proved so unworkable that it was withdrawn and subsequently destroyed. The examiners were in a dilemma. One of their number had already resigned, indignantly declaring that he "would not be a party to this murder"; and they were unwilling to risk a palpable forgery. But this was a routine difficulty. A notary offered his services and guaranteed to manipulate whatever evidence the Friar might offer at the trial with a minimum of falsification and a maximum of effect. His fee was considered exorbitant—400 ducats; but it was made contingent on his success.

The trial lasted ten days and took place behind closed doors; there were fourteen applications of torture; and between the twists of the wrack and the pen a full confession was finally extorted. Nervous, impressionable, undermined by years of strain and anxiety, the victim was without physical resistance; the torturer declared that he had never known anyone on whom the wrack took effect so quickly. With every wrench his convictions snapped, and when he was released he was broken. Deadlier than the wrack, the relentless common sense of his questioners confused him. What if they were right? His prophetic claims were his nemesis; he was vulnerable; he could not be sure. What if they were right? Deliberate imposture he denied; but self-deception—? He remembered his first hallucinations, the occult solicitations of Fra Silvestro, his self-searchings, his reliance on "natural reason," the electrical response to his prophecies, the coming of King Charles . . . and, "Let this question settle itself," he protested at last. "If it comes from God, you will have manifest signs; if it comes from man, it will crumble. Whether I am a prophet or not is no matter of state; and no man has a right to judge or condemn another on his intentions." His intentions! They had been honest; if the means were meretricious, no one could impugn his purpose. Was it right that for one flaw the whole fabric of his faith should unravel? that one drop of adulteration should cloud his clear truth? For that was what was happening. When the examiners had established his impostures as a prophet, they attacked his purpose. "As for my intention and the purpose for which I was working," he testified, "I reply that it was glory and to have reputation and credit; and for this purpose I sought to maintain myself in good esteem in the city of Florence, which seemed to me an apt instrument to increase this glory and gain credit abroad as well, particularly when I saw that I was believed." Such was the handiwork of the notary, a literal transcription of his own words with a mere omission of such redundant phrases as *the glory of God*. "And to further this purpose I preached things which would convince Christians of the abominations that were practised in Rome. And if the Council which I expected had been summoned, I hoped to depose many prelates and also the Pope. And I would have tried to be present and to preach there and to do such things as would have brought me glory." Asked if he aspired to the Papal Throne, "I did not think much of becoming Cardinal or Pope," he said, "because if I had conducted this work without being Pope, I would have been the first man in the world in reputation and in authority; and if I had been made Pope, I would not have refused, though it seemed to me a greater thing to be the head of this work than to be Pope; for a man without virtue can be Pope, but a task of this sort requires a man of excellent virtue." The notary now began to over-reach himself, interpolating wherever the text seemed to call for it such phrases as "this was my pride," "this was my hypocrisy," "this I did for the glory of the world." But the corruption worked its results—even on the Friar. When he was confronted with his testimony, he saw an image of himself which, with all its distortion, could not be wholly denied. Had he really been disinterested? Heavenly ambition was still ambition; pride of character was the most insidious form of pride; and all glory was vainglory. Was the presumption of prophecy worse than that of self-righteousness? His pride of irreproachability—would he have valued it so highly had he been quite selfless? Could he be sure of the purity of his purpose? Everything hung together and with one little rift his whole confidence ravelled. His spirit, like his flesh, succumbed to mortality; and when the examination was over he was heard, in his cell, bitterly lamenting, "O Lord, Lord, you have taken the spirit of prophecy from me!"

After ten days of interrogation and torture, nothing more damaging than an admission of humanity and delusion had been wrested from him; and the Signoria was unsatisfied. "We have to deal," they wrote to the Pope, who complained of their slowness, "with a man long-suffering in body and sagacious in mind, who steels his spirit against torture and envelops the truth in numberless obscurities, and who seems to be determined either to acquire, by simulated sanctity, an everlasting name with posterity, or to endure imprisonment and death. By long and assiduous questioning, for many days and by force, we have barely been able to extort from him something which we will not yet reveal, waiting until the more recondite integuments of his soul begin to open." In spite of them, in spite of himself, his innocence transpired; and with it their true impeachment. They were determined, as they stripped away its last integuments, to force his soul, to probe its secret, to pluck out the heart of a mystery that resisted and exasperated them, the elusive mystery of that moral passion which sustained him and which challenged their humanity. The moralist was on trial. For years the resentment of his pretensions had been gathering to a head, and it rose at last in a grim determination to break his spirit, to humble his pride, to unmask his motives, to reduce him to the normal mediocrity of mankind. The passion of the mob had progressed to the Palace, and the vindictiveness of that mock-trial was inspired by an animal antipathy, a profound temperamental antagonism, which gave it a kind of crude justice. The Renaissance was trying the Middle Ages. Baffled by his faith and unable to force his soul, his judges mangled his flesh and distorted his meaning, persecuting they knew not what, but something that was a fundamental challenge to themselves.

Though the confession was unsatisfactory, it served its purpose. In the presence of eight witnesses, among whom were several of the monks of San Marco, Savonarola signed it, without protest. "My doctrine is known to you," he said to the witnesses, "and known to all. I ask of you only two things: that you watch over the novices and keep them true to that Christian doctrine in which we have so far maintained them. Pray for me to the Lord, whose spirit of prophecy has forsaken me for the moment." Fra Malatesta Sacramoro, with his grim conscientiousness, insisted on knowing whether the confession he had just signed was true or false. His master looked at him in silence, but this time he did not kiss him; he turned abruptly and left the hall. Why protest? What did it matter? Personally, he had ceased to exist. . . .

When the confession was published, however, it created consternation among his followers. "My heart was pained to see such an edifice crumble," wrote one of them; and the sentiment found a wide echo. The monks of San Marco repudiated him and begged the Government not to send him back to the convent. They also wrote a letter of repentant submission to the Pope. "Not only we but men of much greater intelligence," they humbly explained, "were deceived by the astuteness of Fra Girolamo. The penetration of his doctrine, the rectitude of his life, the sanctity of his habits, his simulated devotion, the benefit he obtained by ridding the City of usury, bad customs, and vice of every kind, and the many events which, surpassing all human effort and imagination, confirmed his prophecies, were such that, if he had not retracted and said that his word did not come from God, we could never have denied him our faith." No one distinguished between his principles and his prophecies; and though his work spoke so loudly that, even in repudiating him, they recognized it, no one drew the obvious conclusion. Even his defenders contested the confession only on the grounds of its palpable fabrication. This they did, however, with such vigour and pertinacity that the Government promptly recalled and revised it; and the notary was docked of his pay.

In an effort to bolster up the confession, a second trial was begun; but it was abandoned after three days. Then the process was applied to his accomplices. They were shown the wrack and his confession. Fra Silvestro was quickly convinced; but Fra Domenico, travelling among the ropes and wheels of the torturer, bore them with the unfaltering fortitude of a porter of faith. Incapable of doubt, he was incapable of the final torments which were now besetting his master.

An interval of three weeks ensued, while the prosecution rested, awaiting the arrival of the Apostolic Commissioners from Rome. The daily baiting had ceased; and now the anguish of the mind set in, swelling more sorely than the warped joints which Savonarola, with the aid of his jailer, nursed in his cell. His right arm was whole and he wrote . . . wrote incessantly . . . straining . . . straining to rebuild his faith. The whole fabric of his inner life had foundered. An immense disheartenment, a flooding inrush of fears and doubts, overwhelmed him. The infirmity of his flesh, the disfigurement of his character, the desertion of his flock, left him without faith in himself. He groped feebly for faith in God. Had he ever possessed it? Was that also a delusion? And the last abyss opened before him. God is unfathomable, and every man fashions Him in his own image. Was God only another name for himself? Had he worshipped secretly and darkly hallowed his own reflection in the void? Was his faith anything more than his glorified fear of life? Then he had been rightly broken, the victim of his own vainglory. "Sinner that I am, where shall I turn now? To the Lord whose mercy is infinite? No one can glory in himself; all the Saints say: not of us but of the Lord is the glory. They were not saved by their merit nor by their work, but by the goodness and grace of God, that no one may glory in himself." Now, only now that he was annihilated, could he know God. But how could he know Him without faith? . . . The pen ran on, asserting, asserting . . . He repeated all his formulas, in a long flux of moral delirium, flowing interminably in dazed volubility, and filled the last leaves of the paper with his agony. "Have you faith?—Yes, I have it.—Good: this is a great grace of God, for Faith comes of His gift, not of your works, that no one may glory in them." But under all his assertion ran a constant implacable counterpoint: the Demon of Melancholy plied him with doubts. "Everything happens by chance and nothing exists but what we see with our eyes. Our spirit will vanish in smoke. Who has returned after death to confirm one thing of all that are told us will befall the soul after death? Fables, fables, old wives' tales!" He was doomed. "Do you not see that you call on Heaven and Earth and no one helps you? Do you not see that your only refuge is death?" And the feverish prompting wooed him to the only solution: "Follow my counsel. Heaven denies you, Earth will have none of you, it is better to die. Choose death, and if no man will give it, take it with your own hands." And he followed and suddenly paused. On the brink of extinction, he peered for his reflection in the void. He was alone, in the last solitude, and the silence of those infinite spaces appalled him. Would the after airs know his identity? Or was there nothing? He recoiled; he roused himself. "How long will you be a weakling? How long before you learn how to fight? You have been so often in battle, and are half now in the shadow of death, and you have not learned yet how to fight! Take courage, coward!" He struggled for faith. But faith was a gift of grace, and the old insane round began; neither reason nor will nor works could obtain it; he had only his need and his nothingness. . . . But those sufficed. Benighted, with the instinctive movement of humanity in the dark, he found his faith in his need of it. "If armies are arrayed against me, my heart will know no more fear, because You are my refuge and will lead me to my goal . . ."—and he broke off; for at that point the paper was taken from him and he was called to his third trial.

The ecclesiastical examination repeated the charges and methods of the civil, and with renewed fortitude he made an effort to retrieve himself. In questioning him on the Council, an attempt was made to implicate his protector, Cardinal Caraffa, but he steadfastly denied having conspired with him or any other supporter in Rome. When he was stripped for the torture, he became hysterical. "Hear me," he cried, grappling with temptation. "God, You have caught me! I confess I denied Christ for fear of the torture, I told lies. Signori Fiorentini, be my witnesses: I denied for fear of the torture. If I must suffer, I want to suffer for the truth; what I have said I have had from God. . . . God, You are punishing me for denying for fear of the torture: I deserve it." And, pointing to his broken arm, he repeated over and over, "I denied God for fear of the torture." The pulleys revolved, the long gaunt body was hoisted like a sheep, and he was asked why he had said this. The head sagged, the delirious eyes eluded them. At last he stammered: "To seem good." Like a carcass being weighed, he slowly spun. "Do not hurt me, I will tell you the truth, truly, truly." Presently the examiners asked why he had contradicted himself. "Because I am a fool." Then he was let down. "When I see these torments," he confessed, "I am lost. When I am in a room with a few peaceful people, I speak better." The Court now returned to its original question, and he admitted having sounded the Cardinal of Naples in respect to the Council, though he insisted that he had received only a vague reply. Then, under pressing questioning, he conceded that Naples was "the leader" and was to have brought in the other Cardinals; and, menaced once more with the rope, he broke down and cried in an excruciating spasm: "Naples, Naples, with him and with others I have practised." But it was lost labour: on the following day he recanted again. The

Apostolic Commissioner, realizing at last the futility of such testimony and having ascertained nothing, wrote to the Pope that the crimes he had unearthed were "so enormous that it does not seem right to reveal them at present"; and proceeded to pronounce sentence.

It was communicated to the accused that night and was to take effect in the morning. Fra Silvestro, on learning it, became hysterical and declared that he would protest his innocence to the people. He repudiated the prophet, whose presumption and fallacies he had suspected long before the wrack proved them; but his retraction only won him a place on the left hand of his master. As for Fra Domenico, the Apostolic Commissioner, finding no fraud and much courage in him, had been inclined to spare him; but he was reminded that such qualities would only perpetuate the influence of the master, and he signed the warrant with the remark: "A mischievous friar more or less matters little." Fra Domenico, on learning that the sentence was hanging and burning, also made a demonstration and begged for full measure—burning alive. Savonarola received the sentence impassively, asking merely that he might speak with his disciples whom he had not seen since the night of their arrest. Late that night, in the spacious obscurity of the vacant Hall of the Grand Council, the three met without privacy. Turning to Fra Domenico with a new authority, Savonarola said: "I know that you have asked to be burned alive, but that is not right. Do we know our own strength? Do we know how we will meet the death to which we are doomed? That depends, not on us, but on the grace which the Lord will allow us." Then, with the same chastened calm, he turned to Fra Silvestro. "As for you, I know that you wish to defend your innocence before the people. I command you to abandon such a thought and to follow the example of Jesus Christ, who not even on the cross would speak of His innocence." Standing between his two disciples, he looked from one to the other, from all that he might to all that he hoped to be, with unfathomable reserve; and so he left them. In his cell a confessor was waiting; and his full confession was the sleep that followed. Laying his head in his lap, he fell into a light slumber in which, as in a mute rehearsal of the morrow, nature seemed to measure and mould him for the earth; and in his transparent tomb he smiled; then—was the tomb itself but a womb?—he slipped beyond the ken of his confessor, and the restless sleeper peered perhaps into the void where, in perpetual motion and mutation and travail, worlds upon worlds jarred and stunned.

SAVONAROLA

He was already beyond the pale when, on the following morning, during the public ceremony of degradation, a Bishop confused the formula and said, "I separate you from the Church militant and triumphant." He raised his head and corrected him calmly: "Militant, not triumphant: that is not in your power." Then the death-march began and the three figures advanced slowly along the narrow causeway, under which the children lurked, prodding their passage, toward the gibbets which had been lopped to dissimulate their likeness to the crosses of Golgotha. Fra Silvestro was the first to suffer; Fra Domenico, who could not be restrained from chanting a lusty Te Deum, followed; and his turn came. As he ascended the ladder, a voice cried: "Now is the time, Prophet, for a miracle." He stepped off, the void clutched him, the vital nerve yearned, and the multitude which had watched the ordeal of so many vanities followed voluptuously his convulsive abdominal dance in mid-air. By ten o'clock all was over. The slack thing swung in the breeze, and the flame crept up and loosened its bonds. The boys stoned it and the crowd dispersed slowly. When the embers, soaked in a slow deglutition of blood and viscera, cooled, the faithful gathered and grubbed in the cinders in silence; and the women, rising suddenly, spirited away the heart, which was found whole. To prevent further demonstrations, the Signory ordered the ashes to be strewn in the river. This was done promptly; but at dusk furtive figures were still seen creeping along the Arno, groping in the swiftening waters, sifting and searching them obscurely for no man knew what.

Four weeks later, no memory remained in the Piazza; it was full of the hurrying feet of the future; and Machiavelli crossed it to take up his work in the Palace.

PART TWO

Machiavelli

16

"If we wish to discuss this matter thoroughly, we must ask whether these innovators should rely on themselves or on others; in other words, whether they should depend on prayers or on force. In the former case, they invariably fail; but when they rely on themselves and employ force, they run little risk. Hence it is that all armed prophets have prospered and all unarmed have perished. The nature of the people is mutable, and, while it is easy to persuade them, it is difficult to preserve them in their conviction; hence we must take such measures that, when they no longer believe, we may compel them to believe by force. If Moses, Cyrus, Theseus, and Romulus had been unarmed, they could not long have enforced their constitutions, as happened in our day to Fra Girolamo Savonarola, who was ruined by his new order of things, as soon as the crowd ceased to believe in him, since he had no means of preserving the loyalty of those who believed or of making the doubters believe." Such was the mature judgment of Machiavelli on the revolutionary value of faith. In the past two months he had seen the most spectacular confirmation of an axiom which, however self-evident, seemed always to be forgotten. The cardinal sin of Savonarola was his simplicity; and in the career on which Machiavelli was now embarking that sin was inexcusable. He at least would not forget it.

Yes, this commonplace could never be sufficiently repeated. For even yet, after that overwhelming demonstration of the futility of faith unsupported by force which Savonarola had left Florence as his last legacy, his hard-headed countrymen had not learned their lesson; or at least they had not applied it to their politics and their warfare. And Machiavelli was touched in the quick of his professional conscience; for he was now a Government official, a humble one, a subordinate, but in his own eyes a responsible one. Four weeks after the execution of Savonarola, on June 19, 1498, he applied for the position of First Secretary to the Signoria; recommended by the chief of the First Chancery, he was elected and immediately assumed charge of the Second Chancery. This office, it was true, admitted of no personal initiative: his duties consisted in dictating dispatches, compiling minutes, digesting reports, making transcripts, and annotating official files; but he was serving his apprenticeship and it would be a poor drudge who, beginning as First Secretary to the Signoria, would not soon become something more than a bureaucrat. Life was opening for him: he was twenty-nine, open-eyed, close-mouthed, industrious, discreet; and his only handicap was the originality of his mind. He rarely agreed with his betters. Not that he was opinionated; but he smiled. In the corners of his mouth lurked a little crease which at least passed for a smile, something slyly subordinate which, if he had permitted himself to smile, would have seemed subtly superior; but he had himself well in hand, as he had all the clerks in the office. They saw his mouth twitch and his nose pucker and his lynx-like eyes quicken; but that was all. In the Palace he kept his opinions to himself. In the pot-house, however, among his intimates, at the end of the day, he aired them. There, in an atmosphere that favoured their unfolding, close, mild, and warm, and saturated with the acrid aroma of the lees of the wine, he held forth to a little circle of devoted admirers, his subordinates in the Chancery and his intellectual inferiors, whom he dominated; there, after office hours, he played, over the cards, that great game of the political cafés which begins and ends with *If I were* . . . ! There, despite his intellectual aloofness, he expanded and became the most sociable of men; and his audience appreciated, or thought they appreciated, his ideas and his jokes—they could not always distinguish between them, both were so startling and sensible—particularly when they were aimed at their superiors. Listening affectionately, while he applied his corrosive criticism to the errors of the better vulgar, they were proud of him; and in that little club, dedicated to high thinking and low living, the foundations of his fame were laid.

From personalities the topic turned to principles; and already Machiavelli had an example of the muddle-headedness of his countrymen to harp on. Five days after the execution of Savonarola another ceremony had taken place in the Piazza. This time it was a martial one. Marcello Virgilio Adriani, the Chief of the First Chancery, pronounced a classical oration and conferred the baton of Commander-in-Chief of the Florentine forces on a competent condottiere, Pagolo Vitelli. It only needed—or so it seemed—the passing of the great visionary for Florence to come to her senses. After listening for so long to the Friar who boasted that "he held Pisa in the hollow of his hand"—how did the song go?—

> O betrayer of the Florentines,
> That have made bitter this state,
> Hoping to recover its confines,
> Fine soil you frittered away,

the Pisan War was at last to be prosecuted in earnest. After negotiating for four years with the French, the Republic had emerged in four days from its delusions and begun to rely on itself. So far so good. But it had only begun. The oration which celebrated this step, and the oration alone, was classical; the step itself was but a half-step which begged the question of self-help; and a long stride was needed actually to emulate the example of ancient Rome. Pagolo Vitelli was an able condottiere, one of the best in Italy, but he was a mercenary, and the breed was, in the very nature of things, unreliable. The true test of self-help was a national militia, the citizen-soldiers of ancient Rome: there was no other solution. This, however, was one of those ideas which earned Machiavelli the name of an academic thinker among practical men; and in the pot-house it passed for one of his jokes. He could not seriously expect a nation of traders to bear arms, when they could buy them. He could not seriously expect Florence to break with a custom which every other state in Italy followed. But the retort was prompt. Where had it brought Italy? Why was it impossible there when the Swiss practised it so successfully? Not only did they owe their independence to military service, they supplied half the armies of Europe with crack troops. Or, to come nearer home, what of Pisa where, under the stress of necessity, the whole city had taken up arms? But that was pushing too near home. His friends nodded and sighed. They did not argue, or only for sport, to lead him on by close reasoning to a new round of liquor.

For Machiavelli, however, the idea was not academic. The whole conduct of the Pisan War was in his hands; at least, it passed through them. In addition to his work with the Signoria, he had been appointed secretary to the Ten on War as well. He was in close touch with the camp, transmitting orders, munitions, and money, receiving confidential reports, travelling about the territory; nor was this all. The military campaign had to be accompanied and covered by a diplomatic one, for the Pisan War again dictated the foreign policy of the Republic and the international situation was once more becoming alarming.

How rapidly history repeated itself! Charles VIII had died suddenly and his successor, Louis XII, was preparing a new invasion to wipe out the disgrace of Fornovo, recover Naples, and take in Milan. This time it was not talk, nor was the invasion likely to prove a mere seasonal visit or a military promenade. The new King had none of the flighty ambitions of his late cousin; he was cautious, shrewd, parsimonious, and tenacious, a conservative middle-class monarch, and he meant what he said. When he said that he would rather reign one day in Milan than a lifetime in France, he made the only romantic remark of his life. He was determined not only to have but to hold; the new invasion would not pass like a bad dream; and the proof of it was the conduct of Lodovico Sforza in Milan. He was facing his old nightmare again. The League which he had fashioned at Fornovo and which he had preserved for four years had suddenly disintegrated with the defection of its central member, the Pope. The patriotism of Alexander had yielded to other considerations. King Louis was seeking a divorce and a dispensation to marry the widow of Charles VIII, Anne of Brittany. In August 1498, the Pope sent his son Caesar to France with the coveted dispensation, and Caesar, who had recently renounced ecclesiastical orders, returned to Italy under a new name. Henceforth he was known as Valentino, as the Italians insisted on naturalizing his French title of Duke of Valentinois. From that day Lodovico Sforza slept fitfully. Once more he was isolated in Italy. He attempted to arrange a new scheme of alliances but he met everywhere with a cold shoulder. In public he was careful not to appear crestfallen. With easy assurance he showed the Florentine ambassador a fresco representing the map of Italy covered with Gallic cocks and a figure of himself with a broom sweeping them away—*per nettare Italia d'ogni bruttura*, as he said, "to cleanse Italy of all filth." It was a device of his own invention, as the ambassador immediately recognized. The literal Florentine saw little in the fresco. He observed bluntly that Lodovico might sweep himself away in the dust that he raised; and the *mot* had an immediate success in Florence.

So Lodovico discovered when he negotiated for an alliance with the Republic. He offered money and troops for the Pisan War; but the

Government remained wary and evasive. After preserving its neutrality for so long and at such cost it saw no reason to risk it on the eve of another invasion. It was too prudent, however, and too civil not to temporize. The effect of this policy on the Pisan War was immediately apparent. Vitelli also temporized and it was suspected that he was suborned by Lodovico. Nothing definite could be ascertained, however, and the mere fact of a protracted campaign was too normal with mercenaries to be conclusive proof of disloyalty. Secretly he was held under surveillance; publicly his explanations were accepted He complained of his pay and his supplies, compared them to those of his colleagues, and demanded an increase. Explanations of this nature could only be met by accepting them; but the Ten on War had already squandered so much money without results that they were known among the people as the Spending Ten. Morally and financially they were acutely embarrassed. Their secretary, sitting over their correspondence and digesting it, listened and said nothing. Looking over the Piazza and reflecting on how rapidly history repeated itself, Machiavelli silently nursed his faith that "the ruin of Italy has been caused by resting all her hopes for many years on mercenaries . . . and the man who told us that our sins were the cause of it spoke the truth, but they were not the sins he imagined."

Out of this situation grew his first mission. To supplement the forces of Vitelli it was decided to engage a contingent of mercenaries from Caterina Sforza, the Countess of Imola and Forli. Their value was not so much military as political, for the Countess was a neighbour, her states were a buffer, and the Signoria was willing to sink some money to gain her good will. But only a little; it was essential to buy it cheaply. Here was a perfect problem for a young diplomat. His instructions were clear and he had only to follow them:

(1) gain her good will;
(2) engage her troops;
(3) hire them cheaply;
(4) present the question as a favour on the part of the Republic.

As an exercise, involving nothing of vital moment but requiring some skill for its successful execution, it was well designed to test his practical capacities. His young reputation depended on it, for his appointment caused some jealousy in the office, notably in a certain Ser Antonio; but his friends wagered on him. As a parting word of advice, they reminded him of the first principle of bargaining—to keep cool, assume indifference, and lead the lady to make all the advances. In his case such advice seemed superfluous, but he jotted it down, pocketed his instructions, and set forth for the wide man-raising plains of Forli.

The Countess was herself a virile character. She was known throughout Italy as a virago and she gloried in the name. Beleaguered during a rebellion, she made herself famous by her retort to the besiegers who were holding her children and threatening to slaughter them. "I can make more," she flung back from the battlements; and her sally made the rounds of Italy. She married three times. In the same virile spirit she conducted her diplomacy: hard-mouthed, hot-tempered, hard-headed, and blunt, the very match for a young diplomat, for with her Machiavelli had every reason to expect plainspeaking and plain dealing. Memorizing his instructions—to keep cool, to lead her by studied indifference to make the advances—he pushed on through the auburn fields of Forli.

No sooner had he alighted than he learned that an agent of her uncle, Lodovico Sforza, was in Court negotiating for her troops. The agent, moreover, was present at his first interview with the Countess, and this made it difficult to broach Points 2 and 3. But if Point 2—engage her troops—and Point 3—hire them cheaply—were the real points of his mission, Point 1 was the first. His instructions were explicit. Point 1: gain her good will. This required address. The Countess was forbidding. A robust mastiff of a matron, gruff with the lifelong habit of authority, she turned on him an august stare which warned him that here was a woman unaccustomed to making advances. Nevertheless, he followed instructions and wrapped himself in official reserve and well-feigned indifference. The first point was the *condotta* of her son, Ottaviano Riario. This young condottiere had been engaged for three months' service against Pisa; his contract had not been renewed; he was angling for a re-engagement, but he demanded an increase in salary. Machiavelli's instructions were plain; he was to remind the Countess that "the Signoria was under no obligation to entertain this proposal and that, if they did so, it would be only as a personal favour and in consideration of past services." He did so. No approach could have been more unfortunate. The suggestion of condescension immediately antagonized the maternal virago; and, though he attempted some perfunctory compliments, dwelling on the affection the Republic bore her for her many merits, and repeating that, if she served it, she would not find his Government ungrateful, he had no sooner concluded than she picked up his speech sharply. The actions of his Government, she declared roundly, had always dissatisfied her; though—she relented as she looked at him—their words always pleased her. Then her face hardened and in the map which she turned on him he read no encouragement. She contradicted him sternly. His masters had never recognized her merits, and she proceeded to enlarge on them with a rough but loving hand; and as she did so she became indignant. She hoped, she sincerely hoped that his masters would not be so ungrateful as to dispute whether they were under obligation to renew her son's contract; and she settled that point with a glare which allowed of no rejoinder. The sun was setting when she concluded, and by then she had corrected and revised the whole message of the Signoria; she desired time, she now said, to consider their *request*. And there the first lesson ended. In his initial manoeuvre for position Machiavelli had been completely outplayed; not only had she made no advances, she had adroitly taken offence and placed him at a disadvantage; and to add to his discomfiture, the little scene had taken place under the watchful eye of the Milanese agent.

It was galling; but tomorrow was another day, and he spent the night planning how to repair his errors. On the morrow, however, she did not even receive him, and the next day she sent her secretary to pump him. She had apparently taken his measure. Far from recovering ground, he lost it. The two secretaries sat down together for a chat and, while the tyro was guarded, the veteran played with him. Assuming a tone of disarming frankness, the Forlese let him into the secret of the Milanese offer and succeeded in raising Machiavelli's bid to its limit— 10,000 or, at most, 12,000 ducats. Then he paused, looked worried, and suddenly changed the subject. He had been secretly informed, he said, that the Signoria meant to ask for a treaty of alliance in defence of its frontiers, and to that, of course, "Madonna would never consent." The significant gravity with which he made this warning remark, the tone of friendly reproach with which he coloured it, impressed Machiavelli: he thought it prudent to hedge and replied that of such a treaty he knew nothing—he would write home about it. Thereupon the Forlese smiled. "It does not matter," he said lightly. Provided they could agree on the other points, Madonna would accept this one willingly, but *not* in writing. And, waiving the treaty lightly aside, he reverted to the question of money, redoubling his unsatisfied pressure.

Machiavelli was honest with himself. How it had happened he hardly knew but it had happened. He had offered everything and obtained nothing, he could not outbid Milan, and all that he would bring home would be the verbal good will of the Countess. The next day, however, she sent for him and received him with a sudden cordiality which flew to his head; he flew to his pen and wrote home urging the Signoria to accept all her demands. Her smile had completed what her frown had begun. As he cooled off, he realized it and became uncomfortable. He felt lurking smiles behind him wherever he turned. All this professional cat's play, in which he was cast as the cat's paw, irked him; and he begged the Signoria to recall him. He longed for the wine-room where he could develop his theories or the Chancery where everything was what it was. To be recalled—recalled to the Palace, to his drudgery, to anything, but to his self-confidence! To be standing again at his tall desk, chatting with his clerks, surrounded by his friends! To be listening to Biagio! Biagio Buonaccorsi, true to his name, always of good help! The comfortable humdrum life of the office rose before him, as he reread the letters which his chief clerk and bosom friend had stolen time to write him. "We all long for you and most of all your Biagio, who talks of you every hour and for a year in an hour, as you would not do, if he were away! I have no doubt Madonna honours you and receives you gladly as you write, for many reasons which I will not repeat or I should soon bore you. In my opinion you have performed your mission with great credit so far, which gives me the greatest pleasure; because others will realize that, though you are not so seasoned, you are no whit inferior to Ser Antonio, who is so puffed up. Continue as you have begun, so far you have done us great honour." Biagio at least—Biagio, good Biagio with his dog-like devotion, his comfortable mediocrity, his candid simplicity—believed in his success—and perhaps Biagio was right. The world was satisfied with seeming success; and he alone knew how baffled he was in that Court, how outwitted and fleeced and humiliated and unseasoned; he alone perceived his failure. But when, after days of fretting and chafing, the reply came from Florence, the Signoria agreed with Biagio. The terms of the Countess were accepted and he was granted his recall. Machiavelli congratulated himself, but only on his luck.

Nevertheless, he was too young not to be elated. With the final arrangements successfully completed, he was composing his last report, when he felt a touch on his shoulder and turned to find the Milanese agent standing beside him, "It will not be necessary to write," he said. He explained that Madonna had changed her mind, her troops were going to Milan. Machiavelli stared, rose, and bounding out of the room, abounding in words, expostulated breathlessly to the Countess "both with gestures and words." But in vain: she calmly confirmed her decision, without explanation or apology. All that she consented to say was that she had slept on it and "the more one turns a thing over the better one decides." As she was suckling a young child who was sick, she curtailed the interview. The scales fell from his eyes. Not only had she hoodwinked him, not only had he played blind man's buff in her Court, buffeted, beckoned, browbeaten, deluded, and at last dismissed; he had been untrue to himself, he had been satisfied like the vulgar with seeming success and contented with saving his face. That was what rankled; and riding home through the wide man-raising plans of Forli he felt the most insufferable of all sensations—he felt like an innocent.

In the Chancery, however, he was welcomed with open arms. He had accomplished nothing, it was true, but he had reported the process admirably, and his skill as an observer was recognized even by his superiors. His letters, with their terse, lucid style, their marshalling of all the evidence making for a decision and their scrupulous caution, were commended. And now another field for the exercise of those qualities was awaiting him—the battle-field itself. Before he had time to brood on his defeat at Forli, he was plunged into the feverish activity of the Pisan War and employed in vigilantly reporting the conduct of Pagolo Vitelli. It became daily more suspect. The delays continued; the demands for money, munitions, guns, continued; if they continued much longer, Machiavelli wrote to the camp, phrasing the remonstrances of his superiors with a vigour all his own, "it would be impossible for half of Italy to support these artilleries. So far we have spent 64,000 ducats for this expedition, we have mulcted everyone, and to send you the sum herewith we have emptied our coffers." And he rammed in the conclusion: unless something were done promptly, "we shall undoubtedly be stranded, for if we have to furnish 6000 ducats more, we shall despair of the victory." For a moment these protests produced some effect. Vitelli went into action; a tower and a portion of the walls of Pisa were captured, and the fall of the city was hourly expected. The next news was a shock. An attack was launched, but, as the Florentine troops poured through the breach, Vitelli and his brother—so the report ran—recalled them and even beat back with the flat of the sword those who refused to obey. A frenzy of indignation swept through Florence. The Signoria ordered an immediate investigation, declaring that they would no longer be "led blindfold." In reply the Commissioners wrote from the camp that Vitelli insisted that he was certain of taking the city by treaty. "Either you will not write us the truth or you do not know it," wrote Machiavelli; and he did not know which was worse. "We do not know what to say to this people, nor how to excuse ourselves; we seem to have been feeding them on fables, deluding them from day to day with vain promises of certain victory." He was bitter, and he had reason to be. Within an inch of victory the prize had been snatched from them; their resources were exhausted, the campaign languished, fever broke out, and it was reluctantly decided to raise the camp. But someone had to foot the bill. The treachery of Vitelli was now confirmed by a report that papers had come into the hands of the French, proving his complicity with Milan and containing his promise to Lodovico to "drag out the war." Lodovico, always Lodovico, everywhere in the background! The smouldering fury flared up. Commissioners were sent to the camp, ostensibly to pay off the army, but with sealed instructions the secret of which was in Machiavelli's hands. He was cool now. He urged them "to move prudently, not to err through too much courage or too much caution, neither hurrying unduly nor showing more circumspection than the occasion demands." Vitelli was invited to dinner; the table was cleared; and he was quietly put under arrest. Next, his brother, Vitellozzo, who was sick of fever, was seized; but he asked permission to dress and made his escape. The campaign had lasted fifteen months and this was the end of it. On October 1, 1499, Vitelli was executed and his head was displayed on a spear, with torches to light it, on a parapet of the Palace, about which a crowd had gathered, greater than any that had been seen since the execution of Savonarola.

As for Lodovico, the French were approaching Milan and he was in flight.

In that pointed spectacle, with the mercenary head on the spear and the sanguine torches to light its sallow corruption, had the people at last seen the truth? Machiavelli doubted it. The justice of that act was public and apparent, yet there were those who remained wilfully blind to it. The truth was the last thing which the world recognized. Here was the proof, in a letter intercepted on its way to Pisa, which came into his hands. To make matters worse, it was written by a Chancellor of Lucca and described the execution of Vitelli on official paper as a high-handed act of Florentine ill-faith. Out of his burning patriotic pain Machiavelli undertook to reply to it and in his most scathing style. "A letter addressed to M. Jacobo Corbino, a Canon of Pisa, having come into the hands of one of my friends, he brought it to me and I opened it, in virtue of my office. I was not so much surprised by its contents as by the fact that you should have written it, for I believed that we might expect a serious man and a public official like yourself to write in a manner not unbecoming his profession. Now, how it becomes a secretary of your *Magnifici Signori* to tax such a Republic as this with dishonour, I leave you to judge. since whatever you say against any power in Italy must arouse the resentment of your masters more than anyone else, as you are their mouthpiece and it will be assumed that they approve you, thus breeding hatred against them through no fault of theirs. I have undertaken to write, not so much to clear this city of your calumnies as to warn you to be wiser hereafter; and this I feel bound to do as we pursue the same profession." And he reminded him of its first rudiments. "Among many things which prove what a man is, not the least important is to note how easily he believes what he is told or how cautious he is in feigning what he wishes others to believe: so that whenever a man believes what he should not or feigns badly what he would have others believe, he may be said to be shallow and devoid of all prudence. I shall pass over the malice of your spirit as it is revealed in this letter and confine myself to showing how foolishly you have either believed what you have been told or feigned what you wished to see disseminated to the discredit of this state." The pen, so long poised, suddenly shot out. "First, I thank you for congratulating the Pisans on the glory you think they have won and the shame we have acquired, attributing all such remarks to the love you bear us. Next: how is it possible, let me ask you, that this city should have spent a treasure past computing and that the Pisans should have defended themselves successfully, as you imply, but for the betrayal of Pagolo Vitelli?" The slander that Vitelli had himself loaned his employers money he lanced promptly. "I ask you: what man in his senses, what healthy mind, would believe that Pagolo Vitelli lent us money and that the reason we took it was not to pay him? Do you not see, poor man, that this completely excuses our city and condemns Pagolo? For anyone who believes that Pagolo lent us money must also believe that Pagolo was a rascal since, as all the world knows, he was in no position to advance us money, unless he had received it by corruption to betray us or had saved it from the pay of his men. He has been the cause of infinite disasters to our enterprise and in either case deserved infinite punishment. To the other parts of your letter, since they rest on these two points, I feel it unnecessary to reply; nor do I feel called upon to justify his arrest, since this does not concern me, and if it did there is no reason why it should be explained to you. I merely remind you that you will do well not to congratulate yourself too soon on the plots you say are going on about us, as you know nothing of our counter-plots; and let me advise you, *fraterno amore*, if you mean to indulge your ill nature hereafter and offend without profit, that you do so in a manner more prudent."

But it was not only the malice of slander abroad that he had to puncture, it was the mischief of credulity at home. There were actually those in Florence who still believed in Vitelli and who were unconvinced of his guilt: and they included his closest friends. Biagio persisted in calling him "an excellent man." But that was like Biagio: like all average men, he never went beyond personalities. Biagio had been something of a Piagnone and still believed Savonarola an excellent man; and so, no doubt, he was; but what did that matter? It was not the man, it was the system; and Vitelli had been justly decapitated. Guilty or not, he was a product of that vicious mercenary system which, by making a traffic of warfare, inevitably led to betrayal and failure. What was a mercenary? A man without attachment to his employer, without animosity toward the enemy—the enemy of today was the friend of tomorrow—with only a trifle of stipend to march for, for whom a decisive action meant the end of his pay and victory was worse than defeat. Hence all those sham battles when, as at Anghiari, two armies left but one casualty on the field at the end of a hard-fought day, and that one an accident. Hence the victory of Fornovo, when the French slipped through while the mercenaries were looting their baggage. Hence all the disasters of Italy. And Machiavelli punctuated the argument with indignant pauses, while Biagio walked meekly beside him, and the theme carried them slowly from the Chancery to the wine-room. Hence it was that Charles VIII passed from one end of the peninsula to the other, chalk in hand, choosing his billets; and now the French were returning, and the same thing would repeat itself. There was only one solution. How long before the Republic saw the light? Even yet it did not appreciate the real significance of that mercenary head on the parapet. Vitelli was the victim of their own folly, and, having beheaded him, they would begin with another. How long would they muddle along in half-measures? There was only one solution. Impractical? But practical men, in their short-sightedness, were the most visionary of all. Only one solution—the militia— and that brought them to the wine-room.

In the wine-room the discussion continued. Who expected honour, honesty, or patriotism of a mercenary? Sentiment was essential to force; it was a potent factor in action; that imponderable element was the most practical of all, perhaps, and must be included in any working political philosophy. And in the wine-room the argument mellowed. Force without faith was nothing. Yes, Savonarola was right. That obstinate wrong-headed man was right. Though everything in the world was accomplished by force, nothing was achieved without faith. Faith without force, force without faith, were equally futile. Biagio listened, as he had long ago listened to the Friar, devoutly. Machiavelli, too, had something of the prophet, the same burning zeal, the same passion for the absolute and the antithetical, and he also was a voice *clamans in deserto*, and his piercing eyes were big with vision. But Biagio could not lead him to talk of the Friar. Why was it that the Friar crept into every discussion, into every taproom? Machiavelli merely called for a new deal of cards and a fresh flask of wine. He had no opinion of the Friar, except what he had always said, that he was a very astute man; and a simpleton. And Biagio accepted the old paradox with a submissive, uncomplaining, uncomprehending smile, and was silent.

But silence was the last word of the Friar and, when they walked home through the Piazza where he was so mute now, they paused, and the persistent prompting rose anew. Faith, yes. The experiences of the past year—the faithlessness of Vitelli, of mercenaries, of Lodovico, of Caterina Sforza, the mutability of fortune, the deception and self-deception of men—everything led Machiavelli by the logic of his own thinking to the need of faith. But faith in what? Overhead in the void the stars spanned the ultimate uncertainty. No, not in God; but in man. Maybe they were one. But one thing was certain. All was dark, and the only clue in Nature, the one guide of man, was self-confidence.

17

On October 6, 1499, King Louis entered Milan and virtually occupied Italy. In his train rode Caesar Borgia, representing the Pope, the ambassadors of Florence and Venice, the Duke of Ferrara, and the Marquis of Mantua—the representatives of the principal Italian powers with the exception of Naples. Naples was his next objective; but it was distant and he was slow and sure-footed. To protect his line of march and ensure the permanency of his occupation he was prepared to favour the respective interests of the peninsular states which would henceforth be his neighbours. He spent a month in Milan, reorganizing the

Duchy and the peninsula and laying down the lines of a far-sighted policy which was to convert the invasion into a permanent protectorate over the Italian powers. Penetration was the password of his progress. Accordingly, at the end of the month, each of the political clients who had accompanied his triumphal progress into Milan left his headquarters, satisfied. Mantua and Ferrara, his minor neighbours, accepted friendship; Venice and Florence were his allies; and Caesar Borgia left for Rome to begin, with the aid of French troops, the conquest of Romagna, where he proposed to strengthen the states of the Church and carve a principality for himself. Having drafted these preliminaries, the King returned to France.

In Florence the Chancery was humming. A new impulse had been given to the Pisan War. On October 19 the Florentine ambassadors had concluded a treaty with the King by which he undertook to supply them with troops and pledged the recovery of Pisa before proceeding to Naples, the Republic agreeing in return to supply him with money and men when he went south. This contract promised a short and rapid campaign; it necessitated it, in fact, for nothing else would justify its exorbitant cost; and in this hope the Government was making a heroic effort once more to raise money. Machiavelli worked at his tall desk with compressed lips. It was as he had foreseen. The Vitelli affair, which had bitten so deep into his mind, had taught Florence nothing. The only remedy for one mercenary was another: after the native, the foreign; after the Italian, the French. But at least the French were professional fighters; and there was a chance if the campaign were begun promptly and prosecuted with speed. But everything depended on speed. Not only the financial strain, not only the bitter experience with Vitelli, incited it but something more exciting—a sound to which Machiavelli and all Florence were listening, the sound of a furious cannonade on the frontier where another campaign was in progress.

Its rapidity was amazing. On October 19 Caesar Borgia was still in Milan. A week later he left it. On November 1 the Countess of Imola and Forli sent her children to Florence for safekeeping. On November 27 the town of Imola had fallen and the furious bombardment of its citadel could be heard on the Florentine frontier. On December 10 it ceased. On December 13 it began again from the direction of Forli. On December 21 the fall of the town was reported; on January 13 the fall of the citadel and the capture of the Countess. Florence listened for the next move. That daily din travelled across the frontier and filled the Chancery with its echo, drumming in men's ears, drilling their minds, and rattling the casements with a relentless rhythm that made the Palace quiver like a house of glass. The name of Caesar Borgia boomed throughout Florence. Little was known of him. He was barely out of his teens. His youth had been obscure with the brilliant obscurity of the Church; but ever since he had sloughed off the irksome robes of a churchman he had emerged in his true colours. He had the talents of a condottiere, and the death of the Duke of Gandia had revealed them. In connexion with that mystery a cloud of sinister rumours still clung to him, but they only served to mark him as a coming man. He had speed. His military début had been startling. In two months he had taken in two states and laid the foundation of his principality in Romagna; and all this, as the wise men repeated in Florence, had been accomplished overnight by the aid of the French. But Machiavelli was listening for the next move. It was a full stop. On January 27 the French were recalled to Milan. On February 27 Borgia returned to Rome. He returned in triumph, it was true, bearing Caterina Sforza, laden with gilded chains, amid his trophies and spoils, and was welcomed with immoderate honours by the Pope, who bestowed on him the Golden Rose, symbol of the Church Militant and Triumphant. Others might be dazzled by these vainglories; but surely the Golden Rose was premature. The Chancery might hum the faint strains of the Papal Te Deum and go through the august gestures of pontifical congratulations, but Machiavelli shrugged. Why so much jubilation? Borgia was in the same quandary as Florence. What he had won he won by the aid of the French; and no sooner were they withdrawn than he was halted. The French, like the Lord God, gave and the French took away: to them Te Deum was due. That was the lesson which that booming young man should teach Florence, that and the example of his conduct. What was admirable was that, forced to use the French for his purpose, he employed his uncertain auxiliaries so swiftly and with such self-confidence.

For, meanwhile, the Pisan War had not yet been resumed. The City Fathers deliberated, but the lubricant to set the wheels moving was lacking; time was required to raise money; weeks passed, months passed, and at last a tentative beginning was about to be made, when the whole situation changed in the north and the emergency which recalled the French and halted the progress of Borgia also suspended that of the Republic.

In three months the French had made themselves hated, feared, and despised in Milan. Before his departure Louis had done much to conciliate his new subjects, consulting them in domestic questions, respecting their institutions, preserving their administration of justice, practising economy, and pursuing, in short, an enlightened colonial policy; but what he could not provide against in his absence were those minor problems which are more prolific than major disputes in breeding friction between peoples. With nations, as with men, the real animosities spring from manners, and those of the French outraged the most civilized people in Europe. All the ambassadors spoke of them, and of little else. The ambassador of Ferrara recognized but one question of consequence in Milan: "The French are detested for their overbearing rudeness." The Venetian ambassador complained of their vandalism. "The French are a dirty race. The King goes to Mass," he wrote in the first days of the occupation, "without a single taper and eats alone in public. In the Castello there is nothing but filth, such as Signor Lodovico would not have tolerated for the world. The French captains spit on the floors of the chambers, and their soldiers insult women in the streets." Moving sullenly among their desecrated glories, the Milanese regretted Lodovico and became restive. The fuse was laid and the explosion followed when a group of children who were ridiculing the King in effigy were shot down by the French. There was an uprising, and, while the Governor was attempting to suppress it, Lodovico crossed the border at the head of a Swiss army. He was welcomed with frantic acclaim as he entered Milan, which the French had hastily evacuated. But his return was short-lived. Louis was tenacious, and two months later (April 1500) another Swiss army emerged from the Alps, flying the French colours. Lodovico was willing to try the fortune of arms until he learned that his Swiss refused to fight their countrymen; then he fled, was recognized, arrested, and returned to Milan. He was deported as a dangerous alien and passed through France, a man without a country. Riding through Lyons, he raised his bonnet to the Italian ambassadors, but they ignored him. Manners so French in men of his own race pained him profoundly, for the pride which had precipitated the first invasion to snub Naples had lost none of its sensitiveness. Nevertheless, he learned patience. He was confined for ten years where he could nevermore take umbrage, not even at his stars. He died in an underground dungeon, the walls of which were decorated by his princely hand with primeval scrawls and primitive sentiments. At that depth he discovered the wisdom of the savage, putting it, as was fit, into French: *Celui qui ne craint pas fortune n'est pas bien sage* [1] And the earth closed over him. Milan regretted him.

This sudden spin of Fortune was not merely an interlude which re-

---

[1] He who does not fear fortune is not very wise.

NICCOLO MACHIAVELLI, by an unknown painter
From the portrait in the Uffizi Gallery, Florence

stored the *status quo*. The French were restored, but their tempers, and not their manners, had changed. The reoccupation was harsh, a heavy indemnity was levied, and the Milanese groaned under the yoke. Nor were they the only ones to suffer. The necessity of supporting a large force in Italy was a crushing burden to the parsimonious King, and he was eager to share it. He took up his contract with the Florentines for the Pisan War. He would not take no. Money: they could always find money; and a contract was a contract. He was ready to supply all the men they required and more: 500 lancers, 4000 Swiss, 2000 Gascons; but of these he would pay only the lancers, the Republic to advance the rest one month's pay—24,000 ducats—before they started and to reward them with a similar gratuity when they returned. The Republic reluctantly consented. The troops left Milan with their pay in their pockets and travelled slowly, wasting the country through which they passed. At Piacenza they were joined by 1200 more who volunteered, would take no denial, and had to be paid at the same rates and on the spot by the Florentine Commissioners. One of these paymasters fled incontinently, the other was swept along struggling to pacify the riots and satisfy the complaints with which he was hourly bullied on account of the lack or the poor quality of the victuals. Every stage of the march was disputed, and the wrangling and extortion were still in progress when the army drew up before Pisa. There, indeed, after some delay, an active bombardment began; a breach was made in the walls, and the French poured through, but only to find themselves blocked by fortifications which the besieged had thrown up within. They retreated in disgust and disorder and their commander, Beaumont, unable to control them, laid the blame for everything on the unconscionable stinting of the Florentine Commissioners. It was a repetition of the Vitelli affair and the Government was exasperated. Amid this confusion Machiavelli was sent to the camp to assist the Commissioners and report to Florence. He found them bewildered and paralysed and the camp rapidly disintegrating. A week later the Gascons deserted; the Swiss followed but before leaving they broke into the Commissioner's quarters, demanding their pay and threatening his life. Machiavelli found it difficult to write; but after catching a last glimpse of the Commissioner expostulating with his captors, he concluded his report: ". . . after much quarrelling they carried him off as their prisoner. Of what happened since I know nothing, as I remained here in our lodgings at San Michele, to send word to Your Worships, who will take steps to save your subject, with so many of his servants and yours, from falling into their hands; and what hands!" The French refused to intervene. That night the luckless Commissioner was still disputing his life, and his captors, raising the price by the hour, imposed on him a new contingent of 500 Swiss who had just drifted in from Rome. Days passed without relief, and the prisoner only bought his way out by paying the Swiss out of his own pocket. Then the last mercenaries melted away and the silence of desolation and betrayal settled over the camp.

This time there was no culprit on whom the Republic could vent its indignation. Beaumont had betrayed the Government in the most baffling of all ways, by incompetence; moreover, he was immune, a Frenchman over whom they had no jurisdiction, and an influential one, a protégé of the King's minister, the Cardinal de Rouen. The people could not be appeased by a head on a spear, but satisfaction of some sort they demanded. Pisa, so long a thorn in their sides, had become a sore spot; they were the laughing-stock of the world; and the fear of ridicule, so lively in the Florentine people, so potent a motive with all the world of that time, leading so often to the most desperate courses, rose from the Piazza to the Palace. The Government was resolved on desperate courses. In reality, as they well knew, they could do nothing but pocket their losses; but they dared not face public derision; the dignity of the Republic demanded that something be done; and they did the weakest of all things under the circumstances: they protested to the King. Naturally, this only made matters worse. After an exchange of letters, neither side understood the other; both became equally incensed; and it was decided to send ambassadors to France who would lay the facts of the whole disgraceful misconduct of the campaign squarely before the King; for this purpose eye-witnesses were wanted; and one of the Commissioners was appointed, with Machiavelli to assist him.

Politicians, no doubt, cannot afford to be philosophers; but statesmen cannot afford to be poor psychologists. Machiavelli read the instructions blankly. What did the Government expect? What had it to offer but a grievance and what redress could it claim, without force to support it? In sober earnest—when the heat of feeling had died down—what was the object of this most futile of missions? After the tragedy of weakness, the farce! And to make matters worse, the instructions did everything to defeat their effect. Beaumont was untouchable. The ambassadors were not to accuse him, or only after feeling their way: "If you find a disposition to hear him ill spoken of, then do so vigorously and charge him with cowardice and corruption." Otherwise, they were to "lay everything to his insufficient authority and to his being of so gentle a nature that he did not know, perhaps, how to make himself feared." They were to minimize his mistakes as *well-meaning* and blame the malpractices of the Italians in the camp ("whose misdeeds you may aggravate without scruple") but on no account were they to name the true culprits "except in a slip of the tongue." Could official futility go further? or senile unscrupulousness? Scanning those instructions, the ambassadors wondered what, after crossing the Alps to nag the King, condone the culprit, and blacken their countrymen, remained for them to do.

Here was a test of patriotism yet undreamed of in Machiavelli's philosophy. To complain, to cringe, to wheedle, to protest, to be indignant, cautious, lame, sly, and ridiculous all in one breath, and to employ on a fool's errand the arts of a beggar and a backbiter!—But it was not for him to question his duty. He loved his country too well to count the cost, even in self-respect. He loved his country, yet for a moment it pained him to bear its name, for no love could blind him to the weakness and folly of his countrymen. He set forth on his mission, fully prepared for its only possible result—mortification and failure.

Nor was he wrong. The long journey to France had made the subject three weeks staler when they arrived. They laid their complaints firmly and tactfully before the Cardinal de Rouen, only to receive the expected reply. "These justifications are not very pertinent," the Cardinal remarked dryly, "the matter being already past." Time smiled at their grievance over his shoulder. The point was, what was to be done now? But on this they had no instructions. Was the Republic prepared to sign a new contract? On this too they had no instructions; they had come with a claim, not a contract. The Cardinal stared at them incredulously; he found it difficult to believe that they had come so many hundred miles for no practical purpose. Nor did they receive much satisfaction from the King. He cut short their explanations with the remark that he did not care "to pursue the subject, it being a matter on which much might be said on both sides." He was willing, however, to divide the responsibility. The Gascons, he promised, would be punished; as for the Swiss . . . he could not answer for the Swiss . . . the seizure of the Florentine Commissioner was undoubtedly a brutal indignity, but the Swiss "were accustomed to acting in that manner and were much inclined to extortion." There the matter would have ended but that the King also insisted on a renewal of the contract. He had pledged himself to recover Pisa for Florence; the failure of the campaign was a disgrace to his arms; he would never rest till he had redressed it; he must have a new contract. The ambassadors respectfully agreed to consult their Government.

When, after another three weeks, the reply came, it was, of course, a refusal: the only suggestion which the Republic offered was that the King might take Pisa at his own expense and be reimbursed upon its surrender. From that moment Louis cooled and the position of the ambassadors grew daily more uncomfortable. Their few friends fell away, they were everywhere shunned. They lost even their personal credit at Court. They were men of a modest social condition, sent on a special mission, without the rank, the means, or the authority of resident ambassadors; and the King asked that they be replaced by an envoy with full powers to negotiate with him. Thereupon Machiavelli's colleague took a chill and returned to Florence. He was now left, not so much to carry on as to bear the brunt of his mission, alone. The King no longer received him and he avoided the Cardinal, making only perfunctory visits to Court. To be noticed at all was ominous. One day an Italian at Court called him to heel and gave him a secret appointment at his quarters. Shut out from all consultation, living on rumours, and depending as he did on the beck and call of official eavesdroppers, Machiavelli followed. The personage received him in silence and went into a brown study; nor would he say anything, when his visitor ventured to ask the reason of this mysterious summons, except to ask if the ambassadors were coming, Machiavelli replied that he thought they had started; whereupon his informant studied him impressively and said: "If they come, they may accomplish some good and prevent something which would not be at all to the interest of your masters." He would say no more. Alarmed, Machiavelli ferreted out from other sources the danger so darkly hinted at and learned that the King was planning to take Pisa, add the Florentine fortresses to it, and constitute an independent state on the Tuscan border. In transmitting this information to his Government, Machiavelli put it to them bluntly "how they were to temporize these matters, without a single friend at Court, in disfavour with the King, and beset by so many enemies who make new proposals daily to His Majesty, showing how weak you are and how useful it would be to build a state about Pisa . . . so that Your Worships, being surrounded, would come, without waiting for force, with the yoke on your necks and a blank contract in your hands." He apologized for speaking so plainly and begged them to lay his presumption to his affection; but he could not speak otherwise: authority sprang naturally to his pen, his spirit revolted: he was a clerk no longer.

Nevertheless, the Government continued to temporize—they were too weak to do anything else—the weeks passed, and there was no sign of the ambassadors for whom the King was waiting: no one wanted so thankless a mission. And Machiavelli, lost in a vacuum, living in alternate trepidation and tedium, continued to temporize and eat his heart out. Some little comfort he found in the letters which Biagio and his friends in the Chancery wrote him regularly. "Believe me, Niccolo, you know that flattery is not my style," wrote Biagio, "when I read your letters to some of our first citizens, they commended them highly, which delighted me, and I tried to confirm their opinion adroitly with some words of my own, proving how easily you write them." But praise bored him, cheap praise, praise without results, mere personal appreciation; everything irritated him, even Biagio with his clinging devotion, his good humour, his possessive jealousy. . . . "To tell you the truth," his doting friend ran on, "the letter I received from you this morning puffed me up with pride just a little, when I saw that you think a little more of me than of the other Stradiots in the Chancery; and lest I forfeit my opinion, I did not inquire whether there were any letters from you for the others. I was extremely contented, I seemed to be talking to you intimately again, as we used to do; for I had been a little hurt when your first letters came and I found no mention of me in them, and I wondered whether the old saying, *out of sight, out of mind,* were true of you; but this letter has laid my fears, and I hope you will continue when you have time, and I will never fail to do my duty by you." But Biagio had his uses. To add to his discomforts, Machiavelli was without money. On his departure, he had been allowed a salary less than his colleague's; the remittances had ceased; he had spent his economies, he had borrowed right and left, he no longer knew where to turn. His brother wrote that he had been dunning the office in Florence every day—"I have been at their heels night and day for two weeks"—and Biagio had seconded him obstinately; between them they had finally succeeded in scraping up some *scudi* and Biagio, in sending this little relief, felt that he could now make a modest request. "Spend a *scudo* for gloves and two cloth purses, the smallest you can find, and a few other trifles, and I will reimburse anyone you may name. Also I beg you to send me a rapier, but I want it as a gift, for I never received the one you promised when you went away." Machiavelli had the extravagance of the poor, he loved nothing more than spending, and he loved those who made him do what he loved; with Biagio's plea his spirits revived. For a moment, the pleasure of giving dispelled the gall of a mission without honour or profit or pay; but only for a moment. The dull ache returned, quickened by the postscript which another of his Chancery friends wrote on the back of Biagio's letter: "A thousand plagues on you, Machiavelli mine! You make us live such a worried life here, and what with our other work, we are wasting away. Ser Antonio suffers from his stomach again, I believe because he misses Madonna Agostina to play see-saw with him and warm him. Nevertheless, we often laugh in the First Chancery; and sometimes we have a supper in Biagio's house. Marcello is living with Signor Gigliozzo now and takes his ease, and a few days ago we had a great celebration there: I covered myself with glory. So prepare, prepare! The moment you arrive, *she* will be waiting for you, wide open; Biagio and I saw her several nights ago like a hawk at her window—you know who I mean: *Lung' Arno delle Grazie.*" Those memories—the Chancery drudging—Ser Antonio nursing his colic —supper with Biagio—the Lung' Arno at night—the harlots like hawks at their windows, sniffing their pots of sweet basil—the scented air—the Tuscan stars—were too much for him. He was as homesick as a cat; and he wrote to the Signoria, once more a mere clerk, pointing out that his father had died a month before his departure, that a sister had died since, that he was bereaved, that all his domestic affairs were unsettled, that he was consuming himself in more ways than one, and that he would go anywhere they pleased hereafter if only they would let him come home for a month.

But he was not to be relieved so soon; for now another problem had arisen which demanded his diplomatic skill. The name of Caesar Borgia was booming once more. For four months he had been inactive, and inactivity did not agree with that dynamic young man. Even in the doldrums of Rome he contrived to find exercise and to make himself talked of, and always in the same way. In June it was for a bull-fight; he had piled up a record for Rome—five bulls lanced and a sixth decapitated single-handed—but in July the weather grew hotter and the bull-ring was deserted. In the Vatican gardens he was shot at; such, at least, was the official explanation of what followed. He was said to suspect the young Duke of Bisceglia, his third brother-in-law by Lucrezia. For a month they avoided each other. Then the dog-days began. It was August. One day before dawn Bisceglia was discovered on the steps of St. Peter's, with five wounds in his body. He was carried into the Vatican and the last rites were administered. Rome immediately hummed with sensational rumours, but the Venetian ambassador, an inveterate scandal-monger, was circumspect. "It is not known who wounded the Duke of Biselli, but it *is said* that it was the same who killed and threw into the Tiber the Duke of Gandia." To everyone's amazement, the victim, nursed by his wife and sister, recovered. By the end of September he was convalescent. But September is a treacherous month in Rome. Suddenly he expired.

The malaria was no worse than usual. The Venetian ambassador could no longer contain himself. He had the authority of the Master of the Papal Household, who entered the death of the Duke in his diary with the bald statement: "Not dying from the wound he had taken, he was yesterday strangled in his bed at the nineteenth hour." The Venetian followed his nose and named Caesar; the Florentine ambassador repeated the story; and the physician of the Duke of Bisceglia, arrested and released, retired to Naples to confirm it. The Pope denied it, though faintly. "The Duke says," he said, "that he did not do it, but if he had wounded him he would have been justified." Everyone knew, however, that the Holy Father quailed under his son. The scion who had sprung from his loins was a stranger to him. Caesar maintained a proud silence. The sensation subsided but the impression remained. Caesar was spoiling in Rome, he was cramped, he was caged; inactivity sickened him; he needed an outlet for his genius.

These rumours produced little effect in France, where the political significance of the domestic tragedies of the Borgias was not yet fully appreciated. It needed an Italian like Machiavelli to feel it. Whether rumour made the man or the man made the rumours which clung to him was a moot question; but certain it was that the suspicions which dogged Caesar were rapidly swelling his fame. The value of crime as a political principle was enormous. In Italy nothing was accomplished except by fear—even Savonarola had understood it. Caesar had grasped that fact. He ignored but did not discourage a reputation which was so useful to him. With the instinct of a bull-fighter he had gauged the impressionable nature of his public and realized how vulnerable the Italians were in imagination. In the political arena the glamour of crime, the reputation of mystery, swiftness, and ruthlessness, was an immense asset; and the death of the Duke of Bisceglia could not have been better timed from a political point of view. For now the restless spirit of Caesar had slipped out of Rome and was once more laying its sulphurous trail in Romagna. It was fall, and sulphur ripened the vintage. Pesaro and Rimini fell without a blow; for, though these states were under Venetian protection, Venice abandoned them under French pressure. All the border states trembled. "Harsh in his vengeance, he is great of spirit and ambition and thirsting for eminence and fame," reported the Ferrarese envoy who was sent to study him in action. Ferrara, Urbino, Mantua, Bologna followed his progress with growing anxiety, for though they were under French protection they were uncertain how far or how long they could trust it. The uneasiness spread to Florence, and, when a report rose that the Pope was planning to restore Piero de' Medici, the City Fathers assembled; a resolution was in order; it was unanimously adopted; and they determined to protest to the French.

But to control Caesar it was necessary to control the King, and to control the King there was only one man available at that moment—Niccolo Machiavelli. He obeyed instructions and broached the subject to the Cardinal de Rouen. The Cardinal was not a man of much delicacy. Taking Machiavelli by the hand, he led him toward the Grand Chancellor of the Realm and a group of curious bystanders and, assembling his audience about him, vehemently rehearsed all the injuries he had borne from the Republic, reminding them how His Majesty had been fleeced and dishonoured, how Florence had violated its engagements, and how, now that it dreaded the Pope, it needed the royal favour, which the King would certainly not grant until he knew whether the Florentines were his friends. After this public humiliation, the accumulated bitterness of Machiavelli overflowed. He minced no words with his Government. "The French respect only those who are willing to fight or to pay," he wrote, "and, since you have shown yourselves incapable of either, they consider you *Ser ZERO*." Nonentity, ignominious nonentity, was the just penalty of the weak. He had earned the right to speak plainly, and he did so with grim relish. The weak were always wrong, they had no right to complain; they had only themselves to blame; it was the natural law. But though he was scathing, he was sad; his bitterness gave way to the overmastering need of his country; and he returned to the Cardinal, drilling his lecture into himself. He dared not fail. Ignoring his previous rebuff, he reopened the subject of Borgia. The Cardinal, in a calmer mood and a little contrite, explained that His Majesty had been practically compelled to consent to the enterprise in Romagna, "because, considering what may arise in Italy, he respected the Pope more than any other Italian power, partly because he is the head of the Church, and partly because he is more powerful in arms than any other state, less fatigued, and with fewer impediments." On the face of it this argument seemed unanswerable; but only on the face of it. How easy to crack its cogency! Still in his seething mood of exposure, Machiavelli stripped it of its plausible shell and found its fundamental fallacy. Cornered, he forgot that he was a nonentity and attacked the Cardinal with political theory, lifting the question at once to his own plane. Could not the King see that he was digging his political grave? In a year he had gained a grip on Italy which he was now undoing by a series of elementary errors. And he enumerated them. First, he had absented himself from his seat of government; secondly, he had antagonized his subjects; and now he was fostering a power in Central Italy which, growing by leaps and bounds, would perhaps equal and check his own unless he curbed it in time. And recovering his composure he concluded coolly: "His Majesty should beware of those who seek the ruin of his friends for no other reason than to strengthen themselves and to retrieve Italy the more easily from his hands. Against such an eventuality His Majesty should provide by imitating those who, in the past, have possessed themselves of foreign provinces; which was, to diminish the strong, to conciliate their subjects, to maintain friends, and to beware of *colleagues,* that is, of those who aim at an equal authority in the land. And if His Majesty would pause to consider who are his colleagues in Italy, he would realize that they are neither Florence nor Ferrara nor Bologna, but those who have always sought to dominate Italy in the past, that is, the Venetians and, above all, the Pope." The minister listened patiently to the little Florentine secretary playing his hand for him; he was impressed; he nodded. He begged Machiavelli to believe one thing. "His Majesty is a very prudent man, whose ears are long and whose credulity is short, and he listens to everything but believes only what he knows to be true and holds in his hand." And he opened his own hand. Though he had given permission to the French captain, M. d'Allègres, to join Valentino with a hundred lances, he had given him instructions "to favour your affairs." He went further and confessed that "the prosperity of Valentino is annoying the King." Then the statesman merged in the politician again and he shook his head, insisting that the Italians knew nothing of warfare, to which Machiavelli quickly retorted that the French knew less of statecraft—"if they did," he said, "they would never have allowed the Church to reach such power."

It was the turning-point in his mission. Alone, unaided, by the exercise of his wits, he had wrung from Rouen a vital admission. The self-interest of the French would protect Florence. Moreover, the ambassadors now arrived with authority to negotiate a financial settlement; and Machiavelli returned to Florence.

It was a sad homecoming. He was congratulated on his reports, and they were filed and forgotten. His friends were curious to see, as they said, if he had become *Frenchified*; and they saw no change in him. He refused to admit it himself; it was too painful; but there it was. After eight months abroad he had seen his country in perspective and recognized with the rest of the world the full ignominy of its weakness. But no one else saw it in Florence and he felt an alien in his own land. Nothing had changed there, nothing would change; and he himself, slipping into the old routine, found himself acquiescing by mere force of habit in the customary half-measures, compromises, hesitation, and temporizing of the Republic, and almost resigning himself to its debility which would always be a prey to incompetence, betrayal, and extortion. But in the depth of the slough he revolted, a revulsion of feeling rose in him, a moral need of strength. When the name of Borgia was mentioned, his blood quickened. In Florence it was unpopular, and the old men sanctimoniously repeated the well-worn rumours of crimes. But the only crime was weakness. At the end of the day, when the office was closing, he would linger by the window, looking off over Florence, far away, to the smouldering horizon beyond which lay Romagna. The clerks wondered what he saw, though they saw the same thing; and he would stand alone and admire how confidently rose the young stars.

18

Throughout the winter and spring of 1501 Valentino, as the Italians now called him, no longer to naturalize him but to remind themselves that he was the creature of France, was detained by the siege of Faenza. On April 26 it capitulated. On April 27 he swept into Bolognese territory, demanded the surrender of its frontier fortress, obtained it three days later, and on May 2 crossed the Florentine frontier on his way to Piombino. His lightning-like movements allowed of little formality, but a perfunctory request for permission to pass preceded him. It reached Florence together with hordes of terrorized peasants, complaining of the atrocities of his soldiers. The city was panic-stricken, the shops shut; there were demonstrations and riots, martial law was proclaimed, and the citizens were called upon to bear arms. For ten days confusion and indecision reigned. On May 12 the requested permission was sent to him, but he now had other business to discuss. He offered the Republic his services as a condottiere, at a salary of 36,000 ducats a year, without obligation to active service, except in an emergency, the contract to take effect immediately and to last for three years; and he refused to evacuate the territory until it was concluded. When the Commissioners protested against such extortion, he threatened to sack Campi in the immediate vicinity of Florence. Some of his men were already entering the city on leave, others were brought in by the peasants as prisoners, many were slaughtered, there were retaliations, and the whole countryside was swarming with guerrilla troops. Under these circumstances the contract was accepted and signed. When, however, Valentino demanded an immediate payment he met with uplifted hands and an obstinate *non possumus*. From that ritual gesture of the robbed he concluded that the Republic had no intention of observing its contract, and acted accordingly. The plunder and atrocities continued. The Government sent its mace-bearers to demand his withdrawal; they were beaten and robbed of their emblems of office. In Florence the popular indignation broke out in tumults and protests against the "asinine patience," as everyone called the pusillanimity, of the magistrates, and the magistrates responded by arresting their own subjects, when they found them loitering along the roads, to prevent further friction. The artillery which Valentino had demanded was thrown into the Arno.

At this juncture Valentino was recalled by the French, who were about to march on Naples and to whom his service was pledged. The menace passed away, but the shock lingered. In the state which he had violated without provocation and ravaged without subjugating, he left the resentment and fear of a clumsy and unfinished operation. The reports of torture and rape perpetrated on the peasantry made his name and that of his leading captain, Vitellozzo Vitelli, by-words for inhuman cruelty. The Borgias were now mentioned in Florence with execration.

To Machiavelli too this sudden irruption was a shock, but a pregnant one. At the moment he was too much of a Florentine not to recoil with the rest of his countrymen before the reality of the Borgia; but when the menace had passed, his insight was quickened by it. The pusillanimity of the magistrates, which so excited the indignation of the people, he accepted henceforth as normal; the people had seen it at last; but he owed it to himself to stride ahead and see further. Now that Florence had recognized what he had so long seen alone, his only satisfaction was that of contradicting the general impression and maintaining his intellectual superiority. He absolved his masters from all blame; they had acted weakly; but weakness was a democratic vice. In the Republic of Florence weakness appeared to be its one constitutional attribute. It was a question, in fact, whether vigour and efficiency and even freedom were compatible with a republican form of government. Those qualities were the attributes of the individual, and in delegating them to the conglomerate incompetence and shifting responsibility of his constituted authorities, the citizen defeated his own ends. Democratic government was a fiction: only the individual could impart freedom, vigour, and efficiency to the state. In Florence liberty had always begotten an eventual tyrant. Even in ancient Rome the same thing had happened; the Republic had produced its dictators, the dictators developed the Empire. It was the natural law: all Nature was a tyranny, a perpetual struggle of one kind with another for prepotence, and the most peaceful life was a series of accepted shocks and forgotten violences. And Caesar, in inscribing on his sword *Aut Caesar aut nihil*,[1] was merely obeying the natural law.

But such foresight or such prophetic bodings he kept to himself. The time was not ripe for them. The name of Borgia was anathema in Florence. When the boy tyrant of Faenza, Astorre Manfredi, was brought to Rome and imprisoned in Sant' Angelo, where he was subsequently murdered, despite the promise of Caesar to spare his liberty and his life, detestation of the "diabolical" Valentino, as he was called in Florence, flared up again. But Machiavelli kept his head. He refused to follow the vulgar error: he viewed the act in a moral void, and judged it as the political application of a natural law. Astorre Manfredi had been popular with his people, Caesar was bent on conciliating them, and the apparent contradiction of his conduct was none. In preserving a newly acquired state, and particularly one where the late ruler had been popular, "two points," he argued, "are important." "In the first place, care should be taken to extirpate the family of the former sovereign; in the second, laws should not be changed nor taxes increased." Caesar understood. He could shock, conciliate, forget, and obliterate, precisely like Nature; and indeed the more Machiavelli considered him, the more he felt there the workings of a natural force.

Yet it was curious that others could not see it. Even his frivolous friend, Agostino Vespucci, who was always ready to go whoring with him on the Lung' Arno, wrote now from Rome in scandalized tones. Valentino was in the Vatican and Vespucci overflowed. "Benefices are cheaper here than melons at home or than cakes and water in Rome. The Rota is disregarded, because *omne jus stat in armis*,[2] and in these infidels, so that it seems necessary that the Turk should come, seeing that Christians will do nothing to extirpate this carrion of mankind: *ita omnes qui bene sentiunt uno ore loquantur*.[3] In conclusion I must tell you what I have been told about Someone: not to mention the Pope, who has his illicit flock every night from Avemaria to one in the morning, XXV

---

[1] Either Caesar or nothing.
[2] All right lies in might.
[3] So that all who feel rightly pray an hour a day.

women or more are brought into the Palace to serve Someone, so that the whole Palace has openly become a brothel full of all filth. Other news I will not give you today, but if you reply I shall tell you more." It was the heat, no doubt, the heat that excited such prurient horror, for Agostino only wrote because he was hot "it is midday and I am dying of the great heat, and to keep awake I am writing these few lines"—and he was honest enough to admit that the debauches of his friends bothered him— "I envy them, I must gnaw my chains up here in my room, which is under the roof, and hot, and often I find a tarantula in it." But the summer which always put the Borgias in heat produced, in that sweltering season of 1501, a crop of scandals more lurid than usual. It was then that the world first heard the legend of the Chestnut Supper. The Roman friends of Vespucci did what they could—"good God! what meals they have, *et quantum vini ingurgitant!*"[1] he wrote, "Vitellius, the Roman, and Sardanapalus, if they were alive, would be nothing to them: they have musicians of various instruments and they dance with their women and leap *in morem Salium vel potius Bacchantium.*"[2]—but they could not emulate the vision that leaked from the Vatican of fifty naked courtesans and valets grovelling on the floor—gambolling for chestnuts, and copulating at the feet of the Holy Father, Lucrezia, and Caesar; nor of that matinal scene when the Pope brought Lucrezia to the window to watch the mating of a herd of stallions and mares in the courtyard. Machiavelli was not the dupe of such myths—they were obviously propagated for political purposes—but as myths they had their mysterious truth. The importance of sex in politics was not to be under-estimated; it was perhaps at the root of the impotence of the Republic. The energy with which the Pope seconded his son was not so much an act of political support as of political procreation. The old man was over-sexed, and so was the young one; but their genius lay in their superabundant vitality. Well might they watch the act of life with insatiable satisfaction, it was their political function; and while the spasms of arms were intermittent and the orgies of intrigue slow, those of the flesh stimulated and recharged them. They were natural forces and it was because they obeyed all the promptings of life that they mastered it. They *were* life, summer-born, incandescent, spawning, lusty, and indefatigable.

But, alas, the world was prosaic, and these myths achieved the political results for which they were propagated. They found credence, and from beyond the Alps an anonymous German made himself the mouthpiece of

---
1 And how many wines they guzzled!
2 In the Salic mode or, better, of the Bacchanti.

outraged humanity. In a notorious pamphlet, the *Letter to Silvio Savelli*, he enumerated the crimes against God and religion of "that infamous beast, that betrayer of the human race," Alexander VI, including these stories, accusing Lucrezia of incest, charging the death of the Duke of Bisceglia and the ruin of Romagna to Caesar, and summoning the conscience of mankind to rebel against such abominations. The Pope, when this pamphlet came into his hands, shrugged. He was used to abuse; but he knew Caesar. "The Duke," he said, "is good-natured but he has not yet learned to bear insult." Caesar, in fact, when he returned from Naples, took prompt and harsh measures to suppress the libels which were running wild in Rome. Up to a certain point they had a political value but beyond it they were an impediment; and that point had now been reached. The suspicion of crime was one thing, the notoriety of scandal another, and he punished sternly any libel on the honour of the Holy See and his family. He had his reasons. The Neapolitan campaign was over and it had ended in a division of the Kingdom between France and Spain, a fertile source of international dissension, as he foresaw and as the future soon proved. The French would henceforth have their hands full in Naples; he was anxious to slip off their fetters and to act by himself. But until he had established himself in Romagna he saw the necessity of conciliating his anxious neighbours; and as a first step in this new phase of his diplomacy the Pope offered the hand of Lucrezia to the heir of Ferrara, Alfonso d'Este. The Este were an old and respectable race, who looked with distaste on a match with a family of unsavoury Papal parvenus; and only under paternal pressure did Alfonso reluctantly consent, on the promise of a huge dowry, to the marriage. During the months preceding it, an unusual decorum was observed in the Vatican.

This policy of conciliation was extended by Caesar to all his near neighbours, including Florence. The force of nature had made his peace with human opinion, but in the nature of things that peace could not be permanent; and it was only a question of time before the claims of nature reasserted themselves. What surprised observers was the length of the truce. But at last it broke. His activities were seasonal, and in June 1502 —exactly one year after his first irruption into Florentine territory— while the harvests were about to be reaped and the peasants were singing all the way from Florence to the Val di Chiana, word reached Florence that Arezzo, the key to its southern frontier, had revolted, raised the banners of the Medici, and received Piero de' Medici with Vitellozzo Vitelli, the brother of the executed condottiere. The latter had long boasted to revenge that death; and as the leading lieutenant of Valentino he was thought to be responsible for the atrocities which had marked the previous inroads of his master. The Chancery made its calculations rapidly. Where the man was, the master could not be far; and in fact the next report was that Valentino was following with another army, ostensibly bent on the siege of Camerino. Panic again threatened in the city; the first shock, almost forgotten, throbbed once more through all the arteries of the capital and the nerves of the country; and the rankling bitterness of an unfinished mutilation revived when it was learned that the Pisans had offered their city to Caesar. Before these mounting apprehensions could take shape, the Government acted. Ambassadors were sent to Rome to protest to the Pope and to Milan to appeal to the French. Amid this agitation came a message from Caesar, asking that ambassadors be sent to him immediately. The choice fell on Bishop Soderini, whose brother Piero was negotiating in Milan, and on Machiavelli. Their destination was uncertain, as Valentino moved swiftly; they were to find and to follow him. They left promptly, for the Duke wrote that he had received permission from his ally, the Duke of Urbino, to pass through his territory; and they rode rapidly.

19

Urbino is perched on a spur of the eastern Apennines, where they fork between Tuscany and Romagna. Its mountainous character constitutes its military strength. From the rugged backbone of the Apennines the country descends like a landslide, in a long precipitous incline of slipping hills and clinging shelves which subside abruptly in the plain below; and there the main arteries of the peninsula swing to the right and left of its long reef-like promontory. The mounting road leading to the capital winds slowly amid the lurching confusion of the land in long spirals that are visible from afar, and finally reaches a city secreted amid tilted hillocks in an upland pocket. Like the whole land, the capital hangs on a precarious slope, commanding an interminable approach. In this isolated recess it bespeaks its character. The approaching traveller is at once struck by a huge, barrack-like palace forming part of the walls and blending with the town which clings to it; but far from being fortified this vast bulk faces the world with a single fabulous tower, flanked like a minaret by slender, fluted spires and spanned by two decks of delicate *loggie*.

It was the boast of its builder, the late Duke Federigo di Montefeltro, who was one of the best condottieri of his day, that he had never lost a battle nor fought one on his own soil, and in the evening of his life he raised this monument to that achievement. It was wrought of his dreams and his deeds, of Istrian stone quarried and carried across the Adriatic and a faith equally far-fetched in his sovereign immunity to the vicissitudes of his neighbours below. Vast as a city and one with the town, his house bespoke his confidence in his subjects; they had never betrayed him; while on the side of the world Nature provided. In this monument, inlaid with semi-precious substances and encrusted with trophies of art, he had bestowed as his last labour a choice library where, like the sound conservative that he was, he never admitted anything so vulgar as a printed volume. Such, when he died, were the state, the home, and the ideals inherited by his son Guidobaldo.

Guidobaldo honoured them. An invalid, he was not ambitious; a scholar, he lived in his books; a pious man, he trusted in Providence. His career as a soldier had been interrupted by gout, and he was more of a valetudinarian in young manhood than his father had been in old age. Everything weaned him from the world—his infirmity, his studious tastes, his childlessness, his gentle nature, his calm contemplative domestic mind, and the love of his wife, Elizabetta Gonzaga; and in that singular retreat, closeted with his thoughts, he became as self-contained as his state. When he sat for his portrait, he offered a transparent character—a long sallow face, composed and patient, and listless eyes in which, as he gave audience to posterity with calm indifference, were reflected the *alta quieta*, the *vita dolce e lieta* of Urbino.[1] His spirit inhabited the mansion; it was peopled with echoes and soundless with the quiet decorum of a household moving with that clock-like regularity which abolishes all notion of time; and no part of it more so than his private study which commanded an illimitable vista where his dominions ended and a cloud-laden void where they began. His house was himself, and he had never forsaken it save on one occasion, a few months before, when he moved out to accommodate Lucrezia Borgia, as she passed through Urbino on her way to her wedding. The sister had passed, the brother was passing, and he was alone now, his wife having followed their guest to Ferrara.

On the night of June 20, 1502, he spent the cool of the evening at the

---

[1] The lofty quiet, the gentle and joyous life.

Convent of the Zoccolanti, two miles outside the walls. The vineyard was one of his favourite haunts, with its green grapes budding huskily in the dusk, the low-lying haze clinging to the hot soil, the shadowy cattle switching their tails in the fields, the fireflies, the chimes of the little church, and the measured conversation of the monks. From there, the town was almost invisible; only the huge outline of his home hugged the horizon. There the world waned, in the thickening dusk, to a mere adumbration of its reality—and what was its reality? The fireflies paled, and the stars multiplied, and the gnat-like lives of men subsided in silence and space, and his dominions extended beyond the gloaming. A rider, clattering toward town, did not disturb him. The monks retired and he remained alone, listening to the innumerable small sounds of the night, inhaling the good smell of earth, the hard dry scent of dust in the dark, a steady odour of perdurable reality; and as he listened, and as he breathed deep, his dominions contracted. The clatter returned, there was a movement in the leaves, and the rider pushed through with a tale that brought him to his feet. "I have been tricked!" he cried, striking the ground. He climbed into the saddle and clattered back to the Palace. There his friends were consulting and he took their advice. What else could he do? He had mended the roads and even loaned his artillery to Caesar, who had swerved from his route and by forced marches pushed within striking distance of Urbino: he would be there in the morning. Resistance was impossible, his few soldiers were scattered in distant garrisons. There was no time to lose, nor was Guidobaldo a man to repine. His chamberlain brought his valuables; he sent for his adopted son, Francescomaria della Rovere, who was sleeping upstairs the sound sleep of thirteen; and with a small escort he set off for the mountains. It was eleven: they had five hours' start. The passes to the east were already held by Valentino, and their one hope was to make for the north and the impregnable fortress of St. Leo. Once more he approached the little church of the Zoccolanti, where his father lay buried. His father had paved the way for this flight, as he had paved that of Caesar; the earth shed those who were irrelevant to it; and for a fleeting second the untroubled sleep of his father was filled with his dust. Then the little church lay behind him and the measured sleep of the monks, and in the deepening hush of the country the thud of hooves rang out like a quick tap of betrayal. Through the hoofbeats bearing him away he heard his muffled heartbeats and listened to the child galloping doggedly by his side; and, following the warning of his friends, he left the highroad and followed the beds of dry streams and the trails of the shepherds in the hills. It was hard going; but Elizabetta at least was not with him, and he rode easier. In the twisting gullies and crumbling ravines he did not slacken his pace. By now the long spiral loops of the road from the plain to Urbino would be gliding with life; and suddenly the horses stretched in a new burst of speed. The night was strangely alive; they were struck by the number of shepherds watching from every viewpoint in the hills. Before long they were halted and accosted by one of these shepherds without flocks and invited to change their direction. As they followed him, slipping through the bright southern dark which is no more than a brief lunar day, their guide told his story. His master, suspecting their plight, and noticing toward nightfall the concentration of those curious vigilants with their foreign faces—he knew every face in the district—had sent out his own men to watch for the fugitives. For hours spies and counter-spies had been eluding each other. By devious ways their guide led them through the rising hills, which closed about them in a vast enveloping movement, to the shelter provided for them; but there they received news which forced them again to shift their direction. Valentino had already seized the passes to St. Leo; there was just time to swerve and gain the Florentine frontier. By hard riding they reached it that evening. But the Duke refused to cross. With the Florentine Government he had had some small differences; but his apprehensions were unreasoning; the sense of betrayal had crept into his marrow, and he awaited it everywhere. The boy, however, was exhausted; and he sent him with the escort through Tuscany to his uncle, Cardinal Giuliano della Rovere. That inveterate enemy of the Borgias, it was true, had recently been reconciled to them; but he had not forgotten his own blood; and he was tenacious and resourceful.

Then the lamentable flight began again. With his chamberlain the Duke pushed on, in disguise, toward the Venetian border. Toward sundown, as they were passing through a waste plain of sulphur-beds, the ground gave up a gang of peasants who brandished their scythes and gave chase; but the chamberlain, by falling behind and spilling his money and blood, gave the invalid time to outride them. The sun sank in the sulphur-beds; beyond it lay Castelnuovo di Romagna, on the Venetian border; and when the Duke reached it he immediately sent a courier to Ravenna to claim the protection of the Venetian authorities. In the morning, before dawn, he was roused by a peasant woman who brought him a warning that his message had been intercepted by the Papal troops, that his whereabouts were known, and that Castelnuovo was too small to answer for his safety. He put off his disguise and climbed back into the saddle. The long enveloping movement of Valentino had foreseen and closed every outlet, but he pushed on, weary with the extent of his dominions, skirting the frontier toward a point where he could make a shorter dash for Ravenna. In the fourth night of his flight he saw the northern slopes flushed with signal fires and heard the village bells tolling, but by some slip of Providence which no longer knew him in his nakedness, he slipped through unnoticed and reached Ravenna at daybreak. He paused only long enough to sleep and, with the impulse of flight still working blindly, pressed on in a daze toward Ferrara. Then he swerved. His wife had left Ferrara to spend the summer with her sister-in-law, Isabella d'Este, in Mantua. He laboured on aimlessly, aimlessly rehearsing the past: tricked—tricked by a library, by Livy, by Borgia, by life! And on the seventh day he joined his ladies in Mantua, having saved, as he said, "only his doublet, his shirt, and his life."

His wife was dazed. Only a few months—she could not believe it—only a few months before she had followed Lucrezia Borgia over the route of his flight, nursing the little bride's headaches, those headaches which were the bane of her life and which she laid to the weight of her hair; and she had found her pious and sweet and had conceived a better opinion of the Borgias, far better than her sister-in-law's. Isabella was not reconciled to them yet: not even when a feeling letter came from Lucrezia, declaring that she would give 50,000 ducats for this not to have happened—the very letter of a parvenu. Isabella received the Duke with generous indignation; she preserved, however, the serenity with which she always bore the misfortunes of others; for her own life had been fortunate and she cultivated a sensible philosophy. Her husband had no philosophy and spoke loudly of avenging his brother-in-law; unfortunately, Francesco Gonzaga still thought of himself as the Victor of Fornovo; but she pacified him. Time would tell and for the moment the refugees were safe in their own family; her house would henceforth be their home. It might not be as large as their own, but in many ways it resembled it; it was a shrine of art, for Isabella was also an insatiable collector and not the least of her griefs was the loss of the treasures of Urbino, which she had so often envied. Who knew into whose hands they would fall? Guidobaldo had forgotten them. He was deep in a letter to Cardinal della Rovere, setting forth in exact detail the facts of his flight and fall; and when it was written, he sank into a deep sleep—but a sleep that twitched with fugitive spasms, like that of the hound after the hunt, dreaming, still dreaming of the chase.

20

Travelling rapidly, Machiavelli and the Bishop reached Urbino three days after the flight of the Duke. On the rising road they passed the Papal troops far from the city, where there were no signs of the occupation except a slow line of mules descending the mountain, laden with the spoils. The town was calm, there were few soldiers in the streets, and it was only on entering the Palace that they found it heavily guarded. Valentino received them at night—it was then that he worked and he was now working for effect. Of that there was full proof in the preliminaries—their slow progress and impressive halts in the network of noble corridors where soldiers sprang to attention in every passage—and in the interview itself. Stooping through the last of many deep doors, they passed into the ducal study and found themselves facing the Duke. He was surrounded by his officers, who formed a dense foil for him. The little den, the sultry air of the summer night, the vista through the loggia of a precipitous drop where, far below, lay the kingdoms of the world, everything was calculated to create an indefinable impression and quicken their nerves. In the dim light Machiavelli could discern no more than the common report—he was *biondo e bello*; but that blond beauty was glamour to an Italian, and after nightfall Caesar was a stunning condottiere. He was not merely fair. Lounging among his lieutenants, he was tall and sinewy, and his movements had the supple grace of a bull-fighter and the practised unction of a churchman. But for his muscular bearing he might have seemed dapper; but he was obviously, like his raiment, changeable silk over steel. Rising promptly, after the preliminary compliments, he rose straight to the height of his argument. What he wanted of Florence was an explanation. He addressed himself to the Bishop, while Machiavelli lurked in the background, watching intently. If the Republic valued his friendship—and if it did not it was at liberty to reject it—he expected it to sign a new contract with him as a condottiere; but this time he must have guarantees that the bond would be observed. "I must have explicit assurances," he concluded, moving restlessly about. "I know only too well that your Government bears me no good will and will desert me like an assassin, and has already attempted to create every difficulty for me with the Pope and the King of France." Then he paused abruptly: "This Government does not suit me, you must change it, or if you will not have me as a friend you shall have me as a foe." The Bishop replied coolly that Florence had the government it chose and that no one in Italy could boast better faith: it observed its engagements and honoured its contracts. To these generalities the Duke listened humourlessly. The Bishop went on imperturbably, however, suggesting that if His Excellency wished to prove his friendship for Florence, nothing was easier: he had only to call off Vitellozzo Vitelli, who was his man and in Arezzo. Then, if not humour, something like delight dawned in the Duke's eyes. Sitting down slowly, he reflected. He disclaimed all responsibility for Vitellozzo; he had no connexion with the enterprise of Arezzo; yet he was not displeased that the Republic had been taught a lesson. He admitted it frankly. Then his relish grew grimmer. He studied his muscular hands and, folding them slowly, suggested that a vengeance entirely satisfactory to the Republic might be arranged, if they came to terms. His level eyes rested on the Bishop, who made no reply; then he raised them, gleaming prosperously in their own animal light, and peering into the dark quarter met the scrutiny of Machiavelli. It was a moment of electrical impact, unblurred by reflection, undimmed by afterthought; and the Florentine Secretary stored away that impression. Valentino left him little time for inspection, and looked away, through the loggia, into the night, over the dizzy sea of space below; and the air in the room grew closer. Machiavelli studied him, fascinated. There was power in the level eyes, the vised lips, the long square feline jaw; but there was a hint of impotence, too, in the whippet-like skull and the tapering elegance of the profile; and a suggestion, ambiguous and insidious, of something hollow and histrionic in the man. But this immediately yielded to another impression, far more compelling. The Duke sat looking into the dark with vacuous guile, allowing his offer to rest and exerting a pressure which everyone felt but no one could name—his magnetism. Motionless, he waited. He might have been posing for his portrait, but no portrait could convey the numbing power of his beauty, that blond and baleful beauty to which no Italian was insensible; and the night worked its spell. Then Caesar broke the pose. There was a sudden clank of arms in the study as his captains rallied around him like trained *bandollieri*: he was saying that Vitellozzo had twenty or twenty-five thousand men—they nodded and confirmed the figures—that he himself could count on France —and they nodded again—and he urged the Bishop to impress on his Government the necessity of a quick decision. He gave him four days to reply, and rose brusquely. The interview was over.

Machiavelli and the Bishop were still under its spell when they composed their report. "It is the way of this person," they began, "to be in other men's houses before they know it, as befell the late Lord of this place." In the Bishop, Machiavelli had at last found a Florentine who saw eye to eye with him and who appreciated the genius of Caesar. The Borgias, said the Bishop, "recognize opportunity and know how to use it wonderfully"—it was the whole secret of their success. And Machiavelli concluded the report with a personal panegyric which for once had the stamp of official approval: "So spirited is this prince that there is nothing so great but seems small to him, and in the conquest of glory and states he never rests, nor admits either risk or fatigue; he appears before one knows where he comes from; he is loved by his soldiers and has recruited the best men in Italy; and all these things, added to his perpetual good fortune, make him victorious and formidable."

So convinced was the Bishop of the need of dispatch that he sent Machiavelli back to Florence to hasten the reply of the Government. But the Government refused to be hurried. The city was so uneasy that a decree had been issued imposing severe penalties on anyone who divulged the contents of Valentino's letters or those concerning him. To avoid public gatherings and demonstrations, the races had been suppressed, for the first time since Savonarola's day. The Piagnoni, in fact, were stirring and pointing to Caesar as the scourge and the tyrant predicted by their prophet; there were some even who called him the Anti-Christ. But the Government was calm. In the accurate report Machiavelli laid before them, the Signori, far from the influence of Caesar's sinister magnetism, saw only the shifting strategy of his uncertainty: he raised too many bids and threats; the variety of his arguments, their urgency, and the ease with which he shuffled and dropped them—everything proved it; and they waited for the report from Milan. Nor were they deceived. Piero Soderini, the Bishop's brother, wrote that the King had warned Borgia not to molest Florence; and the warning went far. Valentino not only subsided; two months later Vitellozzo Vitelli relinquished Arezzo, and the rebellious city reverted to Florentine rule.

Machiavelli, however, was still haunted. It was no time to preach Borgia in Florence; but when the Government penalized Arezzo by arresting a number of its leading citizens, confiscating their property, and deporting them to Florence, he took the bit in his teeth. Standing at his tall desk, he composed a harangue, in the classical manner, to the City Fathers. "Lucius Furius Camillus, after conquering the rebel peoples of Latium, entered the Senate and said: I have done what I could by war, now it is for you, Conscript Fathers, to protect yourselves for the future against revolt." And he drew his parallel. "The Senate generously pardoned the conquered, excepting only the cities of Veliterno and Anzio.

The first was demolished and the inhabitants were sent to Rome; the other, on the contrary, was repopulated with new and loyal inhabitants. The Romans knew that we must always avoid half-measures and either win our subjects with benefits or put them out of case to offend. . . . I have heard that History is the master of our actions and the best teacher of princes, and the world has always been inhabited by men who have had the same passions, and there have always been those who obey and those who command, and some obey willingly and others unwillingly, and rebel, and are recaptured. Your policy toward the people of the Val di Chiana in general may be approved, but not your conduct toward the Aretini in particular. They have always rebelled and you have neither benefited nor extinguished them after the Roman example. Instead of benefiting, you have exasperated them by deporting them to Florence, confiscating their property, and depriving them of their honours; and you have not made sure of them, since you have left their walls standing and five-sixths of the inhabitants in the city without sending others to subdue them. Hence Arezzo will always be ready to rebel again: which is of no little moment, as Caesar Borgia is in the vicinity and is seeking to form a strong state by including Tuscany in his dominions. And the Borgias," he concluded, "know neither scruples nor half-measures." Then with a melancholy smile he laid the lecture away among his personal papers.

21

Meanwhile, the lesson of Urbino was working in other minds. In Mantua the Marquis was incensed by the treachery, and the Marchioness by the vandalism, of Valentino. Of the two the woman was the more practical idealist. When Isabella learned that the treasures of the Montefeltri were being dispersed to defray the expenses of the Papal army and that among them was a Cupid by Michelangelo, she wrote to his brother, Cardinal d'Este, to rescue this prize of the collection if it came on the market at a price within her means. The schemes of her husband were more extravagant. With his brother-in-law he went up to Milan where, in that summer of 1502, the French headquarters had become a Court of Appeal for all the dispossessed despots of Romagna. Led by Giovanni Sforza, the late Lord of Pesaro, they formed a little society of ex-rulers, without visible means of support, who lived on each others' misfortunes and their common dreams of redress. Guidobaldo of Urbino was a welcome recruit, and even more so was his champion. Though the Marquis, it was true, was still in possession of his state, no prince in Italy was ineligible to that growing society of uncrowned expatriates, and his adhesion was vigorous. He proposed at one moment publicly to insult Caesar and at another to form a League against him. The agitated group, living on hope and on hearsay, was suddenly aroused by a rumour that the King, realizing at last the folly of fostering a strong state in the centre of Italy, was about to undo it; and they prepared to present their claims in concert. Excitement was at fever-heat, and they had met in the Castello for an audience when they saw a dust-covered horseman race into the courtyard, dismount, and hold the stirrup of the King. In that obsequious posture they had difficulty at first in recognizing Caesar Borgia, who to their common knowledge was at that moment in Urbino; but it was obviously he—who appeared like the devil when he was mentioned—who was in the house before one knew where he came from. The King embraced him and on the following days received him, both publicly and privately, with such pointed honours that the little society dissolved and slowly melted away.

Not so the Marquis, however. He held his ground, to the alarm of his wife. The Court of Appeal had adjourned—what was he doing in Milan? "It is generally believed here that His Majesty has some understanding with Valentino," she wrote from Mantua, "so I beg you to be careful. In these days we do not know whom to trust. There is a report here that Your Excellency has insulted Valentino before the Most Christian King and the servants of the Pope; and whether true or not it will undoubtedly reach his ears. Valentino has already shown that he does not scruple to conspire against his own blood, and he will not hesitate, I am certain, to plot against you. And being jealous of your life, which is dearer to me than my own, and knowing how your natural goodness leads you to take no precautions for your safety, I have made inquiries and have learned that you allow all manner of persons to serve you at table. My dearest Lord, do not laugh at my fears and say that women are cowards and always trembling, for *their* malignity is greater than *my* fears or *your* courage." At first it was difficult to make him hear more than the sound of his own fury; but gradually that affectionate voice found its cooling way to his heart. He was fond of his wife, to whom he was not always faithful, as she well knew; and under the circumstances her constancy touched him. He owed her some consideration. Moreover, on political questions he consulted her, for she had a steadier head than his own; and little by little she convinced him that this was a political, not a personal, question. Between her persuasions and those of the King he finally consented to a public reconciliation with Valentino. The peace was sealed by the betrothal of his infant son, to whom Valentino stood godfather, to the infant daughter of Caesar; and the political question became once more a personal one.

It developed rapidly. Returning with the Marquis to Mantua, Guidobaldo found a surprise awaiting him there. A pleasant surprise it was, on entering Isabella's rooms, to see, newly unveiled and exquisitely set off, the lost Cupid of Michelangelo; and he might have committed the blunder of thanking her for this delicate attention, had he not been warned in time by his wife. That gem now formed part of his sister-in-law's collection. What he regretted was the loss, not of the Cupid, but of the opportunity to offer it to her himself, for he undoubtedly owed her some token of gratitude; but that pleasure was denied him, not only because he was now a poor man, but because Valentino had forestalled his gallant gesture by offering it to Isabella himself. She was beginning, in fact, slowly and reluctantly to reconcile herself to the Borgias. That process, however, had only begun. Valentino was now taking a domestic interest in his late enemies. He was willing to countenance the residence of the exiles in Mantua on one condition—that his title to Urbino be formally legitimized. In a conversation with the Mantuan ambassador, Caesar proposed that the Duke renounce his claims. He alluded to what was perhaps a painful subject, but after all a matter of common knowledge: Guidobaldo was childless. If he entered the Church, he would lead a life suited to his tastes, and he would be looked after—a Cardinal's Hat was mentioned. To be sure, there was the Duchess, but a divorce could be arranged, and he undertook to find her a husband in France: a solution to which she could not object in view of the notorious physical infirmity of her present mate. She was still in the prime of life.

These overtures were received by Guidobaldo with less indignation than his wife expected. He was even tempted to entertain them. His infirmity preyed on him, and its open secret startled him. His impotence was a judgment perhaps: in the natural world he had no rights. That he loved her, that she loved him, was one of those irrelevances which Nature ignored. It was just. But the indignation of Elizabetta answered for both of them. "Sooner than repudiate Guidobaldo," she replied, "she would live with him as a sister." And she smiled at the Cupid rearing its captive wings beside her: she would not miss it. Isabella admired it because it was a pseudo-antique; but Elizabetta was a veteran sentimentalist, and herself a genuine antique. At such devotion something quickened in her invalid lover. A fundamental, long-dormant instinct rebelled. He foresaw the futility of renunciation. The first concession led to the last. With the loss of his state he was losing everything, even the respect of his friends—whenever he looked at the Cupid he realized that. The world respected nothing but property; without possessions he was entitled to nothing; and he clung to his wife and his title to save his self-respect. It was folly to be philosophical and ignominy to yield; and together husband and wife sat down, in the shadow of Eros unconquered in strife, to dictate their reply to Caesar.

Then Valentino, having been accommodating, became peremptory. He could no longer tolerate the residence of Guidobaldo in Mantua. Guidobaldo packed, and the Marquis and Isabella reluctantly watched him leave. They pleaded with Elizabetta at least to linger, since she had not fallen under Caesar's fiat and was herself an invalid in constant need of attention. But the Duchess was stubborn. "She would rather die in the public hospital than live without him," she said. She followed her husband to Venice. Venice was an asylum for political refugees whose presence there made them valuable to the state as pawns in the international game, and they were granted a pension; but before it was paid they knew the poverty of a public hospital. Their straits were so desperate at one moment that the Duchess thought of taking service with the Queen of France; but one glance at her suffering husband convinced her that he could not afford such abnegation. They persevered in their genteel poverty. With Mantua they maintained a regular correspondence, but the letters of Isabella turned more and more on small matters, domestic nothings, innocuous trifles, and rarely mentioned politics. From other sources, however, they received encouragement.

The landless despots were dispersed and forgotten as only the inoffensive can be; but another movement of revolt was now afoot among Valentino's own captains. The lesson of Urbino had not been lost on them. The treachery he practised so easily did not come hard to them; and at least five felt themselves cheated. They only needed a leader, and he arose in the person of Vitellozzo Vitelli. Ever since he had relinquished Arezzo, disgorging under pressure the two ambitions of his life, his vengeance on Florence for the death of his brother and a principality for himself, he had not looked his master in the eye. Moody with syphilis, he nursed a sullen venereal anger against the man who had betrayed him; and he roused other malcontents. The tyrants of Bologna, Siena, and

Perugia, and the two Orsini, Paolo and the Duke of Gravina, with Cardinal Orsini to back them in Rome, felt themselves threatened by the rapid course of Borgian ambition and were sore in its harness. In October 1502, a Diet of the disaffected condottieri was held at La Magione near Perugia, and the articles of a League were signed for the extermination of Valentino. Between them they could muster 10,000 men, a force far outnumbering that of Caesar; but before moving they sounded the states which would have most interest in supporting them for his suppression. The first of these was Venice. Cramped between Romagna and the French, it had every reason to fear Caesar; but his name was inscribed in the Golden Book, he was an honorary citizen, a palace had been allocated to him on the Grand Canal, and for the moment the Serenissima confined itself to an expression of benevolent neutrality. The refugees, however, took heart. From Urbino came rumours of a restlessness ready to break into revolt; and though the Confederates did not solicit their support, Guidobaldo and the Duchess waited devoutly for the outcome of that conspiracy of injustices which eventually begets justice.

22

Next, the Confederates approached Florence. But there also they received the Venetian reply. Officially, Florence remained neutral. The Republic looked twice at a League which included, beside its old enemy, Vitellozzo Vitelli, those sworn champions of the Medici, the Orsini; it was wary of antagonizing Caesar; and it hesitated to encourage a conspiracy whose strength existed as yet only on paper. But the Confederates had only to prove their power to tap a latent sympathy; for of unofficial approval there was no lack. The initiative and the brunt of the effort, however, rested on them, and the result was immediately apparent. Ten days after the declaration of the Diet, the tyrant of Siena withdrew, the Orsini cooled, and the League was in danger of collapsing, when it was suddenly reanimated from another quarter. Urbino revolted and recalled its Duke. It was the first crack in Romagna; the Confederates grew gusty and unfurled their banners. Their credit, damped by their hesitation, revived in Florence; and it rose yet higher when, out of a clouding sky, Valentino offered the Republic his friendship. How changed was the tone now! How chastened! Gone were the high-handed demands, the brusque bravado, the cut-throat pressure of a year ago. The Government studied his prospects. By all reports he was outnumbered; he had appealed to the French, but they were occupied in Naples; and he was reduced, for the moment, to recruiting native troops in Romagna, manoeuvring for time, and attempting to conciliate his neighbours. Until the situation developed, the Government determined to temporize; but as their reports came from prejudiced sources, they decided to send an observer to study him on the spot. That observer was Machiavelli.

Never had he undertaken a mission more reluctantly. Too much was at stake. His faith in the genius of Caesar was in jeopardy. For the Confederates he had no respect; they were understudies; and there were five of them—if they had all been geniuses that would have been four too many. Genius worked alone. Caesar trusted no one but himself, and the secret of his success was that he recognized opportunity. But now came the test. Opportunity had favoured him so far. He had been blessed by unfailing good fortune and cursed perhaps by blinding prosperity. Adversity was the crucial test. Was he a genius or an opportunist? What was the difference? What indeed but success? The opportunity to study him at this critical moment was tempting, but Machiavelli shrank from it. The test touched him to the quick, it was too crucial; for on the issue hung, with his faith in Caesar, his faith in himself.

For now, after a long period of pregnancy, the truth had suddenly revealed itself. He had created Caesar himself, out of his secret longings and mortified needs. That young indomitable dynast was the embodiment of his faith in life. He was power personified, a natural force, a medium of life, whose whole virtue lay in his strength. Caesar dared not fail. The alternative was too dismal—the perpetual mediocrity of life, the misery of little men at the mercy of Chance, the futility of old men shirking its dangers and begging its profits—all the abject realities of life in Florence under the Republic; and the alternative came home to him cruelly with his instructions. He was to study the Duke and report his strength; but his real instructions—they were unwritten but he felt them in the pressure of public opinion—were to discover his weakness. He would obey them scrupulously, he was a patriot; but his patriotism, once so unquestioning, had now become almost perfunctory; through it strove a contrary impulse, a stubborn determination to defend and vindicate Valentino. Only by a conscientious effort could he keep his loyalties from dividing. It was, morally, the most dangerous mission of his life.

But these apprehensions, which he hesitated to admit to himself, could not be expressed to his masters. He fell back on other pretexts. The Government was initiating a pecuniary reform which began—naturally—among the drudges of the Chancery; his salary was threatened, he had been recently married, and his wife held the purse-strings. But that too he could not admit. Missions were expensive, he had neither the rank nor the means of an ambassador, and he was anxious to cut a good figure before his hero. That too he could not explain. But it was not merely materially that he wished to cut a good figure; to parley and temporize with the inscrutable Duke who, as he noted, "never speaks and always acts," was morally humiliating—and equally inadmissible. What fatality had elected him for this trying service? But there was no escape. Into the ring he must go, into that vast arena of Romagna where the states of Italy were watching Valentino, at last in the lurch, awaiting the charge.

It was late in October when he left Florence. Though there was no pressing need and he had a long stay ahead, he raced for Imola as if, from afar, the spell of Caesar were already upon him. Over the wide man-raising plains of Forli, along the sere fields where the late harvests were stacked, he scorched the road, outriding the auburn melancholy of the landscape where, on all sides, the last mellowness of summer was yielding to the slow numbing blight of autumn. The latent chill in the air only made him sweat, and he was not a well man when he left Florence, but he was off for faith, and he kept his mare at a breakneck speed. This unreasoning haste spurred him, when he dismounted at Imola, straight to the Duke; and only then did its reason dawn on him. Admitted to the inscrutable antagonist against whom he was to pit his wits and his faith, he rushed in blindly where angels feared to tread. The Duke listened—flattered by the homage of such hard riding—to the perfunctory assurances of Florentine friendship which Machiavelli hurried over quickly. Their hollowness rang dismally in his own ears; but Caesar affected to ignore them and came to the point. He turned the talk from his prospects to those of Florence. With an affability eloquent of his unruffled self-confidence, he initiated Machiavelli into his secrets; he would tell him, he said, "what he had never yet told any man"; and Machiavelli listened. In the first place, the Orsini were committed to the Medici, and Vitellozzo Vitelli had not forgotten the death of his brother; the moment was ill chosen to favour the Confederates: they were divided and would crumble the moment the French came to his aid. Machiavelli, already familiar with these secrets, observed with amazement the vacuous guile with which Caesar pressed them on him. But Caesar was confident of his effect. The League, he laughed, was "a Diet of failures." Piqued to be taken for a fool, Machiavelli insisted on definite reasons for depreciating the Confederates; and Caesar obliged him. "They are worse fools than I thought," he explained, "not having known the time to injure me, the King of France being in Italy and the Pope still living: two things which feed me so much fire that it needs more than their water to quench it." Then the old peremptory tone crept into his voice; he clouded. Now—that monosyllable galvanized him—now was the time for Florence to show her hand, it would not do to delay; if he made peace with the rebels, he would be bound to Vitelli, the Orsini, the Medici; and he crowded a long meaning into the stare he bent on the Florentine Secretary. But his sinister magnetism was somehow damped, and Machiavelli resisted it coolly. Knowing his man, he too came to the point and asked him to name his terms; but at that question—so pertinent, so obvious—Valentino "veered away." Such inconsistency and evasion startled and dismayed Machiavelli; a hideous doubt arose. Was it possible that Caesar did not know his own mind? that, like everyone else, he was weak and uncertain? To stifle that fear, he changed the subject and probed the Duke for the effect which the loss of Urbino had produced on him. Caesar made light of it; it was "a weak state" and, his mouth slowly hardening, "he had not overlooked the means of retaking it." But Machiavelli pinned him down; his logic was now working fast and furiously—if Urbino was a weak state, how did His Excellency account for its loss? "My clemency and the fact that I underestimated matters ruined me," Caesar replied. "As you know, I took the Duchy in three days and harmed no one, with the except of Messer Dolce and two others who were working against His Holiness." He submitted to questioning easily and even went so far as to volunteer that "the natives were dissatisfied and I burdened them too much with my soldiers." Other observers had noted his love of frank men, though whether he valued honesty because he possessed or lacked it himself was uncertain. At all events, with this candid admission of his mistakes, he restored Machiavelli's confidence in him. Whatever else might be true, Caesar lacked the duplicity of vanity: he was not his own dupe.

So ended the first day of his critical mission. It had begun tamely, and as Machiavelli emerged from that perplexing and disappointing interview, his racing mind stopped, and he foresaw a long fruitless stay in the yellowing land of Romagna. The next morning, however, Caesar sent for him. He was in high spirits and received him more cordially than ever. After reading him a letter from the French, in which was promised the prompt dispatch of three hundred cavalry, he handed it to Machiavelli, begging him to verify the signature. "You see, Secretary?" he said, tapping it

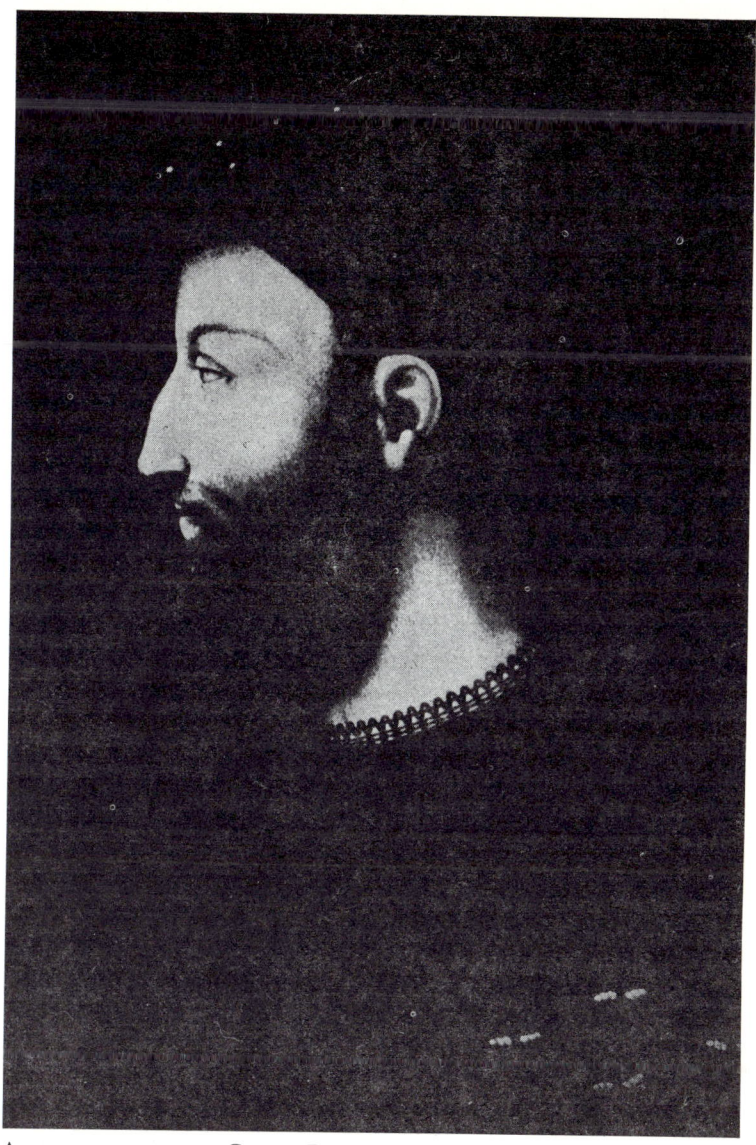

ALLEGED PORTRAIT OF CAESAR BORGIA
From the painting in the Correr Museum, Venice

significantly. "You see how positive it is? Believe me, this revolt suits me well; they could not have discovered themselves at a time which injures me less." Now he was willing to name his terms with Florence—a treaty of alliance and an engagement as condottiere of the Republic; and drawing himself up with a pride that was not histrionic, he concluded: "Write to your masters, tell them that I am *not untrue to myself*, and that I do not lack friends, among whom I wish to number them, provided they declare themselves promptly; but if they do not, I shall set them aside and, though the water were up to my mouth, I shall never mention friendship again." Coming out into the damp November air, which the late sun was fitfully warming, Machiavelli fell once more under the spell. When Caesar laid himself out to be winning, he was irresistible. "Pen cannot tell with what show of affection he spoke," Machiavelli began his report, and he concluded it: "I assure Your Worships that we cannot delay long; if not by the first, then by the second reply, we must decide. I think you should know this and not persuade yourselves, if you decide to consent, that any time will serve."

"If you decide to consent." It was plain where his preference lay and, with all his caution, he could not help insinuating it into the last telling words of an otherwise impersonal report. He would not have been honest, had he done less. But his discreet influence was lost. The Government replied that it could not declare itself until it had consulted the French, and the engagement as condottiere which the Duke solicited had already been offered to the Marquis of Mantua. When Machiavelli reluctantly went to the Duke to communicate this reply and the mute disappointment it caused him, Valentino greeted him gaily. "We have good news from all sides," he said, revealing what was rare in him—a touch of humour, or at least good humour. "The stars are not favourable to rebels this year." And before Machiavelli could open his mouth, he let him into new secrets. The Papal troops had been raiding Urbino and had captured two towns; the Papal Legate had met the rebels at Perugia: Vitellozzo Vitelli was laid up with French boils, Paolo Orsini was sick with scurvy, both were pining to return to his service. If Florence would concentrate a few troops on her frontier, merely as a demonstration, he would remember the gesture as a service. As he ran on in this sanguine mood, Machiavelli forced himself to break the bitter truth he had just received from Florence. The Duke listened easily. The engagement of the Marquis did not trouble him. Francesco Gonzaga, he said, "was an excellent man and his friend, and he would be delighted to have him in the neighbourhood; for his own part, he would serve the Republic voluntarily." And so the dreaded moment passed. But that evening the ducal secretary drew Machiavelli aside with a long face. "It was not necessary for your Republic to engage the Marquis of Mantua at this moment," he said, speaking as a friend of Florence and altogether unofficially. "It seems to me that it has missed an excellent opportunity by giving to another what belonged to my master. I do not see what offers it can make him now, glorious as he is, and so accustomed to conquer, and so supremely fortunate." Even if his master forgot this slight, they could never reopen the question: it was closed—a melancholy word. Machiavelli was worried. "What I understood thoroughly, when I was through," he wrote that night, "was that this article preoccupies His Excellency greatly."

With the Confederates weakening and Valentino daily growing stronger, he no longer understood the diffidence of his Government; but then neither did he understand Valentino. Not only were there no threats or bids for Florentine friendship: the mutable Duke, so accustomed to blowing hot and cold, now maintained toward him an attitude of unbargaining good humour and unwavering and generous friendliness. Machiavelli was so mystified that he consulted his colleagues; and the ambassador of Ferrara suggested, in explanation, that His Excellency might be awaiting the election of the new Gonfalonier in Florence. Then a light broke on Machiavelli and he realized that the influence of Caesar had at last penetrated his country. The election of the new Gonfalonier was, in fact, an event of the utmost significance.

The Republic had finally succumbed to necessity. After so many years of inefficiency, realizing that its deliberations represented a compromise of opinion and its policies a vicious circle of temporizing and half-measures, it had recognized at last that this was an organic disability of all commonwealths. The Republic was constitutionally incapable of the initiative of a personal sovereign, and the example and menace of Valentino had forced it to adopt a constitutional reform, or rather a compromise, so necessary that even Savonarola had foreseen it. It had created a Gonfalonier for life, a permanent executive with powers permitting him to focus, invigorate, and give continuity to its policies. Everything, however, depended on the man. When the result of the election reached Imola, there was an immediate reaction. Piero Soderini, the brother of Machiavelli's friend the Bishop, had been appointed. "His nomination gives the city more credit here than you can imagine," the Ferrarese ambassador said, in congratulating Machiavelli. It was a portent. The reform, deferred for fourteen years lest it lead to a tyranny, had been uncontested, an unprecedented thing in Florence, so completely had Soderini rallied popular confidence. He was a born mediator, an innately constitutional man. He had all the Republican virtues: he was affluent and responsible, childless and disinterested, law-abiding, conservative, public-spirited, and of unquestioned integrity. As a friend of the family, Machiavelli wrote to congratulate him; but his political opinion he reserved. Unlike his brother the Bishop, Piero Soderini was not an admirer of the Borgias. He had all the virtues and none of the vices, and it was a question how far he could go without them. But he had a magnificent opportunity to combine in his person the freedom of the Republic with the efficiency of the autocrat. Between the incompetence of the one and the irresponsibility of the other he appeared, a portent indeed, as a third alternative; but was he more than a compromise? The answer had a peculiar importance for Machiavelli at that moment when his loyalty to Florence and his attraction for Caesar were so ambiguously at odds; and he studied his instructions closely for the indication of a new temper at home.

But as the days passed, it became clearer that nothing had changed, and the attitude of the Duke promptly altered. He was now too busy to receive Machiavelli, though he found time to idle and wrestle with the country people. When the Government complained of the meagreness of Machiavelli's reports, "I am making every effort to win the confidence of His Excellency," he explained, "and to be able to speak to him familiarly, but so far I have succeeded in extracting nothing from him." The same reserve was observed by his subordinates. "An admirable secrecy reigns in this Court," he added. When the complaints continued, he became impatient and asked for his recall. The reply came from Biagio, who used the privilege of an old friend to calm his insubordination. "Niccolo," he wrote, "though you are cautious and clever and it is presumptuous of me to remind you how you should write, particularly of things which occur hourly under your eyes, I shall tell you briefly what I think, although I have done my duty by you everywhere and against everyone who has blamed you. First, let me remind you to write more frequently: your letters are sometimes a week on the way, and this is not to your credit nor to the satisfaction of those who have sent you: you have been reproved by the Signori and others, since, these matters being of such moment, we must hear regularly how they stand. And though you have written fully of the troops this Prince commands, the help he hopes for, and his courage in defending himself, and have reported excellently his muster and that of his enemies, and laid all before our eyes, yet you conclude too surely when you write that his enemies can no longer do him much injury; and I think (though no one else has said this) that you cannot judge so finally since, as you have written and it is fair to suppose, they do not publish the progress of their enemies there nor their exact strength, on which you base your opinion; and here we learn from various sources that the affairs of the League are flourishing: so that, as you have always done hitherto, leave judgment to others and return to your post—and no back-talk. I did my duty as a friend and read your letter to Piero Soderini, because he laughed at your last, in which you asked for a recall." Between Biagio and Soderini, Machiavelli was once more subdued; and suddenly something more compelling than duty riveted him to his post.

In the admirable secrecy of Caesar's Court an event was afoot which he could neither confirm nor disprove nor believe nor fathom. The Confederates were reported to be about to sign a treaty; but it was a treaty at which the ducal secretary laughed as a trick to gain time. Machiavelli was nonplussed. "I cannot believe the Confederates do not know this," he wrote to Florence, "so that I am at a loss, and when I think that something may have been concluded against us, I feel my heart in my mouth at all this secrecy. The secretaries have grown rude, the Ferrarese envoy who used to talk to me freely shuns me, and this evening after supper the Treasurer said something which alarmed me, hinting that Your Worships had been given a chance to treat with His Excellency, but that now the opportunity was lost." All thought of deserting had fled: his patriotism revived in a violent revulsion of fear. The Duke, who kept him waiting for hours—"a thing which never happened before, even when His Excellency was prevented by good reasons"—assured him that the treaty contained nothing against Florence; but denial only deepened Machiavelli's suspicions. He hurried to the Duke's subordinates and his own colleagues, but he was met everywhere with coldness and reserve. All that he could learn from the Ducal Chancellor was that the treaty had not yet been signed: at the last moment the Duke had inserted a clause "touching the honour of the Crown of France." "This clause," he explained, "will either be accepted or not. If it is accepted, it opens a window, and if it is rejected, a door for the Duke to slip out of it; even a child would laugh at this treaty." But if it was so transparent that a child could see through it and was openly advertised as a snare, what lay beneath it? Machiavelli no longer knew what to believe; and a few days later he was completely confounded when he learned that the treaty had actually been signed, and that the Confederates were actually carrying out its conditions. After waiting so long to take the field for themselves, they had now taken it for Caesar and, sweeping into Urbino, had reoccupied it in his name. But now that the rebellion was over and the Confederates, placed on probation, were doing their penance and Caesar's work in the field, martial preparations had redoubled in Imola. The promised French reinforcements were pouring in, the native troops were drilling, and the object of all this post-haste and rummage in the land was unknown. Amid this daily rumour of mustering feet, Machiavelli was summoned by the Duke. In his customary black, Caesar was in one of his mournful Spanish moods. Greeting the Florentine Secretary with the sallow look of an injured hidalgo, he inquired whether the Republic had concluded its engagement with the Marquis of Mantua; and learning that the contract was about to be signed, "And what of me?" he asked. "What condotta will your masters offer me?" Machiavelli turned the question with a compliment—"he had always believed His Excellency a man to hire rather than to be hired"—but the Duke was in no mood for compliments. "What of my honour," he insisted, "being a soldier and a friend of your masters, and having no condotta from them?" Staring him sternly out of countenance, the Duke asked how many soldiers the Republic needed and how many the Marquis of Mantua was supplying; to which Machiavelli replied firmly that the supply was sufficient. "Then there is no place for me," the Duke said curtly and rose and swung on his heel; but he wheeled and returned immediately. "Secretary," he said with peremptory earnestness, "Secretary, tell me, I beg you, whether your masters mean to go further with me than a general friendship. If a general friendship satisfies them, it satisfies me, but I do not wish the hope and the failure to reach a more definite agreement to breed bad blood between us hereafter." And his face was bloodless, as Machiavelli bowed himself out.

The hint worked on him. The nervous Florentine fell sick; his stomach turned. In that atmosphere of latent intimidation and calculated insincerity it was impossible to tell where effect ended and fact began; and his confusion quickened his fear. Somewhere, sometime, it was necessary to believe someone or something; but he believed only what he dreaded. If he could have discerned some purpose in the variations of Caesar's conduct, he could have mastered his stomach; but even Caesar seemed to be the sport of impulse and opportunity, bluffing himself as he did everyone else into the belief that he was the master and not the creature of circumstance. Then Machiavelli became not merely guarded, but critical of him. The glancing irrelevance and intuitive trick of Caesar's mind were deeply repugnant to his own logical habits; yet he recognized that Caesar worked with the instinct, and after the manner, of life. Their latent antagonism declared itself; he recoiled from the fascination of a nature so antipathetic to his own. To be baffled was bearable, but not to be deluded. Intimidation and trickery and temporizing he could admit, if they were means to an end, but not if they were makeshifts without bearing or purpose. And what was Caesar's purpose?

Several days after this interview, he was drawn into conversation by a confidant of the Duke, who took up the theme where Caesar had dropped it. "Secretary," this personage said, taking pity on his confusion, "I have remarked more than once that these general relations between your masters and the Duke are of little profit to him and less to them." And he proceeded to lay a large chart of Caesar's eventual policy before him. "This Prince knows only too well that the Pope may die any day, and that before his death he must find some other support if he wishes to retain the states he has won. His first trust is in the King of France, his second in his arms, and, because he believes that in time these may not suffice, he wishes to make friends of his neighbours and of all those who will be compelled to defend him in order to protect themselves. These are Florence, Bologna, Mantua, and Ferrara, four states which, being adjoining, will command respect if they unite, and the King of France will augment them, because he can trust them." The explanation was plausible. Machiavelli checked it by his own observations. They tallied. In the last three months Caesar had learned much. He had set up a rigid administration of justice in Romagna, he had levied a local militia, and he had begun to reckon with his neighbours. He was developing politically; perhaps this was the turning-point of his career. Machiavelli summed up his conclusions. It was true that Caesar "lives only to advance his own interests or what seem to him such, and since I have been here his affairs have been governed wholly by Fortune." But it was also true that "he is beginning to beware of obeying his impulses and to recognize that Fortune will not pour conquests into his lap. Vitelli and the Orsini have made him wiser than he was. They have taught him to think of retaining his states rather than of acquiring new ones, and the way to retain them is to raise his own troops, to conciliate his subjects, and to make friends of his neighbours; and these are his aims." That much was established; and recognizing his own intelligence in Caesar, Machiavelli began to recover confidence.

But his very intelligence defeated him. Under the influence of fear he had his first revelation of the limitations of the finite mind. Caesar had political foresight; but was he clever enough to develop moral foresight as well? Without good faith how could he command the confidence of his neighbours? While he remained a moral opportunist his political genius was incomplete. The crisis had come; he could no longer obey Nature blindly, he must make his peace with human opinion. But the logic of facts had worked itself out—who could trust him now? In that atmosphere of avowed treachery how could anything be believed . . . until it had happened? Machiavelli, however, was weary of mistrust; he could not go on groping, questioning, speculating for ever; he needed to believe; and there was such a thing as being too cautious. Was it not possible that Caesar, using like a consummate actor his latent personalities as masks, might now be deceiving him by his truth? Might he not be beguiling him by his honesty? Might not all these suspicions be groundless? Machiavelli reasoned his hope, but hope, being reasoned, was hope no longer. All he could see was that perpetual pitfall. Calculation could accomplish so much and no more; without faith it was futile; and what faith could Caesar inspire? He relapsed into indecision and dread.

But he dared not relapse. About him the bugles blew and, as he heard them marshalling the armies to an unknown destination, his mind flew to Florence and the responsibility of his position became unbearable. He could report life but he could not penetrate or cope with it; and he begged again for his recall, urging his masters to send a man of experience, "who knows the world better than I do," and to furnish him "not with incomplete ideas but with resolute views." In reply the Government complimented him on his reports. His friends in the Chancery were amused. "You are never of the same mind for an hour," wrote Biagio; and Agostino Vespucci also twitted him on his restlessness—"see where you are leading us with that spirit of yours, so eager to be riding and roaming and moving!" The strain exhausted him; and he became seriously ill.

He was no sooner in bed than the army was in motion, heading for Cesena. He lagged behind, under the double handicap of sickness and poverty. "I have been ill for the last twelve days," he wrote to his masters, "and if I continue like this I fear I shall come home in my coffin. I leave tomorrow, but I go unwillingly; apart from my health, I have seven ducats in my purse and when I have spent them I shall be reduced to beggary." He might have had his expenses paid by the Court, he explained, but he thought that hardly becoming the dignity of the Republic. He still cared for it; and he packed with feverish patriotism. Cesena . . . Cesena . . . Was Caesar really headed for Cesena? When he started for one place, he usually appeared in another. And after Cesena, what? No one knew. He set out blindly. It was December, it was snowing, and his gloom deepened as he travelled through a country-side impoverished by the long occupation of the army. Its departure had bared what its dense presence muffled, and he passed through the barren land completely disillusioned. When he came up with the army at Cesena, he took in the situation with the feeling eye of a civilian. "The Duke and his troops are quartered in the city and the surroundings, and live to their liking," he concluded his report, "that is, not to the liking of those who lodge them. I leave Your Worships to imagine how things go on here and how they went on at Imola, where the Court remained for three months and the army for two, and where they consumed everything down to the ground. Truly, that town and the whole country have proved their patience and shown how much they could bear. I mention this, so that you may know that the French and the other troops as well behave no differently in Romagna than in Tuscany." It needed no imagination to see those troops, today in Romagna, tomorrow in Tuscany . . . a short dash . . . and Caesar was known for his lightning-like movements. The Duke paused in Cesena only long enough for a summary act of justice. One of his governors, who had brought odium on his name by the harshness of his rule and who was accused of speculating in wheat for his own profit, despite a country-wide threat of famine, was brought up, decapitated, and exposed to the populace on Christmas morning. Immediately afterwards the army resumed its march. The French troops, for a reason which mystified everyone, returned to Milan.

The next destination was Sinigaglia, the last town which the Confederates had taken and with whose capture their term of probation came to an end. There they were waiting to meet Caesar and to surrender it in a formal act of reconciliation. Machiavelli followed slowly, repeating at each stop his complaints—"I cannot go on borrowing three ducats here and four there"—"I can be of no use here, my health is bad, for two days I have had a violent fever, I feel altogether unwell"—and conscientiously accumulating reports which he could not send—"for four days it has been snowing steadily and no one can cross the Apennines." But there was no reason to hurry now. Sinigaglia had surrendered, on instructions from its owner, Cardinal della Rovere, in Rome; the Confederates were surrendering it to Caesar; nothing remained but to celebrate the general surrender. It was a tame end to three months of intrigue and suspense; the triumph of Caesar was too easy, it proved nothing but his luck; and Machiavelli was no longer interested in him. A numbing cold crept into his marrow. The weather was raw, the role of a diplomatic camp-follower disagreeable, the road lay along the bitter Adriatic, and he made it by easy stages. At his halts he replied to the letters of Biagio. They at least carried him back to the Chancery and its small troubles. There were the disputes over backgammon of Ser Antonio and Ser Andrea—"Ser Andrea dealt him a blow that almost broke his rump, and the poor man wears a pillow, and nothing will induce him to part with it"—and the worries of Biagio—"Niccolo, the new Gonfalonier is beginning to disgust the city with his determination to cut the salaries of the Chancery" —and his own—"Niccolo, we have heard no more of the cut, but some say it should apply to the secretaries as well as to the salaries: you should do everything to return"—but his worries were remote, beyond the bleak barrier of the Apennines, and Biagio, with his grumbling but unfailing loyalty, was sure to arrange everything. "Niccolo: we have searched for the *Lives* of Plutarch, we cannot find a copy in Florence, be patient, we must write to Venice: frankly, you are a pest to want so many things. . . ." The *Lives* of Plutarch would have been welcome at that moment. The past had an inestimable superiority over the present: lives that had already been lived were understandable; but Caesar eluded him, as life itself seemed to elude him. He was baffled; but at least Sinigaglia afforded him a respite from his fears, for it lay far from Florence.

And so he toiled on. At Pesaro he heard a rumour which made him quicken his pace; and at Fano he broke into the breakneck speed with which he began his mission. The answer for which he had been waiting so long lay ahead, and he was missing it; but from Fano to Sinigaglia was only fifteen miles. The road lay along the base of the mountains, which it hugged in long loops that seemed never to end; and endless beside it lay the chapped map of the wintry sea on which the winds wrought their will; and between them Machiavelli made slow progress. He was within a mile of Sinigaglia when he saw a thin column of smoke rising from the citadel and heard a muffled din which made the city sound like an exploding den. On the way he had passed the troops of the Confederates quartered at a distance from the town, and he was unprepared for this celebration. As he entered the gates, he found the streets full of the uproar of a sack. Climbing precipitately to the citadel, he met Caesar coming out. The Duke was in full steel and about to swing buoyantly into the saddle. Recognizing Machiavelli, he called him to heel. "This," he said, sweeping his hand gaily over Sinigaglia, "is what I wished to tell Bishop Soderini when he came to Urbino, but I could not trust him with the secret." And he looked meaningly at Machiavelli. "Now that my opportunity has come, I have known very well how to use it, and I have done a great service to your masters." And he galloped off to put down the rioting in the town. He left Machiavelli bewildered. While he pieced the story together from eye-witnesses, the scene recomposed itself under his eyes. Standing on the windblown summit of Sinigaglia, he saw the culmination of a long and elaborate plan, a *beautiful stratagem,* as he called it. For beautiful it was, as every experience that is fully understood is beautiful. He saw the broad poplar-lined meadows through which Caesar approached, at the head of his squadrons; he saw the Confederates lined up to receive him; he saw the salutations and embraces, and the narrow gates, and the pause when Vitellozzo Vitelli was seen to be missing; he saw that sullen syphilitic approaching, with his cloak of green and his hangdog look, yielding now to his premonition, now to a stronger master; and the cavalcade mounting to the citadel; and the closing of the doors; and the prompt arrest; and the pit where the Confederates now awaited their sentence. Beautiful, yes; and an image occurred to him to delineate Caesar—*come il Basilischo fischiando soavemente*—like the Basilisk whistling softly in his den. But he had no time to indulge his mounting mood; the last courier was leaving, and he could only notify Florence of the facts and add: "in my opinion they will not be alive in the morning."

He spent a feverish night, turning over the event of the day. It was so simple, so logical, yet he had not foreseen it. His own fears had blinded him. In the morning a manifesto announced the discovery of a plot against the Duke, and in the chapel of the Communal Palace the bodies of Vitellozzo and another ringleader were laid out. They had been throttled; the next pair—the Orsini—were to be dealt with legally in Rome. In these measures Machiavelli recognized the old Caesar—quickness and caution combined. He was sanguine; his faith was reviving. He saw it all now; his suspicions had been unjust. Caesar had always known his purpose, or at least his opportunity, to which he lent the appearance of a premeditated purpose; and that purpose was legitimate. The manifesto accused the Confederates of laying a snare in which they had been anticipated; whatever the truth of that charge, they had proved themselves capable of it; and it would have been folly to trust them. With the return of his faith, Machiavelli flung his patriotic fears to the winds, the bracing winds of the bitter Adriatic. Now that there was no further need for dissimulation, Caesar could be trusted. He could afford to be honest: he was morally emancipated. And when he was summoned that night by the Duke, Machiavelli went with a light heart, confident that at last he would see the real Caesar.

Caesar was exultant. He received him with a cordiality which "amazed" Machiavelli; moving restlessly about, he congratulated Florence and himself on a blow which had rid them of their common enemies; and he repeated with insatiable relish, "This is the vengeance I promised to perform for your masters when I spoke to the Bishop of Volterra at Urbino." Never, since that night at Urbino, had he been so alive. The eyes were more terrible than ever, for they were the eyes of a man without mystery. He had nothing more to hide or reveal; he was satisfied; and Machiavelli divined in them what Caesar did not suspect. Life and death were one in those eyes, and they were filled with a wanton lust of both. They were alive because they were insatiable; like fire, they lived on what they consumed; and Machiavelli was just sick enough to feel, for a fleeting second, the voluptuous contagion of that bloodlust which, like love, is the supreme satisfaction of reaching the quick of life and transcending it; and he was still troubled when he saw Caesar watching him in hypnotic felicity, and heard him recalling their first meeting at Urbino. Caesar alluded to the Duke of Urbino, who was seeking asylum in Florentine territory. In return for the great service he had rendered the Republic he asked merely that it detain Guidobaldo. "It would not be to the dignity of the City to surrender him and the Republic would never consent," Machiavelli replied. Caesar commended him on so proper a reply and ignored it. The level eyes watched him and the voice went on evenly. Caesar would be satisfied if the Republic agreed not to release Guidobaldo without his consent.

23

In Sinigaglia Caesar lingered only long enough to invite the congratulations of his neighbours. They came, one by one, in a cowed chorus, and only one was tardy and out of tune. From Mantua, Isabella d'Este sent the Duke a gift of one hundred masks, which she begged him to use for Carnival, since "after the fatigues of these glorious enterprises, he would desire some recreation." But relaxation was far from his mind; he had yet to stamp out the roots of the conspiracy. The year began auspiciously; he set out, in the first days of January 1503, for Vitelli's town of Castello, which he occupied without resistance. Thence he passed on to Perugia, which opened its gates to him and from which the tyrant, Gian Paolo Baglioni, fled. He proceeded to Assisi where, learning that Cardinal Orsini had been apprehended in Rome, he put his prisoners, Paolo Orsini and the Duke of Gravina, to death. Next, he dictated the expulsion of the tyrant of Siena; then he abruptly returned to Rome to put down an uprising of the Orsini.

At Assisi, Machiavelli left him. The land, as he rode home, was still hibernating and numb but it was streaked with the seedling green of a new spring. He returned, as he left, with a divided mind. Looking back, he saw the great semicircle which Caesar had swung from Imola to Sinigaglia to Assisi, and now, with Siena, the first nip of his long enveloping movement about Tuscany. But, looking ahead, he saw an exhilarating hope. In his last conversations, Caesar had dwelt on his design of exterminating the tyrants. The petty despots were the bane of Italy; the times were tending toward larger units; and he was in tune with them. Romagna he had already consolidated by conciliating his subjects and his neighbours and levying a native militia; why might not Romagna become the nucleus of a strong Central Italian State and even of a confederacy to deliver the peninsula from the foreigner? There were but two obstacles. Was that ambitious half-breed capable of so patriotic a purpose? His tawny eyes were insatiable; and he was still bound to the French. Nevertheless, Machiavelli, as he looked back, saw Caesar in the ascendant, and he speculated. Infinite and incalculable, the spring lurked about him. The new season would show.

Throughout the spring Valentino was occupied in suppressing the revolt of the Orsini in Rome. The French, meanwhile, were imbedded in a chronic conflict with Spain over the partition of Naples, and in June he was recalled to their service. The flight at this time of one of his creatures, for whom he sent out an alarm, started a rumour that Caesar was planning to go over to the Spanish; but he promptly gave the lie to it by preparing to leave for the French camp.

On the eve of his departure (August 5, 1503) he dined with the Pope at the villa of Cardinal Corneto. The Cardinal was a millionaire—one of the last in the Sacred College—but he was pleased to call his villa without the walls a modest *vigna*. The situation was unhealthy, and the low marshy ground, the treacherous cool of the evening, and the malarial air accomplished what the landless despots and the late League had failed to do. In the morning the host and his guests were among the victims of an epidemic which had been unusually virulent that summer. In the blood of the Borgias it was abnormally violent. The Pope, it was true, was robust and threw off the fever; five days later he was on his feet, celebrating the twelfth anniversary of his reign. He seemed to be his usual sanguine self; his constitution, despite early and late dissipation, was bovine. Nevertheless, he was seventy-three, obese, and uneasy. "It is a bad month for fat men," he sighed, standing at a window and watching one of the endless funerals passing by. He resolved to be careful. He was a frugal eater, it was Friday, and he dined conscientiously on eggs, lobster, peppered pumpkin, preserved fruits, and a small gilded tart. The following morning he was running a temperature; two days later the physicians bled him. He felt relieved, after releasing thirteen ounces of blood, and in the evening was able to sit up and play cards with the Cardinals. But he dealt his hand absent-mindedly; for about him the doors of the Vatican were closing; the orders were those of the Duke; and the old man, listening to these precautions, suddenly felt deserted.

With Caesar, however, the disease was far more acute. This was the one thing he had not foreseen. For the death of the Pope he had prepared carefully, but to be stricken himself at the same time was a coincidence which eclipsed all his calculations. It was a blind, senseless blow of bludgeoning Chance, and it maddened him. He employed desperate remedies. He plunged into frigid water, but the fever, with which he wrestled like a living thing, fastened on him more furiously and, when he emerged, he shed his skin. One thing, however, did not desert him—his presence of mind. Calling in his captains, he gave orders to occupy Rome, recall his troops from Romagna, and close the Vatican; and his trusted Spanish lieutenant, Don Michele da Corella, carried out these measures promptly. Then he turned on himself again. The physicians recommended bleeding; he obeyed; and falling and rising with voluptuous obstinacy the raw body gave and gave, wooing the leech furiously.

In that body, as raw as an infant's, there was but one impulse—the inborn will of an infant to outlive its father. He never mentioned him. Alexander had ceased to be even an accomplice to his being. A few doors away, and worlds apart, father and son lay in rival agonies. The ebbing and the returning life flowed in uneven pulse. For a moment they came abreast. After rallying and sinking, the old man recuperated for the last time. He swallowed emetics like aphrodisiacs, but he was doomed—there was an infallible sign: he never mentioned Caesar. His mind was perfectly clear, but he had forgotten his children. The egoism of death gripped him, the natal egoism quickened Caesar, and in the Borgia apartments there remained only the kinship of the stable. . . . Blood and lust and death, Alexander had borne all. The vital spark was spent: he had littered, he was exhausted, and the labouring carcass struggled now, not to recover, but to succumb. Slowly, in laborious dissolution, the low ultramarine vault with its celestial frescoes grew dim; slowly he lapsed into coma, staring at Isis and Osiris and the Bull overhead; and at last, on August 18, they looked at him. The death-chamber was promptly scoured by Caesar's lieutenants. The keys were surrendered by the Cardinal Chamberlain at the point of the sword; plate and jewels were collected to the value of 200,000 ducats, besides 100,000 ducats in gold. In their haste they overlooked a treasure in the adjoining room; but the servants completed the traditional pillage. When the official visitors arrived, they found the room stripped of all but the chairs, the bed, and the corpse; and they did not linger. No priest watched, no taper burned; only the dim funereal convoy of Isis, Osiris, and the Bull lurked aloft. An insufferable fetor filled the room. The huge carcass seemed to exhale a lingering, fierce, and foul vitality. When the bearers came in the morning, they found that through the long leavening hours of the night it had swollen. The cheeks were enormous, the nose had doubled, the tongue clogged the mouth, the skin was black, and the disfigured face, said an eye-witness, "was hideous beyond anything that man has seen or heard of." The rapid decomposition of the body gave rise to rumours of poisoning and the supper at Cardinal Corneto's villa to fantastic insinuations; but of recent years such rumours had dogged the death of every prominent ecclesiastic whose wealth reverted to Alexander; and they accrued now to his bloated body in posthumous revenue. The bearers shrank from their burden, and while it lay in state in St. Peter's, where a hasty Mass was sung, a riot frightened the clergy, and it was abandoned for twenty-four hours. Then it was transferred to the Chapel of the Virgin of Fevers where the carpenters had prepared a coffin; the box was of ordinary dimensions, the body had outgrown it; rigid, irrepressible, it resisted every pressure; the mitre was removed and replaced with a piece of old carpet; but it was only by dint of strenuously pounding and cramming the obnoxious cadaver that the coffin was finally closed and the hugger-mugger burial completed; and Caesar was free of his father.

But he was oppressed by his own incubus. Time—with time he could accomplish anything—and Time, which he had always outrun, now laid on him its weight of leaden enmity. Out of his fitful sleep he woke, groping through the night for the day, through the day for the night, reckoning every revolution of the hours for one more to breed new marrow in his bones, new skin on his limbs. The dreaded interregnum had begun and he was still charting the changing hues of his flesh when, two days after the obsequies of Alexander, the Orsini rose. The blood feud, quelled at Sinigaglia, broke out with renewed violence, but Sinigaglia had not been forgotten, and his captains did not betray Caesar. Don Michele burned the Orsini Palace and held the revolt in check, while the Duke called in their hereditary foes, the Colonna, and concluded an alliance with them. This led to new complications. As the Colonna were serving the Spanish in Naples, the French ambassador, recalling the recent rumours of the Duke's change of front, called on him and protested. But the sick man protested yet more vigorously; and in return for a solemn promise to send his troops to Naples whenever the King needed them, he was assured that Louis would guarantee the integrity of his dominions. Copies of this declaration were sent to Bologna, Florence, and Venice, and at once checked their support of the returning despots; and Caesar continued to map on his body the spreading patch of flesh, the yellow and the red and the white, that marked his recovery. Time: with time he could manoeuvre. He had gained a month. Rome was restless but under control. On September 13, however, the Conclave was called for the election of the new Pope, and in obedience to the regulation which forbade the presence of troops in Rome during that period, the College invited him to withdraw. He took his precautions, consented, and was carried out of the Vatican in a closed litter and across the Campagna to Nepi. Passing over that desolate plain, populous with tombs, he was surrounded by the unseen powers of the past. There was a power in invisibility. While he had lain jealously secluded in the Vatican, Rome was busy with his myth. The world wove its legends over his struggles, legends as enormous, as monstrous, as the corpse of his father. He was reported to be sweltering in the entrails of a mule; but, the mule being sterile, popular imagination lodged him in the bowels of a bull—a metamorphosis which assimilated him to that Mithraic cult which had been one of the innumerable ancestral religions of Rome. There was an instinctive propriety in the suggestion of the Sun God, immersed in the blood of his victims, renewing his life in the entrails of sex, and mysteriously resurgent from the tomb. The myth had its uses. It followed the exhausted figure across the Campagna, through the tombs of that religious suburb still sacred to the elder gods of Rome; and from Nepi he yet occupied and preoccupied the Eternal City. Unseen, he had almost recovered his gift of ubiquity.

But he had not neglected other precautions. Among the three leading candidates for the Tiara, Cardinal della Rovere, Cardinal Sforza, and Cardinal de Rouen, the latter was his obvious choice, and he pledged him the support of the Spanish Cardinals. But, perhaps because of the Spanish-French conflict in Naples, they were unable to secure a decisive majority; a deadlock ensued; and a compromise candidate was elected. The new Pope, who assumed the title of Pius III, was a feeble octogenarian, suffering from an ulcer of the stomach, who was elected on the tacit understanding that he would not live long. The choice was satisfactory to Caesar, bringing as it did the reprieve of time which he needed. The Pope, knowing his days to be numbered, pursued a valetudinarian policy. "I wish the Duke no harm," he said. "It is the duty of a Pope to bear malice to no man, though I foresee that he will come to a bad end, by the judgment of God." He confirmed him in the command of the Papal armies and recalled him to Rome; then, twenty-six days after his election, he mustered his strength and died. The respite sufficed: Caesar was on his feet again.

Now the situation reopened: the same candidates confronted each other, ready to profit by the slightest change in the political situation. Caesar's prospects had weakened. In Romagna, Umbria, and Tuscany, the dispossessed tyrants were returning, and the rulers of Rimini, Pesaro, Castello, Perugia, Camerino, and Urbino had formed a League for their common protection under the leadership of Gian Paolo Baglioni of Perugia, whom Florence engaged simultaneously as her condottiere. A small nucleus of Romagna—Imola, Cesena, Forli, and Faenza—remained loyal to Caesar, testifying to the wisdom of his rule; but, pledged as he was to the French in Naples, he could not spare troops for their protection or for the recovery of the states he had lost. The Orsini were again in arms, supported by Baglioni and the Venetian condottiere, Bartolomeo d'Alviano, who came to Rome with the avowed purpose of killing Caesar. Moreover, the troops which Don Michele had assembled were beginning to desert. Malaria the Duke could fight with myth, but in this conjunction of circumstances he found it prudent to retire to Sant' Angelo.

Such was the situation when Machiavelli arrived in Rome (October 28, 1503) to present the condolences of the Republic on the death of Pope Pius and to report on the prospects of Valentino. He based his calculations on a rapid process of elimination. On the day of his arrival the betting gave only twenty-six votes to Cardinal della Rovere, although he had the support of Venice. There was every reason to discount him. He was a Genoese, and the support of Venice could not be counted on. Moreover, though of late years he had been reconciled to the Borgias, his hatred of the breed, dating back to the election of Alexander, was notorious; and there was no possibility of circumventing the Spanish clique in the College. The logical candidate was the Cardinal de Rouen. On the following morning, however, Caesar emerged from Sant' Angelo, entered the Vatican, and was closeted with the Venetian candidate; and the betting rose to sixty per cent on della Rovere. A rumour flew that Valentino had traded his votes for a guarantee of immunity and the integrity of his states in Romagna. On the face of it, it was incredible, and Machiavelli, bewildered and sceptical, promptly consulted the Venetian ambassador. He too was sceptical, Cardinal della Rovere had a reputation for honesty, of which he was jealous. Yet it was nothing to bet on, and the Venetian thought it his duty to call on him and ask for an explanation. The Cardinal promptly reassured him—he had not forsaken his friends for his enemies. "See to it that the election succeeds and do not worry," he said in his bluff Genoese way. Then he unlocked: he disliked secrecy. "You see the pinch we are in, thanks to the carrion Pope Alexander left behind him with all these many Cardinals. Necessity forces men to do what they dislike while they depend on others, but once they are free they act otherwise." He depended on the discretion of the ambassador, but the ambassador was a Venetian, and overnight the odds on della Rovere rose to ninety per cent. Machiavelli doubted his ears. Had Caesar taken leave of his senses? Here was a treaty as transparent as that which he contracted with the Confederates at Imola—a child would laugh at it; and Caesar had signed it. The year which had begun so auspiciously and which was ending so darkly seemed to have brought a complete reversal, not only in the fortunes of the man, but in his nature. Was he so infatuated as to rely on the loyalty of his old enemy? Incredible as it seemed, it was apparently true, and on reflection it was perhaps not implausible. Beset on all sides by desertion and scheming, it was not beyond the range of sublunary possibilities that Caesar should prefer to the support of self-interested and temporary friends the integrity of a lifelong and loyal foe. It was a risk; but everything was a risk now, and in this crisis of uncertainty he could trust nothing. It was logical. He had always valued honest men, and perhaps he was obeying his instinct. But he laid a moral responsibility of incalculable consequence on his candidate, and the admission which the Cardinal had made to the Venetian ambassador, if sincere, was not reassuring. The success of Giuliano della Rovere was now a foregone conclusion, for Caesar held the key to it, the Spanish Cardinals being numerous enough if not to make, at least to block, the election. Nevertheless, Machiavelli wrote that "the Cardinals are often of one mind outside the Conclave and of another within," and he sat up, anxiously awaiting the result. "It is now midnight on the eve of November," he wrote that night. "A servant has just come to my rooms to tell me that the Conclavist of the Cardinal has received five messages, one after the other, from his master, informing him of the unanimous decision of the College to elect him. Your Worships should be informed by express courier, but I have no authority to incur extra expense, and at this hour I can neither send nor go out to learn whether anyone else is sending to Florence. It is unsafe to go out here at night. The man who brought this message from the Palace was escorted by twenty armed men."

In the morning Cardinal della Rovere was proclaimed Pope Julius II.

24

By a tragic contradiction the character of the new Pope, who owed his election to such entangling support, was that of a self-made man. Struggle was his native element and independence his backbone. He carried his honesty in his rugged face. Sprung from a stock of Genoese soldiers and sailors, he had proved his vigorous breed in every sphere save the one for which he was fitted. As a boy, he had eked out a living by plying an oar in the port of Savona; at least so ran the story, and it clung to him when he ascended the throne of St. Peter. With his bluff nautical manners, his salt humour, his brusque temper, his square head, and his stocky plebeian build, he tallied with the popular picture of the Apostle who was called from the sea. As a man, he had kicked against the pricks of his ecclesiastical calling. He was honest: it was not his choice. Like his uncle and cousins, he had adopted it because of the facilities for rapid advancement offered by the Church. He was democratic. When his uncle became Pope Sixtus IV, he "arrived" at the top, but he still pushed. Like his cousins, he squandered fortune and health; but though he lived like a sailor on leave he outlived the other della Rovere nephews. His ambition could not be satisfied in the fleshpots. Even in the flush of prosperity he chose to look and to act like an Apostle in fetters. There was that in Giuliano della Rovere which craved outlet; it was more than ambition; with every satisfaction it grew; an inner momentum drove him on, dynamically, toward a goal which he could not name and of which, like a pioneer of his destiny, he perceived only a part at a time.

At first it seemed to be his feud with Alexander. The Papacy was almost in his grasp when Roderigo Borgia slipped in ahead of him. He detested him, not only with the jealousy of a rival, but with the deeper antipathy of instinct. The lawyer he loathed with the contempt of a soldier; the plutocrat with the pride of a self made man; the climber because he was one himself—but how conscientious a one! He craved power, not for personal profit, but to display his public spirit. It was genuine. For years it had been obscured and absorbed by his feud with Alexander VI. Protesting his election, raising the cry of scandal and simony, heading a hostile clique in the College, leading thirty Cardinals to the feet of King Charles, failing, fleeing to his fortress in Ostia, standing a siege, forgiven, driven to France to continue his intrigues, he had put up a long hard fight. Intrigue, however, was not his forte; he hated the French; and, when he was recalled and pardoned by the Borgias, he submitted and bided his time; but now that, after twelve years, his opportunity had at last come, it brought his worst gall. Of all his reasons for loathing Alexander, the greatest was the necessity of following his lead and buying his way to the Tiara. To owe the throne he failed to wrest from his rival to a bargain with his son and a wholesale repetition of his simony was the last mortification. It seemed a posthumous revenge, a sneer from the tomb. He promptly closed the Borgia apartments, effaced their arms, and blackened their name, but he was haunted by the memory of their contamination; and the violence of his revulsion became the motive power of his moral life. They had compromised him; but his honesty had only been in pawn to necessity; he was solvent now, and he was no sooner elected than he struggled with all the vindictiveness of his nature to recover his good name.

Upon this moral knot hung the destiny of Italy. Machiavelli, like the rest of Rome, immediately recognized his dilemma. "The reason for his unanimous election," he reported, "is said to be that he promised everyone whatever he asked, and the difficulty will be to keep his word." But Machiavelli was not interested in the moral difficulties of Giuliano della Rovere except as they affected those of Caesar Borgia. "The Duke Valentino, who has served him better than anyone," he noted, "has received his promise that he will restore him to all his dominions in Romagna, and the Pope has given him Ostia as security. The Duke is lodged in the wing of the Palace called the New Rooms, where he has some fifty retainers; it is not known whether he will leave Rome or remain. Some say he will go to Genoa where he has most friends . . . then into Lombardy to raise troops . . . and from there to Romagna. This is likely, as he has 200,000 ducats in the hands of Genoese bankers. Others say that he will remain in Rome and await the coronation of the Pope, in order to be created Captain of the Church, as he has been promised, and that with this credit he will recover Romagna. Others believe that the Pope is feeding him on hope, and they fear that if he remains he may be detained in Rome longer than he desires, for the Pope's innate hatred of him is well known, and it is incredible that Julius will so soon forget the ten years of exile he endured under Pope Alexander. Meanwhile"—most melancholy of all—"the Duke lets himself be carried away by sanguine confidence; he believes that the word of others is more to be trusted than his own, and that the bond of a bargain will hold."

Amid such divided opinions Machiavelli no longer knew what to believe, and the credulity of Caesar alarmed him; but it quickened his insight. Caesar needed his own perspicacity, and his first impulse was to protect him. He made his problem his own; but the crux of that problem was Caesar himself, and he could not solve it until he had seen him. Unconsciously he shrank from the test, and he began by consulting those who had seen him. They all agreed that the Duke was sadly changed. Cardinal Soderini found him "irresolute, suspicious, and unstable in all his conclusions." Cardinal Herina declared that he had lost his wits and no longer knew what he wanted himself. Machiavelli inquired no further. He made excuses—"it may be because of his nature or because the blows of Fortune, which he is not accustomed to bear, have stunned and confused him"—but he avoided a meeting. Caesar needed to be protected against himself: and who could undertake to do that?

Professional duty, however, soon brought him to the Vatican. The Venetians were advancing on Faenza, and Imola was reported in revolt. Machiavelli was instructed by his Government, which followed the advance of its Adriatic rival uneasily, to protest to the Pope. His Holiness, as a Genoese, could be expected to share their jealousy of Venice. Machiavelli had avoided the Pope as consistently as he avoided Valentino: it was the only way in which he could prove his loyalty, and he went determined to protest vigorously, for at last the interests of Florence and Caesar were one. But his protest produced no effect. Julius listened with such unfeeling reserve that Machiavelli was exasperated and immediately made the rounds of the Cardinals, complaining bitterly that if the Venetians were allowed a free hand in Romagna His Holiness would soon be no better than the *chaplain of Venice*. He repeated the phrase recklessly: let it work! In this mood, hotly championing Florence and Caesar, he found himself in the Belvedere, where the Duke was lodged. He could avoid him no longer. It would have been disloyal to do so, for others were slighting him. The Venetian ambassador had declined to visit His Excellency, when he was sent for, lest "he lend him too much importance!" That was the world, and Machiavelli burned to brave it and atone for the slur of his colleague. But, as he was careful to explain to Florence, he also wished to "sound the Duke and see if there was anything to hope or to fear from him"; for he was a diplomat as well as a champion.

As usual, he put his professional duty first, and the response was electric. Still convalescent and smarting, Caesar was quick to suspect and resent vivisection. Machiavelli no sooner mentioned Imola and the advance of the Venetians than he became "greatly excited and complained bitterly"—but not of Venice. It was Florence that exasperated him. With one hundred men Florence could have saved those states. And, losing all reserve, he railed at his neighbour, breathless with reproach, and worked himself up into a paroxysm of impotent temper. "Since Imola is lost and Faenza attacked," he cried, pacing about in vindictive confusion, "I will raise no more men, I will not play your game. . . ." He swung around and halted, and his voice rose in reckless irritation: "I will put all I have left in the hands of the Venetians . . . it will be my turn to laugh then . . . your state will be ruined . . . the French have their hands full in Naples . . . they will not be able to help you . . ." As he swept on in this tirade, "full of passion and venom," Machiavelli listened, speechless under the charge and appalled by its unreasoning bitterness; and, when finally he made his escape, he reproached himself, first for provoking it and, secondly, for not refuting it. "I did not lack answers, nor would I have lacked words," he explained in his report, "but I preferred to calm him, and as adroitly as I could I took my leave after what seemed to me a thousand years." It was a shock. Not only had he failed to encourage Caesar, he could never do so again. It was too late. "Irresolute, suspicious, unstable in all his conclusions"—"irritable, unsure of himself"—all the reports were true. And all the excuses were true, but they were useless. The mere fact of having to excuse him was damning. The bluster of a boy, the spite of a woman, the fury of a cornered animal—how was it possible to reconcile these with "the inscrutable Duke who never speaks and always acts"? He was disfigured beyond recognition. Here was ruin indeed, lodged in the seat of reason, judgment cracked, passion ranting, self-possession gone, the noble vessel floundering in the trough of despair. Unable to contain his painful impression, Machiavelli reported the scene to Cardinal de Rouen, and in his comment he read

Caesar's political suicide. "God," said the Cardinal, "has never yet let any sin pass unpunished, and He will not overlook those of Caesar Borgia." When diplomats employed the language of moral retribution, it was the end.

But the finality of that word frightened him. He stifled the gnawing doubt. The strongest had their moments of weakness, and he had caught Caesar off his guard. He had touched a raw nerve, and he knew the pain by the kindred pang which that scene caused in himself. At the first opportunity, he rallied to his support repentantly. The Duke announced, several days later, his departure for Romagna; he was only awaiting a safe-conduct through Tuscany, for which application had been made to Florence by the Pope, Cardinal Soderini, and Cardinal de Rouen. To their letters Machiavelli added his own, and it was the only one which was at all warm. Obeying an impulse of compassion—itself a saddening sentiment—he phrased it too warmly perhaps; for it brought an immediate warning from Biagio. "I must not fail to tell you privately," wrote his mentor, "that the mere name of the Duke excites such hatred here that whenever a letter arouses it nothing is more welcome. In proof let me tell you that yesterday, when the question of the safe-conduct was discussed by the Eighty and a number of citizens, those in favour were about ten and those opposed about ninety. Everyone believes here that the Pope wishes to be rid of him and quickly, and that he is sending him into Romagna for no other reason. As for you, writing about him so stoutly, everyone gives you the bird. Some think you are looking for a tip, which you will not receive. You must not mention him here unless you have something to say against him. I thought you should know this, for your own information." Bitter advice, but Machiavelli pocketed it. How cheerfully would he have once faced scoffing and misinterpretation for the sake of Caesar! But now he quailed. He reserved his compassion for himself. He needed it. The homebodies, the mediocrities, were right. Their caution, their neutrality, their pious timidity, were triumphantly vindicated; and he could only acquiesce.

With disillusionment his insight deepened. He saw through everyone now. When he went to the Pope to notify him of the refusal of the safe-conduct, it was with preternatural quickness that he caught the struggle going on in the old man's mind. The Pope received him with his usual guarded reserve, listened negatively to his report, and for a few moments said nothing. But those moments were pregnant. Sitting bolt upright, grasping the arms of his chair, Julius browsed on his thoughts; and they were easy to read. Presently he raised his eyes—so candid, so transparent, so unlike Caesar's—and gave Machiavelli "a meaning look." "It is well," he said in a low voice; "we are contented." Then he studied his lap again; and in the silence Machiavelli watched him, with senile stealth, shifting his responsibility. Though, in that mute passage he recognized the old man's dilemma, it left him unmoved. He reported it calmly. "From this we may conclude what we have hitherto doubted. His Holiness thinks it an eternity till he lose the Duke. He wants to send him away satisfied, with no complaint that his pledges have been broken; but he cares little what you or anyone else may do against the Duke." Next, he went to the Belvedere. When he delivered his message, there was another explosion. Caesar was aghast, his troops were on the way, he had not expected a refusal, and he began to bluster and expostulate blindly. To pacify him, Machiavelli suggested that he send an emissary to negotiate for the safe-conduct; but he did not offer his own services. Caesar stared at him. He understood. With a weary gesture of disgust he sat down and nodded nervously. But immediately he sprang up again, shouting that, if the negotiations failed, he would ruin the Republic, he would make terms with the Pisans or the Venetians or the devil; and he was still hectoring when, under cover of a discreet cough, Machiavelli withdrew. He was unmoved, the scene was familiar, and he was impatient for the end which he foresaw. "If you judge it well to favour him, you may do so," he wrote to Florence, "but the Pope would rather you gave him a kick." The Duke was down.

How do idols fall? "Everyone is laughing at him." Machiavelli admitted it; and he no longer had the courage to face ridicule. For Caesar had at last taken a resolute step. He left Rome to sail for Genoa and begin the recovery of Romagna, and Rome watched his departure with surprise; but the surprise vanished when he returned, ten days later, under arrest and was sequestered in the Vatican. There the Pope now opened negotiations with him for the surrender of his last strongholds in Romagna. While the world laughed, Machiavelli capitulated, with a last flicker of compassion, to the pious. "We see now how the sins of the Duke have gradually brought about his punishment. May God guide all for the best!" But he could not repress a flash of disgust. While the world laughed, he smiled bitterly at its hypocrisy. "Now we may see how honourably this Pope begins to pay his debts, and how he wipes them out with a sponge; yet everyone blesses his hand and will continue to do so, the more firmly he proceeds." In a corner all men acted alike.

Between Caesar and Julius he saw little to choose; yet there was one difference which was radical. Julius was old. Why had his gods not loved Caesar well enough to let him die young? The old man was daily heaping new ignominy on the glamour of the young one. Machiavelli was impatient for the end and averted his eyes from the last stages of that meteoric decline, but he could not close his ears to the daily reports of "this Duke who is slipping into the tomb." In the Vatican, Caesar now led a posthumous life. The living elbowed him aside; he no longer inhabited the Palace, he haunted it. The Borgia apartments were closed, his quarters in the Belvedere were occupied, and he was shunted about wherever a bed could be found for him. The Cardinal de Rouen consented to receive him in his suite, only because he was leaving for France. After the major humiliations came the small ones. Caesar had ceded the strongholds in Romagna and the first concession led to the last. The climax occurred when he was roused one night by a commotion in the courtyard and recognized, ascending the stairs and ostentatiously welcomed by the Pope, the new Captain of the Church, Guidobaldo of Urbino. Summoned to Rome to prepare for the reoccupation of Romagna, he had arrived late and gone to an inn; but the Pope, who was waiting for him impatiently, flew into a temper, sent for him, and insisted on receiving him noisily in the dead of the night. In the morning Guidobaldo was installed in the Vatican. Through that long sleepless night Caesar had been testing his nerve. He was surfeited with small humiliations and rose to a great one. That courage no one could deny him. He requested an audience of the Duke of Urbino. The request was ignored. He repeated it; it was refused; then he took to the secret passage leading to the Duke of Urbino's apartments. Guidobaldo was resting in an anteroom when he was roused by the sight of which he had so long dreamed. The dreaded presence was there in the room, swaying on its knees. Too startled to move, Guidobaldo stared, fascinated by the hooded spell on the floor; then instinct awoke; he rose, advanced, and raising him courteously, granted Caesar the audience he demanded. He listened, while Caesar whispered a long incoherent apology for the past of which Guidobaldo made little save a recurring sibilant . . . *la bestialità* . . . *la bestialità* . . . *di Papa Alessandro*. Caesar cursed his father, blaming everything on his brutality and his own youth; he had been misled and, huskily abhorring his errors, he implored forgiveness; his father was beyond it; but everything would be restored . . . only some trinkets in Forli . . . and the Trojan tapestries he had offered Cardinal de Rouen . . . Guidobaldo finally cut him short "with a few words befitting the request and the occasion," and the bystanders made room for the obsequious figure to depart. In the opinion of one who watched his retreat he was "extremely fearful and well clarified." Guidobaldo, to prevent a repetition of such scenes, had him transferred and confined to an upper floor of the Palace. There, in rooms as unvisited as an attic, the arrangements for the return of the collections of Urbino were concluded by a chamberlain, whom Caesar met, cap in hand, at the outer door and whom he accompanied, at the end of each visit, to the head of the stairs. Below Caesar Borgia never went. When all was over, he was free to depart. But he still lingered, moving from the wall to the window, from the window to the door, from the door to the head of the stairs, back and forth, to and fro, around and about—where was he to go?

Machiavelli had seen enough. He wrote for his recall. Sitting in his inn, by a dying fire, listening to the embers gossiping, he no longer thought of Caesar or Julius or even of himself. He was occupied with more vital matters. Suddenly he felt old, but he did not regret the youth of which Caesar had fleeced him with his false glamour. In Florence a new life awaited him. He was a father. "You have a fine lively boy," his uncle wrote—and the letter was already a fortnight old—and Biagio added only the most meagre details. "Marietta and your little boy are well, and so are all your other kin, and they want you at home. If you can find me a little clay figure (but it must be small) I beg you to buy one and I will reimburse anyone you name; I do not ask this because I believe you will make the slightest effort to find one, but because I am a fool and have not yet learned what you are. P.S. Between us, we shall make something of the little twig; he will honour his name, but he looks like a crow, he is so black." Machiavelli could wait no longer when he heard from his wife. "The baby looks like you, he is snow-white but has a head like black velvet, and I think he is good-looking because he looks like you; and he is so lively, you would think he had been a whole year in the world; and he was born with his eyes open and upsets the whole house with his crying." Born with his eyes open! That boy was himself. To shape this new life was the only way to redeem his mistakes, and there was no time to lose. It was not too soon to teach him that he could not turn things upside down but must take the world as it was. That lesson could not be learned too early, if he was not to see his life spoiled like that of his father. When the recall came Machiavelli had already left.

In Florence, several weeks later, he learned that Caesar had gone to Naples to sell his sword to the Spanish, that he had been arrested by the Spanish commander at the request of the Pope, and that he had been deported, as a dangerous alien, to Spain. He listened without hearing. He was deep in the present and that was the past. The romance was over, he had settled down to realities, his restlessness was gone, he was domesticated, and his world turned about the crib. Already it was a struggle to save that lively little fact from the pampering of his mother and the meddling of his godfather. Biagio and Marietta insisted on sharing him. Piagnoni and women—they were mischievous influences. Watching the crib, he recalled his own childhood. He remembered his mother composing psalms and pulling the wool over his eyes, and his father, like the shrewd lawyer that he was, opening his eyes to hard facts. He was the victim of a divided heritage, he was not well balanced. Even in his love for his fatherland he suffered from contradictions of the heart and the head. One thing and one only his son should learn, and from him: the truth. But what was the truth? To teach a child to live—that was the test. There could be no confusion, no equivocation, no compromise: only absolute honesty. He examined himself with the insight of disillusionment. How could he teach a child to live? He did not know himself.

But who knew? In those first months he was elbowed aside by the women, the priests, and Biagio. Perhaps it was best, after all, that they should have the child. Safe in mediocrity, swaddled in illusions, he would be happy; and what else mattered? To be born with open eyes was not a blessing. To see life too clearly was baffling. It was best to look sidewise at Medusa. But Machiavelli, looking into the eyes of his son, knew that he was cheating him. All that lusty vitality would not go far without faith: it was a necessity: without it life was too brutal and senseless. Savonarola was right, or half-right; for it must be faith, not illusion. Soon that child would be asking questions, and in his confusion Machiavelli quailed from them. His pride of intellect was confounded. The mind could analyse, it could not create faith. But he was forced to rebuild it; the question could not be begged.

To divert himself, or perhaps to grope for facts, he wrote a review of the significant events of the past decade in Italy, rehearsing what experience had taught him, sifting it for what he was sure of: that much at least he could teach his son. He wrote in verse, seeking in rhyme the reason for the meaningless confusion those ten years revealed in retrospect; but he could deduce little save the assonance of sound and sense. Only a few facts emerged. The French invasion of 1494 was "the origin of all our woes," and from it all the others flowed —the loss of Pisa, the great delusion of the Friar, and Florence

> Divided and ruled by the creed
> Of Savonarola who stirred,
> And was divinely moved to lead
> And bewilder us with a word ...

and who plunged the city into dissension which would have ruined it

> Had he not been borne yet higher,
> Consumed by a greater fire.

Then from the good which had wrought so much evil he came to the evil which he had wrought into good, and found himself face to face with his fallacy. Caesar Borgia confronted him, the last bitter fruit of the French invasion. With the rage of a deluded prophet, the old wound reopening, the unrelieved bitterness in his blood rising to his brain, he fell on his false idol. With the fury of an iconoclast, he heaped execration on Caesar's faithlessness and cruelty, compared his struggle with the Captains to a knot of reptiles, the snare of Sinigaglia to the den of the Basilisk, the Basilisk to Anti-Christ, and gloated on his final betrayal:

> crushed by the weight
> That a rebel to Christ deserves.

He exhausted the language of vituperation, but not his unbounded bitterness against the man who had defrauded him of his faith in life. It was only now that he felt the full agony of betrayal. He had believed too passionately, sacrificed too much, immolating conscience and honour to his dark angel, and betraying his own humanity. He had shut his eyes to everything—Caesar's treachery, his ruthlessness, his crimes—dazzled by his unholy brilliance, and the eclipse had come, and he was cheated. Stripped of his power and shorn of his glamour, the man was a mere criminal, and his prophet had blindly glorified Anti-Christ. He had been far more visionary than the Friar. Savonarola had misled none but the credulous, but Caesar had deceived the most perspicacious. To be mistaken in a saint was melancholy, but to be disillusioned in a lost soul was tragic. Delusion, delusion, all was delusion, but this was of all the most sinister, and with aching self-accusation Machiavelli abjured and abhorred his perverse infatuation.

But when the revulsion of feeling was exhausted, after the storm his mind cleared, and through the fumes of failure he saw his faith. The spirit of Caesar was indestructible: it was the spirit of Nature. His only sin was that he failed. The one occasion on which he was untrue to himself and trusted to the honour of others marked his downfall. But if the man failed, his method was sound; and the proof was that Julius only overcame him by using it. And now, when Machiavelli turned to the cradle, when he met that tiny trusting stare which dispelled passion and confusion, illusion and disillusion, and compelled him to be sincere with himself, he could outstare it. If Caesar was a lie, life was a lie; Nature was lawless, all men obeyed but one force—Necessity. And that was the truth.

PART THREE

Machiavelli
and
Castiglione

25

For the class into which Count Baldassare Castiglione was born the luxuries of life were its first necessities, and none more so than loyalty. It was a small and antiquated class, which the new age was rapidly outmoding. It derived its conservative code from the world of chivalry and, though it had lost, both morally and materially, its reason for being, it was in process of discovering another. It was the residue in Italy of a feudal aristocracy. Its roots lay in an abolished world and its traditional employments—military, diplomatic, ecclesiastical—had deteriorated with the rise of the new mercantile civilization of the Renaissance. Warfare had become mercenary, diplomacy an honourable form of eavesdropping, and a career in the Church purely secular; the services which such occupations required were formal. Living on its estates or at the Courts of princes, this aristocracy was economically a parasite, while politically it played an inconsequential part in the national life. Its function was ornamental; its activity had expired with the age that produced it; but something still survived that was indestructible and that lent it vitality—the habit of service; and it clung with conservative tenacity to the feudal tradition of loyalty.

But loyalty to what? Though it had outlived its utility in practical life, it still rendered a moral and ornamental service to society. It patronized the new culture, it fulfilled the functions of a leisure class, it cultivated the luxurious values of life and vindicated its privileges by its breeding; and above all it retrieved the decay of religion by transforming morals into manners. Undermined, on the one hand, by the scandals and worldliness of the clergy and, on the other, by the enlightened and material spirit of the new age, the moral authority of the Church was steadily declining; and aristocracies, as they are the traditional allies of the Church in times of repute, when both are established authorities, are the natural refuge of the religious view of life in its days of decline. There is, in fact, much in common between the religious and aristocratic mentality: they are germane in spirit. For both the conduct of life lies in discrimination and discipline; what they select and reject in life is determined by an aim which transcends life itself; and the faith of the one and the honour of the other is each an assertion of the superiority of man to Nature, which carries as its consequence a code of restrictions on the free play of instinct. But that free play of instinct was the very spirit of the new age. The impulse of the Renaissance, like that of all periods of rejuvenation and vitality, was to live life blindly, without discrimination or question, in obedience to Nature, and to live it whole: an impulse as fatal to religious creeds as to aristocratic codes. It was then that their kinship became apparent, and that an obsolete aristocracy found in the desuetude of the faith the vigour of a new purpose. It set the tone of society; it preserved the self-respect of the race by a standard of manners, which blended moral stamina with worldly amenity, from servility, self-seeking, brutality, and sham—from all the ultimate surrenders to Nature and necessity.

Into this world Baldassare Castiglione was born, at Casatico on the outskirts of Mantua, in 1478. He imbibed its ideals with his mother's milk, grew up in the lee of life, and, immune to mean realities, reached manhood before he realized that all he believed in was alien and obsolete to the generation of which he was a member and not a part. It was too late then: he was formed. He was an accomplished innocent; and his instinct of loyalty, inbred and ineradicable, clung, like a fine and hardy feeler, to one fugitive object after another—his family, his friends, his masters, his class, and, when these were no more, to all that remained of them, their code of life.

The Castiglione were a family of Lombard origin, one branch of which had long been established in Mantua. His father, moreover, was related to the ruling house by his marriage with Luigia Gonzaga, a cousin of the Marquis Francesco. With a palace in Mantua, he preferred, however, to live at his manor of Casatico, as his means were not affluent; and to those early years spent in the country the boy owed a peculiar wholesomeness of disposition and taste and an independence of character which stood him in good stead later. In the world he was never quite of it, and his inner resources gave him moral as well as social poise. He received the conventional education of his class. At sixteen he was sent to Milan to complete his schooling at the Court of Lodovico Sforza—the Court of the *cognoscenti*, as Isabella d'Este called it. It was then at the height of its brilliance, on the eve of the French invasion; and the *cognoscenti* soon discerned the makings of a model courtier in the son of Count Cristoforo Castiglione. He had an aptitude for everything—letters, music, art, athletics—and proficiency in nothing; the facile versatility of the social man; the smatterings of that universal culture which was then the craze; and the well-bred instinct to remain an amateur in life. He shone with a mild excellence: envy never cost him a friend; mediocrity could mistake him for its own. But he had the strength too of a conventional nature, the well-tempered egoism, the eclectic sympathies, and that sort of generalized individuality which includes everything but the abnormal. He was a general favourite: he possessed to a supreme degree the indispensable gift of pleasing; and that virtue of amiability was to be his *vade mecum* through the uncharted years ahead. "A young man well-favoured in person," wrote the Bishop of Mantua to his father, "learned, elegant, discreet, of the utmost integrity, and so gifted by nature and fortune that if he continues as he has begun he will have no equal." On that prospect his father closed his eyes and died, positive of the only immortality he valued—that of his name.

To the widow fell the management of the meagre fortune and its high-minded heir. Proud of her son, she was worried by his lack of ambition; it was not easy to make ends meet; and she soon began to talk of marriage. He eluded her: seventeen years later she was still talking. He had friendships with women, and he valued them too highly to allow them to degenerate into love. His real passion was for horseflesh. When King Louis XII entered Milan in 1499, young Castiglione was a curious spectator of the pomp and circumstance of that historic occasion; and his practised eye went straight to the point. Soberly, for he had just reached his majority, he watched the French gentlemen ogling the women and making their mounts dance—"good horses but they handled them badly"—and sized up the King's roan—"rather small but a good horse, though a little poor in the mouth." The significance of that day dawned on him only when he found the Castello "where once the flower of the world assembled, full now of drinking-booths and dung-heaps." Those dung-heaps made him a patriot; and the compressed statement expressed his state of mind. Hitherto he had hardly realized that the French were aliens. It needed the sight of good horses misridden and the Castello of Milan turned into a stable to quicken his race-feeling; and the discovery made him misanthropic. His appreciation of horses rose, his opinion of men fell. Of the latter he knew little: he had always judged them by two points, their manners and horsemanship. Two points? They were the same—a pleonasm, his tutor would have called it. Manners were the way a man mounted his animal, and *chevalerie*, as the French should know, meant a world of mounted men. But apparently such ideas were peculiar to himself and his countrymen. He returned to Casatico, where his mother repeated that it was not too soon to think of perpetuating his race.

For four years he eluded the subject, then he went to war. In the winter of 1503 the Marquis of Mantua left for Naples to take service with the French; and Castiglione followed, lamenting the equinity of fate. A horse had delayed him. "I searched the whole state of Milan as far as Piedmont before I found one," he explained. "I hope, however, soon to continue my journey and I desire to be nowhere but where Your Excellency is and to devote my poor life to your service, whether on foot or on horseback. God grant me this prayer! I ask no greater favour in this world." Good horses being so scarce, however, the pursuit of his one ambition here below was delayed; and from that disappointment dated a series of others which were to have a far-reaching effect on his career. When at last he reached Naples, he found that he had missed nothing but weeks of inaction, rain, and discontent. But that was not all. The French general having fallen sick, the Marquis had assumed the supreme command. Victuals were low, the men were restless, and he was unable to enforce his authority. Castiglione found him sulking in his tent, laid up with French boils. Francesco Gonzaga was a small man, and he had the vanity of the undersized. He needed a horse. In bed, surrounded by rumours of insubordination, nursing his dignity and his military disease, he cut a poor figure, and he knew it. But for his big bristles, his bulging eyes, his obstinate snub nose, and his dogged look, Castiglione would hardly have known him. No sooner had he arrived than the Marquis grew worse and had himself carried in a litter to Rome. "He is not sick," said the Venetian envoy. "He is a wise man. I say no more." Castiglione had no choice but to follow.

How wise the Marquis was appeared by the sequel. He had hardly left the camp when the decisive battle of the Garigliano was fought. It resulted in the complete rout of the French and established the Spanish dominion in Naples. Among the casualties was an obscure soldier of fortune, Piero de' Medici. The backwash of the battle reached Rome with droves of sick, starved, and half-naked French soldiers, struggling against the inclemency of the weather and the inhabitants. Hundreds succumbed on the fields of the peasants they had preyed on a few months before; many died in the dung-heaps where they nestled for warmth; those who reached Rome entered wherever a door opened and returned, when they were thrust out, begging for death indoors. The Pope fed, clothed, and deported three hundred, but they continued to struggle in, too numerous to relieve. The Marquis continued to Mantua.

Castiglione, however, lingered in Rome. His first glimpse of war was disappointing—its stagnation and backwash. He was eager for active service and, as the Marquis was *hors de combat*, he looked about for experience elsewhere. The fall of Caesar Borgia offered him an opening. Guidobaldo of Urbino, to whom the Marquis had introduced him, was preparing to recoup the last strongholds in Romagna which Valentino had ceded but which still held out in forlorn loyalty to him. He offered Castiglione a command and himself wrote to his brother-in-law for permission to engage the young soldier. Castiglione added his own request with a solicitousness which he was too tactful not to dissimulate. "Since I must ever remain the servant of Your Excellency, and can never think of anything but serving and obeying Your Excellency, my only desire is to do what you command. I await the knowledge of your wishes before sending my answer, and will obey the will of Your Excellency, to whom I commend myself with the utmost devotion." But all his precautions were wasted. The Marquis read between the lines. He had returned to Mantua a moody and susceptible man. The Victor of Fornovo had outlived his glory: his experience in the French camp had proved that; his reputation, his health, and his spirits were declining, and those of Guidobaldo were ascending. There was no logic in it, no reason, no justice. He who was a born soldier was reduced to a life of inactivity, while the scholarly invalid of Urbino was appointed Captain of the Church. The vicissitudes of Fortune had stimulated Guidobaldo. His flight and misfortunes had improved his health; and when he returned to Urbino, welcomed all along the way by ovations, with fruits and wine and children at every milestone, the good tribute of his own earth quickened his acquisitive instinct. When it fastened on Castiglione, Francesco Gonzaga winced. There was no plausible reason to refuse a request so correctly presented, and he consented, but with a curtness which struck dismay to the heart of Castiglione; and his dismay was deepened by the fact that the consent was communicated to the Duke of Urbino and his own letter was ignored.

For a young man of such scrupulous loyalty and so little ambition this was a discouraging start. Despite all his correctness, he appeared to have blundered, to have started life on the wrong foot. But, having taken the step, he could not withdraw. He prepared to depart. The Pope, to whom he had been presented by the Duke of Urbino, granted him an audience and welcomed him to his service. Castiglione made no allusion to the attitude of the Marquis, but he found some comfort in the sympathy which His Holiness showed him. Julius looked him over—tall, upstanding, with firm features and blue eyes—in obvious approval; and his own eyes, no less candid though clouded, seemed to divine his confused loyalties and to admit, out of sad experience, that it was not easy to choose. The youth, no doubt, was very green and over-scrupulous; but he liked him for it; and with a mind still haunted by the Borgias, Julius gave him his blessing.

26

Hardly had Castiglione reached the camp when his horse stumbled and fell on him, and he was laid up with a foot which made him "see the stars at midday." Decidedly, one misstep led to another. The campaign was short, the fortresses were starved into submission, and, with his spurs still unwon, he returned with the Duke to Urbino. He was still limping, and he had some other troubles, as he had received no pay and his mother had difficulty in supplying him with money. "Nevertheless," he wrote her, "as long as we can keep out of debt, let Fortune do her worst! You must not take these things too much to heart, but try to repair what you can and let the rest go as I do, with a light heart." One thing, however, he could not dismiss with a light heart—the attitude of the Marquis; and to his mother's plea that he return to Casatico he replied: "Nothing would induce me to come to Mantua now. I can never think of it without turning a grey hair, and if it were not for Your Magnificence, I would never give a thought to the place." He had made several efforts to ascertain the cause of the morbid displeasure of the

Marquis and dispel it, but in vain; and the little rift was slowly widening into an open breach. He clung to Urbino, to which he grew daily more attached. A year later Guidobaldo attempted to conciliate the Marquis by sending Castiglione on a special mission to Mantua. But no sooner had the ambassador reached Ferrara than he was advised that he would be arrested if he crossed the border. To keep up appearances, he pushed on; having crossed the frontier, he "went into hiding," as he explained to his mother to whom he wrote, as well as to the Duke, describing his dilemma and asking for advice. He was swayed by too many scruples to act on his own responsibility. "If the danger is not very clear and manifest, I shall willingly come, and I should like the Marquis to know I am here. If I do not proceed, I know that the Duke will be extremely indignant, and I should be distressed to displease him, above all on my account. For my own part, I should not hesitate to come, even without waiting for his reply, as I know his mind. . . . I hope you will do something promptly as the matter is most serious and may have bad consequences, since I cannot admit why I am turning back and everyone knows that I have been sent as an ambassador." The Duke guaranteed his diplomatic immunity by recalling him—"though my Lord writes that he would not dream of doing so because of the Marquis's objections," he reported in his next message to his mother, "and would be glad to see what might ensue; but after hearing the warnings I received, he would not allow me to run any risk as he values me too highly. I shall return, therefore, where I am welcome."

To be welcome: that, after all, was his real ambition in life. The rupture with the Marquis revealed it. It proved a blessing in disguise. Cut off by a chance misunderstanding from his home, his family, and his first allegiance, he elected a new loyalty with the deliberation of a man choosing his destiny. "If, by God's grace, I can live a quiet life I shall be content, and in view of the life I have lived so far, I shall never be regarded as anything but an honourable man," he wrote to Casatico. The *alta quieta* of Urbino was his natural clime. The thin high mountain air, the lofty tranquillity of the remote city, the composure of its Court life, the character of the Duke, the congenial company he met there, and the serenity of spiritual satisfaction he enjoyed in that atmosphere—everything attracted him to his adopted country; and there he discovered himself and developed the art of being welcome in the world.

For that was his talent. He had an ear for the concert of men in society. His whole life was a prolonged act of listening—listening for the elusive tune of existence, for the fleeting, half-heard harmonies in discord, for the chiming-point in man and man, for the quiet that comes of mutual understanding. His eyes, blue and alert, were those of a vigilant listener: their gaze was an echo; and his voice had the subdued modulations of a perfect accompanist. He was a musician without music, a composer whose medium was man, and who developed the art of social intercourse by ear. Only much later did the group of friends gathered about the Duke realize that, in entertaining one another, they had been forming a code of values for which one of their number had been waiting. They were unconscious of it, but for him, as he listened so persuasively, a certain association of ideas emanated spontaneously from a chance association of people. They came from every province of Italy and from every walk of life, nor was it chance perhaps that drew them to Urbino. Soldiers, scholars, prelates, artists, parasites, with all their diversity of temperament, profession, and origin, they found something in common there. Some were exiles like the brothers Fregoso of Genoa or Giuliano de' Medici and his brother the Cardinal, who were frequent visitors, for the Duke made his state a haven for political refugees; and misfortune, as the most refining of influences, was the best title of admission to that society. Those whom misfortune embittered did not linger long, for he expected of his guests what he possessed to an eminent degree—a spirit of detachment, a cheerful indifference to the vicissitudes of life; and though he was not of a sanguine nature, his house was, as Castiglione described it, "the very Mansion of mirth and joy." Good cheer was a discipline, an exercise in self-command, an act of self-abnegation; and the morose and self-engrossed, if they lingered, remained to be the butt of mirth. Guidobaldo asked no more of them than he demanded of himself. On his return from Rome, after the fall of Caesar Borgia, his only comment was the performance of a play, "a Mock Comedy of Duke Valentino and Pope Alexander VI, how they planned to annihilate Urbino, how they sent Madonna Lucrezia to Ferrara, how they invited the Duchess to her wedding, how they came to seize the state, how the Duke returned for the first time and fled, how they throttled Vitellozzo and the other Captains, and how Pope Alexander died and the Duke of Urbino recovered his state." Pictures of the passing world—its shadowy tragedies fading by a winter fire—the embers ruminating—mummers recalling memories—what else was the past? A pageant in which men went through the same motions, repeated the same patterns, and invented the same untutored antics, unwittingly. But it made a good play; and then a song, the evening prayer, and sleep. . . .

If the Duke, with his detachment, lent something unreal and dreamlike to that life, the Duchess balanced him in her own more prosaic way.

The influence of women in that Court seconded and corrected that of the men. They worked for detachment too, exercising their privilege and making of life the pastime of an amateur. That was their service to society. Nothing too serious, or too studied, or too zealous was tolerated in their company: war, letters, love, life—everything was smiled down into amenity and unimportance. Whatever pretension raised its head, whether the pedantry of scholars, the affectation of fops, or the self-esteem of soldiers, was immediately pricked; and under the guise of levity they accomplished much—they disintegrated the man-made world by the insidious common sense of women. No one who sojourned long at Urbino could ever again value anything very much: steeped in its wholesome humour, the adept was immune to the common fallacies of the male. What mattered there was not the aim of life, nor its aimlessness, but the manner of living it. Of these ladies the leader was Emilia Pia, a widow who mourned her husband disconsolately in secret and was always on her toes in public; but the presiding spirit was the Duchess.

Like her husband, Elizabetta Gonzaga was an invalid. Of a lymphatic constitution, timid and indolent as a child, she had bloomed late. She welcomed marriage with physical reluctance. Her apprehensions passed with the marriage night, but they were followed by others—she dreaded the effect on her young husband of his discovery, in her arms, of his impotence. Her one impulse was to protect and console him; she loved him with maternal tenderness, she promised him secrecy, subterfuges, her own sterility. But the secret soon transpired, and it was common knowledge when Caesar Borgia used it to part them. A matron then, she preferred "to live with Guidobaldo as a sister than to repudiate him." She did neither. On their return from exile, the health of the valetudinarian couple was a matter of much concern to Isabella d'Este, and her ambassador at Urbino kept her closely informed. "Because of the great press of business left over from the past, I know that they have not slept together. The Signor Duca is very well but does not run or play ball. The Duchess visits him every day, and is very much afraid that he may attempt her and that she may be the cause of his relapsing." Like Isabella, he was worried. Elizabetta had returned from a pilgrimage to Loreto "with the intention of falling into no more follies with her consort nor sinning for his sake. But truly, Madonna, I fear he will come to it, being so accustomed to it. I often say to her: Mind, Madonna, mind what you are doing." The eroticism of the Duke left its mark on her constitution. Debilitated by organic disorder, she led a sedentary life; after two or three turns about the room, she would be forced to sit down; and seeking strength in food she developed the little vices of a glutton. Isabella often scolded her; but she could not overcome her craving for fruit and she was subject to recurrent attacks of dysentery. Observing her frayed and warped life, Isabella was seized with compassion, and her compassion was always practical. When her sister-in-law went to the baths of Viterbo, she gave her some sound advice: "I must remind you, because of the affection I bear you, of one thing: and that is, that your first plunge be the firm determination to avoid everything depressing and to live and thrive on such things as bring health and substance; to force yourself to take exercise, either on foot or on horseback, and to enjoy pleasant conversations, driving away melancholy and care, which come of the indisposition of the body or the mind; and to attend to nothing but, first, the health of your mind and, then, the comfort and respect of your person, for we have nothing else in this poor world, and those who cannot regulate their lives spend them with much pain and little credit." This advice was effective. Elizabetta took the salutary vow and kept it; and the result was the Court of Urbino. It was her creation even more than her husband's. The self-command of a sick woman, the lapses and denials of a sensual one, and the protective passion of a childless one, inspired the society over which she presided with sanity, cheer, sobriety, and profound devotion.

Of all her devotees Castiglione was the most faithful. She was ten years his senior, an invalid matron, with a heavy pale face and listless eyes; her drooping lids, like hardening petals, betrayed her age; but she touched the secret chords of his being. If love is the image of ourselves we ask of another, he missed none of its essential rapture. He kept her portrait, concealed by secret springs, behind a mirror and with it a whole treasure trove of sonnets *To Elizabetta Gonzaga singing,* and madrigals and songs *in grazia della Signora Duchessa.* She stimulated him in his own sense, and his feeling for her was one of unalloyed veneration. He loved her for her fidelity, with that intellectual love of love, that passion for perfection which, though it produced so many fine-spun sentiments and poetic conceits, was not an affectation but a genuine feeling with the Renaissance man. He loved his idea of her which, reflected in his cool depths, he allowed nothing to break or blur; and her shrine was a mirror.

But the delight he found in the Duchess, and only less in the Duke, was merely the crowning pleasure he found in their Court. The circle of their friends, living with them in domestic intimacy, seemed to take on, by association, a family likeness and a spiritual kinship. It was a Court of charming, accomplished, and commonplace people; and not the least of their charms or their accomplishments was their commonplaceness.

What seemed obvious was, like the manner of Castiglione and Raphael who portrayed them, deceptively simple. It was the expression of an urbane, mellow, and balanced spirit, of an exquisite mean which only a ripe culture could produce. A singular sanity was the achievement of that society; and in the evenings; when the company met for conversation, Castiglione, listening for its common spirit through the rapid variations of an impromptu symposium, heard something far from commonplace—something familiar yet elusive—the fundamental undertone of the Normal.

But what indeed was so rare? The circumstances which begot so normal a life were exceptional—the character of the Duke and Duchess, the well-attuned company, the isolated, irresponsible life of Urbino. It was a carefree and charmed life in the lee of the world. The loud world, in its turmoil, had paused for a moment as if to foster the virtue maturing in that mountain retreat. But this precarious calm depended on the good will of Pope Julius; and Pope Julius was not a man of peace.

27

To that robust old man struggle was the breath of life, and the satisfaction of one ambition could only lead to another. His first goal was attained—the obliteration of the Borgias: no trace of their contamination remained in the Vatican or in Romagna; he had expunged their memory by two years of irreproachable conduct. The states of Romagna he had restored to the Church, and his public spirit he had proved by his personal life. Nepotism, scandal, and corruption were conspicuous by their absence in Rome. But those two penitential years had been a period of inactivity, and in the summer of 1506 he was stirring again. To the Sacred College he announced a forthcoming campaign against two unreclaimed vassals of the Holy See, Perugia and Bologna. The College was aghast, and protested; Cardinal Caraffa, as the Dean, reminded His Holiness of the damage to the prestige of the Church if he failed. But no protest availed. The Curia had already attempted to check him by a constitutional curb: at his accession he had signed a pledge to make no war and contract no alliances without the consent of two-thirds of the College; but when, after his first months of power, he had been invited to countersign his signature, he put the pen to two or three articles and then tossed it aside: he had no time for formalities. He had the true interests of the Church at heart and was determined to make the Papacy the dominant power in the peninsula. He refused to recognize either the possibility of failure or another danger of which those who also cherished the true interests of the Church warned him. Was he not risking his spiritual credit by so belligerent a policy? His pressing duty was to repair the moral authority of the Holy See, which a succession of venal stewards—Alexander VI, Innocent VIII, Sixtus IV —had undermined. Julius agreed. But to his positive mind there was only one way of restoring it. Moral authority rested on material power; the world respected nothing else; and, when the Temporal Power was invigorated, extended, and consolidated, it would be time to attend to the rest. His conservative advisers shrank from an adventure whose success, even more than its failure, would further alienate the faithful. But he went his way, undismayed and alone; and they knew that his policies were his character. Already they foresaw in this adventure the beginning of another. Beyond Romagna lay Venice, and Venice was grasping and hankering after its share of Romagna. Julius was a Genoese, born with a grudge. His polititical ambitions were but another name for his personal antipathies, and his dynamic energy was the energy of hatred. From hatred to hatred he progressed in an ascending scale. Beyond Romagna, Venice, beyond Venice . . . what? No doubt new vistas beckoned. How far would his *furia* carry him? It was impossible to set any bounds to it; and, while there was yet time, the College made a stand. But it was useless. Julius put on his San Pietro in Vincoli look. Surrounded by reluctance, alarm, and mistrust, he completed his preparations, negotiated for French aid, raised a little handful of troops, and left Rome late in August 1506. The College he carried with him in his baggage-train; only eight members, too old to travel, too feeble to intrigue, being left behind.

At Nepi, Machiavelli met him. He came as the official observer of the Florentine Republic, and he came reluctantly. Machiavelli too had his grudge, secret, inadmissible, stubborn. Following the Pope along the route which Borgia had blazed, he was critical of the conqueror and betrayer of Caesar. He compared, only to contrast them. The memory was mightier than Caesar had ever been. Julius, with his male vigour, his indomitable will, his reckless self-confidence, and his rapid movements, had Valentino's best qualities, but they left Machiavelli cold. If anything, they made him mistrust Julius the more. The old man was still cheating: without the indispensable vices of the young one he could not go far.

Besides, the virtues of youth were grotesque in a septuagenarian. Where Valentino leapt, Julius pushed; and he pushed everything too far—his impetuosity, his ambition, his hoary high spirits. At Montefiascone the wines were heady, the floor of his lodgings dilapidated, and he narrowly missed the cellar. He escaped with a little joke. The Cardinals laughed dutifully. The attendants smiled obsequiously. The Pope chuckled alone. He was grotesque. But he was in high glee. His eye twinkled indomitably. Machiavelli was glum. The next day, at Orvieto, His Holiness was yet more elated. The Duke of Urbino joined him with a small force and the French promised a reinforcement of five hundred men-at-arms. The effect of this forced march was immediate. Gian Paolo Baglioni, the tyrant of Perugia, came to make his submission. Machiavelli's interest began to quicken. He knew Baglioni. "If he does not injure a man who comes to take his state," he wrote, "it will be because of his good nature and humanity." Good nature and humanity were the last things that Baglioni was known for. Unscrupulous, steeped in crime, he was an ex-Captain and disciple of Valentino; and it would not have surprised Machiavelli if he had repeated the snare of Sinigaglia in Perugia. The Pope reached Perugia, impatient to take possession, and pressed in with the College, without waiting for the Duke of Urbino to come up with his troops. In the narrow streets a dense crowd brought him to a standstill. Here was a Heaven-sent opportunity—the Pope and the whole College bottled up—but Baglioni missed it. The troops marched in, the Pope and the Cardinals were quietly extricated, and the occupation was completed. With a deepening contempt for the irresolute criminal who had allowed himself to be over-awed by the Vicar of Christ, Machiavelli noted his superstitious submission as a capital error. But his opinion of the Pope did not improve.

The capitulation of Perugia was, indeed, a signal victory for the prestige of the Church, and Julius exulted in it. Machiavelli, however, was unmoved. Julius lacked glamour. Neither his nerve nor his luck impressed the disabused observer who, once scorched, was determined to remain cool now. Nothing about that hard-bitten old man touched his desolate imagination; it was seared, and Julius merely nettled it. He could not compete with the perverse fascination of Valentino, which had appealed so deeply to the secret strain of romanticism in Machiavelli and to his intellectual love of contradiction; and it was a curious fact that the most compelling qualities mattered little without magnetism.

The Pope himself realized it. Of all the difficulties with which he had to struggle, the greatest was that of touching the imagination of his countrymen—perhaps because they were his contemporaries. But with the persistence of a self-made man he attacked that problem too. Before the effect of Perugia could cool, he planned, by a giant stride which would stagger the imagination of Italy, to burst on Bologna. But it needed a giant's stride: the Apennines lay between. He left at once for Urbino. The roads were bad, the country was impoverished, progress was slow; but nothing could stop the fretful old man, twelve years behind his destiny, from stealing a march on his mortal enemy, mulcting him of his golden moment, and confounding the incredulous. Time—time was the enemy. At Urbino he paused for three days, reluctantly, though it pleased him to lie under the silken covers he loved and to receive from the townspeople—plain people like himself—a substantial gift of victuals. Then, to the relief of Machiavelli who was happier in camps than in courts, he pushed on. Already the snows of September were on the mountains. The roads were frozen with sleet; the mules, balancing their baggage and Cardinals, clambered and balked and slipped and sulked; the drivers congregated around them, kicking, brandishing the lash, and blaspheming; the Pope came up, scattering absolutions and cursing them forward; but their progress was sluggish. The army was still in the mountains when it met the first envoys from Bologna; but, when the Pope learned that they came not to capitulate but to parley, he arrested them, and they joined the clambering, balking, and boggling mule-train. At Forli, where he was almost mobbed by the boisterous welcome of the Romagnoli, and had to abandon his mule to the multitude and elbow his way to shelter, Julius paused only long enough to thunder anathema against the Bentivogli and threaten Bologna with a major excommunication if it had not expelled its rulers within nine days. At Imola he was met by relays of envoys announcing the flight of the Bentivogli and the submission of the city. It was one more triumph for the spiritual arms and he celebrated it fittingly.

"Ah, would to God you had seen me borne aloft in Bologna! The horses and chariots, the marching battalions, the galloping generals, the flaming torches, the pretty page-boys, the steaming platters, the pomp of Bishops and glory of Cardinals, the spoils and trophies, the heaven-splitting huzzas and the blare of trumpets and the thunder of cannon and the largesse flung to the multitude, and I borne aloft, head and author of all. Caesar and Scipio were as nothing to me!" It was a nightmare to Erasmus, and in these words which he put into the mouth of the Pope he proved how deeply his imagination had been moved by the spectacle of the Papal triumph. He addressed them to St. Peter: no one else in

Bologna heard him. The din of profane jubilation deafened him, and he had a right to be splenetic. He had just reached Bologna, to begin a year of study in the great university town—his lifelong dream—when the Pope launched his Bull, threatening to close the Academy. Erasmus had not been warned. Tense, motionless, sucking the classical stalk without a quiver, he heard nothing till he was roused by the tramp of the Papal legions through the narrow, vaulted streets. Then he reluctantly brought his proboscis out of doors. A scholar, a cosmopolite, a pacifist, and a Rotterdam Christian, it was only natural that he should be shocked by the sight which met his eyes. "I could not but groan," he informed the Netherlands, "when I compared to the majesty of the Apostles converting the world by their heavenly creed these triumphs, which would have brought the blush to a secular prince." Liberal though he was, he was an alien in Italian latitudes, and he was a precursor of many more less tolerant than he. Four years later Luther came to Rome.

But Julius knew his Italians. He was elated and also alarmed by the volatile loyalty, the facile and effervescent enthusiasm of his race; and before returning to Rome he took measures to perpetuate his triumph. The impression of power was the secret of sub-alpine success. Though he conferred substantial benefits and flattering privileges on the Bolognese, these would soon be forgotten; he determined to confound their imagination in perpetuity. After the awe of arms, the awe of art was the most potent hold on the Italian soul. But to body forth the heroic image he conceived of himself needed a kindred genius to his own, and he knew but one master in Italy equal to it—Michelangelo—and Michelangelo had quarrelled with him, fled to Florence, and refused to return. Usually Julius was proud of the fear he inspired, but not of Michelangelo's. It hurt him. The neurotic timidity of the artist, like that of a pregnant woman, was big with life and he needed its robust creations to insure his heredity. He could subdue everything with the thumb of that man—his contemporaries, posterity, Time itself. And the man was as temperamental as a mule. It was a struggle of wills between them, and Julius knew that he had met his match. In Michelangelo he saw his own spirit—pride, stubbornness, loneliness, a strenuous and sublime ambition; coercion was useless and coaxing came hard to the old man. He passed the trying duty to Cardinal Soderini, who wrote to his brother the Gonfalonier in Florence; the combined efforts of the Papal and Florentine Governments were concentrated on the intractable sculptor, who was wooed, pushed, badgered, shamed, and finally teased into submission. "We cannot go to war on account of you," said the Gonfalonier Soderini. Michelangelo, "his neck in the noose," at last left for Bologna, muttering that he would as soon start for the slave-marts of Stamboul. Cardinal Soderini had volunteered to smooth the way for his first audience with the Pope, but, as luck would have it, he fell ill, and this duty devolved upon a Bishop of Lucca, who had a provincial respect for the *bienséances* of the occasion. He was more useful that he knew. With trepidation he saw the Pope glare at Michelangelo and heard him growl: "So! Instead of coming to us, you waited until we fetched you." And his trepidation increased when he heard Michelangelo reply with a statement of his own side of the case. The fidgety Bishop could bear no more. He promptly intervened, apologizing for the presumption of the artist and explaining to the Holy Father that such men knew their own trade but nothing of the proprieties— and the explosion came. Snatching his stick, Julius fell on the Bishop of Lucca, shouting that he had insulted a great artist and might return where he came from—to Lucca, to Limbo, to the bottomless pit of the ever-correct. The luckless man, trepidating in every direction, was unceremoniously hustled out by the servants; the tension was broken; and the Pope; overwhelming Michelangelo with his benediction, put him to work. What he wanted was a colossal figure in perennial bronze to loom above the portals of San Petronio. A question of interpretation arose. The figure was to be represented seated, with the right hand raised in menace; in the left Michelangelo proposed to put a book. "No, a sword," said Julius. "I know nothing of books." It was one of his little jokes. In reality, he had more culture than he cared to admit; but he was moulding his legend.

With his genius in harness, the Pope left Michelangelo in Bologna and returned to Rome. On the way he paused in Urbino. Now he had time to spare but he remained only three days. Despite the solicitous hospitality with which he was received, the life of a lotus-eater made him impatient. He had no imagination for its delicate values. In that atmosphere he no longer felt formidable, he was grotesque, for even he could see the futility of ambition there. He was unhappy, he missed his *terribilitá*. He missed too a face he had hoped to find, the young soldier who had started out so promisingly from Rome two years before; and, when he inquired what had become of him, he was told that Castiglione was on a mission to England. The old man whiled away the time fretfully—what did they do with their time there? One day, watching Ottaviano Fregoso, the Duke's Genoese nephew, toying absent-mindedly with a sword, he lost his temper and ordered him from the room. A Genoese and a carpet-

POPE JULIUS II, by Raphael
From the portrait in the Pitti Palace, Florence

knight! It was exasperating. He growled out his orders to pack. The life was well enough, no doubt, for those who like it and, when many of his entourage asked permission to linger, he made no objection; but so many availed themselves of the privilege that, when he left, he felt deserted. No sooner was his back turned than the company returned to its pleasures. It was as if he had never existed. His nephew, Francescomaria della Rovere, the heir adoptive of the Duchy, accompanied him part of the way; then he too turned back; and under the frosty stars the old man continued alone. No one in Italy understood him, no one but Michelangelo; and Michelangelo . . . he could not be sure . . . Michelangelo perhaps was pursuing his own vision.

28

Insensible though he was to Julius, Machiavelli was inflamed, in spite of himself, by his martial mood; and, when he returned to Florence, it was with a new determination to pursue his own dream. For many months he had been laying the foundations for an experiment. His own vision was at last to be tested. Since the disastrous attempt, six years before, to recover Pisa with the aid of the French, a desultory campaign had been carried on by the Republic: everything had been tried, mercenaries, alliances, blockades, even Leonardo da Vinci. In these efforts Machiavelli had collaborated loyally, particularly with Leonardo. Their acquaintance dated from the days when da Vinci served Valentino in Romagna as a military engineer. They discovered that they had enough in common—a scientific spirit and an admiration for Caesar Borgia—to echo and re-echo each other's approval of his principles: Leonardo writing

> Seize Fate, if you would hold her enthralled,
> By the forelock, behind she is bald . . .

and Machiavelli rewriting

> Chance is my name, whom few men know:
> Hair have I none upon my nape;
> Who toils after me toils too slow:
> Whom I overtake I escape . . .

and when chance made them collaborate on the problem of Pisa they fell into step. Leonardo proposed to reduce Pisa by diverting the course of the Arno. Like so many of his other schemes, this one remained uncompleted. After months of trial and error and expense, all that was left of the laborious experiment was a network of ditches from which the water had seeped back into the river-bed and a page of labyrinthine calculations—an incoherent record of mathematical delirium—scribbled by the amazed surveyor. Everything had been tried but the militia.

Now came Machiavelli's turn. He approached Soderini. He offered him his opportunity. This was the test. If the Gonfalonier recognized and seized opportunity, then perhaps he might yet prove the alternative to Caesar. Soderini listened and allowed himself to be won over. He made the scheme his own and presented it to the Government; and the Government, after a lengthy process of elimination and failure, at last recognized that the solution proposed by Machiavelli was less visionary and extravagant than evasions and half-measures. But there were obstacles. The patronage of Soderini was a political liability, and the militia immediately became suspect as a scheme for the re-establishment of tyranny. The traditional policy of employing foreign mercenaries had its origin in civic jealousy and the fear of creating a force of which ambitious citizens might take advantage; but the character of Piero Soderini carried the day. The Government eventually authorized the experiment on a small scale, withholding its official sanction until the results seemed to warrant it.

It began under serious handicaps. The citizens of Florence were exempted from conscription, the militia had to be recruited from the country districts, and among the peasants patriotic spirit was lacking. But Machiavelli was ready to supply everything. He turned himself into a recruiting sergeant, travelling through the country, supervising enlistments, organizing the conscripts on the lines laid down by Valentino in Romagna. The command of these raw troops was given to Valentino's lieutenant, Don Michele da Corella, who was later dismissed for excessive brutality, but who whipped them into shape. In the midst of these exertions Machiavelli was called away by his legation to Julius; and when he returned it was with new determination and vigour. Involuntarily he seemed to have been stimulated; and from that date everything went well with him. The militia progressed, and the Government showed a spurt of energy. On December 6, 1506—a month after his return—it adopted the constitution of the militia which he had drawn up, and created a new department —the Nine of the National Militia—of which he became the First Secretary. Congratulations poured in on him. "It really seems to us that this militia *sit a Deo*,"[1] Cardinal Soderino wrote from Bologna, "since it grows every day, despite opposition and spite. We have learned with singular pleasure of the new magistracy, and we pray God that its composition may be such as to give it a solid basis, for we believe that the City has done nothing so serviceable and honourable in many a day, if only it is well used, which it is the duty of the good to provide for. They must not let themselves be misled by those who have other aims and who do not cherish the welfare of the City as they should in this new liberty, *dono divino et non humano, nisi corrumpatur malitia aut ignorantione*[2]; and you who have had so great a share in it must not fail." There was no danger. Machiavelli was no longer a prophet unarmed; and with the first hint of recognition his confidence, his courage, and his energy redoubled. He poured them all out in a letter to the Cardinal—a churchman after his own heart—explaining eagerly how the militia worked and why it could not fail. "The copiousness of your letter gave us great pleasure," the Cardinal benignly replied, "because we have clearly understood the development of this military principle, which corresponds to our hope *pro salute et dignitate Patriae.*[3] The only reason that other nations today are superior to ours is that they still maintain discipline, which has long since disappeared in Italy. It should be no small satisfaction to you that you have been the one to begin so worthy an enterprise; persevere and bring it to the conclusion we desire."

29

While this ferment of activity was at work in Florence, another was seething in Urbino. When Castiglione returned, two days after the passage of the Pope, he found the huge mansion overflowing with guests. He had been absent for over six months on a mission to England, to thank the King on behalf of Guidobaldo for the gift of the Golden Fleece, and he felt half a stranger in the great building, as vast as a town, which the influx of the world had turned into a caravanserai. Beside the old familiar faces—Emilia Pia, the Duke, the Duchess, Francescomaria,

[1] comes from God.
[2] a gift divine and not human, and not to be corrupted by malice or ignorance.
[3] for the welfare and dignity of our country.

the Fregoso brothers, and his kinsmen Cesare Gonzaga and Lodovico da Canossa—there were new ones. Giuliano de' Medici was now a permanent guest with a wing of the Palace to himself; Bibbiena, the secretary of Cardinal de' Medici, and Bembo, the Venetian humanist, had settled there; and the Court was crowded with new recruits, who had lagged behind the Pope, declaring themselves converts to its life. Bembo, the slippery-footed dilettante, was beckoning to all his friends to join him. "Come here"—to one—"everything invites you: we will laugh for a week and drive away care"—and to another—"What do we do here? There is little to tell: we laugh, we jest, we play games, we invent new tricks and practical jokes, we study and sup, and now and then write verses. Farewell, in hot haste . . ." In hot haste to do nothing. The life was more brilliant than ever, the visit of the Pope seemed to have stimulated it, to have made the company more conscious of itself, more detached from the strenuous outer world, more exuberant and yet more self-contained; for, despite the numbers which at first shocked the returning traveller eager for rest and seclusion, he found that Urbino had triumphed over its guests and not its guests over it. That choice society was a living organism which accepted and rejected those who were fit or unfit for it, and it had lost none of its fastidiousness. No, Urbino had lost none of its charm: it was he who had changed.

For he saw it now with travelled eyes. He had passed through England, through France, through a Milan that was French, and returning to Urbino with a new perspective, just as the shadow of the bellicose Pope passed over it, he saw the light mottled and the brilliance overclouded by reflections that were sombre though they might be passing. It needed so little to dispel that idyllic world—a mere breath of struggle—and how many of those amateur sages would have the moral stamina to meet the test of reality? They existed on sufferance, and their privileged charter read, as Bembo phrased it, "a home of joy and common brotherhood, a shelter where troubled minds find peace and freedom from care"—but how long does the world overlook the inoffensive? Such reflections, however, were fugitive. The sun was shining and Bembo was rewriting Horace, and Castiglione succumbed to the present. In an eloquent letter which he read aloud to the company, Bembo complained of the surprise which his family showed at his lingering so long in Urbino. Why had he been born with a family? "All I can say is that I am amazed they should think me so senseless as not to know what I am doing. . . . Let them think what they will. Those who fancy themselves wise and who think they can manage our lives better than their own are imbeciles. If God grants me a few more years of life, and if the world does not move out of its courses for a month or two more, they will appreciate how wisely I have chosen. Even if the Pope dies and the face of the world is changed, I shall not be worse off than I am today." Why borrow trouble? He was not ambitious.

Castiglione agreed with him. He too had the genius of contentment, he too was unambitious, and he too had a family that had never known Urbino. His mother was again worrying about his future. She had conceived a bold scheme—a scheme which served the double purpose of reconciling the Marquis to her son and her son to marriage, and which consisted in making the Marquis the matchmaker. So bold was this plan, in fact, that she advanced it not as her own but as the suggestion of a friend and his brother-in-law. But all her circumlocutions and circumventions were in vain: he nipped the preposterous idea in the bud. "I am sure that it is very good of these gentlemen to concern themselves with my welfare," he replied unfeelingly, "but I believe their idea would bring me, not only no benefit, but injury and ridicule into the bargain. Never—not till the end of Time—will I consent to such a thing! If God puts a good marriage in my way, I shall accept it gladly, without assistance from others; but it seems strange to expect a man who has always tried to persecute me suddenly to mend his ways." His scores with Francesco Gonzaga had risen since his journey to England, for the Marquis had done him a shabby turn. Guidobaldo, wishing to offer the Majesty of England a horse from the famous Mantuan studs, had requested one of his brother-in-law; the Marquis had demurred, objecting that the large ones he bred were unsuited to foreign taste; but he had finally consented and sent an animal to Milan, where Castiglione was to call for it. It did not occur to the Count to look this gift in the mouth; when he was about to start, he discovered that it was blind in one eye; he sent it back, begging his mother to administer the only rebuke possible under the circumstances and to return it "exactly as we received it or perhaps in better condition"; and the error was rectified; but neither his temper nor that of the Marquis improved in consequence of it. When, therefore, his mother made her bold proposal, he replied with a bolder one; and his was not a suggestion but a decision. It silenced her, for it was nothing less than to exchange his ancestral acres at Casatico for an estate which he had been offered in the vicinity of Bologna. After that, no more was said of marriage. Fortunately for the old Countess, the negotiations for the exchange fell through; but she realized that her son was an expatriate, no longer by accident, but by choice. The world was too small for him while he had an enemy in it; and for a man of so susceptible a spirit there was no choice but vagabondage or Urbino.

The encroachment of the world, however, had begun. The summer of 1507 was torrid and it brought on a tragedy. Slowly the landscape turned tawny; under a cruel sky the rivers dwindled, the crops failed, the vines shrivelled, the wells gaped, and for the first time within memory even the great basin of Urbino ran dry. Day after day, in the windless air, little clouds lay belee'd on the horizon, their shapes never changing and, as the sun travelled through them, slowly becoming transparent. The incandescent glare consumed everything but the shadows it cast, and the very shadows grew livid in the vast luminous trance. The sour grapes yellowed, the smelted vines rusted, and the numb silence of the canicular season settled over everything. In the Palace, life dwindled to a sigh in the morning, a siesta in the afternoon, and a long convivial night. The company assembled on the loggias, breathless for a whiff of the far Adriatic, listening, now that the fountains were mute, to the cooling melodies of the lute; and for some the music was a relief and for others a strain on the senses. More and more often one couple was missing. The man was a soldier of humble origin and a favourite of the Duke; the woman was a sister of Francescomaria, the widowed Countess of Camerino. The drought, which had drained everything else, fired their blood; but the Court was discreet and there was no scandal until her brother caught wind of the affair. Francescomaria was a true della Rovere. A quick-blooded lad of eighteen, he had been tempered at Urbino, but he was too young to appreciate the tolerance of maturity. He lured the lover to his rooms, murdered him in a fencing match, and fled. The tragedy was hushed up, and the Court ignored it as discreetly as it overlooked life. Within a few weeks Francescomaria reappeared. "There has been some disturbance here because of an unfortunate event in our house," Castiglione informed his mother, but he would say no more. When she insisted, he raised the veil just enough to show the depth of his courtly devotion. "You need not distress yourself about the death of Giovanni Andrea. God pardon him! Such things, when they are done, cannot be undone. Everything has been settled by the wisdom and skill of the Duke. The Lord Prefect[1] is here again, and is restored to favour, and the dead man is already forgotten."

---

[1] Francescomaria della Rovere.

Like everyone else, he bore the blow with perfect amenity; it had been a shock, but it was immediately muffled. Life might strike: they were proof against it. The wisdom of acquiescence, the wisdom of the world, to bear, forbear, and forget, was enough: for tomorrow the sun also rises.

But that muffled blow was only the prelude to another. During the autumn the Duke was in poor health; to avoid the rigours of winter he removed with Elizabetta and his intimates to the lower altitude of Fossombrone; and there he seemed to improve. But he had no tenacity of life and, when April came, he looked over the meadows and in the furrow of the harrow welcomed the hearse. "Why, my friends, would you deprive me of what I most desire?" Guidobaldo appealed to them with his long pale face, his nerveless hands, and suffering eyes. "Is not death, that delivers us from such cruel pains, the best and mildest of friends?" And his old friends prepared to meet his new one. The vigil ended one April morning. He took his leave with studied serenity and, turning to Castiglione, quoted the Georgics:

> Me circum limus niger et deformis arundo
> Cocyti, tardaque palus inamabilis unda
> Alligat, et novies Styx interfusa coercet. . . .

But there was no coercion. His listless eyes, dimming steadily, steered straight for the dark passage. For an hour he lay floating; then, grounding suddenly in the swiftening void, he turned over and eased one hand under his cheek, as if to sleep; and—as Bembo noted, pen in hand—"very quietly, without any sign of fear, he passed from this life."

Elizabetta, who had controlled herself up to the last moment, flung herself after him, caught his face in her hands, and fell back in an abandoned swoon. The room was filled with lamentation and clamour; the attendants flung water in her face, squeezed her arms and wrenched her fingers so vehemently that one was injured; but it was two hours before she revived. For several days she passed from stupor to convulsions and from hysteria to apathy. She no sooner recovered her composure than she lost it at the sight of a new or a familiar face. But, at last, rousing herself to her duties, she sent Castiglione to Gubbio and other deputies to the various towns in the Duchy to control any demonstrations which might arise with the death of the Duke. For the murder of Giovanni Andrea and the violent character of Francescomaria had roused an indignation among the people which the Court did not venture to share or to voice. The publication of the Duke's will, leaving the regency of the state to his widow until the heir reached the age of twenty-five, restored confidence, however; and she was welcomed on her return to Urbino with unmistakable demonstrations of loyalty.

In private she cultivated her grief incessantly. She devoted the remainder of her dowry to the celebration of ten thousand Masses for the soul of her husband, and though his body was laid in the little church of the Zoccolanti, it was not there that visitors to Urbino saw his real tomb. If they saw it at all, it was where the Mantuan ambassador did. When he brought the condolences of Isabella, he found the widow, at night, seated on a little mattress, veiled, in a room draped in black, the windows bolted, with a single candle on the floor. "I was led in by my cloak, like a blind man. She offered me her hand, and I stood for a time like a mute, unable to speak, for we were both sobbing. . . . The young Duke was present, seated on a low stool among the women. When the Duchess called him, he rose and I gave him the message of Your Excellencies. He replied in a few words, which were sensible and circumspect. I thought him a little taller and more self-possessed than I had been led to expect, but on account of the darkness I could not form much of an opinion. The Duchess speaks of him highly and he treats her with the respect of a son and a servant." Into that lugubrious gloom he hesitated to venture, but he served a lady who loved life, and Isabella had already taken her measures to prevent her sister-in-law from indulging a morbid grief. Accordingly, he returned to the Duchess, to cheer her if he could with a message from Mantua, reminding her of a balm for all their hearts—the forthcoming marriage of Isabella's daughter, Eleonora, to that violent shadow, Francescomaria. The ambassador was amazed at his success. "Today we spent more than three hours together, and I drew her into agreeable subjects and made her laugh, which no one has done yet. I urged her to open the windows, a thing which no one has had the courage to suggest, and I think she will open them the day after tomorrow. When Madonna Eleonora comes to be married, she will put off her mourning for joy, for, if this happens, which she so deeply desires, she says that she will no longer feel herself a widow." A bride out of Mantua, a bride in Urbino, a bride come to meet her by the road she had travelled so many years before—it was her youth returning on primrose feet; and she opened the windows.

But the prospect of that marriage only made her more faithful to Guidobaldo. The bridegroom had not sprung from his loins, and she turned to her niece for a daughter, but she could not cheat her blood with illusions. She ached for the man who had satisfied her so completely and barrenly, and who had left her no one to live for. Yet he would have been the first, as she realized, to chide so abject a surrender to nature; and one legacy she determined not to neglect. "The foreign gentlemen who lived at her husband's Court," Bembo was relieved to inform his friends, "will all, I believe, or almost all, continue in the new Duke's service at her request, since she feels that, out of respect to her Lord's memory, this honourable company which served him should not be broken up." But it was no longer the same: the settled melancholy of the Duchess made it difficult to revive the old carefree spirit. The Court had been the joint creation of the Duke and Duchess, and the disappearance of one partner immediately affected its harmony. The virtues of the woman had seemed to gain a superior authority in those of the man: the resignation and self-effacement of one sex had a rarer value in the humanity and magnanimity of the other. Something indefinable but essential to the charm of Urbino had fled. The inner circle did not break up, but its members were called away more and more frequently by duty . . . a melancholy word there. Even Bembo went place-hunting in Rome.

One devotee of the Duchess, however, did not desert her. Not only choice and necessity but duty and the imperative partiality to the dead which he bore in his blood now bound Castiglione to Urbino; and his devotion to the widow redoubled. Into the inviolable gloom of her first bereavement he had not ventured to intrude; but, when the eclipse was over and she emerged into a twilight zone where he could reach her, he watched over her, as she struggled to recover her self-command, and kept her from faltering. He joined her in her cult for Guidobaldo and helped her to fulfil his will. It was then that, as a tribute to the late Duke, he began a memoir of the life that had been, while its memory was yet fresh. In a modest attempt to stem the corrosion of time, to hold old friends together, and to perpetuate a past that was but yesterday, he collected some half-remembered, half-imaginary conversations to which he gave the title of *The Courtier*, and which he dated at the apogee of that life—the brilliant days immediately succeeding the passage of Pope Julius through Urbino in March 1507. But he had hardly begun this pious labour when he was called away from it. The mottled light, the passing clouds which he had felt on his return to Urbino were gathering again, and a wind of war was rising through Italy. Pope Julius was about to open his long-planned and far-reaching campaign against Venice: his nephew Francescomaria della Rovere was called out as Captain of the Church; and with him went Castiglione in 1509 to win his spurs.

30

Approved by Niccolo Machiavelli . . . approved by Niccolo Machiavelli . . . approved by Niccolo Machiavelli . . . The words, scrawled over sheaves of military documents, were no longer the formula of a Chancery clerk: they bore the stamp of authority. The First Secretary of the Signoria, of the Ten on War, and of the Nine on the National Militia, had left his prentice years behind him; a career of initiative, activity, and public service opened before him. The militia which he had been so instrumental in creating now made him. In two years it had developed sufficiently to be employed against Pisa, not indeed independently, but as an auxiliary to the mercenaries, and in some minor operations it had acquitted itself creditably. Machiavelli was now constantly in the camp, and so thoroughly in his element that an order to return to a base behind the lines moved him to protest: "If I dreaded peril or fatigue, I should not have left Florence: I beg Your Worships to let me stay among these camps and work with these commissaries on whatever arises; here I can be of some service, but there I should be good for nothing, and would die of despair."

In the spring of 1509, under cover of the Papal campaign against Venice which cut off all foreign aid from Pisa, Florence began a concerted attack on the city which had resisted it for twelve years. Three camps were established, surrounding the enemy and blocking its supplies from the sea, the mountains, and the inland; and the militia devastated the adjacent territory with a vigour to which the famished peasants bore witness. Machiavelli, passing from camp to camp, delivering munitions and pay, inspecting troops, reporting, advising, pushing, was invested with discretionary powers—"You are prudent, and as you hold the secret of everything it is not necessary to inform you further of our wishes." So ran his orders, and he used them to the full. His confidence sometimes brought him into collision with his superiors in the field, and on one such occasion Biagio was alarmed. "The office is displeased," he wrote. "The stronger are always right and we must respect them." But Machiavelli had left Biagio far behind. He was strong enough to be right himself, and he went his way unperturbed.

In March 1509, proposals of surrender were made by Pisa, and it was Machiavelli who received them. The Pisan commission was composed both of citizens and peasants, and, while the former refused to capitulate unconditionally, the hungry farmers surrounded him, shouting, "Peace,

peace, we want peace, Commissioner!" He exploited their division, pointing out to the peasants, over the protests of the townsmen, the advantages of peace and promising them considerate treatment; and, leaving the leaven to work, turned and rode off. The citizens, who had shown some surprise at being received by a Secretary, watched him depart in consternation. But Florence was now in a position to dictate: after fourteen years of heroic resistance, Pisa was exhausted. The end was so near, in fact, that the foreign powers recognized and hastened to exploit it: the French put in a claim for indemnification to the amount of 50,000 ducats; the Spanish, not to be outdone, demanded a like sum; and Florence was forced to satisfy these extortions before the negotiations could be completed. Then, at long last, in the final week of May 1509, Pisa surrendered.

The day on which the news reached Florence marked the zenith of Machiavelli's career. His friends turned themselves into a claque. "Tongue cannot tell the joy, the jubilation, the ecstasy, this people feels in the news of the recovery of Pisa," Agostino Vespucci wrote him. "Everyone is mad with joy, there are bonfires all through the city, though it is only the twenty-second hour. Think what it will be by night! All that is wanting is that Heaven itself should show some sign of joy: men can do no more, great or small. *Prosit vobis*,[1] you were present at such a glorious triumph, *et non minima portio rei*.[2] If you will deign to reply by a line, given by your hand in Pisa, nothing will please me more, nothing will be more acceptable. *Vale. Tuus si suus Augustinus.* P.S. *Nisi crederem te nimis superbire*,[3] I might make bold to say that, with your battalions, you led the good work so well that, *non cunctando sed accelerando*,[4] you recovered the property of Florence. Do I know what I say? I do not. I swear to God, I would dance you a jig if I had time, so great is our joy." "A thousand, thousand blessings be yours for the capture of this noble city," wrote an older crony, Filippo Casavecchia, "for truly we may say that you have been in great part responsible for it, though I have no fault to find with the diligence or the skill of these noble Commissioners. And though I have taken a marvellous joy in it and wept and capered and done everything that staid and hidebound men do, nevertheless and notwithstanding, now that I have recovered my reason, I am still insanely fond of my joy; and I cannot believe, and nothing will ever convince me, that I was wrong in saying that weighty

---
1 Thanks to you.
2 and in no small measure responsible for it.
3 If I were not afraid of making you too proud.
4 not delaying but speeding.

minds run to the centre and subtle ones to the surface of things. Niccolo, this is a time, if ever you were wise, to be so. Your philosophy, I believe, will never please both the fools and the wise: of these you will never find as many as you need. You understand me? Every day declares you the greatest prophet that ever the Hebrews or any other people had. Niccolo, Niccolo, verily I tell you: I cannot tell you what I mean. Come, then, come, I beg you and visit me." He offered inducements. "I shall offer you—not to mention our conversations—a stream full of trout and a wine that has never been broached. This pleasure will eclipse all my others. Ah, Niccolo, my friend, do me this favour, if only for four days; if you do not come, I warn you, you will hurt me; and I am not asking so much but that I deserve to be satisfied; and whether I deserve it or not, I impose this pleasure upon you. . . . If you do not come, I shall come to you and that will be my ruin, since the laws do not allow me to quit my post under pain of 500 florins' fine: I say no more." But Pisas do not fall every day, and Niccolo was not to be had for the asking. Three weeks later, his friend was still posting letters into the void. He resigned himself, asking only an occasional letter on "the affairs of the world." "But do not send me an oration like your last, of which I deem myself unworthy, but something fit for a plebeian and an ignorant man; and I may add that, as the friars read their office morning, noon, and night, so do I recite yours, and by now I believe I know it by heart."

In that chorus of congratulations one voice was conspicuous by its silence. Dazzled by the apotheosis of his partner, the drudge of his dark days was mute; and it was only six months later, when a cloud threatened the radiance of that glory, that Biagio again raised his voice. The crowning tribute to Machiavelli's success was the jealousy it inspired. The favour which he had won with the Gonfalonier, and without which he could not have promoted the militia, had earned him the nickname of Soderini's pet, his *mannino;* and when that name lost its sting, the gossips hatched another. In the autumn Machiavelli went north to report the Papal campaign against Venice. In his absence, bastardy charges were secretly preferred against him. By an obsolete statute such charges could be used to disqualify him for public office. Biagio begged him to trust him: it was no laughing matter. "Do not make light of it and do not neglect it, and do as I tell you," he wrote. "Your enemies are many and they leave no stone unturned; and the affair is public, even in brothels, and is aggravated by many circumstances. Believe me, Niccolo, I do not tell you half of what is afoot, and, until I produced the law, the judgment was considered a foregone conclusion. I am doing everything to help you. . . . I have just been asked by someone who loves you, and whom you trust, to write and advise you to stay where you are, and on no account to return yet, as the matter is dying down, and will certainly end better if you are absent: besides, I do things which you would not do and which must be done. Everyone expects to be flattered and entreated and honoured, even when the case is clear, and a man who does another a service wants to be thanked both before and after and to be wheedled over and over; and how apt you are in such things I leave you to judge for yourself. In short, one of the best ways of curing this trouble is for you to keep out of it. . . . If I told you that I have not slept since this trouble began, I should be telling the truth; there are so few who are willing to help you, and I do not know why." By dint of soliciting lawyers, buttonholing magistrates, and currying favour right and left, Biagio succeeded in unearthing an exemption which quashed the case; and, when Machiavelli returned, Biagio met him rubbing his hands like a happy fly over his own triumph.

But the apogee is the beginning of decline. The tutelary drudge was doomed. For years he had complained of the unequal gait of their friendship; and a day was bound to come when he would fall behind. The way to Machiavelli's heart lay through his mind: his nature was cerebral and sensual, and sentiment held a small part in it. Biagio had only his personal devotion to offset his mental inferiority; and Machiavelli, now that he had won a recognized place in public life, found full scope for his intellectual development in the impersonal life of the state. He had reached maturity. The friends of his youth receded, yielding their intimacy to a new confidant. Francesco Vettori, who had been his colleague on a recent mission, was his intellectual equal; Vettori stimulated his powers and kindled his heart; and it was the friendship of Vettori which now bore the stamp: *approved by Niccolo Machiavelli.*

31

While Biagio was fighting the bastardy charges, Machiavelli was in Mantua on business. The Papal campaign against Venice, under cover of which Pisa had been captured, now compelled Florence to look to its own position in the peninsula. In a mighty suction Julius had drawn the attention and the forces of all Italy and of the three foreign powers interested in Italy upon Venice. The Papal army had been supplemented by French, German, and Spanish troops; the minor powers had fallen into line—Francescomaria of Urbino taking the field, the Marquis of Mantua accepting the title of Captain of the Church, and Alfonso of Ferrara lending the Papal army his artillery. This sweeping drive culminated, two weeks before the fall of Pisa, in the battle of Agnadei where the Venetian army was crushed. It was a staggering victory for the Pope. Venice lay at his mercy, the armies of the Allies advanced to the very verge of the lagoon, and he was eager to proceed; but the Allies, though they had pledged themselves to the extermination of Venice, held back. By the Treaty of Cambray they had been promised compensation at the expense of the Venetian territories on the mainland, and they immediately proceeded to occupy these claims. The French expanded from Milan, absorbing Brescia, Bergamo, Crema, and Cremona, and promptly lost interest in the prosecution of the Papal campaign. The Spanish indemnified themselves with the Venetian ports on the lower Adriatic, and sank back into their slumbers in Naples. The Emperor Maximilian occupied Friuli, Vicenza, Padua, and Verona, but in the latter towns he met with resistance and was forced to send troops for their reduction. During the lull which lasted through the summer of 1509 it was only around these cities that the war flickered up. Such was the situation to which Florence awoke after the capture of Pisa. Amid the general upheaval and confusion into which the Pope had plunged the peninsula, the Emperor, impecunious as ever and with one foot in Italy, approached Florence for an indemnity; and the Republic agreed to pay for protection. Machiavelli was sent to pay the first instalment to the Imperial agent in Mantua; after which he was instructed to follow and report the Papal campaign and its prospects.

He began by collecting information in Mantua; but within twenty-four hours he decided that "this is a place where lies breed, nay, where they rain, and the Court is more full of them than the town." Machiavelli was not a courtier or he might have discovered that the Court of Mantua, which he found so full of lies, was merely an accurate sounding-board for Rome, and that Rome was full of confusion. The Pope was perplexed, no one knew what turn the war would take next, and it was this uncertainty which reached Mantua. No town in Italy was closer at that moment to Rome, for Isabella had her Curial friends close to the Pope, and they kept her informed. Isabella, in fact, was the one person to sound in Mantua, but for obvious reasons Machiavelli did not approach her. It never occurred to him that she counted politically. To be sure, she corresponded with eminent people, advised her husband, and carried on a little petticoat diplomacy, and she was known as *la prima donna del mondo*, but that was only a pretty courtly compliment. The first lady of the world was well connected politically, related as she was to the Este in Ferrara, the Montefeltre in Urbino, the Bentivoglio late of Bologna, the ex-Sforza of Milan, the Arragonese in Naples, and the royal house of France; but after all she was only a woman, though by all accounts she was a sensible as well as a clever one, content with her domestic sphere, her children, her Court, and her collections. She collected art, in which Machiavelli was not interested; she dabbled in politics, and he had no use for women in politics. He had only one use for them, and he preferred trulls to great ladies. It was the rainy season, and Mantua, girdled by stagnant lakes, was damp; the town was teeming with lies, the Court breeding will-o'-the-wisps and mosquitoes; and Machiavelli moved on, after one night, to look for the truth, which no one knew, elsewhere. If anyone had told him that that woman would have a fatal though remote influence on his own destiny, or that within the next three years the destiny of Italy would be decided by that illustrious provincial dilletante and model materfamilias, he would have shrugged and nipped the idea as one more of the miasmic lies with which the place was infested.

And indeed such fantastic possibilities were beyond all foresight, even that of Isabella herself, and she was far-seeing. Like Pope Julius, however, she perceived only a part of her destiny at a time and, unlike him, she pursued it under the goad, not of initiative, but of necessity. But the circumstances were already in motion which were to bring her into the national struggle and to make her, not merely the most brilliant woman in Italy, but the champion in politics of the instincts, the principles, and the loyalties of her sex.

The fuse had been laid the previous summer, when her husband the Marquis, on his way to join the Emperor, had been ambushed by the Venetians, chased into a haystack, and carried to Venice, where he was imprisoned under conditions of exceptional severity. Isabella immediately pulled wires and moved heaven and earth for his release; but the Venetian Government was vindictive. The Emperor and the King of France both offered their good offices. With singular prudence she declined them. Already her political tact was developing; and she was well posted in Rome. She preferred to appeal to the Pope. Her advisers saw a new policy taking shape. The Pope's crushing victory over Venice was, in fact, his first failure, and it confounded him. He realized too late what it cost.

Lombardy in the hands of the French, Venetia in those of the Emperor, Naples and the Mezzogiorno in those of Spain; of Italy there remained only Rome, Florence, Romagna, Bologna, Urbino, Mantua, and Ferrara. When the Allies forsook his campaign, he cursed his rashness. For the futile satisfaction of a parochial hatred, he had squandered his patriotic patrimony and plunged Italy deeper into foreign bondage; but he was not too proud to admit his mistake. "If your country did not exist," he said to the Venetian envoy, "we should have to create it." But it was not too late: he would re-create what he had ruined. He recoiled and reversed himself. Never, since his bargain with the Borgias, had he reproached himself more bitterly or repented more robustly; and out of his mortification he rose with a new vision. The scales fell from his eyes, the veil rose, and he saw the full scope and the goal of his destiny. All his hatreds died and were reborn in a new one—a great patriotic purpose, the last dream of his deepest animosity—the expulsion of the barbarians and the emancipation of Italy. He made secret overtures to Venice; they were declined, but he persisted. He would not take no, he was inspired, his purpose lent him magnetism, and for the first time glamour in his own eyes; his only regret was that for the moment he must conceal it. When he learned of the capture of the Marquis, he flung his cap on the floor and cursed St. Peter; and to Isabella's appeal he replied with a word which cost him an agony to utter—Patience.

Isabella was risking her husband's liberty on the Pope's new patriotism; and she was not a gambler. Though she recognized that he could do nothing until he had weaned over Venice, patience was a word too mild from so impetuous and headstrong a man. It was like a betrayal. To bind him she knew but one knot—to make him a member of her family. The marriage of his nephew Francescomaria della Rovere and her daughter Eleonora had been celebrated by proxy five years before; the children were past puberty; and the whole value of the marriage was the blood-tie. Accordingly, one misty morning in November, a week after Machiavelli's departure, the bride left Mantua, blessed by Isabella and shepherded by Elizabetta Gonzaga. The journey to Urbino was rigorous: bad roads, bad weather, swollen streams forded with many mishaps—and the Dowager Duchess was gouty; but she was indefatigable. She loved her brother, she loved Isabella, she loved the bride, and she was leading, not a nuptial progress, but a family campaign; and with responsibility her temper became commanding. At Urbino, Francescomaria met them with music and they made a state entry which pleased him so much that he insisted on repeating it; but she lost her temper and bade him behave "like a Christian and not like a Turk," and after some words under cover of the drum and the fife, he yielded. There was no time for ceremonies. The marriage was immediately consummated.

Then Elizabetta faltered. The bridal night was an ordeal for her. The joy she had invoked so long had come and she was greedy for it. Her niece renewed her own youth in Urbino; and the memory of those years, so impotent and unlived, filled her night with ambiguous heartburnings. In the morning the Mantuan ambassador met her leaving, long before he reached the bridal chamber. "God be praised," she said, "all is well." He had himself risen early, but, though he had been "nosing about like a foxhound," it was from Elizabetta that he heard and through her eyes that he saw the scene on which they both dilated. "She told me," he reported to Isabella, "how she went to the room and rapped on the door and said:—Well, well, it is time to be up! They were alone in the room and in bed, and the Signor Duca was obliged to rise and open the door; and he rose stark naked, forgetting his shirt, and suddenly flung back to bed. The poor little bride was deep in the bedclothes, and the Duchess said:—Where is the bride? The Duke said:—Here she is, see! and uncovered her; and she was shamefaced and tried to cover herself as she could; and the Duchess said to her:—Daughter, is this a proper thing, to sleep with men? And she answered:—No, Madonna, but Your Excellency bade me do it. And the Signor Duca said:—Go now, God bless you, we want to sleep. And the Duchess left, and the Duke rose and bolted the door; and so they have begun life together, and a good life, without impediment of any sort." The maternal lubricity of Elizabetta was the last pang and the first joy of her widowhood. Nature overcame her. How could she hurry that idyll? how could she strain the ties which were knitting for a lifetime? She gave them a month and then, with the young couple in tow, she set out for Rome to besiege the Pope.

For a month Isabella had been waiting impatiently; and she grew yet more restless when the letters from Rome spoke of nothing but banquets, plays, bull-fights, and races, and the compliments the Pope paid the bride on her elaborate trousseau and the magnificent taste of her mother. That elaborate trousseau had been a folly, and Isabella had thought it unfeeling of her daughter to accept it, with her father in prison and the treasury impoverished; there had been a little coolness between them; and she was obliged now to remind Eleonora that she was not in Rome to exhibit her clothes. The little bride braced herself and mentioned her father; the Pope put her off kindly, bidding her have patience.

Isabella had been long-suffering, she appealed to Elizabetta, who prompted Francescomaria, and the young Duke, taking advantage of his uncle's good humour one day at the races, when the Gonzaga horses came in with flying colours, broached the subject. The Pope's patience was exhausted. Under an intolerable strain himself, he was goaded by an importunancy which he could not, and which he longed, to satisfy. He was beside himself. He did not curse; he did not complain; he did not expostulate; he did something far more terrible. He hunched his shoulders and, his ashen face tense, asked his nephew if "he meant to play the part of a Valentino!" Francescomaria knew what that meant—he had touched the nerve—and he said no more.

The suspicion of nepotism was, in fact, sufficient to excite all the contradiction and confusion in the Pope's mind: it was the one thing against which he was perpetually on guard. He would hear no more of the Marquis, and Isabella suddenly realized that, in counting on the Pope's family feeling, she had entirely miscalculated. This was a serious error, for her own life was wholly inspired by family loyalty. It was not merely for her husband that she was alarmed: the rebuff was a challenge to all that she felt and believed. If blood-ties were not binding, what bonds were? She was offended as a woman; she was goaded by the unfeeling denial of Julius, because it was so masculine. Already she scented her eternal enemy. She appealed again to the King of France and the Emperor, but only to receive a new shock. Both offered their good offices but, in view of the uncertainty of the international situation, they demanded, as a guarantee of the loyalty of the Marquis, the surrender of his son. His son? Her son! Federico was hers: he was ten years old. The suggestion left her speechless with indignation; she dropped all negotiations; and, when the Emperor repeated his proposal, she instructed her agent to communicate her sentiments to him. "As for the demand for our dearest first-born son, Federico, besides being a cruel and almost inhuman thing for anyone who knows what a mother's love means, it is impossible for many reasons. Although we have no doubt that he would be well cared for and protected by His Majesty, how could we risk him, at his tender and delicate age, on so long and difficult a journey? You must understand what a solace and comfort, in his father's unfortunate situation, we find in the presence of this beloved son, the hope and the joy of all our subjects. To take him away would be to deprive us of life itself, of everything we value. If you take Federico, you might as well take our life and state as well; so that you may reply plainly and finally that we will suffer any loss rather than lose him; and this is our deliberate and unchanging resolution."

Adamantine, she recoiled, and, inflexible, she appealed once more to the Pope. His prospects, in the meantime, had improved. Venice was about to make terms with him. He approached the Republic on behalf of the Marquis; but the Republic demanded, as a guarantee of the loyalty of the father the surrender of the son. There was no alternative, unless she chose to surrender him to the Pope: to that His Holiness thought that he might bring his ally to agree. She recoiled again, aghast. She cast about her desperately in every direction; and in every direction she saw the same enemy multitudinously leagued against her. The Pope, whom she mistrusted; the Emperor, whom she abhorred; the King of France, whom she suspected; the Venetians, whom she dreaded —all were obdurate variations of the abominable species, man. It was a conspiracy. By what irony had she been called *la prima donna del mondo?* The world had promoted only to ruin her. She retreated into her Grotto, as she named her museum, but she found no comfort there. Her Grotto was merely the lair of a female now. A siren, her friends called her; but, if she was one, she was stranded. Lies, lies, the world, like Mantua, was full of lies, lying ambitions, blind delusions, false greeds, fallacious lusts and senseless schemes of men; and there was only one truth, so clear that only a woman could recognize it. And hugging her son, who had her eyes, her hair, her humanity, she shrank into herself and at last saw her destiny.

32

She was Isabella d'Este. What that name meant she was the last to realize; but it dawned on her now. For years she had been unconsciously creating her destiny. From the beginning her domestic life had been a struggle, though a muted one. She had tamed her husband. Francesco Gonzaga was man in the raw; there was nothing else the matter with him; but that was enough. He was a virile nonentity, with the normal attributes of the male. His animal coarseness, his primitive vanity, his complete unawareness of himself, were a perpetual provocation to the civilized woman he had married. She understood him now; but once she had loved him. When she came as a bride from Ferrara, she was not yet civilized. During her first confinement, however, she discovered that he was carrying on an intrigue with one of her women. Leaping from bed, she caught the creature by the hair and haled her up and down; for the first time in her life she indulged in a scene of primitive jealousy, and it was the last. Her pride asserted itself. She withdrew into a life of her own—a life of fastidious feminine sophistication. Collecting books and pictures, corresponding with crowned heads and literary celebrities, cultivating the humanities, she became one of the most brilliant women of her time. Though the Marquis was impervious to culture himself, he was impressed by her prestige when he discovered that it had a political value. Her celebrity assured him a consideration which he needed in his diplomatic dealings. Since the days of Fornovo his reputation steadily declined, his military engagements grew fewer and their results more unfortunate; but his consort was a loyal helpmate. Her influence, her charm, her social diplomacy recovered what he lost. She made herself indispensable to him: she thought for him, eased his burdens, repaired his blunders; and, when she had quietly effaced him, she loved him for his need of her. She forgave his infidelities: they had made her the first lady of her time.

As her vigour grew, his languished. He was the parasitic partner. Isabella, everyone told him—and he believed everything that he was told—was a brilliant woman; but how brilliant she was he never knew. In his own eyes he remained the Victor of Fornovo and never suspected that she had eclipsed him. The amicable misunderstanding essential to marriage was firmly established. They lived their separate lives side by side; he occupied his wing of the Castello, and rarely intruded on hers. As his periods of inactivity grew longer, he became more and more domesticated. The *morbo gallico* which he brought home from the wars, and which broke out recurrently, impeded his pursuit of sport; he had no other resources, time hung heavy on his hands, and he would sit for hours, lonely and morose, with his pets, by the fire. He did not understand what had happened to him. Visitors were glad to escape from his company to that of Madama, and when they returned they found him where they left him, surrounded by falcons and hounds and buffoons; and all—the hooded hawks, the dozing dogs, the silent freaks, and the stranded man—staring into the fire in a mute Areopagus of boredom, and dreaming together a unanimous animal dream.

Meanwhile, in Madama's apartments, an animated life went on. The apartments were small, like the cells of a hive; and similarly they seemed to be wrought of the substance of their occupant. Isabella had lavished her wealth, her taste, her dreams, and her philosophy on her chambers. The walls were elaborate with alabaster, the vaults were florid with allegories; and everywhere, above and about and below, peeped one or another of her mottoes—a musical staff or a pack of playing cards or the cryptic numeral XXVII. These symbols were a part of the charm of the rooms; they were like the fond repetition by a lover of the beloved name; they were worked into the walls by a woman enamoured of her own meaning. And it was simple. These rooms were her whole world, and she made them a universe after her own heart, snug, bright, regular, and beautiful; permeated in every part by her lifelong aspiration toward that ideal of triumphant harmony lurking overhead in the cryptic numeral XXVII—*vinte-sette*—the sects overcome. In that play on words, for a moment, like a somnambulistic musician, she seemed to play on the world. But her eyes were open and she prolonged the moment expertly. Here, in her close *camerini*, the loud discord of the world was hushed, and a harmony which it never knew awaited the visitor. Amid stucco and marble and music and meditation and congenial company, she was never bored. It was true that, with the culture, celebrity, and curiosity of a cosmopolite, she led the life of a provincial. She longed to travel, but the radius of her journeys was small—Venice, Milan, the Lakes. But the world came to her. Everyone of account eventually found his way to her *camerini*. In the depths of her Grotto, she presided, a middle-aged vigorous siren, courted by visitors who came from everywhere, who went everywhere, and who carried her fame wherever they went. And where her fame went her influence followed. With correspondents in all the Courts of Italy, she was in constant contact with the movement of the great world. Its echoes lingered in her little one, like the hum of the main in a sea-shell. She assembled its drift, diligently sorting and storing whatever was of value to herself. And everything novel—whether a new fashion or a New World, a new antique or a new diplomatic intrigue—was of value, for everything fresh nourished her curiosity, her zest of life, her youth.

To youth she clung, not so much with coquetry as with conviction. It was the age of innocence. At least, it seemed so in retrospect and she determined to perpetuate it. She did not indulge in dreams, she was practical, and laboured actively for her ideal. In this design she hired artists as her collaborators. Art was a chastened life; but artists, after all, were men, and she found them intractable and difficult to inspire. So few understood her. When she commissioned a picture, it was to illustrate her faith, and she was partial to allegories of an edifying nature. Invariably she selected the subject, described the composition, specified the measurements, and was surprised when the result disappointed her. She employed the best masters; and the better they obeyed her, the less they succeeded. Perugino, under her dictation, produced his worst potboiler; Bellini, after pondering her ideas for a year, decided that they were unpaintable, and threw up his commission. Only one master satisfied her—Mantegna—but he was her Court painter and enjoyed the advantage of her intimacy. His *Revels on Parnassus*, with Minerva leading the measure and Vulcan cowering in a corner, delighted her in its bleak jocundity; it almost atoned for the wretched failure which Perugino made of *The Triumph of Virtue over the Vices*.

But the allegory of all allegories was herself, and her portraits were the test. They were in great demand, and when she sent them to her friends, it was with the explanation that they did her scant justice. Not that she was vain; but no artist ever saw her as she saw herself. Her best likeness was by Francia, who painted it, with apologies and a compass, from her suggestions, a working copy, and the advice of her friends; he never laid eyes on her. The others, ah . . . the others who worked from life made what they pleased of her. Leonardo lent her his glamour. In his noble drawing of the young Isabella, the fleeting crayon, in its light adumbrations, evoked her in a vague aura of pensive composure and almost transformed her into one of his mysterious women—almost, but not quite. Her spirit was too positive. Sitting with folded hands, serene, without an afterthought, there was a hint of complacency in her poise. But she was not complacent. And Titian, who painted her in maturity, saw her as a magnificent, matter-of-fact matron with great staring eyes, a virtuous complexion, and an air of competent queenliness; he too was dazzled by her apparent aplomb. But they were all misled.

There was a good reason why she could not be complacent: she was not self-confident; she was a woman in a man's world, and she could not harden herself to its brutality. Though she had tamed her husband, though she had built an alabaster domicile, though she was surrounded by the sublimated life of art, she was not immune to the treacherous blows which life still dealt her, through all her frail defences. The most recent of these had been the most cruel, and it had roused her. A fratricidal feud had broken out among her brothers in Ferrara. Inflamed by a woman, one brother had blinded another; the victim had appealed to a third and, failing to obtain redress, had conspired against him; and the latter—Alfonso—had executed the conspirator and imprisoned his accomplice, a half-brother, for life. This tragedy shook her faith in the basic sanctity of the blood-tie. It was from such defeats that she retreated into her *camerini* and her studied composure; but her equanimity was cultivated; and in her inmost sanctuary she was haunted by the helplessness of women. After that tragedy, however, she faced life with a deeper faith in the secret trust of women to maintain humanity among men; and she added to her walls one more motto, which expressed the cheerless wisdom with which she now surveyed the world: *Nec spe nec metu . . . without hope and without fear.*

Against that world she had one weapon. Like simpler women—for she was neither a bluestocking nor a wallflower—she found her real strength in her children. She was more partial to the sons than the daughters—their future was of more moment. She controlled their education closely, particularly that of Federico, whom she had to dispute with her husband. Though the Marquis grumbled, threatening to take the boy over and make a man of him, she waved him aside. She had called this child into being with a classic purpose: she was determined to make him a humane and enlightened prince; he was hers; and she would tolerate no interference. Federico was her living image, with his silken hair, his innocent eyes, his tender and manly nature; and at eight he was already singing Virgilian hexameters at her knee, in a thin, high, childish treble. And now, at his most impressionable age, the world was wresting her one weapon from her. It was Federico or his father: she was expected to choose between a man who appreciated her on hearsay and this child who already divined her instinctively. But the choice had to be made: the world had violated her Grotto; and with an indignant murmur and an aroused rustle the siren rose and emerged to meet its challenge. It was her destiny.

33

She yielded. Weighing her step carefully, she chose the lesser evil and surrendered her son to the Pope; for the more her nimble mind explored it, the more she realized that she could turn the risk to account. In Rome Federico would be removed from the influence of his father; he would complete his education, under the best auspices, at the expense of the Pope. The child was charming. Though she never flirted, she was not above attracting influential men legitimately, through her son. Accordingly, in July 1510, when the Marquis was released from his Venetian prison, the boy left for the Papal Court accompanied by tutors, a majordomo, a lutist, and a provision of sacred relics. The Pope received him kindly and the tutor wrote reassuringly: "His Lordship is lodged in the finest rooms in the Palace, and takes his meals in a most beautiful loggia overlooking the Campagna, which well deserves its name of Belvedere. All day he walks about these halls and the gardens of pines and orange trees, which amuse and delight him beyond measure, but he does not neglect his singing, often sending for his master himself, and he reads the office every day, and will attend to his studies, I am sure, as soon as the teacher arrives." She guided the boy from afar—"you will have every opportunity now of acquiring the experience and knowledge you need in Rome, you can enjoy yourself and at the same time study letters, which are far more important for a prince than a private person"—and she sighed with relief: her intuition had been right. One day the Pope came on the child trying on armour and, shaking his stick at him, cried: "Aha! will you fight me?" Federico burst into peals of delighted laughter and hugged his knees; and they became friends. Her dalliance with the Holy Father had begun; and what she had dreaded as a domestic disaster now appeared to be a political godsend.

But before she could congratulate herself, the situation changed. For a year the Pope had been maturing his offensive against the French; Venice had been won over; everything was ready, when he fell afoul of Ferrara. This state lay between the French and the Pope, and Alfonso d'Este elected a French alliance. The fury of Julius was unbounded and it broke out in a dispute over some revenues due to the Holy See, of which he made a pretext for exacting the allegiance of Ferrara to the Church. No sooner had the Marquis of Mantua been released than the Pope thundered an excommunication against Alfonso d'Este. His armaments were now concentrated on one object: "*Ferrara, t'avro pel corpo di Dio,*"[1] he cried; and his patriotic vision, in narrowing, became intensified. Ferrara was the mote in his eye, the traitor, the backslider, and he saw no further. The old confusion overcame him. He left for Bologna, summoned the Marquis to meet him, made Mantua his base of operations, and sent Francescomaria of Urbino into the field. Francescomaria captured two

---

1 "Ferrara, I shall have you by the body of God."

towns to the south of Ferrara, and the war for the liberation of Italy began.

Suddenly Isabella found herself involved in the far-flung designs of that struggle, with her family divided and embroiled about her. She was devoted to Alfonso, there was an intuitive sympathy between them, and he relied on her to control their relatives in the Papal camp; but her son was in Rome. To save both Federico and her brother appeared, on the face of it, impossible; but, as a woman, she did not recognize the impossible. What she did recognize as a woman was the value of the little things which men overlook or disdain; and trusting to time and her instinct, seizing every opportunity as it arose, following wherever it led, forgetting it when it failed, beginning anew with another, without rational plan but with an unyielding purpose, she began an underhand campaign to retard, to circumvent, and to frustrate the Papal war. She had her friends in the Vatican and she used them to the full; but above all she had the help of women. They recognized her cause as their own and rallied to it, making the protection of her family their common concern; and so well did they work to outwit, to obstruct, to undermine, and to undo the progress of Julius that he had not gone far before he found himself fighting, not the French, not Ferrara, but the covert disloyalty of his captains and the furtive and unflagging intrigues of a league of women.

Naturally, it was among the ladies of her own family that Isabella found her most trusted lieutenants. The two Duchesses of Urbino used their influence with Francescomaria to make his activities in the field as dilatory and ineffectual as possible. But the pivot of the situation was her husband, and to win him over she was forced to accept the assistance of an ally with whom she would have gladly dispensed—Lucrezia Borgia. Her sister-in-law in Ferrara was, for better or worse, a member of her family. Between la Diva Borgia and Francesco Gonzaga there was a sympathy. They were both past their prime and they had both known life; they were a little over-ripe; they met, they melted. It was a sentimental intimacy: Alfonso would have tolerated no other. But his inflammable jealousy never stirred, and Lucrezia, after a lurid past, was too grateful for the peace and respectability she found in Ferrara to risk a scandal. Her one desire was to please, and as she was not very successful with the ladies, she was doubly gratified by the appreciation of the Marquis. Lucrezia was a woman after his own heart, and none of her good points escaped him. She had four charms, not to mention a slight voluptuous cast in one eye. She was vapid, she was virtuous, she smelled of man, and she did not understand art. She had also a fifth. She admired and trusted him. With all the femininity she could command she appealed to all the manhood he could muster. In her company he recovered his faith in the essential rightness of the universe. When Julius launched his excommunication against Alfonso, Lucrezia flowed with distress, and he sympathized. Through a confidant she reminded Francesco Gonzaga of "the love and trust and hope she feels for Your Lordship; she trusts Your Lordship more than any other one person in the world; she commends herself to Your Lordship with her whole heart." This was of no mean moment to Isabella. The womanly weakness which Lucrezia contributed to the campaign was something which she could not supply; and it was essential to it.

Wooed by his sister-in-law, the Marquis made a loyal effort to save his brother-in-law. On reaching Bologna, he did his duty and interceded on behalf of Alfonso with the Pope and, when his efforts as a peacemaker failed, he begged His Holiness to release him from his service. But Julius would take no refusal. With his usual obstinacy and shortsightedness, he forced the reluctant soldier into harness. Venice seconded His Holiness and offered its late captive an engagement, which was at the same time an appeal; for the Doge couched it in flattering terms, promising him immortality for "restoring Italy to her ancient liberty" and urging him to prevent "her perpetual ruin and servitude." But Francesco Gonzaga declined. Then another opinion began to fly through the *calle* of Venice, where the Marquis was dismissed by the populace as a *joto*, a zero, who was ruled by his wife; and to conclude the engagement the Doge wrote directly to Isabella. She advised her husband to evade it, though she urged him to accept the title of Captain of the Church which the Pope pressed on him. He obeyed, and she wrote to Alfonso, reassuring him. Alfonso was a man of punctilious principles and replied in a tone both confidential and caustic: "May the Lord God give him joy of it, but we assure Your Ladyship that if the Signor Marchese had been in our position, nothing in the world would have induced us to accept that dignity, for reasons which *Your Ladyship* will understand. These few words we have thought fit to say for our own satisfaction." It was a thankless role which fell to Francesco Gonzaga; but at least there was Lucrezia. At his age he needed her faith, and for her sake he forgave her husband much. When the Pope offered him secret proof that Alfonso had been more than indifferent to his captivity in Venice, the old soldier did not flinch.

Meanwhile, the campaign was languishing. Francescomaria, after his first successes in the field, had settled down to reflection; and six weeks passed in delays. Then the Pope was informed that a detachment of French troops, on its way to Ferrara, had passed through Mantua. Naturally, there was an explosion, of which the Marquis was the victim; but Isabella supplied an explanation, and her Curial friends closed in and pacified the Pope. His eyes, however, were beginning to open. In Mantua sat Madama, and he needed the state as a base for a flanking movement against Ferrara. A bridge was to be built on the Po; but no bridge could be built until he had come to an understanding with her; and what understanding could they reach? They were fell antagonists, the man and the woman, the patriot and the materfamilias. By an understanding, moreover, he meant a virile argument—coercion. Accordingly, he sent a spy to Mantua to keep one eye on her and the other on the bridge, and in his choice he showed a shrewdness and a malice that were almost feminine. Lodovico da Camposampiero had been a pimp for her husband, and it was safe to assume that the odium he inspired made him immune to her wiles. So far Julius was right. Madama did not molest the informer. He came to Mantua, was frigidly received, learned nothing, and proceeded to the Po; but no sooner was the bridge building than Alfonso raided the Mantuan frontier and destroyed it. The informer began furiously rebuilding, assuring the Pope that such *tricks* would not be repeated under his nose, and promising to make Madama toe the line; but difficulties cropped up at every step—timber, lighters, workmen—there was a shortage of everything. He kept his ear to the ground but his head went round: he heard a story going around that Madama was maligning him behind his back. He hugged his post and protested. "I have heard that Your Excellency is much perturbed and complains of me most abusively," he wrote her, "because I have come to build this bridge." She replied flash for flash. "Messer Vico: whoever has told you that we have abused you lies. We do not hold you of so much account. We have not spoken well of you, because we cannot. We have not spoken ill of you, because it is not our nature to do so. We wish to have nothing to do with you." He put his hands to his ears and kept a sharp watch, and at last he was rewarded. One day Isabella started from Mantua to keep an appointment with her brother, Cardinal d'Este, but the Court and the townspeople, catching wind of her departure and mistaking it for a flight, prevented her. She did not quite know what to make of this incident, but she decided to be flattered by it—"I know that it comes of the love and affection they bear me," she wrote to Alfonso—and she made light of it. Vico saw his opportunity and exaggerated it to the Pope, and the Marquis reported to His Holiness for another lecture; but he bore it patiently and accepted without complaint Isabella's version of the affair. Exulting over "the disappointment of a certain person on the Po, who wrote to the Pope and not to the Marquis, who learned of it first in this way," she was now consumed by a desire to read Vico's incriminating version of the incident and persuaded the Bishop of Ivrea to purloin and bring it to her, at the risk of his life. Apparently it sealed her opinion of its author, for she locked it in her desk and nine years later produced it to ruin him.

Two months had passed, nothing had been accomplished, and already her tactics were rewarded. A French army was advancing on Bologna. For a moment the Pope was panic-stricken and threatened to take poison rather than be captured; but the population of Bologna rallied under his windows, shouting *Julio, Julio*, and the French commander paused, ostensibly waiting for artillery but, in reality, reluctant—as he later admitted—to attack the Vicar of Christ. He had not been long in Italy. The shock, however, was too much for the old man's strength and he collapsed. Isabella was elated. He would not live out the month, she wrote to her brother in cipher. A month, a little month, a woman's month, and all would be normal once more. Nor did these forecasts seem over-sanguine. The Pope disregarded the doctors' orders, consumed quantities of wine and plums, and threatened to hang his servants if they informed on him; and while he lay sick the faint campaign came to a complete halt. He did everything to recuperate except what the physicians suggested. He sent for the Marquis, exhorted him to stand no longer "with one foot in each camp," and gave him his marching orders. The Marquis carried them to Isabella's cronies, the Archdeacon Gabbionetta and the Bishop of Ivrea, who advised the only possible course under the circumstances—a renewed spell of the *mal francese*. He obeyed and took to his bed. On learning of this inopportune attack, the Pope, who suffered from syphilis himself, was immediately sympathetic and sent Gabbionetta to the patient with a friendly message, urging him above all to avoid "the therapeutics of salves." *Non valevano un bel nullo*, said His Holiness: they were not worth a tinker's damn. Then he fell into a reverie and suddenly cursed himself. "By God, the Marquis is kin-sick," he exclaimed; and for that he knew but one remedy—to recover. He promptly did so, and the Marquis, in delirium, was carried to Mantua. The doctors were bewildered.

But it was now the end of November, the fighting season was almost over, and the Pope, though he was on his feet, was far from well. Nevertheless, when he went to his window and looked across the square, he was confronted and challenged by his colossal image in bronze, towering before the Duomo of Bologna. The mighty imagination of Michelangelo invigorated him; glaring at himself, larger than life and with his hand upraised in menace, he sloughed off the feeble snares and impediments of his puny antagonists and felt his pulse. Too much had been spent, both in money and energy, too many preparations made, too little accomplished, to return to Rome with nothing to show for his overweening Italian dream. Before winter set in, something had to be done, and he insisted on advancing. To satisfy and distract him, his advisers suggested an attack on the little town of Mirandola, lying in a strategic position between Ferrara and the French lines, ten miles north of Bologna. This involved the jeopardy of one of Madama's allies, the Countess of Mirandola, but she was a gallant lady and cheerfully risked the assault. The French sent her a company of picked men whom the Chevalier Bayard, in his final inspection, fired with the right spirit. "*Mes enfants, vous allez au service des dames, montrez-vous gentils compagnons pour acquérir leurs grâces, et faites parler de vous!*"[1] The Marquis having finally retired, Julius now appointed his nephew Francescomaria to the supreme command, despite the warning of one of his spies that the malady from which the Marquis suffered was catching. He persisted. Family for family, he was willing to pit the blood of the della Rovere against all comers, Este or Gonzaga or Montefeltre. Francescomaria reached Mirandola and dug ditches. After a month his uncle could stand it no longer—"he has continual fevers," wrote Isabella to her brother, "but with his iron constitution he resists and makes life miserable for others and himself"—and he determined to leave for Mirandola and direct the siege himself.

On a bleak January morning he set out with a train of reluctant Cardinals. The great pall of winter lay over the landscape, and as they advanced they were lost in a blizzard, in the thick of which they missed the road and an ambush which the French had laid for them. When Julius burst on the camp the next morning, pink-eyed, hoary, and discharging like the draughty sky packets of gusts in every direction, everyone trembled and no one escaped: least of all the Duke of Urbino. "That ninny of a Duke," as his uncle called him, was ordered on the carpet and lectured like a schoolboy; and when he opened his mouth the old man, raising his voice with the blast and vying with its infinite vowelling in his fury, cried, "Enough, enough, enough," until he deafened himself and broke off abruptly, "Enough of the past, I want action." Even with his driving presence, however, it was ten days before the guns barked. But the difficulties were real ones: there was no slacking. He was everywhere, looming through the driving sleet like a lumbering bear, wading through the trenches,

---

[1] "My lads, you are serving the ladies, mind your manners, gain their favour, and see to it that you are talked of."

inspecting the batteries, rectifying the aim of the guns, heartening the men, promising them pillage, and drinking with them by the camp-fires. With them he was popular, but the officers found him always under foot. They begged him not to expose himself, but he insisted on moving up to the lines and lodging in a hut under the range of the French guns. "Here I stay until a cannon-ball carries me off," he boasted; and in the night the roof exploded, killing three of his servants. Then at last he consented to retire, hugging the shell which he donated to the shrine of Loreto, and took up his quarters in a ruined convent, where he slept in the kitchen, while the Cardinals made their beds in a stable exposed to the biting winds. But a few days later he was back again in the lines. "Mirandola, Mirandola," he repeated incessantly, loading and reloading the word so regularly that "it was impossible," said an observer, "not to laugh at him." But he compelled admiration also. "Monsignore," said the Venetian envoy to Cardinal Alidosi, "it should be recorded in all the histories of the world that a Pope, lately recovered from a dangerous illness, has come to camp in January, in bitter cold and snow." The Cardinal closed his eyes and agreed. "It is a great thing," he said shortly.

After three weeks Mirandola fell and he was the first to be hoisted, in the buoyant glare of the torches, through the breach. In the morning he was up early, parading the streets and the surrounding country; and this drill was repeated daily, "with the Reverend Cardinals tramping these wretched roads and following him continually." The Duke of Urbino now avoided him and sent his lieutenants for orders. Among these was Castiglione. When his turn came, he was dismissed without urbanity. "You have behaved well," snapped the old man, and sent him about his business; and even Castiglione found the leader of Italy grotesque. But Julius was now fully roused and resolved to push on for Ferrara. He sent for the ambassador of Mantua, to prepare the transportation of the cannon, and announced his imminent visit to Mantua. The ambassador found him in bed and "smelling, in my opinion, not very canonically": the old man was, in fact, extremely unwholesome; and suddenly, amid his musty papers and sour pillows, he fainted. This time the relapse was serious, and when he came to he feebly consented to postpone hostilities to the spring and to retire for the winter to the milder climate of Ravenna.

The winter of 1510 passed peacefully. It was marked by only one event of international importance. The Pope grew a beard. It created considerable speculation. Beginning at Mirandola as a stubble, it grew to a bush in Ravenna, and every eye was rooted on its prodigious development.

ISABELLA D'ESTE, by Titian
From the portrait in the Imperial Museum, Vienna

Like his ambitions, it had a beginning, a middle, and no end. It was "a great ogreish beard," a clump of "terrible hair," and it confounded the beholder. It meant something; but what? Conjecture ran riot, exploring the impenetrable thickets of that ever-ramifying foliage, and was lost in a tangle of confusion. What did it portend? Was it the last brag of the old della Rovere, the final outcropping of his venerable vitality? Or was it the weediness of despair? Was it a bush to brood in? or a beard to brave Isabella? Was it the hirsuteness of Samson snared by Delilah? Was it the bristling of Hercules unmanned by Omphale? Mysteries . . . ! Finally, the Pope set all doubts at rest. It was a consecrated beard. Not till he had driven the French from Italy would he shave.

The relief which this winter brought to Mantua was clouded by a deepening realization of what the struggle was costing. Several towns in Mantuan territory had been raided by the French, despite an understanding which the Marquis had established with them; and, when he complained to the King, Louis cracked the whip, reminding him that "as long as he was Marquis of Mantua he would be esteemed and honoured by everyone, but when he lost his state he would wander the world like a beggar, and find no one to give him bread and everyone to give him a blow." "I am a lost man," Francesco Gonzaga wrote to his brother, "I dare not open my mouth, being in the jaws of these people who overpower me and possess themselves of my property." Under these conditions, when at the conclusion of the campaign of 1509 the King sent him his congratulations, declaring that "he was eternally obliged to him and realized now the importance of the Marquis of Mantua in Italy," Francesco Gonzaga no longer knew where he stood. His only consolation was Lucrezia. The French had been equally overbearing in Ferrara, and she came to Mantua on a visit. She had pawned all her plate to assist Alfonso and at home she was forced to "eat in majolica." In Mantua she learned to paint pottery. It was her compliment to Isabella; and the Marquis repaid it by praising her progress and sitting and forgetting the conundrum of the world and smoothing her hair, as he looked over her shoulder.

Isabella herself was sorely tried by the French. In the course of the winter the Pope returned to Rome, still ailing, grumbling of the Marquis, and hotly threatening Alfonso. The French King, who corresponded with her regularly, assured her that she had nothing to fear from "the hot words of His Holiness, as these are his habit when he is drunk." But he discerned another danger. There was Federico. Louis was worried and thought it his royal duty to warn her that "the Pope often kissed the boy, which displeased him, knowing the Pope to be liverish." This hyperpolitical malice was well calculated to alarm the anxious mother. Had she really risked attracting Julius through her son? Had she forgotten the gossip that Vico supplied him with boys and that Cardinal Alidosi was thought to be his minion? But this danger was part of the complicated intrigue in which she was involved; she could do nothing; and Federico was a valuable pawn. The repugnant suggestion was incredible; she was informed of the life the boy and the Pope led in Rome, and it was what she had always expected. Federico dined with His Holiness; the company knelt, while the Holy Father drank the first draught; then, as the interminable meal proceeded amid a long hum of voices, the boy repeated to him what the day had brought forth. And the day brought forth just what his mother wished. Federico told the Pope, earnestly and proudly, how he had visited the new St. Peter's—and what a fine thing it would be when it was completed, though *that* would not be in the lifetime of *this* Pope—or how he ran after the stags in the little close—and how the Bishop of Ivrea promised to take him again, for he too liked to stretch his legs—or how they both went up to the roof and looked over Rome—or how Raphael of Urbino promised to paint his portrait in the fresco of *The School of Philosophy*. Then, after supper, they would sit and play cards, until the old man began to nod, and all the cards were in the boy's hands. The Pope indeed was outplayed. One day the boy went to the Capitol to see a pageant; the scaffolding broke under the press of spectators; and when the Holy Father saw Federico returning, "he made such holiday," wrote the tutor, "as if life had been restored to him." Though Julius would not admit it and was furious with his own weakness, the hostage had lost all political value for him; while for his parents Federico was now a buffer.

Meanwhile, the peacemakers were at work. The Emperor proposed to summon a meeting of the belligerents at Mantua, and in Rome it was confidently expected that "the women would make peace." The Queen of France, distressed that her consort should be at war with the head of the Church, was working for a truce; and the Pope's daughter interceded with her father. His daughter he sent back to her knitting; to the Emperor he replied that he would talk peace when he had spent a month in Ferrara; and as for the French, there was the beard.

In the spring of 1510 hostilities were resumed. The Papal troops were routed by Alfonso, who performed prodigies of valour, and in congratulating him Isabella confessed that she had had a psychic premonition of victory. But this was only the prelude to a greater triumph. In May the

French launched their long-deferred offensive against Bologna. The army was commanded by a veteran who was not over-awed by the Vicar of Christ, and the assault was completely successful. It was welcomed by the Bolognese, who had been complaining of the rapacity and maladministration of the Papal Governor, Cardinal Alidosi. The Cardinal fled, the population rose, the Bentivoglio returned, and among the spoils Michelangelo's heroic figure of Julius fell to Alfonso d'Este, who broke off the head and made of the trunk a cannon which he nicknamed *La Giulia*.

The Pope was then in Ravenna. He bore the blow with fortitude, but this reverse was followed by others. Francescomaria, who had been in command of the Papal troops, hastened to Ravenna to clear himself and to lay the responsibility for the fall of Bologna on Alidosi, whose unpopularity was the proof of his incompetence. On his heels came Alidosi himself, and the Pope, for once neutral, accepted the explanations of both. With that decision the Cardinal seemed satisfied, and he emerged from his audience smiling; but not so Francescomaria. Infuriated, he fell on the Cardinal and murdered him before the eyes of an approving crowd. "Blessed be the Lord, blessed be the Duke, blessed be this murder," wrote the Papal Master of Ceremonies, voicing the general sentiment, for Alidosi was universally execrated. There was only one dissenting voice. In an agony of grief and rage Julius swore to have the assassin tortured on the spot, but his nephew had already fled, and two hours later, in a closed litter, hiding his tear-drenched face, the Pope left for Rome. He was nearer to defeat than ever before; everything was forgotten—Bologna, the French, Ferrara—and his consuming thought was to avenge his favourite. One defeat he was resolved not to suffer—the moral reverse of condoning the crime. The old wound reopened, the dead rose, the execrable similarity of his situation to that of Alexander and Caesar haunted him, and he felt the old Borgia challenging him to do better. The rain fell in torrents; the journey by ox-cart was slow; and he clung to his litter, hiding his head, hugging his pillow, and vowing not to sink into that quagmire of criminal indulgence. When he entered Rome he mounted a horse; but under the heavy Tiara and the damp sacerdotal garments he was seen to be singularly bowed.

For many weeks this tragedy eclipsed all questions of politics and war. The women were confronted by a new problem and used all their resources to obtain an acquittal for Francescomaria. Elizabetta appealed to Isabella, who did what she could, but what could she do? "We can do little anywhere and least of all in Rome," she explained. "If we were able to help him, we should do so willingly, but Your Ladyship knows that we have little credit at Court." Her concern for her son-in-law was so cool as to be almost perfunctory. She seemed to have forgotten all her Curial friends. But Alidosi had been one of them, and he had served her well. Yet, after all, he was dead, and, as a woman, she had no choice but to be on the side of life. She wrote conscientiously to her sister, Lucrezia Bentivoglio, to collect evidence in Bologna of the late Cardinal's malpractices, and to her son Federico in Rome to plead with the Pope and the College. She did her duty, but she did it without warmth. Francescomaria had served her well, but his violence shocked her, and his neutrality in the Papal war filled her, even while she profited by it, with contempt for the weakness of men.

Julius was deaf to the pleas of family affection: he had suffered too much from it. But Francescomaria was confident. He came to Rome, surrendered himself to the jurisdiction of the Sacred College, and lived, a nominal prisoner, in the palace of one of its members, where he was visited daily and received Roman encouragement. "I cannot convince myself that so just an act should bring me to grief, even though the Holy Father speaks of proceeding against me," he wrote to Mantua. In the Sacred College sentiment was overwhelmingly in his favour: Cardinal di San Giorgio made an impassioned appeal, and another of his friends, Cardinal de' Medici, was appointed President of the Commission created to try his case. A voluminous dossier was prepared, blackening the character of Alidosi: it would take three years to plough through it, the accused confidently declared. Confronted by this universal and damning detestation of his late favourite, Julius found himself alone in upholding the ends of impartial justice. Principles unsupported by passion had never been binding on his nature, and he lacked the vindictiveness to be unbending. He was sick and he fled. He fled to the country to gather confidence from the earth, and pushed back to his origins and the basic elements which steadied his judgment because they underlay his whole life—the soil and the sea. At the Papal lodge of La Magliana, near Ostia, he hunted and fished and tried to forget. Observers agreed that he made a brave effort. "The airs from that quarter are bad, for the sea winds reign there for ever, but His Holiness fears nothing and breasts the breezes, bare-headed." Gradually, day by day, the winds carried away everything—the brief breath of justice, the fleeting crimes of inconsequential nephews—but the winds swept away his health too. The humid gales, an immoderate diet, and the repeated shocks of the last few months brought on another collapse; and he was transported to Rome, a dying man, against the wind. His strength ebbed rapidly, and the waiting hands of women felt for his weakening will. His daughter plied him continually, extorted a promise of pardon; but he was too weak to give it effect. The end seemed so near that the Cardinals sent out couriers announcing it, and the curious began to crowd into the Vatican. They found it already despoiled and half-empty, and they wandered unchallenged, trespassing where they pleased, though they respected the sickroom. There the Pope lay with a couple of flasks and two other friends by his bedside, a Jewish physician, and little Federico, who fed him broth and medicines. When the Cardinals came to pay their respects to the corpse, they found it blinking cheerfully. The windows were open, the servants were bringing in strawberries, and the physician was holding up to the light a flask of curative Malmsey, which suffused his face with a sanguine glow and the death-chamber with sacramental radiance. The Pope improved steadily. One day Federico asked permission to introduce Francescomaria who wished to kiss the feet of His Holiness. The old man refused; but several days later he summoned the College to his bedside and absolved the Duke of Urbino "not by process of justice, as he first proposed, for that would be too lengthy, but by Apostolic grace."

These events consumed the winter and spring of 1511. The convalescence of the Pope was longer than usual, for he was morally as well as physically shaken. The women had subdued his conscience, but he reacted vigorously and put a broader distance between their aims and his. When he resumed his plans, he neglected Ferrara, firmly resolved to keep his eyes on the greater object—the expulsion of the barbarians. His two campaigns against Alfonso had taught him the futility of antagonizing family loyalty: it was the one moral tie to which his countrymen instinctively responded. He must work with it, not against it: that much was clear; but it was equally clear that he could not rely on the patriotism of the Italians: that sentiment had yet to be created. Thus it was that when, in October 1511, he proclaimed the Holy League, in which Spain joined the Holy See and Venice for the expulsion of the French, the Pope was forced to fall back on the foreigner to emancipate Italy. The one independent power in the peninsula, Florence, elected to remain neutral.

Such was the triumph which, out of the little stream of obstacles which she had set flowing, Isabella had achieved—an anti-foreign movement supported by foreign arms. In the struggle that ensued she and her kin— and the circle to which she was related by blood, marriage, influence, or charm, was a wide and ever-growing one—found themselves on the French side. As usual, her husband suffered. Baglioni, the ex-tyrant of Perugia, who had taken service with the Pope, wrote to his brother-in-arms: "It seems too shameful that Italian valour and blood should yield to every demand of these barbarians, who are our capital enemies," and harping on Gonzaga's own experience with the French he continued: "I implore Your Excellency, since you were once the foremost in arms, to rouse yourself and, by your virtue and spirit, show your face openly against these Frenchmen in behalf of Holy Church and the Illustrious Republic of Venice, as you are in duty bound to do; and you have an obligation even greater to Italy, whose name and honour you bear, and which looks for aid and comfort in its liberation mainly to Your Excellency." But the appeal was fruitless; and even Vico da Camposampiero permitted himself to be insolent. He defended the Marquis to his face: "Your Excellency is one of those who least allows himself to be governed by women, and you treat Madama Illustrissima better than any queen or duchess that we have had in Italy for a long time," he wrote, "but you let her attend to her own affairs, and in matters of state you know how to act without feminine counsels."

Hostilities began in the autumn of 1511. The conflict had now entered a broader phase, and it was marked by a warfare more sanguinary than the peninsula had yet known. The sack of Brescia by the French (February 1512) recalled the Apocalyptic terrors which Savonarola had predicted twenty-seven years before. Isabella was moved by it but she kept her head. "About ten thousand people have been slaughtered," she wrote to Alfonso. "Those who have escaped from the tempest and who arrive here do not know whether they are alive or dead. Suffice it to say that the whole city is running with blood; it is pitiful." She added, however: "I feel great compassion for the misery of this wealthy city, but I am glad that it will be an example to others to keep faith and fear the power of France, which will help to insure the quiet of Your Excellency." Three years of commerce with war, politics, and men had hardened her to the inevitable, and there was a faint trace of sandy aridity about the siren. She was herself in close communication with the French commander, Gaston de Foix, and, while the shock of nations ebbed and flowed about her, she enjoyed a brief respite to her anxieties. But not for long. In April 1512, the national struggle culminated in the battle of Ravenna, which broke the power of the French in Italy. They fell back on Milan, lost it, crossed the Alps, and of their dominions retained only Brescia, the Castello of

Milan, and the Castle and Lighthouse of Genoa, as landmarks of what had once been.

At long last Julius had triumphed, and his victory exceeded even his dreams; yet even now the great aim of Isabella's procrastinations was won: he was morally exhausted. The old intractable will yielded: the energy of hatred, satisfied on so much grander a scale, unbent, and he was willing to discuss terms with Ferrara. At first, it was true, the name of Alfonso could not be mentioned; he threatened to exterminate him with Lucrezia and their children; but, as Gabbionetta wrote, "the nature of Our Lord may sometimes seem hard, but anyone who considers his actions will always find his mind inclined to what is good, and in the end he proves a most clement prince. He is incapable of anything mean and whoever says the contrary is ill informed." Whatever fury remained was the fury of joy. It was unbounded. On the morning when he received the news that the French had lost Cremona, Federico and the Mantuan ambassador were admitted to his bedside, and the little lad was the only sedate person in the room. "He had us enter and open the windows," the ambassador wrote, "and, leaping from bed in his shirt, read the letters aloud and began to strut and crow, crying *Julio* and *Chiesa*, and singing—the most extraordinary thing I have ever seen. All day he has done nothing but laugh and jest; he seems beside himself, and such is the exuberance of His Holiness that anyone who purposes to speak to him henceforth should, I think, arm himself beforehand with a stout weapon." In this boisterous good humour he suggested that Isabella should be the intermediary in his negotiations with Alfonso. It was a merited recognition of his real antagonist.

But his mood was too boisterous for that brave lady. To the surprise of her friends, who urged her to come to Rome, she declined. In vain they reminded her of the many opportunities she was missing—"such a splendid opportunity to see Rome, and to accommodate the affairs of your brother, for truly your presence is most necessary to the interests of the Signor Duca Alfonso and would have been of great honour to Your Excellency and would have added to your fame, and then, when the interests of your brother had been settled, you would have taken your son and heir home." But she was overcome by humility. "We are sorry to have missed this opportunity to see Rome," she replied, "but we should not have presumed to think our presence so useful to the Signor Duca." With an exquisite sense of her own limitations, she realized that whatever she might do in Rome would be much better done by Federico. To Federico, accordingly, was committed the care of his uncle of Ferrara and the first introduction of Alfonso to the Holy Father.

On his side Julius entered into this domestic spirit and promised to receive Alfonso *en famille*. "He wishes to lodge him in the Palace in the Jewel Chamber," the ambassador wrote to Mantua, "and to have him eat with Signor Federico, to whom he will give enough money for the steward, so that no one may say, in case the Duke falls ill, that he has been foully fed; and he wants him to sleep in the bed and the sheets of Signor Federico." Alfonso was not altogether reassured by these arrangements, however, and hesitated to leave Ferrara. A domestic reception was not necessarily a cordial reception; and there was at least one grievance, which Julius was nursing, and which would require explanation—the destruction of Michelangelo's heroic statue. Not being a man of much invention, Alfonso denied it, offered to pay for another statue, and awaited the result. The Mantuan ambassador reassured him. "As for the statue, it is wellnigh impossible to get it out of his head that a cannon was not made of it and named *La Giuliana*; but when I told him that the Signor Duca proposed to make a figure and set it up in the piazza, we understood each other, and His Holiness began to laugh heartily."

Alfonso came to Rome diffidently. A thick-set man, with aristocratic, hawk-like features broadened but unblurred by age, he moved heavily with an aquiline sense of his dignity, and he determined to be careful. He did not lack courage, but the legend of Julius oppressed him. Slipping into the city late at night, he notified his nephew of his arrival. In the morning Federico was up betimes, smoothing the way. "As soon as Our Lord was awake, Signor Federico did his duty with all the grace and gentleness in the world. His Holiness replied, touching him under the chin and stroking his head and playing with him: 'We wish you to go to the Signor Duca and visit and encourage him in our name to come confidently and to make up his mind to want what we want.'" The first formal meeting passed off easily, and Alfonso moved through a ceremony of submission with corpulent docility. But he could not make up his mind, when the terms of peace were discussed, to want what the Pope wanted. There were hitches and snarls, and, as the negotiations dragged on, the Duke became uneasy. His nephew did what he could to distract him. Together they explored the glories of the Vatican. Where the boy entered freely, Alfonso followed with awe, and nothing could induce him to enter, even on tiptoe, the private apartments of the Pope. He was willing, however, to visit the Sistine Chapel where Michelangelo, flat on his back, was

FEDERICO GONZAGA, by Francia
From the portrait in the Metropolitan Museum, New York City

spinning his substance on to the vault. He climbed the scaffolding, saw with his eyes and touched with his hands the stupendous population of prophets and sybils with continental limbs, with latitudinous laps, swelling about him colossal and similar to the statue of Julius, and of which he would never make cannon. On the right floated the Almighty, on the left Noah rolled drunken, and both bore the lineaments of Julius: the presence, the power, the inspiration of his enemy, multiplied and magnified by a transfiguring imagination into innumerable, overpowering, and superhuman forms, haunted him; and on taking his leave he hoped that Michelangelo would favour him with "a small picture" from his hand. Imagination, working in his literal mind, took a literal form, and he became daily more restless and nervous. At last, apprehending he knew not what danger, he fled; for six weeks he disappeared completely; and, when he returned to Ferrara, he had no reasonable explanation to offer for his conduct.

Meanwhile, a Peace Congress had been called in Mantua to settle the international situation, and to this body Alfonso referred his treaty with the Pope. It was attended by the representatives of Spain, of the Emperor, and of the Venetian and Florentine Republics. The Holy See was represented only by an observer. Julius resented a Congress which shifted the political focus to Mantua, which settled the destinies of Italy at the dictation of the foreigner, and which robbed him of his patriotic triumph. The power of the French was now replaced by the pressure of the Spanish and the pretensions of the Emperor: the morning was dawning, cold and grey, amid the waning celebrations of a hollow victory. There was a bitter taste in his mouth. Unable to oppose and unwilling to approve the Congress, he vented his irritation on the Mantuan ambassador. Their interviews degenerated into wrangles, into shouting matches, and barely fell short of physical assault. Julius upbraided the Marquis, called him his worst enemy, and threatened Federico. "We shall not send his son home," he shouted one day, lurching about in his chair. "No! We shall send him to the Torricella in Venice where his father was, if he is not careful. I intended to make him the first man in Italy, and he thinks only of doing me every injury in the world." Then he paused abruptly, aghast at his own threat, and continued, breathing quickly and shortly: "No, I cannot have any harm come to Signor Federico. I have reared him, I will not have him a part of this. . . ." And, blinking at the ambassador, he added lamely: "If it had not been for his son, I would have made him suffer for the wrongs he has done me in the past." Noting the

Pope's mood, the ambassador pumped this vein, asking His Holiness if he meant to reward the Marquis by sending his son to captivity; whereupon he brought up a gush of confusion. "I love him too much, too much," the old man gasped, and heaved a long sigh. He was lost. The women had won, and his one dread was the necessity, now that Italy was at peace, of parting with Federico. That evening, after supper, they went to Sant' Angelo to see the artillery. Counting the days until he would be alone, Julius walked slowly, and when they arrived, "he showed him the cannon, one by one, and told him their names: one was the Bull, another the Lion, another the Wolf, another the Dog. Then he showed him a fine piece which he wished to test and said:—Signor Federico, we shall fire this one now, so that you may see it and tell your father that you have seen something he has not seen." The cannon barked, the harmless smoke drifted through the mild evening air, and the boy who was not yet a man and the old man who was once more a child walked home hand in hand.

If Julius in his triumph was baffled, Isabella in her defeat was undeterred. It was not a defeat; she persisted; she went on, a woman, for ever. In Mantua, where the destinies of Italy were to be settled, she entertained the Congress. The *prima donna del mondo* was once more in her element. The world, the great world, was flocking about her in overwhelming numbers. Mantua, its streets crowded with soldiers, clerics, and diplomats, resembled a miniature Rome. The Palace was too small to accommodate all her influential guests, and it required all her tact to decide whom to lodge in the suite of honour on the first floor—Spain or the Emperor. She solved the problem of precedence by a process of rotation, which was her comment on history. The first to arrive was the Imperial delegate, Mathias Lang, the Bishop of Gurk, huge, blond, handsome, and boorish, who made himself unpopular by his overbearing manners. So pleased was he with his rooms that he refused to leave them for three days, holding his Court and receiving his hosts there. When, however, he consented on the third day to make a public appearance, Isabella was waiting for him with a battalion of ladies, recruited from every corner of the province. With this "army of women" he chatted for two hours; the following evening he met them for dinner, presiding at a long table, packed with provincial beauties; and the next day he moved out, and the Spanish Viceroy, Don Ramon de Cardona, moved in. The Spaniards presented another problem with their punctiliousness and their light fingers. Don Ramon and his gentlemen lost no time in paying their respects to their hostess. Half-way down the hall, surrounded by a retinue lighting her with upraised candelabra, Madama received them—so an eye-witness wrote to Rome—"with those beautiful manners of which she knows the secret, and with such charm that the whole household of the Viceroy was amazed. The gentlemen fell into a lengthy dispute for the place of precedence on the right hand, and Madama was obliged by the Viceroy to accept the more honourable side; and so they went into the Painted Chamber where their Excellencies conversed for some time, while the gentlemen of the Viceroy went to visit the haunts of Madama, which they extolled to the skies, declaring that they had never seen rooms more delightful or more charmingly decorated. Madama then led the Viceroy through them, expecting him to praise them as much as his gentlemen. The Viceroy is grateful to everyone for the immense courtesy and consideration with which he has been received, and Her Excellency will offer him a beautiful and honourable banquet next Sunday or Monday on the other side of the lake." At this banquet the evening passed in music and singing and gallantries and fan-battles; and when she retired she found that her gown, sewn with golden devices, had been stripped of seven embroidered candelabra.

Three questions confronted the Congress: the liquidation of the Ferrarese War, the restoration of the Sforza to Milan, and the settlement of an old score against Florence for adhering to the French and refusing to join the Holy League. Though she was not admitted to its deliberations, Isabella was in close touch with the Congress, and it was in her *camerini* that its essential decisions were prepared. She ingratiated herself with Gurk and captivated the Viceroy; from each she obtained a promise of protection for her brother, Alfonso, and her nephew, Maximilian Sforza. Her efforts in behalf of her own blood proving so fruitful, she was happy to lend her influence to a family which she numbered among her closest friends. The final question before the Congress was the restoration of the Medici in Florence. The Pope favoured it, to bring Florence into the Holy League; the Congress favoured it, to propitiate Julius for its protection of Ferrara; and Isabella favoured it for the sake of Alfonso. The Congress being in unanimous agreement on this question, the freedom of Florence was sacrificed to the security of Ferrara. Giuliano de' Medici, representing his brother the Cardinal, engaged the army of the Spanish Viceroy; and though the Florentine Government, forewarned of its danger, sent envoys to Mantua, they were powerless to prevent the transaction: they were not invited to Madama's functions. When the Congress closed its sessions, the destinies of Italy had been settled to her entire satisfaction.

34

In August 1512, while the Congress was dancing in Mantua, the Spanish army marched upon Prato, the gateway of the Arno valley and the outpost of Florence. Prato was defended by the militia. In the Pisan War it had done little more than picketing and skirmishing duty: it now faced the test of fire. The Spanish were hungry, ill-paid, disorganized, but they were the veterans of Ravenna; a breach was made in the walls, they poured in, the militia fled, and Prato suffered a four days' sack of barbaric ferocity. "The rapid and cruel capture of Prato," Cardinal de' Medici wrote to the Pope, "though it distresses me, will have this advantage, that it will serve as an example to others." Florence immediately capitulated, and the Cardinal received its envoys with shrewd moderation. Bland as the August moon and unflushed by the fires of Prato, Cardinal de' Medici surveyed the harvest pacifically. He would not have been the son of Lorenzo the Magnificent if he had not been mild, and, now that his brother Piero was dead Cardinal Giovanni vindicated the sagacity which his father had discerned in him. For himself and his family he claimed nothing but the right to return to Florence as private citizens and to buy back their property. It was true that he required guarantees of his security, which excited comment among the Republicans; as one of them remarked, "a man who means to live peaceably in a Republic and who requires guarantees that he will not be molested, asks in effect and means in fact to molest the liberty of others." These guarantees naturally involved modifications in the Government. But while they were under discussion, his partisans in Florence anticipated them. Five young bloods broke into the apartments of the Gonfalonier Soderini and forced his resignation. With his usual public spirit Soderini effaced himself. Through the good offices of Machiavelli he obtained a night's lodging in the house of Francesco Vettori, and the next morning he left Florence, under escort, for an exile from which he never returned.

This rapid succession of events—they occurred within a fortnight—marked a crisis in Machiavelli's life. The collapse of the militia was a bitter blow, and the fall of Soderini an even worse disappointment. The flight of the militia he called cowardice; the resignation of Soderini he preferred not to describe. Both were betrayals, and easy to predict, but it was bitter to be a true prophet, and a seer after the event. For now he saw what he had only suspected before. The militia were green fighters, without public spirit; and Soderini, for all his public spirit, was a green fighter too. As the danger approached, he had shown all the symptoms—refusing to suppress the Medici partisans, disdaining common precautions. Moderate, law-abiding, self-effacing, and impartial, he met the normal requirements of a public man in normal times; but in an emergency such scruples had no place in public life, they were a betrayal of trust. He had ruined not only himself but the Republic. Machiavelli did not blame him, he blamed himself. This disappointment was deeper than his disillusionment in Valentino; for Soderini was the only alternative; and for his sake Machiavelli had renounced his romantic aberrations and accepted, with reluctant logic, the solid orthodox virtues of the average man. He had been untrue to himself: he had championed a man in whom he did not believe; Caesar at least had inspired him. But this time he showed no bitterness: he was too weary, too mature. He did his duty and saw Soderini safely through the gates; and when he was gone he did his duty as a friend. "I know the compass by which you navigate and if it could be condemned, which it cannot, I would not condemn it, seeing to what port it has brought you," he wrote him. "But looking at it, not with your glass, in which we see nothing but prudence, but in that of the many, I find we must judge matters by the purpose which governs them and not by the means through which they are accomplished." He defended Soderini in Florence, recognizing the humanity with which he had attempted "to extinguish infections by patience and goodness, never daring to quench them by force, though his enemies often gave him the opportunity; and this he justified by saying that it would have been necessary to violate the laws, which would have bred bitterness and endangered, after his death, the office of Gonfalonier for life, which he believed useful to the City. Nevertheless"—it was now his only conviction—"one should never sacrifice evil to good, when evil can easily get the better of good."

That axiom was the conviction of a man who had been ruined by moderation. The Medici entered Florence as quietly as Soderini left it. Giuliano, who was the first to arrive, retired to a friend's house, shaved his beard, and changed his clothes to conform to Florentine fashions, appeared on the streets unattended, and made an excellent impression by his unassuming manners and liberal views. He remembered and respected all the local prejudices. Cardinal Giovanni, who followed him, was equally tactful; he had an even longer memory than his young brother; and the reorganization of the Government went on effectively. A board of sixty-five members, appointed by the Medici to co-operate with the existing departments of the Republic, was ratified by a popular Parliament, the first since Savonarola abolished the institution, and while the Republican façade remained intact, the city reverted insensibly to the constitution under which it had been governed prior to the revolution of 1494. When the Medici brothers re-entered their ancestral palace, after eighteen years of exile, the past was annihilated with the irresistible ease of the old motto, still rippling in a regular, pliant, even rhythm on their walls: *Le Temps revient*. There were no reprisals; there were merely readjustments and precautions. Soderini was banished for five years and the members of his family for two—time to forget and be forgotten. His friends were lightly treated. Francesco Vettori, under suspicion for favouring his flight, was imprisoned for a few days; but as his brother had been one of the five Mediceans who forced the Gonfalonier's resignation, he regained not only his freedom but the confidence of the Medici and was appointed ambassador to Rome. The only victims of the change of administration were some minor officials, without influence or consequence, who were politically suspect, and whose posts were part of the spoils of office. Among these were Biagio and Machiavelli. Both were dismissed, and Machiavelli, compromised by his intimacy with Soderini, was confined for a year to the territory of the Republic and forced to give bond for his obedience. He was also forbidden to set foot for a year in the Palace, though this order was suspended from time to time to permit him to draw up his accounts and hand over the business of the Chancery to his successor.

It was ruin; but amid so many instances of the moderation and liberality of the Medici, Machiavelli refused to believe that his ruin was alone irreparable. He was insignificant, but he had a friend. Like Vettori and with his aid, he expected to recover the confidence of the Medici; and he resigned himself to a period of probation. "January does not vex me," he said, "provided February favours me." February came and a new blow fell on him. An abortive conspiracy for the overthrow of the Medici, hatched by two young Republicans with whom he was distantly acquainted, was discovered by a Government informer, who picked up a list of names, among which was that of Machiavelli. He abhorred conspiracies in principle and was too prudent to engage in them in practice; but with the other suspects he was arrested, imprisoned, and put to the question with several turns of the wrack. The ringleaders confessed to a nebulous plot, but they exonerated their supposed accomplices: the names were those of possible sympathizers, who had not yet been approached. "The ringleaders and almost all the other suspects to the number of ten have been seized," Giuliano wrote to Isabella, "but so far nothing has been discovered beyond a mischievous intention of some sort; they are men of noble but small name, without support, and of no danger to the state, even if they had succeeded." The two Republican plotters were executed, and Machiavelli paid for their acquaintance with three weeks of confinement and anxiety. In the harrowing uncertainty of his situation, lying in a lightless cell, listening to the litanies for the dying, he studied his sensations. An unflinching realist, he described them with wry humour in a ballad which he addressed to Giuliano de' Medici. He implored that liberal and life-loving young man to identify him, for he was unrecognizable in the dark, worried by vermin "as big and plump as butterflies," by horrible stenches, by the rattling of chains, the cries of the tortured, and the prayers of the condemned, and he frankly confessed:

> But what worries me most
> Is that, sleeping, at break of day
> I heard one sigh: For you they pray.
>   Let them give up the ghost,
> If only you hear me and I,
> Good sir, may escape from this sty.

Though his wrists and ankles were swollen, he was agreeably surprised, when he came out, by the fortitude with which he had borne the ordeal.

This misadventure was a setback, but he refused to believe it anything more, for he recovered his freedom at a moment when it was impossible to despair in Florence. In three weeks the world had moved: Pope Julius had died, and Florence was celebrating the election of his successor, Cardinal Giovanni de' Medici, who assumed the title of Leo X. Long before the news was confirmed, the city was delirious with enthusiasm. For four days and nights the incessant booming of cannon and bells, the crackling of bonfires, the blazing of illuminations on the Cupola, the shouts of *Leone, Leone*, the long-drawn din of the Medici cheer, *Palle, Palle*, filled the city with an exploding conflagration of joy. Bonfires burned before every door; the wooden roofs of the shops were torn down for fuel; and the authorities had to issue an edict to save the tile ones. "I came out of prison to the universal joy of this city," Machiavelli wrote to Vettori, associating himself irresistibly to these celebrations; the past was a bad dream. "I shall not repeat the long tale of my misfortunes; all I shall say is that Fate has done everything to injure me, but, God be thanked, it is over. I hope to incur no more trouble, because I shall be more cautious and the times will be more liberal and less suspicious." Then, with Vettori in Rome, his mind began to wander. "Keep me if possible in the mind of our Lord, so that he or his family may begin to employ me for something, for I believe I should be of credit to you and of service to myself." The universal delirium in Florence, which hailed the election of Leo as a godsend and made everything possible, went to his head; but with Vettori's reply the truth began to penetrate.

Vettori was sympathetic but sober. "My dear crony: For the past eight months I have had the greatest sorrows in my life, and some which you do not know; but the worst was to learn of your arrest, for I understood at once that you would be tortured, as you were. It grieves me not to have been able to help you, as your trust in me deserves. At the creation of the Pope, I asked him for only one favour, your freedom, which I am happy to hear you have already obtained. Now, my friend, what I have to say to you today is this: bear this persecution bravely, as you have borne your others; and now that things have quieted down and that the fortune of these people surpasses all imagination, let us hope that you will not be confined to the territory for ever; and when you are free to travel, I want you to visit me, if I stay here, for as long as you please." And that was all. As for Machiavelli's hope of employment, Vettori was too tactful to mention it; for it was clear that his friend was still a little light-headed. The sudden alternations of his fortune had no doubt touched him. But Machiavelli denied it. "As for facing Fortune, I want you to find this much pleasure in my pain," he wrote; with the quick ear of the unfortunate he had already caught the first hint of discouragement. "I bore it so squarely that I have grown fond of myself and seem to be a better man than I expected; and if these masters of mine decide not to confine me to the territory, I shall be pleased, and I believe I shall conduct myself in a manner which will please them also; but if not, I shall live as I used to, for I was born poor and I knew stinting before I knew plenty." As quickly as Vettori he changed the subject. "The whole band sends you greetings, beginning with Tommaso del Bene and ending with Donato. Every day we are in the house of some wench to recover our spirits, and only yesterday we watched the procession from the house of Sandra del Pero; and so we pass the time amid this universal felicity, enjoying what life is left us, and I feel as if I were dreaming."

Dreaming indeed: for in Florence, where the endless celebrations still continued and where everyone was preparing, like the pigeons rising and wheeling about the Piazza, to follow the Florentine Pope to Rome, the life that was left him was too little not to eke it out with hope. The more he veered away, the more obstinately it returned to his pen. "I am determined not to desire anything passionately," he began his next letter.

POPE LEO X WITH GIULIO DE' MEDICI AND CARDINAL ROSSI, by Raphael
From the portrait in the Pitti Palace, Florence

"Of all the things I have ever asked of you, I beg you once and for all to take no trouble, for if I do not have them I shall not suffer at all." He hoped merely that they might continue their political discussions ... if those did not bore him. "If you find it tedious to discuss affairs, seeing them fall out so often quite contrary to our expectations and conceptions, I agree with you. The same thing has happened to me. Nevertheless, if I could talk to you, I should be bound to fill your head with cloud-castles; for I am so made that, being unable to discuss the wool trade or the silk, or profit or loss, I must talk of statecraft; and I must either cork myself up or run on. If I could cross the frontier, I too might come to Rome and ask if the Pope is at home; but amid so many bounties mine flags, through my own neglect. I shall wait till September." But all these stoic resolutions were, after all, only evasions, and he concluded: "I hear that Cardinal Soderini is very active with the Pope. I wish you would advise me whether I should write and ask him to recommend me to the Pope, or whether it would be better for you to speak to the Cardinal, or whether we should do neither the one nor the other: send me a word of reply."

Of these suggestions Vettori preferred the last; but he gave the others due consideration. "I have been reflecting whether it would be good to mention you to Cardinal Soderini," he replied several days later, "and I have decided that it would not because, though he is exerting himself with the Pope and seems to be in great favour with him, at least judging from appearances, yet many Florentines are opposed to him, and if he put you forward I do not think it would do you much good, nor do I know if he would do so willingly, for you know how cautiously he acts. Moreover, I do not know how apt an intermediary I would be between you. He has shown me some good demonstrations of affection, but not such as I expected; and by saving Piero Soderini I seem to have reaped ill favour on one hand and little thanks on the other. But I am satisfied. I have served the city, my friends, and myself." But he had learned his lesson.

After that there was no more to be said. Vettori knew the world, and to forget it Machiavelli returned to his boon companions; but a change had come over them too. "The old crew, as you knew it, seems to be lost. All the leaders have been cooked or have flown the coop," he complained to his crony in Rome. "Tommaso has become strange, boorish, tiresome, and so mean that you will think him another man when you return. I must tell you what happened to me the other day. He bought 7 lbs. of veal last week and sent it to Casa Marione. Then, thinking that he had spent too much and looking for someone to share the expense, he went about begging us to dine with him. Out of pity I went with two others, whom I found for him. We dined and the bill came to 14 soldi apiece. I had only ten with me and owed him four; and every day he duns me, and only last night he nagged me on the Ponte Vecchio. Whether you think him wrong I do not know; but this is nothing to the other things that he does." Even conviviality was overcast by political eclipse. In the evening the little group gathered, no longer in the wine-room, but on the street-corner, at the bench of the Capponi, to bask in the late sun, to watch the passers-by, and to gossip. Machiavelli gossiped stoically, but the *tedium vitae* was too much for him. Lacking the caution of Vettori, he returned, at the risk of importunacy, to the attack; and this time he was reckless. "The Magnifico Giuliano is going to Rome and you will find a natural opening to favour me, and so will Cardinal Soderini. I cannot believe that, if my case is handled with some skill, I shall not be employed in some capacity, if not in the service of Florence, then of Rome and the Papacy, where I should be less suspect. I do not write this," he added hastily, "because I desire these things too much, or because I wish you to be at any trouble or expense or inconvenience or worry on my account, but because you know my heart, and if you can help me you know that my welfare will always be identical with yours and that of your house, to whom I owe whatever remains to me."

The reply was a long political letter, discussing the international situation.

Then at last Machiavelli understood. He took the cue. Regularly, every Saturday night, he wrote Vettori a long political letter, discussing the international situation. These letters were his last link with the world, and he clung to them with anxious tenacity, in a stubborn effort to ward off extinction and stagnation. He wrote voluminously, writing to talk, talking to think, thinking to live; when the correspondence was interrupted he caught his breath; when it was resumed, he confessed his relief. Indefatigably he spun the last thread that bound him to life, and every tremor that threatened it threatened his existence. The speculative life with which he began his career was all that remained of it; but in that resource he forgot, for a few hours every week, his defeat. "If I were Pope . . ." he began, and plunged into the mazes of Papal diplomacy, changing his skin now with Leo, now with the Catholic king, now with the Emperor; and Vettori replied; and the two statesmen without portfolio settled the destinies of Europe between them, or rather, like their superiors, they left them hanging, for they were insoluble. Whatever happened, the outlook for Italy, overrun by the foreigner, was dark. Carefully as they charted the probable course of events, events followed their own haphazard, illogical way. Vettori, even more than Machiavelli, was baffled, for he insisted on seeing enigmas where there were none and was never satisfied that things happened as they did. Only of one thing was he sure—"If you ask me what I would have the Pope do, I reply: the contrary of what he does"—and that merely deepened his confusion, for the Pope, in his foreign policies, seemed to be pursuing the most contradictory courses at once, and all with equal caution and sagacity. Vettori gave up in disgust. Politics were fascinating but futile; he enjoyed them as an intellectual game, but he did not take them to heart; they were not in his blood, they were not his genius: Vettori had no genius. Machiavelli, on the contrary, poured his full powers, his ripened thought, into these weekly analyses, lavishing on them a logic, a detail, a conscientious and exhaustive accuracy worthy of an official report; it was habit and it was illusion; and there was always the chance that they might be passed around and read by appreciative eyes. But Vettori was no Biagio. He appreciated Machiavelli's genius and preserved it for himself.

Even this resource began to shrink, however, when for reasons of economy Machiavelli retired to his farm at San Casciano. Cut off in the country from all information, he was doubly dependent on Vettori. "In my happiest days," he now wrote, and Vettori was delighted to hear it, "I never enjoyed anything more than your discussions, because I have always learned something from them. Now that I am far from every other advantage, you can imagine how welcome your letter was—it lacks only your presence and the sound of your voice—and while I read and reread it, and I reread it many times, I forgot completely my wretched condition and felt myself once more in harness, where I spent so much labour and time in vain. And though I have vowed not to think or to talk of state matters, yet I must break my vow to answer your questions, for no other obligation weighs against our old friendship, above all when you do me so much honour as in this letter, for, to tell you the truth, I have taken no little pride and vainglory in it. I am sure my opinions will seem to you to have lost their savour, which you must excuse, since I have stopped thinking of these things, and, besides, I hear nothing of what is happening; and you know how difficult it is to judge things in the dark, especially these. . . ." Even in Rome Vettori knew that; and in San Casciano, Machiavelli was reduced to hearsay and guesswork. But, after all, what were politics but hearsay and guesswork? Was it possible to discuss them with scientific accuracy? His diplomatic missions—what had they been but eavesdropping and conjecture? He had always been in the dark; and his masters also. Practical politics were a blind groping from a shifting present to a problematical future, a continual process of makeshift, improvisation, and experiment. The only political facts were political principles; and now from the past—for only the past was sure—Machiavelli began to collect, out of his reading, reflection, and experience, a few general truths, the little residue of wisdom which remained of his career, and to put them on paper. With everything else drying up, his life shrank to its centre. Alone, forgotten, and obscure, he ended his retreat and, writing to infuse the meaningless confusion of life, veering for ever under the vagrant gusts of Chance, with what little order, regularity, and scientific stability the mind could lend it, he discovered himself, rebuilt the world that had rejected him, and outgrew Vettori.

Suddenly, as if he divined what was happening, Vettori began to feel lonely in Rome. The cautious egotist, though he was not intuitive, was sensitive to his comfort. A married man with the tastes of a bachelor, unsociable, crusty, averse to ceremonies, and critical of the inadequacy of humankind, he preferred to the pomp of the Vatican the unfashionable life he led in his retired lodgings at the foot of the Janiculum; but he craved congenial company. He urged Machiavelli to visit him. The ban had only three months more to run, his friend could safely risk it, and the ambassador painted a meticulous picture of the idle days they would share. "First, I must tell you where I live, for I have moved and am no longer near so many courtesans as I was last summer. My quarter is called San Michele in Borgo, which is very close to the Palace and the Piazza San Pietro, but in a somewhat solitary spot facing the hill which the ancients named the Janiculum. The house is very good and has many apartments, though they are small; and it faces the north, so that the air is perfect. From the house you pass into a church: this is very convenient since, as you know, I am religious. The church, it is true, is used more as a promenade than anything else, for Masses and divine services are held there only once a year. From the church you pass into a garden, which was once trim and pretty but has now gone to seed; but it is being repaired. From the garden you climb the Janiculum Hill, where you can wander at will among vines and along little paths without being seen by anyone, and this was the site, according to the ancients, of the gardens of Nero, of which you can still see the traces. In this house I live with nine servants, not including Brancaccio, a chaplain, a secretary, and seven horses, and I spend my whole salary freely. When I first came, I began to live gaily and delicately, inviting strangers to the house, and serving three and four courses, and eating out of silver, and such things; then I realized that I was spending too much and was none the better for it; so that I decided to invite no one and to eat at an inn, I returned the silver I had borrowed, partly so as not to be responsible for it, and partly because those who lent it expected me to solicit favours from His Holiness, and when I did so the favours would not be granted; so that I determined to be rid of these obligations and to give no bother or annoyance to anyone, that none might be given to me. In the morning, at this season, I rise early, dress, and go to the Palace, but not every morning, only two or three times a week. There, sometimes, I exchange twenty words with the Pope, ten with his cousin, six with the Magnifico Giuliano; when I cannot speak to him, I talk to his secretary, Pietro Ardinghelli, and then with whatever ambassadors may be in the rooms; and I learn some little thing of no importance at all. When this is done, I go home, except that sometimes I dine with Cardinal Giulio de' Medici, the Pope's cousin. At home I eat with my own people, or sometimes with a stranger or two who come uninvited. After dinner I would play cards if I had anyone to play with, but as I have not, I walk in the church or the garden. Then I ride a little beyond Rome, when the weather is fair. At night I come home. I have ordered a quantity of histories, mostly of the Romans, such as Livy with the epitome of Lucius Florius, Sallust, Plutarch, Appianus Alexandrinus, Cornelius, Tacitus, Suetonius, Lampridius, Spartianus, and others who have written of the Emperors, beside Herodotus, Ammianus Marcellinus, and Procopius, and with these I pass the time; and I ponder on what rulers unhappy Rome, which once made the world tremble, has suffered, and I no longer wonder that it has borne two Popes like our last. Once every four days I write a letter to the Signori and tell them some stale news that means nothing, because there is nothing else to write, for reasons which you know. Then, when I have supped and chatted with Brancaccio, I go to bed. On Holy Days I go to Mass, and I do not neglect it as you sometimes do. If you ask me about courtesans, I reply that, when I first came, I kept some; then the summer air frightened me, and I contained myself. Nevertheless, I had one who comes to see me often of her own will; she is fairly pretty and pleasant to talk to. I have also in this place, though it is solitary, a neighbour whom you would not dislike; and though she is of noble family, she does a little trade. *Niccolo mio*, to this life I invite you; if you come, you will give me pleasure, and we will return to Florence together. Here you will have nothing to do but to see the sights and come home and tell stories and laugh. And you must not think that I live like an ambassador, because I insist on my freedom. I wear long or short clothes as I please, I ride alone except for my servants, I never go to the houses of Cardinals, because I have none to visit but Medici and Bibbiena, when he is well. People may say what they please; if I do not satisfy them, they may recall me; for the truth is, I want to turn back the clock a year and be in the capital again and sell my horses and clothes; and I wish to spend no money of my own, if I can avoid it. And one thing you must believe me, for I say it without flattery. The concourse of the world is so great here that, though I have made little effort, one cannot help meeting people, and few have satisfied me, and I have found no better judgments than yours. *Sed fatis trahimur:*[1] for when I speak to some of them for any time, or read their letters, I am amazed that they have won any promotion; there is nothing to them but fables, lies, and formalities, and few rise above the common. Bernardo da Bibbiena, who is now a Cardinal, has a charming talent, it is true, and is humorous and discreet and has done much in his day; but he is ill now and has been so for three months, and I do not know if he will be what he was. And so often we labour for rest and never find it; let us enjoy ourselves, and come what may. . . . Christ be with you!"

To this invitation Machiavelli replied with *The Prince*.

35

That the genesis of *The Prince* was defeat, Machiavelli was the first to admit. In reply to Vettori's invitation he described the life he led, contrasted its idleness with that of his friend, and announced its fruit. "By the way of thanks, I can only describe my life to you and, if you think it fit to exchange with yours, I shall change it willingly. I am in the country, and since my last mishaps I have not spent twenty days in Florence to settle them. I have been bird-snaring: I rise before dawn, dress, and wander off with a bundle of cages on my back, looking like

---

[1] But we are in the hands of fate.

Geta loaded with the volumes of Amphitryon; and I bring home two or at most three pigeons. This is how I spent September; then this sport gave out, much to my regret, mean and outlandish though it is; and what my life now is I shall tell you. In the morning I rise with the sun and go to a wood that I am having felled, where I spend two hours looking over the work of the previous day and killing time with these woodchoppers who are always in trouble among themselves or with their neighbours. I could tell you many fine things about this wood and the trouble it has cost me with Frosino da Panzano and others who wished to buy my timber. Frosino sent for several piles without notifying me and, when it came to the payment, he wished to hold back ten *lire* which he said I owed him from a card game, four years ago, in the house of Antonio Guicciardini. I would have given him the devil and called the carter a thief, but Giovanni Machiavelli came between us and made peace. While this ill wind was blowing, Battista Guicciardini, Filippo Ginori, Tommaso del Bene, and several other citizens each took a load. . . . I told the others I had no more wood, and they were very much offended, particularly Battista who numbers this among the other disasters of Prato.

"From the wood I go to a spring, and then to one of my bird-traps; I take a book with me, Dante or Petrarch or one of the minor poets, Tibullus or Ovid or such; I read their loves and tender passions and remember my own, and for a time I find joy in such thoughts. Then I take the road to the inn, chat with the passers-by, ask the news of their villages, hear all sorts of things, and note the various tastes and tempers of men. By then it is dinnertime. After I have dined with my family on whatever food my poor farm and meagre patrimony afford, I return to the roadhouse. There, beside the host, I usually find a butcher, a miller, and two furnace-makers, with whom I cheat time for the rest of the day, playing flush or tric-trac, both games which breed infinite disputes and insults, and as we generally fight for a farthing we can be heard shouting as far as San Casciano. And this is how, thick as thieves with these lice, I relieve my brain and forget the malignity of my fate, bearing these bruises to see if, at last, Fate will not take shame.

"When evening falls, I go home and enter my study. On the threshold I slip off my day clothes with their mud and dirt, put on my royal and Curial robes, and enter, decently accoutred, the ancient Courts of men of old, where I am welcomed kindly and fed on that fare which is mine alone, and for which I was born; where I am not ashamed to address them and to ask them the reasons for their actions, and they reply considerately;

and for two hours I forget all my cares, I know no more trouble, death loses its terror: I am utterly translated in their company. And since Dante says that we can never attain knowledge unless we retain what we hear, I have noted down the capital I have accumulated from their conversation and composed a little book, *De principatibus,* in which I probe as deeply as I can the consideration of this subject, discussing what a principality is, the varieties of such states, how they are won, how they are held, how they are lost; and if any of my fancies ever pleased you, this one should not displease you; and to a prince, and particularly to a new prince, it should be acceptable; and for this reason I have dedicated it to the Magnifico Giuliano. Filippo Casavecchia has seen it; he will tell you something of its contents and of our conversations, though I am still enlarging and polishing it.

"You would have me, my honoured ambassador, leave this life and come and enjoy yours. I shall do so, you may be sure; but for the moment I have some business which will detain me another six weeks. What makes me hesitate is that the Soderini are in Rome, and if I come I shall be obliged to visit them. I should not be surprised if I alighted in jail on my return, instead of at my own door; though this state is very firmly established, still it is new, and being new it is suspicious, and there are plenty of pedants who, as Pagolo Bertini says, would invite others in to dinner and leave me in the cold. If you can settle this apprehension, I shall certainly come in six weeks.

"I have discussed my little book with Filippo and asked him whether or not to present it; and, if I should present it, whether I ought to bring it myself or send it to you. Without recommendation I doubt whether Giuliano would even read it, and his Ardinghelli might take the credit for this latest labour of mine. But present it I must, for necessity hounds me, I cannot remain like this without becoming importunate in my poverty. Besides, there is my desire to be employed by these Signori Medici, even if only in rolling a stone; if I did not win their confidence I should not think much of myself. They have only to read this little book to see that the fifteen years I have spent studying statecraft have not been spent sleeping or idling; and anyone might welcome the service of a man who has won his experience at the expense of others. My loyalty they should not doubt; I have always been loyal, and it is not now that I would begin to break faith; a man who has been good and faithful for forty-three years, as I have been, cannot change his nature; and the proof of my goodness and faith is my poverty. I wish you would write me what you think of these things. *Sis felix.*—December 10, 1513."

The Prince was thus, in its immediate object, a bid for employment by the Medici. It was a final appeal—all else having failed—through the medium of his ideas; and it was for his ideas, above all, that he craved employment. Italy, slowly sinking under the domination of the foreigner, was facing servitude; and the Medici were in a strategic position to determine its future. Controlling both Florence and the Papacy, they held a nucleus of power which might easily control the peninsula, if they extended their dominions; and this was known to be the cherished ambition of Leo. "His object," Vettori wrote in one of his moments of lucidity, "is to maintain the Church in the prestige in which he has found it and not to diminish its states, unless he does so for the benefit of his family, that is, his brother Giuliano or his nephew Lorenzo, on whom he is thinking, in any event, of conferring states. . . . That he intends to confer states on his family is plain. All our past Popes, Calixtus, Pius, Sixtus, Innocent, Alexander, and Julius, have done so; those that did not, could not. Furthermore, his family is concerning itself little with Florence, a sure sign that they are thinking of other established states, where they will not have to humour their subjects continually. What states he has in mind I shall not discuss, as he will change his mind with occasion." Here, then, was a lever to move Italy. The paramount need of the hour was national union—a forlorn hope: "As for the union of the Italians," Machiavelli wrote in despair, "you make me laugh; there has never been union among them for any good purpose." The one collective principle which that race of obstinate individualists recognized was the family; it was only out of the family that patriotism could grow. It had been the cardinal error of Julius to undervalue that principle, but his error was the opportunity of the Medici. In pursuing their family ambitions they might become national leaders—on two conditions: first, that they identify their interests with those of Italy; and secondly, that they acquire and maintain their new states successfully.

To those two objects *The Prince* was dedicated. The first inspired the glowing exordium: "This opportunity must not be missed to reveal to Italy, after so many years, her liberator. Nor can I say with what love he would be welcomed in all those provinces which have suffered from these foreign floods, with what thirst for revenge, what stubborn faith, what devotion, what tears! What gates would be closed to him? what people would refuse him allegiance? what treachery would resist him? what Italian would deny him homage? For this barbarian domination stinks in all our nostrils. Be this, therefore, the mission of your Illustrious House, assume it with the courage and hope of a just enterprise, so that under its banner our fatherland may be ennobled, and under its auspices the words of Petrarch may be verified:

> "Virtue over against Rage
> Will run to arms, and brief be the shock:
> For yet the antique courage
> Is not dead in the Italian stock."

The second object inspired the book itself, with its systematic analysis of the principles by which new states are secured and retained.

But beside the personal and patriotic inspirations of *The Prince*, there was a third, which combined them both. The Medici had a forerunner in their Messianic mission—a man "who had given Italy a gleam of hope that he had been sent to redeem it, but he was rejected by Fortune, so that it still waits for one to come to heal its wounds." Such was the singular transformation which Caesar Borgia had undergone in his mind. In retrospect Machiavelli saw him prophetically. Like the Medici, he had been on the point of forming a strong state which might eventually have become the focus for national union; and, though that state had been reared for his own aggrandizement, it had reverted after his death to the Church; on that basis Julius had built for the expulsion of the barbarian; and it was now for Leo to achieve what Valentino had begun. In that pyramidal design Machiavelli saw the synthesis of the past; and he surveyed the future with confident lucidity. The success of the Medici reconciled him to the failure of Valentino; and it was his method which he proposed to them as an example. *The Prince* is Caesar Borgia, resurrected in a glorious avatar, to redeem Italy by his *virtù*.

But his method was useless without his spirit; and if his spirit was that of Anti-Christ, such was the gospel of patriotism. Christianity was possible only in private life; it was inconsistent with patriotism, since "it leads us to depreciate the love of the world and makes us mild. The ancients, on the contrary, made the love of this world the supreme good and were more fierce in their actions and sacrifices. The ancient religion beatified only men of mundane glory such as generals of armies and founders of republics; ours glorifies meek and contemplative rather than active men. For us the supreme good lies in humility and submission and in the contempt of the world, whereas for them it lay in greatness of spirit, in strength of limb, and in everything that makes men bold. Ours teaches men to be strong in enduring rather than in doing; and thus the world has become the prey of scoundrels who have found men willing, in order to gain Heaven, to endure injuries rather than to avenge them." The virtues of Christ could only survive under the protection of Anti-

Christ: antithetical, they were complementary. Each had its own sphere, the error lay in confusing them, the common error of judging a public man by his private character. Even he had slipped into it and, in a moment of sentimental weakness, had heaped moral obloquy on his fallen idol. But after the failure of Soderini he reverted to Caesar; and *The Prince* was an apology, a monument of reparation and apotheosis to the memory of a man whom he had wronged. Over against the virtues of Christ the stamina of Caesar, the classic virtue which made the liberation of Italy the mission of Anti-Christ; and Machiavelli invoked and extolled it with the mortified longing of the defeated.

The first requisite, therefore, was to inculcate into the new Prince a robust public conscience; his education was ethical as well as political. "I do not see how one can censure him," he concluded a recapitulation of Caesar's career. "On the contrary, it seems to me that I should offer him as a model to all who, by fortune or the support of others, rise to power; for, being great in spirit and lofty in ambition, he could not have governed himself otherwise than he did. . . . Therefore, he who must secure himself in a new principality, win friends, overcome by force or by fraud, make himself loved and feared by his people and revered and obeyed by his soldiers, exterminate those who have power or reason to harm him, change the old order for the new, be severe and gentle, magnanimous and liberal, destroy a disloyal soldiery and create a new one, and maintain friendships with sovereigns in such a manner that they must help him with zeal and offend him with caution, cannot find a more living example than the actions of this man." The blood which that career cost was not wasted: Machiavelli pauses to make the point, citing the example of a tyrant of Syracuse who built his career on wanton brutality: "Yet it cannot be called talent to slay fellow-citizens, to deceive friends, to be without friends, without faith, without mercy, without religion: such methods may gain empire but not glory." The difference was obvious. "Harshness, properly used, if of evil it is lawful to speak well, is that which is necessary to one's security and which is applied at one blow and not persisted in afterwards . . . Harshness improperly used is that which, though small to begin with, multiplies rather than decreases with time. . . . Injuries should be done all at once, so that, being felt less, they offend less; benefits should be given little by little, so that the flavour of them may last longer."

Nevertheless, the virtues of a prince must be martial ones. "A prince should have no other aim or thought, nor select anything else for his study, than war and its rules and discipline; for this is the sole art that belongs to the ruler, and it is of such value that it not only supports those who are born princes, but often enables men to rise to that rank from a private station; and, contrariwise, we see that when princes have thought more of ease than of arms they have lost their states." The only exceptions are the rulers of ecclesiastical states; "for they are sustained by the ancient ordinances of religion, which are so all-powerful and of such a nature that the principalities may be held no matter how their princes behave and live. . . . Such principalities are secure and happy . . ." and they prove nothing. The Prince being a militarist, the question arises of the type of military he should employ; and Machiavelli returns to his obsession. As the Medici had abolished the militia, it was necessary to remind them that "in mercenaries cowardice is the danger, in auxiliaries, valour; and the wise prince has always avoided these arms and turned to his own, choosing rather to lose with them than to conquer with others, for a victory won by the arms of others is never a real one." And he pointed the principle, despite the disastrous experience of Prato, with a proof that was always conclusive: "I shall never hesitate to cite Caesar Borgia and his actions. . . . The difference between one arm and the other can easily be seen by comparing the prestige of the Duke: (1) when he employed the French; (2) when he employed Vitelli and the Orsini; (3) when he relied on his own soldiers, on whose fidelity he could always count and which was constantly growing: he was never more highly esteemed than when he was, and was seen by everyone to be, completely master of his own forces."

The Prince being now, by the methods of Caesar Borgia, in possession of his state, "it remains to be seen what should be his rules of conduct toward his subjects and friends. And as I know that many have written on this point, I suppose I shall be considered presumptuous in raising it again, especially as I shall depart from the methods of other people. But, if what I write is to be of use to those who understand it, it seems to me more profitable to pursue facts than fancy: many have portrayed principalities and republics which have never been known in reality, but the difference between how we live and how we should live is so great that to neglect what is for what should be is more likely to ruin than to save us: the man who would act entirely in obedience to virtue can only be ruined among so many who are evil. To hold his own, the Prince must learn, therefore, how to be unrighteous, and to use evil or not according to necessity. . . ." From this principle of expediency the whole moral code of the Prince derives.

The first accepted virtue to be revalued is liberality: a quality of peculiar importance at a period when wealth was prized primarily for its moral revenue—for show, for patronage, for reputation, rather than for material satisfaction; and for the Prince therefore the essential is "to be *reputed* liberal. Liberality exercised in a manner that does not bring you the reputation of it injures you; if you exercise it honestly, as it should be exercised, it may not become known, and you will be censured for the want of it. . . . Therefore, a Prince should not shrink from the reputation of meanness . . . he will in reality be exercising liberality toward all those from whom he does not take, who are numberless, and meanness only toward those to whom he does not give, who are few. . . ." And for the benefit of the lavish Medici: "Nothing wastes so rapidly as liberality, for even while you exercise it you lose the power to do so and become either poor and despised, or, in avoiding poverty, rapacious and hated. Above all things, a Prince should guard against being despised and hated, and liberality leads you to both."

The next problem is the use of clemency and cruelty. "Every Prince should desire to be considered clement and not cruel; but he should be careful not to misuse mercy. Caesar Borgia was considered cruel; nevertheless, his ruthlessness reconciled Romagna, unified it, and restored it to peace and loyalty. He was more compassionate than the Florentines who, to avoid the imputation of cruelty, allowed Pistoia to be destroyed by the factions. . . . And of all princes it is impossible for the new Prince to avoid the charge of cruelty, since new states are full of dangers. . . . Upon this a question arises: whether it is better to be loved or feared. . . . In general, this is true of men: they are ungrateful, fickle, false, cowardly, and covetous, and, as long as you succeed, they are yours body and soul; they will offer you their blood, property, life, children, while the need is distant; but when it approaches, they turn against you . . . and they have less scruple in injuring a man who is beloved than one who is feared, for love rests on the bonds of obligation which, owing to the baseness of men, are broken at every opportunity for their advantage; but fear preserves you by an unfailing security—the apprehension of punishment. Nevertheless, a prince should inspire fear in such a way that, though he does not win love, he avoids hatred . . . which is always possible, provided he does not touch the property of his subjects and their women. Above all, he must keep his hands off their property, for men forget the death of a father more readily than the loss of their patrimony. . . . Among the many wonderful deeds of Hannibal, this one is recorded: that having led an enormous army, composed of many races, to fight in foreign lands, no dissensions arose either among them or against the

Prince, whether in his good or bad fortune. This was due to nothing else but his inhuman cruelty . . . without that cruelty his other virtues were insufficient for his purpose. Short-sighted writers admire his deeds from one point of view and from another condemn the principal cause of them. . . . I conclude, therefore, that, as men love according to their free will and fear at the will of the prince, a wise prince should build on that which he and not another controls, seeking merely, as I have said, not to be hated."

The emancipation of the Prince from the bonds of private morality is now carried one step further, in a yet more radical innovation. "Everyone admits how laudable it is in a Prince to keep faith and to live with integrity and not with craft. Nevertheless, the experience of our times has shown us that those princes who have accomplished great things have set little store by good faith, that they have circumvented the minds of men by craft, and that in the end they have overcome those who have based their conduct on good faith. . . . There are two ways of combating, by law or by force: the first is proper to man, the second to brutes, and as the first does not suffice we are compelled to resort to the second. The Prince, therefore, must know how to use the brute and the man: which is what the ancients signified by the fable of Achilles reared by the Centaur. And among the brutes the Prince should adopt the lion and the fox, for the lion cannot defend himself against snares nor the fox against wolves. . . . To rely on the lion alone is to know nothing. Therefore, a wise prince cannot, nor should not, keep faith to his disadvantage, when the reasons which caused him to pledge it no longer exist. If men were entirely good, this precept would not hold, but since they are bad and will not keep faith with you, you are not bound to observe it with them. . . . But it is necessary to know how to colour such conduct, and to be a great dissembler, and men are so simple and so subject to present necessities that they are easily deceived. One recent example I cannot pass over in silence: Alexander VI never did anything else but deceive, nor ever thought of anything but deceiving, and always found dupes; yet he succeeded, for he knew this side of the world."

And now, to seal and secure these qualities of calculation, economy, cruelty, and cunning, one thing more is needed—a shining coat of hypocrisy. "Though a prince need not possess all the good qualities I have mentioned . . . to seem to have them is useful: as, for example, to seem merciful, loyal, humane, religious, and sincere, and to be so, but to be so with a mind so flexible that, if the need arise, he can change to the contrary. . . . He should be careful to let nothing fall from his lips that is not instinct with the five qualities I have mentioned, and must appear to those who see and hear him all compassion, all faith, all humanity, all religion, all integrity. Nothing is more necessary than to seem to have these last qualities, because in general men judge by the eye rather than by touch, for it is given to everyone to see and to few to touch him. Everyone sees what you appear to be, few know what you are, and those few dare not oppose the opinion of the many, who are protected by the prestige of the state. Let the Prince consider the conquest and security of his state, the means will always be found honourable, and everyone will commend them, because the vulgar always judge by appearances and by results; and in the world there are only the vulgar, for the few find a place there only when the many have no ground to rest on."

But Machiavelli was in a mood too austere to indulge in baiting the vulgar; he owed the common conscience of mankind an explanation of this code which contradicted all its accepted opinions; and he proceeded to vindicate it. A beacon for the future, his Prince was a rebuke to the past, to the improvident princes who had betrayed Italy to the barbarian by their political sins—their shiftlessness, temporizing, and sloth, their common disunion and individual helplessness, their abject dependence and blind speculation on the only providence they knew—the mutable divinity of Fortune. And suddenly the theme deepens, the discussion broadens, the subject is thrown up against the illimitable vista of man buffeted by his fate, and its basic impulse rises in an effort to rally and pit the will, the courage, the intelligence of man against the overbearing power that builds and unbuilds his being.

"It is not unknown to me that many men have believed, and still believe, that the affairs of this world are so governed by Fortune and God that the wisdom of man is powerless to direct or stay them, and that it is useless therefore to give them too much thought, and that we should let chance rule them. This belief has gained credit in our time because of the great changes we have seen, and still see, every day, beyond all human conjecture. In thinking of this, I am sometimes tempted partly to agree with this opinion. Yet, not to forfeit our free will, I hold that Fortune may be the arbiter of half of our affairs, but that she lets us govern the other, or maybe a little less. I liken her to one of those ravaging torrents which, when they rage, flood the plains, ruin trees and houses, and carry the soil here and there; everyone flees, everyone yields to the onrush, unable to resist; but it does not follow that, when the weather clears, men should not make provision, with defences and barriers, against a return of the flood by drawing it off in channels, so that its force may be neither so unchecked nor so dangerous. So it is with Fortune, who shows her power where virtue has not prepared to resist her, and vents her fury where she knows neither bulwarks nor barriers have been raised to contain her." This is the sanction of that code of unscrupulous efficiency: it is a creed of self-preservation. Buffeted by fortune, overborne by blind chance, man controls a fraction of his destiny—half, or maybe less—only by the constant exercise of courage, will, and intelligence; and even these do not suffice. Into his positive gospel there now creeps a mystic element which Machiavelli is forced to admit. The Prince must develop a flair for the Time Spirit: "He who acts in accordance with the spirit of the times, I believe, will succeed." But, with his usual repugnance to mysticism, Machiavelli frankly prefers self-confidence. "For my part, I think it better to be bold than calculating, because Fortune is a female, and to down her we must beat and bully her; and we see that she yields more often to the bold than to those who go to work coldly. And so, woman-like, she is always a lover of young men, because they are less cautious and more violent, and with more audacity command her."

It is the Time Spirit, however, that inspires the synthesis and coda of his gospel. "Considering, therefore, all the matters of which we have treated, and reflecting whether the present time in Italy would be favourable for a new Prince, and if there would be an opportunity for a prudent and able one to introduce new forms which would bring him honour and to all men advantage, so many things seem to me to conspire in his favour that I never knew a time more fit than the present. If it was needful that the people of Israel should be captive to manifest the virtue of Moses, that the Persians should be oppressed by the Medes to discover the magnanimity of Cyrus, and that the Athenians should be scattered to illustrate the ability of Theseus, then at the present time, to discover the virtue of an Italian spirit, it was necessary that Italy should be reduced to the extremity in which she now is, more enslaved than the Hebrews, more oppressed than the Persians, more scattered than the Athenians; without head, without order, beaten, despoiled, torn, overrun, and enduring every kind of desolation. . . . We see her imploring God to deliver her from the cruelty and insolence of the barbarian. We see her ready and disposed to follow a banner, if only someone will raise it. And we see no one at present in whom we can hope if not in your Illustrious House, which with its virtue and fortune, favoured by God and the Church, of which it is now the ruler, can lead this redemption. This will not be difficult if you recall the lives and actions of the men I have mentioned. Though they were great and remarkable men, yet they were men, and none of them had more opportunity than the present affords, their enterprises were no easier nor more just, nor was God more their friend than He is yours. Justice is on our side, a necessary war is a just war, and arms are hallowed when there is no hope save in arms. . . . Moreover, how remarkably, and beyond all example, have the ways of God been manifested! The sea is divided, a cloud has led the way, the rock has poured forth water, it has rained manna, everything has contributed to your elevation: you should do the rest. God is not willing to do everything and deprive us of our free will and that share of glory which is rightly ours." And with that mounting and Mosaic exhortation, in a final rally Machiavelli joins the prophets. He had published his substance, he had climbed Sinai; and from San Casciano he surveyed Florence and revealed his whole vision and his full stature as an armed prophet. Across the years he challenged at last, in a supreme counterblast to Christianity, the spirit of Savonarola; and the second great lawgiver of the Renaissance confronted the first.

Inspired by the Time Spirit, he even assumed the tone, the mystic exaltation and imagery of his predecessor; but, though his creed was the antithesis of that of his forerunner, something visionary seemed to mislead him too. The very realism of *The Prince* defeats his own purpose. The redeemer of the chosen people is the outcome of their defeat: his one goal is success, his one virtue efficiency, his only principle expediency. His morality is the martial law of the soul, in which the normal rights of humanity are suspended. But as politics are a perpetual emergency, either latent or actual, expediency becomes his normal law. He is emancipated from common prejudices; he exists in a moral void; his conduct is to be judged by the mind alone; he is a scientific creation; that is his strength; and it is also his weakness.

In the political philosophy of *The Prince* there is no mention of his social responsibility: his functions begin and end with war. He is an isolated figure in a hostile world, with which his relations are defensive and offensive. He is one more manifestation of Italian individualism—the self-made man raised to political power for the satisfaction of his own ambition, and his subjects benefit, at best, indirectly by his success. It is logical that, with this premise, his principles should be anti-social; but it is also logical that in the long run the systematic practice of cunning, cruelty, and hypocrisy should undermine the confidence upon which the social compact and the stability of the state depend, and perpetuate the abnormal and unsettled conditions of which he is the outcome. This unresolved inconsistency is a radical defect, which makes the realism of the system specious and short-sighted; and Machiavelli himself seems to suspect it by the insistence with which he qualifies principles which, fully developed, could only lead to the ruin of his Prince. But compromise is only begging the question; for a like inconsistency underlies the basic assumption on which the book is built—that public morality is one thing and private another. The distinction is artificial. How is it possible for the Prince to separate his private and public conduct in hermetic selves, to change his nature with his functions, or that in the constant interaction of ruler and ruled one should not affect and demoralize the other? To isolate political phenomena and study them scientifically in a moral void is, after all, a fallacy which gives a taint of academicism to *The Prince*. In the end the choice between personal and political morality, between Christ and Anti-Christ, could only be made for life as a whole; and in making it Machiavelli was the victim of his own defeat.

Men who practise unscrupulousness do not write books in praise of it. Machiavelli preached what he deplored, and professed what he could not practise; but only at the cost of a profound self-division. He recognized reality and subdued his own conscience to it; it was an act of discipline, but also of insincerity toward himself. He surrendered to Nature, and his gospel, while it seemed scientifically sound, was morally vulgar. But was it even scientifically sound? For the salvation of Italy he prescribed a code of cultured savagery, which was too primitive to be successfully practised by a race which, for better or worse, had outgrown barbarism, and which could only ruin its civilization. *The Prince*, in fact, like all such manuals of cultured perversity and anachronistic sternness, was the product of a high civilization in decadence; and its creed, sprung from defeat, could only beget defeat.

In the last analysis, Machiavelli had proved the opposite of what he set out to demonstrate. If his gospel proved anything, it was that moral expediency was a contradiction in terms, that the moral law was absolute or nothing, that moral values were intrinsic and could not be subordinated to self-interest without sapping and destroying them. Unwittingly he confirmed Savonarola. They had much in common. Both started from the same disabused view of life, the same radical recognition of its brutality, and both developed their faiths to an extreme and uncompromising conclusion. Like all spiritual rebels Machiavelli was akin to what he repudiated and confirmed it by his apostasy. He too, like his forerunner, was a victim of his temperament and the Time Spirit. Religious faith was decaying, undermined by the corruption of the clergy, classic culture, material ease, and the fanatical failure of the Friar; but the need of faith was undying; and the substitute which Machiavelli offered was the choice of his own temperament—the religion of the State. His gospel was merely the logical creed, developed to its extreme limits, of the sacred egoism and arid virtue of patriotism. *The Prince* is a melancholy book.

36

To be enrolled among the prophets it only remained for Machiavelli to be unrecognized by his own countrymen; but if ever a creed was destined for recognition, it was his; for it merely codified, in effect, the common practice of mankind. The only handicap was that it was too candid; and that was perhaps a real difficulty, as he had dedicated it to the gentlest of the Medici, Giuliano. But Giuliano was the representative of the Pope in Florence. As a test, Machiavelli decided to submit his book to the searching eyes and level judgment of his intellectual equal, Vettori, and it was a mutual friend, Filippo Casavecchia, who carried the theme to Rome, where he was to spend the winter with Vettori.

Then the difficulties began. With the arrival of Casavecchia, who was not a little censorious, the ambassador found himself under criticism for the life he led; and to make matters worse, his steward, Brancaccio, also objected to it. For the moment Vettori was too involved to think of anything else. "If I have not replied before to your letter of the 10th and perhaps will not reply as I should today, the reason," he explained, "is that Brancaccio and Casavecchia annoy me every day, reminding me of the dignity of the city and the duties of my office. You know that I find some pleasure in women, though rather to chat with them than for any other satisfaction; for I am now of an age when I can do little else but talk, but Filippo as you know is averse to their company. Before he came, as my lodging is somewhat unusual, courtesans would often visit me, to see the church and the garden adjoining the house; and it never occurred to me, when Filippo arrived, to send and warn them not to be so bold as to show themselves here; so that the day before yesterday one entered the room, just at dinnertime, and was freely admitted by the servants as usual. She sat down and made herself at home, so that I could neither dismiss her nor explain her presence to Filippo, who opened a pair of round and disdainful eyes at the sight of her. We sat down to table, dined, and talked, and after dinner she went as usual to walk in the garden. I remained with Filippo, who began his philippic somewhat as follows: 'I trust, Your Honour, you will not take it amiss if I who, from our childhood together . . .' Foreseeing a long lecture and scenting its drift, I interrupted him and said that I understood from the beginning what was to follow, and wished neither to listen to correction nor to justify myself, for I had always lived a free man and meant to do so for the rest of my days; whereupon, though reluctantly, he consented that women might come to my house as they pleased." With Brancaccio Vettori's difficulties were of another order. Brancaccio disapproved of the visits of a certain Ser Sano, a Roman broker of unsavoury repute, whom Vettori received only on business, his predecessor having undertaken a suit for him. The ambassador was nettled. Between these two censors, "you see my position," he went on, "and how I must account for whatever I say and whomever I receive. I wish you would tell me whether you think Filippo or Brancaccio has the more right to scold me; I am fond of them both, but for all their reproofs and reminders I shall continue to do as I please." Then he bethought himself of *The Prince*. "You write me, and Filippo has told me, that you have composed a book on statecraft. If you will send it to me, I shall be pleased; and though I am not an expert, I think I should judge your work: what my judgment and competence lack, my affection and faith will supply; and when I have read it I will give you my opinion, whether or not you should present it to the Magnifico Giuliano." But what he really wanted at this moment was not the book but its author. "Your objection to coming here seems to me easy to dispel. Nothing will happen to you if you pay a single visit to Cardinal Soderini. Piero Soderini is in a settled mood, and I do not think he would care to be visited, particularly by you; and if you avoid him I do not think it will be imputed to ingratitude; for I have been thinking it over and I do not find that he or his family have done you any unusual favours. You did not owe your position to them, you had been employed for three years before he became Gonfalonier; and in whatever capacity he used you, you served him faithfully and received merely the usual compensation. We have been trying to find something for you here in Rome. There has been some talk of Cardinal de' Medici[1] being made Legate to France, and I have thought of speaking to him, since you have been there and have some experience of that Court and

---

[1] Giulio de' Medici, the Pope's cousin.

knowledge of French ways. If we succeed, so much the better; if we fail, we shall have lost nothing."

While Vettori was thinking of speaking to the Medici, Machiavelli, however, was thinking of his friend's plight; and his reply, overflowing with gaiety, brought Vettori back to his own business. "I must say, it is marvellous," wrote that expert friend, "to see how blind men are to their own sins, and how bitterly they persecute the vices they lack. I could cite you examples in Greek, Latin, Hebrew, and Chaldee, and press on into the land of Prester John and the Sophy to prove it, if there were not so many homegrown and recent examples. I am sure Ser Sano could have come to your house from one Jubilee to another, and Filippo would not have minded. . . . I am sure, on the other hand, that, if the whole bordello of Valenza had the run of your house, Brancaccio would not have batted an eye; nay, he would have lauded you more highly than if he heard you haranguing the Pope more eloquently than Demosthenes. And if you wished to prove it, you needed merely to pretend, without letting one know the complaint of the other, to believe them both and to obey their precepts, shut your door to the hussies and Ser Sano, looked solemn, and pondered your ways; and I guarantee that not four days would have passed before Filippo would have been saying: 'What has become of Ser Sano? Why does he never come to see us? It is too bad, such a decent man, I cannot understand what people have against him; he knows all the ins and outs of this Court, he is a useful busybody; you should send for him, Your Honour.' As for Brancaccio, I need not tell you how pained and surprised he would be by the absence of women. If he did not bring up the subject, like Filippo, as he warmed his backside by the fire, he would have told you in private. And the better to convince you, I should have dropped in while you were reforming and exclaimed: 'Your Honour, you will fall sick, you take no recreation: there are no boys here, no women; what is this house? an infirmary?' My dear ambassador, this world is full of fools, and few know that to follow the advice of others leads us nowhere, for no two men are ever of one mind. Nor do they know that a man who passes for wise by day will never be accounted a fool by night! If he is considered respectable and trustworthy, whatever he may do to gladden his heart will do him honour and no shame; and instead of being blamed as a humbug and a wencher, he will be called a good fellow. And something else they do not know: that what he gives is his own and he takes nothing from others; he is like wine when it ferments; it lends its aroma to the vessels that smell of must, and takes no mould from the vessels. Therefore, my dear ambassador, forget the mould of Ser Sano and the tongue of gossip and follow your ways and let Brancaccio talk, for he does not realize that he is like one of those wee wrens, that is the first to scold and squawk, and when the owl comes the first to be caught. And our friend Filippo is like a buzzard which, when there is no carrion in the country, flies a hundred leagues to find one; and when he is gorged perches on a pine and scolds at the eagles, falcon, and other such fowl as, being dainty of their food, go hungry half the year round. So, Your Honour, let the one gorge and the other squawk, and mind your own business."

With this letter Machiavelli precipitated an unforeseen and far-reaching imbroglio. Vettori, hungry for approval, promptly acted on his advice, dismissed the women and Ser Sano, and reported to his *dearest crony:* "I have always praised your genius and approved your judgment in little things as in great, and the advice you gave me in your last about Filippo and Brancaccio bore fruit in a few days. As you know, I have more faith in others than in myself and am always anxious to please everyone but myself. I yielded, therefore, to their persuasions and agreed to believe them. . . . We lived in this way for about eight days and no one came to the house except a few people on business and a certain Donato Bossi, who is a grammarian by profession, a man with a strange austere face; and he never speaks of anything but the root of a word and the derivation of a name and whether the verb should come at the beginning or the end of a clause, and similar matters of no moment and which are very tedious to hear; and I did nothing but ply him with questions on his hobby, to draw him out; and, though such a life vexed me, I bore it as best I could, to convince Filippo and Brancaccio of their error. Nor did I have to wait long; for, one evening, as we were seated by the fire, Brancaccio began by saying that I should invite a certain lady who is one of my neighbours, and that not to invite her was unsociable, a quality which many people take amiss, and that men who are so reserved are considered peculiar and ill bred. But first I must tell you what the condition of this lady is, so that you may understand why both urged me to invite her. As I wrote you before, my lodging, though close to the Palace, is a little out of the way, in a street that is not much frequented and among neighbours of a lowly class; but next door, in a very decent house, there lives a Roman widow of good family, who has been and still is pleasant company, and though she is past her prime she has a daughter of about twenty, who is exceedingly pretty and who does a little trade on the side. She has also a son of about fourteen, well bred and gentle, but of good morals and decent, as a boy should be at that age. And, as our houses are next door and our gardens adjoin, I could not avoid some acquaintance with this lady, though I made it a distant one; and she has often come to ask me for favours with the Pope and the Governor and I have helped her whenever I could, as we are bound to do with widows and minors. This, then, was the widow whom Brancaccio persuaded me to invite to supper; and Filippo, with his eye on the boy, added his pleas, so that I finally told them that I consented to do whatever they wished. It was about nine o'clock in the evening when we reached this decision, and I did not suppose that they would call in my neighbours at that hour; so, when they left me, I sat down to write a letter to the Ten, and I was reflecting on how to compose it so as not to disclose all the plans of His Holiness because I did not know if it would please him, and yet not to write so barrenly that they should think me lacking in diligence or ability or that I did not show them the proper respect, being as they are the first men in the city. And while I was in this quandary, in came the widow with her son and daughter and a brother, who came as a chaperon. I rose and received her as agreeably as possible, given my nature: you may have noticed that flattering phrases and effusive welcomes are not my habit; but I made an effort and finished the letter abruptly, saying that I could form no opinion until I knew the decision of the Swiss at the Diet of the Epiphany. Meanwhile, Brancaccio sat down to chat with the daughter and Filippo with the boy, and to give them more liberty I called the widow and her brother aside and inquired about a law-suit of theirs, so as to occupy them and give time to the others until we sat down to supper. But I could not help listening from time to time to what Brancaccio was saying to Costantia, for such is her name, and you never heard such blandishments: he praised her breeding, her beauty, her conversation, and everything that can be praised in a woman. Filippo was as glib with the boy, asking if he studied, if he had a master, and, as he warmed to the subject, if he slept with him, so that the lad often hung his head in confusion without replying. By then it was suppertime and we sat down gaily; afterwards we gathered about the fire and spent the time telling stories and playing games. And you would have laughed when, shortly before supper, Piero del Bene came in, interrupting their sport but not mine: I should have preferred not to have him enter, but I do not know how to offend or to feign, so in he came; but he had so cold a welcome from Filippo and Brancaccio that he soon withdrew. We spent the evening pleasantly and about midnight the neighbours retired, and we went to bed. But, *Niccolo mio,* now I must complain of you: for, in pleasing my friends, I have been captivated myself by this Costantia.

Previously, when women came here, I never lost my heart; I merely whiled away time with them. Now this girl comes, and I venture to say that you never laid eyes on a lovelier, a more fetching creature. I had seen her before, to be sure, but only from a distance; and on closer acquaintance she delights me so much that I can think of nothing else; and, since I have sometimes seen you in love and known what you suffered, I am resisting as well as I can at the start. I do not know whether my efforts will suffice, and I doubt it, but whatever the outcome, I shall write you. I have seen the chapters of your book, and they please me beyond measure; but until I have the remainder I do not wish to give a final opinion. . . . Filippo does not like what you say about his battening on carrion; he says that he always covets perfection and that it is you who take everything that comes, without discrimination."

How, at such a moment, could Vettori form an opinion of *The Prince*? Agitated, distracted, confused, he skimmed a few chapters, was impressed beyond measure and, shelving the bomb, returned to more important matters. And Machiavelli approved; he thoroughly appreciated their importance; in fact, "when I think over this story from beginning to end," he replied, "truly, if I had not lost touch with everything, I would insert it among my memories of modern life, for it seems to me worthy of being told to a Prince, as something which I have learned this very year." He entered into the drama with ardour, for he had created it, and re-created the scene as he pictured it in San Casciano. "I seem to see Brancaccio squatting on a footstool, the better to contemplate the fair face of Costantia, and with words and gestures and laughing and attitudes, and with ecstatic mouthings and eyeings and spitting, drool and pine and hang on the words, breath, looks, odour, and soft ways and womanly charm of Costantia.

> Next, turning to my right hand, I behold
> The boy and Casa yet nearer his goal,
> Grazing his cheek with a bald head and bold.

I see him gesticulate and shift from one side to the other; I see him shake his head sometimes at the bashful replies of the boy; I see him talking now as a father, now as tutor, now as a lover; and the poor lad wondering where he is leading him, at one moment fearing for his honour, at another trusting to his gravity, at another impressed by the fine mature appearance of the man. I see you, my dear ambassador, coping with the widow and her brother, but keeping an eye on the boy, the right one, and the left on the girl, and one ear for the widow and one for Casa and Brancaccio; I hear you reply vaguely and like Echo to the last words; and at last break off the conversation with those little, long, quick strides of yours, a trifle stiff in the hams. I see Filippo, Brancaccio, the boy, and the girl, rise as you approach, and I hear you say: 'Sit down, sit down, do not rise, go on talking'—and after many formalities, a little fulsome and home-bred no doubt, they all sit down again and begin some delightful conversation. And above all I seem to see Filippo when Piero del Bene came in; if I could paint, I would send you his portrait, for certain of his familiar attitudes, certain sidelong glances, certain supercilious poses, cannot be described. I see you at table, flourishing the bread and the glasses, and the trestles quivering, and everyone brimming, nay, running over with joy, and at last deluging everything in a flood of mirth. And lastly I see Jove yoked to the chariot, I see you in the toils of love; and because green wood burns best, your flame is the hotter for the resistance it meets. Here I may be permitted to exclaim with Terence: *O coelum, o terram, o maria Neptuni!*[1] I see you at war with yourself, *et quia non bene conveniunt, nec una in sede morantur maiestas et amor.*[2] Fain, fain would you be a Swan to leave an egg in her lap; fain turn to Gold to lie for aye in her pocket; fain be any animal, so you might never leave her. And since my example alarms you and you recall what the shafts of Love have done to me, I am bound to report how I dealt with the blind bow-boy: the truth is, I let him have his way and found more mercy than if I had denied him. Off, then, with the bit, off with the reins, close your eyes, and say:—Lead on, Love, be thou my guide; thine be the honour if I win, thine the shame if I lose: thou art the master. This is what I have to say in reply to your letter."

Then, for a moment, he glanced at his own life: "Here there is nothing to report. . . . When I go to Florence, I spend my time between the shop of Donato del Corno and the house of La Riccia, and I seem to bore them both; one calls me a shop-pest and the other a house-pest. Still, I make myself useful to both as a confidential adviser, and this reputation has served me so well that Donato lets me have a warm seat by his fire and Riccia sometimes lets me steal a kiss on the sly. Their favour, I think, will not last long, for I have given each some advice, and neither, apparently, the right counsel. Only today Riccia said, pretending to address her servant: 'These wiseacres, these wiseacres, I do not know where they belong; they seem to tell you the contrary of everything.' You see, Your Honour, where the devil I belong." And he concluded:

---
1 O Heaven, O Earth, O Neptune's seas!
2 For Dignity and Love do ill agree or share one throne.

"I should like to keep their favour; for me there is no cure; if any should occur to you or to Filippo or to Brancaccio, I should be grateful if you would write me."

But this muffled appeal fell on deaf ears. The comedy he had started in Rome had entered a new phase, it was turning serious. Vettori complained of his conscience, and for himself too he saw no cure. Little he cared for his dignity—"I think I have more dignity when I am Francesco in Florence than His Honour in Rome," he replied. "But I have been reminding myself that I am forty years old, that I have a wife, that I have married and unmarried daughters; that I have no money to squander; that it is only fair I should save all I can spare for my daughters; that it is cowardly to succumb to the flesh; that she is my neighbour; that I would be spending money on her every day and would be gaining in return only endless trouble. Besides, as she is young and lively and pretty, I tell myself that she is bound to attract others of a very different sort than myself as she attracts me, so that I should have little pleasure and would be in continual jealousy; and turning these thoughts over I resolved to put her out of my mind; and in this infatuation I remained for two days and already felt so firm that nothing could shake my resolve." But he reckoned without the Roman widow, who had everything of a lady but the income. "On the third day, it so happened, the mother came to see me in the evening and brought her daughter along with her; and I who had sworn to defend myself like a man in armour was captivated by her words and gestures. The mother talked of her affairs and then left the room, leaving her alone with me by the fire; and I could not refrain from speaking to her and touching her hand and her throat; and she seemed so lovely and charming that I forgot all my resolutions, and I decided to yield and be her prey, and to be guided and governed as she pleased. What followed I will not tell you: suffice it to say that I have known more jealousy and vexation than I expected. So far the expense has been slight, but my mind has been in continual anxiety. The more I speak to her, the more I wish to speak to her; the more I see her, the more I long to see her. It might be of some help if my nephew Piero came to the house; once he came to supper whenever he pleased, but now he comes no longer; and this might put out the fire, for I do not believe that it has caught so badly yet but that water would damp it. But, *Niccolo mio*, you never laid eyes on a lovelier creature: tall, well proportioned, rather plump than lean, a white skin, a warm complexion, a face oval or round, I do not know which but I like it; seductive, delightful, merry, always laughing, without fluids or ointments on her face, and not very careful of her person; of her other beauties I shall say nothing, for I have not tasted them yet, much as I long to. Naturally, I have not escaped scolding or, let us say, some friendly admonitions from Filippo and Brancaccio: to which I replied what seems to me true, that a man should never be rebuked when he knows that he is wrong: this only serves to increase his suffering and not to cure or lessen his error. And it so happens that Filippo is caught in the same toils as those for which he blames me; but in his case it is the errand-boy of a goldsmith, who in his opinion is peerless but inviolable, for he is sacred to the Host, that is, the goldsmith. Nevertheless, Filippo has been roaming around and feeling his way. Knowing what these Romans are, I tried to restrain him before he went much further, but I failed, and finally the goldsmith threatened to injure him and would have done so if Filippo had not been frightened away, and now he no longer looks at the boy or even passes through the Banchi where his shop is. Whatever stronghold he besieges next will have to be weaker and less well guarded; and hence he is continually consorting with Ser Sano, so that Brancaccio is disgusted and refuses to walk with him in the streets of Rome; and when I am at home they are always quarrelling, and they appeal to one of my secretaries as an arbiter, a fellow as big as Piero Ardinghelli, but not very experienced in such things, who has rather been training his hand, which is the first thing required of a writer, than his mind. . . . We live and learn and many things happen to us in a lifetime: I am not surprised that Riccia in her wrath should have cursed your wisdom; but I should not conclude that she does not love you and will not welcome you whenever you wish; for I should have to think her ungrateful and I have always found her kind and humane."

The wind of love was blowing in all quarters and Machiavelli began to itch. He made a feeble attempt to draw Vettori back to politics and the problems of *The Prince,* but Vettori made no mention of *The Prince,* and in a brief and despairing review of the situation in Italy observed, with the resignation of a lover of Costantia: "My friend, I know that these kings and princes are men like ourselves, and I know that we do many things, even those which are of very great importance to us, by chance; and so I believe they do too." Chance! If that were true, of what use were reason, theory, thought? Men reasoned, life went its way. He had written a book; if it made so little impression on Vettori who appreciated him, what would it mean to those who ignored him? Was it not better to drift? There was a lethal release, an irresponsible bliss in abdicating will and effort, in surrendering to the irresistible force of life: love at least brought a few hours of relief. "Follow your love *totis habenis*,"[1] he replied to Vettori. "The pleasure you have today you will not have tomorrow; and if the affair stands as you say, I envy you more than I do the King of England. Follow your star, I implore you, and do not lose one iota of your pleasure for anything in the world, for I believe, as I always have, and as I always will believe, that what Boccaccio says is true: better to do and regret it than to regret not having done it." His only regret was that he could not take his own advice; and sooner than be a spoilsport he became a hermit. For a few weeks there was silence; then he could bear it no longer; there was an involuntary murmur, despondent and submerged. "Here I am among my vermin, I find no man who remembers my servitude or who believes that I can be good for anything. It is impossible to continue like this much longer; I am wearing out; I see that, if God does not relent, I shall be forced to leave my house and find work as a constable's clerk, if I can do nothing else, or bury myself in some forsaken hole and teach children to read, and leave my friends here, who already think me dead; and they will be better off without me, for I am an expense to them now, being unwilling to spend and unable to see them without spending. I do not write this, because I wish you to take the least trouble or thought on my account, but merely to relieve myself, and so as never to mention the matter again, since it is as odious as it well can be." And he returned to his vow of silence. The days passed, monastic, stagnant, mute; nothing happened; Chance itself ignored him. Then, a month later, he broke his vow; he was a hermit no longer: he was released: he had found himself a widow. "You, my friend, with your Roman love," he wrote gratefully to Vettori, "have kept up my spirit, and I have eased my mind of infinite vexation, reading and thinking of your pleasures and pains, for they are inseparable; but now Fortune has brought me to a point where I can make fitting return. For here in the country I have found a creature so kind, so delicate, so noble, that I cannot praise nor love her enough. Following your example, I should describe the birth of this Love, telling you in what toils he took me, where he laid them, and how strong they were; you would see that they were toils of gold, laid amid flowers, woven by Venus, and so gentle and soft that, though a churlish heart could have broken them, I had no heart to, and though I have dallied but a little while, the tender bonds have become hard and have tightened

---

[1] With all your might.

into unbreakable knots. And do not believe that Love caught me by his usual snares; I knew them and they would not have sufficed: he used lures extraordinary, against which I neither could nor would defend myself. Suffice it to say that, at an age close to fifty, the August sun does not scorch me, these rough roads do not tire me, and the black of night does not frighten me. Everything seems easy and to every appetite, however contrary to what mine should be now, I adapt myself. And though I seem to have entered into a great commotion, yet in the heart of it I find such ease, both because of this rare and smooth phase of Fortune, and because I have forgotten all my cares, that for nothing in the world would I free myself if I could. I have forsaken all thought of great and serious things, I find no pleasure now in reading of ancient or reasoning of modern life; everything is transformed into sweet themes, for which I thank Venus and all Cyprus. So that, if you care to write about your lady, write and, as for other matters, you may discuss them with those who value and understand them more than I do, for I have found nothing but bitterness in them, and in this pleasure and profit."

It was his farewell to *The Prince*.

A long silence ensued—from August to December—and Vettori began to feel lonely again. His infatuation was waning and his conscience troubled him more than ever: he had perhaps neglected his friend. "You may say that you have had a great many words from me without result," he wrote uneasily. "For this my excuse is easy. As I have not been able to help myself, you cannot be surprised that I have not helped you, and I am sure that you understand that it was through no lack of good will." What worried him most was that Machiavelli no longer talked of love; what was love if not something to talk, and, above all, to complain of? Vettori tactfully avoided the subject and tried to wean his crony back to serious things. He sympathized with him assiduously, he thought of him incessantly, he bore his misfortune bravely, and he read him a philosophical lesson. "Believe me, we are led by Fate. I was reading, the other day, a book by Pontano *On Fortune*, which has just appeared, and which is dedicated to Gonsalvo da Cordoba. He proves clearly that neither genius nor foresight nor fortitude nor any other virtue is of any avail against Fortune. Rome offers us daily examples of this. Here we find men without breeding, education, or talent in the highest positions. We must acquiesce; and you in particular should do so, for you have known afflictions, and have passed through worse ones than this. God will bring this one too to an end. . . . I am sufficiently in favour with the Pope and the other Medici, I believe, but then I ask nothing of them. I spend the salary which the law allows me and at the end of the month nothing is left of it. I am free of love and I have returned gratefully to my books and my card games."

Machiavelli acquiesced. He thanked his friend for "all the thoughts and efforts you have bestowed on me; I can promise you no reward for them, because I do not believe I shall ever be able to benefit either myself or others; but what must be, must be." He was as stoical as Vettori; and he too shelved *The Prince*. If Vettori could read and forget it in favour of the gospel of Fortune—well, he could write and forget it, quite as philosophically, in favour of the gospel of Fortune.

But Vettori, now that he was "free of love," was plagued by the thought of it. He viewed his friend's growing bondage with deepening sympathy and concern. Unable to inveigle him into serious subjects, he wished at least to make him take a serious view of love. He turned and turned about the subject, unable to find an opening. At last he tapped lightly. "Truly, Ovid is right in saying that love is bred of idleness," he began; but there was no response. This idea obsessed him, and after ruminating it for a fortnight, he returned to it. "My dear friend," he wrote, "there are no letters which I read with more pleasure than yours, and I wish I might write you many things which I know cannot be committed to correspondence. For several months I have understood only too well how you loved, and I was tempted to say to you: *Ah, Corydon, Corydon, quae te dementia caepit?*[1]—Then, reflecting that this world is nothing but love or, to put it more bluntly, liver, I forbore; and I have been thinking how far men are at heart from what they say. A man has a son and says that he means to bring him up decently; yet the first thing he does is to give him a tutor, who spends the whole day with him, and has every facility for doing what he likes with him, and lets him read things which would put life into the dead. His mother washes and dresses him well to make him more attractive; when he begins to grow, he is given a room on the ground floor, where he has a hearth and every other convenience, so that he can live freely and bring home whatever company he pleases. We all do this, and those of us who seem to be the most strict are most at fault; it is no wonder, therefore, that our youths are as lewd as they are: it all comes of their wretched upbringing. You and I, old as we

---

[1] Ah, Corydon, Corydon, what madness has mastered you?

GIULIANO DE' MEDICI, by Allori
From the portrait in the Uffizi Gallery, Florence

are, still keep some trace of the habits we contracted in youth; and there is no help for it. . . ." And to steady his friend and win his confidence, he associated himself with his weakness. "I wrote you that idleness made a lover of me and I repeat it, for I have almost nothing to do. I cannot read much, because age has weakened my eyesight; I must be accompanied when I go walking, and that is not always possible; if I occupy myself with my thoughts, they bring me for the most part nothing but melancholy, which I shun; and so, of necessity, I think of pleasant things, and I know nothing more pleasant to do or to think of than fornication. Men may philosophize as they please, but this is the plain truth, which many know but few will admit."

But the silence in San Casciano was unbroken. It was the silence of consent. With reason baffled, effort defeated, and friendship itself uncomprehending, the prophet subsided and let thought languish into the sensual soliloquy of instinct. What else was left? For, after all, Vettori was right: men may philosophize as they please . . . And *The Prince* was forgotten.

37

But his thought was his life: it might languish, it could not die. Machiavelli might quarrel with his genius, neglect and repudiate it; he could not kill it: he was its creature. Even in exhaustion, it needed little to revive it—a mere hint of interest and encouragement; and Vettori now made a contrite attempt to lure him back to politics and, putting to him certain crucial problems of Papal policy, carried his replies to Court. Italy was languishing deliciously in a lull to her chronic disturbances. But the war-clouds lay low on the horizon. The storm-centre was Milan, which the French were bent on retaking. The Spanish and the Imperialists were bolstering up their weak and inexperienced puppet, Maximilian Sforza; and Leo, committed to maintaining the *status quo,* was temporizing, preserving an overt neutrality and intriguing covertly with all sides. Machiavelli immediately put his finger on the fallacy of this traditional Italian policy. Effacing himself and letting his ideas speak for him, he fed Vettori the doctrines of *The Prince* in their application to the national problem. It was, he said, the gravest which had arisen in the past twenty years, "and I know none more difficult to analyse, more dubious to judge, and so dangerous to decide and to act upon"; but the greatest of all dangers was to shirk it. "I think that neutrality has never been useful to anyone, who finds himself in a position in which he is weaker than any of the combatants, with his states interspersed among theirs; and you must understand, first, that nothing is more necessary for a prince than so to conduct himself with his subjects, his friends, and his neighbours, that he will be neither hated nor despised, but, if he must choose, let him choose to be hated rather than despised. Pope Julius did not care if he was hated as long as he was feared and respected; and by the fear he inspired he upset the whole world and raised the Church to its present position. I tell you that to be neutral means to be hated by the loser and despised by the winner; and, when once a man begins to forfeit respect, and to be thought a useless friend and a negligible enemy, it is to be feared that every insult and injury will be done to him. . . . If we consider all the states of His Holiness, where they lie, what minor powers they include, and the combatants, we must conclude that His Holiness is one of those princes who, under no circumstances, can afford this neutrality." And after weighing all the probabilities and supporting his argument with a meticulous analysis of the contingencies throughout Europe, he concluded that "inasmuch as there are more odds of victory on the French side than on the other, and as the Pope by his adhesion can assure the French victory but not that of the others, and it would be less formidable and more tolerable to have France as a victor and friend, and it is impossible to remain safely neutral, I think that His Holiness should either adhere to France or else to the others, provided the Venetians join them, but not otherwise." These letters made an impression. "Both your letters on the questions I put to you have been seen by the Pope and Cardinals Bibbiena and Medici," Vettori reported, "and they were all astonished by the talent and praised the judgment they showed. And though we can draw nothing but words from them, because of our bad fortune and because I am a man who cannot help his friends, nevertheless, to win the good opinion of the great may some day be of use to you."

This little puff sufficed to rekindle Machiavelli's spirit; and it was fanned a few weeks later by a report that the Pope was about to form the long-predicted state for his brother Giuliano. This state, it was rumoured, was to comprise Parma and Piacenza in the Milanese, and Modena and Reggio in Emilia, a composite principality which would form an Italian bulwark on the Lombard front and might become, with Florence and Rome, a nucleus for national federation. Immediately he wrote to Vettori, and in a tone which showed how quickly he recuperated and how deeply, in the curative springs of instinct, he had already recovered his courage and resiliency. Once more his spirits bubbled; and in reply to Vettori's "epistle on the liver" he enclosed a facetious sonnet as a proof of his practical philosophy. "Anyone who saw our letters and their diversity, my revered crony," he smiled, "would be very much surprised, for at one moment we would seem grave men, utterly wrapt in great things, and not a thought in our heads that was not lofty and proper. But then, turning the page, he would think us frivolous, fickle, lewd, and utterly wrapt in vanities. And this manner of acting, if to some it seem shameful, to me seems laudable, for we imitate Nature, which is various; and he that imitates Nature cannot be rebuked. And though we usually indulge this variety in several letters, I wish to display it today in one, as you will see if you turn the page. Now, sir, spit and listen:

"Your brother Pagolo has been here with the Magnifico Giuliano, and in talking to me of his hopes, he mentioned that His Lordship had promised to make him Governor of one of the states which are to be conferred on him. And as I have heard, not from Pagolo but from common report, that the Magnifico is to become lord of Parma, Piacenza, Modena, and Reggio, this seems to me a fine and powerful principality and one which can surely be held, if it is governed properly in the beginning. But to govern it properly one must understand the nature of the subjects. These new states, occupied by a new prince, present infinite difficulties in the holding of them. And if there are difficulties in holding states which are homogeneous, such as the Duchy of Ferrara, how much more difficult is it to hold those which are composed of various fragments, like this one of Signor Giuliano! One part of it is a member of Milan, the other of Ferrara. The first thing that the new Prince must do, therefore, is to unite his subjects . . . by residing there in person or by appointing a deputy with supreme authority. . . . And should His Lordship still wish to reside in Rome, if he will delegate one who is thoroughly familiar with the nature of the place and local conditions, he will lay an excellent foundation for this new state of his. . . . Duke Valentino, whose work I should always imitate if I were a new prince, knowing this necessity, made Messer Ramiro President of Romagna: a decision which made his people united, fearful of his authority, affectionate to his rule, and confident in it; and all the love which they bore him, which was great considering his newness, sprang from this policy. I believe this could be easily proved, because it is true; and, if Pagolo is appointed, it would be a position which would win him recognition not only from the Signor Magnifico but from all Italy; and besides profit and honour to His Lordship, he could also bring reputation to himself, to you, and to your House. I have broached these ideas to him; he was pleased and thinks he may use them. I thought I would write you so that you might know our ideas, and, if need be, smooth the way for them."

He had learned the flexibility of Nature. He presented his ideas to Vettori. Unpacking the contents of *The Prince*, stripping its ideas, disclaiming his pride and his parentage, he smuggled them to Rome, offering them to whoever would appropriate and provide for them, and scattered them, like pollen on the wind, to fertilize the destiny of the Medici. It was a final attempt to outwit misfortune and his friends and to reach, in an anonymous form, the ear of the Magnifico Giuliano. But Giuliano was not the Medici of the future. Gentle, easy-going and pleasure-loving, and too liberal for the stern responsibilities of government, he had retired to Rome where he found a brilliant social life for which he had every aptitude; and there his ear was caught by the voice, not of *The Prince*, but of *The Courtier*.

PART FOUR

Castiglione

38

In the autumn of 1513, while Machiavelli was writing *The Prince*, Castiglione was working, in the intervals of his official duties in Rome, on *The Courtier*. The book, which he had begun five years before, as a memorial to Duke Guidobaldo and the Court of Urbino, had grown into a profession of faith, embodying the social and moral code of his calling; and he had his reasons for writing—though he really had no time for it—the theory of the leisure classes.

He had found his vocation. After a brief and perfunctory experience of war under Pope Julius—shivering through the siege of Mirandola, sharing his goose-quilt with an ailing Cardinal, composing a pacific elegy in the night-watches—he had exchanged a career of arms for more congenial service. War was a trade. "I did as little harm as possible and I see everyone enriched but myself, but I am content," he confessed in the thick of it; and he plodded on only because it was the conventional duty of his class and a necessary part of his profession as a courtier. On the death of Julius, he was sent to Rome as ambassador *pro tempore* of Urbino. He was influential in promoting the election of Leo, much to the delight of Francescomaria, who immediately began to speculate on the hospitality which the Medici had received, in the days of their exile, at Urbino. As no one was better fitted to win their confidence, Castiglione remained in Rome to pursue, amid the crowded scenes of the Papal

Court, his only ambition in life and his natural vocation—that of being welcome in the world.

He was conspicuously successful; but to be conspicuous distressed him. At the Vatican he was *persona grata,* and his popularity carried its penalties. He was constantly over-taxed with commissions and compliments from the Duke of Urbino, the Duchess, the Duchess Dowager, their friends, and the friends of their friends, his family in Mantua, distant relatives and remote acquaintances and prospective parasites, all pressing forward for favours of every description—pensions, privileges, promotions, monopolies, exemptions, recommendations, introductions—until even his patience faltered and he confessed that his profession of official begging was "devil's work." To a man so reserved this side of Court life was irksome; and it would have been intolerable had he not found, in the seats of power in Rome, almost all the old members of the inner circle of Urbino. There was, in the first place, the Pope, who showed him every consideration; there was Giuliano de' Medici, "his dearest brother"; and there was their *alter ego,* Cardinal Bibbiena. "Beside all the rare virtues that endear you so deeply to me and to all who value the humanities and mutual affection, your devotion, apart from all other reasons, will always make you first in my heart," Bibbiena assured him, "and I remain the same *bel Bernardo* as of old." That genial prelate, who had become Treasurer of the Papal household and who dispensed patronage like another Pope himself, went out of his way to prove that he remembered Urbino. A climber, he kept his head and his friends in the hour of success, and he prided himself on his nicknames more than on his titles. He was still their "booby" and always at their service. Nor were these protestations the mere *cortigianerie* of which people accused him: he was as good as his word. And so were the other Urbinati: Bembo, the slippery humanist who had settled down as a Papal Secretary; Federico Fregoso, who had been created Archbishop of Salerno; Bernardo Accolti, the *improvvisatore,* who had the influence of a buffoon at the Vatican; and Castiglione's kinsman, Lodovico da Canossa, whose house he shared in Rome. In the capital of the world he was still among his old mates; and to them he owed his success.

That debt he repaid in his own way. Prosperity filled him with misgivings. Despite those eager protestations of fidelity, he was under no illusions. How long would such devotion endure? How long would it outlive the corrosion of Time and the corruption of the world—the estranging influence of new ties, the self-satisfaction of success, the divorce of high responsibilities? To hold old friends together, to keep alive the memory of a past which he, for one, would never forget, was the only return he could make; and at the same time it was a posthumous service to Guidobaldo and a living tribute to his widow: a perennial memorial to their achievement. They had created, that childless couple, a Court which had the intimacy of a family; and it was so that Castiglione conceived of society, as a sort of loose, shifting, elective family, enlarged and diffused through the world. Society was the transitional stage between the family proper and the state, between private and public life; it was the matrix of all forms of impersonal association; and, as a collective principle, it embraced and surpassed them all, relating the individual as it did, not to a particular group, but to the human family at large. So it had been at Urbino. "I doubt whether the charm that emanates from a dear and loved company," he wrote, "was ever felt anywhere more than we enjoyed it at one time there"; the inspiration of the Duke and Duchess "seemed a bond, holding us so united that there was never cordial love or concord of will among brothers greater than that which existed among us." Though the memory and influence of Urbino were bound to be dimmed and diluted in Rome, if the graduates of that social school carried something of the principles of conviviality—conciliation, adaptability, self-discipline, and humanity—into the commerce of the world and the practice of politics, then perhaps—despite the corrosion of Time —the life that had once been lived in Urbino would not have been lived in vain; and he sat down to complete *The Courtier*.

But the pen soon slipped from his hand. The present pushed out the past; the world left him no leisure to remember or to write. The pressure of his social duties was as unremitting as that of his official service. Pleasure, at the Papal Court, was an exacting, an arduous, a never-ending routine. "Let us enjoy the Papacy which God has given us," Leo was reported to have said to Giuliano; and pleasure became an essential part of his policy. He had been elected on a programme of peace; by that law of alternance which seemed to govern the succession of the Papacy, after the turbulent reign of Julius, Italy and the Church turned with one accord to the candidate whose nature, like his motto, was SOAVE. The international situation was dark, but by dint of vigilant vacillation and patient temporizing he preserved peace, or at least a truce—and what more could anyone do in the condition of chronic warfare which was settling on the peninsula? The war-clouds lay low on the horizon, but within their radius lay a broad expanse where the sun still shone brilliantly on Rome; and in that brief halo he cultivated assiduously the arts of peace. An opportunist, like his father, Leo was blessed, in lieu of other qualities, with a kind of tact which made him exquisitely sensitive to the spirit of the times. Intuitively he perceived that the development of Italian genius was neither toward religion nor politics but toward art; and he made it his mission to foster its real glory. Swarms of artists, scholars, and poets flocked to Rome, lured by his prodigal liberality, and few were turned away. Among these few, it was true, was Ariosto, who complained that the Holy Father, now that he had grown great and given up his eye-glass, no longer knew him, while scores of mediocrities flourished in his near-sighted favour. But there was only one Ariosto, and the literary tastes of the Pope, who boasted that he had been born in a library, were comprehensive. In music his ear was surer: he was a melomaniac; and there was no bad music. Doting on the fine arts from his cradle, he carried on the policy of his predecessor and beatified Rome by beautifying it, though always in the spirit of the times. The *furia* of Julius was over and with it went the *terribilità* of Michelangelo, who was sent to Florence to work on the tombs of the Medici. In Rome his place was taken by Raphael of Urbino, whose graceful facility Leo appreciated. In art he loved ease and charm; life was strenuous enough, and much too harsh. But of all the glories of peace the one for which he had most aptitude was the art of life; and he brought the social life of the Vatican to a brilliant pitch with a constant round of suppers, concerts, plays, pageants, regattas, races, hunts, bull-fights, balls, and vivacious Masses. In this whirl Castiglione revolved with the rest of his world. He was in constant demand, now to stage a play, now to improvise a symposium, to swell a concert or grace a supper, so that he rarely had time for what he preferred—a quiet chat in a literary academy or an hour of collaboration with Raphael on their plans for the excavation of ancient Rome—let alone for completing *The Courtier*.

But that only made the claim of his book more compelling. The present, in pushing out the past, was rearing magnificently and whinnying without direction. The munificence of the Medici had attracted such an influx of climbers, particularly of Florentines, that the Romans complained of being colonized; and all had been welcomed with such indiscriminate bounty, that the influence of those officials "without breeding, education, or talent in the highest positions," of whom Vettori complained, gave a motley tone to Roman society. Money and the tastes of the *parvenu* dominated it. The notorious extravagance of the Pope—"he could no more save a thousand ducats than a stone could fly upwards," sighed Vettori—paved the way for the bankers who abetted and emulated his orgy of spending; and not all of them had the background, the tradition of wealth, and the mellowness of the Medici. Forging the Age of Gold at forty per cent, they poured the horn of plenty into the fleshpots. Chigi, the Sienese banker, was not satisfied until he had eclipsed the Holy Father at the housewarming of his new villa on the Tiber. In what seemed to be a hall hung with priceless tapestries the guests were served in gold plate emblazoned with their own armorial bearings; the plate was then tossed into the Tiber, where nets had been laid for it; and when the Pope felicitated his host on the splendour of his saloon, the hangings were drawn, revealing the stalls of a stable. Nor did such exhibitions displease the Holy Father; he was fastidious only in the daily care of his beautiful hands. Papa Gianni, as he was fondly called, was too sure of himself not to enjoy, with sovereign simplicity, vulgarity in others. It was part of his generosity. He positively refused to discriminate in his pleasures. He passed with the same ease from a learned conversation or a session of chamber music to the sixty-five courses of Cardinal Cornaro's suppers and the deafening din of a table band comprising every known instrument and commanded to perform without flagging, so that the grey dawn found the puffing cheeks still blowing and the sagging elbows still sawing. He was equal to everything but boredom. But he was easily amused. He had the succulent risibilities of an infant, and everything tickled them—a pie that popped into twenty-four blackbirds—a monster pasty—Fra Mariano Fetti swallowing forty eggs on a wager—a regurgitation—an elephant: *the* elephant, which knelt at his feet, saluted three times, and, dipping its trunk in a bucket of water, performed after the manner of one pachyderm to another. A true Tuscan, Pope Leo enjoyed horseplay. Fra Mariano was his own joke and a broad one—a barber who began life as a convert to Savonarola and who ended as the "Cowled Buffoon" of the Vatican, where he was courted by the very men who made game of him. Many were shocked when a feeble old man who aimed at Petrarch's laurels was paraded through Rome on the elephant; but not Leo. He watched the sport from a window with puckering mouth and flabby chuckles. His mirth was not loud, for he suffered from indigestion. He sucked in his laughter and let it relieve him. An inner effervescence suffused the bland moon-like face, which was no sooner overcast than it became sallow and extinct. Buffoons, who were his pet pleasure, mingled with boon companions, who were Castiglione's pet abhorrence, in the Papal anterooms. Elected by the "young Cardinals," and himself the youngest of the Popes—he was under forty—Leo brought youth into the Vatican. Castiglione, who was no older, already felt the approach of age there. *Manca il fior gentil dei miei primi anni,* he wrote. If at thirty-five he complained of the passing of "the sweet flower of his first years," it was neither a sentimental affectation nor that uneasy anticipation of maturity which is itself a conceit of youth, that set him apart and aged him in the Rome of Leo X: it was his conservatism. Though he was too much a man of the world not to conform to the time, the place, and the people where his lot was cast, he did so with reservations. At heart he harked back to Urbino, where he had spent his youth in acquiring the accomplishments of a courtier, only to find them wasted amid the promiscuity, the gilded vulgarity, the laxity or total absence of standards in Rome. In the sumptuous civilization which the Medici were promoting a favoured place was reserved for social life: but who realized that it was an art? He was no purist, but he respected his calling. It might be, and it was not, an Italian glory. He was moved by the pretensions of upstarts and the untutored assurance of parasites, if not to protest, at least to draw an ideal portrait for those "many fools who, because they are presumptuous and inept, think to acquire the name of a good Courtier," which would remind them that there was more to their profession than place-hunting and fleshpots, that it required a lengthy culture of mind, body, and character; and he returned once more to *The Courtier*.

Character—because that profession was so easily demoralizing—character was of imperative importance. Manners, after all, were but the convivial form of morals, the minor modulations of a major principle, modified by custom and adapted to conventional practice; but, however pliable to social fashion, they derived from a principle that was elementary and unchanging. Self-respect and mutual consideration were the whole code of the Courtier. He was the social man, and the art of convivial life required a sedulous self-discipline, a constant abeyance of impulse and tempering of egoism. That rudimentary law might be disregarded only by the privileged few who had mastered it or the inferior who were exempt from it; but within the social pale moderation and modesty were binding on the initiate. Like the fountains of Rome, the Papal Court was overflowing with an exuberant life in which formal animals neighed unbridled and riderless through a glittering spray. And Castiglione sat down to claim for his profession, as the preserve of an aristocracy, the chastening discipline of the aristocratic view of life, for which the aim of life was the manner of living it. If such moral elegance was ornamental, it was not useless. In the vast confusion and futility of life, which no man could comprehend or control, one could answer for nothing and no one but oneself; and to perfect oneself was perhaps the only service which anyone could render to his kind.

As the manuscript approached completion, it was shown about among his friends, among whom was Giuliano de' Medici. He played a prominent and flattering role in its pages; and it was to the voice of Castiglione that he was listening when Machiavelli made a final attempt to catch his ear for the doctrines of *The Prince*. To the many elusive factors which had thwarted Machiavelli was now added one whose potency he was the first to recognize. "The Prince," he had written, "will be successful who acts in accordance with the spirit of the times, and he who does not will fail." And at that moment, as it seemed, the spirit of the times was propitious to *The Courtier*.

39

Of all the Medici, Giuliano was the most sympathetic to Castiglione. They had been friends in Urbino, and the fragrance of Urbino still clung to Giuliano in Rome. Modest and unambitious, cordial and sincere, the Magnifico was prepossessing because he had the politeness of the heart. He cut a figure as refreshing in the Vatican as he did in the foreign clothes which he favoured. They were the acme of fashion. But his elaborate dress, the *bandeau* on his hair and the French hat tilted at a rakish angle, only underlined the unassuming nature of the man, and the contrast would have been faintly comic, had it not been for his swarthy beauty and the air of languid dissipation which he cultivated and which lent him the look of a *beau ténébreux*. Even in display he was diffident and, though he was susceptible to environment, he had the sense, the elegance, and the pride to remain natural. Where Leo was ingratiating, Giuliano was winning. He was the amateur among the Medici. He was devoted to metaphysics, music, and women; as a gallant he was ingenuous, as a musician he was judicious, and as a philosopher he philandered. In this prince of courtiers Castiglione saw the making of a courtly prince; he had the first requisite of both a courtier and a prince: he listened well. The third son of Lorenzo de' Medici seemed born to give and to enjoy felicity; but the shrewd father who called him Giuliano the Good had not destined him for public life. The paternal role had now fallen to Leo, and he soon realized that his younger brother was too lenient to rule Florence. When he called him to Rome, it was not, however, to lead the mere life of a courtier: Giuliano was a pawn; and the Pope was making plans for him which interrupted those of the author of *The Courtier*.

At the same time these plans gave a new turn to those of the author of *The Prince*. To replace Giuliano in Florence the Pope was grooming his nephew, Lorenzo, the son of Piero; and Machiavelli had already inspected the newcomer. "I must not neglect to tell you how the Magnifico Lorenzo is acting," he wrote to Vettori. "So far he has shown a mettle which fills the whole city with hope; and everyone seems to recognize in him the happy memory of his grandfather. His Magnificence is painstaking in business, liberal and gracious in hearing suits, slow and earnest in replying to them. His manner of conversing is such as to distinguish him from others but not to show arrogance; nor does he mingle with them in such a way as to lose reputation through too much familiarity. With the young men of his own rank he conducts himself in a manner not to estrange them nor to allow them any youthful impudence. In short, he makes himself loved and respected rather than feared; which is the more to be praised in him as it is the more difficult to accomplish. His household is so ordered that, though there is much liberality and magnificence, it does not surpass the life of a citizen; so that neither in his outward nor inward progress do we see anything which offends or which is reprehensible; and everyone is extremely pleased. And though I know that you will hear this from many, I thought I should describe him so that, with my testimony to prove it, you may share our pleasure; and, if you have the occasion, you may repeat this on my part to His Holiness." This judicious young man was, in fact, literally observing the instructions which the Pope had laid down for him and sedulously imitating the example of his uncle Giuliano; but he was after all the son of Piero. He had his father's self-will and ambition; and Leo curbed only to train his bent. When Machiavelli realized this, he began to weigh the prospects and the character of Lorenzo against those of Giuliano de' Medici.

Both were the creatures of Leo, however; and it was on the Pope that the future depended. As a first step in his plans, Leo created Giuliano Captain General of the Church. There was an immediate reaction in Urbino. Seeing himself superseded in a rank he had confidently expected to retain, Francescomaria della Rovere recalled other slights which he had not expected from his old friends, the Medici. He, at least, had done his duty. On the election of Leo, he had written to Castiglione: "We cannot tell you how delighted we are, and we hope that our services to this good and holy Pontiff will now receive recognition. You will commend us cordially to His Holiness and assure him that we shall be no less zealous in his service than in that of our uncle of blessed memory." Shortly afterwards, Francescomaria bought himself a town. He borrowed the money and put in a claim on the Papal Treasury for the arrears of his salary under Pope Julius, a sum which as it happened exactly covered his debt —twenty thousand ducats. To his amazement Bibbiena, as Papal Treasurer, demurred. Francescomaria was outraged. "Of all men in the world we should have thought that M. Bernardo would be the last to break his word to us," he wrote to Castiglione, instructing him to convey his sentiments to the Treasury; but they produced no cash. Then the old ungovernable della Rovere blood flared up. It had never occurred to him that his claim could be questioned; but apparently there was money in Rome for everything but past services. And how was he to satisfy his wife's uncle from whom he had borrowed the money? He was a man of honour himself. Such were the indignant complaints he vented on Castiglione; for, with his heart confounded by ingratitude and his head confused by miscalculation, he had to abuse someone. By dint of patient negotiation, Castiglione finally effected a settlement. A Papal fief was conferred on the relative from whom Francescomaria had borrowed the money, and the Duke was appeased. After that, however, the Pope felt that he had repaid the hospitality he had received at Urbino. His visits had been brief and occasional. Accordingly, when he appointed Giuliano Captain General of the Church, he did so without compunction: he owed nothing more to Francescomaria, least of all an explanation. Francescomaria complained *sotto voce* to Castiglione; and *sotto voce* Castiglione pacified him. But with the recurrence of such incidents, the composition of *The Courtier* languished.

The appointment of Giuliano was, as all the world knew, merely a preliminary to the next step, and in the spring of 1514 Rome was again speculating on the state which the Pope would confer on him. A rumour arose that charges were to be preferred against the Duke of Urbino on the basis of his absence from the battle of Ravenna two years before and that he would be deprived of his Duchy. This brought Francescomaria posting to Rome. Bibbiena, who had been forced to investigate the Duke's record in connexion with his claim on the Treasury, had a plausible case if he chose to make use of it; but as an old friend he preferred to shelve it. At a meeting in the house of Castiglione he reassured the Duke, who returned to Urbino. The rumour persisted, however, and the friends and family of Francescomaria became uneasy. Isabella decided to conduct a quiet investigation of her own. She sent her secretary to Tuscany to ferret out the facts. At the baths of Viterbo he discovered a reliable source of information and reported: "In the dilemma of finding a state for the Magnifico Giuliano, Ferrara is out of danger, but Urbino and the rest of the territory once occupied by Valentino are less so. Nevertheless, my informant believes that Urbino will be safe, as the Pope would be too notorious for ingratitude. He is more apt to turn to Siena, Lucca, and the Marquisate of Massa. The Sienese and the Lucchesi are very suspicious." The multiplicity of these suggestions alarmed her. Viterbo, after all, was a mere breeding-ground of gossip; Rome was surer, and in Rome the next rumour was that His Holiness was reverting to his original idea of forming a composite state of Parma, Piacenza, Modena, and Reggio. The fears of Francescomaria were allayed, but hers redoubled, for, whatever form the scheme took, it threatened some member of her family. Parma and Piacenza affected her nephew, Maximilian Sforza, the puppet Duke of Milan; Modena and Reggio threatened her brother, Alfonso of Ferrara. It was time for her to take command of the situation.

But the situation had changed since the days of Pope Julius, and it was no longer so easy to command. Her new antagonist was as oblique and reserved as herself, and of her old Curial friends only one remained—the Archdeacon Gabbionetta. A year before, when these rumours had begun to rise, she had put him on the trail, and he had caught a glimpse of the truth. Biding his time, he had broached the theme one evening, after listening dutifully to a concert "of violins, which lasted a long while," and seized the moment when the Pope sat entranced listening to the dying strains of the music. His mind still dilated with the melody, Leo had answered with the utmost candour. It was true, he said, that he was thinking of Parma, Piacenza, Modena, and Reggio—he would hide nothing from his friends in Mantua, he would speak to them as to himself—and he proceeded to soliloquize to Gabbionetta. "It was true that he was thinking of giving those states to the Magnifico Giuliano, but one difficulty checked him: having determined to do everything to maintain the Duke of Milan in his state, as this seemed to him the way of securing Italy, and likewise to keep peace with France, he did not wish to endanger Giuliano after his own death, either on account of Parma and Piacenza or on account of the Duke of Ferrara"; and he had decided therefore to abandon the idea. Gabbionetta remarked, however, that in discussing it "he bit his lip and clenched his hands in the pleasure of such subjects." But that was a year ago. Now, when Gabbionetta revived the subject, he could learn nothing. "His Holiness," he replied, "swears everyone with whom he negotiates to silence, under pain of excommunication." With

BALDASSARE CASTIGLIONE, by Raphael
From the portrait in the Louvre, Paris

the hovering hand passing over Urbino, Milan, and Ferrara, Isabella was too restless to remain in Mantua. With Julius she had been on the defensive; with Leo she was forced to take the offensive. Besides, the Marquis was insisting on renewing their marital relations; and this was her opportunity to see Rome. She did not reason; she followed her instinct.

In the summer of 1514 she visited her nephew in Milan; then, Genoa being so near, she went a little farther; and in Genoa where the winds and the shipping of the world converged and the shining horizons which she had always longed to explore expanded on every side it was impossible to linger: she took the road to Rome. As she approached the capital, she notified the Marquis through her son. "*Federico mio,*" she wrote gaily to Mantua, "it seems to me too shameful that you who are so young should have seen Rome and I, your mother, should not, so I have decided to visit it also and not to envy you." She was travelling *incognita,* and no one would have suspected her destination but for the fact that she had brought her women along. But who could keep the approach of Isabella d'Este a secret, or respect an *incognita* which, as she confessed, was dictated only by reasons of economy? At the gates of Rome she was met by a bevy of Cardinals, who escorted her to the Palace of the Cardinal of Aragon. Her expenses were paid by the Papal Treasury and Bibbiena immediately sent her, with the Pope's compliments, a purse of five hundred ducats with a promise of more to follow. Her first audience with the Holy Father was a gala solemnity. He raised her from her knees and seated her beside him; and with that introduction to Roman society she was launched on a dazzling round of festivities. "Day after day I visit these Right Reverend Cardinals," she wrote to Mantua, "our cronies, I mean, for I should have too much to do, visiting them all." Though she had hoped to combine devotion with pleasure, she was forced to abandon that idea. "We are so busy with these Right Reverend Cardinals that we have no time to recite the major office; take 3 ducats," she wrote to her secretary, "to the Reverend Mother of San Paolo and ask her to say it for us, while we are away."

But it was not only devotion, it was business, which she hoped to combine with pleasure; yet, whenever she approached the difficult subject, the Pope invited her to hunt or Giuliano to a banquet or a bull-fight. An iridescent sheen of pleasure descended between her and the Holy Father. Whenever she trespassed, he was impenetrably affable; but as she studied the familiar face, seeking at least to divine what lurking ravages time and ambition had traced in its habitual expression, she was baffled. She found herself face to face with the Man in the Moon. With her instincts asleep, she became dissipated. Revolving with the rest of the world in a hypnotic round of revels, she spun farther and farther from the centre; and there were moments when, even socially, she felt herself an outsider. Among the festivities which the Pope commanded in her honour was a performance of Bibbiena's comedy, *Calandria*. The subject was equivocal, and the eminent author had larded it with innuendoes which made her change colour; and though she applauded with a straight face, she scolded him lightly when it was over. And quite as lightly the incorrigible Tuscan teased her and, himself turning player, mimicked her provincial prejudices and her north-country accent: "*Vuuu che ti viegna la fievra, Mozicon? son queste commedie da presentare a una mia pari?*"[1] And again she changed colour. Meanwhile, her women were at work. Bibbiena insisted that the presence of women was all that was wanting at the Papal Court; but the Mantuan ambassador did not agree with him. "Rome is no proper place for women," he wrote to the Marquis, "although the perfection of mind and purity of life of Madama are so manifest and unmistakable that this remark does not apply to her." He could not say as much for her ladies, however; and it was with embarrassment that he forwarded a joint letter from them to young Federico, each claiming a little kiss, one on his right hand, one on his left, one on his upper lip, one on his lower and one on his moist tongue. The Marquis agreed and recalled his wife; but the Pope pleaded for a reprieve. Unwilling to abandon her purpose, she lingered, invoking the antiquities—"every day we visit the antiquities, and every day they seem more wonderful"—and blindly exploring the secrets of the living. Three months had passed in this way when she learned, with a shock, that the Pope had purchased from the Emperor Maximilian his rights to Modena. In acute mortification she left for Naples.

Little as she approved the manners of Rome, she liked those of Naples even less. Though she was welcomed extravagantly, though her fame and her portraits had preceded her and she was cheered in the streets, though the Queen Mother devoured her with her eyes, though the local saint was excited and his blood liquefied in January instead of in June, though she was fêted furiously all about the blue bay and admitted that she had never known such magnificent festivities, yet the native manners with their mixture of Spanish punctilio and southern extravagance were not to her taste: she had only one word for them—*napoletanerie*; and six weeks later she was back in Rome. Meanwhile,

---

[1] "Booby, Booby, will you run up a fever? Are these proper plays for a lady like me?"

the world had passed on: King Louis XII had died, and Giuliano de' Medici had left for France to congratulate his successor, François I, and to receive from him the title of Duc de Nemours and the hand of his aunt, Filiberta of Savoy. What this French alliance forebodcd she could not discover; but it bore an ominous resemblance to the political début of Caesar Borgia. And, her quick mind travelling back, she remembered Urbino and Romagna and the gift of one hundred masks she had once sent Valentino for Carnival. She needed as many now to hide her confusion. No amount of personal adulation could disguise the fact that she had failed; something was afoot which she could neither circumvent nor divine; if Julius had revealed to her the power of women, Leo had made her feel their helplessness. His aim was hers, and he protected and promoted his family with feminine patience and tact. With her enemies she could cope, but not with her friends, and he seemed to take a malicious pleasure in befriending and eluding her. It was she now who was anxious to return to Mantua, and the Marquis again recalled her, but Leo once more intervened and Bibbiena played the booby about her, persuading her to remain until Carnival. She yielded, resigned to the role of a woman and nothing more: it was her pre-Lenten penance. Carnival came, with its intoxicating tintinnabulations; and on the last night she sat in her carriage in the Piazza Navona, surrounded by her admirers, surveying like a stranded siren in that Roman arena the dazzling spectacle—the fire-works flushing the gloom with a phosphorescent glare, the fountains glistening in multicoloured glory, the rockets suffusing the sky with siphons of effervescent stars, the fluttering showers of confetti, the revelling multitudes milling about her, and the naked obelisk erect in the night. . . . It was her parting impression of Rome.

Three weeks later, a housewife in Mantua, she was balancing her accounts. The trip had been costly: she had borrowed right and left, she detested debts, she would have to cut down on her collecting, she could not travel for years; and she had accomplished nothing. It was a cruel blow to her self-esteem. Leo had accomplished what the Marquis had failed to do: he had tamed her; and the Marquis was wooing her back into leading-strings. Her mind was haunted by Rome and its venerable Carnival, and the obelisk, symbol in perpetuity of the procacity of pleasure, reminded her of the defeat of her sex. She had lost even her hard-won self-confidence; but at least she was no longer a provincial.

Henceforward she let Francescomaria and the future take care of themselves. What the alliance of the Medici with the royal house of France foreboded no one knew. Giuliano had returned to Rome, more fashionable than ever, his French clothes fuller, his French hat tilted at a more rakish angle, and looking now like a world-weary fop or a wilted mushroom, for his health was poor. What the future held for him he did not know, except that the determination of his state depended on the international situation. It was a political pause, pregnant with embryonic schemes, with everything vague and in flux, swimming with tentative aims, shifting plans, and hovering hands, and shot through with ghostly reminders of the past—the first steps of Valentino, the first strides of Julius—but these only accentuated the difference of the present and led nowhere in its confusion. Everything rested on the Pope, and he was not the man to precipitate any situation, much less so uncertain and dangerous a one. With the accession of François I, a new personality was rising on the horizon. In many ways he resembled Giuliano, he was cultured, magnanimous, fashionable, rakish; but he was enterprising, and he was committed to the recovery of Milan. The marriage of Giuliano was a move on the part of the Pope to avert, or at least to delay, this threatening danger. To delay—it was all that Leo could do. Though many blamed his procrastination on his short-sightedness, he was paralysed, in reality, by his foresight. To move in any direction, in the precarious international truce, was to court disaster. He carried the problem of his country in his crutch. A fistula, often operated but always returning, made motion painful and exertion agony, and his politics were sedentary. The French, like the Spanish, like the Germans, were in the blood of Italy, breaking out intermittently, subdued for a time, and always returning when they were expelled. It was only by inaction, by studiously forbearing to irritate the endemic disease, that the peninsula could enjoy an invalid peace.

From afar Machiavelli followed this pregnant pause closely; but it was now from very far. He no longer had the satisfaction of sending his advice to Vettori, seeing it submitted to the Pope's advisers, commended, and ignored, for Vettori had returned to Florence. Together they deplored the Pope's supine neutrality; but it mattered little. As Machiavelli said, "I know that my opinion has against it a natural defect of men which is, first, to live day by day; secondly, to believe that what has never been ever can be; and lastly, to judge a problem as if it were always the same." All that was clear was that neither the Pope nor Giuliano was capable of initiative and that the Medici state, on which he had based his hopes for Italian emancipation, would be chosen, not by the Medici, but as Vettori had always insisted, by Chance.

That half-partner in human affairs now sat on the throne of France. In the summer of 1515, after two years of neutrality, two years so successful in avoiding a miscalculation that the Imperial Legate left Rome in disgust, complaining that "the Pope weaves everything into a labyrinth," Leo was at last jostled into a decision. François I was no sooner on the throne than he was in the saddle and the invasion of Milan was prepared with the speed of a raid. The sore was swelling again, and the Pope joined Spain and the Emperor for the defence of the peninsula. The Papal armies assembled in Bologna, and Giuliano left Rome to assume the supreme command. On his way he passed through Gubbio, in the state of Urbino, to persuade Francescomaria to join the forces of the Church.

To these advances Francescomaria listened at first coldly and, with his usual outspokenness, he alluded to the old rumour of the Pope's designs on Urbino. Giuliano vigorously denied it, assuring him that he for one would never be a party to such a crime; he was never more sincere or more winning; and the young della Rovere, like his late uncle, was quick to anger but easily appeased. He invited Giuliano to spend a few days in Urbino, where his old rooms were waiting for him: that was the test, he would not violate the *genius loci*. Giuliano declined, but so reluctantly that his host was mollified and consented to take service under him against the French. From Bologna, Giuliano reported this little victory to Rome, and there the engagement was regarded as settled. The Duke of Urbino was supplied with money to raise troops and join the Papal army in Bologna. But the contract was no sooner signed than Francescomaria began to reconsider. His mind had been too deeply unsettled by the suspicion which had lodged in it. He was still wavering in moody indecision when he learned that Giuliano was ill and had resigned the supreme command to his nephew, Lorenzo de' Medici. That settled him. Under Lorenzo he declined to serve. Castiglione vainly attempted to make plausible excuses for his conduct in Rome; the Pope was highly incensed and imputed this change of front to French influence; nor did the Duke do anything to discourage this impression. Unable to distinguish between his pique and his politics, he was not unwilling to let the Medici know that he was not to be had for the asking when they needed him. After several weeks of negotiation, the Pope ordered him to report in Bologna with his men. The Duke refused, though he placed his men at the Pope's disposal if they chose to follow another commander, which, of course, they refused to do. The Pope took a very grave view of this insubordination on the eve of battle and exacted his service as a vassal of the Holy See; the Duke contended that his service was a business engagement, which he was free to accept or reject; the mischief grew; and Giuliano was urged to warn his friend that if he persisted he was a ruined man.

Meanwhile, with the speed of a French Valentino, François had crossed the Simplon by forced marches and reached the plains of Lombardy. At Marignano, a few miles from Milan, the forces of the League were waiting for him. The numerical strength of the two armies was approximately matched, but Lorenzo de' Medici carried secret instructions from the Pope not to enter the engagement until its issue was predictable. The Battle of the Giants, as it came to be called, was still in progress and the Swiss employed by the League were justifying their invincible fame when, at the end of the day, couriers were dispatched to Rome, announcing an Italian victory. Bibbiena ordered the city to be illuminated, and the Pope communicated the news to the ambassador of Venice, not without satisfaction, for the Venetians had joined the French. The next morning His Holiness was roused from sleep by an urgent request for an audience from the Venetian envoy. Drowsy and dishevelled, with his official face still uncomposed for the day, Leo entered the room and stared. The unconscionable diplomat was dressed like an illumination and wore a gala smile. "Holy Father," he said, "last night Your Holiness gave me bad news and false; today I bring you good news and true: the Swiss are routed." In confirmation he handed him a dispatch announcing the overwhelming victory of the French. For once the bland fat man was caught off his guard. He clasped his hands, cracked his knuckles, and blinked in naked dismay. "What will become of us?" he exclaimed. The question was not addressed to the ambassador, but the ambassador answered it. "Nothing will happen to us, as we are the allies of the Most Christian King, and no harm, no harm at all, will come to Your Holiness." Summoning all his near-sightedness, Leo stared at him without seeing him and made his escape. The next day they met again and the Pope reproached him with his unfeeling behaviour, but the ambassador was still unabashed. "Holy Father," he reminded him, "the rejoicings the other night were confined to your Palace, there were none in my house." "It was all the fault of Bibbiena," the Pope replied; "he acted without our knowledge." Then, peering sagely at his tormentor, he added: "We shall place ourselves in the hands of the Most Christian King and trust to his mercy."

François followed up his military triumph with an even more rapid and brilliant diplomatic success, detached Spain and the Emperor from the Pope, and persuaded them by adroit compensations to recognize his victory. With the Pope isolated, François invited him to Bologna to conclude a treaty of perpetual alliance. Leo saw his opportunity. Summoning all his resources, he prepared to dazzle the victor. Overnight he evolved a sartorial policy for the solution of the international crisis. French fashions were discarded and a heroic effort was made to impress the foreigner by the prestige and pomp of Italian elegance, splendour, and taste. Tailors and traders swarmed into the Vatican, money rose to sixty and seventy per cent. "If ever the bankers have enriched themselves, it is this year," Gabbionetta wrote to Isabella, begging her to lend her tapestries for this patriotic occasion. Everyone was volunteering, and as her styles were copied in France she contributed cheerfully and sent an expert observer to Bologna. When all the arrangements had been completed, the Pope passed through Florence in a dress parade. The enthusiasm with which he was welcomed testified to his prestige; the city outdid itself to honour him. Two thousand workmen had been busy for a month, erecting triumphal arches, shrines, obelisks, and figures; the principal churches were built over, externally, with false façades and internally with pseudo-choirs, tabernacles, and galleries, and divine services had to be held elsewhere. When the Papal procession entered Florence, it passed through a mimic mythological city which reproduced, at a fabulous cost, the Golden Age in plaster and gilt. Preceded by fifty youths in silk and miniver with long silver wands, the Pope was borne through the streets by the Signoria, himself a glittering idol under a huge baldacchino, "amid such a crowd that it made one's eyes ache to see," said an eye-witness. "Perhaps there had never been such a multitude assembled in Florence before." Silver was flung to the bystanders as Leo smiled blandly and scattered benedictions over the insistent acclamations which exalted him; and the effect was so persuasive that he might have passed for the Liberator of Italy. It was with genuine regret that the population watched him depart and saw the triumphal arches dismantled.

After so successful a rehearsal, the performance hardly equalled it. When the Papal cortège entered Bologna on a gloomy December day, the population was unfriendly and the gorgeous pageantry made no impression except by contrast with the appearance of the French, who were insultingly shabby. There were hardly four golden chains or a whole suit of brocade between them, noted one close and scandalized spectator, and the state entry of the victorious army resembled nothing so much as a municipal councillor taking office. The King himself, to be sure, was a commanding and spectacular figure, but his soldiers looked and his gentlemen acted like bargemen. "There is not one of them that may be likened to, or that looks like, a gentleman," Gabbionetta reported to Isabella. "It is unbelievable," wrote her observer, in describing a fracas which occurred at High Mass in the Duomo, "it is unbelievable how little respect they showed to many noble Italians, and how they hustled and beat them, respecting neither the Pope's people nor the others; even the Venetian gentlemen came in for their share of abuse." The King, however, was an exception. The courtly Valois displayed the most feeling reverence for the Vicar of Christ, who leaned on his arm, worn with the weight of his triple Tiara, his fabulous cope, and his fistula, whenever they appeared in public together. But François allowed him no time to dazzle or blandish him. He remained in Bologna only four days and they were constantly closeted in secret conference. When the terms leaked out, the treaty, however, was seen to be a handsome one. The King pledged himself to respect the integrity of the states of the Church and to preserve the authority of the Medici in Florence; while the Pope in return ceded Parma and Piacenza, which the French had already occupied, and promised to restore Modena to the Duke of Ferrara. This clause, which cancelled the original project for a Medici state, sealed the doom of Urbino.

Francescomaria, warned that the Pope would indemnify himself at his expense and realizing that he had an excellent pretext to do so, sent Castiglione to Bologna to appeal to the King. So successfully did he plead that François consented to intercede with the Pope; but Leo was inflexible. Urbino was a Papal fief, the Duke was guilty of a flagrant felony, and he reserved the right to deal with him as he chose. Castiglione, however, insisted; but the friends of the Duke were sceptical. "As for Urbino, matters look bad," Gabbionetta wrote to Mantua, "and though the King has promised M. Baldassare Castiglione to approach our *Saint Père* once more, those who love the Duke fear the worst." That François consented to renew his appeal was due to the personal impression which Castiglione had made on him. The young Valois was a new phenomenon, an enlightened foreigner who fancied the art and the manners of Italy. He had already asked the Holy Father for the famous Laocoön, a request with which Leo hastened to comply, though he promptly had a copy prepared. But in one respect François was a connoisseur who could not be put off with a clever facsimile. He flattered himself that he knew a gentleman; and Castiglione fascinated him. He was not surprised to learn that he was writing a book on *The Courtier*. The subject was fallow and no one was better fitted to treat it; he urged him to complete it "for the benefit of future generations," and intimated that he would not be averse to accepting the dedication: and, as a proof that he deserved it, he condescended to solicit the Pope at a farewell supper on the eve of his departure.

In the morning he left a message explaining that he had done his royal best but that, after a second rebuff, as Castiglione would be the first to understand, he could not insist.

40

The class instinct awoke in Castiglione. To fight to the last for lost causes was the fundamental tradition of his breed. Moreover, his loyalty to Francescomaria was a legacy from the dead Duke, and, if anything more was needed to spur him, it was the prospect of Elizabetta resuming, in her declining years, the life of an exile. But who could cope with Leo? François had failed, and the Pope had returned to Florence. There remained Giuliano, but Giuliano was lying in Florence gravely ill. Castiglione determined to consult Isabella. On her visit to Rome he had renewed his boyhood acquaintance with her and made himself agreeable in a number of ways, above all by persuading Raphael to work for her; and on her return to Mantua she had promoted his reconciliation with the Marquis. For some time Francesco Gonzaga, impressed by his success in Rome, had shown signs of relenting; he was willing to forget and forgive the injuries he had done Castiglione; and Castiglione was now at liberty to visit Casatico whenever he pleased. Accordingly, when the Congress of Bologna dispersed, it was the road to Mantua which he took.

On the way, he stopped in Modena to please his mother. The old Countess was only half impressed by his success in Rome: he was thinking of everyone but himself and of her and of Casatico; and when he wrote, in the prime of life and in the full radiance of Rome, that "the flower of my first years is fading, and this life which we cherish is a shadow, a fleeting dream, a vapour, a wind," the old lady decided to marry him without further delay. She took the necessary steps and begged him to return by way of Modena and look over the "merchandise" which she had chosen for him. He did so and was satisfied. Ippolita Torelli had all the proper qualifications—money, character, beauty, and connexions. There were only two possible clouds: she was fifteen and he was thirty-seven; and her mother had murdered the first man she married. But in the eyes of the daughter he detected an eager tolerance of man. Fresh from the convent, she was already counting the days, when he left Modena, to their reunion. "When I think that I must live without you for fifteen days," she wrote him post-haste, "I feel as if fifteen swords pierced my heart." The marriage was announced on his arrival in Mantua.

But Ippolita was destined to wait. He had more urgent business on his mind than marriage, and in Mantua he paused only long enough to consult Isabella before returning to Urbino. He found the great lady rusticating in a suburban villa, because, as she said, "in the solitude of the country it is easier to remember the pleasures of Rome than in the small and narrow society of Mantua." But it was not the pleasures, it was the baffling impermeability, of Rome that his appearance recalled to her. He seemed to bring the dreary winter landscape with him. Nevertheless, she set her slender threads of influence in motion, though without conviction. She mobilized her French nephew, the Constable de Bourbon, who was governing Milan; but without much success. Then she thought of better. Federico had been sent to France as a hostage for the politics of his parents, and there was no reason why he should not become, once more, from a hostage an influence. He was fifteen and popular with the King. Federico pleaded manfully for his brother-in-law Francescomaria, and the King promised to write to the Pope. At the same time he suggested that he would be pleased to have a portrait of Madama who was still, as he understood, one of the comeliest women in Italy. But—was she growing old indeed?—the thought of playing on his royal gallantry revolted her, and she replied rather shortly that she had no more portraits of herself. Then François suggested that she might send one of her daughter, the Duchess of Urbino: everyone told him that she was one of the beauties of Italy; but she replied even more shortly that the reports of her daughter's beauty were greatly exaggerated. And François, unwilling to risk a third rebuff, forgot the promised letter to the Pope.

Meanwhile, time was passing and the blow was approaching. The Pope no sooner returned to Rome than an indictment was drawn against the Duke of Urbino, not only on the basis of his desertion, but also on the old charge which Giovanni de' Medici had himself helped to quash five years before—the assassination of Cardinal Alidosi. Castiglione hurried back to Urbino with a Mantuan Captain, Luigi Gonzaga, whom Isabella sent as a military expert. She begged her son-in-law, however, to do everything to avoid war and "to consult with the Signor Marchese and his other friends and relatives." "Because of our love for Your Lordship and our daughter, we are bound to give you our opinion," she explained, "and though we believe Your Lordship to be prudent, yet in his own affairs a man should always consult with others." Fearing, however, that like most men Francescomaria would ruin his affairs by himself, she made one more effort in another direction.

The last hope was Giuliano de' Medici. Her courage quickened when she learned that, rallying from his illness, he had protested to the Pope against the spoliation of Urbino and had induced him to abandon it. But there was an obstacle—Lorenzo de' Medici. The nephew who so studiously imitated Giuliano in Florence was bent on succeeding him in Urbino; and behind him, restlessly urging him on, was a scheming mother. Everything hung on the life of Giuliano, and his life hung by a thread. He was in the last stages of galloping consumption, and the hectic rally was followed by a relapse which brought the Pope hurrying to his bedside at Fiesole. Isabella snatched at the critical moment and sent her confidential agent, Agnello, to Florence.

Agnello was permitted to see the patient, though only on the express condition that he would avoid all painful subjects; and Giuliano, "in so feeble a murmur that he could hardly be heard," was barely able to acknowledge his greetings. Bibbiena, who was at his bedside, was deeply discouraged: the Pope, he said, was obdurate. Nevertheless, Agnello took his courage in his hands and obtained an audience of the Pope. Throughout it Lorenzo lurked within earshot. The Holy Father was extremely ruffled. Growing greyer as he grew angrier, he broke into a hubbub of bitter complaints, rehearsed all the offences of Francescomaria and, rapidly scolding in nervous volubility, exclaimed that "he did not know how he could be expected to wear the double horns of injury and indulgence: others would ape his example, others would trick and abuse him, presuming on his lenience, and he would be no better than an owl." But, after all—better an owl than a parrot—he ended by making a proposal. "We shall punish the scoundrel, we shall punish him, we shall take his state," he went on, rising and hooting carefully about, "and to show that we desire, not revenge, but a warning example, we shall give the state to his son; or the Marquis of Mantua may govern it, provided that rogue does not." Agnello leapt at this suggestion and asked if he might submit it to his master, the Marquis; the Pope nodded; but at this point Lorenzo approached and drew him aside, and after a whispered conference Leo abruptly ended the audience.

Agnello, knowing his business, immediately put the proposal in writing and had it witnessed by two Cardinals before sending it to Mantua.

The reply, when it came, was entirely satisfactory—Francescomaria consented to place himself and his state in the hands of his relatives—but it came with a delay which made it clear that he had weighed the proposal with mature deliberation. The Pope, in the meantime, had also weighed it with mature deliberation and when the reply came he had completely forgotten it. He insisted on summoning the Duke to his trial immediately. Agnello appealed to Cardinal Riario, who had witnessed the offer, and the Cardinal protested to the Pope, declaring that his personal honour was involved; but all he could obtain was a promise that proceedings would be deferred until the return of the Papal Court to Rome; and even this Leo granted reluctantly: it was only wasting time, he said. Meanwhile, someone else was wasting time. Giuliano was dying; yet "though everyone believed he had not three hours to live," as Bibbiena remarked with amazement, "he has lingered miraculously for six days, without being able to take nourishment." It seemed as if something sustained him —as if, after tasting all the pleasures of life, he could not part with it until he had known its full pain. With a last consumptive effort, he appealed to the Pope. Leo was fond of his brother, but his family feeling was masculine: what he loved was not persons but posterity; and as Giuliano was doomed, he urged him gently "to think of nothing but to get well," and hurriedly departed with Lorenzo for Rome.

The dying man sank rapidly, but he succeeded in communicating his effort to Bibbiena, who hovered over him in sleepless solicitude. Bibbiena whispered the final inspiration to Agnello, "both because I wish to satisfy so many gentlemen and in behalf of the honour of Signor Giuliano and my own"; and Agnello wrote to Isabella: "As completely as I had given up hope, so completely am I now cheered." And Isabella, gathering the last breath, wrote in turn to Elizabetta: "As you are of such venerable authority and the House of Medici is so deeply indebted to you, you will soften the heart of our Lord, even if it were the most hardened in the world." The widow rose, surrounded by the moral support of all those who were inspired by lost causes—Giuliano, Isabella, the Marquis, and Francescomaria—and set out for Rome, accompanied by her gentlemen and escorted by Castiglione.

On the day of her arrival, she found the summons to the Duke of Urbino already posted. The coincidence seemed to her deliberate; and she did not hesitate to say so when she was received by the Pope. He replied that it had long been decided, that he was extremely occupied, and that, as the subject was so painful to both of them, they might well defer its discussion. She was immediately discouraged; but a little group of friendly Cardinals rallied around her and urged her not to relax. She returned a second, a third, a fourth, a fifth, a sixth time, and always with the same result. With each visit the Pope became "more difficult and severe," but his patience never wore out: he was determined to exhaust hers. He lacked the moral courage to dismiss her and he was too diplomatic to deny her. Deploring the difficulty of finding a solution and entreating her to suggest one which he could accept, he left her dumbfounded by his ingenuity and his disingenuousness. He was extremely careful of appearances; and on this trait Bibbiena counted. Unwilling to champion the Duchess openly, Bibbiena lurked behind the scenes, prompting, suggesting, directing the manoeuvres, and attempting to marshal public opinion against the Pope. In the intervals of her visits, her gentlemen, Castiglione, Luigi Gonzaga, and Alberto Carpi, took up the theme, harping now on the sentimental, now on the legal, now on the personal, now on the pastoral, sides of the question; but Leo eluded them all. He played the comedy consummately and never flagged with repetition. Only occasionally could they score a point. When he challenged Luigi Gonzaga to suggest an honourable solution, "Holy Father," that blunt soldier replied, "I do not propose to lay down the law, but so far as I can understand, nothing would be more generous or more becoming to the Holy See than pardon." He was rewarded with a compassionate stare. Alberto Carpi was more aggressive. He cleared the Duke of the original charge, claiming that his contract, which he had examined, made his service contingent on his pay and that Francescomaria had been legally free, therefore, to withdraw by forfeiting it. The Pope, manifestly annoyed by such quibbles, denied all knowledge of this clause and, remembering that it was the hour of the matutinal office, called in the Cardinals and retired, as Carpi described him, "subterfugaceous as Proteus." Amid these spiritless evasions, Isabella had a bold inspiration and proposed to carry the appeal over the Pope's head to the Lateran Council; but on reflection she realized that this step was too rash: the Cardinals were willing to intrigue with her but not to make a public stand, and an adverse decision of the Council would be irreversible. And the futile farce continued.

Elizabetta's patience was at last drained; she broke down on her *via crucis* and rose only to announce her retreat. But when she took her leave of the Pope, he would not hear of it. He had just been informed of the death of Giuliano, which caused him less pain than he expected; he was disappointed in himself and with lugubrious compunction he made an effort to revive his deadened feelings. The form which this effort took was a *faux-pas*. As a proof of his personal sympathy, he warned Elizabetta that if she returned to Urbino she would incur the excommunication which he was about to lay on the Duke. But the simple lady completely misunderstood this friendly warning and replied sharply that "it seemed very strange to her that she could not do her duty as a Christian." To pacify her, he promised her and her ladies a special exemption; whereupon her tears began to flow and, her indignation rising with them, she reminded him bitterly of the benefits he had received in his exile at Urbino; he braced himself, folded his arms, and paid her the terminal courtesy of a blank silence. Still talking, still weeping, she showed herself out; but it was with one satisfaction at least that she disappeared: she had reduced him to speechlessness. There was a kind of honesty in that.

But, alas, Elizabetta Gonzaga was too simple a woman to be satisfied with so little; like her clever sister-in-law she was tempted to go on for ever; she dared not take no. The Pope went to hunt at La Magliana and, as it was well known that when the bag was good he gave any thing to anyone, she followed him, waiting patiently while, with monocle in one hand and sword in the other, he edged into the bush and dispatched the dying stag; and when he returned she approached him once more. The bag was good but the lackeys and courtiers assembled in the hall watched her pass out flushed with displeasure—"at which," wrote Agnello, "no one who knew the ways of FORTIS was surprised, though everyone showed the greatest sympathy and distress at the plight of a Lady who might well have moved the most venomous or savage beast." Yet her failure was not unfruitful. Irritated by the resistance and criticism he encountered on all sides, Leo made a public statement that "his aim was neither money nor a state but only the satisfaction of the honour of the Holy See." The unwearying siege of intercession had served Bibbiena's purpose: public opinion was aroused and hostile, and the Pope recognized it by promising to suspend sentence if the Duke gave an example of submission and came to Rome. He would give him a penance, he said, which "at first might seem hard, but afterwards he would invest his son with the title." Isabella immediately perceived the importance of this concession and wrote to her sister-in-law to "do everything to obtain this promise in writing." Castiglione was elected to undertake this delicate commission.

His turn had come. It was the critical moment in the lost cause and it demanded a supreme delicacy for which he seemed to have been reserved. The contest had shifted to a plane of manners and the last hope of the defence was to manoeuvre the Pope into a position so conspicuous and inescapable that he would be compelled either to defy public opinion or to submit to that decent hypocrisy which was the last moral refuge—a conventional semblance, a ghostly reminder of honour—and keep his word. It was a slender chance and required an expert hand. Castiglione was on the alert. Ushered into the Papal study, he began carefully to feel the subterfugaceous soul, but only to find it changing colour under his hands. The Pope was flushed. Understanding only too well the mistrust he inspired, he played on it and, abruptly reversing the roles, complained that these continual delays were nothing but a subterfuge to trick him; and with nervous bravado he attempted to usher his suitor out. Castiglione gave ground, returned, and insisted; Leo sat down, looked bored, and resisted. He had granted too many postponements, he repeated curtly, and he studied his nails with pointed impatience. No doubt, Castiglione agreed, no doubt the delays had been many but they had certainly been short; and then, with the door in sight, he made for the point. If the Duke came to Rome and made his submission, he would expect some guarantee of his safety; but Leo, lighting up, parried with a masterly feint. The submission must be unconditional; it was beneath him to bargain; moreover, the Duke himself "would never trust him unless he realized that he had the power and not the will to harm him; nor could he ever trust the Duke until he had some proof of his confidence." He stared at his antagonist conclusively, and suddenly remembered that he was Baldassare Castiglione. He was Baldassare Castiglione; and something—some magnetic candour in the man perhaps—moved Leo to be frank. He offered a spontaneous proof of his good will. No harm would come to the Duke, the Pope said, "he would pledge his personal word to him and to the Marquis and to as many Cardinals as they pleased, but not in writing; for if he wished to deceive he would do so by Bulls and Briefs; but his personal word could be trusted." And the mask, so courteously raised for a moment, slipped back on the official face, leaving Castiglione at a loss. It was the only point he had scored; and he reported the interview to his master without comment, except to remark that His Excellency would have to decide for himself—no one could advise him.

Francescomaria immediately raised troops and made his preparations to defend Urbino.

Six weeks later all was over; he was in flight with his family to Mantua; and Lorenzo de' Medici entered Urbino at the head of the Papal troops (June 1516). Old observers, whose memories went back fifteen years, speculated on the similarities and the differences of the past and the present. "Lorenzo is clever and capable of great things," the Venetian ambassador to the Vatican believed, "and though he is not the equal of Valentino, he is little inferior to him." Was he the Medici of the future? Machiavelli believed so; and, effacing the name of Giuliano from the dedication of *The Prince*, he replaced it with that of Lorenzo de' Medici, Duke of Urbino, and waited. Certainly, Lorenzo had the ambition which his uncle lacked; he was already talking of a French marriage which would give him a place among the crowned heads of Europe, and of making himself master of Italy. Francois I sent him his congratulations. In a private conversation with the ambassador of Ferrara, however, the King pointed out that, "as this conquest had not cost him a single man nor a single drop of blood," Lorenzo would do well, "if he were wise, to content himself with this one state of Urbino." "I doubt," he added, "if he will succeed in holding it, for remember, he is, after all, only a shopkeeper."

41

For Castiglione the fall of Urbino was a providential calamity. It ended his career, and he relinquished it with relief. It had yielded him the only satisfaction he cared for—ten years of disinterested service. That record served him well when with the refugees he returned to Mantua. The Marquis welcomed him home; a new service awaited him; and his ruin, like his rise, was made easy for him. But he preferred to retire. His real vocation was society and the society of Urbino, which had once been so essential a part of his being, had now completely disintegrated. Some of its members were dead, others were changed, all were scattered, and each had carried away a fragment of himself. Suddenly he found himself stranded—a middle-aged sentimentalist evicted from a dream. His whole life had been a vicarious one; it was time to think of himself. The service of princes was precarious, the life of society ephemeral; sooner or later the new ties would break like the old; and he had no heart to court fresh disappointments. The futility of his profession, the evanescence of his friendships, the aimlessness of his existence, left him bewildered; and retracing his steps to Casatico, he settled down to recuperate, to recover his bearings, and to reorganize his life on his own acres.

His life . . . but had he ever really lived? Everything had always been made easy for him and he had missed the experience of life itself. He had no vital attachment to anything, nothing whose loss left him inconsolable, nothing to inform the new emptiness of his days. He had lived correctly, conventionally, and barrenly. Of all his accomplishments, what achievement remained? Reputation; by his code that was enough; it signified; yet it left him lonely. It was not possible to build a complete and well-tempered life on the amenities alone; in the end Nature exacted her due, and he craved some basis more substantial, more fundamental. But it was not too late to begin anew; and that start too was made easy for him.

Ippolita Torrelli was waiting. The fifteen days to their marriage had stretched into six months, and the gossips in Modena commented venomously on his prolonged absence, but she would not admit that he had neglected her. "Those cruel tongues with their slanders have not prevailed," she wrote him, "I have given them to understand that there is no happier girl in the world than I, which is no more than the truth, my dear Lord, and the best of revenges. And now that they can no longer abuse Your Lordship, they turn on me and say that I am nothing but a lump of flesh with two eyes." So sensible, so young, and so enamoured! She touched him. Her devotion was doubly welcome, because he deserved it less than he needed it. She was destined perhaps, that girl of fifteen, to lead him back to his lost youth; there was no reason to defer the wedding longer and he promised to bring her to Mantua. At the last moment, however, he was detained by business and sent her brother instead. She could not contain her disappointment. "I have just learned that I am to come to Mantua without your company," she wrote him, "and I want a few words with you on that subject, but I shall wait until I can use my tongue"—and she sealed the note with a nuptial pout. But all was forgotten when, on the outskirts of Mantua, she was met by her husband, the Marquis, and a deputation from Court, and escorted to the Castello where Madama and the two Duchesses of Urbino welcomed her. She passed inspection triumphantly: "No lovelier girl has been seen in Lombardy," said the clergy; "the bride satisfied everyone," the laity agreed; and the Count, immediately responsive to public opinion, warmed to the general approval of his wife. He had married correctly, and the couple now settled down at Casatico to make each other's acquaintance.

She was twenty-three years his junior, and at first she seemed like a child in the old manor, but she did her best to grow up to him and to efface the disparity of their ages. Longing for the day when a child would make a woman of her, she sat by the fire with her mother-in-law, embroidering baby-clothes and begging for reminiscences of his boyhood. The Count became very fond of her, and so did his mother. The old

Countess was satisfied: the prodigal had returned and was leading the life she had always planned for him. Her own life was easier now: there was a man at Casatico to cope with its problems—the neighbours who diverted their water, and the peasants who refused to cart their crops to Desenzano, and the hungry mouths to be fed when the market at Mantua was bad—though, to be sure, he had no head for business, and she still had to check his accounts. But she no longer worried over his welfare; he was always within call to answer questions or, if not, Ippolita knew where to find him—in his study or in the stables or inspecting the melons or roaming the fields—doing all the things he had done as a boy, and apparently perfectly contented. Marriage and the management of his estate absorbed him completely. The world saw him rarely and he seemed not to miss it. The most sociable of men, he was now the most self-sufficient. Solitude had no terrors for him, certainly not the solitude which one man and one woman make between them; and Ippolita was almost a woman, and he found it pleasant to fancy himself half a young man again.

Half, but not wholly. The past divided them. It was the one thing they could never share; and, the fonder he grew of her, the more painfully he realized it. With Ippolita a new life began, real and substantial, which reminded him of the futility of the old, and he could not forget the years he had wasted without her. They were the best of his life. The one illusion of youth he could not recapture was his confidence in the future; he had already consumed it, and he was haunted by regrets for the past. Its fibres had been too recently severed, and in that phase of sentimental convalescence, though new ties were knitting, the old scars still smarted. There was still an aching void which she could not fill. The angel of annunciation hovered over Casatico, and tomorrow Gabriel might triumph —tomorrow—but today—today was sacred to memory. Phantoms, more real than the flesh, clung to him like the mists that hung about the old house in the dank hours before dawn. He was restless. When he went up to Mantua, he found himself in the world but not of it, and the solitude of the multitude was intolerable. He returned with relief to the placid monotony of Casatico, the thriving hush of the country, the stealthy fall of the leaf, the mute rumination of his memories, and the patient expectation of the unborn. But he was still restless. He walked through the calm fields and his mind wandered back to Urbino and its vicissitudes— the fugitive succession of Guidobaldo and Valentino and Francescomaria and the Medici—and here, among the young crops, the vengeful chafe of kings seemed a little thing. Guidobaldo and Borgia both lay, the conqueror and the conquered, with a spear of grass in their hands; Francescomaria and the Medici were mute under the spiral song of the lark; and he found a fleeting composure in resting his memories under the sun. But when evening fell, and the vapours stole over the meadows, once more the void within him reopened and, taking the rushlight, he withdrew to his study and surrendered to his nightly nostalgia of the past.

It was the hour for drawing up his accounts; and it was then that he completed *The Courtier*. Now, at last, he had leisure to write, and the many delays which had stayed his hand had served merely to mature the book and lend it final meaning. Beginning as a sentimental memoir and developing into a professional creed, it was completed as a vindication of his vocation and an apology for his life. The time had come for a final accounting with himself. It was too painful to weigh his life and find it wanting in lasting value, and he wrote to redeem its futility, to lend it, in his own eyes at least, some illusion of achievement and purpose.

But what purpose could so ornamental a profession as the Courtier's serve?—a profession which, though it included the service of a soldier or a diplomat, was essentially that of a social companion? Precisely. Was there no service in perfecting social life, in developing a type of man in whom the habitual exercise of all the qualities it required became second nature and, holding the natural man in abeyance, bred a social conscience and fostered civilized life? To fuse men was the secret of the convivial ideal; in the intercourse of men of the world, their natural differences and irremediable antagonisms were suspended; and society, with its code of courtesy, achieved, in a truce of convention, a semblance of that solidarity which was the aim of religion or patriotism. Its polite fictions kept alive the memory, and the aspiration, of their common humanity; and a code of manners might dissimulate the mission of a moral lawgiver—a mission the more necessary that the demoralization of Italian life in religion and politics made society the last refuge of its self-respect—and a mission the more easy that nowhere was the power of public opinion so potent as in the domain of manners and customs. Of all laws, the unwritten law of social usage was the most binding on the average man: the claims of his God or his Government were remote and occasional, those of his neighbour familiar and unremitting; and the standards of the society to which he belonged were perhaps the one compelling influence on his conduct.

But those standards were variable; they were constantly modified by the shifting forms of time and place. "I know how difficult it is," he wrote, "amid the various manners that are observed in the Courts of Christendom to select the best and, as it were, the flower of Courtiership;

because custom makes us favour and disfavour the same things; manners, habits, forms, and fashions that once were esteemed become debased and, vice versa, the base become prized. It is clear, therefore, that custom rather than reason introduces innovations and abolishes old forms, and he that seeks to determine the best often errs." Nevertheless, by the comparison of many models it might be possible to deduce something which all had in common and which might be accepted as normal; and was not the happy mean of the normal the whole aim of worldly morality? The superhuman ideals of religion strained nature; the material ideals of patriotism surrendered to it; those of the world were a compromise, a *modus vivendi* of the soul. It was the function of society to hold the balance true, to maintain the wholesome average proper to man; and it was for that norm of beautiful living, that recurring undertone, that he had been listening all his life, ever since he first heard it fitfully in the old days at Urbino.

To suggest it he had only to return to the past, to convene the old circle in memory, and to let them speak for themselves. But it was with diffidence that he ventured to trace "a portrait of the Court of Urbino not by the hand of Raphael or Michelangelo, but by a mean painter capable only of drawing the main lines." To do it justice he needed the manner of Raphael; for Raphael, who had painted so many of its courtiers and who was himself a son of Urbino, had caught the quintessence of that society in a manner whose mellow elegance—so deceptively simple, so nobly mediocre—was the sublimation of the normal, the pink of its perfection. There was more than a touch of the same consummate urbanity in the limpid flow of his own prose; but after all neither of them could vie with the originals. He made himself their medium; effacing himself and recollecting their own words, he convoked them to one of their favourite pastimes—an impromptu symposium on the virtues of their own vocation—and created the social man by a social act.

For such a man there might be a future. François had urged him to complete the book "for the benefit of future generations." His interest was a symptom of the changing times. The process by which an old and civilized race subdues its conquerors through its culture had begun, and certainly it was only through its culture that the dignity of Italy could survive: politically it was lost. To transmit, not merely to his countrymen but to the foreigner, not only to his contemporaries but to future generations, the Italian ideal of a gentleman—to send that quickening inspiration through the veins of men unknown and times yet to be—would be to commemorate Urbino and assure the triumph of Time over the Medici. They might triumph in Urbino today, but tomorrow . . . *Le Temps revient*: it was their own motto.

The return of the Medici to Urbino was a chance shock which set a man searching for his faith, and, through the long even nights at Casatico, Castiglione laboured till time ceased to exist for him. The mists of the present dissolved, and the past returned in its pristine clarity. Once more the old faces came crowding about him—Bembo and Bibbiena and the Magnifico Giuliano and the Duchess and her nephews, the brothers Fregoso of Genoa, and Emilia Pia and Pallavicino, the misogynist, and Cesare Gonzaga and Canossa and the rest—as they once were, before the world touched them. Once more it is March 1507, and Pope Julius, pursuing his mole-like upheaval of the peninsula, has paused in Urbino and passed on; and after his departure the company, stimulated by the brief intrusion of the alien world of war, has reassembled for its normal diversions. Once more they meet in the Duchess's rooms after supper; once more they range themselves in a semicircle around her chair; the voices rise; various topics are proposed, bandied about, and dismissed; someone proposes the perfect Courtier as the theme of the evening; and Count Lodovico da Canossa begins.

42

At the outset the question of caste comes up. "I would have our Courtier well born," Canossa begins; but not because of class prejudice. Though he comes of an old conservative family, he keeps abreast of the times and prides himself on his open-mindedness. He is a man of the Renaissance and he reasons, resting his conviction of the value of blood on the eugenic value of heredity and the traditional value of *noblesse oblige*. "A man of low birth," he contends, "incurs less discredit than a noble if he swerves from the path of his ancestors; for nobility is like a clear lamp, revealing and illumining good conduct and bad and kindling and inciting a man to virtue, both by the dread of disgrace and the hope of praise. . . . Hence it almost always follows that in arms and other actions of repute the most notable men are noble, for Nature has secreted in everything an occult seed which lends a certain power and property to whatever derives from it and makes it resemble it, as we see not only in the breeding of horses and other animals, but also in trees, whose shoots almost always resemble their stock, and, if sometimes they degenerate, it is because they have been badly cultivated." But this argument is at once challenged. "This nobility does not seem to me so necessary," a voice protests. Gaspare Pallavicino is a young man who for reasons of his own recognizes no ancestor but Adam, and in the spirit of the new age he protests such feudal ideas. "I could name many who, born of the best blood, have been vicious and others who, despite their low birth, have ennobled their posterity by their virtues. If it were true, as you say, that everything reveals the occult virtue of the original seed, we should all be alike, as we all have the same origin, and no man would be better than the next. ... Nature knows none of these subtle distinctions, and, as this nobility is acquired neither by ability nor power nor art, it is rather to the credit of our ancestors than to our own; and it seems to me altogether unfair to say that, if the parents of the Courtier are lowly, all his other qualities count for nothing." Canossa is chagrined that his open-mindedness should not be recognized. It is one of his best qualities and he has been at pains to acquire it; but it counts for nothing with the new generation. He is of an excitable nature but he is unwilling to appear reactionary and he compromises between the feudal and Renaissance views of the value of blood. Maintaining that birth constitutes an initial advantage, but conceding merit and talent as titles to social recognition, he opens his vocation to the natural gentleman and sustains the liberal tradition of Italian aristocracy and that Renaissance cult of reason and humanity which tempers even the conservative tenets of class pride—submitting them to discussion, defending them on rational, and opposing them on generous, grounds—to the enlightening influence of the New Birth.

But he has the instinct of privilege, and he now claims a natural one: beauty. "I would have our Courtier well favoured, and he should be born not only with beauty and ability but also with a certain grace and, as we say, a *blood* which will make him, at first sight and to everyone, pleasing and welcome." Birth, beauty, ability, and charm: why should he not be exorbitant? When he is temperate, he is immediately misjudged. But no one demurs: the aesthetic sense of the age accepts these claims without question.

His next point also meets with general consent. "I believe that the principal and true profession of the Courtier should be arms"—though, of course, only as an amateur. "I should not expect him to show so complete a command of military affairs as a Captain must possess: this would be to wade in too deep, and we shall be satisfied with an undaunted spirit and integrity of faith, which he must manifest on every occasion; for courage is more often recognized in small than in great things; often in major perils where there are many witnesses we find men who, though their hearts weigh like lead, are spurred on by shame or companionship and push forward blindly, doing their duty God knows how, while in less tight corners, where they can avoid danger without dishonour, they willingly look to their safety. But those that, even when they expect neither to be seen nor recognized, show spirit and shirk nothing, however slight, that might tax them—these have that virtue of soul we seek in our Courtier." And one thing more: "The soldier we seek should be fierce, harsh, and always among the foremost before the enemy, but everywhere else modest, reserved, and humane, avoiding above everything ostentation and insolent self-praise, which always arouse distaste and aversion."

This leads to a larger question. Pallavicino objects that he has found few who are not given to self-praise if they are proficient in anything, and for his part he is willing to condone so human and democratic a failing—"because a man who knows his own worth, when the ignorant do not recognize it, is bound to be irked if his talent is buried; and he is compelled to disclose it or be defrauded of honour, which is the true reward of all virtuous exertions." Suddenly the discussion has fallen on a pregnant theme—on the great craze of the age, its passion for fame, its unblushing cult of celebrity, its inordinate appetite for praise, the meed of all virtue, the motive of all effort—vanity. Vanity; it is vanity in all its forms and under all its pseudonyms—glory, honour, learning, virtue—that makes the world go round, vanity that distinguishes man from the animals, vanity that is his sixth sense and of all the most lustful and insatiable; and if its satisfaction is the accepted object of virtue, why expect men to be superior to it?

But there is a way of civilizing vanity, to admit and smile at it; and Bibbiena illustrates. The facetious prelate captures the conversation as it threatens to founder beyond its depth, and steers it lightly back into the shallows. "I remember that you said our Courtier should be gifted with beauty of person and feature," he begins swimmingly. "Now, I believe I am blessed both with grace and beauty of feature, that being the reason, as you know, that so many ladies pine for me, but I am in some doubt as to the beauty of my person, above all of these legs which, to tell the truth, are not as well turned as they might be; though I am very well satisfied with the bust and the rest of me. I wish, therefore, that you would define this beauty a little more minutely, so that I may resolve my doubts and rest my soul in peace." A ripple of laughter rewards his self-immolation and with the distant look of a masterpiece among sightseers he submits, body and soul, to public scrutiny. "Certainly," Canossa agrees, "certainly you may truthfully claim beauty of feature, and I need no other illustration to define it; your appearance, we agree, is exceedingly pleasing, it delights us all: the lineaments are not very delicate; nevertheless, it is gracious and manly enough. And of such would I have the countenance of the Courtier: not so soft and womanish as that of many who curl their hair and pluck their brows and sleek themselves with every trick that the most wanton and disreputable women use. These should be banished not only from the Courts of every great prince but from the commerce of gentlemen." Then, like an expeditious guide, he returns from the successful diversion which Bibbiena has created to his subject and, to take the taste of effeminacy out of his mouth, rehearses the sports of the Courtier, sports which are not only training for war but the civilized substitute for it; and he urges his countrymen to excel, first, in their own sports, secondly, in those of the French, thirdly, in those of the Spanish; and in all to display that native grace which, in this as in everything else, is the crown and criterion of strength.

Grace. "It seems to me," Cesare Gonzaga remarks, "that you place it everywhere as a condiment, without which all the other properties and qualities are of little value." And he asks, a little self-consciously, whether, if it is not inborn, it can be acquired. He is near enough to the awkward age to listen for the verdict with a long face and a beating heart. "I should not undertake to impart this perfection," Canossa replies, "particularly as I said a moment ago that the Courtier should wrestle and vault and do many other things which I cannot teach, not knowing them myself, but which I know you have all mastered. Nevertheless, having often reflected whence this grace arises, I find one rule that is universal: and that is to avoid, as far as possible and as a most fatal and destructive reef, affectation; and if I may employ what is perhaps a new word, to use in everything a certain carelessness which conceals art and makes what is said and done seem to come without effort and almost without thought. Therefore, we may say that that is true art which does not seem to be so, and to nothing should we bend our study more than to conceal it. . . . In painting, a single stroke of the brush drawn easily, so that the hand seems to travel without apparent calculation or art in obedience to the painter's design, clearly discloses the mastery of the artist. And so it is in all other things."

A condiment, did Cesare Gonzaga call it? It is the very marrow of the matter. There is nothing which that seasoning essence does not affect. Facility, the outward and visible sign of an inward and spiritual grace, informs the whole creed of the Courtier. It is his final sophistication. The mastery of life or—what amounts to the same thing—the illusion of its mastery, lies in living it gracefully. To preserve the consummate carelessness, the becoming detachment, of an amateur, to forfeit anything but that serene appreciation of the vanity of life and that handsome dissimulation of its difficulty, which are the secret of moral elegance; to deprecate whatever is too studied, strained, intense, or earnest—conviction, ambition, passion, success—these habits mark the seasoned mind and distinguish the well-born soul; or, as a disciple of *The Courtier* put it, *Un honnête homme ne se pique de rien.*

So far the development of the Courtier has followed the fashion of his class in all countries, but now the Italian ideal begins to emerge. As grace is the outcome of balance, physical accomplishments must be matched with moral and mental ones to produce that versatility of the universal man, which is indispensable to normal life in general and to social success in particular. As for moral grace, "I believe that the only true moral philosopher is the man who tries to be good," says Canossa, settling the question with summary ease, "and he needs few other precepts but the will to be so." "But, beside goodness, our true and spiritual grace I believe to be letters, though the French recognize nobility only in arms and think nothing of all the rest; indeed, they not only do not appreciate letters, they detest them and hold all lettered men in abject contempt; and they think it the worst affront in the world to call one a *clerk*." "You are right: this error has long reigned among the French," Giuliano de' Medici agrees; though he hopes for an exception in François of Valois. A shadow of patriotic pain comes over the company, as Canossa resumes: "To say this to you is superfluous, I know that you all understand how mistaken the French are in thinking the pursuit of letters detrimental to that of arms. You know that the true incentive of great and hazardous actions in war is glory: the man who makes war for gain or any other motive not only achieves nothing but does not deserve the name of a gentleman, he is no better than a shopkeeper.... What soul is so humble, timid, or sluggish that, reading of the greatness of Caesar, Alexander, Scipio, Hannibal and so many more, he is not inflamed by a burning desire to emulate them and will not risk this fleeting life of two days for a fame that is wellnigh perpetual? But unless a man know the charm of letters . . . he measures fame by the span of one or two generations, since his memory goes no further; and he cannot value that brief span so highly as the other which is wellnigh perpetual; and valuing it less, he will probably risk less for renown than a man who is enlightened." But Canossa is only half convinced by his own argument; in reality he is pleading, and he grows pensive; and the shadow deepens. "I would not have some opponent, to refute this opinion, adduce the contrary effects and say that we Italians, with our cult of letters, have for some time past shown little valour in arms, which is only too true; but we may honestly say that the fault of a few has been the cause of great ruin and shame everlasting to the rest of us; and the true cause of our ruin, and of the decay if not the death of virtue in our souls, lies with them; and it would be far more disgraceful for us to publish this than for the French to misjudge letters. It is better to pass over in silence what we cannot recall without pain and, leaving this subject on which I have entered unwillingly, to return to our Courtier, whom I would have more than commonly learned, especially in those studies we call the Humanities."

Shadowy under its mop of black hair, livid under its glowing black eyes, the face of Canossa holds for a moment the mortified pride of his race; the company watches him in tacit agreement. Then he leads them into happier pastures. The culture of the Courtier, of course, must be catholic and classical; but as a philological patriot Canossa champions the colloquial tongue: it is the living speech that forms style, good writing being but the graphic form of good conversation. Next, there is music . . . music . . . his hobby; and he is about to mount it when a voice, growing restless in Utopia, interrupts: "But . . . But . . . In all the wide world no vessel so vast could be found to hold all you would have in your Courtier. . . ." "Wait a little," smiles the Count, "for much more is to follow." This is his answer to hecklers, his Italian retort to the gallery. He smiles; but his eyes are still big with their patriotic vision and his face is still drawn with suppressed feeling; and it is all he can do to speak calmly of music. He would rather keep silence and with a tense effort he contains himself, remarking merely that, "rightly considered, there is no repose from fatigue, no balm for an ailing mind, more honest in idleness nor more laudable than this." But this is to say nothing: what music means to him and how eloquent he can be on this theme everyone knows; and to draw him out Pallavicino pricks him. There are prigs in virility as in other things, and the young man plays the part of one. "Yes," he says, "music, I have no doubt, like many another vanity, is fit for women and maybe for some who pass for men but not for men indeed; they should not emasculate their minds with delights that may lead them to dread death." But he gets no further. "Never say it," cries Canossa, bridling with indignation, and his black eyes flame, and his black beard bristles—"never say it"—he protests with peremptory pain and catches his breath—"never say it"—and drawing himself up he threatens him with instant multiloquence: "for I will enter into a great ocean of eulogies and remind you how music was always vaunted by the ancients and held for a holy thing, and in the opinion of many philosophers the world itself is composed of music, and the heavens in their motion make harmony, and our very soul is formed of the same element, and moves and stirs and takes on life and virtue through music." He is launched; rage makes him rhapsodic; and he marshals the ancients from Plato and Socrates with their metaphysical scales to Lycurgus and the *Lacedaemonii bellicosissimi* with their martial marches; and he appeals to the harmony of the spheres to manifest in the mystic sonority of music our one intimation of immortality; and he blasts the man who has no melody in him—"look, if he does not delight in it, for a dissonance in his soul"—and banning him to a melomaniac's limbo, irredeemable by the lute, the viol, the flute, and the omnipotent organ, he confounds him for ever with the proclamation of a world sustained everywhere and always by song. He is still brimming, still breathless with lyrical volubility when that accomplished musician, Giuliano de' Medici, agrees with him, in behalf of the company, unconditionally.

But the smouldering soul of Canossa is now fully aroused; from one outlet it veers to another; from music of which he knows much he turns to art, of which he knows less. "Truly," he exclaims, "the man who does not value art seems to me far wide of wisdom." He apostrophizes the company with an injured expression; but no one challenges him—what Italian would deny his birthright? He is too elated, however, and he proceeds dithyrambically, likening "the great machine of the world" to "a great and noble picture composed by the hand of Nature and God, which deserves imitation and praise"; and it is only when he has ransacked the ancients and appealed anew to the universe that he is winded. Society varies little, and the subject of art leads to the customary ineptitudes. A dismal discussion ensues on the relative merits of painting and sculpture. Canossa favours painting; a sculptor is present—Cristoforo Romano—but he is mute; and that contentious minx, Emilia Pia, has to stir him up. "And what do you think?" she asks him point-blank. "Signora, I consider sculpture more exacting, of greater art and dignity than painting," he replies patiently. "Maybe," Canossa admits with his usual open-mindedness, "maybe, as statues are more durable, they may be said to be more impressive; as memorials they serve their purpose better than painting; but painting is also long-lived, and while it lasts it is much more delightful." The sculptor turns this categorical verdict tactfully, though the tact is adamantine. "I think you maintain the contrary of what you believe, and all for the sake of our Raphael; perhaps you consider his mastery of painting so supreme that the art of marble cannot match it; but consider that this is to praise the artist, not the art." And he proceeds to point out a few elementary facts to the titled amateur. The object of art being imitation, he invites Canossa to compare the superficial two dimensions of painting with the solid three of statuary: "you will not tell me that being is not nearer the truth than seeming!" Then he carries the argument and the initiation one step further: the dignity of an art derives from its difficulty and "I consider sculpture more difficult because, if an error is made, it cannot be corrected, while this is not true of painting." But Canossa is dogged. "I do not favour Raphael and you must not think me so ignorant as not to recognize the mastery of Michelangelo and your own and that of many other masters in marble, but I speak of art, not artists, and as you say both are imitations of Nature, yet it is not true that painting *appears* and sculpture *is*." Somewhat nettled at being misjudged again, he insists on the resources of chiaroscuro and perspective and colour—"and colour? is that nothing?"—and the variety of subject-matter, and the lifelikeness of painting in proof of its superiority; but the sculptor, resigned to the futility of discussing art with musicians, merely stares at him stolidly, and he concludes hastily: "I do not think we should pursue this discussion further. All we need say is that the Courtier should have some acquaintance with painting, since it is honourable and useful and was valued in those days when men were better than they are now." And, by way of coda, he flings out a grace-note: "And if he gained no other pleasure or profit but to appreciate the excellence of ancient and modern statues, vases, buildings, medals, cameos, engravings, and the like, he would have learned to feel at the same time the beauty of living forms." And with that, just as he extricates himself, he stumbles on a fruitful idea. "See now," he exclaims, "what pleasure an acquaintance with painting can cause! And so say all who, when they admire beauty in a woman, delight in it so deeply that they seem translated, though they cannot paint; if they could, they would delight in it yet more, for they would appreciate more completely the perfection that gives them such pleasure." At this Cesare Gonzaga laughs and laughs gracelessly. "I am no painter," he says, "but I am sure I delight more in a woman when I see her than when she is painted, even though your peerless Apelles were to return to earth." Error, cries Canossa, error! "This pleasure does not derive from her beauty entirely, but from the affection you feel for her; confess, when you first saw her, you felt not a thousandth part of the pleasure you knew later, yet her beauty was the same; which proves how much more your feeling stirs your appreciation than her beauty." And suddenly he sees his own meaning. It is for this abstract ideal of pure and intrinsic beauty that he has been groping all along in defining the Courtier. The whole discipline of his creation is dictated by a feeling for form and consonance. He is the complete man, symmetrically developed, purged of personal idiosyncrasy, and fitted for his social role by his versatility, sanity, and poise. Grace is his genius, conviviality his virtue, the normal his nature; he lives to please, to be *persona grata* is his glory; the pink of mediocrity, he is the model of all those primrose people whose common virtue is: *Raphael pinxit*.

But in explaining himself he has exhausted himself, the company is drooping, the night is half gone; and the discussion, therefore, is adjourned until the following evening.

While the roughly moulded model lies wrapped in the night, Castiglione appears for a moment in his own person to defend his age against the *laudatori tempori acti*. This intermission and retiring-room is their sphere, the confirmed bystanders and benighted spectators of life, who complain that "in the Courts of their day reigned such good and honest customs that Courtiers were all like Monks, whereas today, they say, all is contrary; among our Courtiers there is no fraternal affection nor decent living, envy alone prevails, and malice, and immoral customs, and dissolute life, and all manner of vice; the women are shameless, the men effeminate; our dress, too, they condemn as soft and unseemly. In sum, they condemn infinite things among which, no doubt, many merit reproof, for it is undeniable that our age teems with vices more than the one they commend. But I think they mistake the reason for this difference and are foolish, for they want a world of good without evil, which is impossible." And he invokes the moral average. "Who does not know that there would be no justice without injury? no courage without cowardice? no continence without incontinence? no health without infirmity? no truth without falsehood? no felicity without misfortune? . . . I believe that the passions and infirmities of mankind are not visited upon us to make us subject to them; it would not be right that Nature, the mother of all good, should deliberately determine to afflict us with so many evils;

and as she has formed health, pleasure, and our other blessings, so with these she has linked infirmity, affliction, and our other flaws" as a stimulus. "For no evil is greater than that which festers from the corrupt seed of good; and since Nature produces far better spirits now than then, those who turn to good are far better and those who turn to evil far worse. We may say that those who abstained from evil, knowing no better, deserve no praise at all; if they did little wrong, yet they did as much as they could. Let us cease then to censure the faults of our time, for without them we should lack our virtues." Then he resumes his anonymity and, firm in his faith in the law of moral compensation and his creed of conventional optimism, unfolds the wings of his subject once more; but his impatience with the old men prompts the following scene.

The Courtier has been roughly moulded; it now remains to visualize him under actual conditions. By some inadvertence, this duty falls not to the lively Canossa but to Federico Fregoso; but this seeming inadvertence is in fact a part of the finely calculated art of the design. Federico Fregoso resumes where Canossa has left off; and like most disciples he subtly distorts the spirit of the original conception by his fidelity to the letter and the bias which his own temperament lends to its development. He is an old young man, stunted by ancestor-worship; for he and his brother, Ottaviano, are scions of a princely Genoese family and exile makes them acutely conscious of their origin. In deference to their uncle, the Duke of Urbino, they make an effort to live in the present, but in deference to themselves they never forget their past. Their pedigree is their only property and they cherish it. Living on his lineage, Federico at twenty-seven is prematurely senile; by nature he is methodical, prosaic, and positive; and he appropriates the Courtier.

Already in the overture to the second evening he assumes his functions with a painstaking deliberation which nothing—neither the pleasantries of his audience nor the echo of his own platitudes—can ruffle; for the Duchess has put him on his mettle. "Messer Federico," she says as the company reassembles, "this is a heavy burden we have laid on you, and we expect much of you." Burden? Burden? Bernardo Accolti leaps up. The famous extemporizer—a brisk little man—scents boredom from afar; and bristling with the assurance which has won him the name of the *One and Only Aretine*, he boards and braves the incubus. Burden? "And what burden is this?" he bubbles belligerently. With grave civility Fregoso bears down on him. "And does it not seem to you, Signor Unico, a

ELIZABETTA GONZAGA, by Carotto
From the portrait in the Uffizi Gallery, Florence

heavy burden and a weary task imposed on me this evening, to demonstrate in what manner, mode, and time the Courtier is to employ his good qualities and perform all those things which we have agreed become him?" No, l'Unico replies flatly, and proceeds to scuttle him with piratical common sense. "It seems to me no great matter. All is said, I believe, when we say that he should have judgment, as the Count told us last night. Give him tact, and he needs no other precept to use his faculties at the proper time and in the proper manner; to formulate this more minutely would be altogether too difficult and, very likely, superfluous." But such expeditious sense would put an end to the discussion, and Fregoso has something to contribute to it: nothing very substantial, it is true, but he is a young man of discernment and he does what he can: he refines on the obvious. Accordingly, while the extemporizer fidgets, Fregoso inaugurates the discussion with placid self-confidence, rehearsing the premises of Canossa:

"Correct conduct seems to me to consist in a certain circumspection and sense of the fitness of things. I wish our Courtier, therefore, to observe certain general rules which, I believe, contain in brief the gist of my meaning. The first and foremost is that, as the Count well remarked last night, he should shun affectation; then, in whatever he says or does, let him weigh where he is, in whose presence, the time, his purpose, his age, his profession, the best means of attaining his object; and with these considerations discreetly govern whatever he says or does." Upon so compendious a definition there ensues, inevitably, silence. But now someone else becomes impatient. Signor Morello, the senior of the company, observes tartly: "These rules of yours seem to me to teach little; for my part, I am as wise as I was before, though I do recall having heard something of the sort from the friar-confessors, who called it, if I remember rightly, the correct *circumstances*." Fregoso laughs, undismayed by this setback, which he construes as an invitation to elaborate on the rudiments; and, having several points on his mind which he is determined to express, he unloads. He has collected all his predilections and aversions to use them as illustrations of what he conceives Canossa to mean, since he means it himself. In war, for instance, the Courtier will always remember that he fights primarily to shine; he will never risk his life as readily "to bring in a herd of cattle as to scale a wall"; in sport he will nurse his appearance, "knowing that the public and particularly women observe the first comers most closely, he will never be the last to appear"; if his accoutrements are in any way defective, he will sooner not appear at all;

nor will he shine for the vulgar. But at this Pallavicino also becomes impatient and in the name of Adam protests. "In our country, in Lombardy," he says, "we have no such scruples. At popular festivals, our young gentlemen dance with the countryfolk all day in the sun, and play with them at wrestling and running and jumping and tossing the bar; and I see no harm in it; the rivalry is not one of rank but of skill and strength, in which men of the people yield nothing to gentlemen; and this familiarity seems to me to show a certain likeable liberality." He convinces himself with a young careless nod; but not so the punctilious patrician who holds the floor. "This dancing in the sun is not to my taste at all," Fregoso replies, surveying the company for approval, though he is careful to avoid any appearance of consulting them. "I see no advantage in it." And as his audience remains neutral he continues: "If he must wrestle and run and jump with countryfolk, he should do so—in my opinion—in such a way as to show that he is willing to humour but not to contend with them, and he should be sure of winning, or else let him not meddle with them; for it would be too bad and too brutal and undignified for a gentleman to be worsted by a yokel, particularly in wrestling; I think, therefore, he had better abstain, at least in any large gathering; for to win is to win little and to lose is to lose everything."

Pallavicino does not reply. He broods. The man is so exasperatingly correct, so lacking in courtly carelessness, and seems to believe that propriety is an end in itself and the whole purpose of the Courtier, that he is fair game; but he is not easy to trip. Meanwhile, Fregoso is expatiating patiently on his pet aversions, exposing one by one all the pests who have annoyed him at one time or another in his life; and when he has thoroughly ostracized all the cranks, eccentrics, and exhibitionists, or as many as he can recall at the moment, he pauses to dwell again on the exclusive value of reserve. "In wrestling, running, jumping, and exhibition riding, I like a man to shun the common multitude, or at least to show himself very rarely," he confides to his audience, "for there is nothing so excellent but the ignorant soon tire of it and value it little when they see it often. The same is true of music . . ." Canossa turns as if he expected to be challenged; and folds his arms; and his dark face flushes; and he sits in brimming silence. "The Courtier should make music as a pastime," Fregoso continues, "and almost reluctantly, and never in the presence of low people or of a great multitude." But by now Pallavicino is thoroughly exasperated by this obsession and shunts Fregoso into the mysteries of music; and Fregoso proceeds imperturbably, developing its proprieties with methodical nicety, defining the range of music permissible to a gentleman, the branches, instruments, time, place, purpose, age, suitable to this pastime. *"Bella musica,"* he says, "is to sing by the book, confidently and with a beautiful deportment, and most of all to sing to the lute, for the charm lies in a solo, and we listen far more closely to the fine delivery and the aria, when our ears are undistracted by more than one voice; and we detect far better each little slip"—an important point—"than in choral singing where one helps the other." Pallavicino laughs: it was an inspiration, this appeal to music, which reveals Fregoso like a touchstone, exposing all the latent self-preoccupation which warps his whole version of the social man; and Canossa looks solemn, listening in amazement to an appreciation of music in which he hears everything but a feeling for music itself. But before either of them can make the point—it is one of those lost opportunities in which the best conversations abound—the victim has slipped away; and the little conversational drama continues.

Though he may be a musician neither of men nor of harmony, Federico Fregoso is an authority. "What I find particularly delightful is recitation to the lute, which adds so moving a power to the words that it is wonderful. All the key instruments also are harmonious; for their consonances are perfect; and there is charm in the music of four violins, which is very suave and artful. . . ." But what he really has an ear for is the time and the place: the time—"when he is among intimate friends and there are no other occupations"; the place—"I expect him to shun the multitude and the menial." One more point, and he is satisfied: "He will remember his age, for truly it is improper to see a man of position, old, toothless, wrinkled, and white-haired, hugging a viol and playing and singing among women; for most songs are love-songs and in old men love is ridiculous, though sometimes it delights despite years to kindle a cold heart." This rouses Signor Morello who is younger at heart than his years betray; and seeing him grow uneasy, Giuliano de' Medici intercedes. "Do not deprive an old man of this pleasure, Messer Federico," he begins, but he goes no further, for the old man of sixty-three does not need his sympathy, and the young man of twenty-seven does; and neither will have it. "I do not deprive an old man of this pleasure," Fregoso explains, "but I wish to prevent you and these ladies from laughing at his folly. . . . And I say the same of dancing: we should forsake these pleasures before age compels us to leave them unwillingly." "You might as well do away with old men altogether," Signor Morello exclaims, growing as red as his beard, "and say that only young men may be courtiers." Fregoso laughs. "You see, Signor Morello"—and his eyes rest on that trim, apoplectically coloured beard, and suddenly they shine like a mirror

—"you see that those who love these delights, if they are no longer young, study to seem so; they dye their hair and trim their beards twice a week; and all because Nature mutely reminds them that such things are fit only for youth." The ladies laugh prudently; and, seeing the old man look troubled, the young one relents. "But there are other diversions with ladies, which are suitable to age." "What?" snaps the butt. "To tell stories?" "Precisely." Fregoso approves. "Every age, as you know, has its own thoughts and its peculiar virtues and vices," and he draws the classic distinctions to conclude: "Of all ages the most temperate is the manly, which has left behind the faults of youth and has not yet reached those of age." The ideal Courtier had best be a man of middle age or— better yet—a youth touched with maturity: temperamentally twenty-seven. "What I like to see is a lad a little inclined to the grave and the taciturn, superior to his years, and with none of those restless ways which we associate with his age; he seems to possess, I hardly know what . . . something more than other young men have. . . ." And dropping his eyes modestly, he pauses for a moment, a long pensive moment; then he raises them and proceeds, almost with the effect of speaking impromptu. "His calm bearing," he says, completing the portrait of a superior youth, "suggests a certain well-founded pride, inspired by judgment—not temper—ruled by reason—not appetite—and we usually find that manner in men of great heart." Everyone recognizes the original, and his victims swarm on the opportunity to retaliate: Morello, Pallavicino, Canossa, and Accolti rise, when he suddenly cheats them. "I have no other rules to offer," he says, "except those which I have already mentioned and which, it seems, Signor Morello learned as a child from his confessor." And with a gratified smile Federico Fregoso abdicates.

But Emilia Pia leaps up. That inveterate mischief-maker, that widow and tease, feeling the unspoken annoyance of all the men whom Fregoso has antagonized, is determined to provoke it; and even they are ready to bear more of him rather than let the bore go unpunished. "Messer Federico," she says, "you shirk fatigue too much, but you shall not escape till you have talked us to bed." "And if I have no more to say?" he pleads. "Show your invention," she replies prettily, and the mischief in her face almost makes her attractive. "If it be true, as I am told, that men of eloquence have composed a volume in praise of a fly, or baldness, or the quartain fever, will you not take courage and eke out our evening with the Courtier?" Indeed he will; indeed. "We have said enough to fill two volumes," he sighs, "but since no excuse serves, I shall continue until I have satisfied you to the best of my ability, if not of your expectations." He has a surprise in store for them.

So far he has considered the duties of the Courtier to himself; now he proposes to say a few words on his relations with others, and primarily with his Prince. Not unnaturally, as a scion of a ruling house himself, he expects "the Courtier, with all his thoughts and all his might, to love and almost to worship his Prince and to adapt all his ways, his manners, and his will to please him." When, however, someone objects that he has described a sycophant and a flatterer, his reply is unexpected. On the contrary, he contends: compliance schools character, it requires a constant abnegation of self, a habitual deference to another, and makes public spirit second nature and self-indulgence social sin; and he shows an appreciation of social conscience which amazes Pallavicino in a man he had supposed to be completely self-centred. The painful possibility that he may have misjudged him presents itself; but he dismisses it. Pallavicino is too young to be mistaken, but not to be annoyed with himself; and his irritation with Fregoso redoubles. Biding his time, he sits moodily, waiting for an opportunity to express it.

The talk turns on the best methods of winning favour; Fregoso reviews the approved, the dubious, the semi-acceptable, the demi-reputable, the quasi-questionable, and concludes that "the best way to win favour is to merit it." But, at so wild a statement, there is an outcry. "I doubt very much the truth of that rule, experience proves the contrary," cries a poet. "How few win the favour of princes nowadays unless they are presumptuous! For my part, I know none who have risen by modesty and, if you will pause to consider, I believe you will not find many either. Consider the French Court, one of the noblest in Christendom today, and you will find that all those who are popular there are presumptuous." "Do not say so," says Fregoso, quickly contradicting so provincial a prejudice. "In France there are many modest and courteous gentlemen. It is true that they use a certain familiarity and casual freedom which is native and natural to them, but we should not call that presumption." "Look at the Spaniards," the poet insists. "And the French are far worse, though they make a great show of modesty at first meeting; and truly, they know what they are about, for the sovereigns of our time favour such manners." Shocked by his disrespect of royalty and such cynical views in a poet, "I cannot permit you, Messer Vincenzo," Fregoso replies, "so to slander the princes of our time." It is clear that they speak from different experience: the poet and the patrician are worlds apart; but this poet is hard-headed and argumentative; and Fregoso, with his unquestioning faith in human nature and established authority, is too profoundly right-thinking a man not to stiffen in personal offence. His manifest repugnance to the sordid-subversive almost betrays him into a scene; but the Magnifico Giuliano quickly shifts the conversation to the psychology of clothes.

Having no interest in this topic, Fregoso is willing to be liberal about it. "I have no set rule to give you in the matter of dress, except that a man should conform to the majority; and since, as you say, custom is so various and we Italians are so fond of following foreign fashions, I think every man may wear what he likes." But even to a frivolous subject he succeeds in giving a serious turn. "I do not know what fate has decreed that Italy no longer has an Italian fashion in dress; for, though the new styles make the old seem absurd, yet the old were a badge of freedom as the new are an omen of servitude, and the omen has been only too well verified. There is not a nation that has not made us its prey, and little remains to plunder, yet the plunder continues. Let us not enter on so painful a subject," he adds hastily, and wins the sympathy of Canossa. "The clothes of the Courtier, if they are not unusual or improper to his profession, may be what he please. I prefer those which incline to the sober and quiet rather than the showy, and I recommend the reserve which the Spanish prefer, as externals often indicate the intrinsic tastes of a man. Dress may be no small argument of the mind of the wearer; and not only dress, but all his manners and habits, beside his actions and speech, are symptoms of his qualities." Pallavicino throws up his hands: at such redundant detailing of the self-evident he exclaims, "And what symptoms by which we judge a man are not either action or speech?" "You are too subtle a logician," sighs the Uninspired; and changes the subject once more.

Sensitive suddenly to the latent hostility around him, Fregoso speaks of friendship. The plight of his country makes him feel deserted. Too fastidious to make friends easily, he recommends the same circumspection for the Courtier; and suddenly a voice is raised in approval, a voice yet unheard from, the cool, schooled, lymphatic voice of Bembo. The Humanist has composed a whole literature on this theme; and he opens his mouth. What issues forth is a tiny elegy on the frailty of friendship. All his life the great dilettante has deplored, with plaintive self-pity, the shallowness and insincerity of mankind. "This matter of intimate friendship," Bembo begins, breathing on his beard and speaking with exquisite articulation, "is, as you say, one requiring great caution, not only because of the reputation which we may gain or lose by it, but because true friends are all too rare nowadays. There are, I fear, no more Orestes and Pylades in the world, no more Thesei and Pirithouoi, no more Scipii and Lelii...." And he sighs with satisfaction; for he takes as much pride in the purity of his plurals as in the melancholy theme of which he is a master. "Nay, through what fate I know not, it befalls every day that two friends who may have lived in cordial affection for years finally fall out, either from malice or envy or frivolity or some unfortunate reason; and each blames the other; and both may be at fault. To me it has chanced more than once to be deceived in those I loved most and from whom I confidently expected affection; and therefore I have come to the conclusion, in my heart of hearts, that the best course is not to trust anyone in the world, nor to surrender so completely to a friend, however dear he may be, as to communicate to him all one's thoughts unreservedly, as one would to oneself; for there are so many recesses and secret crannies in our souls that it is impossible for human prudence to detect all the dissimulations that may lie concealed there. I believe, therefore, that we do well to love one man more than another, according to his deserts, but not to swallow that sweet lure of friendship so deep, that later we may regret it." But such tepid wisdom appals even Fregoso. "Truly," he says, "the loss would be far greater than the gain, to deprive human fellowship of that supreme degree of friendship which, in my opinion, is our greatest boon in life. Without this perfect friendship man would be more wretched than any animal in creation." No. Moderation in amity means something else entirely. It means, he continues, a due proportion between familiarity and reserve, and he dips into his antipathies for examples. Drawing the distinction between a friend and a good fellow, he fastens on the boon companion, a species which awakens his abhorrence, and dwells with fascinated disgust on that clan of perpetual minors, with their impudent intimacies and public privacies, who profane the name of friendship and disgrace the society to which they truckle—the outlaws of the parlour. Then he veers vigorously to the opposite pole and excoriates those effusive frauds and obnoxious pests who "to ingratiate themselves with a new friend vow, at first meeting, that they have never known a man they loved more and swear that they would give their lives to serve him"—cats' lives—"and other such protestations as pass reason." Between these extremes, he protests, the mean of friendship lies; not, as Bembo believes, in sentimental miserliness. At the touch of a cooler nature than his own, Fregoso almost warms, and his critics are half placated.

But still it is not bedtime; and the mention of improper pleasantries, with which Fregoso illustrates his aversion to boon companions and practical jokers, naturally suggests a discussion of proper ones. This, however, as he is the first to admit, is a theme for which a proper mind is the most unfit. "There is not one of you," he says handsomely, "to whom I do not yield in everything and, above all, in humour, unless the ineptitudes which often amuse us more than wit may pass for humour. Here is the master of that!" And he turns with a smile to Bibbiena. The muffled conversational drama has reached its climax. Fregoso disarms his critics. The offence of the bore is a grave one, to be lifeless is the first of sins, but, from the moment that he recognizes his limitations, the company forgives and forgets him. Immediately the atmosphere freshens: the plot turns; and the movement passes by a natural transition into the hands of an antiphonal figure. With his self-conscious propriety Fregoso has given a bias to the Courtier which only humour can correct—humour which is the instinctive perception of the fitness of things, the natural, not the studied, form of propriety; and of that Bibbiena is the acknowledged master.

A self-made man, with the insinuating good humour of a climber not quite sure of himself—modest, amiable, supple—the popular victim of many a merciless joke—always ready to laugh at himself—no one can better supply the flexibility indispensable to the social man. He slips nimbly into the vacancy which, with an elaborate compliment, Fregoso makes for him: "While Messer Bernardo is reasoning, I shall rest like a weary traveller under his delightful foliage and listen to the murmur of his words as to the flow of a running stream; then, when I am a little refreshed, I may find something more to say." Bibbiena bows and wrecks the simile. Over so laborious and long-winded a pleasantry he makes an effort to climb lightly; but even he trips. He fondles his bald head. "If I show you my pate," he muses ruefully, "you shall see what shade to look for from my delightful foliage. As for the running stream, that may be vouchsafed you, for I was turned into one once, and not by an antique God, but by our Fra Mariano here, and I have been running ever since." He smiles down his tame joke; but no matter, it serves its purpose: the recollection of a famous shower of which he was the victim sets the company in a roar and, while the laughter is dying, he collects himself. "Leave tickling us with your tricks," Emilia Pia says smartly, "and teach us how to laugh, and why, and all you know on this subject. And no more delays: begin, begin!" It is the theory they want, not the practice, and Bibbiena is never more amusing than when he is serious. The gentle, doe-eyed prelate does his best to look thoughtful, and after some preliminary apologies—mere exercises to limber up—begins: "Mirth is so proper to man that we describe him as a laughing animal. Whatever excites laughter exhilarates the spirit and delights it and lets us forget for a moment the tedious cares of which our life is full." The balm of existence, the elixir of life, the buoyant play of reason, the safeguard of sanity and prompt arrest of folly: true enough, laughter is all this, but . . . but . . . "But what this laughter is, and whence it springs, and how it fills the veins, eyes, mouth, sides, and so will out that, though we strain, we cannot hold it, this"— he throws up his hands in despair—"this will I leave Democritus to explain, and he could not tell you either." These, however, they all know, are mere feints; he has the philosophy of laughter at his finger-tips; and with a little more urging he comes to it.

In the first place, laughter is a form of criticism. "The root of the ridiculous is deformity, for we laugh only at such things as are unbecoming and seem amiss, without actually being so. I cannot define it otherwise. Reflect, and you will find that what we laugh at is usually something unseemly which yet is not bad." It is limited by the sense of which it is the expression—the sense of measure. "We do not laugh at the unfortunate or the abject or rascals or public malefactors: these deserve a worse penalty than derision, and it is inhuman to mock the miserable unless," he adds with a swift glance at Bembo, "they glory in misfortune and presume on it and parade it." One other class must be immune—the happy great who are privileged to be susceptible and among whom, alas, he will never count himself. But there are other reasons for restraint. A jest is a suggestion and prospers by what it implies: "We should touch our man in passing, imperceptibly, in such a manner that he who hears and sees may infer from our words and gestures much more than we reveal, and so fall to laughing." The more sober, the happier it is, since it is a demonstration of reason: laughter is a convulsion of common sense. As such, it is a social discipline, correcting the eccentricities of the individual and recalling him to the convivial normal. It can only be exercised on subjects which are amenable to control: physical deformity is barred, though it offends our native sense of symmetry and "the faults of the body are meat for laughter, if they are scored discreetly; but in this we should follow the manner of Messer Roberto, who imitates everyone and nips his weak points, sometimes even to his face, yet no one minds." Laughter, in short, is sympathetic: even malicious laughter must understand what it ridicules. But the proper subjects for derision are deformities of the mind and the will—prejudice, pride, pedantry, affectation—all the sins against reason, which spring from a warped judgment and reveal a self-obsession, which it is the function of laughter to detect and dispel. Humour enlightens, liberating us from whatever is too personal or partial, transforming us into detached spectators of ourselves, making us self-conscious and self-critical; without it man remains a moral quadruped.

When the discipline of humour is voluntary and a man laughs at himself, then the triumph of social conscience is complete. To him much may be forgiven; he may indulge his infirmities and cultivate his eccentricities, if he smiles at them: nothing, indeed, is more delightful. If to err is human, to recognize one's error is the triumph of humanity; the combination, by flattering both our weakness and our strength, is sheer comic virtue: and Bibbiena, so human, so alert to his foibles, and so disarming in his facetious innocence, is the living illustration of it, seeming at every moment to demonstrate, under the attentive eyes of Fregoso, how much more sociable it is to be fallible than correct.

As he makes his points with an enormous repertory of anecdotes, Bembo challenges him to tell one at the expense of Florence. "And why do you not tell the tale about your Florentine Commissary?" the Venetian begins, always quick to twit the Tuscan on his parish pride. "Messer Pietro, if you do not keep still," laughs Bibbiena, "I shall tell all I have seen and heard of your Venetians, and that is not little: above all, when you sail a horse." "Do not, do not, I beg you," cries Bembo, "and I will suppress two more which are perfect gems." The brisk gale which greets his retreat allows Bibbiena to make his next point: the element of surprise in laughter. The unexpected startles reason and upsets balance; and this panic mirth, which ranges from the violent shock of practical jokes and physical mishaps to the mild surprise of slips of speech and the literal trickery of a pun, makes laughter an act of recognition and recovery. Such humour appeals to the quick-witted, since it develops self-possession; conversely, the slow-witted laugh at the unfamiliar, which disturbs their habits and nettles their complacency; in one case, laughter being flexibility, in the other, inertia.

From the psychology Bibbiena turns to the technology of laughter, sorting jests into *motti, detti, bischizzi, burli, facezie,* until the anatomy of mirth threatens to leave only the corpse of the Comic Spirit on his hands; but he is nimble and the lecture never develops into a wake. No sooner does a mouth open to yawn than it is locked in a spasm of laughter, for he keeps up an unflagging fire of stories: flippant, farcical, nonsensical, enormous, abdominal, dry, ironical, quizzical: they run the whole gamut of the ridiculous, with two exceptions. The blasphemous and the obscene are barred; and he grows genuinely grave. "This is abominable;

and those who show their wit without reverence to God deserve to be driven out of the society of every gentleman. And so do those who are obscene and filthy in their speech and who have no respect for the presence of women, and who find no greater pleasure than to make them blush, and who are constantly collecting such jokes and stories. As, for example, this year in Ferrara . . ." And he illustrates under his breath. "You see," he concludes regretfully, "the joke was ingenious, but in the presence of women it was obscene and not proper." "Women love nothing better," says Pallavicino, "and you would deprive them of their pleasure." Still spoiling for the argument he has missed with Fregoso, he fastens on Bibbiena. "For my part, they have put me to the blush oftener than men." "Of such I do not speak," says Bibbiena, "but of virtuous women, who merit respect and honour of a gentleman." "You shall need a subtle rule to discover them," Pallavicino persists, "for those that seem the best are usually the worst." He squares himself; this subject lies close to his heart: he was a misogynist long before he reached his majority, and he is just twenty-one. Bibbiena laughs the uneasy laugh of the cornered mild and appeals to Giuliano de' Medici. "If we had not here our Signor Magnifico, who is known to all the world as the champion of women, I would undertake to answer you; but I shall not do him that wrong." Emilia Pia intervenes briskly: "Women need no champions, where their critic is of so little weight. Leave Signor Gasparo to his perverse opinion, which comes of his knowing no woman who will look at him and of no other fault on our part; and proceed with your argument." Bibbiena resumes: "To stain the honour of a gentlewoman is despicable and deserving of the gravest punishment, for in this women must be numbered among the miserable, and should not be attacked, since they have no arms to defend themselves." "Truly, Signor Bernardo, you are too partial to these women of yours," says Pallavicino. "And why would you have men show more respect to women than women show to men? Should not our honour be as dear to us as theirs is to them? Do you think it right that they should taunt us without restriction in everything, and we be mute, and thank them into the bargain?" There is such a thing as being too fair with women; it will not do to make a superstition of chivalry. But Bibbiena thinks it will not do to humour young heretics; and, to settle the argument at once, he drops in the double standard. "I do not deny," he says blandly, "that women should observe a due respect with men in jesting and teasing, but I do say that they have more licence in nipping those of little virtue than we with them; because we ourselves have decreed that in us loose living is no fault nor vice nor shame, while in women it is so extreme a scandal and disgrace that, let a woman once come by a bad name, be it truth or slander, she is eternally shamed." Pallavicino stares, uncertain whether this is banter or earnest; and, while he is deciding, another voice speaks for him. Ottaviano Fregoso, like his brother, is a man of settled opinions and, being more mature, is yet more dogmatic in their expression; and delicate subjects have an irresistible attraction for him. "Signor Gasparo might reply," he says, turning to Bibbiena with a satisfied air, "that this law you say we have made is not so unfair as you suppose. As women are most faulty animals, of little or no consequence compared to men, it was necessary, since they are incapable of virtue themselves, to curb them with the fear of shame and forcibly to endow them with some good quality; and continence being the most essential for assurance of issue, we were obliged to make them continent by every art, method, or device we could conceive, and to concede that in all else they might be of little use and behave clean contrary to what they should." "Is this how you speak of women, Signor Ottaviano?" says the Duchess. Embarrassed by such raw banter—at least she hopes it is banter—she tries to blunt it with mild and matronly humour: "No wonder they do not love you." "I do not complain," laughs her nephew; "on the contrary, I thank them; if they will not love me, I am not bound to love them." But he laughs alone; then, vaguely aware of his solo, he falters. "But this is not my opinion, I merely say what Signor Gasparo might say." Bibbiena covers the painful pause: "A great gain it would be if women could convert two such arch-enemies of their sex as you and Signor Gasparo." "I am not their enemy, but you are the enemy of men," Pallavicino retorts; and he baits Bibbiena: "You will find few men of value who think much of women, though sometimes for reasons of their own they profess the contrary." This is more than Bibbiena can ignore. "You not only insult women, you offend every man who respects them," he replies sharply and for a moment, a long moment, he considers whether or not to take up the challenge. "Nevertheless, for the moment, I do not propose to leave my chosen subject and embark on so difficult a task as their defence against a great warrior like you. Seeing the ladies so silent and suffering your insults so patiently, I must conclude that a part at least of what Signor Ottaviano said is true, that they do not mind how much we abuse them, provided we spare their honour." And with that he rises, still flustered and mopping his brow, and the ladies swarm about Pallavicino. The bedlam swells; the drowsy wake; the company rises: it is bedtime. "Look, look," cries Pallavicino out of a stridor of women; "they cannot reason, they appeal to force." "You shall not escape," says Emilia Pia, pitching her voice a little higher. "You thought, because Messer Bernardo was tired, that you could abuse women as you pleased, and no one would contradict you; but we shall put a fresher knight in the field." And turning to the Magnifico Giuliano, she appoints him their champion for the following evening. "I hope your argument will be such as no one can contradict," says the Duchess, rising. "So turn your mind to this one theme and form us a Lady such as our adversaries shall shame to say she is not the peer of the Courtier, of whom Messer Federico need say no more, for he has adorned him all too well if our Lady is to equal him." Whereupon the company takes leave of her; and through the tranquil Palace in every direction the tapers burn to bedward.

Meanwhile, at Casatico, where night after night his light burns to the past, Castiglione appeals from the critics of the present to those of the future. "From this fragment you may judge how superior was the Court of Urbino to every other in Italy. I venture to affirm this confidently and I hope to be believed, for what I praise is not so remote that I could take the liberty of inventing it, and I have witnesses in many men of great credit who are still living, and who have seen and known the life which once flourished there; and I feel myself in honour bound, to the best of my ability and with every art in my power, sedulously to redeem from oblivion their bright memory and to perpetuate it in the minds of posterity. Hereafter, perhaps, someone may envy our age for their sake; for there is no one who, when he reads of the marvels of antiquity, does not form a higher opinion of those characters than books can express, no matter how divinely they may be written." The obscure lobby of his study now becomes a shrine, for his pious devotion to the past is inspired by an impulse which is religious, in the original sense of the word as the binding power of association, from which a common spirit springs. Where two or three are gathered together, there the spirit quickens; and it is to social life that the spirit of the times, baffled in religion and politics, now turns for a source of union and concert. The Humanist spirit, with its longing to embrace and fuse the variety and confusion of life, fills that courtly Renaissance conversation—at once so formal and so free, so schooled and spontaneous, so disciplined in design and convivial in movement—with an ardent vision of the one virtue of which human nature is normally capable: that of moral urbanity. And it is this virtue which women lend to society. They are the custodians of the social covenant. In the code of the Courtier the Renaissance woman comes into her own, and the mission which Isabella pursued amid the strenuous turmoil of actual life is realized, in these animated pages, by her passive sister-in-law, Elizabetta. Though she takes no active part in the conversation, she presides over it and her presence permeates its conduct. The men defer to her, above all in their conduct with women—"with whom we had the freest and most blameless commerce, but such was the respect we bore to the will of the Duchess that that freedom was the greatest restraint." The concert of the sexes which she inspires is a happy compromise between polite and personal feelings—a relation which constitutes for Castiglione the true charm of society. A cordiality neither conventional nor intimate is the sentiment he prefers, for his is the genius of friendship rather than love; and he is the champion of the sex because he is that happy anomaly, a friend of women. Neither the lover nor the misogynist can treat the equality of the sexes; for that a third person is needed; and the only expert is the amateur. The pious hand returns to the page, the medium resumes, merging once more with his visions; and, as the company reassembles, the misogynists and feminists meet, and the champion advances.

Giuliano de' Medici is an amateur, however, of an ambiguous sort. A veteran philanderer, he has sacrificed his health to women, but he has never contracted the cynicism of the alcove; he is that rare type of *roué*, a rake who respects women. Familiarity only deepens his chivalry; and he rises to their defence with a gallantry which is partly the easy generosity of the self-indulgent, partly the gratitude of a graduate of the sex, but above all the benevolence of a nature genuinely sympathetic and disinterested. He is so sentimental a libertine, indeed, that he does not believe himself a libertine at all. He is a connoisseur; and he combines the aplomb of an expert with the guileless idealism of an amateur. "Signor Magnifico," says the Duchess, "we all expect to see our Lady well graced, and if you do not manifest her beauties we shall think you jealous." There is no danger: the risk lies in another direction: he does too well.

The Lady he creates is, in fact, point for point, the counterpart of the Courtier; and he lavishes accomplishments on her so liberally that when he has finished Pallavicino can contain himself no longer. "I wonder," he says scathingly, "now that you have granted women letters, continence, magnanimity, temperance, and what not, that you do not give them the government of cities and lawmaking and the command of armies, and set men to cook and spin." The Magnifico is not disconcerted. "This too might not be amiss," he admits. "Do you not know that

BERNARDO DOVIZI DA BIBBIENA, by Raphael (?)
From the portrait in the Pitti Palace, Florence

Plato, who certainly was no friend of women, gave them the custody of cities and gave to men all other martial exercises? Do you not think that many might be found who would govern cities and armies as well as men?" He presses the point and, since Pallavicino disdains to reply, he prods him. "I know that you would like to bring up the calumny Signor Ottaviano raised against women last night, saying that they are very faulty animals, incapable of virtue, and of little or no consequence compared to men; but you are in error, great error, both of you, if you believe it." Pallavicino tries to beg the question; he is thoroughly unhappy; as a democrat, he inclines to equality, but as a son of Adam he has a grudge which dates back to the Fall; he finds it impossible to be consistent; and he begins by hedging and ends by exploding. "I do not wish to bring up what has already been said," he protests. "You wish me to say something which will offend these ladies and make them my enemies, just as you flatter them to gain their good will; but they are so much wiser than most women that they prefer truth, though it does not flatter them, to false praises. They do not mind if we say that men are of more consequence, and they will agree that you have been arguing prodigiously, attributing to the Court Lady things which are impossible and ridiculous, and so many virtues that Socrates and Cato and all the philosophers in the world count for nothing." Then, indignant at so preposterous a conclusion to so unfair a premise: "I marvel how you exaggerate, I wonder you are not ashamed. You might be satisfied with a Lady who is lovely, affable, virtuous, and entertaining in music, dancing, games, and the various diversions of Court life; but to make her acquainted with everything in the world and to attribute to her virtues which men themselves, even in times past, have rarely revealed, is more than one can endure or even listen to." He stifles; but, remembering the advantage which the Magnifico will take of his speechlessness, he collects himself and continues more calmly: "That women are imperfect animals I do not say: the merit of these ladies would give me the lie; but I do maintain that some very wise men have left us their opinion that Nature, which is ever striving to produce more and more perfect things, would, if she could, continually bring forth men; and, when a woman is born, it is an error or slip of Nature, and contrary to her purpose, like children that are born lame or blind or fruits that never ripen. Nevertheless, since these defects are the fault of Nature, we should not hate them; we must show women the respect they deserve; but to rate them higher than they are seems to me a manifest error."

Even with men Giuliano de' Medici is chivalrous, and with so green an antagonist he shows himself generous. He plays with him and begins, with an air of weighing the theory seriously: "Of the imperfections of women you seem to me to adduce a most unconvincing reason: to which I might reply, though this is not the place to enter into such subtleties..." But subtleties have an irresistible attraction for Giuliano de' Medici, and on second thought he decides to metaphysicize the misogynist before he fells him with plain common sense. Accordingly, he leads him into a dialectical labyrinth with a long-drawn definition of Form and Substance and the essential entities of things, and, when the young man appears to be thoroughly dazed, he concludes: "As no stone can be more perfectly stone than any other, insofar as it is stone, nor one piece of wood more wooden than any other, so no man can be more perfectly man than the next, and consequently the male is not more perfect than the female, with respect to formal substance, since both are included in the species MAN, and that in which they differ is accidental, not essential." Pallavicino is still groping and grasping and digesting the point, when the Magnifico leads him on to the next step. "If you tell me that man is more perfect than woman, if not in essence, at least in accidental qualities..." And he pauses, waiting for the classic argument of the physical and mental inferiority of woman, which he expects Pallavicino to raise; but Pallavicino is still swimming in the void, unable to reach or even to recognize solid ground; and Giuliano has to supply the argument himself in order to demolish it. "If you tell me this, I reply that these accidents are either of the body or the mind: if of the body, men being more robust, agile, and better able to bear fatigue, I say that this implies little superiority since, among men themselves, those who possess these qualities are not more valued than others, and in war, where most of our strenuous duties lie, the bravest are not always the best. If of the mind..." He smiles: really it is too easy... "Have you never heard the maxim in philosophy that those who are soft of body are apt of mind? Hence women are more given to thought than men. In science, do you not remember reading of some who knew philosophy? of others who excelled in poetry? of others yet, who prosecuted or defended law-suits most eloquently?" He shrugs. "If man is not superior in substance nor in the accidental attributes, I do not know where his superiority lies." And, picking up what remains of the theory, he blows it lightly away and drops to mere common sense: "And since you say that it is the purpose of Nature to produce more and more perfect things, I do not see how you can claim that Nature does not mean to produce women, without whom the human race could not be preserved." "Let us not enter into these subtleties," says Pallavicino quickly. "These ladies would not understand us; and, even if I replied with excellent arguments, they would believe, or pretend to believe, that I am wrong, and would render sentence in their own favour."

Pallavicino is not yet worsted, however. After clinging to the theory like the tail of a kite, he has landed it, and he shows Giuliano how well he has grasped it. "As we have entered into this subject, however, I shall say merely—and this, as you know, is the opinion of some very learned men—that man resembles Form and woman Substance; and, as Form is more perfect than Substance, man is superior to woman, and I remember having heard a great philosopher ask in one of his problems: Why is it that women always love the first man to enjoy them? and why do men almost always hate the woman who initiates them into love? And the reason he gave was that in that act woman reaches her consummation in man, whereas man finds imperfection in woman; moreover, all women want to be men, by a natural instinct which teaches them to seek their perfection." But the veteran makes short work of such chop-logic. "The poor creatures do not wish to become men in order to be more perfect, but to have freedom and escape the bondage which men have imposed on them by their own authority"; and there are no metaphysics in the physiology of love: "the cause of the perpetual love of a woman for her first lover and of the aversion of a man for his first mistress is not what your philosopher offers in his problems; it lies in the constancy and stability of woman and in the fickleness of man, and there is a natural reason for it: the male, being hot, naturally runs to volatility and fickleness, while the female . . ." But Emilia Pia, who has been watching the subject vanish in the metaphysical empyrean with a lengthening face, now puts her foot down. "For the love of God, Signor Magnifico, leave your Form and your Substance and your Male and your Female, and speak to be understood. We have understood very well the evil that Signor Ottaviano and Signor Gasparo have spoken of us, but we cannot make head nor tail of the way you defend us; and this will only confirm the bad opinion our enemies have of us." Her large square jaw trembles at the thought of one more abstract compliment. But her felicitous brusquerie serves only to excite the enemy—the friendly enemy, as Pallavicino now protests himself. "Do not give us that name, Signora," he cries; "it belongs to the Signor Magnifico. He proves by the false praise he bestows on women that there is no true." And he returns to the attack, rallying his followers, and the fray becomes general. The misogynists bring up their heavy arguments and ram in Mother Eve; and Frigio, an old soldier who has been primed with the doctrine of Original Sin, swings into action: "The fault of the first woman made us all fall from grace, and she it was who left us our heritage of death and pain and sorrow and all the woes and calamities which the world suffers today." "If you invade the sacristy, you shall carry something away," retorts Giuliano. "Do you not know that that same sin was redeemed by a woman? But I will not mingle divine matters with our light talk," and he turns to other resources, fluttering the annals of history and recalling an interminable line of martyrs, saints, and heroines of antiquity; but Pallavicino refuses to be impressed. "Ah, Signor Magnifico, God knows what happened then," he exclaims, "those times are so remote, many a tall tale might be told and we could not deny it." But Giuliano sweeps on, heedless of the infant cry of historical criticism: "And if we come down to the present, we need not seek far; we have them here beneath our very roof"; and the memorable roll-call continues, marshalling all the famous ladies of the day, recruiting an illustrious galaxy, and culminating at last in one "to whose most excellent virtues we should do wrong, reporting them so soberly as we must do here"—Isabella d'Este. The overwhelming evidence of that name silences everyone; and in that triumphant supererogation Giuliano rests his case.

The enemy, wavering, makes a last stand, gives ground, and grudgingly admits the necessity of woman to our being. "To our well-being too," cries Cesare Gonzaga, and launches into an impassioned panegyric of the Muse of civil living, which completes the rout. When Pallavicino makes an effort to rally the breaking ranks, Ottaviano Fregoso checks him. "For the love of God," he laughs, "give up, give up, you will make no headway; you will only have these ladies for your enemies and most of the men as well." Pallavicino throws up his hands and saves his face. "Thank me, ladies," he cries, "if I had not contradicted the Signor Magnifico and Messer Cesare, you would not have heard all the praises they have bestowed on you." "All the praises the Signor Magnifico and I have bestowed on women," says Cesare Gonzaga superbly, "and many more, were well known: they were superfluous."

The very completeness of the victory is disappointing, however; the company sits in unsatisfied silence; and Federico Fregoso voices its unspoken thought. "Signor Magnifico," he says, "to prompt you to something more, I should like to ask you a question about what you have said is the principal profession of the Court Lady; and that is, that you should enlighten me on a point which seems to me of the utmost importance; though the excellent qualities you have bestowed on her include wit, knowledge, judgment, skill, modesty, and so many other virtues, yet I think that what she most needs to know is something about love and conversations about love." But at this the idealist becomes extremely guarded; of love he will not speak at all, and of conversations about love his one recommendation is to believe all men liars. Federico Fregoso protests: he has the sensuality of the serious and the curiosity of the conservative; and he insists; but the expert philanderer refuses to gratify him with anything but his own precepts of circumspection and propriety. Pallavicino also protests: "Will you not let this excellent lady of yours love, Signor Magnifico, at least when she knows that she is sincerely loved in return?" Hopeful of revealing the man in the feminist, he persists, but the Magnifico remains discouragingly discreet. "On this subject I do not wish to advise her: all I say is that love, as you understand it, is only proper to married women." "This opinion of yours, Signor Magnifico, seems very austere," says Federico Fregoso, sucking in a satyric smile. "I think you must have learned it from one of those preachers who rebuke women to keep the pick for themselves; it seems to me you lay too hard a law on married women." And to lead him on, he deals out indulgences with charitable *finesse*, dwelling on the causes of unhappy marriages, the impossibility of divorce, and the injustice to the mismated; but Giuliano declines all his bids. "If the Court Lady finds herself in this unfortunate situation, I would have her yield nothing to her lover but her soul." Then someone else makes an effort—Roberto da Bari, the mimic of Urbino. "I appeal from your sentence and I believe, Signor Magnifico, that I shall have plenty of company; but since you insist on teaching your married woman such churlish manners, what of the unmarried? Are they also to be so hard-hearted and uncivil and not favour their lovers in anything at all?" Giuliano corrects his plural: "I want my Court Lady to love one man, whom she can marry." He is invulnerable to a mimic who will not be his pupil; and the company sees that further effort is hopeless. "Well, you cannot complain that the Signor Magnifico has not formed a peerless Court Lady," says Pallavicino, "and for my part, if you can find one, I am willing to agree that she is the equal of the Courtier." "I undertake to find one as often as you find a perfect Courtier," says Emilia Pia; and when that grim coquette speaks there is nothing more to be said.

The hour is late, the contest is over, and it is resolved as the unanimous sense of the evening that the Courtier is a man who is for ever courting a Lady who is never compromised. This moves Bembo to make his one contribution to the evening—a sigh. He rises, perpendicular but drooping, and steals on his long uneasy feet toward Emilia Pia. Ever since he came to Urbino, he has been lamenting her obduracy and punning passionately on her name, and he still finds her charm as positive as her virtue. Everyone knows the nightly manoeuvre in which he now engages. He hovers over his Emilia Impia like a devoted question-mark, elastically inquisitive, and shuffling his feet and his sighs. But between himself and herself stands Ottaviano Fregoso explaining, in a series of flat statements, that he is not her enemy. "I am not your enemy," he says positively, "and this contest has displeased me, not because the victory has gone to women, but because with so long a discussion we have lost the opportunity to debate many other fine points, which remain to be made about the Courtier." At that the company stares and the sleepiest eyes open wide. "You see, you see," exclaims Emilia Pia no less flatly, "you are our enemy. You would not have us form so excellent a Court Lady, not because there remains anything to be said of the Courtier, for these gentlemen have told us all they know and neither you nor anyone else, I am sure, could add anything more, but because you are jealous of the honour of the Court Lady." He ignores her as blandly as she ignores Bembo. "Certainly, besides what has already been said of the Courtier," he proceeds, "I expect much more." The Duchess voices the amazement of the company. "In that case we must see if your talent is such that you can give the Courtier a greater perfection than these gentlemen have already done." He offers to satisfy her, for after three evenings of frivolity the main point remains untouched. As the hour is late, however, the Duchess rises and dismisses the company, including her nephew in a gracious but dry good-night.

The night that follows is a long one, the long night of Time that has swallowed that light company; and, before convening it for the last time, Castiglione takes leave of the friends who so soon will disperse and go their own ways for ever. Some are to vanish beyond recall. Pallavicino and Cesare Gonzaga and Roberto da Bari and the Magnifico Giuliano will die in their prime; but not too soon to honour the house that bred them. "If they had lived, I believe that they would have risen so high that everyone who knew them would cite them as clear proof of how praise worthy was the Court of Urbino and how graced with noble gentlemen, for this has been true of all who were formed there.... For, as you know, M. Federico Fregoso became Archbishop of Salerno; Count Lodovico da Canossa, Bishop of Bayeux; Signor Ottaviano Fregoso, Doge of Genoa; M. Bernardo Bibbiena, Cardinal of Santa Maria in Portico; M. Pietro

Bembo, Secretary of Pope Leo; the Signor Magnifico, Duke of Nemours; and Signor Francescomaria della Rovere, Prefect of Rome and Duke of Urbino, though it was a far greater honour to the house where he was bred that it produced so rare and excellent a gentleman than that he became Duke of Urbino; and of this I believe no small reason was the noble company, in whose daily conversation he has always seen and heard admirable manners." In the long view those idle and frivolous days were not futile. Urbino has contributed something to the time, which Time could not disperse except, on its long even currents, to sow it anew. And now, as the last evening approaches, the shadow of the future falls across it, lending a new breadth and gravity to the final movement of the convivial concert; the theme deepens and develops the consummation of the Courtier—his value and his responsibility to life at large.

Ottaviano Fregoso has the qualities of his defects. Like his brother, he has the solid substantial genius of the Genoese. Though he is too dogmatic for playful debate, he is impressive when the theme grows grave, and shines in a monologue. He has spent the day preparing and puts in a late appearance; he finds the company dancing and Pallavicino leading the measure; and, though he cannot bring himself to apologize for his attitude of the previous evening, he makes a subliminal effort to efface it. "I expected to see Signor Gasparo abusing women again," he observes jocosely to his aunt, "but, seeing him dance with one, I conclude that he has made his peace with all, and I am pleased that the dispute, or rather the debate, of the Courtier has ended as it has." "It has not ended yet," says the Duchess, amused by his furtive contrition. "I am not such an enemy of men as you are of women, and I will not deprive the Courtier of the honour due him or the ornaments you promised to bestow on him." She watches the dance and lets him stand, for a penance, nursing his sheepish jauntiness, until the measure is ended; then she calls the dancers to heel and, as the music dies, they settle like a flock around her. "Signora," he says, "since I desired many other good qualities for the Courtier, and you construed my wish as a promise to contribute them, I am willing to speak of them; not that I propose to exhaust the subject, but merely to dispel the impression that, as someone objected last night, I said what I did to detract from the credit of the Court Lady." And, the hour being so advanced, he solemnly promises to be brief.

"I believe that the perfect Courtier, as Count Lodovico and Messer Federico have formed him, may be good not merely intrinsically and for his own sake, but also for the purpose he serves; for, if he served no other purpose than to exist for his own pride and satisfaction, I should not advise a man to spend so much labour and study in acquiring this profession as it requires; on the contrary, I should say that most of his pursuits are mere frivolities and vanities, and as such rather to be blamed than praised in a gentleman; for these fashions which belong to the service of women and love serve merely, though many may disagree with me, to effeminize our minds, demoralize our youth, and reduce it to lewd living; and to this we owe the fact that the Italian name has been dishonoured and few dare, I will not say to court death, but even to face danger. . . . But if his activities are governed by the good purpose I propose, then, it seems to me, they are neither harmful nor futile, but extremely useful and worthy of infinite commendation. The purpose, then, of the perfect Courtier, I submit, is this: that he should win, by the qualities these gentlemen have bestowed on him, the favour and confidence of his master so completely that he may, and always will, tell him the truth in whatever concerns him, without fear of his displeasure. . . . Hence I should say that music, games, pleasure-making and the other graces of the Courtier are the flower of his calling, but its fruit is to induce and aid the Prince to govern well, and to dissuade him from misrule."

But this, as someone immediately objects, is to transform the Courtier into a minister. Fregoso shrugs; it matters little by what name he is called. He is determined to redeem a profession that is so easily demoralizing, to dignify its futility, and to vindicate the identity of manners and morals, even if that transformation smacks of prestidigitation and the claim which he makes seems strained. It requires an effort; for the moral trust of the Courtier as the ingratiating mentor of his master is the utmost development of which he is capable; and his growth is limited by the same fundamental flaw which vitiates his profession—his lack of initiative and responsibility. He remains a parasite, whether healthful or pernicious; and the discussion naturally shifts, therefore, to the master whom he serves.

At this point, *The Courtier*, as it emerges into the political sphere, becomes the counterweight, in the moral evolution of the age, to *The Prince*, marking the hour with antiphonal finality. Inevitably the disciples of Caesar Borgia and of Guidobaldo of Urbino disagree; if the *Prince* is an irresponsible individualist, the patron of the *Courtier* is the apotheosis of the social man, and his character, so far from being governed by political expediency, is the source of it. "Of the many errors which we see in our Princes today," Fregoso continues—for, more outspoken than his brother, he is critical of princes—"the greatest are ignorance and self-infatuation; and the root of these two evils is nothing but falsehood, a vice rightly odious to God and man, and more harmful to princes than other men; for more than other men they lack what they most need, that is, advisers who will tell them the truth; their enemies lack the affection to tell them the truth and their friends become flatterers and for the most part pave their way with lies which inflate the mind of the Prince with ignorance not only of external things but of himself: and that may be called the greatest and most enormous lie of all. Hence it is that princes, never knowing the truth about anything, and drunk with that licentious liberty which power breeds, are so deceived and corrupt; finding themselves always obeyed, they pass from this ignorance to excessive self-conceit and, transported by self-will, become overbearing; and one error leads to many; for their ignorance leads them to occupy states, whenever they can, by any means, fair or foul. If they were wise, they would strive, not to rule, but to avoid ruling, because they would know how monstrous and pernicious a thing it is when the subjects, whom they propose to rule, are wiser than the prince who governs them." It is here that the Courtier finds his consummation as the link between ruler and ruled, the confidant of the one and the interpreter of the other; and to betray this trust is to become a social outlaw, "for, as there is no good so universally useful as a good prince and no evil so universally pernicious as a bad one, no penalty, however atrocious and cruel, is a sufficient punishment for those unprincipled Courtiers who use their good qualities and pleasing and amiable manners for a bad purpose; for of these it may be said that they infect not a single vessel, from which one alone must drink, but the public font, which feeds an entire people, with a mortal poison." And he rests his case with the formal satisfaction and the sigh of relief of a Jehovah on the final day of Creation.

But, precisely, Pallavicino detects a flaw in the ideal: it is supernatural. Our natures, he reminds Fregoso, are not our own: virtues and vices are dispensed from on high. "Signor Gasparo," the lawgiver replies with judicial compassion, "would you make men so miserable, so perverse in judgment that, though they have found means to tame beasts and can teach a wild bird to fly at the bidding of a man and willingly forsake his woods and native liberty for the fetters of service, they cannot do as much for themselves and with study and diligence better their own natures? I do not believe the moral virtues are wholly inborn," he continues, vindicating the freedom of the will and the perfectibility of human nature with the passionate conviction, the generous rejuvenescence, of a man of his time, but with the sobriety of a mature, a Genoese, realist. "Men never elect evil in the belief that it is evil, but because they are deluded by a certain semblance of good. The art which teaches us to distinguish false from true can be learned; and the virtue by which we discern what is good from what merely seems so, may be called true knowledge, and it is more profitable to human life than any other, since it dissipates that ignorance which, as I have already said, is the source of all evil." To the objection that we must take man as he is, he replies that, if he cannot be remade, he may be modified: the normal ideal for a creature that neither crawls nor flies is that balance which excludes neither the natural instincts nor the claims of the will, and which is the goal of worldly wisdom. "I do not say that temperance should completely abolish and uproot the passions from the human soul; it would not be good that it should do so, for the passions contain some part of good. . . . This would be as though, to avoid drunkenness, we made a law that no one should drink wine. The passions, when they are tempered, favour virtue; anger stimulates strength; hatred of wrongdoing promotes justice; and so with all the others which, if they were entirely removed, would emasculate us and make reason so feeble and languid and inane that it could accomplish nothing, like the helmsman of a vessel in a dead calm." "Truly, Signor Ottaviano, we cannot deny that your precepts are good and useful," says Cesare Gonzaga, "but, if you formed your Prince on them, I believe you would be described as a good schoolmaster rather than as a good Courtier, and he as a good tutor rather than a great Prince." "You cannot give a greater or more becoming compliment to a Prince than to call him a good tutor," Fregoso replies.

In magisterial silence, Ottaviano Fregoso packs up the tables of the law; turning to the Duchess, he says: "This is what I had to say, Signora, of the purpose of the Courtier, and I shall let the others continue, if they have anything further to add." Suddenly he sees her looking at him gratefully: she is proud of him. "The hour is so late that it will soon be time to put an end to this evening," she says, "and besides, I think we should not mingle another subject with this one, for you have collected so many various and beautiful ideas that we may say, not only that you are the perfect Courtier we seek and capable of teaching your Prince, but, if Fortune favours you, that you may become an excellent Prince yourself, which will be a great comfort to your country." He laughs with honest grace. "Perhaps, Signora, if I were in that position, I should be like many others who know how to preach better than they practise." She rewards him with a trusting smile, and the company crowds around him in congratulation. Whatever grace he may lack, he has made amends by his generous vision of their vocation; its value has stirred them, like a personal service, for which they are secretly grateful; they are roused, excited, and exhilarated, and no one can think of sleep yet. "So much honour I did not expect for our Courtier," says Pallavicino, "but since Plato and Aristotle are his companions, no man, I dare say, will disdain the name." Then the gravity of the moment makes him flippant. "I seem to recall," he adds slyly, "that these gentlemen said last night that he should be a lover; and since, if he is to lead the Prince into the strait and narrow path, he must be an old man, for knowledge rarely comes early, especially in matters which we can only learn by experience, I do not see how he can decently be a swain." And he laughs a long delighted young laugh, like a cock-crow. The company echoes him; everyone snatches at the objection to prolong the evening. Bembo takes issue, the epilogue develops, and the Duchess for once is ignored.

Bembo is on his toes, quivering with contradiction from the tips of his long, fibrous beard to the toes of his long, slippery feet, and insisting that an old man not only need not forgo love, but that he alone is apt to know it. But suddenly he sees the Duchess smiling wearily, and with a quiver of compunction he subsides. She makes a bid for his secret. "You have taken no part in our discussion this evening, Messer Pietro," she says, "and I am glad, since it gives us more right to enlist you, and we hope that you will teach the Courtier this happy love, which bears with it neither blame nor sorrow; so tell us, on your word of honour as a gentleman, all you know." And she looks as mysterious and discreet as if she were begging for a choice morsel of gossip. He laughs nervously and his spine tingles. "Signora, if I say that it is legitimate for old men to love, these ladies may mistake me for one myself; perhaps you had better pass this subject to someone else." "Young in years, old in wisdom," she reminds him, "you have nothing to fear. Speak. No more excuses." She stifles a yawn, and with a lean flattered smile he risks one more evasion. "Signora, to treat this matter properly, I ought first to run home and consult the hermit of Lavinello." "Messer Pietro, Messer Pietro," exclaims Emilia Pia impatiently, "there is no one in this company more disobedient than you: the Duchess ought to punish you." She is so peremptory that she startles him into fluent speech. "For the love of God, Signora, do not be angry, I will tell you all you wish." And he flows steadily into an elucidation of Platonic Love.

"Love, in the sage definition of the ancients, Love is nothing but a certain longing to enjoy beauty; and, since desire craves only what it knows, knowledge must precede desire; and since we have three modes of knowledge, that is, through the senses, the reason, and the intellect—the senses breeding appetite which we have in common with the brutes, the reason breeding choice which is the attribute of man, and the intellect, through which man may commune with the Angels, breeding will . . ." The liquid syllables flow on, in orderly eloquence, until Emilia Pia begins to wonder whether she did well to release his loquacity. "The soul, then, lured by this longing to enjoy beauty, if it is misled by the judgment of the senses, falls into grave error and believes that the body in which it beholds this beauty is the principal cause of it and that an intimate union with it is necessary to enjoy that beauty"—and, stealing an oblique glance at her, he concludes: "which is false. These lovers are most unhappy, for either they attain their desire, which is most painful, or they do not satisfy it," which is more so. And now the plaintive note of which he is master creeps into his voice, as he dilates on the satiety of satisfaction, the delusion of desire, and the vanity of carnal love, whose throes he likens to a form of teething; only when the fretful infancy of love is over can the soul find pleasure and peace; and with sidelong sighs he pursues, in obbligato to the theme, his abstruse courtship. She listens, uncertain whether he lingers on this point to display his passion for perfection, for her, or for the sound of his own voice; and he labours it at great length and reluctantly concludes: "When the natural heat begins to cool, we are no longer deceived and possess beauty perfectly; and this love always leads to good, for beauty is good; and of this love old men are far more capable than young ones."

Signor Morello has been polishing the arm of his chair with a restless hand. "It seems to me," he objects, "that to possess this beauty you admire so much without the body is a dream." Canossa seconds him. "Do you believe, Signor Morello, that beauty, as M. Pietro Bembo says, is always good?" "I do not," the old man rejoins promptly. He cites to the contrary instances of unfeeling, fickle, and supercilious beauties; and Federico Fregoso heartily agrees. "Beautiful women are for the most part either proud and cruel or else wanton; though this might not seem a flaw to Signor Morello." But at such flippancies the lean vacant face of Bembo lengthens. "Gentlemen, gentlemen," he says earnestly, "I would not have any of us incur the wrath of God by maligning Beauty, which is a holy thing. By way of warning to Signor Morello and Signor Federico, lest like Stesichorus they be stricken blind, the fitting penalty for those that despise Beauty, I say that Beauty is of God: it is the circle of which Goodness is the centre; and as there can be no circle without centre, there can be no beauty without goodness. Behold the great mechanism of the world, made for the welfare and preservation of everything created by God. The round Firmament, adorned with so many divine lights; in the centre the Earth, surrounded by the elements, sustained by its own weight; the Sun circling all, that illumines all, skirting the nether pole in winter and then rising again toward the upper; and the other five planets that likewise describe the same course. We praise the world every day, calling it beautiful; we praise it whenever we say, a beautiful sky, a beautiful country, a beautiful sea, beautiful rivers, landscapes, gardens, trees, cities, temples, armies, houses. In short, this gracious and holy beauty is the supreme ornament of everything; and in some sort we may say that the Good and the Beautiful are one and the same, and above all in the human form, of whose beauty the original cause is, I believe, the beauty of the soul." He is winded; but Canossa inflates him once more. "Many believe that reason and love cannot agree." "Too wretched, too wretched would our nature be," cries Bembo in esoteric despair, "if the soul which so easily conceives this ardour were compelled to subsist only on that which it shares with brutes and could not enjoy that nobler love which is ours alone; and, since you urge me to enlarge on this lofty theme, I shall not decline but, knowing myself unworthy to treat these holy mysteries of Love, I entreat Him to touch my mind and tongue, that I may teach the Courtier to love unlike the vulgar." His tongue is touched; voluble and vapid, it develops the hallowed theme; and Emilia Pia is left far behind as he soars, spiralling out of the gross errors of sensual infatuation into the serene, rational, and refined realms of spiritual affinity, to which he points as "the true communion of Beauty with Beauty and the generation which some believe to be the end of Love." "To breed beauty from beauty would be to get a handsome boy on a lovely mother," Signor Morello objects, "and I should take this as a much surer proof of her affection than the amiability you favour." Bembo laughs and, rebounding buoyantly, balloons along more anti-umbilically than ever. "We must not digress, Signor Morello," he flings him in adieu, as he vanishes into his native void. Not only will the rational lover be for ever immune to the afflictions of the flesh; not only will he eventually be insensible to the lady he loves; with a final effort he may subtilize her out of existence altogether, "if he will use this love as a stepping-stone to one more sublime; and this he can accomplish by considering how confining it is to contemplate the beauty of one form alone; and to escape this confinement, he will gradually collect every charm and accumulate every beauty in his mind until he conceives a universal Idea, transforming multiplicity into that unity which pervades Nature, and so will contemplate, not the individual beauty of one woman, but the universal beauty that adorns all forms. Then, blinded by the greater light, he will no longer love the lesser." Nor is this happy consummation all.

Bembo draws a deep breath and gains altitude. "This degree of love, though it be very lofty and such that few may reach it, is not yet to be called perfect. When our Courtier has reached this degree, I would not have him rest but boldly press on, pursuing the sublime path which will bring him true bliss. . . ." In the small hours of the night the most rarefied sensations become plausible, and he advances with clairvoyant confidence. "Instead of emerging from himself, as he must do to contemplate corporeal beauty, he will enter into himself to contemplate that which only the inward eye can see, for it becomes keener as the eye of the body becomes jaded; and thus, purged of sin, emancipated by the study of true philosophy, initiated into the life spiritual, and exercised in the pursuits of the intellect, the soul, turning to the contemplation of its own substance, and awaking as it were from a deep sleep, opens those eyes which all possess but few use and beholds within its depths a gleam of that radiance which is a true reflection of Angelic Beauty, and so eagerly pursues it that it becomes almost intoxicated and transported with longing to unite with it, for at last it seems to have found the trail of God, in the contemplation of Whom, as in its blessed end, the soul seeks to rest. This is that Beauty indistinguishable from the Supreme Good, whose light kindles and draws all things to it." There is momentary pause, which might well be final but that the company grows uneasy, watching him stare into space. In a mystic sense it may be true that whatever can be conceived to be, is; and in that sense the intensity of his vision almost convinces them; but they are torn between their twin passions of idealism and common sense, and he has to strain in a final effort to elevate them. "O Most Holy Love," he murmurs, "what mortal tongue is worthy to praise you? Most Beautiful, Most Good, Most Wise, bred of the union of Divine Beauty, Goodness, and Wisdom, you in these and these in you abide, and you return upon yourself as in a circle. O most sweet bond of the world, you unite the elements in concord, you move Nature to breed, and whatever it breeds you prompt to perpetuate life; you assemble together what is apart, you lend perfection to the imperfect, likeness to the unlike, love to the inimical, fruits to the earth, calm to the sea, to the Heavens their life-giving light. Deign, O Lord, to hear our prayers, enter into our hearts, and with the splendour of your celestial fire illumine our darkness and, like a faithful guide in this blind labyrinth,

CASTIGLIONE

show us the true path. Correct the error of the senses . . ." and his voice trails away, still leading in prayer; he is translated; his glassy eyes are uprolled in beatific hebetude; at last, he sits in stupefied abstraction, his lips moving without a sound. Emilia Pia becomes alarmed and plucks him by the sleeve. "Be careful, Messer Pietro," she murmurs, "lest we lose you." "Ah, Signora," he sighs breathlessly, "this would not be the first miracle Love has wrought in me. Ah, Signora . . ." and he can go no further. The company urges him, but the spell is broken, he is exhausted. Accordingly, at the suggestion of the Duchess, the discussion of Platonic Love, the theme of all our morrows, is deferred till the following evening. "This evening, you mean," says Cesare Gonzaga. "This evening?" echoes the Duchess. "It is already day," he replies, pointing to the pallor lying like a faint film on the window-panes.

The fatal moment has come, the dawn that dissipates ghosts; and Castiglione strains to grasp and visualize for ever, in the half-light, the last substantial glimpse of those phantom figures of the past. "Then everyone arose in great surprise, for no one thought that the conversation had lasted longer than usual; but, as it had begun much later and had proved so delightful, no one had perceived the flight of time and not an eye was heavy with sleep, as almost always happens after a white night. Opening the casements on the side of the Palace which overlooks Monte Catri, they saw the East flushed with a rosy dawn, and all the stars fled save the mild sovereign of the Heaven of Venus, which guards the confines of the night and day: which seemed to exhale a smooth halo, filling the air with a nipping chill and stirring amid the murmuring woods of the neighbouring hills the sweet concerts of the birds. Thereupon everyone, respectfully taking leave of the Duchess, retired without tapers, the light of day sufficing." And, as the morrow invaded the shrine of his vision, at Casatico the pen slipped from Castiglione's hand.

43

There it lay, the substance of his life, compressed into a little sheaf of shining pages. Of the men and women who had once constituted his being and to each of whom he now restored some quickening part of himself, nothing remained but the ideas they represented. Everything had vanished but the Platonic reality, the pregnant psyche which it was for him to disseminate, as his final service to Urbino. But, partly from modesty, partly from reluctance to violate the privacy of his memories, he hesitated to publish a volume which was at once so personal and so ambitious. He consulted various friends. Canossa urged him to print it; but Canossa was partial, and he preferred to approach an authority who had not been a familiar of the Court of Urbino. The reply being favourable, he doubted again and appealed to Bembo. "Do not trouble about the style," he wrote him, "that can be touched up by another hand, and if the form and substance of these dialogues do not satisfy your taste, I shall alter, omit, or add whatever you may suggest." A Platonic dialogue in the form of a *jeu de societé* was manna to Bembo, but he was a very busy creature: the Papal Secretary was sampling the fleshpots of Rome, rearing a prolific family, fostering literary cenacles; it was many weeks before he replied, and the letter went astray. A year later Castiglione again applied to him for advice. Bembo was then enjoying a well-earned holiday in Venice, and, when he finally composed his opinion, it was no longer needed. Castiglione had consulted himself, lifted the blindfold, maturely considered *The Courtier*, and locked it away in his closet.

For in that year something had occurred, something which had long been maturing and which now came to light. He had outgrown his past. The life of the Courtier was a phantom existence, not only because he had outlived it, but because, as he now realized, it was a pose. All its aims—culture, ideals, friendship—were mere semblances of life, refined illusions of reality, eclipsed at last by a genuine experience. For the first time, a profound and uncultivated feeling possessed him; and beside it the conventional sentiments of his youth paled into insignificance. The self-sufficiency of virtue, the disinterested pursuit of honour, the fugitive pleasures of society, the half-measures of friendship, now appeared no more than green conceits, fond infatuations, and the book based on them a literary exercise without vital meaning. He was passionately in love with his wife.

Love came to him late, and with consuming intensity. The precious sentiments of the past had sealed his latent affections: his devotion to his friends, his idolatry of the Duchess, had shielded the slow secretions of his sensibility; and when love came, charged with the pent-up force of years, it fired a nature whose passion had never been tapped and devoured to its roots a heart that was whole and intact. The only portion of *The Courtier* which still rang true to him was its defence of the mellow love of maturity; he could vouch for it not merely with seasoned serenity but with all the unbroached ardour of his springtide. He was rejuvenated. The years which separated him from his wife were forgotten. Everything had returned into the appointed order, his life resumed its unbroken continuity, and with the birth of his first child he was born anew. "I must inform Your Excellency," he wrote to the Marquis Francesco Gonzaga, in announcing the event, "that you have one servant more, and among all the reasons I have for rejoicing none gives me more pleasure than the fact that I have a son to devote to your service." Another Castiglione would now live over his past; for himself there was only the future; and for the rest of his life he settled down to embrace, in a belated but vigorous prime, the one joy that had come to him uncourted.

44

Three years slipped away. The Marquis Francesco Gonzaga was on his last legs. The ravages of syphilis, of inactivity and boredom, of long years of domestication and political insignificance, had played havoc with his constitution, and his spirit was broken. He had lost all his self-confidence. When the refugees of Urbino first came to Mantua, though he welcomed his sister, his daughter, and his son-in-law, he sent them to live in the outskirts of the state. Their arrival had been preceded by that of his infant grandson. "On the one hand, Nature stifles my fear, but love, on the other, revives it," he confessed. From that day he was doomed: the shock of discovering himself hastened his decay. Though he had solicited and received permission of the Pope to receive the exiles, he was menaced from time to time with an excommunication for befriending them. Isabella advertised her contempt for it; but it troubled his conscience. His courage ebbed with his animal vigour, and he shrank visibly into the shell of a man. He lived in constant apprehension of nameless dangers, and above all he dreaded his own fear. He came to resemble the figurehead in the abandoned fountain of his courtyard, the stranded Triton about whose feet the frogs formed at night. Lying in the twilight, he listened to their lugubrious gulping, monotonously memorizing, like ventriloqual oracles of the gloaming, a muffled reminder that it was time to die; the blood pulsed as sluggishly in his veins as their nightsong; and in 1519 he closed his eyes and died, leaving his state and his heir to the capable hands of Isabella, whose ability he recognized with his last breath.

But her self-confidence was also impaired. Federico Gonzaga was now a youth of nineteen. In many ways he answered her expectations. The chubby child with silken hair and innocent eyes had grown into a chubby man with vacuous eyes, close-cropped hair, and the silken whisper of a budding beard under his adolescent mouth. His amenity, his munificence, and his culture manifested her maternal influence; but after all she had loaned him to the world as a hostage. The best years of his boyhood had been spent in foreign Courts, and when he returned she discovered that other hands had been at work. Plunged prematurely into a hardening world of pleasure and intrigue, he had completed his education alone. Shortly after his father's death, a tutor to whom he had taken a dislike was murdered, and rumour connected his name with the mystery. A violent scene ensued between mother and son. "Before God, Marquis, tell me the truth," she demanded; but the truth never transpired; and she recoiled. The unsettled suspicion made her study her son as a stranger; but a stranger who was hauntingly familiar. Whether it was his father's spirit or her own untamed Este blood that she recognized in him, it troubled her. The leading-strings were broken. When he took a married woman as his mistress, she could only disapprove with a rigidity, a violent reticence, which aged her visibly; but lest age estrange them, she did her utmost to dissimulate it. She bloomed obstinately and unwillingly. The futility of her efforts to form Federico according to her fastidious feminine tastes gnawed at her heart and spoiled her complexion; she was forced to fly a flag of distress and she attempted to surround him with courtiers whom she could trust; and she trusted no one but Castiglione.

And so, with her fading charms, Isabella invaded Casatico and wooed the friend of women from his retreat. He was reluctant to leave it, but he could not deny that name or her appeal to it. What she offered him was an opportunity to achieve their common ideal of a man whom women approved and to convert literature into life. The role of mentor to his prince was the supreme responsibility of his calling, and the instinct of duty was in his blood. So, too, was his duty to his wife; but he reconciled both claims. It was for her sake as much as for Madama's that he consented to take up his duties as a companion to Federico. The young Marquis was impressionable. At one moment his eyes, brilliant without belladonna, were as feminine as his mother's; at another they were insipid, opaque, and masculine; his face, like his nature, was passive; and, though he was fully fledged, he was not unamenable to a strong and sympathetic masculine influence. Castiglione won his confidence and became something of a friendly paternal adviser, not only to the heir of Isabella but to her younger sons, Ercole and Ferrante, and insensibly he began to live anew the book which he had laid aside.

45

Within a few months of the death of Francesco Gonzaga, another political figurehead and eminent syphilitic passed away—Lorenzo de' Medici, Duke of Urbino. The hopes of the exiles of Urbino revived, and there was a gathering of the family clan in Mantua. For three years the refugees had lived a genteel life of ever-deepening distress. Elizabetta, after selling her last keepsakes, including her cherished plate designed by Raphael, had taken to travel, sojourning at intervals with her nephew Ottaviano Fregoso, the Doge of Genoa. Francescomaria, however, had made an unsuccessful attempt to recover Urbino by arms, which had won him credit and sympathy, and his spirit was unbroken. Isabella, gathering them under her wings, took the lead and wrote to her friends in Rome to learn what effect the death of Lorenzo, the last legitimate member of the Papal family, had produced on the Pope.

Of these friends the most practised and skilful was still the Archdeacon Gabbionetta. He went straight to the Pope, whom he found in a state of phlegmatic resignation, and to sound him remarked that "it was the common opinion that God had stricken him for his own good." Leo took him by the hand, looked into his eyes, and gratefully agreed. "God Himself, the Blessed Virgin, and the Holy Apostles have always known our good intentions," said His Holiness, "though sometimes, like other men, we have yielded to the frailties of the flesh, and we thank God for His mercies." Pleased with this chastened spirit but not satisfied with it, the Archdeacon hurried backstairs to interview the Medici factotum, Pietro Ardinghelli. To him too the Pope had opened his heart. *"Dominus dederat, Dominus abstulit,"*[1] Leo had said, admitting that "as a Medici he was deeply distressed to see his posterity extinguished, but as Pope he was extremely relieved that God had delivered him from the service of

1 God has given, God has taken.

princes, of whom he now had no further need while they still needed him; with many other words all tending to indicate that he was determined henceforth to think only of the profit and promotion of the Holy See." Gabbionetta, accordingly, sent an encouraging report to Mantua, and Canossa confirmed it. "His Holiness shows every disposition to accept the will of God," he wrote, "and to conform to his own better instincts." Isabella did not count too confidently on this chastened mood, but she weighed it with other factors and made her calculations.

For some time past the Pope had been making surreptitious overtures to Mantua. Too prudent to let the resentment of the Gonzaga, the Este, the Montefeltre, and the della Rovere fester there, he applied on every occasion the emollient salves of his softest phrases to the sore spot. He regretted incessantly the unfortunate necessity which had estranged him from his old friends in Mantua; for his own part, his feelings had never changed; and the mere mention of the name of Gonzaga set his mouth flowing with unctuous saliva. These advances had begun even before the death of Francesco Gonzaga. "Archdeacon, Archdeacon," His Holiness said one day to Gabbionetta, "I shall show the whole world the love I bear the Signor Marchese and his children and his illustrious House, although"—and he paused in eloquent confusion, clasping and unclasping his hands—"although the Devil . . ." And, wiping his lips, he let the unfinished phrase speak for itself. Although he avoided all mention of Isabella, he attempted to mollify her indirectly by suggesting that her second son, Ercole, should come to Rome to complete his education, and he hinted at the tasselled Hat. Nor did he overlook her youngest boy. Looking one day at his portrait, "Our little godson has a sharp little face, a wicked little face," he chuckled. "Let the Marquis look to him, we shall take care of the other." The death of Lorenzo de'Medici seemed to open the way to a *rapprochement*; and putting two and two together, compounding his policy and his repentence, Isabella felt that the time had come to appeal, or at least to prepare the ground, for the restoration of Francescomaria to his state. Accordingly, as the man most designated for this mission was Castiglione, he was sent to Rome to convey the condolences of the Gonzaga to His Holiness.

But already the chastened mood was wearing off, or rather the conscience of the Pope was working itself out in a manner strictly consistent with his character and his responsibilities. The death of his nephew and the extinction of his line frustrated the family ambition which was the mainspring of his life; it was a profound shock and he accepted it as a Divine visitation; and when he recovered he cheerfully sacrificed the ambition he could no longer satisfy to the superior interests of the Church. But some men are ruined by reform. In his disinterested zeal he sacrificed both his own interests and those of Francescomaria to his Apostolic duty and determined to annex Urbino to the Holy See. But, though the purity of his motives made him impenitent, his conscience worked slowly and, before he reached this conclusion, he kept Castiglione in suspense for five months. Patience, he reminded him when the Count grew pressing, was the greatest and most salutary of virtues.

The delays of the Pope, Castiglione was prepared to bear, for they were traditional; but what really taxed his patience were the delays in his letters from Casatico. Often as Ippolita wrote, she never wrote frequently enough to satisfy him; and when he grew restless he remarked with a smile to the Pope that it only rested with His Holiness not to make him the one man in the world who found patience unfruitful. To cheat his heart, he composed an imaginary letter from Ippolita to himself in the form of a Latin elegy; and to kill time he lent to her inarticulate longing his own elegiac eloquence, prompting her to lament her loneliness, to confess her jealousy of the charms of Rome, her dread of its disorders, her relief when Canossa brought her good news, and to conclude with a prayer to Leo and the other divinities to send her husband home. The Elegy consumed so much time that her next letter echoed its complaints; and then he lost no time in replying in prose. "If you complain, my dear wife, that you have been without letters from me for eighteen days, I have certainly not spent four hours without thinking of you. Since then I have made amends with many letters, which you must have received by now. But you are really much worse than I am, for you never write unless you have nothing else to do. Thank God, your last letter was a long one. You say I should make Count Lodovico tell me how much you love me. I might as well tell you to ask the Pope how much I love you. All Rome knows it, and everyone tells me I am sad and out of sorts because I am not with you: I do not attempt to deny it. They all wish I would send to Mantua for you. Think it over and tell me if you would care to come. Jesting aside, tell me if there is anything you would like in Rome, and I will not fail to bring it; but you must tell me what you would like most, for some morning I shall arrive when you least expect me and find you still in bed, and you will vow that you were dreaming of me, though there will not be a word of truth in what you say! I cannot yet name the day, but I hope it may be soon. Meanwhile, remember me, love me, and believe that I never forget you: I love you infinitely more than I can say and commend myself to you with all my heart." With her letter in his pocket, he found patience then to sit for his portrait by Raphael, to elaborate with him their scheme for the restoration of ancient Rome, to study his frescoes of Cupid and Psyche in the Chigi villa, and to visit his new gallery of *grotteschi* in the Vatican. And two months later he was called from that dainty gallery into the Pope's study, overwhelmed with personal compliments, and sent empty-handed home to Mantua.

In consequence, the relations between Mantua and Rome once more became strained. With chagrin Leo learned from the informers he kept at the Court of the Gonzaga that he was openly abused even in the presence of the Marquis and his mother. One incident particularly distressed him. His godson, Ferrante, teased by the courtiers on his affection for the Pope, picked up a lance—so the report ran—and attacked the Apostolic arms. The Pope read this report with pain. "The Devil makes those whom I most love love me least," he complained; then his grief turned to anger, and he protested against the continued residence of Francescomaria in Mantua; but this outburst was only a peevish flash, and his natural bonhomie soon reasserted itself. Nevertheless, the incidents continued. Several months later, it came to the ears of the Mantuan Court that an expedition, manned by Ferrarese exiles and secretly supported by Rome was being levied against Alfonso d'Este, who was then lying critically ill. The Marquis and his mother acted promptly, patrolling the Po, arresting suspects, unearthing munition camps, with a vigilance so searching that the scheme remained abortive. It was only when it was thwarted that Leo took cognizance of it; it left him aghast: he threw up his hands in dismay. "What will they think of me?" he exclaimed; and, as their opinion was no secret, he became bitter; and in his bitterness he resolved to dispel the suspicion and animosity of his old friends by a palpable proof of his good will. The international situation was such that he could not afford to let the tension develop. At the same time, Isabella and her son, also recognizing its dangers, determined to make overtures on their side and sent Castiglione once more to Rome to negotiate a better understanding with the Pope.

It was with more than usual reluctance that Castiglione accepted this mission. He had no confidence in its success; his wife was expecting a third child; the heat was intense; he was not well; and the one face which he would have welcomed in Rome lay moulding in the grotesquery of the grave. "I arrived safely, very tired and overcome with the heat, but not ill," he wrote to Casatico. "I am well but do not feel as if I were in Rome, now that my poor Raphael is gone. God rest that blessed soul!" He was warmly received, however, by the Pope, who startled him by proposing, of his own volition, to make Federico Gonzaga Captain-General of the Church. "If I may venture to advise Your Excellency on the strength of my long service," Castiglione wrote to his client, "I should urge you to thank the Pope warmly, to express your great desire to accept his offer, and to close quickly, so that we may know what it means, for I am certain that it conceals something." The Marquis needed no prompting; he accepted precipitately; and Castiglione suddenly found himself in a critical impasse.

On the one hand, he had to satisfy a young man who leapt at the glittering bait and who behaved unaccountably when he was disappointed; an ambassador who failed Federico Gonzaga paid for it with his life and his property. Though such caprices might be unlikely in the case of a man like Castiglione, yet it was within the range of sublunary possibilities that his nest at Casatico might be the stake of his failure or success. And failure was by no means improbable, for on the other hand he was dealing with a man whose duplicity was notorious, and the offer was no sooner accepted than the Pope began to reconsider and procrastinate. "This is the house of change and variation," Castiglione warned his master, "and it is too difficult to discover its secrets. I say no more, I believe I have said enough." From audience to audience he groped his way in a tragic quandary. Leo insisted on his affection for the Marquis and his desire to "take him as a son in place of the poor soul who was dead"; but he also insisted on his fear that Federico Gonzaga might not serve him wholeheartedly, "because of Francescomaria." When Castiglione attempted to allay this fear and protested that the Marquis valued his honour, the Pope looked dubious. The moon-like face clouded with an expression at once somnolent and wary, an expression which stole over it when he suffered from heartburn or prandial fatigue, and which gave a touch of cruelty to his pursed lips. But he did not press the point. He revealed his motives slowly, in covert glimpses, one by one; and his determination to break up the family nest at Mantua by detaching the Marquis was only one of them. Beyond lay others. The appointment of the Marquis was bound up with the development of the international situation.

The election, in the previous summer, of Charles V to the Imperial Crown had unsettled the balance of power which it was vital to the peace of Italy to preserve. In his person Spain and the Empire were united; his dominions embraced Naples and the Lowlands as well; and his preponderant place on the map made a conflict for the hegemony of Europe with his rival, François I, inevitable. The preparations had already begun; the theatre of war was, as always, to be Italy; and Leo was busy shuffling his cards. With France he was already bound by a perpetual alliance, but the Emperor was pressing him with a tempting offer to restore Parma and Piacenza, to subdue Ferrara, to protect Florence and the Papacy, and to reinstate the Sforza in Milan. When Leo continued to hesitate, the bid was raised. Charles threw in the Lutheran heresy, offering first to suppress it and, when this proposal was ignored, threatening to protect it. The Pope, who had hitherto taken little interest in the schism, began to look with a worried and astigmatic eye into the book of Brother Martin. He was not slow to recognize the political capital which Charles could make of the Protestant movement; but still he could not bring himself to a decision: it was a temperamental impossibility. He vacillated like a delicate instrument, vibrating nervously to every atmospheric disturbance, and the complex uncertainty by which he was agitated left the appointment of Federico Gonzaga in suspense. Mantua was the gateway of Italy; it was essential to secure it; but as long as he was allied to the French, Leo was unwilling to make a decision which they disapproved, and they had protested against the appointment to so responsible a post of a young man "so inexperienced and pleasure-loving." On the other hand, Mantua was an Imperial fief, and he did not wish to antagonize the Emperor. Lastly, he shrank from disappointing the Marquis and making his state a hotbed of disloyalty. He continued to vacillate.

Amid the shifting mysteries of Papal diplomacy Castiglione moved in suspense, through a land of shadows; but he had one inspiration to guide him. He saw enough of the Pope's problems to appreciate his perplexities and his indecision, but under his calculations he divined something else—an honest reluctance to break his word to the Marquis. A core of simple good faith, which Leo had done everything to discredit, still steadied the mutable Medici; the world had corrupted but not destroyed it; with Castiglione, whom he respected, he was sometimes sincere, and the Count gambled and trusted him. He trusted him at the risk of deception, ridicule, and worse—trusted him despite his notorious duplicity—trusted him because of it. For Castiglione felt the loneliness of the man whom everyone mistrusted; he knew that Leo valued his good opinion; he understood the hypnotic power of opinion to create what it suggests; no one knew better that half our lives are lived in others' minds and half our character is the judgment others form of it; and he offered the Pope his faith. Only a simple man could have been so shrewd.

Often, as the days passed, his confidence seemed forlorn but he clung to it: it was not more shadowy, after all, than the elusive political realities among which he found himself groping. But the suspense was trying and he longed for the quiet constancies of Casatico. "I always mean to write, though I do not always do so," Ippolita wrote, "I am happy to hear you are well. Please take care of yourself and be of good cheer. I am well and I pray God that I may be safely delivered of a child. If He had done me the grace to allow you to be with me, I should not mind how much I suffered." Then there was a pause, and at last a letter from his mother, enclosing a short one from his wife. "I have given birth to a little girl," she wrote. "I do not think you will be disappointed. But I have been much worse than before. I have had three bad spells of fever; I am better now and I hope it will not return. I will write no more, as I am not very well yet, and I commend myself to you with all my heart.—From your wife who is a little exhausted with the pain, from your Ippolita." He was not seriously alarmed. "My wife must be coming on well; if the fever had continued you would have let me know," he wrote to his mother a few days later. What distressed him was that he could not remember the name he had chosen for his daughter, "but you can wait until I write again," he concluded and signed himself, "your obedient son, B. Castiglione, who is very, very tired." The following evening he dined with Bibbiena, who was just recovering from a serious illness. In the mirth of his friend, who avoided his eyes and stared at the other guests, he felt something forced which he attributed to his illness. The following morning, however, the Cardinal appeared in his room and, producing a letter from the Marquis, gently broke the news. The fever had subsided at last: his wife was dead. Castiglione did not realize that Bibbiena was weeping; he did not hear what he was saying; he felt a strange sensation. Life, at last, had become hard for him.

46

"We broke the news as best we could," Bibbiena wrote to the Marquis, "and Your Excellency will understand how great was his grief. We could not check our tears and wept with him for some time; but at last we succeeded in comforting him a little, and his own courage and wisdom enabled him to resign himself to the law of Nature and the will of God, although very painfully. His grief, however, goes deeper than we see." Some part of it Castiglione revealed to the Marquis in reply to a letter of condolence which touched him. "My dear, my only and most honoured master, I never thought," he wrote, "that I could feel a greater sorrow than to see my wife die, nor expected that she would have to take this journey before me; but what I feel, and shall continue to feel, even more bitterly, is that I was absent at the time of her cruel death. But it is the will of God and I can only pray that He will have compassion on that blessed soul and not leave me here too long without her. May He grant me the grace, also, to do some service for Your Excellency, so that I may satisfy my natural obligations to you and, above all, prove my gratitude for the tender and affectionate sympathy which you have shown me in my heavy sorrow. If anything could comfort me, it would be the kind words of Your Excellency. May Our Lord reward you, since that is beyond my power." And he roused himself to resume a service which was a relief and whose successful issue was the only consolation he awaited.

But that service consisted of standing and waiting, and of something worse—of a perfunctory round of official pleasures which he could not escape, and which he pursued with grim mortification as a discipline, determined not only to bow to the will of God but to dance to it. The Pope expressed his sympathy by granting him a pension and commanding him to a hunt. Leo also had his troubles, and his only cure for them was his favourite sport; cantering across the Campagna, he dismissed all his cares and forgot the claims of the living, which were so much more haunting than those of the dead; and he urged the Count to follow him. The international situation was growing more pressing every day, and he was organizing a monster hunt at Palo, to last four or five weeks or even longer, if necessary. As the hunting season was his giving season, Castiglione could not afford to remain behind and be forgotten. Accordingly, on All Souls' Day he rode out, in mourning, with a mob of gentlemen to the Papal lodge. The party numbered over a thousand and resembled a small army on the march; and, though such mass sport was not to his taste, he was grateful for the solitude of the crowd. At Palo, in the desolate landscape swept by the stinging gales of the Tyrrhenian Sea, he could lag behind, while the abundant game thinned the multitude straggling gregariously in every direction, and indulge his melancholy; or he could ease it by joining the chase, pitching in and scouring the compound where the stampeded quarry were corralled and exterminated, glutting himself with the will of God among the red deer and subduing the leaping hare and the rolling boar to the natural law. An enormous beat of wolves, boar, hares, goats, stags, and hedgehogs, had been provided for the Pope, who sat on his palfrey, starched and smiling, waving his handkerchief, as the rout poured pell-mell into the pale; and, amid the bedlam of tumbling riders and lunging beaters and a crazed menagerie bewildered by horns and explosions and dogs, the mourning hunter stalked oblivion and returned with his trophies. At night the day was lived over by the fire around the heaped-up bag, one Cardinal laughing at his mishaps, another lamenting his miscalculations, a third explaining bibulously how he had spitted his favourite hound by mistake. But, though Castiglione steeped himself day after day in wholesale slaughter, he could not glut himself. When he learned of the death of Isabella's brother, Cardinal Ippolito d'Este, the old ache revived. "One such sorrow would have sufficed to upset a whole life," he wrote to Madama, "and I have had so many in such a short time." The hunt lasted five weeks. Then the Pope's cousin, Cardinal Giulio de' Medici, arrived with a new mob, bringing the party up to two thousand and, as Palo was denuded, the migration moved on to the Papal preserves at Corneto and Montalto. There word was received of the death of Bibbiena. The Pope took it lightly and did not let it interfere with the sport. He had cooled toward Bibbiena ever since he knew that he was dying; the thought of death distressed him, except in the form of a great hunt, when he found the sociable slaughter of so many miscellaneous creatures exhilarating. Neither did he allow business to interrupt the chase, though Cardinal de' Medici had brought the French ambassadors with him; and, when Castiglione broached the subject of the appointment of the Marquis, he found the Pope engrossed in venery. Game was plentiful, the weather was good, the political situation was bad, and a *caccia grossa* was organized to surpass all the others. The canvas enclosure was spread over a wide area, but two thousand sportsmen and menials engaged in the *mêlée*, and in the seething confusion there were many daring exploits, ludicrous accidents, and hairbreadth escapes, including that of the Pope from a wolf—a thrilling moment which brought a light sweat to his face, though he assured his rescuers that he felt as safe as if he had been under the protection of Mars. Yet, incredibly, one man slept through the day. The Archbishop of Mantua napped under a tree, only waking when the sun was setting and the oxcarts were lumbering home with the kill. That night, at supper, however, he gave a glowing account of the sport he had missed, to the intense delight of the Holy Father. In the exhilaration of those scenes Castiglione found a fleeting forgetfulness, but not for long. His mother insisted on reminding him of practical problems connected with the death of her daughter-in-law: there was the question of her resting-place in the family chapel, and the question of the disposal of her wardrobe, and of his return, and of his children, questions which she could not settle alone. "I cannot say any more about the things which belonged to my poor wife," he replied, as soon as he could find a quiet corner in the crowded house in which to reflect and to write. "I will only beg Your Ladyship not to throw them away on any account. As for the black velvet gown, if you cannot find anyone who would like it, you might keep it for the house. The tailor might advise you what to do with the other clothes, or you might write to Madonna Costanza in Milan, telling her to keep the name of the owner a secret and explaining that these are only a part of the wardrobe. You might also write to Verona and Brescia and Ferrara, if there are any persons there whom you can trust, and get what you can for them; but I leave all this to you to settle. As for S. Agnese, I think you are rather hard on our chapel in that church, although it is true that the poor child sometimes said that she did not wish to be buried there. I trust that, when God sees fit to end my life, my bones may lie with hers, and both for the honour of the living and the peace of the dead I hope some day to restore our chapel in S. Agnese. As to my return, I beg you not to distress yourself: there are many reasons why I should remain here. God knows with how heavy a heart I should enter the house now! I hope, too, that my mission may bear good fruit this time and be of more use than my last one. Would to God it had not brought me all this sorrow!" And he returned eagerly to the grand business of hunting, from which his personal life was a digression.

The season lasted so long that when the Pope returned to Rome the gaieties of Carnival had already begun. The Eternal City was crowded for the races, and the Marquis entered two of his best horses. Castiglione felt his interest in life revive. The Mantuan horse won the first race but was disqualified on a technicality. In the second race the jockey was within an inch of the goal when a bystander stepped in front of it, forcing him to swerve, and in spite of the foul, the banner was awarded to his competitor. The loss of his wife, of his friends, of Urbino, Castiglione had borne stoically, but now the self-command of a lifetime broke down. Nothing could convince him that the culprit was an innocent bystander, and he protested violently to the Pope. "I asked that he should be hanged or sent to the galleys or at least given four or five turns of the rope," he assured the Marquis, "and I promise Your Excellency that he shall not escape unpunished." The rare opportunity to wring justice from death excited him; and to offset this outrage he wrote hopefully of the probable issue of his mission. There were signs: the Pope had spent three hours looking into Luther, he was anxiously awaiting the outcome of the Diet of Worms and the attitude toward the heretic of the Emperor, and he was daily cooling toward the French. He had promised to confirm the appointment of the Marquis *soon*, and Castiglione confidently believed that "this *presto* would not be as slow as the others."

But after this flare his spirits sank again. The Carnival was the dullest in his experience. The plays were poor, the scenery magnificent, the actors mediocre. That description applied to the whole social life of the Vatican now. It was, no doubt, the death of Bibbiena. He had been the life of the Court, and his *Calandria* was still the best comedy of the Leonine Age, though, to be sure, the Pope had been highly amused by another, which he had read in manuscript and of which he had commanded a performance. This was *Messer Nicia*, or *Mandragola*, by one Niccolo Machiavelli. The author was identified at the Vatican as an unsuccessful place-hunter and obscure political pamphleteer, who had at last conformed to the spirit of the times and turned his talents to farces. His comedy was a caustic fable, founded on fact, in which a gullible doctor, his virtuous wife, her scheming lover, a pimping parish priest, and a mythical love-potion furnished a lively painting of popular life, which had met with instant success in Florence. A local connoisseur had recommended it to Bibbiena, shortly before his death, for performance at the Vatican. To this suggestion Bibbiena had replied with his usual courtesy or, as the connoisseur preferred to express it, "with his usual *cortigianerie*." He had passed it on to the Pope, and the Pope had read it with rising feelings. He was moved by the prologue with its apology for the frivolity of the author—

> Forgive him if he strives
> With these idle fancies
> To while his heavy time away,
> For he has nothing else to say
> Nor hope for. Being forbidden
> To show his wit in other ways,
> He must keep it hidden. . . .

He was impressed by the sequel:

> There is no possible cure for our evils now; we must resign ourselves to seeing everyone turn away, snickering and backbiting; our age has lost its ancient virtue, for, since everyone censures it and laughs, no one labours for a generous aim which the winds will

> disperse and the mists efface; but if anyone hopes to alarm the author by abusing him, I warn him that he too can abuse, in fact, it is his greatest art, and he respects no man in Italy, although he bows to those who seem to wear a better cloak than he....

And by the comedy itself, which fully redeemed the author's vaunted power of bitter raillery, he was so thoroughly amused that he directed Cardinal de' Medici to find him some employment as a writer. The Cardinal thought the matter over and awarded him a contract to write the History of Florence.

The robust sense of humour of Leo had scandalized stouter tastes than Castiglione's. Believing as he did that nothing reveals a man more than what he laughs at, Castiglione, whose own humour was mild, drew the line at many things—at boon companions and practical jokes, at sacrilegious ridicule, at personalities, and even at malicious gossip: that was one element of social life to which he never reconciled himself and which he deplored as a peculiar vice of Courts. Yet he was forced to recognize that it was the lifeblood of Rome and more prevalent now than ever. Whether it was that he had lost his mirth or that the society of the Vatican was degenerating, he found the wit like the men, and the men like the meats, "high" and over-seasoned. There was a touch of rottenness in the facility with which men laughed at themselves and the lust with which they laughed at each other. The laughter of the satirist, the laughter of *Mandragola*, had a stinging gall and a bracing abuse; but there was another laughter even more in favour there and far more effective in forming public opinion—the laughter, rampant, vulgar, insolent, and venal, of Pasquino. For years Pasquino had been an accepted tradition of the Papal Court. The little statue in the Piazza Navona to which anonymous writers affixed their squibs was a mouthpiece of public opinion, whose drifts it caught, echoed, and disseminated; and no one had taken him seriously. But Pasquino was no longer a statue, he was a man who had captured his trade and his power and was using them for his own ends. Pasquino could not be ignored, now that he was the trade-name of Pietro Aretino.

Unless the ageing courtier looked upon the world with too spectral an eye, the rise of Pietro Aretino was a portent of its decay. That lean and famished adventurer, with his prying eye, his cadaverous look, and his eavesdropping gait, was everywhere in the Vatican, the epitome of its promiscuity, the living symptom of the disintegration of society. He had sprung up no one knew how, and had become a force as anonymous as his name. His origin was a mystery. By his own account, he was born in Arezzo in a public hospital "with the spirit of a king"; and he had grown up in the gutter. His mother was a whore, his father either a cobbler or a gentleman—he was not sure which—and his name that of his birthplace. He had been a vagrant ever since he could remember, until his vagabondage ended in Rome, where he became a lackey or a poet—there was little difference—in the household of the banker Chigi. Then, one day, he gained a foothold in the Vatican and began to climb. He clung to a compatriot, Bernardo Accolti, the extemporizer of Urbino, until *l'Unico Aretino* discovered that his *protégé* had stolen his name. He was no longer the only Aretine: there was Pietro, who had become a power by identifying himself with another anonymity—Pasquino. The little god of gossip protected his prophet. His were the liveliest lampoons and the deadliest, the most licentious and the most libellous; and his pasquinades were not only tolerated but applauded and rewarded at Court. Cardinal de' Medici took him up, and the licensed scandal-monger underwent another transformation and emerged as an inspired publicist. Lodged in the official world, he fattened on its laxity, finding favour in its affinity, for he was the familiar creature, the vital parasite of a system. In that promiscuous, pushing Roman world, where everyone was on the make, he was at home, impudent, unprincipled, and venal, exploiting and satirizing it. His success was the measure of its culture and its mockery; and he himself was a living lampoon on the society which accepted him.

Castiglione ignored him, as he did everything that was unpleasant and incurable. When the Marquis asked him to collect his pasquinades, "the verses you ask for," he replied, "do not appear until the second of May; of those of the past I have not been able to find a single copy; they appear in a flash and are sent out and never seen again." But what was lasting except the ephemeral? Certainly there was nothing ephemeral about that persistent impostor worming himself up in the Vatican; he was there to stay, and he could not be ignored with impunity. But life had grown too hard for Castiglione to adapt himself to it. The world was changing, and he was standing still. These were the accepted fashions of the day; to be captious was to join the elder generation. He remembered Urbino, and its manners seemed those of a bygone age. Pasquino was the new Courtier. Castiglione brought out his manuscript once more and submitted it diffidently to his friends. It would soon be outmoded, it would soon be meaningless. His whole life had been governed by his respect for public opinion, and public opinion was now governed by Pietro Aretino.

47

With the contract to write the *History of Florence*, Machiavelli had no sooner obtained, after nine years, his coveted connexion with the Medici than his past protested. Piero Soderini, who had not communicated with him for years, immediately wrote from Rome offering him a position as secretary to a Roman nobleman, "which I consider much better than living there and writing histories for a pittance." Machiavelli declined. Writing history for the Medici might annoy Soderini, and he himself would have preferred making it, but he had fasted too long to despise even its dead bones. It was a beginning; it meant work, recognition, self-respect, a new lease of life; and, as he told Vettori, he would have thought little of himself if one service had not led to another. And so it did. He had no sooner begun his researches than Cardinal de' Medici offered him a mission. It was a small one, but it required a serious-minded man.

Cardinal Giulio de' Medici was himself a serious-minded man, the only one in the family, in fact—and that was a telltale reminder of his illegitimacy, despite the Pontifical legitimization which his cousin Leo had conferred on him. Conscientious, efficient, hard-working—working even at his pleasures—he drudged for his cousin Leo, taking over his official chores, assuming the routine of his responsibilities, supervising the government of Florence, and attending to the multifarious details of ecclesiastical administration, in which the Pope left him a free hand. In this connexion a delicate problem had arisen. The Franciscans were in need of a reform as drastic as that of the Dominicans in the day of Savonarola; and to effect it he felt it necessary to follow the example of the great Friar and separate the Tuscan from the Lombard Congregations of the Order. The Lombard Franciscans had shown some reluctance, however, to accept this division; and what he needed was a man whom he could send to their headquarters at Carpi, a man who would handle them with the patience which he could not devote to the question himself. To facilitate his task, he combined it with another. The Wool Guild of Florence wanted a Franciscan preacher for Lent, and was particularly anxious to secure one of the brothers of Carpi, a choice which would no doubt do much to conciliate the Chapter. This mission he offered to Machiavelli.

Among all the caprices of Fortune, Machiavelli had never foreseen a practical joke so enormous as to find himself wheedling a chapter of friars, picking a preacher for Lent, and treading in the footsteps of Savo-

FRANCESCOMARIA DELLA ROVERE, by Titian
From the portrait in the Uffizi Gallery, Florence

narola. He accepted the mission unsmilingly, until he reached Carpi; then he could contain himself no longer. He could not open his heart to Vettori, for Vettori had suggested his name to the Wool Guild; but Carpi was only a few miles from Modena, and at Modena there was someone better—there was the Papal Governor, Francesco Guicciardini. Guicciardini was an old friend, who possessed everything that Vettori lacked, who had a deeper sympathy, a richer culture, a bolder mind, and a wider experience of the world, and to whom he could speak as freely as to himself, at least when he forgot that Guicciardini was, after all, His Excellency the Apostolic Governor-General of Modena and Reggio.

In nine years Machiavelli had learned to laugh, and Guicciardini was the man to laugh with him. "My dearest Machiavelli," the Governor wrote, as soon as he learned of his predicament, "certainly it was good judgment on the part of our venerable consuls of the Wool Guild to select you to pick a preacher. I am sure you will not disappoint their expectations or your own honour, which would be tarnished if at your age you gave yourself to the life spiritual, for, as you have always pursued the contrary profession, everyone would attribute your conversion not to your goodness but to your dotage. I urge you to dispatch your business as quickly as possible, for you run two risks in remaining there: the first is that those holy friars may compromise you as a hypocrite; the second is that the air of Carpi may make a liar of you, for it has had that property for many centuries. And if, for your misfortune, you were lodged in the house of some Carpigiano, your case would be incurable."

Machiavelli reassured him by return post. "I was in the privy when your courier arrived, sitting and thinking of the absurdities of the world, and trying to conceive a preacher after my own heart for Florence, and one who would please me, for in this I wish to be as stubborn as in my other opinions. And as I have never failed our Republic when I could serve it, if not with acts, at least with words, and if not with words, with signs and gestures, I do not intend to fail it in this either. It is true that I am contrary in this as in many other matters to the opinion of our citizens: they want a preacher to show them the way to Heaven, and I want one to show them the way to the Devil; they want a man of prudence, loyalty, and integrity, and I want one madder than Ponzo, more artful than Savonarola, more hypocritical than Frate Alberto, because it would seem to me a fine thing, and worthy the goodness of these times, that we should experience in one what we have suffered in so many friars, and I believe the right way of finding the way to Heaven is to discover the road to Hell to avoid it. Moreover, when we see how much reputation a rascal wrapped in the cloak of religion obtains, we may easily conjecture how much credit a good man, who followed the footsteps of St. Francis in truth and not in simulation, might expect. And finding my fancy a good one, I have decided to choose a man by the name of Rovaio, and if he resembles his sisters and brethren, I think he will serve. I wish you would give me your opinion in your next letter. I am staying here without a thing to do, because I cannot complete my mission until the General of the Order and the arbiters are appointed, and I have been pondering how I could sow as much trouble here as seems to be the lot of these Franciscans elsewhere; and if I do not lose my mind I think I shall succeed; and the advice and assistance of Your Lordship would be valuable. If you were to go out for a walk and wander over here, it would not be a bad thing, or you might at least write me and suggest some masterstroke; if you were to send me an express courier every day, as you did today, you would do me several good turns: for one thing, you would give me some ideas, and for another, you would make my reputation rise here with the arrival of so many couriers. I can tell you that when the archer arrived this morning with your letter, bowing to the ground and saying that he had been sent expressly and in post-haste, everyone rose with so many murmurs and salutations that the whole convent was in a flutter, and many asked me what was the news; and I, to boost my credit, said that the Emperor was expected in Trent, and that the Swiss had called a new Diet, and that the King of France wished to consult with the Emperor, but that his counsellors were dissuading him; so that they all stood around, open-mouthed and cap in hand; and as I write there is a circle about me, marvelling that I can write so long and thinking me inspired; and I, to make them gape yet more, raise my pen sometimes and ponder and swell, and then they begin to drool; and if they knew what I am writing, they would be even more astounded. Your Lordship knows that these monks say, when a man is confirmed in grace, the Devil no longer has power to tempt him; so I have no fear that these friars may lead me into hypocrisy, for I think that I am already confirmed in it. As for the lies of the Carpigiani, I can hold my own with all of them, for it is many a day since I have taken my degree, and I never say now what I believe nor believe what I say, and if I sometimes tell the truth I conceal it among so many lies that it is not easy to discover it. Tomorrow I expect one of those archers of yours, and be sure that he claps spurs to his horse and arrives in a sweat, to make the company drivel; you will be doing me honour and also giving these archers a little exercise, which is healthy for horses at this season."

"Not having, my dearest Machiavelli, either time or wit to advise you," Guicciardini replied, "nor being accustomed to offer advice unless you ask me, I wish to help you at least by boosting your reputation, so that you may accomplish your arduous mission. I am sending you a courier who looks like an archer, whom I have told to ride with the utmost speed on a matter of the highest importance, and not to let his cloak touch his ankles till he dismounts. I am sure, what with his haste, and the things he will tell the eavesdroppers, that everyone will believe you a great personage and your business of everything but monks' cloth; and to convince your hosts that you are a big gun, I have enclosed some dispatches from Zurich, which you can use by showing them or holding them in your hand, as you think best. I wrote yesterday to M. Gismondo that you were a very rare person; he replied asking me to specify in what lay your rarity; I have not answered yet, to keep him in suspense and make him observe you closely. Profit by this reputation while you may: *non semper pauperous haberitis vobiscum*.[1] Tell me when you are through with those friars, and if you can sow some discord among them or at least plant a seed that may pullulate later, it would be the most excellent action you ever accomplished, and it should not be difficult, given their malice and jealousy."

Then the sport began to spoil for him; he was filled by a bitter compassion for his friend, and he wrote, on the same day, another letter, not to the missionary this time but to the historian. "Machiavelli, my dearest: when I read your title of Ambassador of the Republic to the Friars and recall with how many Kings, Princes, and Dukes you once treated, I remember Lysander who, after so many triumphs and trophies, was put to work distributing meat to those same soldiers whom he had so gloriously commanded, and I say: See how the same things happen over and over, only the faces of men change and the outward form; and we see nothing today that has not happened in times past. But since the names and forms change, only the wise realize this; and that is why history is so useful. It puts before us and compels us to recognize what we have never seen or known. From which it follows, by a monkish syllogism, that we should be thankful to the man who put you to work writing history, and exhort you to do your duty diligently, nor do I believe that this legation will prove useless, for in these three days of idleness you will have sucked the Commonweal of Fools dry, and you may be able to make use of their model, comparing it to some of your other forms. . . . I have sent the courier; if he serves no other purpose, he may at least procure you a cake the more tomorrow at supper. I must warn you, however, that M. Gis-

[1] the poor ye will not always have with you.

mondo is a foolish soul and given to gossiping or, as the Lombards call it, chatting; you had better be cautious, therefore, or the geese may turn into drakes and cackle too much. That Rovaio is not willing to go to Florence does not surprise me, he does not care for your wine; and I cannot approve your choice; it does not agree with your own judgment or with that of those who commissioned you, particularly as you have always been known as a man inordinately wide of ordinary opinion and an inventor of new and unfamiliar things, I suppose that the Wool Consuls and everyone who knows of your commission will expect you to bring home a friar of a kind that never walked the earth. So you had better make up your mind, put an end to the joke, and return home, where you are so eagerly expected."

Machiavelli agreed. The joke was wearing thin; even his host, M. Gismondo, was growing suspicious. "I think he suspects something, because he is on the alert and cannot understand why I should write or receive such long Bibles here in these deserts of Araby, where nothing grows but friars; and I doubt whether he thinks me as rare a man as you described, since I remain indoors and sleep and read or do nothing. But he feels me out, and I reply with a few incoherent words, basing my opinion on the Flood that is bound to come, and on the Turk who is sure to appear, and wonder whether we should launch a Crusade in these times, and feed him with such shop-talk until I am sure he cannot wait to talk to you and understand what it is all about, or maybe to quarrel with you for putting such a burden upon him, that encumbers his house and keeps him tied down here; but I believe he does not expect it to last much longer, and he continues to serve good food and oceans of noodles, and I gorge like six dogs and three wolves, and at dinner I say: Today I shall win three *Giulii* from you; and at supper: Tonight I shall win four. Nevertheless, I am obliged both to him and to you, and, if ever he comes to Florence, I shall repay him, and you may tell him so when I am gone. That traitor of a Rovaio will have to be dragged to Florence. He says he does not think he can come, because he does not know how to preach there, and that he has had no honour in Florence: the last time he preached there he forbade the prostitutes to walk in the streets without a yellow veil, and he has had a letter from his sister saying that they wear what they please and wag their tails more than ever; and he complained of this very bitterly. But I have consoled him, telling him that he should not be surprised, for it is the custom of great cities to be constantly changing and doing one thing today and another tomorrow; and I cited Rome and Athens until he was comforted and has promised to come: I shall tell you the sequel tomorrow. This morning the friars appointed as their Minister-General Soncino, who is first a man and secondly a monk, and a good and human man. This evening I am to address Their Paternities, and tomorrow I expect to be gone, and till then every hour seems a thousand. I shall spend a day with Your Lordship, *quae vivat et regnet in saecula saeculorum.*"[1]

The next day, however, he was still lingering, though very unwillingly, for his host was putting questions to him about his secret business which made him extremely uncomfortable. "My backside was throbbing, and I was afraid that he might seize a broom any moment and send me back to the inn; so let us call a holiday tomorrow, or this joke will breed mischief, and I do not want to lose the good it has done me, the magnificent meals, the glorious bed, and the other things in which I have been wallowing like a child again. This morning I raised the question of the separation, today I shall push it through, and tomorrow I hope to be finished with it. As for the preacher, I am afraid he will do me no honour, for my man is backing out; the father superior says that he is promised elsewhere, and I shall return home, I suppose, in disgrace; and that worries me, for I do not know how I shall face Francesco Vettori and Filippo Strozzi, who wrote particularly requesting me to do everything so that this Lent they might be sure of some spiritual food which would do their souls good. . . . I hope you will write them a line or two and excuse me as best you can. As for History and the Commonweal of Fools, I am sure that my time has not been wasted, for I have found much that is good in their institutions and orders, which I may yet make use of, particularly in drawing comparisons, for when I describe silence I need only say: They were as quiet as monks at meals. And I could name many other things which this little experience has taught me."

In Modena, on his way home, he spent a few hours with Guicciardini, gathering information of the great world, discussing the coming conflict, and threshing out the questions which were still, after nine Lenten years, his spiritual food. The Pope had just concluded an alliance with the Emperor, and Machiavelli was anxious to get at the bottom of his motives for abandoning the French. It was, of course, a choice of necessary evils, but to choose the preponderant power and make common cause with the Emperor was, Machiavelli insisted, a political error of the first magnitude. He had already consulted Vettori, and Vettori believed that the Pope was tempted by the offer of Parma and Piacenza and his undying desire to

---

[1] May he live and may he reign till the end of time.

reconstitute, with Urbino and Ferrara, the Medici state. But Vettori was as far from Rome now as Machiavelli himself. Others believed that Leo had joined the Emperor because he was alarmed by the Lutheran heresy; but they were the pious few who were alarmed by it themselves. What did the Governor-General think? He was in a position to know. Machiavelli came from Carpi, laden with problems and as mystified as the friars.

Guicciardini, however, admitted that he was as much in the dark as everyone else. Everything was conjecture. As for the Lutheran heresy, it was undoubtedly dangerous. The scandalous sale of indulgences, the frivolity, the extravagance of the Roman Court, were not understood on the other side of the Alps as they were in Italy; and the Pope underestimated the menace of the Protestant movement. As for his political motives, who could say? "Perhaps," he concluded, "the Pope was moved by the desire to have Parma, Piacenza, and Ferrara"—that possibility could never be excluded—"perhaps by the fear of seeing the two sovereigns combine to his disadvantage"—that was probable; but there was a third explanation which deserved to be weighed—"perhaps also by the hope of doing something great before his death. Cardinal Giulio de' Medici, who knows all the secrets of the Pope, told me that His Holiness hoped first to drive the French out of Genoa and Milan with the aid of Charles V, and then, with the aid of the French, to drive Charles V from Naples and gain the glory of freeing Italy, to which his predecessor had aspired." That possibility, at least, was exciting; but was it really his purpose? Cardinal Giulio was too serious, perhaps, to know all the secrets of the Pope. The risk was too enormous, Leo was too cautious, and in any case the liberation of Italy would never be accomplished by political chicanery and juggling foreign alliances. On this Guicciardini and Machiavelli agreed: the salvation of the country lay in self-help and of all hopes that was the most desperate. They agreed, also, in their anti-clericalism. The Church was the great obstacle to the union of Italy. Lying in the centre of the peninsula, Rome was just strong enough to disrupt and not strong enough to unite it; the policies of the Holy See changed with every Pontiff, and in the case of Leo with every shift in the wind. It was idle to look to Leo for national leadership or to any of the Medici, in fact. Was there one of them who had the vision, the tenacity, the resourcefulness, and the longevity to attempt it? They had all been tried and found wanting—Giuliano—Lorenzo—Leo—and who was left? The drudging hack Cardinal Giulio? Was he the Medici of the future? Machiavelli grimly agreed with the Papal Governor. In nine years he had learned to laugh at all his faiths; and he returned to Florence to write its history.

48

Meanwhile, the Papal and Imperial alliance had been published in Rome, together with the appointment of the Marquis of Mantua as Captain-General of the Church, and preparations for the campaign had begun. Federico Gonzaga immediately offered Castiglione the command of fifty lancers, which he declined, much to the dismay of his mother. He had reached a time of life, however, at which he was bound to consider himself, he explained. "His Excellency has done this with a very kind intention, and I am very grateful to him. But being so deep in debt, I foresee that the post would do me more harm than good, as it would entail heavy expenses. Besides, I am no longer a boy, and I find exertion more fatiguing than of old, and I know by experience how difficult it is to manage a body of men. If the Marquis ever thinks of rewarding me for the labours which have brought him these honours, I should like his gratitude to take some other form, for I do not regard this as a reward but a burden, and if I chose to seek work elsewhere I could easily find it. But during the short time that is left me in this world I do not mean to eat any more bread of sorrow. Therefore, since the Marquis is pleased to say that he needs me equally in camp, at Mantua, and in Rome, indeed, wherever he has business, and begs me to choose the place and the employment I prefer, I have decided to remain in Rome." His decision was final. "I am quite as anxious to see you and all my family again as you are to see me, although, when I remember that I shall not find the dear one I left there, my whole soul recoils at the prospect. But this cannot be otherwise. I do not know when I shall return."

His mother was disappointed. He was growing old: he had never thought of himself before or of his ease; but she could not begrudge him the meagre contentment he found in Rome. "I am living in the Belvedere," he wrote her, "which is a great relief. I wish you had as delightful a place to live in, with this beautiful view, these lovely gardens, and all these noble antiques, fountains, basins, and running waters.... All who enter Rome on this side pass through the street below, as well as those who walk in the fields, and after supper I amuse myself watching the crowds of boys and girls at their games." To sit and rest and watch the world go by—it was all he asked; but to rest in Rome, in that summer and autumn of 1521, was difficult. The world went by too rapidly; and even to sit and watch it was strenuous.

Now that he was lodged in the Palace, the Pope consulted him constantly on the reports from the camp. The Allied forces were concentrating slowly, too slowly to satisfy him, for he was in a fever of impatience, of incertitude, of fear. "His Holiness is almost beside himself with anxiety," the Count wrote to his master, "and would like to hear what is happening in camp every hour, if possible." Leo could not understand why Parma had not yet been taken, and Castiglione had to initiate him into the technical secrets of military delay. His mother was very much mistaken if she fancied that he had nothing to do. "I have enough to do all day and every hour, and spend my time reasoning with these people who have never seen a battle, and think it the easiest thing in the world to take a fortified and garrisoned town, and who expect men to fly on wings!" But Leo, after a lifetime of procrastination, was thrown into a panic by decision, and lived in hourly dread of betrayal by the Emperor and of vengeance from the French; and Castiglione was the only man who appreciated what it meant to live in daily suspense, hanging on the will of a power which he could not control. The Holy Father favoured the Count with his intimate confidence and with flattering attentions which excited some jealousy. But "I no longer value his attentions as I once did," Castiglione admitted to his mother, "though some people think I value them more." At last, after three months of agitation, the strain told on Leo's health, and he broke down. His old complaints returned: everything hurt him, his fistula, his eyes, his liver, his heart, but not even illness could calm his anxiety, and it galvanized him into life again. He rallied irritably; he worried himself into convalescence; and he went to La Magliana to recruit. It was November. The chill in the air had killed the mosquitoes and cooled the malarial flats; the house was empty and draughty, and he felt well enough to venture out in the sun. He wandered through the mews, inspecting his hawks; he strolled on, feeding the rabbits and peeping at the ferrets; he ran his hand over the glistening cage of the great *gazzara*, whistling to the hundreds of jays, doves, and herons, which were also enjoying the sun and which watched him obliquely; and soon he felt strong enough for a little hunting. On the last day of the month, returning from the chase, he met Castiglione who brought him news which restored him completely. The French had evacuated Milan, and the fall of Parma and Piacenza was a matter of hours. "This pleases me more than the Papacy," the Pope exclaimed and ordered an immediate celebration. As he had caught a slight chill, he hugged the fire, but the exuberance of his joy made him restless, and he hurried again and again to the window to watch the bonfires buffeting the damp night wind in the courtyard. The weather was so raw that, on his return to Rome the next day, he dismounted and walked a part of the way to keep warm, tramping along martially, at double-time. For a week he was a little under the weather, but he insisted on working; he played cards briskly, promptly paying his losses and flinging his winnings over his shoulder, and he felt his old self again. On the Saturday night, he listened to music, closing his eyes, as usual, and beating time with his beautiful hand; then, suddenly, his hand fell and he fainted. He did not recover consciousness for two long hours. The physicians put him to bed. He revived and relapsed and revived with his normal vacillation for twenty-four hours. During the night he woke to find Fra Mariano Fetti clinging to him and begging him to remember God. "Jesus, Jesus, Jesus," Leo murmured, and sank back into coma. In the morning Castiglione entered the room, which had already been dismantled, and looked at the face from which all sensation had fled; and he too felt nothing.

49

"To obtain the Papacy and the profit and glory of our House, we should pledge our very selves," Isabella wrote to her brother-in-law, Cardinal Sigismondo Gonzaga. She had suffered too much from too many Popes to feel safe until she controlled the Papacy herself: Fate had made her a woman, but she had a brother-in-law; and with all the abnegation of consuming ambition she dedicated herself and all she possessed, including her jewels and the services of Castiglione, to the candidacy of Cardinal Gonzaga. The services of the Count as a lobbyist had already been bespoken by Cardinal de' Medici, but he responded to her appeal and laboured in a cause which he knew to be hopeless. Though Cardinal Gonzaga spent money freely and shaved his beard to obtain that effect of age which, as he said, "was worth hard cash in times like these," no one took him seriously. Pasquino was railing at "the Mantuan baboon." And Pasquino was boosting Cardinal Giulio de' Medici. With serious opposition Castiglione could cope, but the terrible ridicule of Pasquino, anonymous, irresponsible, remorseless, and vulgar, he could neither answer nor silence. Nevertheless, his client continued to hope. In the betting Cardinal de' Medici had the lead, supported as he was by the Emperor, but when François I declared that, if Giulio de' Medici were elected, neither he nor his subjects would obey the Roman Church, his odds fell from 50 to 12. As eighteen of the thirty-nine members of the College were candidates for the Tiara, and the confusion of bargains such that anything might happen, a compromise candidate was the likeliest result, and Gonzaga entered the Conclave commending himself to the Holy Ghost.

The doors were sealed, and Castiglione took up his station as one of the Noble Guards. The vigil was longer than he foresaw. As the days passed without result, the interregnum, always a lawless period in Rome, caused more concern in the Vatican than the Conclave itself. The canons of St. Peter's, accompanied by flocks of children and processions of barefoot friars with banners, congregated daily before the Palace, kneeling, praying, and chanting the *Veni Creator*. Castiglione at his post grew mildly flippant with fatigue as he listened to their electioneering litanies. "Every morning we expect the Holy Ghost, but, if I may say so, the Holy Ghost seems to have forsaken Rome," he wrote to Mantua. "These poor priests and friars have sung the *Veni Creator* so long in vain that the heart of the Holy Ghost must be petrified." The doors behind which the Cardinals were immured seemed to have buried them alive: once indeed they opened in the dead of night and he saw "all the Cardinals with tapers in their hands," slowly advancing, not with a decision but with a dying member, whom they released. Then the doors were sealed again, and the vigil continued. It became necessary to apply the usual pressure: their rations were reduced to one dish apiece, and after three days more to bread and water. The doors opened again, this time to emit Cardinal de' Medici, who was called away on business to Florence, and with his elimination it was certain that a compromise candidate would be elected. At the end of a fortnight the Noble Guards were finally relieved, the College filed out in confusion, and to the little knots of friends who gathered about him the secretary of Cardinal Rangone made no secret of the fact that he had lost his soul: the treacheries, the broken pledges and perjuries, which he had witnessed in those two weeks, without a single spark of piety, had destroyed what little faith and religion he still possessed. Meanwhile, an enormous crowd had gathered under the window waiting for the proclamation. As the Cardinals appeared, the restless interregnum ended in a tense hush; but the name was read so faintly and was so unfamiliar, that at first no one caught it; then someone recognized it but could not pronounce it—it was the name of a foreigner; gradually it spread, and the bewildered multitude began to murmur the sound of Adrian Dedel of Utrecht.

The response was a riot. As the Cardinals appeared in the streets, they were followed and jeered, and the mob was particularly ugly with the Mantuan baboon, so ugly, in fact, that he found it necessary to harangue those at his heels. "We deserve the most severe punishment," he agreed, "and I am glad you do not avenge your wrongs with stones," and, thanking them for their forbearance, he hurried on, betting on his lead. In the morning the walls of the Vatican were chalked with the popular verdict: *Roma est locanda*.[1] It was the great betrayal. The Papacy had been betrayed to the barbarian; the one institution which was traditionally Italian, the last birthright, was profaned, the unwritten law was broken; and Pasquino awoke, echoing the general groan, and booing the thirty-eight traitors who had betrayed Christ because not one of them was fit to represent Him.

"The Court is disappointed by this election," Castiglione wrote to Mantua, "although the Pope is said to be an excellent and holy person, and we hope for all that is good from His Holiness. But what distresses everyone is that Rome must remain for some time without a Pope, as he is absent in a distant country." This aggravated the situation. The Pontiff was then in Spain as Viceroy of the Emperor, whose tutor he had been, and his election came as a complete and most unwelcome surprise to him. Born and bred in poverty and piety, he had, like his compatriot Erasmus, a Flemish aversion to the Roman Court, which he had never seen and never wished to see, having learned quite enough of its corruption and extravagance from his friend Erasmus and other good Flemings; he was in no hurry, therefore, to reach Rome; and he made no secret of his determination to drive the moneylenders from the Temple and initiate a radical reform of the Church.

When this news, travelling with the proverbial swiftness of bad tidings, reached Rome, there was a general exodus. The Leonine Age was liquidated overnight. Four thousand Papal officials and servants found themselves unemployed and destitute, and unable even to recover their arrears in salary, for the Papal coffers were empty. The Florentine traders who had swarmed into the city at Leo's accession packed and vanished. Commercial life languished, rents fell, and banks closed. The artists migrated. The Court disbanded, the clergy retired to their estates or their dioceses, and finally the Cardinals appointed to administer the city in the interim were forced to forbid further emigration.

Then, like an empty building, the grandeur of Rome, now that it was no longer populous, dawned on the Romans, and became more imposing

---

[1] Rome is for hire.

as the coming shadow stole over it. There, on its seven hills, rose the achievement of the Popes, which had reached its magnificent culmination under the Medici; and the unpopularity of the Pedant Adrian, as he was already known, lent a new and almost mystic prestige to the last member of the Papal family. Cardinal Giulio de' Medici fell heir to the posthumous popularity of his cousin and the accumulated glory of the Leonine Age. He cultivated his advantage. Though he was neither very sociable nor generous nor art-loving, he knew what was expected of a Medici: he dispensed patronage and made his house a centre for what social life remained in Rome, with the result that in the six months before the new Pontiff appeared, he came to be regarded by the populace as the virtual Pope.

Meanwhile, the conditions of the interregnum had been aggravated by the prolonged absence of the titular Pontiff. The depleted Treasury brought all the activities of the Vatican to a standstill. The war had come to a halt for lack of money; the soldiers, the captains, even the Captain-General himself, were threatening to desert. Federico Gonzaga, unable to obtain his pay, had already started for Mantua when he received a long and fatherly letter from Castiglione, pointing out that he was jeopardizing his career and sacrificing a hard-won opportunity which might never recur; and he realized that his mentor was right. In Rome, to add to the general gloom, the plague had broken out. The edict forbidding emigration was rigidly enforced, and those who could elude it in no other way escaped by dying. The mortality rose alarmingly. Under these conditions Pope Adrian, who had the zeal of a reformer but not of a martyr, was more loath than ever to leave Spain.

Finally, however, in August 1522, he arrived. He was welcomed by the Court and the populace with becoming pomp and even with a flicker of forced enthusiasm, which soon expired, however, as the city settled back and observed his peculiar behaviour. So averse was he to the dignity of his office that he proposed to rent a small house as his residence in Rome; and when he finally consented, under protest, to occupy the Vatican, he succeeded in converting the enormous palace into a very small house indeed. He took up his quarters in a remote wing, where he dispensed a ducat a day to his Flemish housekeeper, a spinster, who made his bed, cooked his meals, and lent him her moral support. His predecessor had kept a hundred grooms; he reduced them to four. In vain he was reminded that the Papal Court had an economic function to fill; he was a theological economist, and economy, the rigid, unreasoning economy of the Gospels and the Dedels, became the order of the day. "All Rome is horrified," wrote the Venetian ambassador, "at what the Pope has accomplished in one short week." The Vatican, with half its personnel discharged and its apartments closed, echoed like a house to rent, over which His Holiness presided as a caretaker. He lived, not merely in retirement, but in hiding, inaccessible and almost undiscoverable among his books. He gave audiences reluctantly, and his invariable answer to every problem was the cautious wisdom of inexperience: *Videbimus,* We shall see. The most prolonged vacancy of the Holy See would have been preferable, Bembo wrote, thanking his stars that he had retreated in time to his Paduan villa; and, though he wrote from hearsay, he had heard enough to horrify him at the degeneracy of the Roman Court.

A hundred fountains still flung the liquid pulse of the Eternal City aloft incessantly; incessantly the glistening spires rose and fell; the gushing cascades broke in braided jets; the jubilee of waters surged and sang; but they sang to solitude. The lavish, rushing, rising, buoyant life of Rome, quelled at its source by a clot of foreign matter, sank underground. The memory of Papa Gianni haunted Rome like a waning mirage, and all the refugees of the late regime flocked about Cardinal Giulio; but even he found the plague and the Pope too dismal and fled to Florence. Then the gloom deepened. But one champion still resisted. One voice still rose, railing, bubbling, sometimes breaking, but never relaxing its incessant squirt of ridicule, indignation, grief, and scorn. The unquenchable mockery of Pasquino vented the popular contempt of a Pope who was everything that the vulgar abhorred, a plebeian, a pedant, and an alien. It penetrated even the hermetic seclusion of the Pope's study, wearing his patience away, and goading him slowly into constipated fury. At last he exploded and threatened to fling the nagging statue into the Tiber; but even his friends reminded him that public opinion could not be submerged. Pasquino, said Don Juan Manuel, the Imperial envoy, Pasquino would continue to croak under water. The baffled Fleming subsided, but he was obstinate, his anger rankled phlegmatically, and one day, unexpectedly, Pasquino was silent; and Aretino followed Cardinal de' Medici to Florence.

One more reform had been accomplished, and Castiglione breathed a sigh of relief for the Pope. He, at least, had some sympathy for the alien. But he was anxious to be gone. The diplomatic corps had dispersed; he was almost the last survivor; the death-rate was rising to 100 and 150 a day, and the Vatican was not under quarantine. "Death seems to stare one in the face," he wrote to a friend, "and it is not pleasant to find oneself without money and with a large household of hungry mouths, all clamouring to be fed. It is unsafe to engage new servants, so I am in great need of help, and have already asked my mother for 100 ducats, which I shall need if I leave Rome, as I think I must do. . . . It is nonsense to say that a man can always protect himself from infection: one must send out servants for provisions. And I am here in the Vatican, where there is no guard except in the Pope's apartments. All I can do is to wash in vinegar, perfume my hands, and commend my soul to God—at home, not in church. The Angel of the Castello stands with his sword drawn! May God have mercy on us all. To tell the truth, I should be glad to be out of this, or at least to feel free to go, for the sight of so many dead bodies borne to the grave without priest or cross is a strange and cruel thing. Not a day passes without some horrible spectacle. Just now I saw a poor girl, about ten years old, whose parents had both died, left alone with the bodies, without another soul in the house. I found her at the door crying, and there was not a single person who would take her so much as a cup of water. But it is vain to speak of such miseries." He held his ground until he could leave with a clear conscience. He was practically alone in the Belvedere, sitting by the window and watching the world go by. When he took his constitutional, he walked from the Belvedere to the Vatican and back without meeting a soul or, what was the same thing, a soul that smiled. He had the great court, with its trim gardens, its fountains, its basins, its antiques, its acres of statues, all to himself, and he could not be sure how long they would survive either, for the iconoclast upstairs had frowned on the Laocoön and the Apollo Belvedere as pagan images. But two duties kept Castiglione at his post. He took his place daily in the line of petitioners who formed before the little window in the *Sala del Papagallo,* where the Pope manifested his presence by an economical syllable: *Videbimus.* Gradually, despite the barriers which divided them, despite all the impediments of temperament, of race, of language—for the Pope spoke no Italian, and few Italians understood his Latin—Castiglione penetrated to his confidence. Something sweet-smelling in his service, some fine aroma of gentility in his devotion to a thankless duty, appealed to the lowly Fleming. Here was one Italian who did not look at him critically, who understood his Latin, his difficulties, and his good intentions, and who listened to him intelligently; and for the first time he no longer felt a stranger in a foreign land. He warmed to the ambassador of Mantua, whose eyes were blue, and whose petitions he could conscientiously grant. He lent him his hand to kiss and dismissed him with more than *Videbimus.* Castiglione at last informed his master that the Pope had confirmed his commission and promised him a part payment on his salary.

POPE CLEMENT VII, by Sebastiano del Piombo
From the portrait in the Palazzo della Pilotta, Parma

He was also able to inform the Duke of Urbino, who had recaptured his State immediately after the death of Leo, that the Pope consented to confirm him in its possession. He was now free to leave, and he set his face homewards.

A year before it had seemed as impossible to him to return to Casatico as to turn back the hands of time and return to Urbino, but now that Rome had become uninhabitable he had no choice. A year had passed, and in the last few months the daily spectacle of death had made it almost impious, while unnumbered multitudes went the immemorial way unmarked, to nurse his single sorrow. The plague, falling like the gentle rain of Heaven, had blurred and slowly obliterated the fading traces of his personal life; and Ippolita, after the brief and poignant experience of love she had brought him, took her place among his placid memories. Love had been an interlude, too intense to last, in a life essentially passive and detached; and he reverted to his old habits and became once more the impersonal spectator of his own existence. He was forty-two: everyone assured him that he was still in his prime; and he resumed his life as a courtier in the pretty painted museum of Isabella's *camerini* in Mantua.

He was just beginning to feel at home there when a familiar face appeared in Mantua. Pietro Aretino arrived, armed with a letter of introduction from Cardinal de' Medici, a glib tongue, a lean look, and his enormous Roman assurance, and established himself on a footing of intimacy with the Marquis. His triumph amazed everyone but himself, though even he was impressed by it. "I am in Mantua with the Signor Marchese and so high in his favour that he leaves food and sleep to talk with me," he wrote immediately to Arezzo. "He declares that he has no other pleasure in life, and has written very honourably about me to the Cardinal. If I decide to remain with him, he will allow me 300 *scudi*. He has lodged me in the very rooms occupied by the Duke of Urbino, when he was turned out of his state, and has given me a steward. There are always *gran Signori* at my table, and no gentleman could live better. The whole Court worships me. Happy the man that has one of my verses! The Marquis has them copied, no matter how many I make, and I have composed a few in his honour. So I stay on, and every day he makes me presents, which you shall see in Arezzo. . . . At Easter I think we shall go to Loreto. On this journey I shall satisfy the Duke of Ferrara, and the Duke of Urbino, both of whom wish to make my acquaintance, and the Marquis will present me to their Illustrious Lordships." Suddenly the challenge came home to Castiglione. Rome was commodious and cosmopolitan and promiscuous, but Mantua was too small to accommodate the old and the new Courtier. He decided to publish his book. His friend, Bandello, announced it as a public service, deploring "how few understand what this name of Courtier means"; and he added: "We hope that our Signor Conte Baldassare Castiglione will show the error of these lean courtiers, when he publishes his book of *Il Cortegiano*." Then the Count reconsidered. If an Aretino was accepted, flattered, pampered, lionized, the whole code of his life had no meaning. Why should the Courtier be versed in arms, in culture, in responsibility, in honour, when an upstart without principles, education, or name could do as well? And when Isabella invited Castiglione to join her on a trip to Venice, he accepted.

Aretino was soon recalled, however, by Cardinal de' Medici. The Marquis parted with him reluctantly, but it was for their mutual advantage. The Pope had written to the Cardinal demanding that Aretino be sent to Rome, "because of certain new things that had appeared there," and his presence in Mantua might be compromising to his new patron. It was embarrassing even to his old one, and Cardinal de' Medici advised him to disappear for a time. To disappear—the Pope himself could have pronounced no more cruel sentence—to disappear and be forgotten and untalked-of was more than he could bear in silence; he vanished but he continued to bubble. He kept in touch with the Marquis, epistolizing him and sending him little gifts, trifling tokens of his gratitude, like those four combs which he had picked up second-hand and whose only value lay in their sentimental associations, though they were also of rare ebony; the blackest "Venus must have used to comb her golden locks, but opinions are divided, some say it belonged to the royal concubine of Cardinal de' Grassis, others other things, but I believe it belonged to the most Holy and Religious Laundress of the Pedant Adrian. The other three Pasquino gave me." The pedigree of the combs was a problem he left to the pedants to settle; he presented them to his patron with the blackest reputation he could manufacture and his compliments, and trusted that Federico Gonzaga would accept them for his sake. Meanwhile, Pasquino, the giver of all good things, had been officially suppressed in Rome; but Aretino had not long to wait for his reprisal.

A few weeks later, after a reign of eighteen months, the Pope died. A votive wreath was hung on his physician's door, gratefully inscribed: "To the Deliverer of his country, S.P.Q.R." On his tomb the College inscribed a compassionate epitaph: "Here lies Adrian VI, whose greatest misfortune was that he became Pope." And even his compatriot, Cardinal Enkevoirt, concurred in the general verdict and reminded posterity in Roman capitals graven deep in the sepulchral marble "how much it matters, alas, in what times even the loftiest virtue appears." The world surged back to Rome, and with Cardinal de' Medici came Aretino to work for his election. Though he arrived too late for the Pontifical obsequies, he hastened to bury him also: "Here lies Adrian VI, a holy man, that is, a German, the son of a tailor; the Emperor made him a Cardinal, because he taught him to read his primer."

50

The brief Pontificate of Adrian VI had been not a reign but an interregnum; and a reaction to the legitimate traditions of the Papacy was the foreordained outcome of the next Conclave. On November 19, 1523, Giulio de' Medici was proclaimed Pope under the title of Clement VII. The Conclave had lasted fifty days, the struggle had been bitter, but when it was over opinion was unanimous: he was the logical successor of Leo, and the interloper had made his election inevitable. Now the palmy days would return: the blight was over, the sun was shining, everything was the same again. The Vatican was alive with solemnity and bustle, crowded with courtiers, musicians, artists, actors, and scholars; yet there was a perceptible difference, a lingering chill that persisted like a faint foreboding that nothing could be the same again. The long Renaissance day was verging on evening. The old zest was gone. The irresponsible gaiety and lavish splendour of Leo's day flowed freely once more, but they were vaguely diluted and adulterated. The difference was almost indefinable but it was troubling. It was something less than lassitude and more than moderation. It was like the return to an interrupted revel, the unconscious resumption of its aftermath. After an interval of eighteen months, the Medici revival, welcome as it was, seemed belated, and diligently as he promoted it, it was only too clear that Clement was not Leo.

He did his utmost to maintain the Medici tradition and emulated his cousin studiously, but he was performing a role of which he was the heir only because he was the understudy. He knew what was expected of him, and he did it, with the perfunctory cheer of a man who had learned to play but not to enjoy himself. He patronized art rather because it was the thing to do than because he loved it, though he was partial to fine jewellery and goldsmithwork, to whatever was ornamental, ingenious, and minute. Leo had been myopic but he saw; Clement saw but he squinted. He was devoted to music; yet he never thrilled the musicians as Leo did by listening voluptuously, with eyes closed, humming the melody and beating time with his hand. Clement listened to music as if it were a secret. Actors he encouraged as if they were scholars, and his entertainments were marked by a becoming decorum. They were handsome but not prodigal. He spent what his position demanded but he did not believe that it demanded extravagance or that a Medici was not entitled to full value and a fair price; and merit he rewarded only when he was convinced that his bounty would not be misplaced, for God had given him money—and a great deal of it—to spend where it would do the most good. And so, at the Pontifical banquet, heaped up but not running over, the meal seemed slightly warmed-over to those who described the host as parsimonious and reserved, and who reminded each other, as the wine went round, that he was after all a bastard.

Illegitimacy had lost its conventional stigma in most quarters, but Clement laboured under a peculiar disability: he was himself impressed by his irregular origin. The son of Giuliano the Elder, the brother of Lorenzo the Magnificent who perished in the Pazzi conspiracy, he had been brought up with his cousins without discrimination, but he never forgot that he owed his success to their favour rather than to his right. And the women of the family were less generous than the men, particularly his cousin Clarice, Leo's sister, who seemed to take a stiff-necked pleasure in snubbing him. If he had been a robust love-child, he would have laughed at nagging women; but, though he had inherited his father's beauty, he had none of his buoyancy. His vitality was low; he was anaemic and easily impressed by respectability. He came to care for it with a consuming and sterile sensitiveness. The consciousness of inferiority not only impaired his will; it chilled a nature that was amiable but timid, and he went through life apologetic and self-effacing, fortunate but friendless, and instinctively and always on the defensive. Circumspection became his second nature, and the satisfactions of the head replaced those of the heart. His cousin Leo protected and promoted him, finding him clever and hard-working, and leaving the irksome details of official routine to his hands, but Leo never relinquished the initiative and control of a master; and the little assurance and will which Giulio displayed were constantly undermined by the habit of subservience to which he owed his career. It showed even in his appearance and carriage. He was tall, slender, lithe, and well built, a handsome ecclesiastic with the chiselled features of a flaccid Apollo in skirts, and he would have been an elegant and commanding figure if he had thought himself so. But from the days when he stood beside Leo's chair in the attitude not obsequious but self-deprecatory of an understudy, he had contracted a stoop which not even the Tiara could correct. Now that he had no one to depend on but himself, his dependence was even more conspicuous, and in his magnificent supremacy he resembled an over-dressed and self-deferential lackey. This impression was enhanced by his propriety, which was uncomfortably like the studied respectability of a steward.

The constitutional inferiority of the new Pope was even more apparent in political than in social life. With no superior to consult, he depended on his subordinates, dividing his confidence and his mistrust between his secretary Gian Matteo Giberti, the Bishop of Verona, who was partial to the French, and Nicholas Schömberg, the Archbishop of Capua, an ex-friar of San Marco, who was as staunch an Imperialist. They neutralized him completely. He was already committed to the policy of Leo, a policy of semi-neutrality, of dilatory duplicity; but with all his vacillation Leo had a political flair and in a crisis was capable of decision; Clement had no intuition about anything; he had only advisers, and apprehensions, and the enigmatic precedent of Papa Gianni. Clement VII was a posthumous statesman, and he came to power when the mortal conflict between François I and Charles V was about to reopen.

At La Magliana, through the waning days of November, the gamekeepers waited in vain for his visit. The weather was mild, the autumnal skies were clement, the game was plentiful, but the lodge remained vacant; and the idle beaters agreed that the new Medici was not, like the old, a sportsman.

51

The election of Giulio de' Medici was an occasion of quick concern and prompt congratulation in Mantua. The Marquis had befriended him in the past and at this moment his military career needed diplomatic support. The authority of the young Captain of the Church had been so continually hampered by the Imperial captains who were his colleagues, that he had followed the time-honoured example of his father and retired on a pretext of illness to Mantua. Accordingly, Castiglione was sent to Rome to congratulate the Pope, to complain to him, and to sound his advisers on the probable turn of his international policies. Within twenty-four hours of his arrival at the Vatican the Count had completed his mission. He had visited Giberti and Schömberg: the one had advised him to see the Pope after eight in the evening, the other before eight in the morning; and that was as much as anyone in Rome knew of the relative influence of the French and Imperial champions. He had kissed the feet of the Holy Father and reminded him that, as the services of the Marquis had always been at his disposal before he rose to these heights, so they would be entirely at his command now that the dearest wish of his heart had been realized; to which the Pope replied gratefully that "as His Excellency had shown him so much kindness in the dry tree, it was unnecessary to repeat these assurances in the green." He withdrew the kissed foot and thrust the other forward. He hoped to show that the love and kindness of the Marquis had not been misplaced and repeated that he could never discharge his obligations to His Excellency. After these preliminaries, when Castiglione referred to the friction between his master and the Imperial captains, the Pope folded his limp hands, leaned forward, and suggested solicitously that the Marquis should think of nothing but of getting well. Unwilling to be foiled so tamely, Castiglione insisted that his master would decline to serve under the Imperial Viceroy, unless His Holiness declared by a Brief that his authority was not to be interfered with. His Holiness promised to bear this in mind. Then, with a delicate hand he proceeded to describe circles about the subject as lightly as if he were sketching a nimbus, and ended by placing his finger on the point. "First of all, His Excellency must get well and allow these Captains to make use of his troops." Beyond this he would not go. He was a peacemaker at heart, and with this negative cordiality his suitor had to be satisfied. No man in Rome could obtain more of him. The Marquis, accordingly, continued to nurse his military career in Mantua; and Castiglione resumed his duties as his ambassador in Rome.

Before long he found that he had an unofficial colleague. If Pietro Aretino did not actually elbow him out of office, he supplemented his efforts, officiously singing the praises of Federico Gonzaga in the Pope's ear. For Aretino now had his *entrée* there. Clement had created him a Knight of Rhodes, a dignity full of sentimental associations for the Holy Father, who had begun his own career with it. Aretino lived up to his new dignity. Recognition developed his independence, and he paraded it with the easy port of a flunkey for ever ushering in himself. The Pope never looked more like a steward than when Aretino presided over him like a major-domo. Of the two, the poet was the more imposing figure if only because of his assurance, and the remarkable feature of their relation was that it was not at all surprising: the dignity of neither compromised that of the other. Prosperity had not made Aretino unmindful, however, of old friends; and in every letter he reminded the Marquis of the good character he was giving him, whenever he had occasion to speak to the Pope.

Under these conditions Castiglione gratefully accepted a mission which the Pope offered him six months later. The Emperor was pressing for a renewal of the alliance he had concluded with Leo; François was negotiating for the same object; and, as Clement was dickering with the French, he determined to send a Nuncio to Spain to reassure the Emperor. Competition was keen for the post; but it was not an easy one to fill. What His Holiness needed was a rare man, a diplomat versed in all the blandishments of his trade, seasoned, resourceful, capable of beguiling the Emperor, yet of a character such that Charles, who was a keen judge of men, would trust him, and guileless enough himself to countenance the duplicity of a policy of which he would be half-agent, half-dupe, and wholly the pawn. Character was half the battle, and he knew no one who carried it so transparently in his face as Castiglione. Besides, it was a pleasure to patronize a man of such impeccable respectability. To Castiglione the offer came as a complete surprise. He was flattered by it, though, as he wrote to the Marquis in asking permission to accept it, he was more eager for rest than for fresh exertions. But had he the right to rest? The role of a peacemaker was arduous but it was the fitting culmination of his life. To labour in one of the pivotal positions of the world for the amity of nations was the final transfiguration, the apotheosis, of his social career; and he set forth, leaving the Vatican and Mantua to Aretino.

Almost at the same moment Aretino left the Vatican in disgrace. He had stumbled suddenly on the Pope's sense of propriety. His friend Marcantonio Raimondi had brought out an album of engravings from plates by Giulio Romano, illustrating the Twenty-Six Modes of Copulation, for which Aretino had supplied a series of graphic sonnets. The appearance of this album created an unexpected scandal. Giberti was outraged; the Pope censured it severely; and the authors were prosecuted. Giulio Romano was in Mantua, but Marcantonio Raimondi was arrested and imprisoned, and Aretino found it expedient to disappear for a time.

He had recently fallen out with Giberti, but he could not trace the storm entirely to the Datary; it was too widespread; public opinion was aroused, and both his friends and his enemies had joined the hue and cry, making an issue of it, a protest of public decency. An issue? He accepted it as such. Whether the outcry was simulated or sincere, it was equally hypocritical, and his critics stung him into self-consciousness. From that day he assumed a title which only he could confer on himself: *Il Veritiero*, the Truth-Teller. He had discovered himself and his purpose in life. He was born to strip his fellow-men of their pretences, to expose the naked truth of Nature—Nature without sham or shame, without restraint or refinement—Nature elementary and supreme, the sole criterion of truth. And what question could serve his purpose better than that of obscenity and sex? It contained, in germ, his whole gospel. What question was so webbed in confusion and hypocrisy? The monstrous superstition that sex was vulgar or sinful was a notion so repugnant to his nature that it made him despair of human sanity, a blasphemy so enormous that it would be appalling if it were not so puny as to be ludicrous; and the only sensible retort was derision, the bludgeoning derision of which he was master, the sane, searching enormous laughter of the natural man. That man was perhaps not a natural animal, that sex was a cruel reminder of that fact, that it was too deeply involved in cultivated sentiments to be capable of rational treatment, that the conventions of manners, morals, and taste rested less on hypocrisy than on reserve, naturally meant nothing to a man for whom the distinction between what is public and what is private had never existed. He saw the question of obscenity *sub specie aeternitati*. Later he explained himself to a dispassionate authority, a physician. "Since poets and sculptors, both ancient and modern, have sometimes shown their skill in composing lascivious things (the marble Satyr in the Palazzo Chigi, for instance, the Satyr who is violating a boy), I amused myself by writing these sonnets below the figures, the wanton memory of which I beg leave to dedicate to the hypocrites, for I am out of patience with their vile judgment and the nasty custom that denies the eyes what most delights them. What wrong is there in seeing a man possess a woman? Why, the very beasts are freer than we! It seems to me that what Nature has given us for our own preservation should be worn about the neck as a pendant or on the hat as a medal. It is the very source from which gush interminable rivers of men; which has produced you, the first of living surgeons; which has begotten the Bembos, the Molzas, Fortunios, Varchis, Martellis, Lorenzo Lenzis, Dolcis, Titians, Sansovinos, Fra Bastianos, Michelangelos, Popes, Emperors, Kings; which has produced the prettiest children, the loveliest women, with all the *Sancta Sanctorum;* so that we should ordain Feast Days and celebrate Holy Days in its honour, instead of wrapping it in a piece of cloth and silk." For the moment, however, he could only fume, a muzzled and exasperated martyr to pornography, and make a skirmishing stand for truth by turning tail and showing his back to Rome.

But to whom was he to show his face—that face famished for truth, lean and livid and pugnacious with unmerited disgrace? Giulio Romano was in Mantua, building a pleasure-palace for the Marquis; but Aretino avoided Mantua and the Marquis. He was in a mood, not for pleasure-palaces, but for camps; and, surveying the horizon, he elected a martial patron, Giovannino de' Medici or, as he was popularly named, Giovanni delle Bande Nere.

This young condottiere, whom many regarded as the hope of Italy, had at this moment a supreme merit in his eyes. He was a Medici, and the Pope had no use for him. They were related, remotely by blood and closely by circumstances; and the young soldier was more of a Medici, though he was only half a one, than the illegitimate priest. Giovannino de' Medici was a member of the collateral branch of the family, which the elder and official line had always ignored; but he could not be ignored: his mother was Caterina Sforza; and the daredevil spirit he had inherited from that illustrious virago, combined with the liberality, intelligence, and resourcefulness of a true Medici, gave him a temperament to which anything was possible—even genius. He was hardly out of his teens before he carved himself a fortune with his Black Bands, into whom he instilled a discipline and devotion that made them more than bandits, a militia. His exploits were constantly having diplomatic consequences, which the Pope was forced to explain away, and his irregular military activities filled the chanceries of the Vatican with the flurry of a maternity ward. Whether or not he was the hope of Italy, he was the hope of Aretino at this moment. In the days of his vagabondage, the aimless poet had rubbed up an acquaintance with the reckless freebooter, holding his horses and riding them; sharing his adventures, if not of the field, of the alcove; keeping him company whenever he was smitten or wounded; and becoming the most sentimental of his camp-followers. In the arms of his Mars dei Medici, as he called him, he found a soldier's welcome. Giovannino caught him on the rebound as lightly as one day he caught his infant son when he was tossed to him from a window; and he hauled in Aretino, overflowing with gratitude and gossip and the courage of his convictions and the breathlessness of his fall. They were kindred spirits, brothers-in-arms; the old friendship flared up again, and Giovannino provided for him liberally. Aretino did not flatter, he spoke no more than the truth, when he said of his patron that "the man who was not a coward shared not only his heart but his authority." "How many," he testified gratefully, "how many have I seen appear before him, in rags, alone and hungry, and three hours later lodged, mounted, clothed, served, and fed!" Together they clattered through the streets of Reggio, and together they drank to the truth and each other until they forgot what the truth was. Listening to his Roman adventure, Giovannino de' Medici recognized the genius of Aretino, introduced him to it, and baptized him *The Scourge of Princes;* and Aretino recognized the justice of that title and made a career of it.

Together, too, they took the field. In October 1524, François crossed the Alps, recaptured Milan, and bottled up the Imperialists in Pavia. Giovanni joined him with his Black Bands and Aretino; and Aretino, introduced to the Majesty of France, immediately made an impression on him. At the same time Castiglione passed through the French camp on his way to Spain. Extraordinary honours were paid to the Papal Nuncio—honours which Castiglione did his best to avoid, in view of his destination and the situation of the Imperialists, besieged in Pavia; and at his interview with the King he was careful to explain the true nature of his pacific and impartial mission. "I gave the King the Pope's Brief," he wrote to Giberti, "and explained that the sole purpose of my visit to the Emperor was to further the common peace of Christendom without respect to any particular person, and that His Beatitude has as sincere a regard for the honour and greatness of His Majesty as for those of any other prince. The King replied with the utmost courtesy and assured me with many well-chosen words that he felt certain His Holiness had the most excellent objects in view and would be a good Father to all mankind; and that he on his part would be his most obedient and affectionate son, and would not fail to place all his affairs in the Holy Father's hands. . . . He spoke in this manner at great length, always showing the greatest reverence for His Holiness, and expressing a confident hope of victory." That the royal cordiality was anything more than diplomatic courtesy did not occur to Castiglione until he was gone. Then he learned what everyone, apparently, but himself already knew, that an alliance was on the point of conclusion between Venice, Rome, and the French. As the truth dawned on him, he was deeply disturbed; but it was too late to turn back. His mission in Spain would not be easy; but he pushed on, leaving Italy and the easy life to Pietro Aretino.

52

The scandal of the *Modi* was soon forgotten. Within a few weeks of his flight—it only needed his disappearance for any scandal to subside—Aretino had returned to Rome and was once more hymning Clement—

> A better Vicar Christ could not privide
> For the honour and welfare of His Bride—

and Giberti—

> No mortal God
> Could find beneath the terrene firmament
> Better Datary or better Clement.

Though he had not recanted his convictions, he was young enough to forget them when they were not crossed, and truth, like every cause from that of Pasquino to that of the Pope, could triumph only by time-serving. Once more he was buzzing in the fat of things. But his first breach with the official world had inflamed his independence; it was inborn and irrepressible; and it only required another occasion to provoke it.

In February 1525, the battle of Pavia was fought; the French were annihilated and the King was captured and subsequently transported to Spain. The Pope was bewildered. A French victory he could have borne, if it had not been overwhelming, but a French defeat so irreparable surpassed all his expectations and broke indefinitely the balance of European power. He himself, and the Holy See, and Florence, and Italy, lay at the mercy of Charles, and Charles had been incensed beyond measure by the treaty which the Pope had concluded with the French. The shock had its immediate repercussions in the Vatican, setting the careful equilibrium of its counteracting influences oscillating and unable for several weeks to recover their balance. The credit of Giberti, as the sponsor of the French alliance, wavered, though it did not break; and Pasquino echoed the fluctuations of public opinion. Personalities, not politics, were the staples of Aretino's trade, but he was too sensitive to public opinion not to reflect its mercurial temper. If ever he responded to an impersonal passion, it was then. It was impossible to breathe the air of Rome without inhaling the gravity of the situation. The menace of Imperial retaliation and Italian servitude was no longer a remote diplomatic prospect, it became overnight a patent reality; and no one in Rome, however insignificant, self-centred, and apathetic, but felt himself for a moment a member of the national life. There was no longer any such thing as private apart from public life; and Pasquino vibrated inarticulately to the universal anxiety and the stirrings of patriotic passion. His mockery spared Giberti but it grazed him, pursuing with deadly persistence his incompetent advisers and unpopular subordinates. From a time-server Aretino turned suddenly into a censor, and the moment was ill chosen for his political growth. Giberti was bending every effort to retrieve his credit, to revive the French, to regain his ascendancy over the Pope, and to obtain as a public proof of it a Cardinal's Hat; he was sorely tried; but he was patient for a season, patient through the spring, patient until midsummer.

In the small hours of a July night Aretino was attacked in the street by thugs and left for dead. The business was botched; his vitality was enormous, his destiny unfulfilled; he was lugged home, scotched in the head, the chest, the arm, and the leg, his pen-hand crippled, but alive; and, as soon as he could speak, he began, of course, to recover. The excitement was intense, his house was crowded with sympathizers, and the story travelled. Federico Gonzaga, learning it from his ambassador, passed it on with thin discretion: "The cause of the quarrel is ugly and known to everyone." Giberti at last lost patience. He had ignored political sniping; but the whispered charge of political assassination was an attack on his personal character; and he promptly issued his own version of the affair. According to this account, Achille della Volta, one of his creatures, had quarrelled with Aretino over the affections of his cook; and Achille della Volta, to prove that he bore no malice, went so far as to visit his victim. But the story was hard to kill· while Pasquino lived, it could not die. It reached the Pope, who was inclined to credit it; but the authorities did not move, and even Achille della Volta was unmolested. Aretino let the damning inference speak for itself, while he recovered; nor did he protest then. He was too disgusted with Rome, where impropriety was persecuted and murder was protected; and, as soon as he could carry his guts, he shook the dust of the infamous city from his feet and headed for the camp of Giovanni delle Bande Nere to earn the name which the freebooter had given him—*The Scourge of Princes*.

53

After Pavia, the Pope had averted immediate reprisals against Rome by paying a subsidy to the victorious but impoverished Imperial army. But the situation remained critical and he redoubled his efforts to conciliate the Emperor by sending a Legate to Spain to supplement the efforts of Castiglione. In a crisis two heads were better than one. Far from resenting this collaboration, Castiglione welcomed it. He had won the Emperor's confidence, or rather his sympathy, for Charles had no confidence either in the Pope or Giberti. The latter he blamed for the French alliance which had led to Pavia; and as he was informed that, even since Pavia, Giberti was still pursuing a pro-French policy, Charles made no secret of his resentment. "I am grieved to note the Emperor's bad opinion of the Datary," Castiglione wrote to Schömberg. "It is even worse than I imagined. He calls him a scoundrel and uses language very unlike His Majesty's usual moderation. He will certainly be deeply incensed if the Datary should be created a Cardinal; but you will, of course, keep this to yourself and act with your usual prudence. What you write from Rome fills me with concern; I fear that all we do here is undone over there. For God's sake, remind His Holiness how much more Caesar is to be trusted than anyone else; for my part, reason and experience convince me of the Emperor's good faith; I am as sure of it as I am of my own existence. I beg Your Excellency, both for the Pope's service and for the general good, be vigilant and do not allow His Holiness to act rashly." What with the Pope's susceptibility to influence, his indecision, his timidity, and his ambiguity, the situation was more than Castiglione could handle alone, and he awaited eagerly the arrival of an expert.

The Legate whom the Pope selected was a Florentine, Cardinal Salviati, and, when the choice of a secretary to accompany him came up, the name of Machiavelli was suggested. For a moment the possibility of his association with Castiglione arose; but the appointment as usual passed to another. Contrary witnesses to their age, they were destined, from motives equally patriotic, to work at cross-purposes and apart.

Machiavelli, in the meantime, had completed his History of Florence, or rather, he had brought it up to the death of Lorenzo the Magnificent. "I have been living in the country, writing my History," he wrote to Guicciardini, "and I would give tenpence, but no more, to have you here and to show you where I am, for I am coming to certain details in which I need your advice, whether I offend too much by heightening certain things and reducing others; but I shall be circumspect and try to write in a manner such that, though I tell the truth, no one can complain." Those details which required discretion were the living; and he preferred to conclude with the death of Lorenzo, for beyond it what could he say that would be both truthful and acceptable to the Medici? He needed money, however, and he wrote to Vettori asking if it would be advisable to come to Rome and present the book to the Pope. "My dear friend, I cannot advise you whether to come with the book or not," Vettori replied, "for the times are not favourable to reading and giving. On the other hand, on the first evening of my arrival, the Pope himself inquired about you and asked me whether you had finished the History, and when I said that I had read part of it, that you had reached the death of Lorenzo and that it was satisfactory, and that you wished to bring it yourself, but that in view of the times I had dissuaded you, he said: But he should come, I am sure his books will be acceptable and pleasant to read.—These were his very words; but I would not have you rely on them too much and come and find yourself empty-handed, which, given the present mood of the Pope, might well happen; nevertheless, I did not want to fail in my duty. I write you what he said. God be with you." It was the history of *The Prince* all over again. Vettori, with his failing eyesight and feeble insight, was once more at his weevil-like work of subtle defeatism; his blood was running cold, but his age and apathy failed to deter his friend. Machiavelli came, not merely to present his History, but to suggest to the Pope the sequel which the last of the Medici might yet write.

For the past had taught him one thing—the truth of *The Prince*. The passage of the years had tempered some of his ideas, or maybe it was Guicciardini, who was so much older than he, though he was fourteen years younger—Guicciardini who grasped them so completely that sometimes he stifled them—Guicciardini who, judging them by his vast political experience, modified the conclusions which were too doctrinaire, too absolute, too true to be quite true. But Machiavelli, in writing his History, had been groping for the roots of Italian decay, and the more he bored into the past and compared it with the present plight of Italy, on the brink of national fusion through defeat, the more profoundly he believed in the saving principles of *The Prince,* or at least in its basic doctrine of self-reliance and efficiency. Time had withered what was extravagant and matured what was sound in his ideas; and to none did he cling more tenaciously than to the Militia. In a series of interviews with the Pope, he laid before him a proposal to arm the citizens and reorganize the Militia for the defence of Florence; Clement listened; Machiavelli extended the idea, drafting the scheme of a national Militia to be raised in the states of the Church; and Clement nodded. It was a time for heroic measures; and the cautious Medici was so far convinced that he referred the project to the President of Romagna.

Nothing could have been more fortunate, for the President of Romagna was Guicciardini, who had never questioned this idea, at least in principle. The reply was prompt. "I should have no fear of arming the people," Guicciardini reported, "if it were any other people than this. But Romagna, torn by bitter feuds, is divided into two great factions, which still call themselves Guelfs and Ghibellines, and which rest, the one on France and the other on the Empire. The Church has no real friends here, and hence it would be extremely dangerous, when we declared war on Caesar, to have armed his partisans in the hope of using them for our own advantage. This enterprise should be founded on the love of the people, which the Church entirely lacks in Romagna. No one is sure of his life or his property here, and everyone looks to the foreign powers, on whom the whole peninsula depends, for protection. To compose the Militia, as Machiavelli proposes, of men independent of either faction would be to find no one at all. Nevertheless, if the scheme is to be attempted, I shall devote every effort to it, and so His Holiness should do, for, once undertaken, we should trust to it more than anything else." Guicciardini had spoken, and the Pope dismissed the idea. It was heroic but impractical.

Machiavelli returned to Florence. He was used to rebuffs, but this one shook for the first time his faith in himself. The idea which was the backbone of his thought had been vetoed by a man whose competence he could not question and whose sympathy he could not doubt. It was a more deadly defeat than the apathy of Vettori. Vettori was his equal; but with Guicciardini he had the sense of being not only a social but an intellectual inferior. The President belonged to the oldest nobility in Florence; he had held high posts from the beginning of his career; and, though he would not admit their social inequality, he could not disguise his intellectual rank; it transpired, in spite of himself, in the sophistication of the aristocrat. Guicciardini's judgment reflected his breeding in its poise, its experience, its disillusionment. He was detached; his only principle was that there were no principles; and he had not so much ideas as an intellectual tone. Though he admired Machiavelli, he made both the cynicism and the enthusiasm of his friend seem raw and ingenuous. He understood Machiavelli too well. Sympathetically, calmly, judiciously, he neutralized his ideas, developing them so logically that he defeated them, sapping their audacity, taming, transforming, and destroying them. The process had been going on ever since they met, but what made it so rapid was that Guicciardini was so many years the junior of Machiavelli. He was the younger generation overtaking him. With his alarming levelheadedness, his scrupulous fidelity to the prosaic truth, he made his elder feel a rash and dogmatic tyro. And now, when Machiavelli hoped at last to return to active political life, the younger generation had discarded him, regretfully but firmly, as an impractical theorist, an academic patriot. It was too late; he had waited too long; and with that sentence Machiavelli's intellectual pride was broken. It was his last refuge, and in the innermost recesses of his being he felt himself eclipsed by an *alter ego.* His whole faith had been founded on the feasible, and his friend was more of a realist, more of a Machiavelli, then himself. Guicciardini completed what the Medici began: he extinguished him.

But Machiavelli struggled. His intellectual pride was his backbone, and, though he deferred to the judgment of Guicciardini, he secretly nursed his own conviction and continued to correspond with the Governor on personal and political subjects, though with a formality on which Guicciardini rallied him. "My dearest Machiavelli," the great man finally protested, "I must tell you that if you honour my letters with the title of Illustrious, I shall honour yours with that of Magnifico, and with these reciprocal titles we shall give each other a pleasure which will turn to grief when at last we find ourselves all—all, I say—fly-blown. As for news I know nothing with nerve in it, and I think we are all wandering in darkness, but with our hands tied behind our backs, so that we cannot ward off the blows." Machiavelli said nothing. He let Guicciardini continue to convict himself out of his mouth; such admissions merely confirmed the need of a Militia; and with each new letter the President's prognostics became gloomier. The truce with the Emperor continued, lulling the country into false security. "Caesar means to become master of Italy and can never be the friend of those who are bound to oppose him,"

Guicciardini wrote. "It is useless to trust to an agreement with France, which is prostrate, because it can only be to our injury. No agreement would be stable without the liberation of the King, who would not observe a pact with us if he had to bear the brunt of it. The truth is that Caesar will make his own pacts, while the rest of us are sleeping, and will defeat us all, not by superior strength, but by our fatal improvidence." Nor was Guicciardini convinced by a formal treaty of peace which was concluded between Charles and the Pope. "In any event the Emperor will be the arbiter of Italy. The Pope will have only the name of a ruler, and will be tantalized for the present with proposals which will turn out to be dreams." Machiavelli agreed in silence, and finally Guicciardini himself spoke his unuttered thought. "Those that are afraid of war must be shown the perils of peace. Too much prudence is imprudence, and no enterprise now would be rash. We must run to arms to escape a peace which will make us slaves." The fact was so obvious that it leapt to his lips irresistibly; but he had not changed his mind about the Militia; and Machiavelli returned to his History. "I am beginning to write again," he replied, "and I relieve myself by accusing the princes who have done everything to bring us to this pass."

Then, in March 1526, word reached Florence that François I had been released by Charles in return for the renunciation of all his Italian claims and his perpetual alliance with the Emperor; and Machiavelli could no longer keep silence. "Whatever happens," he wrote to Guicciardini, "I believe we shall have war in Italy, and soon; hence we must have France with us and, if we cannot, we must decide what to do. In that case, we must follow, it seems to me, one of two courses: either submit and buy ourselves off, or arm and help ourselves as we can. Buying ourselves off will not serve, I believe; if it did, I would say, let us go no further. But it will not, for either I am stone-blind or they will take our money first and our lives next, so that it will be a kind of justice to find ourselves destitute and destroyed, when we would be no worse by defending ourselves. Now I propose something which will seem to you insane. . . ." And he flung himself recklessly against the sanity of Guicciardini. "You may think this scheme ridiculous or dangerous, but these times require bold, strange, and unusual resolutions. You know, as everyone who thinks knows, how fickle and foolish the populace is; nevertheless, it sometimes suggests what should be done. A few days ago it was said in Florence that Signor Giovanni de' Medici was raising a company to make war where he liked. This made me think that what the people were saying was what should be done. I believe every thinking man agrees that there is no leader among the Italians whom soldiers follow more willingly, or whom the Spanish more fear and respect; everyone agrees also that Signor Giovanni is bold, fiery, large in his views, and a man of great decisions. We could engage him secretly and have him raise this company, giving him as many horse and footmen as we can. The Spanish will suspect some purpose in this and will fear both the Pope and the King, since Giovanni is a soldier of the King; and if this were done it would soon turn the heads of the Spaniards and make them change their plans, for they expected to ruin Tuscany and the Church without opposition. It might make the King change his mind and decide to break his treaty and make war, if he found himself dealing with live men, who offered him action and not merely bribes. And if this remedy will not serve, I do not know what will. I can see no other; and put this under your thinking cap: unless the King is moved by strength and life and authority, he will observe the treaty with the Emperor and leave you in the lurch, because, having come more than once to Italy, and you having either opposed him or stood and watched him, he will not wish to repeat the experience."

At the same time he laid this new suggestion before the Pope, on his own initiative, through a friend in Rome. The reply was that "it is not acceptable, as it would amount to a complete exposure of His Holiness, since such a soldier of fortune could not operate without money or obtain any effect, with the opposition that he would encounter in Lombardy, and, if His Holiness supplied him with money, the enterprise would become his." But the idea was one which not even the advocacy of Machiavelli could curse. It was popular: it sprang from the people; it travelled to the highest, pregnant with a passion too strong for Guicciardini, for the Pope himself, to discourage. A month later an offensive and defensive League for the preservation of the integrity of Italy was concluded between Rome, Florence, Venice, and Milan, under the protection of France and England, and Giovanni delle Bande Nere was engaged as a Papal General.

And so it had come at last. If not the Militia, here was its spirit at least —a confederation of Italian arms, united by a nascent national sentiment, and led by the one captain capable of commanding general confidence. The Liberator invoked in the exordium of *The Prince,* so long and so vainly awaited, had appeared with the need for him, and with one accord he was renamed, in a popular apotheosis, Giovanni d'Italia. Here, at last, was the Medici of the future. About that consecrated head converged the prenatal yearnings of a nation and the last ardours of Machiavelli's decline. Giovanni delle Bande Nere was the hero of his old age, a Valentino with none of his infamy and all his fascination and nerve and—greatest token of all — his good fortune—a fortune which he owed neither to his family nor to the foreigner, but to himself and the faith of his followers. Time, in its interminable groping for heroes, had at last turned up the type, the archtype who atoned for all the trials and failures that had gone before. An aura of associations hung about that young man, lending him a glamour that transformed the soldier of fortune into a son of destiny. He seemed to fuse in his own person the beginning and the end of an age. He was the great-nephew of that Lodovico Sforza who had brought the barbarians into Italy and who had said:"Italy? What is Italy? I have never seen it." He was the Sforza born to see Italy. Young with dreams and hoary with memories, he seemed to span and recall Machiavelli's own life. Almost thirty years before, on his first diplomatic mission, Caterina Sforza, to whom he owed his first diplomatic defeat, had been nursing a sick child who had grown up to become this Giovannino de' Medici, and to revive Machiavelli, in spiritual defeat, with the cheering vigour of an autumnal enthusiasm. He was the liberator from everything alien and oppressing— from doubt and despair and moral humiliation and the bloodless wisdom of submission. He was his last romance with himself.

Meanwhile, Machiavelli had been employed in supervising the fortification of Florence, a work which advanced slowly, because of the procrastination and uncertainty of the Pope. His duties frequently took him to the camp in Lombardy, where Guicciardini was occupied in keeping peace among the bickering captains and restoring the cracks that threatened to appear in the living ramparts of the armies of young Italy. One of these trips brought Machiavelli to the camp of Giovanni delle Bande Nere, under the walls of Milan. For a few hours his vicarious life reached its apogee. He exchanged military ideas with his host—for Machiavelli had written a little treatise on *The Art of War*—and, the talk turning on the Romans, Giovannino invited him to demonstrate his ideas of classic drill in practice. He accepted with alacrity. Three thousand men were waiting for review. For an hour, for two hours, he himself was Giovanni d'Italia; for an hour, for two hours, under the scorching sun and the critical eyes of the staff, he manoeuvred the battalions of young Italy—marching, counter-marching, wheeling, halting, dividing—into such confusion that at last Giovanni stepped up and, courteously reminding him that armies marched on their stomachs, gave a few orders and to the roll of drums put his legions through their wonted paces and dismissed them. "Signore," said Machiavelli, as they sat down to dinner, "I firmly believe that, if you had not relieved me this morning, we should still be in the field under the sun." But he had other talents, and he proceeded to upset the table with one of his best camp stories. He had not been so gay in years.

54

Under Milan, not once but ten times o'er,
He said to me: Pietro, if from this war
God and good fortune bring me home again,
I shall make you lord of your countrymen.

It was a promise: *Pietro Aretino, Lord of Arezzo.* Giovanni de' Medici had made it with his usual liberality, and Aretino celebrated it by imitating the prodigality of his patron. "I yield to no man in generosity," Giovanni observed one day to Guicciardini, "unless it be to Messer Pietro, when he has the means." And though at that moment the means were not very plentiful in the camp of the Black Bands, Aretino reminded the world that he had been born in a hospital with the soul of a king and proved himself a prince by living like one. He shared everything with his patron—his bed, his board, his debauches, his heart, his purse, his promises—but what he prized more than all these, more even than the prospect of ruling Arezzo, was that with Giovanni he shared what he had never shared with any man before—his sorrows.

For the hero was often heartsick. The Pope stinted him . . . of money, of supplies, of confidence, of authority. His colleagues would not co-operate with him. Francescomaria of Urbino, who had assumed the command of the Venetian contingent, insisted on completing the siege of Cremona before joining the Papal condottiere in the siege of Milan. Everyone was working at cross-purposes and for himself, and the Pope compromised everything by delays, indecision, and diplomacy. Giovanni grew moody and restless. His grievances preyed on his temper; and it was then, in those black hours when the forces of inertia and confusion ate away the impulse of action, that Aretino repaid his protector. When Giovanni, in the cups of his wrath, longed for death, Pietro was there to echo and re-echo his bitterness until he relieved it. He outdid himself: he became more than a boon companion or a bedside crony, he transformed himself into a spiritual director, sympathizing, stimulating, tempering, curbing his impulses, restoring his patience, and when the crisis was over resuming his usual jovial role and doing his own patriotic duty by keeping the national hero in love with life. Loving him with the ardour with which men love, not those who befriend them but those whom they benefit, Aretino discovered the one sincere, profound, and disinterested sentiment of his life. He made it his duty to keep the great man, amid the petty vexations which enfeebled him, a hero.

And Aretino reaped his reward. His relation to Giovanni was a service to Italy, a moral liaison between the high-strung tension of the leader and the slackness of the led; and the more he inspired his master, the more he inspired himself. He gave and he drew, he drew and he gave, until by a facile and imperceptible metamorphosis he himself began to acquire the heroic traits. He disclosed a new fortitude, independence, and self-respect; and who could say that those qualities had not been dormant in him all along, needing only an ideal to excite them? He was impressionable, he was what men made of him. Exhorting the hero to magnanimity, he forgot his enemies in Rome and sacrificed his personal rancour to a patriotism which was fired and personified in Giovanni d'Italia; and Aretino idolized him as devoutly as Machiavelli himself.

55

The publication of the Italian League roused the Emperor to action. Castiglione had warned the Pope. He had strained the proprieties to preserve the peace of Europe and addressed a personal remonstrance to his master, imploring him not to take the aggressive, staking his life on the pacific intentions of the Emperor, and reminding Clement that Charles was in a position to do irreparable harm not only to his temporal power and dominions but to his spiritual jurisdiction by supporting Luther and abetting insurrection against the Roman Church in Germany. "Therefore, Blessed Father," he wrote, "I do not see that we have sufficient resources, nor yet do I recognize any just cause for making war on the Emperor. To defend oneself is always legitimate, but to begin a war is not only wrong for everyone but most culpable in those whose duty it is to promote the welfare and prosperity, the peace and tranquillity, of nations, and above all of a country that has suffered so many calamities as our unhappy Italy. If once she is plunged into this fire, she will be at the mercy of those barbarians who have always hated her and are eager to return to a land where many of their race have perished, less from thirst for conquest than from a lust for revenge. Therefore, Holy Father, watch over Italy as your obedient child and servant. If God wills to send us a new war as a punishment for our sins, at least let it not be said that Your Holiness was the first to kindle it. Surely, the high reputation for goodness and piety which Your Holiness has acquired throughout the world, and which to my joy is nowhere greater than in Spain, demands that you should not be the first to sow war or declare yourself the enemy of a prince who has never shown you anything but kindness and good will. . . . I feel that I must, once and for all, deliver my conscience by addressing this letter to Your Holiness, not in order to seem eloquent or to use fine phrases, nor yet out of hatred or love to any monarch in the world, but solely from a sense of affection and loyalty. I humbly kiss Your Beatitude's holy feet." It was not with impunity that Castiglione had left Italy; in Spain he had acquired an international perspective on patriotism; and this appeal was his diplomatic last will and testament. It was ignored, and when with the publication of the Italian League for the defence of the peninsula the Pope placed himself at the head of the national movement, the Emperor promptly retaliated.

At the instigation of the Imperial envoy in Rome, the Colonna rose, raided the city, and forced the Pope to take refuge in Sant' Angelo. This outbreak of the feudal Barons whom five Popes had laboured to suppress, was an argument which struck home; and Clement reluctantly consented to a truce with the Emperor, by the terms of which the forces of the League were withdrawn south of the Po. Guicciardini was indignant. "I would rather abandon Italy," he wrote to Giberti, "than to live in Rome as our Lord will have to live, if he continues in this course. *Tu ne cede malis, sed contra audacior ito.*"[1] But the truce was signed, the armies withdrew, and there remained in Lombardy only Giovanni de' Medici, with four thousand of his Black Bands and secret instructions to continue the war under colour of being in the employ of France. The hero had a free hand at last, if he consented to play a lone hand—but was that not the test of heroism? Giovanni was sick of the role, however, and

[1] You yield to evils. I oppose them the more boldly.

threatened to go over to the enemy unless he were given a state, as the Pope had so often promised—"and he is quite capable of doing it," Guicciardini wrote, after interviewing him. But better counsels prevailed. Twelve thousand German Landsknechts were concentrating at Bozen, about to descend upon Italy; and the theatre of war was his.

Clement had appointed Giovanni de' Medici with congenital misgivings. He admitted Giovanni's virtues, but he insisted that "they were far outweighed by his vices." A hero? No doubt; but he was also a cousin. He regarded him with the reserve of a relative. He would have preferred someone less heroic. When the engagement of the Marquis of Mantua as Captain of the Church expired, the Pope was eager to renew it, but his eagerness was not reciprocated. The Marquis pointed out that, by the terms of his original contract with Leo, he had been dispensed from serving against his feudal overlord, the Emperor, and, as his state would bear the brunt of the invasion, he was under a moral obligation to his subjects to remain neutral. But Clement would not take no. Finding persuasion useless, he called for his files. He had a long memory; and he recalled that, five years before, when Castiglione had negotiated the appointment of the Marquis with Leo, a secret clause had been appended to the contract, neutralizing the dispensation which Federico Gonzaga now invoked. The contract was found; but the secret article had disappeared. Clement doubted everything but his memory; an investigation was set afoot, and it was discovered that Ardinghelli, the Papal Secretary, had been bribed, four years before, by Castiglione to abstract the secret clause. Ardinghelli fled to Florence and committed suicide—rashly, in the opinion of the professionals of the Vatican, who were certain that he would not have been prosecuted. The Pope, in fact, contented himself with complaints that the man had "sold us and our friends for money." The Marquis he did not blame: it was only to be expected; and the Mantuan ambassador officially denied the whole story, though not without embarrassment, since he had himself received the purloined article from Ardinghelli. As for Castiglione, the Pope spared his sensibilities and never alluded to his part in the scandal; but he became more critical of the Count's service in Spain and permitted himself to complain occasionally of his inefficiency. Though Clement swallowed the Marquis's denial, he would not accept his refusal to renew the contract. His heart was with the weak; he felt safe with them; and he was determined to have Federico Gonzaga on any terms. He persevered, and in an aberration that was the very logic of his soul signed a contract with Federico Gonzaga which countenanced his neutrality, gave him the honours and emoluments of his office, dispensed him from its duties, and completely neutralized his value to his employer.

Giovanni delle Bande Nere had never shown much respect for the Marquis. He was now skirmishing in Lombardy, harrying the German hordes which were pouring from the passes of the Alps, until he could strike a decisive blow. These German armies were formidable, aflame not only with martial but religious ferocity, composed in large part of rabid Lutheran Landsknechts, and led by a general who made no secret, though he was a staunch Catholic, of his sympathy for the Protestant prophet. "*Mönchlein, Mönchlein,*" Georg Frundsperg had cried at the Diet of Worms, "*du gehst jetzt einen Gang, dergleichen ich und mancher Obreiter auch in der allerernstlichsten Schlachtordnung nicht gethan haben. Bist du aber auf rechter Meinung und deiner Sache gewiss, so fahre in Gottes Namen fort und sei getröst: Gott wird dich nicht verlassen.*"[1] As a military man, Frundsperg valued the fighting spirit of the Lutherans and encouraged the legend of their Schrecklichkeit and his own—he was reputed to be carrying a halter to hang the Pope. Though they were ill paid and ill disciplined, they were sustained by a superior power: their goal was Rome, and the march of the Landsknechts was a migration of Messianic vandals. As they debouched from the Alps, the Black Bands kept up a rapid guerrilla warfare, attempting to divide and raid them before they could concentrate in overwhelming numbers. At Seraglio on the Po, Giovanni planned to surprise them, as they forded the river; and to intercept them he crossed the Mantuan frontier. On the border he was at first refused passage and then delayed with formalities until the Germans slipped through. His indignation was unbounded. There were diplomatic consequences. The Marquis complained to the Pope that the *gran Diavolo* had slapped and beaten one of his courtiers, plucked the beard of one of his chancellors, and threatened to hang four of his gentlemen. The Pope dictated a letter of reprimand to the *gran Diavolo,* but its only effect was a fresh series of incidents. Giovanni assumed that the Marquis was in connivance with the enemy and acted accordingly.

Nor was it only Federico Gonzaga who neutralized Giovanni's lone efforts to check the German advance. Frundsperg, in desperate need of supplies and munitions, negotiated with Alfonso d'Este and obtained both victuals and artillery. Thus reinforced, the Landsknechts resumed

---

[1] Little monk, little monk, you are taking a step which neither I nor many a Knight have ever undertaken even in the most desperate battle. But if you are sure of your cause and your reason, go forth, in God's name, and have faith: God will not forsake you.

their march and Giovanni and his guerrilla troops prepared to engage them at Governolo, a few miles from Mantua. The Marquis wrote to the Pope. What was the difference between a hero and an outlaw? Merely a point of view: the difference between being for or against him; and from the point of view of Federico Gonzaga, the conduct of Giovanni and his Bande Nere was that of patriotic blackguards. "They do all the damage they can, they rape women, rob men, kill cattle, burn houses and hayricks, rifle strongboxes, and live as they please without paying for anything. They behave worse than if they were in the land of the Turks." He was still dictating when he was interrupted by the issue of the battle. Through the flying snow of a bleak December day a line of stragglers approached Mantua, bringing in the wounded outlaw; and Aretino appeared before the Marquis, to do his last duty as a liaison between the living and the dying and beg a death-bed for Giovanni d'Italia.

56

The battle had begun briskly in a sweeping attack on the entrenched Landsknechts, when the cannon borrowed from Alfonso d'Este came into action. Giovanni, unwarned of it, and leading with his customary intrepidity, was struck in the leg. It was his game leg, which had been broken at Pavia, and his followers were stunned. The attack slackened, his captains rallied about him, he was carried to Mantua, where quarters were provided in a private house, and the death-watch began. Aretino induced the Marquis to visit him. Then he sat down to celebrate the passion and death of the hero in a letter which marked at the same time, with the accent of a spiritual testament, the passion and death of the hero-worshipper.

Every sensation of his master, every sensation of his own, was observed and embalmed with graphic publicity for the inspiration of posterity. From the moment of the explosion and the consternation of the captains, "lamenting the calamity which had felled so noble and excellent a leader, surpassing all memories and all ages, on the eve of superhuman events and in the utmost need of Italy," Aretino sleeplessly interpreted each significant phase of the scene. He watched the arrival of the Duke of Urbino, "who loved, or rather who worshipped him, respecting him so deeply that he dared not speak in his presence." He noted the perplexity of the patient, scratching his head, putting his finger in his mouth, and whispering, "What will happen now?" and frequently repeating, "I never did anything cowardly." He observed his own self-command as he approached Giovanni and urged him to let his wrecked limb be amputated. "So be it," said Giovanni. And Aretino suffered the operation. "Then the surgeons came in and congratulated him on his strength of mind and completed their duties for the evening; and after giving him a medicine they went to prepare their instruments. At suppertime vomiting began. 'The omens of Caesar,' he said, 'we must think of other things than life.' And folding his hands, he made a vow to go to the Apostle of Galicia. When the surgeons returned with their instruments, they asked for eight or ten men to hold him, while the worst of the sawing lasted. 'Twenty,' he said smiling, 'could not hold me.' Lying there with a firm face, he held up the taper to light them, and I fled and stuffed my ears and heard only two or three cries and then his voice calling me. As I reached him, he cried: 'I am cured.' And, threshing about, he exulted and, but for the Duke of Urbino who protested, he would have had the leg and the foot brought him, mocking us who could not bear to see what he had borne. But, to be brief, the pain which had left him returned two hours before dawn with every variety of agony; and, hearing him beat against the wall, I was alarmed and dressed hastily and hurried to his room. As soon as he saw me, he said that what plagued him more than the pain was the thought of cowards, and he talked to me to take his mind off his troubles. When the day broke, he was so much worse that he made his will, leaving many thousand *scudi* in coin and chattels for those who had served him, and only four *giulii* for his own burial; and he made the Duke his executor. Then he prepared himself for confession, like a good Christian, and said when he saw the friar: 'Father, I have always lived like a soldier, since it is my trade, as I would have lived a religious life, had I worn your habit; and if it were not against the rules, I would make my confession in public, for I have done nothing unworthy of myself.' After Vespers the Marquis, moved by my prayers and his own innate goodness, came and comforted him with words so feeling as I, for one, would never have expected of any prince but Francescomaria. And His Excellency concluded with these words: 'Your mighty heart would never condescend to use anything of mine, give me my wish now, ask me a favour fitting your quality and mine.' 'Love me when I am gone,' he replied."

With that appeal, Giovanni d'Italia had already outlived himself. "His whole household, forgetting fear and respect, surged about him, mingling with their betters around the bed, and wept the bread, the hope, and the service they lost with their master, everyone trying to catch his eye to show him his grief. Amid this turmoil, he took the hand of His Excellency and said: 'You lose today the best servant and the greatest friend you ever had.' ... And so he resisted until about the third hour of the night; and, because his suffering was unbounded, he begged me to read him to sleep; and as I did so I saw him consumed by sleep in sleep. After a quarter of an hour he woke and said: 'I dreamed I had made my will, and I am cured, I feel nothing more. If I continue to improve like this, I shall teach the Germans how to fight and show them how I avenge myself.' Then the light which bewildered his eyes paled before the perpetual shadow. He called for Extreme Unction and after receiving the sacrament said: 'I will not die in these swaddlings.' So a camp cot was prepared and he was laid on it, and as his soul slumbered he was occupied by death."

Completing the service which he had rendered to the hero in life, Aretino concluded with a panegyric, in which his feeling, exasperated by the numbness of death, rebelled and broke into extravagant hyperbole; but hyperbole was the only sincerity, for "if God had granted him his allotted span, everyone would have known his goodness as I knew it, and I praise him for his merits, not from flattery." Then, as the last legacy, he seized the scourge and cracked it with prophetic fury over Italy. "Everyone may envy and no one imitate him. And Florence and Rome (God make me a liar!) will soon learn what they have lost. Already I hear the screams of the Pope, who thinks he has gained by losing him." The date was December 10, 1526.

57

In the life of Aretino, as in the life of Italy, that date marked a crisis. He confounded his own loss with that of the nation. "I should have died when I saw him breathe out his illustrious soul, and died when his features were cast by Giulio Romano, and died when I closed him in the tomb," he wrote to the widow in sonorous abandon. "Only the comfort I find in the eternity of his memory keeps me alive, and my sustenance is to hear the great say: He is spent, the spurt of Nature; he is fled, the exemplar of antique faith; he is gone, the true brawn of battle. For, truly, no one ever raised so high the hopes of Italian arms. Lo, he is hardly interred, and already the boasts of the barbarian, swelling sky-high, appal the most bold; and already fear rides Clement, who made the one man who could give him life long for death." He was inflated with a universal feeling and so dilated that he vented it as his own. With Giovanni something went out of his life which had transformed it. The hero swept through him, a wind, and was gone. And now—? The spirit that had soared was the spirit that sank; under the wintry sod it was laid away in the slow obsequies of December. On a raw and blustering day the Marquis and his Court had borne the Liberator, amid billowing mantles and clinging litanies, in a lingering death-march, to the tomb; and there the bystanders knelt, unanimous, empty-handed, facing the future without a champion.

The destiny of Italy, for a supreme moment, had hung between Giovanni and Giulio de' Medici, between those two incompatible cousins who composed its alternate soul; and now that the future had slipped from the grip of the soldier to the lax hand of the priest, the only alternative was servitude. The death-watch had begun for the nation. With the coming of winter the war subsided and the Germans hibernated; but the lifeless season was the last reprieve. The plain of Mantua is bleak. The winds rush to their trysts; the land is numb; nothing moves in the vast trance of winter but the trees, incessantly teased by the breeze, hazed by the gale, quizzed by the blizzard. Greedy draughts raise and bandy the dust, like a foraging host, blindly scouring the soul in insatiable need and spewing it in baffled fury. Three months—three months before the first grass blade—three months of barren husbandry—three months of watching and waiting and wondering and wind.

Those airs full of overtures and obituaries dissipated and blurred the gladiatorial sonority with which Aretino buried the Redeemer of Italy. He faced his own future. He was stranded; and the death of the hero was the knell of the hero-worshipper. He returned to the Marquis, but the shadow of Giovanni lay between them, and the Marquis had cooled. He consented to receive him for a week; and Aretino repaid this hospitality with his soul. The perfervid affection he had lavished on Giovanni he now offered to Federico Gonzaga for bread. He was only half cynical. *A tout seigneur tout honneur*. Though the Marquis had done much in his inglorious neutrality to thwart the hero, he had been formally reconciled to him at the end; and Aretino was consistent. The sycophant is to the hero-worshipper what the prostitute is to the lover; and he had no choice.

He was homeless; the Marquis was humane; and the week grew into months.

Meanwhile, Aretino was busy. He cultivated the memory of Giovanni as closely as he cherished his death-mask. In the last impression of those features, strenuous and lean like a streamline of energy, he found inspiration to equivocate with the face of the Marquis, which was more vacant and no mask. It amused him to compare them, like the masks of Tragedy and Comedy, and to pass from one character to the other himself. He resumed his laughing role. Better than by sentimental lamentations or windy rhetoric, he could serve the memory of Giovanni with the lash of bitter raillery; and he prepared to lay it on those who had brought him low. The new season was opening: it was time for his Almanac. Every year he brought out a compendium of *giudizii*, flying leaflets couched in the form of mock forecasts and filled with miscellaneous comment on public events, which he circulated throughout Italy as a vehicle for whatever amused his mind or irritated his bladder. He set to work and for weeks exuded copy with such prodigal industry, verve, and facility, that the Marquis was once more impressed with his genius. The contents amused him and he accepted the dedication; and in due time there appeared in Rome, blown on a great gale of jocular gloom, the *Giudizio or Prognostic of the Fifth Evangelist, M. Pietro Aretino, for the year 1527*. It opened mildly enough. *Chapter I: the Disposition of the Air and the Entrance of the Sun: according to the judgment of modern interpreters of the planets, the Sun will enter the first pothouse he reaches and reappear a week later, at the meridian of your sun-dial in Mantua, reeling drunk. The Atmosphere may be foul, what with the heavy breath of the Germans swilling Italian wine and the mild emanations of their feet. The fourth Quarter of Spring (according to Tommaso the Philologue of Ravenna) will be as windy as the sex of Giacomo di San Secondo.* But this was only the preamble. Under cover of buffoonery Aretino had smuggled into the Almanac a bombful of personal allusions which exploded in Rome with the effect of an enormous discharge of sour wind. As this effusion was dedicated to Federico Gonzaga, the Papal Confessor called on the Mantuan ambassador and made representations; and the wind promptly veered.

Under the gale which now blew from Rome, the Marquis immediately yielded and explained. "When Signor Giovanni dei Medici came here to die," his Chancellor wrote, "the Marquis was requested by this Aretino to give him shelter for six or eight days, which he could not refuse, particularly as he assumed him to be in good odour with His Holiness, since he was in the service of Signor Giovanni. It is true that both then and since then he has attempted to slip into the service of His Excellency, who would not have him, as he does not fancy such swine. His Excellency sometimes found pleasure in his compositions, but he never approved of his speaking or writing abusively of the Pope or the Cardinals or the clergy; on the contrary, as soon as he discovered his malicious tongue, he detested him so heartily that he could not endure him, and for many days he was cold to him and refused to receive him. Finally, since he had asked to stay eight days and had remained five months, he told him to be off; whereupon the beggar began to bluster and threatened to speak as ill of the Marquis as ever he did of any man, adding that he would not lack matter if he set his mind to it; but His Excellency sent him a message which made him as meek as a lamb, and he has left with our maledictions. With his usual liberality and kindness, however, my master gave him 100 *scudi* and some other gifts." Two days later the Chancellor wrote more anxiously: "If His Holiness is not satisfied by his dismissal, he has only to send a secret message or drop a hint, and, though the man has escaped others, he will not slip through our hands." But Rome was satisfied, and in Mantua the incident was considered closed.

But Aretino had yet to be heard from. Dismissed by the Marquis and persecuted by Rome, he was driven to extremities; he dropped compromise and emerged in his real colours. It was no mock-prophet that left Mantua; it was a true one. He was the Truth-Teller, born to strip men of their pretences; and of all their pretences the most transparent were their pretensions to honour, truth, loyalty, courage. Princes, like parasites, knew no law but self-interest, and he was their Scourge. The hero had christened him, and he would yet be heard from. Life was inglorious, he was its prophet; and he dedicated his future to the proclamation of its ignominy. But the lash of the prophet was futile and the sting of the satirist risky: truth could only triumph by hypocrisy. There was but one way to scourge princes: to lodge in their vitals, to fasten on their vanity, to pander to their craving for fame and their fear of abuse, to flatter and intimidate, by falseface and plainspeaking, until he brought them under the sway of public opinion, and to use that power for his own ends. And those ends—were they not holy? When he had wrung from the world, by its own methods and at its expense, the living which it owed him, when he was free to live as he pleased, in obedience to his instincts, in imitation of his betters, and in defiance of his censors, he would accomplish his full mission and champion the rights of the natural man; for he was the prophet of a new age, the forerunner of the modern world, where

GIOVANNI DI PIER FRANCESCO DE' MEDICI
(GIOVANNI DELLE BANDE NERE), by Bronzino
From the portrait in the Uffizi Gallery, Florence

men were accountable for their faith and their conduct to no Power but the Power that made them what they were.

But to accomplish that mission, where was he to turn now, with every tie severed, every door closed, and war over Italy? The March winds roared by and he followed them. The last haven lying in the lee of the deluge was yet to be heard from, the liberal asylum of the outcast, the expatriate, and the freethinker. The level immensity of the plain blended with the illimitable boundaries of the sea; the horizon shimmered and grew reedy; about him the marshes murmured, steeped in the mournful soliloquy of the waters; the winds spent their dust over the dunes and swept on in insatiable transiency. But within the sea-wall the waters were calm and, liquidating all his cares, a faint reef of domes, like the monumental mirage of some submerged Ark, lay snug on the lagoon. Venice loomed before him.

58

In Mantua the gardens of Madama were blooming under the vernal equinox; and she had not seen them for two years. "I have been in your Court and seen your *giardinetto*, which is as lovely and green as Heaven," her maid wrote her. "The little trees are bearing large apples, my friends the figs are ripening, the jasmines are clambering to the sky, everything invites us to joy. The divine Grotto and the *camerini* would make Hell itself brilliant and delightful. The beautiful loggia and the lawn, laid out with new fruits, tempt us to lay away sorrow and put on new garments of joy. *Signora mia,* everything is thrice lovely and invites you to enjoy the fruit of your labours." But the gardens, the loggia, the Grotto, and the *camerini*, remained empty. Madama had been away for two years, and it was rumoured that she would never return; for the reason was autumnal.

The Mantua of Isabella d'Este had become the Mantua of Isabella Boschetti, and its Court was too small to accommodate more than one Isabella at once. The late *prima donna del mondo* had ignored her son's mistress until even in Rome it was known, and from no less an authority than Giovio, the Papal historian, that "the inamorata of the Marquis rides proudly, surrounded by all the gentlemen who once flocked about his mother, and there remain with her only one or two old gentlemen who refuse to forsake her." Her husband at least had never flaunted his women, and he had accepted her political tutelage; but Federico . . . To be disgusted with Federico would have been to be disgusted with life, and she loved them both too much; but she cherished her dignity. At first she had withdrawn into her Grotto and consoled herself in the halflife of art; but the most aesthetic of her instincts was her *amour-propre*, and she soon emerged. Of youth she still had the secret, her blind faith in herself, and she proved it by departing for Rome.

That had been two years ago. Since then the Marquis had repeatedly attempted to coax her home, but in vain. Whenever he visited her vacant apartments, he was reminded of the cause of her absence by two cryptic devices which she had added to her walls. They mystified him. One, in which the Papal historian had collaborated, represented "a triangular candelabra, like those used in Holy Week, from which the priests mysteriously remove the tapers one by one, until only the topmost is left, signifying that the light of faith cannot fail." But what faith—what mysterious feminine faith—surmounted the eternal triangle? The darkness was clearer than the light. Her trust in God? She needed it, after a life of exemplary virtue, and she had piously adopted the motto which Giovio proposed: *Sufficit unum in tenebris*. But apparently she was not satisfied, for she supplemented this device with another and a more profane one—a sheaf of lottery tickets tumbling from the urn of Chance, signifying that "she had tried everything and lost, but that she would yet triumph over her rivals and return to her former greatness." But since when did Fortune favour the old? In Rome, however, her mysterious faith, whether in God, in Fortune, or in herself, was amply rewarded. There she was still the first lady of her time, and everything favoured her. She obtained from the Pope a Cardinal's Hat for her second son, Ercole, and a dispensation for her third son, Ferrante, to serve with the Imperial army; and for herself she found time to visit the shrines she had missed on her first visit under Leo and to make her devotions. Mantua had only one charm for her now—she was missed there; and she indulged her maternal coquetry, promising and always putting off her return, until the Marquis, finding all his pleas in vain, dutifully desisted.

But in the winter of 1527 he became anxious. He was in the position —the lofty position of a weathervane—to scan the map of Italy and discern the drift of the morrow. Behind him, between Mantua and Ferrara, lay the German hordes, hibernating and restless for plunder or pay. Frundsperg was feeding them with promises. In Milan a Spanish army, commanded by the Constable de Bourbon, was in the same situation. Both commanders appealed to him for supplies, which he refused on the plea of poverty and neutrality. He was willing, however, to play the peacemaker and, when his cousin the Constable de Bourbon appealed to him to avert a possible disaster, he used his good offices to promote a truce with Rome. But the terms which Bourbon proposed were considered exorbitant in Rome and progress was slow. It was also circuitous, for the Italian League viewed these negotiations with suspicion and finally refused the intermediary a safe-conduct through their lines. The winter passed without result. With the coming of spring the disaster became every day more probable. The Emperor had balanced the international situation but not his budget: the German Diet and the Spanish Cortes refused the necessary credits to keep his armies in the field; Frundsperg with his unpaid Lutherans and Bourbon with his unpaid Spaniards were forced to live off the land, and the land was cropped close. The Marquis was uneasy. He walked in his mother's gardens. Her maid was tending the jasmine and nursing the old gentlemen who longed for Madama, as she said, "like the Messiah." She was dandling the dwarf who was clamouring for Madama—all the little people loved her. Without Madama there was no joy in the gardens. Everything invited her to return, and she . . . The Marquis agreed. It was a dismal spring. Giovanni de' Medici was underground, and Clement was in the Vatican, and Madama was in Rome. No one in Italy was in the right place. He wrote to his mother, urging her once more to return; and once more she declined gaily, though she promised to be prudent. "As we are not more courageous or more martial than we are," she wrote, "at the very first alarm we shall mount and ride off in search of refuge." But she was not alarmed. Why should she be? She was in Rome.

Under the mild spring skies it was impossible to realize any reality beyond what the sun shone on; and Rome, like herself, was basking in an impregnable glamour. Above all, the weathervane of Rome was calm. After months of vacillation, Clement was calm. Giberti had been complaining that they were on the brink of ruin, and washing his hands all winter of the outcome. To clear himself, he had filed all the suggestions which the Pope had ignored or rejected. "The irresolution of the Pope," he said to the Mantuan ambassador, "is something incredible. . . . I doubt whether anything can overcome his natural bent, or whether we can hope for any good from him—not that he is not full of goodness, there is not a better man in Christendom—but he is *dead to the world*." Guicciardini likened his apathy to the infatuation of the doomed. All his intimates were mystified; but what did his intimates know? Who could be intimate with Clement? He guarded his secret. The long strain of anxiety had ended in exhaustion, and he had found relief. Peace reigned, wherever else, in his mind, the peace of a man intolerably tried, and tired, relaxing in fatalistic indifference. Who could begrudge him the numb ease of the drowning? He enjoyed his pleasures now. Secretive and lonely, he listened to music, and the dissonant world was muted: the drum met the viol, and the flute trilled between them in sudden successful inspirations; and he hung on the artful modulations—which was the truth? this harmony or that discord? He sat entranced, and around him Rome stood spellbound, and Isabella who attended these concerts devoutly was calm.

With the first thaws of March, the Spaniards were in motion; they were joined by the Germans; and the hungry armies swept southward. The forces of the League, under the command of the Duke of Urbino, kept pace with them, diverting them into a narrow channel, and turning them aside first from Piacenza and then from Bologna. The famished hordes then swung toward Florence, but the Duke intercepted them, and, swerving once more, they headed for Rome. There the sacred concerts were abruptly suspended, and the Pope hastily concluded a truce with the Spanish Viceroy in Naples. But this was a mere gesture, an instinctive precaution dictated by habit; what he really relied on, in an emergency, was the venerable prestige of the See. The uneasiness of the Vatican had seeped into Rome, permeating the whole city, and so many were fleeing that the Pope issued an edict making mistrust illegal and forbidding flight or the removal of treasure; and he gave a serene example of confidence by disbanding his troops. The sacred concerts were resumed. It was Easter; under the mild Paschal sun Rome dozed, manifestly eternal. The sacrosanct city solemnly honoured Divine Providence. In her temples Christ rose, in clouds of balm, in sacramental psalms, in mystic wine, in hallowed wafers; in her meadows, in one more resurrection of spring; and in the chanceries of the Vatican, in one more truce: *Te Deum, Te Deum laudamus*. But the hunger of the Imperialists knew no truce. On the proclamation of the armistice, the Landsknechts mutinied and, swarming through the camp in maddened thousands, promulgated the Imperial law: plunder or pay. Overnight the march of Empire was ordained by its pawns. Their commanders were stampeded. Frundsperg, arguing gutturally, succumbed to an apoplectic stroke. The riot spread, the Spaniards broke loose and sacked the tents of their captains; and Bourbon only regained control of them, after hiding for three days, by complying with all their demands. Plunder or pay, plunder or pay . . .

The dunning cadence rocked the camp and set it in motion like a marching-song; but it was not a march, it was a migration. Multiplying insubordinately, they pressed the land, pullulating like locusts and digesting its dearth in the long wake of bleakness they left behind them. But, once in motion, order reappeared—the predatory order of the pack. Through torrents of rain in the tireless momentum of numbers they tramped, fording swollen streams in gangs, hand in hand, chanting their last hardships, and cheering their leader. Bourbon marched by their side, singing their songs, taking their jokes, sharing their privations, and recovered a semblance of authority by fraternizing with them; but his authority was so feeble that it bore no strain; he was hurried along by a force he could not control, and he led it as the first boulder leads the landslide. When the Viceroy attempted to stem them with pay, it was too late; their trade was to take, and the unearned increment of slaughter was too tame. Too tame, too, the excommunications launched against them as Lutherans and Moors; they gloried in the names; and the hungry were heathen, and the heathen unharnessed when, on the evening of May 5, 1527, they swung their pickets and camp-fires in a wide semicircle under the walls of Rome.

In a last effort Bourbon had forwarded a proposal to settle for an indemnity. He shrank from a sacrilegious assault on the Holy See; but no answer came. Surveying the walls from his headquarters on the Janiculum, he stood with Ferrante Gonzaga, knee-deep in vines, and surrendered the Eternal City to the morrow. But he was reminded by his cousin that Isabella was in Rome and he sent her a message that, whatever happened, she would be relieved, if she fortified herself against the first shock.

59

Between that rapacious hemicycle lying in the night and his pastoral duty Clement did not hesitate. As the danger approached, he rose to it. He refused to compound the crime and bargain under pressure; he wrapped himself in his sacerdotal robes and prepared to meet the morrow in state and succumb, if need be, on his throne, with Giovio, the physician and the historian of the Popes, beside him.

The attack began at dawn. Rome was blanketed in mist, through which the bugles blew in ghostly ubiquity. The walls had been manned with a hasty levy of volunteers—menials, seminarists, artisans, and a sprinkling of professional soldiers—but the walls themselves were in an advanced state of disrepair; in places great seams ran down to the ground; in others they housed dwellings; vines nestled about their base; and the fortifications had long served, in fact, only to raise the customs' tolls. In the first pallor of dawn, under cover of the mist and the vines, the enemy groped toward the nebulous hulk of the Holy City. The attack began tentatively in a series of reconnaissances and skirmishes. At one point, a group of prowlers stumbled on a window boarded up under rubbish and broke into the street beyond; at another, a sentry stumbled on the enemy and in fleeing led them to the breach he was guarding. But as yet these inroads were few. The defence was furious, the seminarists of the Collegio Capranica particularly distinguishing themselves; and, though they fired blindly into the fog, guiding themselves by the din, the besieged beat off the attack for over two hours. Bourbon led the next wave. He was clad in white to rally his men and made a conspicuous target as he scaled a ladder; and a great shout went up from the walls when he fell and the assault slackened. The defenders dispersed in droves through the city, claiming the victory; others followed, clamouring for food; and those who remained on the walls had a breathing spell. Bourbon was borne off the field, but his men were maddened by his loss, and, as he passed away, groaning: *A Rome! A Rome!* they returned to the attack and swept over the top into the Borgo. *O Madre!*—with the first Spaniard the cry leapt the walls—*O Madre! que hoy será vengada!* On their path lay a hospital. They swarmed in and with shouts of *España! Amazza!* exterminated the inmates, but as they came out they were overtaken by a rumour that the army of the League was a day's march away and, finding themselves alone, they paused. Two hours sooner, the rumour might have halted the assault; now it merely speeded the sack. With the next wave came the Germans, furious at being outstripped, and a jealous race for the spoils began. Groping their way through the deserted Borgo, they met a detachment of Pontifical troops, who joined them, while at their heels came the rabble, opening the jails, and the whole pack, interlopers, Spaniards, Germans, Romans, and jailbirds, made for St. Peter's. The Pope was at prayer. There was just time to gain the gallery to Sant' Angelo; and as he strode along, striding but not running, with his historian at his heels raising his robes, the slaughter kept pace with them below. The white Papal rochet made a target for snipers, but with a gesture historic Giovio threw his own mantle over him. Visions flashed by, through the narrow apertures of the tunnel, glimpses of pandemonium which haunted the fugitives, one of whom, in recalling "the clatter of steel, the wails of the maimed, the frantic neighing of horses, the sudden explosions, the crackle of fire, the howling of dogs, the roll of drums, the blare of trumpets, and the crumbling of masonry," dreamed long after that through that din thunder would hardly have been heard.

The agony of his flight and its ignominy only dawned on Clement when he found himself in the fortress. It had elapsed like something unreal, independent of his will. A moment before, he had made up his mind to die, but it was the mysterious machinery of the body, the irresistible viscera, that superseded the brain in an emergency, and that thought. Giovio as a physician knew that, and as a historian. Amid the miserable throng struggling into Sant' Angelo, crowding, kneeling, swarming up the ramps, jostling through the corridors, disappearing and reappearing in every recess of the triple-walled fort, Clement VII vanished. The capacity of the castle was soon over-taxed. The drawbridge, rusty with disuse, was raised slowly; the portcullis could not be lowered completely; and so dense was the crowd wedged under it that many were mangled as it fell. In the confusion several of the enemy had slipped in and were butchered. The latecomers eddied about the walls, the bolder edging along the towpaths and scaling the joists. A belated Cardinal was hoisted to the ramparts and dropped, more dead than alive, among three thousand refugees; and the bewildered multitude continued to churn about the bastions. Another crowd, caught on the bridge of Sant' Angelo, waited in convulsive congestion; the Landsknechts charged; and the bedlam turned to a shambles. It was midday, the sun came out, and through the long muggy hours of the May afternoon the watchers huddled under the Angel followed the progress of death through the doomed city. A tense silence reigned: "No one spoke, everyone betrayed his fear in his face," said one of them. The intensity of terror created a dazed sense of detachment. "We watched," said a gunner, "like spectators at a play." Leaning on their guns like gods translated beyond life and like men stunned by its godlessness, they seemed to dream what they had so long foreseen. Strange to themselves, alien to each other, they followed the unfolding of the terrible spectacle. From that viewpoint, as in the perspective of eternity, it unfolded like some infinitesimal pantomime in a serene panorama, for the first onslaughts were over, and after the first infernal din an unnatural hush muffled the sounds that still punctuated it—the sporadic screams, the distant detonations, the remote hum of invisible turmoil. The sack had settled down to the methodical business of pillage and slaughter. Knots of soldiers passed through the streets shouldering their spoils; little figures rolled on the ground, locked in the ambiguous embraces of lust and death; but otherwise the scene, save for its silence, seemed almost normal, for the city had absorbed its invaders. They had burst into its wealthiest quarter, the Borgo San Pietro, where most of the Cardinals had their palaces, and they were teeming like glutted bees. But toward sundown a change appeared. The Imperial commanders came on the scene. The dense city lying beyond the Tiber was untaken, the bridges were guarded, the guns of Sant' Angelo had been trained on them, and, if the army of the League advanced, their position was critical. It was essential to complete the occupation before nightfall. Accordingly, amid a revival of bugle calls, the gods on Sant' Angelo saw the bridges, their last line of defence, systematically attacked. To destroy them would have been easy, had they not been Romans: but the bridges were noble and old; and the enemy poured over them. One by one they were carried. The Papal troops made a last stand on the Ponte San Sisto where, as the Imperialists pressed forward, they were jammed in the chains that barred them and trampled underfoot, as they attempted to vault them, by their own horses. The guns of Sant' Angelo were silent: munitions were lacking; there were but seven gunners to man them, and they were watching the pantomime. Meanwhile the enemy advanced slowly through the darkening streets of the city, alarmed by the ease of their victory and dreading an ambush. The Spanish began to substitute ransom for slaughter; the Germans baited them on their backsliding, and a battle was only averted by the timely arrival of their commanders. Thus it was that, when night fell and Rome was completely overrun, the dead numbered no more than eight thousand. They alone slept through the night that ensued, a night of exploding shrines, of delirious din, of lurid brilliance, of sulphurous gloom. The havoc was wholesale; neither religious nor diplomatic immunity nor age nor sex had been spared; women, children, masters, menials, clerics, laymen, lay pell-mell in the streets, in the churches, in windows, in portals, and in pieces, like the garbled litter of a mimic Doomsday, stumbled over by scavengers, worried by dogs; and the survivors lived to envy them.

For Rome was not unbuilt in a day. On the morrow a systematic sack began. An administration was set up: the city was divided into districts, and the harrow passed over it slowly, exhaustively. Day after day the industry of destruction progressed, and the dying city was slowly galvanized into posthumous life. To meet the needs of the army, banks reopened and notaries reappeared, drafting inventories, registering bills of ransom, cashing notes of exchange, and storing loot. Like maggots on a charnel-pile, they digested the disaster. The annals of Rome in those days were written in their ledgers, in columns of figures that codified the atrocities by which the wealth of nations changed hands. A whole science of extortion sprang up, revealing an infinite genius in an infinite field for ingenuity. The mildest methods were sleeplessness and bone-cracking; to be hung, head down, from the windows or, hands up, from the rafters, to lose an ear and be fed with it, was horseplay; the quick of agony was touched in obscene probings which treated the pregnant parts of man as impregnable places and tactical problems; and money flowed over the counters. Reluctance to pay meant torture, but so did alacrity, in the greed for more; and all bargains were provisional, ransoms being paid four times over to the Germans, the Spanish, the Epirotes, and the Italians. To preserve their authority, the officers truckled to their men and were always willing to split with them; and the demented victims who appealed to them found them powerless or complaisant. There was neither redress, nor relief, nor escape. Those who fled to the Campagna found it full of lurking peasants waiting to waylay the fugitives. Some fled to the catacombs, seeking Christ in the sepulchre a month after He had risen, and in the tortuous crypts where the quick dogged the dead searching for a hypothetical hereafter, for above ground there was none. Day after day, slowly, methodically, interminably, the sack progressed, engulfing the city acre by acre; and it was only then that the magnitude of the calamity came home to the trapped population of Rome.

A few palaces belonging to the Imperialist Cardinals and crowded with refugees who could pay for protection had been spared, but they succumbed one by one; and it now became a question how much longer the last strongholds could hold out—Sant' Angelo and the Colonna Palace of SS. Apostoli where Madama of Mantua was immured.

60

Isabella had prepared for a longer siege than the two hours which Bourbon and her son Ferrante had promised would be the limit of her ordeal. When the deluge broke and engulfed Rome, she had already stocked her Palace with provisions, received three thousand refugees, hired soldiers, and walled up the gates. Toward evening, her son sent two captains to reassure her, and with their appearance she had to stand an internal siege. They brought her protection at a price. An indemnity was levied on the refugees and, amid the evasions, the haggling, and the recriminations to which it gave rise, it became her duty to arbitrate, to persuade, and to compose. She tasted the bitterness of benefaction. She moved among blessings, but she moved among 2200 women, and a story got about that Ferrante had lined his pockets with a share of the money. As he had sent the captains to relieve his mother, the inference was natural; but what the facts of the case were, Ferrante explained in a letter to his brother in Mantua. On reaching the Palace he had been refused admittance by his colleagues until he consented to the indemnity; he complied—"my greatest desire being to save Madama, which I did only with the utmost difficulty, as a rumour had spread through the camp that, what with goods and money and noblemen, there were over two millions in gold in that palace; and this was due solely to the compassion of Madama in sheltering 1000 gentlemen and 2200 Roman gentlewomen, who contracted for their persons and property with the two captains to the amount of 40,000 ducats, and I did not see a penny of it."

The rumour of these millions travelled quickly, and, as the plunder grew thin elsewhere, the Imperial Generals found it more and more difficult to guarantee protection. Terror seeped through the walls. Madama herself was a prey to it. "I have heard her wish many times over for death," said one of her friends. "She recalled the prudent and affectionate appeals of our Signore to leave Rome, and I am sure she would have given all she possessed to have followed his advice." Terror was all she possessed now, and she offered it in an agony of propitiation to whatever gods there might be. Why had she lingered in Rome? She herself no longer knew. Was it some prescience that she would be needed there? Or was it pique? Or was it pleasure? The pleasure of piquing Federico? The delicious thrill of reviving his affection had made her foolhardy, perhaps, but she did not regret her imprudence. It would have been folly, when absence and danger made her so dear, to return to her Paradiso, and she was no fool, even in risking the sack of Rome. In every camp she had family connexions, and she felt herself capable of circumventing an army. She was not reckless; she gambled with system. But Bourbon was dead; she had failed; she had tempted Providence; and after trifling so long with Fate, Fate was now flirting with her. Her pride, however, sustained her. There were others more agonized than she, who claimed her compassion or who quickened her shame. There was Domenico Venier, the Venetian ambassador, who had concealed himself in her secretary's room and who, even there, even *incognito*, seemed to feel, as she said, "that everyone was watching him, as if the walls were as transparent as glass." But there were others who steadied her faith in human dignity. There was Luigi Gonzaga, the Mantuan ambassador, who, amid those scenes of abysmal disaster, with the world listing and humanity slipping headlong, was a prey to professional scruples. In that unprecedented situation he insisted on being *en règle* and felt it his duty to visit the Pope; and, when he found that impossible, he continued to compile his reports, though he did not know when or how he could send them; but they occupied his mind and gave a salutary example of self-possession. He did more: he went out and, forcing his way into the Imperial camp, collected opinions and brought them home and reflected on them and wrote them up. "In this total ruin and extermination of Rome, having forced my way into the Imperial camp, I write to Your Excellency to say that it is an extreme compassion to see this calamity.... A man must be superhuman to preserve his senses.... We must believe that our Lord God wishes to scourge Christendom, for this will not be forgotten for years and years. ... I believe, in fact I am certain, that there will be no more captains and soldiers of the Church, and that the Pope will be reduced to the Spiritual Power.... This shabby Pope has been governed by others rather than by himself, and hence this has happened, but I believe God has willed it, to punish these ministers of the Church, which will be purged to His will, if ever it raise its head again." The future? The world ended today. "The majority of men desire not to live, so as not to see such horrible and impious sights. For the past eight days Madama has wished a thousand times over that she had followed Your Excellency's advice and returned to Mantua."

But in the very extremity of her straits Isabella found salvation. Provisions were dwindling; she was reduced to garlic and bread, and the refugees to a diet of herbs; and despite the indemnity, the exertions of Ferrante, and a cordon of Landsknechts, the Imperial Generals were so uneasy for her safety that they proposed flight. She hesitated only long enough to make sure of protection for the women she left behind; and she was a little impatient with the Mantuan ambassador who hesitated to desert his post until he had smuggled a note into Sant' Angelo and consulted the Pope. In reply His Holiness sent his benediction and a safe-conduct. Everything was *en règle*, and the little party picked its way, under an escort of Landsknechts, to the Tiber, where boats had been provided. The soldiers lugged a cargo of her antiques, and, thanks to their predatory appearance, they reached the river unmolested; but once launched, progress was slow. Down the sallow tide, amid drifting corpses, between banks grim with ruin, they floated, patiently wooing the current as it swam through a vacant metropolis of cavities. For hours they could not clear Rome, the weather squalled, and in the tentacles of the gale the river retracted its flow and the suction of disaster seemed to draw them back to a doom from which there was no escape; but Fate, ruthless to others, was only flirting with Madama. They reached Ostia. There, in the purgatorial port of Rome, under filthy skies, amid inhospitable inhabitants, they were windbound for eight days, and in such scarcity of food that Ferrante had to supply them out of the maw of Rome. The Venetian ambassador, looking forward to the crossing to Civitavecchia, was seasick, and the Mantuan ambassador, looking backward to Rome, was heart-sore. "Here I am with tears in my eyes and sorrow in my heart," he wrote, "as Your Excellency may well imagine, and I assure you that I am overpowered with grief to be living in these times, so prodigious and violent and full of disasters and calamities, and in which we have every reason to believe that each day will disclose new tribulations and exterminations, and that the whole world will crumble and be annihilated." And, still apologizing for his existence, he boarded the ship. The crossing was negotiated in safety, but the galley which followed with the antiques was captured by corsairs.

The return to Mantua was triumphal. The population turned out, the bells pealed, the Marquis rode on one side of her, her son the Cardinal on the other, and cries of *Isabella* filled the air; nor was there any doubt as to which Isabella they acclaimed. "Surely," a sympathetic observer noted, "Madama may now be convinced of the love her two illustrious sons and her whole loyal people bear her; and her beauty seemed to prove how little she had suffered from her terrible trials." She bloomed; the sack of Rome seemed to have rejuvenated her; but she was tired and, while her sons proceeded to a solemn service of thanksgiving in the Duomo, she and her women retired to a less conspicuous church to make their devotions. In an intimate sense she recognized the especial mercy of Providence for women. Her escape had been miraculous but no more than she expected. She had been preserved for a purpose and she could not have perished with her faith. But what faith? The topmost taper burned in the darkness, mysterious even to herself. To name it was to quench it. In herself? In Fortune? In God? it was all these and more: the faith, blind and holy, of women in life, their unquestioning constancy to its will, their unreasoning trust in its value, their unfailing labour for its survival. She believed in her own vitality. But it was not what it had been. After the excitement, she was exhausted and was confined to her bed. Lying there, amid her familiar surroundings, everything seemed strange but the fact that she was there, nothing was changed when she recovered but her longing to travel. She craved quiet; she was content with her Grotto; and she moved through her garden, remembering and forgetting. The jasmine clambered to heaven, everything invited her to joy, and she was happy with a happiness as unmeaning as grief. Life was a dream ... of horror in the night, of peace in the sunlight. ... She was an old lady.

61

Meanwhile, though the Castle Sant' Angelo still held out, the passion and death of Rome were transforming it from a fortress into a mausoleum. Like all the Papal fortresses, it was unprovided for a siege, and famine was making inroads. There were three thousand mouths to feed; the Mole was infested on all sides, and every meal meant a victim. The children who crept around the walls, filling the baskets that were lowered to them, were picked off by the enemy, and only their faith reached the besieged. But for faith they were even more famished than for bread. For what no blockade could cut off, what the enemy on the contrary encouraged, was rumour, the deadly, daily, demoralizing rumour seeping in of an orgy of sacrilege and vandalism in Rome, of a fury of fanatical iconoclasm, of St. Peter's turned into a stall and the Landsknechts stabling their horses in the Stanze of Raphael in the Vatican, of Pope Julius rolled out of his tomb, of the Heads of the Apostles bandied about, of the Lutherans parading the Lance of Longinus, of the Veil of Veronica displayed in a brothel, of the Holy of Holies invaded—and the nightly rumour of subhuman brutalities—a Cardinal bluffed with a mock-burial and borne in his coffin to bed—a priest killed for declining to sing Mass to a mule—rumour upon rumour of abominations redounding to the crack of Doom and verified daily under their eyes in processions of priests passing in leash through the streets to their stations of auction, and culminating one night in a conclave of drunken Landsknechts under the walls of the Castle mimicking the Mass and proclaiming Luther

Pope. And to vouch for everything there was the silence of Rome where the bells no longer tolled and the faith was stifled. An exemplary piety reigned in the fortress, where the change of guard was observed less punctually than the liturgical hours. The Pope celebrated Mass regularly. In Rome with the tolling of the bells Time had ceased; but the hourly murmur of litanies in the Mole maintained a feeble respiration of faith . . . of faith . . . in Time. Time always returned for the Medici, and Clement was punctual in his genuflections to Eternity.

But as the days passed without relief and the famine grew, the Pope pined. The greens on his table reminded him of the woman who had brought them and who had been hanged by the enemy. Faith—the slaughtered innocents lying moth-like below the walls testified to its efficacy. They stank; and he did not smell sweet. An odour clung to him, an odour of sanctity, an aroma of mould, of undernourishment, of melancholy; and as a cat licks itself, he wept himself, clean; but the morbid odour remained. He nursed his regrets. One day he surprised himself by voicing them. "If Pietro Aretino had been with us," he sighed, "we should not be here, worse than in prison; he would have told us freely what Rome was saying of the Treaty with the Viceroy, and we should not have trusted ourselves to such hands." He directed his secretaries to compose an appeal to the Emperor, but on scanning their letters he tossed them aside, complaining that Aretino alone was capable of treating the matter. And gloom, the gloom of the old mausoleum underlying the fortress, seeped through its walls, transforming it once more into a tomb.

Day after day, the watchers under the Angel scanned the horizon; night after night, they sent up flares, and at last, on the eighteenth, relief loomed on the horizon. It was the thirteenth day of captivity when the scouts of the League appeared on the Janiculum and turned back. An urgent appeal was smuggled through to the Duke of Urbino, who lay at Monterotondo, only ten miles away. But he refused to stir. As he lay there so tantalizingly near, Clement in his long memory travelled back listlessly to the occupation ten years before of Urbino, and began to believe that he was the one Medici for whom Time returned only to expiate its memories. And inhaling the gloom of the old mausoleum, he watched the sepulchral horizon in vain.

Meanwhile, Guicciardini, who accompanied the army of the League, was expostulating with the Duke of Urbino, but he received only a flimsy explanation and an impatient reply, and the army retreated to Perugia. The meddling civilian, shaken off with military strides, then appealed to the Cardinal-Regent of Florence for aid in a desperate attempt to deliver the Pope. "The poor man is shut up in the Castle with no hope but your aid," Guicciardini wrote, "and he solicits it with words that would move stones. But you do not even reply. May God never help me if I would not rather be dead than see such cruelty. You think so much of the Piazza and the Palace there that you forget all the rest. But if the Pope is lost, your prudence will serve you nothing, because you will lose the soul of your body politic." The desperate scheme was that of a surprise attack, and, when Machiavelli was sent to him to inquire what could be done, Guicciardini sent him to Civitavecchia to consult the Papal Admiral, who considered the scheme and found it too rash to attempt. At this moment Machiavelli was recalled to Florence by an event which he had never believed that he would live to see. A revolution had broken out, the Medici had fallen, and the Republic was restored.

He lived to see it but nothing more. On the return journey to Florence his travelling companions heard him sigh, more than once, like a man short of breath. His old post was vacant and he applied for it. On June 10, F. Tosinghi was appointed. The shock was too much for him. He took to his bed, treating himself with hepatic aloes, a nostrum for indigestion in which he had complete faith. At least, it had done him no harm; and it was the only thing in which he believed that had done him no harm. After fifteen years of adversity, the revolution had come too late. His past was forgotten and only his service with the Medici was remembered. He was repudiated as a time-server. If he had been a successful one, how soon would that have been forgotten! But he had made only the minimum of compromise necessary to survive, and he had survived only to be ruined by his expediency. Even as a time-server he was a failure, and failure was unforgivable—who knew it better than he? It was just. His whole faith was based on the philosophy of defeat; but it was the tragedy of his life that he could never reconcile his creed and his conduct. He was a sheep in wolf's clothing; however unscrupulous his principles, his integrity was so flagrant that only a politician could doubt it, only a partisan could question his patriotism; but his patriotism had outgrown party: the form of government was immaterial, the life of the state alone mattered; and all he solicited, of the Republic or the Medici, was an opportunity to serve it: for that he had made every sacrifice, even of consistency. "I love my country," he had written to Vettori only a few weeks before, "better than my very soul."

Deeper than politics, deeper than sentiment, deeper than racial partiality, deeper yet, his patriotism was religious. Every man fashions his god in his own image. The state was everything he was not—strong, self-sufficient, successful, and permanent—its life was a compensation for his own; and it was all a delusion. His country was a fiction, it did not even exist. What was the state but the aggregate of all the little egoisms which constituted and controlled it? That corporate person had no identity; it was a figment of the brain, a fetish created in his own image to magnify him, an idol which had consumed him and cast him away.

In that hour of supreme disillusionment, if he had returned to the faith of the world-weary and his childhood, he would only have been following the example of Florence and his friends. Vettori turned to the supernatural to account for the conturbations of Italy, and the Piagnoni were reviving and pointing to the sack of Rome as the vindication of their prophet. And Guicciardini was arguing that faith was not inconsistent with reason. "Faith," he wrote, "is nothing but to believe firmly, and almost with certainty, what is not reasonable or, if it is reasonable, to believe it with more resolution than reason warrants. He that has faith becomes stubborn in what he believes and proceeds on his way intrepid and determined, despising difficulties and dangers, and prepared to suffer every extremity. And as the affairs of this world are subject to innumerable accidents and chances, at many milestones, in the length of time, unforeseen aid may greet those who persevere in this obstinacy; and since it proceeds from faith, it is well said that faith can accomplish great things. A remarkable example of it in our days is the obstinacy of the Florentines, who contrary to every reason in the world have prepared to meet the war of the Pope and the Emperor without hope of help from anyone else . . . and this obstinacy arises in large part from the belief that they would not perish, according to the predictions of Fra Jeronimo of Ferrara." But faith could not be built on the finite calculations of the mind. Machiavelli, however, held firm. He resisted spiritual defeat. The test of a faith was its fruits, and he had served his lights, however fallacious, with an abnegation and constancy which no Christian could better; he was too much of a Christian himself and his self-disgust made the virtues of the spiritual pauper abhorrent to him. As he grew worse, a friar was called in; but for the friends by his bedside he repeated, or invented, a dream which he left as his legend. Slipping into sleep, he had met a great multitude of paupers and was told that they were the Blessed in Heaven; then they vanished, and, as he slept on, he was surrounded by a host of grave men reasoning of statecraft, among whom he recognized many pagan philosophers, and these were the damned; and he was given his choice. And sleeping on strenuously, he made it: "Sooner to Hell and reason of state with those great souls than to Heaven with that rabble I first saw." But when at last the smiling eyes grew obtuse, the friar hovered over him and sealed them.

He died of his life, of a surfeit of failure. The date passed unmarked, like his life—to whom did it matter? not even to himself—what was there to remember?—and Time triumphed over his complaints in a last dose of hepatic aloes; and on June 22, 1527, he was interred.

62

The expulsion of the Medici from Florence, following the desertion of the Duke of Urbino, roused the Pope to a forlorn resolution. He opened negotiations with the Imperial Generals for surrender. The terms which they offered him—an indemnity of 400,000 crowns, the surrender of all the Papal fortresses, hostages, and the continuation of his captivity in Sant' Angelo until all the conditions had been fulfilled—were not a solution of his situation, but they offered a reprieve. He gave what he could not keep and retained what he dared. To hostages he consented readily enough; a portion of the indemnity was raised by smelting the Papal jewellery, but to the commanders of his fortresses he sent secret instructions to disregard his orders for their surrender, thus prolonging his captivity deliberately and indefinitely. But its rigour now became bearable. Food came in and visitors; it was a stagnant life but it was life; and his faith in survival revived—survival by his usual methods—evasion, procrastination—how did life ever survive?—how but by refusing to recognize finalities? On June 7 the treaty was signed and forwarded to Spain for ratification. The future had been transferred, at least, from the hands of Providence to those of the Emperor.

The first news of the catastrophe reached Spain two weeks after the signing of this armistice and six weeks after the sack. Charles, in Valladolid, was about to enter a tournament and, after listening to the report with impressions ranging from smiles when he heard of the fall of Rome to gravity at the account of the atrocities and sympathy for the plight of the Pope, he ordered the sports to be resumed. It was only when the clergy, accompanied by the grandees, called on him to protest, that the festivities were cancelled. The churches were closed, and Charles made a formal declaration to the diplomatic corps, absolving the Imperial and Catholic Crown from all responsibility for the catastrophe. The sincerity of these expressions impressed the British ambassador, who voiced the diplomatic consensus of opinion—"we all thought he spoke very heartily," he said—and Castiglione himself was convinced of the good faith of the Emperor.

In the enormity of the calamity Castiglione believed what it would have been a more crushing calamity to doubt. He had always believed what he wished to believe and, now that the power of Providence had devolved upon the Emperor, he needed to trust its benevolence; he could not break the habit of a lifetime. In a personal interview, Charles repeated his regrets, laying the blame entirely on the lawlessness of the soldiers and the incompetence of the commanders, and Castiglione, taking him at his word, urged him to lose no time in releasing the Pope; but on that subject the Emperor maintained such sovereign reserve that the Count found it necessary to supplement his appeals with those of the clergy, and organized so many public demonstrations that they were finally forbidden as a public nuisance and a disturbance of the peace. For several weeks the quiet gentleman from Mantua was one of the most conspicuous figures in Europe. Fortunately, with the eyes of the world focused on him, he was supported by the opinion of the world. There were rumours that the Pope would be deprived of the Temporal Power, and more than rumours that he would be brought to Spain to duplicate the spectacular captivity of François I; but, however tempting such prospects might be, Charles was too shrewd to outrage public opinion. He had no love for the Lutherans, and the French and English Crowns were already negotiating an *entente* to temper his triumph. After mature deliberation and an impressive delay of twelve weeks, he appointed, in September 1527, two plenipotentiaries to negotiate the release of the Pope; and Castiglione wrote to the Holy Father announcing his success.

In the interval, the situation in Rome had entered a new phase. The first furies of the sack had spent themselves, but its force had not subsided, and the Imperial Generals were powerless to check it. With authority paralysed, religious life stifled, and economic life arrested, the continuation of these conditions, sanctioned by the inaction of the Emperor and the Powers, threatened to subvert every basis of civilized life and to convert the sack into a social revolution. The Pope, as he paced the battlements of Sant' Angelo, surveying those scenes of infinite desolation, cast about blindly for something or someone to blame. The Emperor had written him sympathetically, reminding him, however, that his disloyal diplomacy had done much to precipitate the catastrophe; but it was more than one man could bear, as it was more than one man could cause. It was the outcome of a long historic process, which he was born to expiate—of economic and religious and political causes, underpaid armies, overpopulated countries, national rivalries, royal dreams of prestige, ecclesiastical corruption, moral revolts, all conspiring and festering together until the sore had burst; but there was no comfort in accusing historic processes. Castiglione had his enemies in Rome and some of them were in Sant' Angelo. He was suspected of being in the Emperor's pay; and Giberti, though he did not go so far, complained of the credulity and negligence of the Nuncio so adroitly that Clement, with a mind stunned and stale, took up his pen and re-echoed the reproach gratefully.

His letter of reprimand crossed that of the Count announcing his success. It cut Castiglione to the quick. He bore it in silence for three months, but everyone noticed a change in him. Ever since the sack, he had been under a cloud. He lived it over in imagination, and every new report preyed on his mind, passing through him in a constant tremor of muffled shocks, which at last undermined his impressionable constitution. He was a sick, a heart-sick, a broken man. At last he replied. "This letter has greatly increased my already profound distress. It shows me that my one remaining comfort has vanished, together with all the rest. Amid these overwhelming griefs and anxieties, I thought, at least, that Your Holiness was satisfied with my services, to which the very stones in Spain can testify. . . . Truly, Most Blessed Father, the reverence I owe you should make me keep silence and accept your reproof without vexing you with explanations, which are themselves another form of opposition, hardly becoming one who is your servant, but my own conscience and the pain these charges cause me compel me to say that I do not believe the condemnation passed on me is merited." Of the repeated and explicit protests he had raised against the Papal policy he said nothing; and after rebutting the charges of negligence and apologizing impenitently for his credulity, he concluded: "Would to God the Bishop of Verona[1] had come here himself or could still come with the permission of Your Holiness! Then he could judge my present and past conduct and testify that if, as Your Holiness deplores, it was lacking in industry and ability, it was inspired at least by good faith and excellent intentions. . . . These failings being those of Nature, which has made me so, it seems to me that I deserve to be forgiven, particularly as I recognize and confess my defects.

[1] Giberti.

I beg Your Holiness with all due reverence to forgive me if I have said too much in this letter, and hope you will impute it to the extreme distress I feel under the weight of so many sorrows; indeed, it would be impossible to bear so heavy a burden unless I felt sure that Your Beatitude would accept my excuses and would no longer be dissatisfied with me, for, though all sorrows are bitter, those which are unmerited are intolerable. True, when I see Your Holiness, my own master and the Vicar of Christ on earth, bearing such great and unmerited afflictions bravely and patiently, I feel that I should shoulder my own, which are little compared to his, without complaining, but my weakness is not to be likened to the fortitude of Your Beatitude. I trust that, together with Divine aid, this magnanimity will enable Your Holiness to overcome this fierce tempest of fortune, and to live many years in glory and tranquillity, for the service of God and the welfare of Christians, as all your loyal servants desire, and I most of all. Humbly kissing your most holy feet . . ."

Clement was capable of delicacy on second thought. He recognized the transparent good faith and incurable good intentions of his Nuncio; and it mattered little by what virtues Castiglione had failed; nothing mattered now. He manifested the magnanimity which was expected of him. He was grateful for the appreciation which Castiglione showed of his patience; it was long-suffering; but it had been sorely tried by the moral support which he received from another quarter. From Venice Aretino had addressed a public letter to the Pope, reminding him that "he that falls, like Your Holiness, should turn to Jesus with prayers and not against Fate with complaints." From an adequate distance the poet discerned and proclaimed the manifest workings of Divine Providence. "It was necessary," he wrote, "that the Vicar of Christ, by suffering these misfortunes, should pay for the errors of others; and the justice with which Heaven corrects errors would not be clear to the whole world if your captivity did not testify to it." He too touched a sympathetic chord. "How great will be your glory if, girt in patience, after having surpassed yourself in industry, strength, and prudence, you permit the will of God to promote you yet higher! Collect yourself, consider all the virtues of your supreme soul, and tell me if you may not rightly hope to rise many degrees higher than you have already risen? Never doubt but that God will maintain the religion of His Church and, in maintaining it, will maintain you; and if He maintains you, your fall is only apparent, not actual. But what must be actual and not merely apparent is the attitude of mind of the Pontiff, thinking of pardon and not of vengeance; for, if you will pardon rather than punish, you will pursue an aim becoming the dignity of your office. . . . And so from the trial to which the licence and sins of the clergy have brought you, you will wrest with honour and glory the prize of patience, for whose sake these sufferings have been visited on your most constant Holiness, whose feet I devoutly kiss."

The moral triumph so unanimously urged on him was not easy, however, even for a nature as magnanimous and passive as Clement's. The more his situation seemed to improve, the more desperate it became in fact. Famine and pest had followed the sack; the city was exhausted; and the armies plundered it no longer for gold but for bread, searching even the sick-beds. "The silence, the solitude, the infection, the corpses scattered here and there, putrefying, chilled me with horror," said a visitor. "The houses were open, the doors broken down, the shops empty, and in the deserted streets I saw only the fleeting figures of some savage soldiers." This witness was a collector who had come in search of antiques, but the only antiques were the corpses. The living were primitives. Between famine, pest, feuds, and desertions, the armies were rapidly depleted—the Spaniards had dwindled to half their number—but the survivors were tenacious and clung to Rome like the plague. Victims of their own havoc, destitute amid the wealth they had destroyed, they found themselves, seven months after the march on Rome, in the same straits as those which had precipitated it, and the tragedy repeated itself. Once more, and more desperately, they raised their imperial and insatiable cry, *Plunder or Pay*; but, when their commanders proposed to march, they threatened to mutiny, demanding before moving the arrears of their pay before and after the sack. These sums reached a total which the Imperial Treasury could not satisfy, even in part, except by bleeding the Pope; his resources were exhausted; and, as the armies refused either to release him or to withdraw, the situation turned in a vicious circle. Thus it was that, when the Imperial plenipotentiaries reached Rome and the treaty of peace was formally ratified in December 1527, the Imperial Generals were unable to give it effect. The situation had developed into an insoluble deadlock, and it no longer mattered how patiently it was borne. It was more than man could cause or bear or undo: it was a cataclysm.

Responsibility was meaningless and Clement was no longer haunted by it until, one day, a pamphlet in popular doggerel, printed in Venice, was handed to him by the Chamberlain Deacon. It bore the title *Pax Vobis;* but it was signed P. Aretino. As the Holy Father read it, he was so troubled that he broke down and wept. "Is it possible to lash a Pope so heartlessly?" he sighed, letting it slip from his hands. As he dropped it, the shocked Chamberlain took it up. "Messer Pietro," the Deacon wrote to the author, "I can hardly believe that I am alive. I felt as if I had leapt from the window when I, myself an Aretine, handed our Lord the *Pax Vobis* which the persuasions of the wicked and your own malice moved you to write. It is such an outrage that His Beatitude wept and let it fall from his hand. By God, though I am the Chamberlain Deacon, I tremble and dare not go in to him, so cruelly have you cut him to the heart with this strange form of revenge, and I pray God it may pass without harm or discredit to you." But a more painful scene was to ensue. When he returned to apologize for his countryman, he found the Pope still haunted by the rhymes in which the Scourge of Princes lashed the victims and authors of the cataclysm; and Clement seemed at last to discern in its enormity the obscure workings of Providence. "We admit the wrong done to Pietro Aretino," he said with a conviction of guilt which brought him relief, "and we tolerated it because Giberti was the minister of our confidence and mattered more to us than he, whom we regarded as a friend rather than a servant." He did not complain; in fact, he was patient.

63

If the Pope found peace in expiation, his fellow-victims had neither his sense of guilt nor his patience to sustain them. The *Pax Vobis* roused a storm of indignation, and they had but one answer to make to its salutation:

> *Pax Vobis,* good people,
> And God give you to choose
> Between heathen and Jews
>   And the Germans,
>
> Who want, without sermons,
> New wine and a saddle
> To sit and to straddle
>   Both women and men,

> And each column and garden,
> O people of Rome, wears
> The affliction it bears
> > In submission.
>
> Without your permission
> I will tell you all now
> Who caused the sack, and how,
> > And when, and why.
>
> My name too will I cry,
> Or this much at the least:
> I was never a priest,
> > Nor loved one. Nay!
>
> Now mark well what I say:
> I was never the fool
> Of that plebeian arch-mule
> > Gian-Matteo Giberti.

But to reply to it a super-Aretino was needed, and one arose in the person of the poet Berni, who rushed to the defence of the Pope and Giberti in a frenzy of vitriolic vituperation:

> So much, so much you will yet spew,
> Slimy tongue, grimy tongue, tongue without salt,
> A knife will yet call you a halt,
> Quicker than Achilles' could do.
>
> The Pope is the Pope, you are a slave
> Fed on backbiting and refuse,
> Half in the grave, half in the stews,
> Crippled, ignorant, arrogant knave.
>
> Gian-Matteo and his men, fool,
> Thank God, they are alive and well:
> They will drown you in a cesspool.
>
> Beware, bully, beware your knell:
> If you must tell tales out of school,
> Read what your head and your hands spell.

While the gloom of the Mole crackled with these retorts, there was at least an illusion of liberty: freedom of speech still survived in Rome; but the illusion soon faded under the pall and silence of the sempiternal siege. Finally, the Imperial Generals took the initiative and connived at the Pope's flight. He was conveyed in disguise to Orvieto, where his situation was *aliqua mutatio soli sed nulla libertati*.[1] Such at least was the opinion of the English ambassadors, who visited him there to negotiate the divorce of Henry VIII and Catherine of Aragon, and who had it from his own mouth. "The Pope could not deny to Mr. Gregory that it were better to be in captivity in Rome than here at large." There was liberty indeed in the dilapidated palace in which he was lodged, but it was the liberty of a poorhouse. The roofs were caved in, the walls were bare, and they counted "thirty persons, riff-raff and others, standing in the chambers for a garnishment." It was raining and bitterly cold; there was freedom for the damp to soak in overhead and the draughts to leak through underfoot, for the floors were decayed and, as the ambassadors waited for their audience, wrapped in cloaks loaned by the servants, they decided that "it was of little consequence who were lords of this country, unless for a penance you would wish it to be the Spaniards." The Pope's bedroom— for the audience was informal, as he was spending the winter in bed—was yet more dismal: they gave it a rapid glance and appraised the furniture, bed and all, at 20 nobles. Then they discovered the Holy Father. Almost mummified by calamity, Clement looked like a relic: emaciated, his wan face melting into the long unkempt beard he had grown in mourning, his air of hieratic misery lent him a spiritual dignity which was the last disguise. They groaned and turned away—"it is a fall from the top of the hill to the bottom of the mountain."

There, at the bottom of the mountain, four months later, he received a presentation copy of *The Courtier*. It was privately printed and sumptuously bound in hand-tooled leather, which he appreciated; and the handsome volume, with its gilded characters and ornamental clasps, upon which no expense had been spared, lent a touch of charm to the cheerless room, into which the pale rays of spring were beginning to penetrate. It was doubly welcome because it was so incongruous. The Pope gave it a place of honour among his drab and well-worn books of piety. Several weeks later, however, he was obliged to separate them. A story reached his ears which pained him. He sent for the ambassador of Urbino to learn whether it was true that Emilia Pia had been so rapt in reading and re-reading *The Courtier* that she died without receiving the rites of religion? The ambassador was shocked. "Oh, what wicked tales people invent!" he protested. He made a gallant attempt to clear the memory of that good lady, but "Who knows?" he added. "For my part,

---

[1] somewhat of a change of ground, but none of liberty.

I cannot believe it, but everything is possible. God rest her soul nonetheless!" The Holy Father, however, did not countenance levity. *The Courtier* continued to occupy a conspicuous place in his room, where the damp would not rot it, but his books of piety stood alone in the tepid spring sunshine. He had left frivolity behind him in the sacked Vatican.

Castiglione had at last been compelled to publish his book, through the indiscretion of an admirer to whom he had lent the manuscript and who had circulated it, against his express request, among her friends in Naples. It had been copied, and to prevent a garbled edition from appearing, he issued it himself. He was annoyed, but she was without regret. The Marchesa Vittoria Colonna was happy to have forced his hand. "I do not wonder that you have formed a perfect Courtier," she wrote, "since you had only to hold up the mirror to yourself and reflect what you saw there." It was true; and it was a matter of elementary justice to himself and to the life he had lived to recognize it. The censure of the Pope had shaken him, and, though he had regained his confidence, he felt himself an alien in a world which recognized only the virtues of efficiency. After believing in everything and everyone else, Castiglione was at last forced in self-defence to believe in himself; and he withdrew in a moral recessional through ever older and older selves to his first fundamental faith. *The Courtier* contained it; he had carried it through life; and the hesitations and delays which had retarded its appearance seemed to have reserved it for the moment when it was most needed. For the hour was supremely apt. After a cataclysm which had swept away the basic sanctities and the commonest decencies of civilized life, it was time for a gesture of moral luxury, time to declare his faith in the amenities of life, because of their very futility. The hour of abysmal brutality was the hour to repeat that what mattered in life was not its object but the manner of living it. And *The Courtier*, so long in maturing and so often remoulded, underwent one more transformation in his mind and emerged with a new value and its last moral meaning. It was his religion.

Nor was he alone in recognizing it. After practising worldliness with an almost religious decorum, it was logical that he should bring his social amenity to the service of religion itself. In the summer of 1528, Alfonso Valdés, a secretary of the Emperor with Lutheran leanings, wrote a Dialogue justifying the Sack of Rome as a Divine Judgment on the corruption of the Church. Circulating at Court, it was widely discussed and approved, and many of the Emperor's advisers urged him to promote the reform of the Church by reducing the Pope to the Spiritual Power. Castiglione protested and demanded an apology and a retraction; but Valdés, though he offered an apology *pro forma* and was willing to tone down his language, refused to retract the argument and prepared to publish it in Germany and Italy. The argument was thoroughly Lutheran; it attacked the duplicity of the Pope, the corruption and venality of the clergy, the worship of relics and images, the practice of granting dispensations, and the effusion of money on ceremonial vanities. Castiglione challenged it in a public reply, burning with indignation but tempered by a moderation which made it a spiritual consummation of the Courtier and a model of Catholic piety. "You say in the very words of Martin Luther that your purpose is to open the eyes of men and enlighten their ignorance, for the glory of God, the good of Christians, and the honour of the Emperor. To this end you proceed, first, to show that what happened in Rome was the fault, not of the Emperor, but of the Pope; and, after declaring that you do not wish to abuse the Holy Father, you charge him with fraud, calumny, and a long list of crimes, making him appear the most unprincipled man on the face of the earth. Secondly, you assert that the ruin of Rome was the manifest judgment of God on this city, where the worst vices flourished under the cloak of Christian religion. After describing the corruption and hypocrisy of the clergy, you see fit to censure those who honour the relics of saints and the images of Christ and the Blessed Virgin, and say that under these pretences the priests fleece ignorant and simple souls of their money and even allow them to worship false relics. You are at great pains to prove that neither God nor the saints care for gold and silver or any worldly goods but ask only the sacrifice of a pure and contrite heart and that it is far better and more pleasing to God to relieve the necessities of the poor than to adorn His altars or raise holy shrines. You descant on the awful wickedness of a priest who, being in mortal sin, celebrates Mass and receives the Blessed Sacrament, and pour contempt on indulgences, dispensations, and canonizations. Thus, in all these questions, you take care to bring forward only the evil and forget the good, and you add that those bad priests who receive Christ into their bodies, which ought to be pure and undefiled temples, are guilty of a worse crime than the German soldiers who stabled their horses in St. Peter's. . . . No sane person would deny that priests who deceive the ignorant, and receive the Holy Sacrament in a state of mortal sin, have erred grievously. But I cannot conceive, as you seem to do, how these things afford any excuse for the spoliation of relics, true or false, for the massacre of the clergy, the profanation of altars and churches, and the stabling of horses in holy places. Surely no one is so ignorant as to believe that two wrongs make a right, and I hold this, which is your chief contention, to be sufficiently answered. But I maintain, moreover, that, if there are bad priests, there are also good ones, true lovers and servants of God, who honour the relics of saints not for themselves, but for what they represent, and seek by means of things seen to raise the thoughts of men to the unseen. Even if these relics were false, the worshipper would not be an idolater, for whatever stirs the heart to devotion, and leads men to God with the faith that works miracles, must of necessity be good. Therefore it seems to me the utmost impiety to excuse sacrilegious acts by this means, and that the arguments you advance are both foolish and blasphemous. We all know that God and the Saints have no need of our offerings. But since men cherish riches as they do, clearly the motive which prompts them to offer gifts for the love of God must be pleasing to His Divine Majesty, who cares little for fasts and mortifications or to see us go barefoot and live like hermits on acorns and water, but who delights in the burning love that moves all those who do these things from a longing to serve Him. For the same reason it is fitting that gold and silver and precious gems should adorn the vessels that are used for Divine Worship. When you say that it would be better to give the money to the poor, you remind me of Judas's speech: 'To what purpose this waste? Might not this ointment have been sold for three hundred pence and given to the poor?' Christ rebuked him saying: 'The poor have ye always with you, but Me have ye not always.' And St. John the Evangelist adds: 'This Judas said, not because he cared for the poor, but because he had the bag.' . . . I cannot drive away the vision which haunts me night and day of the grief, the horror and amazement, the lamentations and groans, that must have torn the hearts of those old Canons of St. Peter's, who had spent so many years in that holy church, when they saw armed men violate those altars and chapels, slaying women and children and young and old in their mad lust for gold, and scattering sacred relics and the bones of holy martyrs, who had shown by their constancy that they loved Christ more than their lives. Anyone with a spark of religious feeling in his breast must realize what those priests suffered, and can only wonder that their hearts did not break and their minds give way at the sight. Many of those ruffians, no doubt, were lawless and godless soldiers, and there were many heretics and Jews among them, but to think that in the Emperor's own house, in the palace of a prince so truly Christian, so just and so virtuous, we should find a secretary who not only dares to excuse these outrages but commends them and openly declares himself the enemy of Christian rites and ceremonies, this is a thing so intolerable that I can hardly believe it. In those terrible hours when even dumb creatures—nay, the very stones themselves—were moved to pity, you alone, and a few like you, rejoiced at the destruction of the world, and with a refinement of cruelty have sought to stir up hatred against the miserable remnants of Rome and of the Church that have survived the general conflagration. The Pope and the Emperor may perhaps extend their clemency to you, and pardon the injury you have done them; but neither of them can forgive the insults which you have heaped on Christ and His religion. The people of this land would rise up to drive you out of Spain, because this Christian country hates the name of heretic. Go, then, to Germany where your Dialogue has paved the way for you, and Luther and his followers will welcome you, for you may be sure that the Inquisitors whom you revile as Pharisees will show no respect of persons, and that Christ whose protection you invoke will not stretch out His Hand to save you from the sword of justice and the chastisement your obstinacy deserves."

His temper was dangerous when it was roused, and he had not been so stirred since the day the Marquis's horse had been disqualified by a foul. The Emperor refused to prosecute Valdés, but he pressed on Castiglione the title and revenues of Bishop of Avila, renewing an offer which the Count had declined while the relations of the Pope and the Emperor remained strained. Now, however, the situation was in process of liquidation, the armies had left Rome, and Charles was about to sail for Italy to receive the Imperial Crown from the Pontiff; and he accepted the benefice as a recognition of the true bent of his nature, the religious core of his worldliness, and the identity in his life of morals and manners. It was the culmination of his career; it was also its close. He was worn out with exertion, anxiety, and ill health; he had borne his full fruit; and with perfect propriety, a week after his appointment, he expired.

Amid relics, amid shrines, amid altars and tabernacles, amid a venerable muster of transcendent idolatries—towering tapers and gilded *reyas* and hieratic banners—amply accoutred in the gorgeous harness of ecclesiastical pomp, accompanied by the dignitaries of the clergy, escorted by the grandees of Spain, travelling in time with his pallbearers and supported, as his life had been, in the last stage of its passive progress, by hierarchies of witnesses and galaxies of images, he was borne through the thoroughfares of Toledo to the most sumptuous church in Christendom and laid away in the innermost shrine reserved for the heroes and saints of Castile. When the multitudinous vainglories had filed by and the commemoration was over, the Emperor remarked to his courtiers: *Yo vos digo que es muerto uno de los mejores caballeros del mundo.*[1] In later years Charles kept three books by his bedside: *The Prince* and *The Courtier*, and between them the Bible. The remains were subsequently transported to Mantua to lie with those of his wife in the family chapel; and his mother lived to see his son ride away, in his turn, a mounted man.

---

[1] I tell you that one of the best gentlemen in the world is dead.

Aretino

> Take your laurels, Caesar and Homer. Nay,
> I am no poet nor prince. I am known,
> And own a style and a state of my own,
> Because I do not feign truth, for I portray
>
> ARETINO, censor of the proud world
> And nuncio and prophet of truth. Here
> Virtue wears a countenance of good cheer;
> Mark what the hand of Titian has unfurled.
>
> But if vice you adore, vice you should fear,
> Shut your eyes and shun my face evermore;
> For, though I be painted, I speak, I hear.
>
> Federico Gonzaga I adore,
> And Signor Giovanni yet I revere;
> But, beyond these, I honour no man more.

With this sonnet Aretino signed his portrait by Titian and proclaimed his mission to the world. The poet and the painter were working, hand in hand, to produce a new prophet; new times were at hand; and the new lawgiver, who was rising to confound Italy, only needed to reach Venice and meet Titian to be heard from.

A year after reaching the lagoon, he formally severed his last tie with the mainland. He offered a horse which he had abandoned in Mantua to a friend. "I give the nag gladly," he explained with his customary generosity, "and I expect you to accept it in the same spirit. If you must offer me something in return, wait till I leave and offer me another; but you shall wait long, for I have determined to live here for ever; a man who cannot live in Paradise is a fool." If Paradise was a place where he could be himself, he had found it. "Our country is where we are welcome," he declared, and he adopted the city and made it his state of sovereign independence. In Venice where "the sun warms all alike, the moon gives light, and the stars shine for everyone," he could live his life and speak his mind as he pleased; there he could call his soul his own; and there he found a foothold for his long transfiguring flight. There was only one drawback.

When he reached the lagoon, in March 1527, he was a beggar on horseback. He dismounted and embarked, destitute, footloose, and friendless, for in Venice he had no connexions. With only the parting gifts of the Marquis between him and the fluctuating gutters of Paradise, he could not call his soul his own until he had won material independence. His new-found freedom was dear to him and to sell his soul to the service of princes was inconsistent with his new-found principles; but there was one service in Venice which he could enter with a clean conscience and a margin of profit. He was an artist *manqué*. That was all, perhaps, that stood between him and a soul. Art was the one thing in the world he revered more than the memory of Giovanni de' Medici. As a boy, he had practised it. In his first year of vagabondage, he had dabbled in painting in Perugia; at the end of that term, learning that art was long and life was short, he threw up the brush; but he had learned enough to appreciate art. In Rome he frequented the best masters, picked up the lingo of the studios, trained his eye, and became as conversant with the secrets of the craft as with those of the Vatican. His passionate love of paint, combined with his technical knowledge and his journalistic verve, gave him every qualification for a critic, an agent, or a dealer; and the time had now come to exert his powers. In that supreme hour when the sack of Rome had exhausted the religious, political, and social life of Italy, only one faith remained. The real religion of Italy, the impulse with which the Renaissance had been labouring all along, was the deathless passion of art. It rose from the ruins and followed the fugitive life of Italy to Venice; and there it found refuge in the genius of Titian.

The genius of Aretino was his quick instinct for the times, and to Titian he turned his own talents. The fame of the great painter was still parochial and that of the great *claqueur* was cosmopolitan. Titian was impressed by it. Susceptible to the glamour of the mainland, he concluded a covenant with the plausible poet. They agreed to collaborate, Aretino to receive, in return for his pen and his connexions abroad, a half-share of the commissions he procured for the painter. The graft prospered. Within three months of his arrival in Venice he was in a position to offer Federico Gonzaga, with whom he promptly renewed relations, two portraits by Titian, one sacred subject by Sebastiano del Piombo (not at all depressing: "without *hypocrisy*, stigmata, or nails"), and a Venus by Sansovino which would "make his mouth water." One client led to another, and he was launched.

But it was more than a living that Aretino drew from Titian, it was a soul. Titian was the painter that he might have been, had life not been so short, and Aretino served him as a model and a mentor. They were kindred spirits and between them they shared, half and half, the sould of the dying Renaissance. In Venice, at least, there was no sign that the age was dying; never had life been more lush there; and, celebrating it unanimously, they inspired each other. Aretino divined in Titian what Titian discerned in him—the soul of matter. The painter was fascinated by a model who excited all his powers, because he himself possessed them so abundantly—veracity, voluptuousness, virtuosity. The poet vied with his sanguine virtues, for he had lost the famished look of his Roman days, the braggart stoop and the cut-throat scowl, and was putting on fat, and his fat was a revelation. He now wore a countenance of good cheer, which manifested his virtue. Again and again Titian returned to that portly figure, breathing before him like a living boon, never satisfied that he had plumbed the secret of its broad bravura, its superabundant vitality, and its jovial aroma. He painted everything but the smell of the man. But the smell was the soul, and it was lush and elusive. In portrait after portrait the painter studied that imposing presence, so substantial and so hollow, and those brilliant eyes, so candid and sane but without questions or qualms, searching them for the soul of matter; for who could say that a man so triumphantly alive was soulless, or that, if he were hollow, that was not the ultimate truth of which he was the prophet? But he was baffled by his own genius. While the painter ennobled, the prophet glorified matter; and, when the sitting was over, the model became a mentor. Their tastes were congenial. Both loved generous wines and generous women, succulent food and succulent gossip, high living and low life; in the orbit of their favourite haunts the advent of one was invariably followed by the approach of the other; and over the table Aretino taught Titian. Lying back in jovial digestion, the prophet fathomed his mystery and divulged his virtue; and not merely his abandoned gestures and his honest eyes but his sanguine smell manifested his unquestioning faith that life was enough.

The soul and the flesh were one and indissoluble, but for the complete revelation of one the perfect satisfaction of the other was essential, and with such prodigal habits and an irregular income Aretino found it necessary to supplement the service of art with other resources. A day came when he reluctantly compromised with his principles and returned—temporarily—to the service of princes. Having determined on the step, he took it boldly. He wrote to Federico Gonzaga, proposing to immortalize him and his breed in an epic poem. He had no opinion of himself as a poet and less of Federico as a prince; but there was no need for Federico to know that. Those were trade-secrets. As a poet, he could always help himself to the *Orlando Furioso* of Ariosto, who had performed a like service for the Este and who was the poet he might have been, had he not been the prophet of Pasquino. Accordingly, he borrowed the title of his poem—*Marfisa*—and the general scheme in frank emulation of his purpose. The scheme was fabulous and bore only the most remote relation to reality; and as he drafted it, he realized that his idea was inspired. The *Orlando* was a supreme example of the romantic literature of escape, and he would improve on Ariosto with a mock-epic and confer on the Marquis a mock-immortality: in that medium the poet of Pasquino was a past-master. If ever a prince needed a poet, it was Federico Gonzaga, who had foiled Giovanni d'Italia; his inglorious neutrality cried for apotheosis, and it was with a calm conscience that Aretino reached for the laurels he had laid on the tomb of the hero. He was the poet his patron deserved; and there was no truth without hypocrisy.

Necessity never mothered a more useful invention. The Marquis snatched up the bait by return post. He burned to see the beginning and the end of his epic; and, though the bard laboured, spinning cantos so profusely that he was soon lost in their confusion, yet he laboured Penelope-like to ward off the suitor. Writing at a rate which outran his ideas, he was in no haste to be done, and, while he laboured, he lived at ease. The Marquis refused him nothing, he collaborated in every conceivable way. He sent him an amanuensis to sort and copy his cantos; he furnished a detailed genealogy of the Gonzagas; he supplied him with money, with damasks, with wines, with hampers of delicacies. He went further. Aretino remembered a lad in Mantua and begged the Marquis to sound him. The Marquis replied that, finding the youth reluctant, he did not feel it "decent or just to command him," and regretted his inability to oblige his poet; but, as it happened, he did him a service. Aretino then remembered a Mantuan lady by the name of Isabella Sforza, and this time he congratulated himself on the result and, turning over a new leaf, wrote:

> Be it known hereby and to everyone,
> How Isabella Sforza has converted
> Aretino, who was born perverted,
> Which St. Francis himself could not have done.

And the epic progressed.

With its progress, Aretino became sincerely inspired. Though his foot tapped the floor like a pedal as he laboured the Muse, he found a moral satisfaction in his drudgery. He was accomplishing his mission. The Marquis was a symptom of his generation, and the alacrity with which he accepted his bid for glory was not ludicrous, it was tragic. He craved what he needed. For this generation life was enough, and this meretricious glory. Sapped of religious faith, politically disrupted, dominated by the barbarian, Italy was demoralized; and the deepening despair of its society was manifest, like a phosphorescence of decay, in its lust for fame—fame, no matter how venal—fame at any price—fame however fictitious—an hour's fame before the night. And the Scourge of Princes was there to peddle it. He was fulfilling his function, and it was with the intimate satisfaction of a leech that he catered to his patron. He at least was true to himself, as he laboured like a Homeric humbug, only half-hearing under his tapping foot the steady lapping of the iridescent gutters of Venice; and only when the Muse slumbered did he smell them.

65

Then, suddenly, there was a hiatus. His pension stopped, and for eight months the Marquis neither wrote nor replied to his letters. There was no explanation; his patron was completely irresponsible; and Aretino was outraged. Just as he had won a foothold in Venice and was beginning to establish himself, the ground gave under his feet; not only his mission but his existence was endangered; and feeling himself slip toward the gutter he felt as fictitious as Federico Gonzaga. He protested, he complained, he wrote, he fumed, he sulked; and in vain. He threw up the epic, he resumed it, he dropped it resoundingly; but to no purpose. He threatened to emigrate, and, when he was ignored, he strode to the French ambassador and opened negotiations for a pension in France. Then his heart failed him. Whenever he passed through the port with its crowded shipping, his feet dragged; the plying ferries, the swarming gondolas, the argosies rocking on the lagoon, the pinnaces fleeting in the estuary, made him homesick; he muttered and made motions, but he knew that he would never embark. He preferred to perish in Paradise, even if he had chosen a fool's paradise. Life was enough in Venice, and elsewhere it was too much. He called a gondola and lounged on the buoyant heave of the watery floor and cursed his luck and counted the months he had wasted in the service of Federico Gonzaga, and suddenly he remembered that it was time for his Almanac. He compiled it overnight, and in the *Giudizio* of Pietro Aretino for the year 1529 there was no mention of the existence of a Marquis of Mantua. He sent it at once to the Mantuan ambassador with his permission "to copy and send it wherever he pleased"; and he enclosed the Gonzaga genealogy. "For my part, I consider any obligation and service I had with the Marquis broken, and in proof of this I am returning the genealogy of His Excellency," he informed him. "Tell him that I have changed my mind and do not dare to complete my poem in honour of a man who lets me starve, and that Pietro Aretino will never lack patrons." And having written that letter, he was overcome by its finality and felt as wretched as if he had left Venice.

Several weeks later the Mantuan ambassador visited his French colleague and found that the terrible gossip had preceded him. An incident ensued to which he felt it his duty to devote a detailed report. "Learning from various sources of the gossip and bluster of Pietro Aretino, and how he threatened to talk of all the princes of Italy when he went to France, and how he meant to avenge himself with his accustomed arms on His Excellency, who would afford him plenty of matter, and how he had already begun to nag his servants, saying much less than they deserved," he wrote, "I found the said Pietro in the house of the French ambassador with Count Guido and the ambassador of Florence. These gentlemen began to laugh and joke about what he had told them before my arrival. Besides the matters concerning Mantua, the Florentine envoy told me that the rascal had had the effrontery to boast that he was the cause of the dispute over the question of precedence between Mantua and Urbino, and that he had the power to injure me, which I knew to be a lie, since he had lost the good will of the Duke of Urbino ever since he wrote the sonnet beginning, *The Duke needs a wall for a corselet*. I called the said Pietro into the presence of Count Guido and the Florentine and said that I wished them to hear what I had to say to him. I told him that as long as he had spoken honourably of my master, I had honoured and loved him, but now that I heard he had decided to change his tone, he would forfeit my friendship, and as I had always befriended him with our Illustrious Lord so I would do the contrary now, and he would regret having offended a Marquis of Mantua. Hitherto, I added, I had persuaded myself that he had spoken of His Excellency under stress and because he loved him too well; but seeing him persevere in these provocations and abuse his friends and servants, I was forced to conclude that he meant what he said. To which he replied that he told the truth about his servants and friends, and that he would say whatever he pleased of His Excellency, since he had nothing to do with him now and was no longer recognized as his servant, and that no man could injure him, and that he was not afraid of His Excellency, and that by God he would continue to talk as he pleased. Then I told him that my master was in a position to injure him and anyone who dared to offend his honour, and that he did not show him the respect that was his due, and that if he did what he threatened, he might fare worse than he foresaw and would not be safe even in Paradise. And I turned my back on him in great anger, for we had been quarrelling for some time, and I moved away and began to talk to the French ambassador of other matters. But the said Pietro looked very dejected and alarmed by what I had said, and when I left the room he followed me and begged me not to write to my master what he had said, it all came of his love and jealousy, and he never meant to write or speak of him otherwise than with honour, as a Prince who deserved it, and from whom he had received many benefits, though not so many as he deserved, for he deserved too many for the poem he had made in his honour. I thanked him and exhorted him to persevere in his good sentiments."

The Marquis took an extremely serious view of the incident and threatened to suppress the said Pietro. This produced a startled gurgle by return post. "I am Pietro Aretino," it said, "your servant by nature, not by art, your bosom friend in burning affection and not in frigid bondage, and I remind you that if a tongue could wear out, mine would be threadbare by now with praising you, and that if your angelic goodness hates and despises me, it hates and despises your glorious self. No King, no Pope, no Emperor, but the Marquis of Mantua, incarnate in my soul, confounds me, not for fear of my life but for love of his great merits. And I kiss your hand, if I am still worthy to do so." "Your letter," the Marquis replied two weeks later, "and the stanzas of your *Marfisa*, in which you praise my House, have given me the greatest pleasure, and I have read them with the utmost delight. I cannot deny that to hear myself and my family extolled by such choice and cultivated talents as yours gratifies me, as I know that you have few equals and no superiors in the art of writing."

The ground was solid once more under his feet, but Aretino had suffered too much by the shock not to make his patron pay for it. He made him pay, in the first place, with a gown of black velvet, lined with gold cloth and trimmed with gold braid, a shirt, and a doublet of brocade, to celebrate their reconciliation. Next, he ordered, in return for these cast-off clothes, a damascened dagger of the most costly and exquisite workmanship, which would require six months to make, as a gift for the Marquis—"and perhaps," he warned him, "you will regard this as the most precious of all your precious possessions, if I am not completely bereft of judgment." The reckless generosity which he displayed, when he had the means to indulge it, was even more reckless when he lacked them, and he did not count the cost when it was a case of excelling His Excellency and making him pay for it. Once more the stanzas of *Marfisa* began to flow; once more he begged for an amanuensis, as he was buried in a litter of rhymes of which he could make neither head nor tail; but the poem bored him. He had passed through too bitter an experience. He was wasting his talents on Federico Gonzaga. Why should he not aim higher and enlarge the scope of his poem to embrace the Pope and the Emperor? Why should he not make it a monument to his own fame and a vehicle for recovering the favour of Rome? When the Marquis became impatient with his slow progress, he retorted by putting his patron to work. "Since I have worn myself out with such fervour, making a book that will leave an everlasting memory of you and your family," he wrote him, "Your Excellency must take the trouble to press the Pope for a Brief and the Emperor for a *Privilegio,* prohibiting the unlicensed printing of this book within their domains for the next ten years. These favours, Signore, are granted to anyone who asks for them and cannot be rightly refused to me, particularly as both His Beatitude and His Majesty are gloriously recalled in the poem." It was true, no doubt, that he had given the Pope some cause for complaint in the past but—"but though I have nipped him in idle chatter, in these compositions which will live I exalt him fervently, and since I hope to be rewarded, not by

Princes, but by the Press, I beg you not to deprive me of this profit, which is a small favour but of much importance to me. If you do not condescend to do me this service, or if Caesar or Peter are unwilling to grant it, I shall write twenty stanzas and lampoon them so properly that anyone who prints them will be excommunicated and ruined; so that Your Excellency will be doing a most pious deed in preventing such a scandal. I kiss your hands, and if I do not obtain what I ask, I shall say that my dagger, like all arms that are given, breeds enmity." The dagger brought an immediate response, the Marquis knew the meaning of *noblesse oblige*, and, as the eagerness with which the poet pressed for a copyright seemed to promise the speedy completion of the epic, he lent himself to the scheme and directed his ambassador at Bologna to broach the question to both sovereigns.

The moment was auspicious. The Pope and the Emperor had met in Bologna to settle the peace of Italy, and the Marquis was anxious that the general amnesty should include Aretino. A naturally amiable man, he hoped that a reconciliation might reform the malice of that bitter tongue. His ambassador reported, however, that "it is impossible to obtain anything for Aretino either from the Pope or the Emperor, because both say that, beside his past offences, he has recently written a Testament which is most insulting to both of them." When this reply reached the poet, he picked up the epic and carried it to the pawn-shop; then, his head still whirling, he dashed off a letter in which he vented his mortified feelings on the Marquis; and in exasperated confusion his humiliation, his pride, his injury, his rankling grievances and pent-up gall burst forth pell-mell with the headling effusion of a punctured bladder. Over and above all he rued one thing: "I never regretted anything so much as that I asked you this favour, and your ambassador will testify that he had already sent off my request, when I recalled it." As for the Testament, he had not written it, he knew who had, and "if it was not written by one who eats His Holiness's bread, I have crucified Christ." The copyright was nothing: "I may lose a few *scudi* by this refusal, but my glory is not subject to Briefs, and I can dispense with them." What mortified him was to be misunderstood. "I want no Briefs nor Privileges from anyone. They shall soon see who Aretino is. Genius is not subject to the pleasure or displeasure of princes. The Pope thinks that I deserve no favours; the world thinks I do. He knows very well that, when I was with him, he loved me, for I am a rare man and an honest one, and one day I trust he will open his eyes to my glory. Whatever happens, I am his servant. Continue to use whatever means you think proper, Your Excellency, to defend the innocence of your servant; if you find that I have written the Testament, cut me in a thousand pieces. I know who has written it, but I shall keep my mouth shut lest I be suspected of spite." But if he shut his mouth on one subject, he opened it wide on another. "*Signore mio*, you are not only courteous, you are lavish with everyone: how can you be so close with me who adore you? When will you give me bread? When I am dead? Is it nothing to you that a poem composed to glorify you and all who bear, have borne, or will bear your name, should have to be pawned for 200 *scudi* to buy the bread I have eaten in writing it? I tell you what all Venice knows and I thought, when I sent you the dagger, that you would give me enough to save me from shame, but my luck with you is even worse than with the Pope. I beseech you, send me, in my dire need, 50 *scudi*. You will save my life." Then the thought of the poem in pawn revived his fury. "By the body of St. Francis, if I had the book in my hands now, as I have not, I would burn it, if Your Excellency does not send me the moneys. But I know I shall have them, and I need them to pay a part of the debt on the dagger, which is worth more, by God, than you appreciate, and I doubt whether you would have suffered what I have suffered on account of it. One month from now I shall send you a saddle, the most stupendous thing that ever a King or an Emperor laid eyes on, and of more value in its kind than the dagger, and not even for this do I expect to receive so much as a shirt. May I lie in my gullet!" Licked, sealed, spitted, and slapped, the letter was already on its way when, with a final expectoration, he scribbled a postscript to the Mantuan ambassador: "Tell His Excellency that those who have seen my dagger and his gifts and compared them are no little amazed. Tell him the truth, that I have been much blamed, and that is no jest."

It was too late to murder him. The Marquis was at a loss. It was ridiculous to resent him. The colossal impudence, the outspoken calculation, the wheedling importunacy, the preposterous swagger and petulance of the man had the enormous and transparent candour of a child or a buffoon or an elementary natural force. One could not snub an aboriginal savage. He blunted rebuke. He was a moral primitive, whose cynical integrity made dignity, pride, delicacy, decency, meaningless and irrelevant. He was too disarming to murder, too irrepressible to reform, and too impervious to tame. There was only one alternative: to ignore him; but after ignoring him unsuccessfully for eight months, nothing remained for the Marquis but to humour him.

Aretino now realized, however, that he could not rely on the Marquis to reconcile him with Rome. About this time Giberti passed through

Venice. The poet sought him out, threw himself at his feet, and obtained his forgiveness for the past. Naturally, he was not satisfied with so little, and he immediately wrote to the Marquis, announcing the reconciliation and begging him to write a letter of congratulation to Giberti and to intimate how much he would appreciate some tangible recognition from Rome of the merits of his poet. The tact which Aretino displayed on this occasion did not surprise the Marquis; he had ceased to be surprised by anything which Aretino might do; the acquisitive sense of that aboriginal was capable of anything, even of acquiring delicacy; and, as Federico Gonzaga prided himself on his own tact, he was pleased to exercise it in behalf of his protégé, if only to show him how such things were done among civilized people. He did as he was bid and wrote Giberti a choicely worded letter, which he sent by special courier to Verona. Giberti replied with sly malice and without haste. "I am extremely gratified by the pleasure Your Excellency professes to take in my reconciliation with Messer Pietro, and by your condescending to consider it so important as to send me a courier expressly for that purpose. Being as I am your devoted servant, any little service of this sort will be agreeable to me, particularly one which you consider so great that henceforth I shall consider it such myself." When the Marquis read those words, he winced. An exquisite pang stung his civilized vanity; he had invited the snub by sponsoring a savage. Was it possible that Aretino had persuaded him to write that letter for the sole purpose of making him ridiculous? The Marquis went white at the thought; he suspected diabolical schemes everywhere; and he realized that his patronage of the poet was compromising him in the eyes of the world and that he was paying for his immortality with his dignity. His murderous instincts awoke. Then his eyes fell on the conclusion of Giberti's letter. In his own he had alluded very tactfully and even sympathetically to the attempt on Aretino's life in Rome. The wording was consummate—"while I believed that what you did against him was not done without good cause, yet I always hoped that your kindness and humanity would lead you to do what you have now done"—but even the refined vagueness of that reference seemed a blunder in the light of Giberti's reply. "There is a phrase in your letter which I cannot let pass," the Bishop wrote, "without begging you to rest assured that whatever was done against him was done without my command, my consent, or my knowledge; on the contrary, I was so shocked that, had I not been dissuaded by infinite requests, I would have made a much greater demonstration than I did." The Marquis hastened to apologize for seeming to misjudge him; but on second thought he decided that he had not misjudged him, after all. Giberti had merely learned, like himself, that, if the man could not be murdered, there was no alternative but to humour him; and consoled by that thought, he forgave the Bishop his snub.

With the poet, however, the Marquis became extremely guarded. He no longer alluded to his family epic; he no longer alluded to anything. At thirty, Federico Gonzaga was worn out with dissipation and almost a valetudinarian and, like an invalid, he began to care more for his comfort than his glory. He resigned himself to oblivion and found that, after all, it was perfectly comfortable. The poet, finding his patron unwilling or unable to promote his reconciliation with Rome, also lost interest in *Marfisa,* and began to cast about him for other protectors. In Venice he lacked influence, but he whistled and set to work. One thing he had learned: that, to arrive anywhere, it was necessary to begin, not at the bottom, but at the top. He began with the Doge. The Doge was pious, and to win his eye the chameleon creature once more changed colour. He had always advertised his contempt for the clergy, and it was repugnant to play the hypocrite, at least in public, but there was one priest in Venice whom he sincerely respected, and who stood high in the favour of the Doge. Pietro Vergerio was one of a little band of Catholic reformers, who hoped to stem the Lutheran menace by a judicious reform of the clergy. With these aims Aretino found it possible to sympathize, and he cultivated the reformer in private. But Aretino could conceal nothing, and Titian blinked at the change which came over his crony. Was this the man he had painted? Something was amiss. It was not his veracity, it was not his virtuosity, but his voluptuousness . . . He seemed to be ashamed of it. He had lost or mislaid his good cheer. Aretino blamed everything on his debts—he could not obtain credit—he expected "to die on a bridge." Titian cocked his eye and surveyed the soul of matter. Why was he starving himself? What did he expect to gain? The flesh and the soul were indissoluble. He deceived no one but himself by such austerity. Aretino shut his eyes and sighed. Even Titian misunderstood him. But he persevered. Pietro Vergerio was soon satisfied with his progress, and recommended him to the Doge; and the Doge consented to intercede for him with the Pope on condition that Aretino delete all abuse of His Holiness from his writings, and that he confess, communicate, and mend his life. The poet solemnly took the pledge.

In January 1530, the formal reconciliation of the Emperor and the Pope was solemnly celebrated in Bologna. It was an historic occasion.

The dove of peace hovered, a bedraggled bird, over the peninsula. In the Duomo of Bologna, which had witnessed so many such scenes, Clement VII placed the Iron Crown on the head of Charles V; the Emperor knelt, rose, and restored the Pope to his temporal dominions; and, as the Pontiff went through the feeble motions of a nominal sovereignty, Italy lapsed into a servitude which was to last from the Renaissance to the Risorgimento. It was a peace of exhaustion, and it was fittingly celebrated. The Pope was worn out by ill health, humiliation, and the terrible experience of the Sack; nothing remained but his magnanimity; and when, amid the general dispensation of honours and indulgences, a petition in behalf of Pietro Aretino was presented to him in the name of the Doge, he relented. He had lost his long memory in the Sack; he forgot everything connected with it; but there was only one way to forget Aretino. Accordingly, the Pontifical victim of the Pax Romana bestowed on the penitent poet of the *Pax vobis* his benediction, an Order of Knighthood, the coveted Brief for the *Marfisa*, and a promise of more substantial gifts to follow; and the Emperor followed suit with an Imperial Knighthood and the *Privilegio*.

Little pride as he had left, Clement still prided himself on not misplacing his bounties, and he was deeply relieved, therefore, by the letter in which Aretino acknowledged value received. "Your major-domo, the Bishop of Vasone," he wrote, "handed me the Brief here in the Palace of the Queen of Cyprus, and repeated what he was commanded to say: i.e., that you were not so amazed at rising to the Papacy from the rank of a mere Knight of Rhodes, or at being imprisoned when you were Pope, as you were by my flaying your good name, particularly as I knew why you did not punish a certain person for attempting my life. Holy Father, in everything that I have ever written or done my tongue has always been true to my heart, and in attacking your honour I have always protested that I was not to blame for taunting you. If those who have attained the summits of power and honour through you insulted you with spears, what wonder that I taunted you with tittle-tattle? Two things I repent and am ashamed of. I repent having censured a Pope whose glory was always dearer to me than life; and I am ashamed that, in censuring him, I did so in the depths of his afflictions. Now I thank God that He has relieved your soul of the bitterness of offence and mine of the sweetness of revenge. And in future I shall be your good servant as I was in the days when my virtue, fostered by your praise, fought for you against Rome when Leo vacated the See; and I will so conduct myself that the Serenissimo Gritti, whose perfect modesty has mediated between your patience and my rage, will have occasion to reward rather than to punish me."

Aretino was as good as his word. In Lent the Mantuan ambassador met him in church "with tears in his eyes and his confession in hand." In the dim light the poet had difficulty in reading it, but he studied it devoutly, and when he raised his eyes they were harrowing, and when he spoke his voice was husky. The ambassador was so amazed at the change that he immediately reported it to the Marquis. It was the event of the day in Venice. "He told me that he knew God would not forsake him, and that He would do him more good than he deserved, having been a great sinner, and that he had put an end to the life he was leading, being absolutely resolved to renounce his rancours and hatreds and the rest of his wicked ways, and that he was thoroughly contrite, and that he would confess and communicate with his whole household, which he had not done for many years." On learning of this reform, the Marquis also was relieved. He looked forward now to a little peace himself and did not begrudge the poet his Divine patron. No more was said, on either side, of *Marfisa*. It remained in pawn. Aretino was too busy living the poem of the pure in heart to remember his epic. It had served its purpose. It had brought him a contrite heart and a sincere conviction of the vanity of human glory, including his own, and his one concern now was to redeem his soul. It was still in pawn. He did not haggle with Heaven; he spent Lent communicating, confessing, dieting, mumbling, and mortifying himself; and, when he appeared once more in public, the Doge congratulated himself on having won a soul and rendered a public service to the City.

On a memorable afternoon in April 1530, in the Hall of the Grand Council in the Ducal Palace, Aretino publicly presented his soul to the Doge and the assembled Senate and acknowledged his debt to the City which had redeemed him. The gorgeous hall, fretted with gold, transfigured with frescoes, filled with ambrosial sun and the flickering shimmer of the lagoon, resounded to a grandiose harangue, which the poet pronounced with the sonorous serenity and the grandiose avowal of a man reading his naturalization papers in Paradise. "I who, in the liberty of this great state, have learned at last to be free, repudiate Courts for ever and here build the everlasting tabernacle of my advancing years; for here there is no place for betrayal, here the cruelty of harlots cannot rule nor the insolence of ganymedes, here favour cannot prevail over right, here there is neither theft nor violence nor murder. And therefore," he concluded his inaugural apostrophe, "I who have terrified the wicked and protected the good, give myself to you who are the fathers of your people, the brothers of your servants, the children of truth and friends of virtue, the comrades of strangers, the pillars of religion, the custodians of faith, the ministers of justice, the heirs of charity, and the subjects of clemency." Then with a sweeping and synonymous movement of fluent obeisance he turned to the Doge. "Illustrious Prince, gather my love in the lap of your compassion, that I may praise the nurse of all other cities and the mother elected of God to glorify the world, to moderate manners, and to give humanity to men, and to humble the proud, pardoning the erring. Such," he declared with a gesture which filled the room with a vast rhetorical fresco, "such is its privilege, to usher in peace and to end wars." Then his vision broadened and his pacific inspiration raised the roof. "Therefore the angels lead their dances and assemble their choirs and spin their wheels of light over the field of air above it, extending the ordinances of its laws and the length of its life beyond the terms prescribed by Nature. O universal fatherland! O common liberty! O station of the scattered! How much greater were the woes of Italy, were your goodness less! Here is the refuge of her peoples, the security of her riches, the safeguard of her honour; she embraces her when others abuse her; she supports her when others abase her; she welcomes her when others expel her and feeds her when others starve her and, cheering her in her tribulations, sustains her in love and charity." And associating himself with the celestial city and identifying himself with its destiny, he stood inhaling its sovereign independence and exhaling his own triumphant emancipation. "Be mute, O Rome, for here there are none who could or who would tyrannize over liberty!"

66

Pacific and sumptuous, Venice received and transformed Aretino. The mansuetude and magnificence of the maternal city, sprawling on the warless lagoon, mellowed him like the warm balm of a moral hothouse. His malevolence melted away as he basked in a glory and affluence that accrued every day. For now his fortune turned. His official recognition in Venice and his reconciliation with Rome consecrated his reputation and sanctioned his influence, and they began to assume, in the dying Renaissance, a prodigious development.

Two years before, he had leased the Palazzo Bolani on the Grand Canal. It was there that he starved, and in those days it was all he could do to live up to its front. A crowd at his door meant a special occasion— a gift of wine from Mantua, for instance. Such an occasion he recalled when, in weeding out his past correspondence with the Marquis, he came on a letter which he preserved, if only to compare the past and the present. Even then, he was pleased to observe, his old self had laughed at himself. "If I were known as a saint instead of a devil, or if I were the friend instead of the enemy of the Pope, people would conclude, seeing such a crowd at my door, either that I was working a miracle or that it was the Jubilee. And for this I have to thank your wine: no inn is as busy as my house, my servants fill the flasks of the servants of all the ambassadors in Venice from morning till night. . . . Wherever the world eats or sits or walks, all it talks of is my perfect wine, so that I am more known for my wine than for myself, and I should have been ruined had I not received this solemn vintage. And the little moisture it brings to the eye in drinking it makes me weep in writing of it." His eyes moistened as he reread himself, and with a pleasure more acute than any wine could cause. For now such scenes were an everyday occurrence, the jubilee was perpetual, the miracle a commonplace; and the affluence of visitors was such that his stairs were worn away, as he wrote to a friend, "like the pavement of the Capitol by the wheels of the triumphal chariots. I do not believe Rome, in a manner of speaking, ever saw such a mixture of nations as come to my house; I receive Turks, Jews, Indians, Frenchmen, Germans, Spaniards; as for our Italians, I leave you to imagine. Of the common people I say nothing. It would be easier to wean you from the Emperor than to find me for one moment without soldiers, scholars, friars, and priests around me. I seem to have become the oracle of truth, for everyone comes to tell me the wrong done to him by this prince or that priest; I have become the secretary of the world and I sign myself such in my letters."

How had this miraculous transformation come about? He had broached the solemn and inexhaustible vintage of human fatuity. Patrons multiplied about him, and they were satisfied with less than an epic— with a sonnet, a letter, a compliment, with anything that slaked the insatiable thirst of the age for praise and publicity. He no longer needed Federico Gonzaga, the world was full of his kind, and they came paddling

PIETRO ARETINO, by Titian
From the portrait in the Pitti Palace, Florence

into his canal and crowding through his door. He still corresponded occasionally with the Marquis. He sent him his compliments under glass—Venetian glass blown expressly for him. "This new design has so pleased the master glassblowers of the Serena that they name all the various things I have made there *Aretini*. The major-domo of the Pope has taken some to Rome and His Holiness, I hear, went into raptures over them; and that amazes me, for I thought that in Court they cared only for gold and not glass, as I know Your Excellency also believes. I am your servant." He sent him snatches of *Marfisa*. "Your Excellency asks for some trifle to fan yourself in the great heat of these days. I send you the stanzas composed in honour of the Gonzaga genealogy. They are what they are and I have no weakness for my brain children; as for my opinion of the book as a whole, I refer you to my secretary—the fire." The fire was metaphorical but his opinion was a fact. After another quarrel with the Marquis their relations ended; he made some minor alterations in the epic and disposed of it at second-hand to a patron whose name alone entitled him to it, the Marchese del Vasto.

Aretino knew where his real genius lay. He was composing his reputation, and that was vaster, more fabulous, and more poetic than any poem. He was persuading the world to accept him at his own valuation; and that ambition, common to every man but realized by few, fulfilled a universal dream and was itself a poetic achievement, for which the world envied and honoured him. He was the poet of human conceit and he realized a universal desire by flattering it. His own reputation rested on the common craving for fame. He capitalized and exploited it; he created and controlled public opinion; he dispensed censure and honour and made and unmade reputations; and his clients in turn accepted and spread and created his own credit. He was the lawgiver of the vainglory of life. What poem was as poetic as that mere fact? Nor was that all. Though his reputation rested on nothing more solid than puff, he lived on it. His palace was crowded, like the shrine of a miracle-monger, with admirers bringing tribute. He was emancipated from ordinary necessities. He was converting Venice into an Earthly Paradise. In the celestial city he lived on the love of his neighbour, giving and receiving, instead of the hard barter and sinful sweat of the common lot, the voluntary exchange of free gifts and the noble commerce of mutual admiration. He was eliminating from life the root of all evil—competition. He filled the heart of humanity with a new hope, the old hope the race left behind it in Eden, the lost hope of living on nothing. The feat was extraordinary and he was unique; but he had proved that it could be done; and for that service alone he was pensioned as a pioneer, supported as a prophet, and applauded as a poet.

He became the rage. Fashions are ephemeral, but in the ephemeral he found immortality, and his vogue spread. It ran throughout Italy, throughout Europe, and even beyond—the Bashaw of Algiers and the corsairs of the Barbary coast sent him tribute—it spanned the four points of the compass without breaking; it lasted with the tenacity of a legend which Time could not stale, and of a superstition which it could not explode. That a fame founded on puff, maintained by fugitive correspondence, and warranted neither by talent, service, nor accomplishment, should not eventually have palled on its public, may well have appeared an inexplicable mystery with the passage of time, but time held the secret which explained his fascination—his living presence, his magnetic personality. He was supremely *simpatico*. He had the exuberant spontaneity, the quick responsiveness, the facile and expansive charm of his popular origin, heightened by a brilliant gloss of worldly manner which went with his wardrobe. Success, far from spoiling him, mellowed and brought out his innate geniality. His malice was skin-deep and he reserved it for professional purposes. He bit the hand that did not feed him, but he left no scar that could not be licked and healed. His temper, his petulance, his impatience, his pugnacity, were as effervescent as a child's and passed with the occasion that provoked them; and now, with the world at his feet, his jovial spirits shone forth, unclouded. He was natural; he put everyone at his ease; and it was impossible to doubt, in the company of that irresistibly human creature, that Nature was not sound when it was satisfied. Above all, his zest for life was infectious; he communicated it to an ever-growing public which craved it and which besieged the bubbling spring, clamouring for more and more. His charm could only be felt fully at first hand; yet such was its vigour and exuberance that it overflowed into his letters which remained still warm, after the passage of time, with the tingling sparkle of personal intimacy. And it was his intimacy which made him immortal. He was one of the first to discover the appeal of the personal, the dignity of the familiar and trivial, the significance of the everlasting detail of life. He opened the eyes of his readers to the little unconsidered obvious things which they saw without seeing, and which he revealed by his relish in reporting and reliving them. Conducting his life in a blaze of publicity, he made copy of it; he took the world into his confidence, assuming that whatever interested him must interest it, and rightly, for nothing human was alien to him. And this was the real service he rendered to his generation. Under the bluff and the hollow vainglories, the prophet proclaimed that life was enough.

And certainly in Venice, in those palmy days of the sixteenth century, life was enough; it only needed eyes to see it; and he had the vision. From his window he commanded a view of the Grand Canal and its multifarious life on which he gloated, and his one regret was that, with all his visitors, he still had numberless and unknown neighbours who would never see what he saw. One day that thought was too much for him and he snatched his pen and wrote an open letter to his landlord, who probably did not appreciate it either, for the poor man was born in Venice. "I should think it a sin of ingratitude, gentle sir," he preluded, "if I did not repay with praise a part of my debt to the divine site on which your house is built and where I dwell with the utmost pleasure in life, for it is set in a place which neither hither nor thither nor higher nor lower could better. Certainly, whoever built it gave it the most proper and pre-eminent place on the whole Grand Canal, and, as this is the patriarch of all avenues and Venice the Pope of all cities, I may truthfully say that I enjoy the most beautiful street and the most delightful view in the world. I never go to the window but I see thousands of people and as many gondolas going to market. The *piazze* to my right are the Beccarie and the Pescaria; on the left, the Bridge and the Fondaco dei Tedeschi; while, facing them both, rises the Rialto, crowded with traders. Here I see boats full of grapes, game and birds in the shops, and kitchen gardens on the pavements. Rivers and irrigated fields I no longer care to see, now that I can watch the water at dawn covered with every manner of thing that is in season. It is a joy to study the bearers of this grand plenty of fruits and greens and to watch them dispensing them to the porters who carry them to their stalls. But all this is nothing to the sight of twenty or twenty-five sail-boats, heaped up with melons like a little island, and the multitude thronging about them to reckon and weigh and smell their beauty. Of the beautiful housewives shining in silks and gold and jewels, and seated proudly under the poop, I will say nothing, lest I slight their pomp. But I will say that I hold my sides when I listen to the boatmen shouting, jeering, and roaring at those who are rowed by lackeys without scarlet hose. And what man could hold his water if he saw, as Giulio Camillo and I saw, a boatload of Germans upset in the dead of winter, just as they came out of a tavern? Giulio is a wag and he says that the side-door of this house, being dark, narrow, and brutal to climb, is like the terrible name I have made for myself by venting the truth; but he adds: anyone who knows me finds in my pure, frank, and natural friendship the same calm contentment that he feels when he comes out on the portico of my palace and leans on my balcony. Moreover, to add to the delight of my eye, here are the orange groves that gild the base of the Palazzo dei Camerlinghi on one side, and on the other the *rio* and bridge of San Giovanni Grisostomo; and the winter sun cannot rise without saluting my bed, my study, my kitchen, my chambers, and my hall.... In sum, if I could satisfy touch and the other senses as I satisfy sight, the house would be a heaven, for I enjoy every recreation here that can please the eye. Nor must I forget the great gentlemen, both foreign and native, who pass my door, nor my heavenly rapture when the Bucentaur goes by, nor the regattas, nor the festivals which convert the Canal into a continual triumph for my eye, which is lord of all it surveys. And what shall I say of the lights which appear in the evening like scattered stars? Or of the night music which tickles my ear with sweet harmonies? It would be easier to describe your profound judgment in letters and public affairs than to exhaust the delights that I enjoy merely in gazing. Therefore, if there be any faint breath of talent in the trifles I have written, I owe it to the influence, neither of shadow nor of light nor yet of verdure nor of violets, but to the joy I feel in the airy felicity of your mansion, in which may God grant me to number, in vigour and health, the years a respectable man may hope to live."

The lust of the eye was the first revelation of his gospel. He saw and he made others see by the graphic gift of a pen which translated the vision instantaneously; and the vision in Venice was so entrancing that the puzzle of life seemed to be solved merely by sitting at a window and watching it drift by. Life was a puzzle to those who lived it and a pattern to those who watched it; and all its miseries were no more, maybe, than the aberrations of misguided ambitions and the delusions of sealed senses. It needed so little to enjoy it, and *gaudeamus* was the secret of goodness. Life was simple and good, when it was lived sanely and sensually; but it was perpetually distorted, wantonly and perversely, by the pernicious illusions of human conceit—glory, ambition, honour, achievement visionary ideals which faded like vapours amid the visual virtues of Venice. There the insinuating and hourly circulation of water passed like a pervasive current of oblivion amid the life and handiwork of man, isolating and intensifying their substantial realities. Sometimes that lingering basement of oblivion troubled Aretino; there were hours when sickness or solitude undermined his vitality; but he had only to open his window to recover his unclouded Venetian view of life. "My dear gossip," he wrote on one such evening to Titian, "having in contempt of my custom supped alone, or rather in company of this tedious fever which lets me relish no food, I rose from table, surfeited with the despondency with which I sat down to it. And resting both arms flat on the window-sill, and leaning my whole body on it, I abandoned myself to the marvellous spectacle of the multitude of boats.... And when the crowds had dispersed, I, like a man weary of himself and with nothing to occupy his mind, raised my eyes to the heavens which, since God made them, were never so lovely with light and shadow. The atmosphere was such as men like myself, who envy you because they cannot be you, would render it. First, the buildings in the foreground, although of stone, seemed to be of some plastic material; and beyond them you beheld the air, in some parts pure and alive, in other murky and sallow. Fancy, too, how I marvelled at the clouds, dense with moisture, lying half in the foreground over the roofs and half in the gloaming, for on the right everything was a *sfumato* darkening down into grey-black. I was spellbound by the variety of hues they revealed. The nearest burned with the embers of the sunset; the farthest glowed with a dimmer, leaden hue. Ah, how beautifully the hand of Nature hatched the air, making it fade and recede from the palaces, as Titian does in his landscapes! Here was a blue-green and there a green-blue, truly conceived by the caprice of Nature, that master of masters! She melted and modelled with light and shadow in a manner which made me exclaim more than once: O Titian, where are you? Upon my word, if you had painted what I report, you would confound men with the wonder that astounded me; and in gazing on what I have told you I nourished my soul on it, for the wonder of such paintings does not endure."

The other senses nourished his soul as benignly and he glorified them as eloquently. He composed a whole series of epistles to the Venetians in praise of the table, spending hours of delicious gustation in the recollection and anticipation of food, rhyming it with the Rational Good, and relishing it not only with the palate but with the hand, the eye, the nose, and even the ear. The sound of "that *laf-lof* when the scullions are slapping the batter" immediately thickened his tongue; the feel and form of certain viands intoxicated him; and the smell of new bread augured the goodness of the world. The arrival, one winter's day, of a batch of thrushes set him singing the Franciscan *inter aves* twice over; and as for Titian, the birds blushed for him, as Aretino wrote to the giver: "While the table was being laid, our Messer Titian, seeing and sniffing them on the spit, glanced out at the snow which was falling most unfeelingly, and ditched a crowd of gentlemen who expected him to dinner. And we all praised the bird of the long beak which, boiled with a little dried meat, two leaves of laurel, and a pinch of pepper, we ate for love of you, and because we liked it."

It was a pleasure, it was a privilege, to feed a man who appreciated food as he did; it was a profit, too, as his publisher found; in return for the first and last fruits of the season he received some of the most eloquent letters that ever passed through his presses. "Surely, my good friend, if I plumed myself on my surname of DIVINE as every pedant would do, I should undoubtedly believe (since it was the custom of the ancients to offer their Gods the first fruits of the earth and of their flocks) that I am, if not a demi-God, at least a third of a one, since I am tempted to that fancy by the endless little gifts you make me of the first fruits that issue from bountiful Nature and Art. Recognizing, however, that my meagre merit dilutes my divinity, lest it go to my head, I credit your gifts to your being too kind. You begin by whetting my appetite with orange blossoms, which you mingle, like my servants, with pimpernel, catnip, dandelion, and a hundred or more herbs and send them in little baskets and hampers so well woven of reeds, that I am bound to take the baskets and hampers along with the salads; and your good lady will make such an outcry in not having them back as my girls do in the delight of keeping them. I do not know where you find the variety of flowers, violets and pinks, which you send me, fragrant and blowing, long before they have begun to bud elsewhere. Behold, oh, behold me, with these bunches of mammoth violets long before April: behold me with my lap full of roses, when a rose would be a miracle anywhere else! And what shall I say of these tender little almonds that I dote on like a pregnant woman? Hardly have the cherries begun to puff their red cheeks before you send me the ripe ones to sample. And where shall I place the strawberries, dotted with natural grain and native musk? And the limes, which were hardly in bloom, and the sight of which made Perina and Caterina dance for joy? Who would not drink in a beaker so shining and new? Who would not grease his beard and lather his hands with the soaps and oils you send me so often? Who would not pick his gums with your tooth-picks? I will wager anyone that I was the first to see the figs of the year, plucked in your garden, and will be the first to suck the muscadel pears, the apricots, the plums, the melons, the grapes, and the peaches. But where shall I bring in the artichokes that have graced my table so unseasonably? And where the squash that I ate fried, when I would have sworn they had not a leaf to their name yet? And because in all that you have given me I have seen your heart, I hold your gifts in the core of my heart. And this will follow, and soon: every tuft of violets, the red and the white and the yellow, with which you have charmed and cheered me, I will repay as they deserve."

A sentimental epicure, he was as sensitive to a slight in a salad, and repaid it as promptly, as to a courtesy; for salads were the one field of knowledge in which his taste was sure and despotic. He abhorred citronel; and, when one of his admirers insisted on ignoring his aversion, Aretino lost patience and read him a lecture on the whole subject. The herb left a bad taste in his mouth, and what would not down must come out. "Men wonder why enmities arise among men. Here is the answer: two blades of this grass, which you cannot keep from sending me, and I cannot keep from throwing away. Be so good therefore as to send me the tribute imposed by your courtesy, so that I may enjoy the fruit of the seeds that you sow in March in the tender soil for the profit of hucksters and traders. Fortunio will tell you how I love them and praise them and welcome your dole of mixed greens and the servant who brings them. I observe how you mix the tart and the tender. And no little knowledge is needed to temper the bitter and sharp tang of some leaves with the savour, neither bitter nor sharp, of others, making a compound so smooth that satiety itself would taste of it. The tiny flowers strewn in the green of these good and beautiful herbs whet my hunger; and their beauty tempts my nose to smell and my hand to touch them. In short, if my cooks knew how to season them *alla genovese,* I would forsake the breasts of the wild grouse which again and again, for dinner and supper, to the glory of Cadore, I receive from our incomparable Titian. I forget what pedant it was who, scowling at a salad you sent me the other day, tried to celebrate lettuce and endive, herbs without odour, which Priapus, god of gardens, wroth with them himself, determined to exterminate like vermin; for a mere clump of wild radish with a bit of cat-mint is worth more than all the lettuce and endive in the world; and indeed I marvel that poets do not unlace and sing the virtues of this salad. And we do a great wrong to religion not to praise it, for friars and nuns steal time from their prayers to pick out the sand, and waste hours, like wet-nurses, in washing and dressing it. It was a Florentine, I believe, who invented it. It must be so, for the setting of the table and laying it with roses, the rinsing of glasses, the plums in stews, the millet puddings, the dressing of kidneys, and the fashion of serving fruit after meals, all come from

Florence; and their neat little, fleet little brains have subtly foreseen everything that can foil a spoiled appetite. Tomorrow, therefore, may I return to the favour of your life-giving gardens!"

In a world without citronel, in a world without spite, in Venice, where virtue was easy, his virtue expanded magnificently. He gave with a prodigality on which he prided himself, returning the tribute he received with the redundant generosity of the class which he had scaled. It was his patent of nobility. "One must be born to it," he wrote to the Cardinal de Lorraine. "One must bear the nobility of great blood, like yours, from birth. What generosity can one of these artisans have, who have reached your dignity by money or luck? What manners, what civilities, what princely qualities, can we expect of traders and plebeians? What is more meritorious than to help your neighbour? How much do those who can give owe Heaven? The pleasure of giving is incomprehensible, I am mute." He gave in every conceivable way and from every imaginable motive—for show, for charity, for speculation, for malice—to patrons who paid and repaid his advances—to the poor who haunted his kitchen, to beggars who dogged his passage—to princes in need of publicity—to priests whose niggardliness he never tired of shaming: "to give like a priest" was his favourite taunt. He gave gladly, bitterly, recklessly, shrewdly, compassionately, ostentatiously, and always immoderately, ruining himself over and over. Horses, jewellery, armour, art, passed through his hands unreckoned, like bangles and sequins; and even flattery, the staple of his trade, he dispensed freely, with a genuine pleasure in gratifying and indulging an appetite as native to the mind as concupiscence to the senses. He avowed it as frankly as he did the lusts of the flesh, without false shame, with an immense fellow-feeling, and with perfect simplicity. "I know not what pleasure misers have in the sound of their gold, but I do know that to the ears of the enlightened no music is so sweet as the sound of their own praise, and they feed on it, as the souls in Heaven feed on the face of God. We rise from the world whenever we hear our name glorified, and are transported beyond mortality when it is sung." Why deny it? It was natural and, being natural, could not be mean. The passion for reputation, however venal and unmeaning, was at least lip-service to the ghost of a moral ideal. His ear was enlightened, like his eye. He was no longer the "censor of the proud world": he belonged to it.

Whatever his failings, they did not include those of the snob: his heart was with his own people, and the humble and needy kept him a beggar in the plenitude of prosperity. "On receipt of the five hundred *scudi*, I made out a quittance," he wrote to one of his patrons. "And for your information I add: since Your Excellency keeps me in a rage with writing you so often, I claim and exclaim, *the pension! the pension!* hoping with these complaints to have it doubled. A thousand times this sum would not be enough for my needs, for everyone runs to me with his own, as if I were the heir of the royal treasury. If a poor girl gives birth, my house pays the expenses. If a man goes to jail, I have to provide for everything. Soldiers that are sore in harness, and pilgrims in distress, and all sorts of vagabond cavaliers, come to me for shelter. And no one falls sick without sending for my apothecary and for my physician to heal him. Not two months ago a young man, who was wounded not far from my house, had himself carried into one of my rooms, and, when I heard the disturbance and saw the fellow lying half-dead, I said: 'I knew that my house was an inn, but not a hospital.' Do not wonder, therefore, if I cry that I am constantly dying of hunger. It is true that, if my servants had not stolen hundreds and thousands from me I do not know how many times, I would keep cool. But what of it? Why do we accumulate money? Lie low, lucre, I am satisfied to live, as everyone knows I live, without greed of gold." Born in a public hospital—how often had that taunt been flung at him!—at the zenith of his splendour he continued to live in one. His house was a public infirmary for broken bones, broken hopes, ruined women, ruined reputations, and he ministered to every form of material and moral distress, relieving what he could with comfort and what he could not with illusions. The magical ease with which he had achieved power gave him the reputation in the popular imagination of a thaumaturge who could accomplish everything. He did what he could to live up to it. He lent a helping hand not only to struggling artists, scholars, and poets, but to moral reformers. The Catholic Reform Movement, which was attempting to counteract the attacks of the Lutheran schism, was beginning to meet with official censure and persecution; and he numbered several of its leaders, notably Pietro Vergerio, among his personal friends and was always ready to put in a good word for them, partly in order to rail at Luther, the "Arch-Pedant," and partly in order to protest against the atrocious pedantry of persecution in the name of Christ. "Who has ever been improved by persecution?" he wrote in defence of one of these reformers. "Christ, so far as we know, in His humanity, left no prisons nor wheels nor ropes nor flames to torture those who, if they have misread His laws, confess their error. He punishes with mercy all those who cry, *Miserere!*" Though his influence on public questions was small, he used it to the full to promote tolerance and to testify to the only religion he recognized. "The Christ who has so often saved me from death for some great end of His own, will always be with me, because I keep His truth alive, and because I am not Peter but a miraculous monster of mankind." And was it not true? His only monstrosity was his enormous humanity, which made that of normal men seem stunted and mean. Whenever he sat down to table—that table where the waters of Venice were miraculously transmuted into wine—whenever he relieved need, whenever he glorified life and moved others to adore it, he was ministering to humanity and keeping alive the truth of Christ; his very being was an act of thanksgiving to his Maker. And was that not the purpose for which he had been providentially preserved? Venice had matured him; the pacific and sumptuous city had ripened his last meaning; and he could keep it a secret no longer. Amid the claims of an enormous correspondence, he took thirty days to celebrate his faith and issued a grateful and gratuitous meditation on *The Humanity of the Son of God.*

67

The passage of time slowly consolidated his fame, like the passage of the tide accumulating the sandy foundations of the city, and fused it with that of Venice itself. He personified the city and it perpetuated him. Meditating one day on the amazing multiplication of his name, he wrote to a friend: "By the pinions of Pegasus, I declare that, much as you have heard, you have not heard half the hymn of my fame. I have already repeated and I repeat that, beside medals of coin, putty, gold, silver, copper, lead, and stucco, I live in effigy on the fronts of palaces, I am stamped on comb-cases, on the handles of mirrors, and on plates of majolica, like Alexander, Scipio, and Caesar. Moreover, I inform you that at Murano some kinds of glassware are named *Aretini*; and *Aretina* is the name of a race of colts. *Rio Aretino* they have named the lane that bathes one side of my house on the Grand Canal, and to spite the pedants yet more, not only do they speak of an *Aretine* style, but three of my wenches and chambermaids, who have left me and become ladies, still call themselves *Aretine*." He was a fetish, a charm, a superstition of fashion. The lick of the water under his window, a long lap, lap, lap, like the pulse of his heart, a slow clap, clap, clap, was a regular rhythm of plaudit; and its redundancy never palled, though through it he heard the noiseless circulation of the oblivious lagoon and the monotony that is the immortality of the nameless. The morrow might come, the day was enough; and he laughed and rewrote the letter, with a slight variation: "Laugh with me at the pleasure I feel in seeing myself in medals and cases and combs between Alexander and Caesar. Laugh, I say, and remember the day you scolded my wenches for calling themselves *Aretine*. For my part, I do not believe my name will die out so soon, for I have some fame even in the gutter. I am declaimed by quacks, I sponsor tales that would never sell otherwise, I am pleased even by the legends that she-poets invent against me. I am delighted because the mean think themselves somebodies by quarrelling with me. Meanwhile, my shekels run into the thousands, while they stand by like a Niccolo Franco. . . ." Niccolo Franco, Niccolo Franco. That name gave him pause. It jarred the even digestion of his glory and interrupted for a moment the regular pulse of terraqueous plaudits. Niccolo Franco was his past.

One day his door was darkened by a famished scholar with a look so lean and cadaverous that he reminded Aretino of his vagabond days, and in compassion the poet fed, clothed, and put him to work as a secretary. The man knew Latin, Greek, and theology, and for thirty days his erudition was useful—the thirty days during which he looked up sources and translated texts for his master's *Meditation on the Humanity of the Son of God*. After that his erudition became impertinent. Aretino was about to bring out a collection of Letters. In ten years he had written two thousand, but when he looked up his files only one hundred copies remained. He sat down and rewrote ninety in six weeks, filled in the gaps with duplicates and dedications, threw up his hands, gasped, and gave out. To Niccolo Franco fell the labour of arranging the result for the press and, judging the Aretine style by Aretino's manifest ignorance of Latin and Greek, he proceeded to amend it. His efforts were overlaid by those of the printers, so that, when the book appeared in a medley of misprints and cruel corrections, Aretino groaned. "The errors of printers," he noted for a later edition, "are like the sins of the clergy, and truly it would be easier to find Rome sober and chaste than a correct book."

Nevertheless, the success of the book was enormous; the editions, tumbling from the presses, could not keep pace with the demand; and the furore in Venice was fanned by the frenzy in the provinces. "Never at the opening of the Rota in Rome," one of his correspondents wrote him from Fano, "have I seen such competition among the pleaders pushing in as here at the sale of your book. When a bulletin announced *The Letters of the Divine Messer Pietro Aretino,* people immediately flocked about with such jostling and hubbub that I was reminded of the charity dispensed in some cities to the poor in hospitals on Maunday Thursday." The one person who kept his head in this craze was Aretino himself. He abandoned the profits of the book to his publisher. "God willing, the courtesy of princes shall pay my labour of writing and not the poverty of those who buy me. Let him that loves profit turn merchant," he wrote to his editor, "and, plying the book trade, renounce the name of poet. God forbid that so low a traffic should be the trade of my generosity. A pretty business it would be if I, who spend a treasure every year, were to imitate a gambler who keeps a hundred ducats in his cupboard and then beats his wife for not filling the lamps with fried grease." As for the glory . . . he cast about him for a confessor. "If it were not like cutting off the heads of Hydra, my brother," he wrote to an eminent scholar, "I should want to burn all that I have ever written. I open my mouth and out come some feeble phrases and unprofitable words, and I mark the paper with ink like the white walls of a tavern smudged with charcoal by those who take pleasure in defacing them. It is only lately, I admit, that I have come to know myself. And to prove it, I have disowned everything I have written so far and have begun to learn how to write. My excuse must be that Fortune, which has always been my enemy, has compelled me to earn my bread by the sweat of my pen, my nature being such that I would not have condescended to earn it in any other way. And I assure you that I deserve your favour and that of other learned men, because I know that I know nothing. Modesty is my hidden virtue."

Aretino knew his value better than anyone, and best of all when he depreciated it. He was a journalist and, though he envied the scholar, he was too sensible to spoil his style by schooling it. Its vigour could not be pruned with impunity. Whatever the flaws of the Aretine manner, they were inseparable from its virtues. Hasty it might be, diffuse, trivial, and prolix, but its nervous gusto and graphic naturalism were lively, and he realized the value of his gifts when he attempted to teach others. They could not be imparted; to write as he did it was necessary to live as he did, greedily, recklessly, freely, fully. But he had his disciples—the poor poets whom he employed as secretaries and supported as prentice parasites—and in teaching them he stumbled on his own definition of good writing. "Work as a sculptor of senses and not as a miniaturist of words." He wrote with his thumb, and he thumbed his nose at purists and pedanta, and particularly at Niccolo Franco, for whose benefit he formulated his creed:

"Go to Nature and study her habits, if you wish your writings to astound the very pages on which they are written, and laugh at those who steal hollow phrases, for there is a vast difference between imitators and thieves, and thieves I have always blamed. Look at a nurse suckling a child, see how she slips her nipple into its mouth, how she moves its feet and teaches it to walk, how she lends her smile to its eyes, her words to its lips, and her gestures to its motions until, as the days pass, Nature develops its own aptitudes. This is how a student should study the poets and, taking only the breath of their spirit, develop the music of his own organs. I tell you again, poesy is nothing but a delightful lunacy of Nature and its virtue lies in its own frenzy; without song it is a tambourine without bells and a bell-tower without chimes. The man who writes without being born to write is cold pumpkin. If you doubt it, solve me this: with all the industry of patient avarice, alchemists have never yet produced gold, while Nature, without effort or thought, breeds it beautiful and pure. Learn from the painter who, when he was asked whom he imitated, pointed to a group of men, meaning that he drew his models from life and truth, as I draw mine in speaking and writing. Nature, of whose simplicity I am the secretary, dictates what I compose, and my native speech unties my tongue when it twists itself up in superstitious knots and foreign jargons. And unquestionably I imitate myself, for Nature opens up to us like the broad hussy she is, and Art is the louse that must tickle her. Work, then, as a sculptor of senses and not as a miniaturist of words."

And how had Niccolo Franco repaid this lesson? Young, poor, pushing, and a parasite on a parasite, he paid his master the tribute of a rank imitation and produced an epic of witless and alembicated filth, modelled on *La Marfisa Errante,* which he named *La Putta Errante.*[1] Aretino laughed indulgently—the fellow was young and Nature had only begun to open up to him—and he boosted the reputation of the novice in Venice. With the success of the *Letters,* however, worse ensued. Niccolo Franco completely lost his head. If a mere collection of Letters reaped such remuneration and glory, of what use were Latin and Greek and education and art? He shed his impedimenta and plunged. He borrowed money and brought out on spec a volume of *Vulgar Epistles.* Then Aretino flinched. They were a studious imitation of his own, and they were

---

[1] The Wandering Whore.

dull, stilted, and lifeless. But the feeble copy was like a flawed glass, which distorted a recognizable image, and there was a truth in the travesty which made Aretino tremble. Indignation overcame him, and disgust. Was that he? Suddenly Franco loomed before him like the ghost of his old self, assassinating his self-esteem, exposing and mortifying him, degrading and dragging him down in abysmal discouragement. Niccolo Franco was the gutter, he reminded him of the slime stealthily undermining the foundations of the implausible city and his own incredible fame. His vainglory Aretino laughed at, but the *Letters* were his real self, he was jealous of his one modest achievement, and the wretched imitation was just good enough to appal him. Surely, there was a difference; his own *Letters* were not lifeless, they were not dull; but he could not be sure. Only the world could decide. But he dared not appeal to the public; the verdict was too vital; and he trepidated like a throttled organ in the Palazzo Bolani, and all the walls trembled, and all the windows rattled.

It was a serious fright; but the public vindicated him. The *Epistles* fell flat and Franco was ruined. Then his imitations took a more personal turn. He lampooned the Divine Aretino up and down Venice as an ignoramus, a quack, and a blackguard. In Ca' Aretino there were indignation meetings, and the water boiled about its door. A champion emerged. Ambrogio degli Eusebii was a secretary who handled a stiletto as well as a pen and, meeting Franco on the street, he made a pass at him which left an indelible scar on his face. This attack precipitated another. On learning of it, Aretino threw up his hands, once in gratitude and once in regret, and brought them down on a large clean sheet of paper. He was alarmed by the relief which he felt; it revealed how deeply Franco had wounded him; and to rid himself of so mean a satisfaction, he wrote out his version of the affair and appealed to the world to judge between them. The throttled organ was released, the pedals pumped, and the hands travelled over the paper in a vast sustained wheeze. "I have known mad, insolent, envious, malignant, unjust, spiteful, obstinate, arrogant, villainous, ungrateful men, but such folly, insolence, envy, malice, injustice, vanity, obstinacy, arrogance, and villainy as his—never!" The finality of that phrase left him exsufflicate. But Franco was merely fleshed; to finish him more than a scratch was needed—a vocabulary; and, puffing like a porpoise, Aretino filled himself with compendious wind to deplore and condone with official compunction the conduct of his champion. "Ambrogio has left an everlasting memory of the edge of his dagger on his face; while I regret the manner in which he has served me, yet charity in this case would be an offence to mercy, of which he is unworthy." With his wind he recovered his dignity and with his vocabulary his composure; and he proceeded to recapitulate the whole painful story of his relations with Franco. "The poor wretch stumbled into this divine city and, air being more abundant than bread here, sent me word that if I would accept him as a slave he would serve me as such. To tell the truth, if he had not thrust himself on me with the presumption of those who assault fame, prodigal though I am, I should have been miserly with him. Be that as it may, his good luck and my bad fortune lodged him with me, not only for dinner and supper, but so snugly that one brother could not have asked more of another, nor a son of his father. And one of my wenches would have burst if she had not cried: 'My master who entertains great gentlemen is running a poorhouse,' for he was the leanest and shabbiest pedagogue that ever sucked soup. But in a month Niccolo was unrecognizable. 'Lice,' quoth he, 'be off now and sleep.' And well might he say so, for I had clothed him like a gentleman. The vulgar said I gave the wretch more than he merited, seeing his velvet bonnet and his velvet shoes. No sooner did that personification of a hack know that he had no more to fear of necessity than he began to perform stunts with his sonnets; and when I looked them over and said, 'To my mind, you might sign four or five of these,' he flushed to the roots of his hair and declared that all his sonnets were perfect and that Petrarch himself could not appreciate their perfection. I said nothing and let the boor rumble on, for it is more polite to put up with an offence under one's own roof than to punish it." What followed, however, filled him with such disgust that he could not bring himself to name Franco; and he finished in a fury of circumlocutions which exhausted his ingenuity in inventing synonyms for a man who was now no more than a smear. "Then the sodomite, instead of writing my letters, took to emulating them and made a book of which not a single copy was sold, and which ruined the Frenchman who loaned him the money to print it. I do not deny that he outdid me in the title, the size, the style, the fine paper, the illustrations, and advertising of his book, but not in its humanity. *Ecco!* The backbiter turns on me and rips me, in return for my defiling my pen by naming the blackguard. I thank you for saying that the praise I wasted on him redounds to the credit of my goodness and not to the defect of my judgment. Certainly, it pleases me to praise my acquaintances, even though I rue it as I rue puffing this swindler; but compassion is the core of my soul. Imagine a desert and you will have the image of my long-suffering kindness and the proof of my great liberality; but as those who forget offences, which they have the power to punish, are magnanimous and strong-willed, I shall wait and punish the sot by my courtesy as I relieved him by my charity." But first there were still a few synonyms. "The stray buffalo ekes out his life with two ounces of *pasta* a day; which made Monsignor Lioni say when he gave him a few *lire* for his trash, 'I am not paying these notions, I am relieving a beggar in need.' And I must tell you what the mistress of the ambassador of Mantua said, when she heard the scoundrel scolding at me. She caught him by the shirt I gave him to hide his nakedness and cried: 'Take it off before you abuse the man who gave it to you!' But all this is nothing to the boasts with which the ox boosts his Dialogues above any that ever were written. 'Here is where I pass Lucian,' says the hack. Meanwhile, the stink is raging with hunger. Titian says that when the wretch saw him from afar and had to pass him, he tucked his bonnet in his shirt so as not to greet him; and yet the robber would be choking with hunger if the pity of that most famous man had not found him employment with the Mantuan ambassador. Let the Jew strut in his rags and crown himself with chimeras and scrape his brain dry! The cricket in him made him chirp to Sansovino, the ornament of our age and the wonder of others: 'What would you say if, to the shame of your Pietro who draws 200 ducats from the Emperor, I received 400 from the King?' 'I should be amazed,' Sansovino replied, 'and meanwhile it makes a good story.' When Serlio, the light of our architecture, heard that the cur boasted of making his fame, he said: 'I am happy if he does not rob me of the little I have.' And Marcolini, the most loyal of friends, when he learned that the sot was gloating over the printing of his notions and saying, 'Marcolini has the profit and Aretino the credit of his *Letters*,' gave him his answer: 'But for my profit and my friend's credit, Franco would be a scullion.' But I deserve to have my eyes plucked out by the pen of Pasquino for wasting good ink on such scum." As he concluded that letter with flagging sides, Aretino was completely satisfied. It proved past dispute that his pen was not lifeless.

His past was routed, and he recovered his self-confidence; but he had been severely shaken. After Franco he needed a sedative, and as his successor he chose the champion who had spoiled Franco's face. Ambrogio degli Eusebii was a delightful antidote. Young, poetic, impulsive, and scatter-brained, he was both willing and wanting as a secretary; but it was not primarily as a secretary that Aretino employed him. It was to lay the last lingering recollection of that sordid spectre of the past. If

Franco recalled the squalor of his youth, Ambrogio reminded him of its charm, and he rejuvenated his master. At least, that was the service Aretino expected of him, and he petted and fathered the young poet. Ambrogio, for his misfortune, was a Venetian born and did not appreciate his birthplace; the horizons beckoned; his imagination ran away with him, everywhere, anywhere, nowhere; and whenever he delivered a letter he returned with a mind full of destinations and dreams which he mistook for his destinies. He longed to travel, to marry, to go to war, to grow up; and only the wealth of his whims kept him from ruining his life. Aretino warned him against women, war, and wandering, and secretly hoped that he would never grow up; but he played a thankless part. He laid the sobering hand of sympathetic maturity on the lad; he read him lectures which made little impression on the flighty young fool but which the old one appreciated; and, as they were full of wisdom, he wrote them up as letters. "As for wives, happy the man who takes them metaphorically and leaves them in fact," he warned him. But his wisdom made him uncomfortable. Far from rejuvenating him, Ambrogio made him feel mature and sedate; and he finished in a flourish of fatherly rakishness. "Leave the fardel of wives on the shoulders of Atlas! Leave their laments to traders, and their follies to those who can bear or beat them; leave your house and come home and call it your own; walk in the street and go to church without minding the gossip that follows every man that is married; and if you itch for offspring, get them on any wife but your own." As for war, if anything was more foolish than slaughter, it was to glorify it. "Glory where it belongs! When we are dead, Dame Fame can blow her bagpipes and call her jigs and her galliards, and he that is crowned with laurel hears nothing when he lies dead as the dust of Cyprus. Change your mind, for you will make a better sonnet than a levy, and enjoy life at my expense." He ached with common sense, but what had youth and common sense to do with each other? He ached with something worse than common sense. Ambrogio was hungry for experience, and he was surfeited with it. Finally, as the least of the evils after which the lad hankered was wandering, Aretino indulged him and sent him to France to collect his pension from the King. On the return, Ambrogio gambled it away. Sooner than lose both the lad and the money, his master forgave him; but when he sent him on a similar errand to England, the same experience was repeated. This time the culprit could not forgive himself and, a young man of experience by now, he drifted from England to Portugal and from Portugal to the Indies. His last message was a promise to preach Aretino to the Antipodes, the young end of the world.

Aretino was alarmed. This was a more cruel blow than that of Franco. Youth was deserting him, and his futile efforts to fetter it were a warning sign that he was passing his prime. He refused to believe it. He consulted his memory and his mirror and both returned an accurate reflection. He saw a fine figure of venereal manhood, robust in voluminous velvets, carrying his corpulence with unimpaired vigour. Only the beard was discoloured. He thought of dyeing it, but the experience of a friend, on whom the operation had miscarried, warned him not to dupe Nature. No, he would cheat anyone but not Nature . . . unless Nature cheated him. Was she beginning to betray him? He felt distressed and unsettled. The present was slipping away, as fugitive as Ambrogio, and the future . . . ? What future did Nature hold for him?

The desertion of Ambrogio forced him to choose a new secretary. He experimented with many and none satisfied him. Some fleeced him, some married his mistresses; the safest were the dullards; but the more diligently they served him, the less he liked them. What he abhorred was a secretary who was a mere employee; anything tame in the house made him uncomfortable; and with such men he began immediately to behave. If he discovered any ambition in them, he encouraged them to desert and pursue it at his expense. Such was the case of Agostino Ricchi, who succeeded Ambrogio degli Eusebii. A respectable and studious young man, he came to Venice to learn whatever Aretino could teach; but Aretino could teach him nothing; and anyone inert whom he did not feel and who did not respond to him was a callus in his life. And a callus was not merely uncomfortable, it was a challenge. Agostino Ricchi distressed him more deeply than Franco or Ambrogio; he impeded his well-being, he defeated his life-giving power, he menaced his mission, he undermined his self-confidence. Accordingly, he persuaded the insensible disciple to continue his studies elsewhere. The young man, trusting him completely, accepted a leave of absence and matriculated at the University of Bologna. For a time Aretino was relieved, but then he became aware of a new ache. His conscience troubled him. Was he not deserting his mission? Was he not losing a soul? Surely, he had vigour enough to master an impediment; he could not let Agostino Ricchi worst him. His pride made him even more uncomfortable than a dull pupil, and perhaps the dull pupil was merely numb and could be kindled and reclaimed with a little passion and perseverance. To the discomfort of his conscience was now added that of a torrid summer, and Aretino recalled him. "If science and life were dearer than knowledge, my son," he wrote to him with fatherly solicitude, "I would urge you to work; but life being of more value, I beg you to join us here where, without plaguing yourself with the deviltries of Aristotle, you will learn how to keep well while these dog-days last." He sweated with compassion, and the paper stuck to his hand, but he clung to his resolve. "I wonder these sweltering days do not melt the paper on your pen, your pen in the ink, the ink in your style, your style in the subject, and your subject in your brain." There was something maddening and inhuman about a man who could work in such heat; but he determined to experiment with him once more at a higher temperature. Meanwhile, the only science worth knowing was weather-wisdom, and he invited the young man to consider the curriculum of the seasons. "Summer," he began, "is like a rich noble wanton, languidly sprawling and smelling highly and doing nothing but drink and drink and drink...." But alas, he no sooner drew that alluring picture for youth than he realized that summer no longer meant that for him. It meant only mortal discomfort, and his compassion for Agostino melted into self-pity. "But who can bear the beastly behaviour of the bugs and the fleas and the flies and the mosquitoes, which of all the plagues of summer are the worst? Summer lays you out stark naked on the sheets, and your scoundrel of a servant fans you with great puffs of laughter, and leaves you the moment he sees your eyes close, so that you no sooner doze than you wake and sweat and drink and sigh and twist about, as if to shed yourself, if that were possible." This was not at all what he meant to say, but it was the truth. He was too seasoned; the plenitude of life was too much for him now; he cared more for his comfort than for wantonness. Even his weather-wisdom was deserting him, and he no longer knew what to teach Agostino. He longed for winter; he was growing tame; it was only then that he felt alive. But no matter. "You must return," he repeated. "I have had a little room prepared for you where you can sleep in your skin, a room that calls little libertines home from thousands of miles."

Sprawling on his bed, lethargic but not listless, sluggish but not inert, Aretino awaited the return of Agostino Ricchi with misgivings. He surveyed himself with a critical eye. The joints of the elbows and the hinges of the knees were thickening, the toes were ageing, and the belly, once as hard as a melon, was sagging. The prophet appraised his body of doctrine and groaned. But he stretched and refused to succumb. No. The tame disciple was on the way but Pietro Aretino was still lusty, and, while manhood remained, Time could not quell him.

68

No, A thousand times no—against the dread advances of age Aretino mustered all his animal spirits and shook his whole body in vigorous denial. Despite the great heat, he even roused himself to dictate a letter to an old friend. "Believe me, I am the same good companion as of old, and the weight of years would seem light if I were not so fat, a trick which I never believed Nature would play on a man of my temperament. Many blame my fat on my felicity"—and it was true. "It is not the food, it is the ease of this city that makes me so fleshy, that I am in a continual rage." But the soul was not subdued by the flesh. The rage of midsummer might make him languid, for "it is almost impossible to keep from sleeping in this heat when a soft wind blows or a gentle rain falls," but after a nap he woke with an unclouded mind and a firm resolve. Nothing tame should ever enter his house.

And indeed in Ca' Aretino nothing tame could dwell, for nothing was regular there but disorder. The huge happy rowdy, affectionate as he was brutal, craved a constant response from his familiars, and everyone who entered his service immediately became his intimate. His menials he treated with an indulgence which spoiled them as servants. But though he forfeited their respect, though he was fleeced and robbed, though confusion and neglect reigned from the cellar to the roof, he bore everything cheerfully on principle. If he complained, it was never to them but to strangers, and then only to explain. "Rare are the days in summer or winter when I do not rise in the morning and call this one and wake that one, an incredible thing in this city, though we pay well for poor service. I have envied them a thousand times over and wished to be one of them, or else that they might all become me for a change and a punishment; then I should live in peace and they without pleasure." Sometimes he lost his temper but he hurt himself far more than he did his domestics. "I reproach, I afflict, I devour myself whenever anger gets the better of me and makes me so untrue to myself as to scold, abuse, or strike one of my beloved family of servants; repentance is little, shame is nothing, apology nothing"—and the explanation was simple. He was superstitious. "I who am more feared than loved delight in the little respect my servants show me, for I seem to mitigate my miraculous fortune by tolerating their ill-bred ignorance."

In these conditions, however, he was uncomfortable. What Ca' Aretino needed was a mistress, but that was impossible. It already had too many.

There were five or six in the rooms where he kept his little harem of *Aretine*, and order had to reign among the recognized mistresses before it could be enforced among the others. To choose a favourite was out of the question; they were all charming, and their variety kept him in love with life and himself. "Now that I begin to understand what I am, I laugh and wonder at myself, for as I pass from one folly to another I feel as if my loves would be everlasting. Here is the second after the first, and the fourth after the third, and they accumulate like the debts of my prodigality. Truly, there dwells in my eyes a passion so tender that it attracts every beauty and can never be sated with beauty." There was only one drawback. "If, by means of some necromancy, I could lose the weight of eight or ten years, I should vindicate my wisdom for, changing my loves by the month, I am like a poor but clever courtier who, by changing his servant every two weeks, is always well served and pays no salary. But it is the devil to make these changes in age, for age has good will but weak legs." In Ca' Aretino he led a dog's life. The tail was wagging the dog; but he trusted to Nature. "What in God's name are we to do with the tail? for what purpose has Nature put it between our legs?" he exclaimed. And Nature relieved him. With the pregnancy of Caterina Sandella a change came. When her child was born, there crept over the chaos of Ca' Aretino the dawning and natural order which only a new life could bring to it.

The infant was a girl, and he had hoped for a son; the mother was disappointed, but he consoled her by publishing his satisfaction to the world. "It has pleased God to give me a girl when I, true to the custom of fathers, expected a boy, as if girls, apart from our fear of their frailty, were not far more comforting! What do we lose? A girl is the easy chair of our old age and not an hour passes but her parents enjoy her affection. So that I no sooner saw myself in my seed than I dismissed from my heart all the disappointment that others feel on her account, and was so overcome by the tenderness of Nature that at that moment I felt every delight of our blood. And because I was afraid that she might die, I had her baptized in the house; but Christ has preserved her to be the joy of my old age and the witness of my being, which I have received from others and passed on to her; and I thank Him and pray that I may live long enough to celebrate her marriage. Meanwhile, I must be her plaything, for our children make fools of us. In their innocence they trample on us, pull our beard, slap our face, rumple our hair, and in such coin repay us for the kisses with which we smother them and the hugs with which we bind them to us. But no pleasure could match this one, if the fear of their coming to harm did not maintain us in continual anxiety. Not a leaf falls, not a fluff drifts down the air, but it seems so much lead falling to crush them; and Nature never breaks their sleep nor spoils their appetite but we tremble for their health. So that the sweet and the bitter are strangely mingled; and the lovelier they are, the more we fear to lose them. God keep my little girl, for truly she is so charming that if she suffered I should die. Adria is her name, and well named since she was born by Divine Will in the lap of these waters. And I am proud of it, because this place is the garden of Nature, and in the ten years I have lived here I have known more joy than in Rome I knew despair."

But Adria had one drawback. She was an infant. He found her conversation delightful, for she spoke fluent Venetian from the day she was born, but she was too deep in her liquid gurgles and droning consonants to listen to him. He longed for the day when she would be a young girl; he wanted her as she was and as she would be fourteen years later; he demanded the impossible—and why not? Had life ever denied him? He prided himself on the exorbitance of his demands. Was anything impossible for Pietro Aretino? And Nature replied with Pierina Riccia.

Pierina Riccia was the fourteen-year-old bride of one of his secretaries, who atoned for all the misdeeds of his predecessors by marrying and bringing her home to the house of his master. She was everything that Adria would be fourteen years later—conversational, lively, and virtuous; she had chosen her husband, as Adria would do; she had married for love, as Adria would do; and he wrote to her uncle in brimming delight. "Ecco! God has sent me Madonna Pierina Riccia, and to tell you the truth, if you compounded all the tenderness of perfect love that four of the tenderest fathers feel for their young, it would not mount up to the least part of the affection I feel for this lively and lovely young girl, whose goodness and honour safeguard her beauty in a manner so knowing and charming that it brings tears to my eyes to think of it. How is it possible that a child of fourteen could choose a husband who loves her better than her money? I spend whole days thinking of this, as I watch her cooking, reading, embroidering, fitting the dresses she makes for herself, and doing everything with that well-bred manner with which she was born; and I am ready to swear that I have never seen such gentle manners in anyone. Would to God the others I have helped showed as much gratitude as she does for the benefits she receives from me! She calls me 'father and mother,' and truly I am both to her; and when I am asked how many children God has given me, I reply: Two—including her, since she appeared, for her good fortune and the comfort of my infirmities, before the child of my own blood," What he did for her he did for Adria, and everyone recognized the disinterestedness with which he doted on her. There was no discord. He was not troubled by the husband; on the contrary, "I am happy when I see her continually and playfully caressed by Polo, her discreet husband and my creature." The husband was not suspicious of him, and the mother of Adria was not jealous of her. "And it is a miracle that she and Caterina are always arm in arm, but so it is, and my life knows a peace that it has never known before." It was incredible but he could write with perfect honesty that "I have taken her in lieu of a daughter, nay, I have made her my own daughter, and I cherish her as a guardian against old age, whose evil is irreparable."

But in his paternal affection Aretino was exacting. When Caterina and the infant and the young married couple spent a week in the country and overstayed their leave, he felt so deserted in the lifeless house that he wrote Pierina a letter of gentle reproach. "Women have a proverb, my daughter, which says: a bargain is one thing and a betrayal another. You and Messer Polo and Caterina, with the maid and the man, asked my permission to spend eight days in the country; ten days have passed, and I think it only right that you should return. I am happy that your mother has had the satisfaction of presenting her son-in-law to her neighbours. I am happy that you have been praised for choosing a husband of your own free will. Everyone has seen now how you are both dressed, and the virtue with which you merit my munificence is manifest. And now you will come home, unless the villa seems to you more splendid than this city and the Brenta more smiling than the Grand Canal. To my mind, one should spend a week and no more in the country; for that length of time the open air, the wild landscape, and the uncultivated inhabitants are pleasant because of their novelty; but after ten days the crudity of the place and the peculiarity of the people begin to pall, and we must return to civilization and comfort. I expect you, therefore; for with five mouths less to feed I am as worried as a Cardinal with one more. Not to see you beside me at table seems to me an omen of ruin, and I must say that to watch myself patiently gnawing a bone is the triumph of a generous nature, not of a sumptuous vainglory."

Life in Ca' Aretino became a domestic idyll and in deference to Pierina and Adria a new propriety began to permeate the household. "I am a changed man," he warned a friend who was coming to visit him. "Our house is full of women and nurses and daughters. You will be surprised to find the licence and confusion you left transformed to strict order. Moreover, young man, you will have to suffer my age, which grows daily more disgusted with loose habits. I begin to feel the continual fretting of time, and the peace I need will breed war, if you behave otherwise." With domesticity something tame had at last crept into the house, but so insidiously that he did not suspect it. He was too happy.

Too happy indeed: the idyll could not last. The world which had accepted all his excesses resented his respectability, and just as he was settling down, comfortably, he was attacked. A Venetian nobleman, whose wife he had admired platonically, preferred charges against him of blasphemy and pederasty; and as these were statutory offences, he was forced to flee Venice. To be persecuted for a platonic offence was a preposterous mishap, and he fled under protest, indignantly denying everything, even his flight. He made a visible effort to conceal himself along the shallow edges of the lagoon, and the police shut their eyes as they searched for him. He was reported missing but not lost; time passed; friends intervened; and, when the scandal had blown over, he reappeared. His return was triumphal. On both sides of the Grand Canal crowds cheered his passage; on the landing of his palace he was handed up by a multitude of magnificoes and domestics; but it was only when he held Adria in his arms that he felt the ground solid once more under his feet. He was shaken. The scandal had disfigured him in his own eyes. The ignominy of his flight, the power of persecution, and the infamy of the charges undermined his self-confidence; he had lost his old independence; he needed support. But Adria was an infant and the filial comfort he craved only Pierina could give him.

To Pierina he turned in the critical hour of his unsteady homecoming; but in her attitude he seemed to divine only his disgrace. The suspicion plagued him; he questioned her eyes, but she seemed to ignore or avoid his appeal—he could not be sure which; and the doubt, always dismissed and always returning, became a morbid conviction. The idyll was over and the scandal had ruined it. The injustice of his unmerited plight embittered him; then the justice of it confounded him. The scandal had revived his disreputable past; it was undying; and all his efforts to outgrow it were useless. He succumbed to discouragement, and he blamed his low spirits on the tame domesticity of his life. The unreal respectability of Ca' Aretino weighed on him; he despised its false pretence and its deadening decency; he longed for the old disorder; but he dared not profane the home of Pierina and violate the idyll that had been. He shuffled off to find relief in the labyrinthine and voluptuous vistas of water and wantonness of Venice; but he shuffled home unsatisfied. He no longer found joy in furtive debauches; he craved permanence and stability like an old man, and adventure and novelty like a young one; he was confused; it was the critical age. Longing for love, dissatisfied with it, restless and unsettled, like an animal sloughing its skin, he no longer knew what he wanted. But he knew that life in Ca' Aretino was becoming unbearable. The presence of Pierina was a perpetual reproach; he resented her innocence: she was not his daughter. But he dared not admit that he desired her; the thought was almost incestuous; and he became increasingly miserable. The husband foresaw perhaps what was coming —the wonder was that it was so long coming—and deserted Pierina. It was the only solution. The tension was broken. Pierina was abandoned and Aretino made an effort to console her with fatherly compassion; but nothing could save her from his sympathy; his patriarchal hand slipped to her thighs and he let her console him; and when he awoke, he knew once more what he had almost forgotten, that the only true ties are rooted in the flesh and that all the rest was evasion.

Then for the first time he knew love and it baffled him. In the mingled rapture and remorse of his passion, sensation flowed into sentiment and sentiment into sensation in troubled confusion. He missed the illusion which was half his love for her, he ached for her innocence and could not forgive her his triumph; and at times the lover regretted the father. But he was caught in the toils, he was the creature of Nature, and Nature was inexorable. The sting of the flesh was insatiable, and he consumed what he craved with an appetite whetted and exasperated by remorse. He was doomed: his large lecherous hands withered whatever they touched, and he dreaded the day when she would become merely one more of his *Aretine*. But the mischief was done, it was too late, he could only devour his desire. The common experience of the ageing voluptuary was new to him, and he rebelled against it bitterly, longing for the impossible and cursing his inconsistency. If the senses were innocent, why should he expect any other innocence of her? But he had adulterated desire with an ambiguous dream, it was in his blood, and in corrupting Pierina he felt that he had violated something in himself. He could not explain what had happened to him. Why was love not as simple as desire? Nature knew no distinction between spirit and sense. Why had Nature cheated him?

But his imaginary anguish was soon dispelled by a more pressing anxiety. The purity of Pierina which deluded and exasperated him, the listless ease with which she succumbed to him, the hectic ease with which she took to debauchery, the feverish appetite with which she craved his expert caresses—all was explained by a ghastly discovery. She was sick.

A lingering consumption was devouring her more rapidly than he; and her morbid excitement quickened it. Then he forgot everything—her depravity and her innocence, his illusions and scruples—in his jealousy of her life; with all the vigour of his enormous vitality he struggled to arrest the progress of the disease; and in combating the decay of her flesh he lost for a time his soul-sickness. But it was only a reprieve. His love and her malady came to a climax together. The doctors ordered her removal to the mainland, and he sent her to his villa; but day after day, in all weathers, he crossed the lagoon to be with her, to protect her with his passion, to revive her with his need, and to console her with his despair. Sometimes the weather was too rough for the boatmen, and he risked it alone, plying a reckless oar, and arriving exhausted to study her symptoms . . . and his own. For the canny old creature spied on his passion and watched himself suffer like an artist. He was struggling to subdue something more deadly than her disease. Instinctively he recoiled with all his animal vitality from suffering, decay, and death; but he forced himself to overcome his aversion. He was afraid of himself; he dared not admit that the soul was subdued to the flesh; and he disciplined himself like an ascetic to divorce them. He knelt by her bedside, holding her in his arms and denying, as her eyes grew more hollow and her cough more cavernous, that anything separated them; he fondled her with perfervid endearments which concealed their estrangement; and if the lover sometimes quailed, the father never faltered. He prided himself on the devout passion with which he "kissed her monstrous eyes, her ghastly cheeks, and her sickening lips"; he gloried in "the decay of her beauty, which should have withered my love, but which increased it so intensely that the most loving father could not feel such pain and compassion; and, as she lay there, hour after hour, damp with the tears that tortured me, she could not but see that the anguish of my heart and soul were more deadly than the disease of her body." It cost him a constant exertion; sincerity was a strain; it needed a supreme tension of his loose and dissipated nature to sustain the test; but he dared not succumb; too much was at stake; and day after day he knelt by her side, mortifying himself and craving of the sick woman a soul.

After thirteen months she recovered and he rose from the ordeal, morally whole. His qualms and doubts were no more; the harrowing experience they had shared had welded them together; and he loved her unquestioningly. She was a part of himself. There followed three years of unclouded peace. With vigour and health life became simple once more. But Pierina was not cured, and while the progress of one malady was checked, the other corruption continued its ravages. She eloped one day with a lover. He bore the blow with superb sophistry. Once he had dreaded the day when younger men would profit by her corruption and leave him only its regret; and now that it had come he met it with heartbroken bravado. He told himself that it was inevitable, which was true; that he was well rid of her, which was true; that she would not live long, which was true; that the lover was vicious and would punish her, which was true; but all these truths together were totally dishonest. When a friend traced the fugitives and offered to punish them, he replied: "In robbing me, the man has restored me to myself; in keeping her, he delivers me of a harlot, a harpy, a thief, and of sin, shame, and expense. I do not deny that she deserves punishment, but I leave my vengeance to the deadliness of her disease, which torments her so cruelly that I am almost sorry for her. Thank God, therefore, for what has happened as heartily as you would grieve if I were to lose the light of my mind, the gift of my talent, and the reward of my labour, and not the vile, vain, and rank pleasures of the flesh, for in losing them we gain, and in gaining them, we lose." Of one thing she could not rob him, his moral victory; but he could not bear sympathy, and when another friend was so unfeeling as to condole with him, he burst out fiercely: "I am free of the foulest tie that ever bound human heart. If it were not that I always saw the falsity of my idol in the five years I was forced to adore her, I should blush for not knowing myself, as she should blush for her infamy. But I had no water to quench so mortal a fire; I had to wait till it died of itself, anything else would have done violence to my soul. Truly, it is not in our power to love or not to love, and though love be immeasurably disloyal, yet we must bear it. I shall not tell you how she came into my house without a thing to her name and how she was furnished with all the pomp of silks, brocades, chains, pearls, comforts, honours, and respect; but I beg you to read in the second volume of my *Letters* what I wrote to Don Lope de Soria of my goodness when she was sick and, considering the ingratitude with which she has repaid so many benefits, tell me whether woman, the root of all evil, is not the likeness of the Fiend more than man is the image of God. I congratulate myself on two things, that she has come to the end she deserved, and that I shall learn to love women no longer than the act which subdues them. Anyone who does otherwise is not a man but a beast."

But even that cynical resolution was bravado; he could no longer subdue the soul to the flesh. Four years later, she returned to him to die. After four years of an indifference more desolate than death, he welcomed the agony which she could still cause him and prolonged her life with every comfort and consolation he could provide. He was no longer her lover, no longer her father. Nothing remained but the essence of love, the impulse of one creature to protect another in a universe indifferent to all alike. It was his last privilege to dispense the protection he had won from the world and to guild her waning memory of humanity with an illusion of providence. Her mother, however, insisted on removing her from Ca' Aretino to her own home, where she could pass away among the undivided consolations of religion. He submitted. He had long since recognized the separation of the flesh and the soul.

When he learned that the end was approaching, he took up his pen to write to the few friends who might care, but who cared? He was immediately discouraged and for once speech failed him: "This morning she received the last Sacraments, and I am so moved that I can write no more." Then he took up his pen once more and wrote to the mother, who had excluded him from the supreme intimacy: "I loved, I love, and I will love her till the sentence of the Last Day judges the vanity of our senses and the virtue of our spirit. Live in God, my daughter, and die to the world! You were her mother by blood and I her father by affection, and my heart yields nothing to yours in this sorrow, for which there is no remedy but to submit to the will of God." As a last token, he received a brocaded slipper which he had given her and authority to defray her funeral expenses. He housed her in a magnificent sepulchre covered with voluble angels; but where she rested there was silence and the tomb stood ajar. "Though Time heals every wound," he repeated three years later, "I do not believe that its years will ever cure the malady that my love for Pierina has left in my heart. I may truthfully say that when she died, I died."

69

What remained was a posthumous life. Aretino lived on, apparently the same man as before, but the zest of life was gone. His passion for Pierina, like an equinoctial storm in the autumnal years of maturity, marked a seasonal change. Though he weathered it, his vitality was strained. The veering confusion of feelings which wracked him—

passion and pity, shame and pain, queasy pleasure and uneasy remorse—warped his elementary nature; like an animal he was hurt by a power he could not understand, and like a man he invented a primitive superstition to account for it. He rediscovered the soul. The vanity of the senses made it a necessity. But what was the soul? He groped for conviction and could not find it. He had destroyed the soul of everything.

He had aped every moral attitude. Honour and glory and religion and virtue and patriotism and pride—he had imitated them all and the world had accepted and applauded his counterfeit. He had struck every pose and discarded it and paraded its opposite, and the world had accepted and applauded his performance. He had impersonated every virtue and made it unmeaning. Never again would it be possible to believe in the sincerity of human pretensions; Pietro Aretino had lived, and the success with which he imposed on the world exposed its hypocrisy. Of all the ideals for which men had lived and suffered and died he had made a mockery and a farce; he had voided every creed and discredited every code; his work was done. He had accomplished his mission. He had destroyed all the superiorities of man to Nature. And Nature had tricked him. The spirit was a necessity, and he no longer believed in it. He had defeated himself. But that was his destiny: he was a prophet.

The triumph of life was complete, and life was as unmeaning as everything else; nothing remained but to live and to laugh at it; and with the bravado of a prophet he continued to preach its virtue, though he no longer knew what it was. The huge machine functioned by the mere momentum of custom, with nothing to live for, without a desire that was not a habit. He went through the motions with unflagging will, true to his faith in the sufficiency of life itself. What other aim could it have? what purpose but to repeat itself ad infinitum? But if the will was infinite, the flesh was mortal. His pulse was slackening, age made him sluggish, and he needed stimulants.

And the stimulants were not lacking. His fame and his fortune increased, without effort on his part, like the revenues of a capital investment or the spontaneous multiplication of a natural process. He was pensioned by more sovereigns than he could remember, and every year brought forth some new supererogation of tribute and honour. The Emperor proposed to nominate him for the Cardinalate, but nothing could wean him from the city to which his life was indissolubly wedded. He left it only once to meet the Emperor, with whom he rode for an hour in intimate conversation, while the Imperial escort fell behind at a respectful distance; and on his return to Venice he was welcomed with official salvos. There the lap of the water and the clap of his heart buoyed him up in a regular uninterrupted pulse of plaudits. *Divino, Divinissimo, Precellentissimo, Unichissimo, Onnipotente*—these were the common currency of acclaim: the ascending scale passed from paroxysm to paroxysm of hyperbole; and the delirious chorus of adulation reached the high note of hosanna in the dictum of an Imperial General who declared that the Divine Aretino was "absolutely necessary to human life." It was a recognized fact, and the idol nodded and proposed that the age be known by his name. And why not? He had divined its self-seeking by his own.

These were powerful doses, but he was disillusioned, and instead of recharging him these vainglorious elixirs merely irritated his spiritual impotence. Baffled by the vanity of the soul he fell back on the vanity of the flesh for a stimulant. He fought the deadening triumph of Time with his only weapon—"and if I could not hitch it forty times a month to one or another of these wenches," he confessed, "I would consider myself done for." He followed the example of Sansovino and exhorted him to follow his own. "Though there is nothing so disgusting as to see an old man beginning to live, I praise you for restoring your youth with the recipes prescribed by the punks. I imitate you easily and sometimes strenuously, and regret having urged you to quit the brothel, since it is easier to preach than to practise, and I am so deep in it that the little while I am not there I am eating my heart out. Titian never does this, for *omnia per pecunia falsata sunt*,[1] says the pedant." What did the pedant expect? Pleasure for nothing? It was like a desertion to find that Titian was not game. "What amazes me is that, wherever he is, or whomever he sees, he attempts to fondle and kiss them, and play a thousand young tricks, but he never goes further. But this is a pedantiferous letter, and you will oblige me by a glimpse of the girl you have picked up." The dung-heap had its virtues. It was the mould of life, the fertile sediment of new birth, the marrow of more and more morrows of matter and soul; and it was warm. He nestled into it and the lawgiver succumbed to the law. In the raptureless rhythm of senile mating he lapsed into the even pulse of indifferent Nature and prepared for eternity. One day he was missing and Ca' Aretino was for sale. A black box was packed and slowly borne over the lagoon, while afar on the dunes the sea lavished its unresting surges and in the void of the night the stars reappeared in perpetual motion.

[1] They are all corrupted with money.

Bibliography

P. Villari. *La Storia di Girolamo Savonarola e de' suoi Tempi.*
Herbert Lucas. *Fra Girolamo Savonarola.*
J. Schnitzer. *Savonarola.*
Piero Parenti. *Savonarola nach den Aufzeichnungen des Florentiners. Piero Parenti, von Dr. J. Schnitzer.*
P. de Greysses. *Mémoires sur Jérôme Savonarole.*
Michelet. *La Renaissance.*
De Roo. *Materials for a Life of Alexander VI.*
P. Villari. *Niccolo Machiavelli e i suoi Tempi.*
N. Machiavelli. *Letters. Diplomatic Reports.*
G. Prezzolini. *Niccolo Machiavelli the Florentine.*
J. Cartwright. *The Perfect Courtier.*
Denniston. *Memoirs of the Dukes of Urbino.*
Luzio. *Isabella d'Este.* Articles in the *Archivio Storico Italiano.*
R. de la Sizeranne. *Celebrities of the Renaissance.*
R. Sabatini. *The Life of Caesar Borgia.*
E. Rodoconachi. *Rome sous Jules II et Léon X.*
Luzio. *Pietro Aretino nei suoi Primi Anni a Venezia.*
P. Aretino. *Lettere.*
J. A. Symonds. *The Renaissance.*
Hutton. *Pietro Aretino, the Scourge of Princes.*
H. Vaughan. *The Medici Popes.*

Chronological Table
of principal events between the years 1492 and 1532

1492.	April 9.	Death of Lorenzo de' Medici.
	August 11.	Election of Roderigo Borgia as Pope. Takes the name of Alexander VI.
1494.	September.	The French invasion begins under Charles VIII.
	November 5-28.	Occupation of Florence by the French army.
	November 9.	Overthrow of the Medici in Florence. Flight of Piero, Giovanni, and Giuliano de' Medici.
	November 12.	Revolt of Pisa from Florentine rule.
1495.	January 1.	The new Government takes office in Florence. Beginning of the ascendancy of Savonarola.
	February 22.	Charles VIII enters Naples.
	April.	Proclamation of the League for the defence of Italy between Rome, Milan, Genoa, Venice, the Emperor, and the King of Spain.
	May.	Charles VIII loses Naples and begins his retreat to France.
	July 6.	Battle of Fornovo. The French make good their retreat.
1496.	October.	The Emperor Maximilian invests Livorno.
	November.	The Emperor raises the siege of Livorno and returns to Germany.
1497.	June 14.	Assassination of the Duke of Gandia in Rome.
	June 18.	Publication in Florence of the excommunication of Savonarola.
1498.	February 11.	Savonarola resumes preaching in defiance of the excommunication.
	March 18.	Savonarola preaches his farewell sermon.
	April 7.	The Ordeal by Fire in Florence.
		Charles VIII dies in France.
	April 8.	Attack on San Marco and arrest of Savonarola.
	May 22.	Execution of Savonarola with Fra Domenico and Fra Silvestro.
	June 1.	Appointment of Pagolo Vitelli as Captain of the Florentine Republic.
	June 19.	Appointment of Machiavelli as Secretary to the Signoria.
	July 16-24.	Legation of Machiavelli to Caterina Sforza, the Countess of Imola and Forli.
	October 1.	Pagolo Vitelli is beheaded in Florence.
	October 6.	King Louis XII of France enters Milan.
	November.	Caesar Borgia begins his campaign in Romagna. Capture of Imola and Forli.

1499.	February.	Lodovico Sforza reoccupies Milan.
	April.	The French recover Milan. Lodovico Sforza is captured and sent to captivity in France.
	July-December.	Legation of Machiavelli in France.
	October-November.	Second campaign of Caesar Borgia in Romagna. Capture of Rimini and Pesaro.
1500.	April.	Capture of Faenza by Caesar Borgia. His incursion into Florentine territory (May).
1501.	June.	Caesar Borgia surprises and occupies Urbino. Machiavelli and Bishop Soderini meet Caesar Borgia at Urbino.
1502.	September-December.	Revolt of the Condottieri against Caesar Borgia.
	October-March, 1503.	Legation of Machiavelli to Caesar Borgia in Romagna.
1503.	August 18.	Death of Pope Alexander VI.
	September 24-October 18.	Reign of Pope Pius III.
	November 1.	Election of Cardinal Giuliano della Rovere as Pope. Takes the name of Julius II.
	December.	Death of Piero de' Medici at the Battle of the Garigliano, where the French are defeated and Naples passes under the undivided control of Spain.
1506.	August-November.	Campaign of Pope Julius II against Perugia and Bologna.
1508.	May 15.	Battle of Agnadello or Vaila. Defeat of Venice.
	June 7.	Capitulation of Pisa to Florence.
	December 10.	Conclusion of the League of Cambray between Pope Julius II, the Emperor Maximilian, Spain, and France against Venice.
1510.	July-January, 1511.	Campaign of Pope Julius II against Ferrara, ending with the siege and capture of Mirandola.
1511.	May 22.	Bologna is captured by the French.
1512.	April 12.	Battle of Ravenna. The French are driven out of Italy.
	August.	Congress of Mantua.
	August 29.	Capture of Prato by the Spanish. Return of the Medici to Florence.
1513.	February 20.	Death of Pope Julius II.
	March 17.	Giovanni de' Medici is elected Pope. Takes the name of Leo X.
	August-December.	Machiavelli writes *The Prince*.
1515.	September 13.	Battle of Marignano. François I and the Venetians defeat the Papal and Imperial troops. The French recover Milan.
	December 7-11.	Meeting of Leo X and François I in Bologna. Conclusion of alliance.
1516.	March 18.	Giuliano de' Medici dies in Fiesole.
	June.	Lorenzo de' Medici and the Papal troops occupy Urbino. Castiglione completes *The Courtier* at Casatico.
1519.	May 4.	Death of Lorenzo de' Medici, Duke of Urbino.
	June 28.	Election of the Emperor Charles V.

1521. May 29.	Conclusion of alliance between Charles V and Leo X against François I.
November.	The Papal and Imperial Allies recover Milan from the French.
December 1.	Death of Pope Leo X.
1522. January 9.	Election of Pope Adrian VI.
September 14.	Death of Pope Adrian VI.
November 19.	Election of Giulio de' Medici as Pope. Takes the name of Clement VII.
1524. December.	Clement VII concludes secret treaty with François I against Charles V. François I recaptures Milan and lays siege to Pavia.
1525. February 24.	Battle of Pavia. Annihilation of the French by the Imperialists, who recover Milan. François I is captured and sent to captivity in Spain.
1526.	François I is released by Charles V and concludes a treaty with him, renouncing his Italian claims, which he repudiates upon reaching France. But he remains inactive. Clement VII concludes the Holy League for the defence of Italy between France, England, Rome, Venice, and Florence against Charles V.
September.	Rising of the Roman Barons against the Pope, instigated by Charles V. The "rehearsal of the sack of Rome."
December.	Death of Giovanni delle Bande Nere in Mantua.
1527. May 8.	The sack of Rome.
May 16.	The Medici Government in Florence is overthrown and the Republic is restored.
June 22 (?).	Death of Machiavelli in Florence.
December.	Flight of Clement VII to Orvieto.
1529. August.	Treaty of Cambray between François I and Charles V. François I renounces his Italian claims and Charles V becomes the undisputed master of Italy. The Imperial army besieges Florence.
1530. February 24.	Formal reconciliation of Charles V and Clement VII at Bologna. The Pope crowns the Emperor.
August 3.	Florence capitulates to the Imperial army.
1532.	Alessandro de' Medici, the son of Clement VII, becomes Duke of Florence.

Relationships
of the principal persons in this narrative

I *BORGIA*
Don Roderigo de Lanzol y Borja, born in Xatavia in 1431, was the nephew of Don Alonzo de Borja, Pope Calixtus III, to whom he owed his advancement in the Church. By Giovanozza dei Catanei he had four children: Giovanni (the Duke of Gandia), Cesare, Lucrezia, and Giuffredo.

Lucrezia Borgia was married three times. Her marriage to Giovanni Sforza, the Tyrant of Pesaro, was annulled. Her second husband, the Duke of Bisceglia, was assassinated. In 1501 she was married to Alfonso d'Este of Ferrara.

II *DELLA ROVERE*
Giuliano della Rovere, Cardinal of San Pietro in Vincoli and afterwards Pope Julius II, was the nephew of Francesco della Rovere, Pope Sixtus IV.

His nephew, Francescomaria della Rovere, was the adopted heir of Guidobaldo di Montefeltro, the Duke of Urbino.

III *ESTE*
The children of Ercole d'Este, Duke of Ferrara, were Alfonso d'Este, Duke of Ferrara, Cardinal Ippolito d'Este, Isabella d'Este, married to the Marquis Francesco Gonzaga of Mantua, Beatrice d'Este, married to Lodovico Sforza of Milan, and Laura d'Este, married to Bentivoglio, the Tyrant of Bologna.

IV *GONZAGA*
Francesco Gonzaga, Marquis of Mantua, husband of Isabella d'Este.

Elizabetta Gonzaga, his sister, married to Guidobaldo di Montefeltro, Duke of Urbino.

His three sons, in order of seniority, were Federico, later Marquis of Mantua; Ercole, later a Cardinal; and Ferrante.

His brother, Cardinal Gonzaga, was a candidate for the Papacy after the death of Pope Leo X.

V SFORZA

Lodovico Sforza, known as Il Moro, was regent of Milan during the minority of his nephew, Giangaleazzo Sforza, whose wife, Isabella of Aragon, was a granddaughter of the King of Naples. After the death of his nephew he became Duke of Milan. By his wife, Beatrice d'Este, he had a son, Massimiliano, who held the throne of Milan for a short period under the protection of the Spanish.

Cardinal Ascanio Sforza, the brother of Lodovico, became Vice-Chancellor of the Vatican on the accession of Pope Alexander VI, whose election he had been instrumental in promoting.

Caterina Sforza, sister of Giangaleazzo, the Countess of Imola and Forli, married as her third husband Giovanni di Pierfrancesco de' Medici, a member of the junior branch of the Medici, and by him had a son known to history as Giovanni (or Giovannino) de' Medici, celebrated under his professional name of Giovanni delle Bande Nere.

Family Tree
of the senior branch of the MEDICI

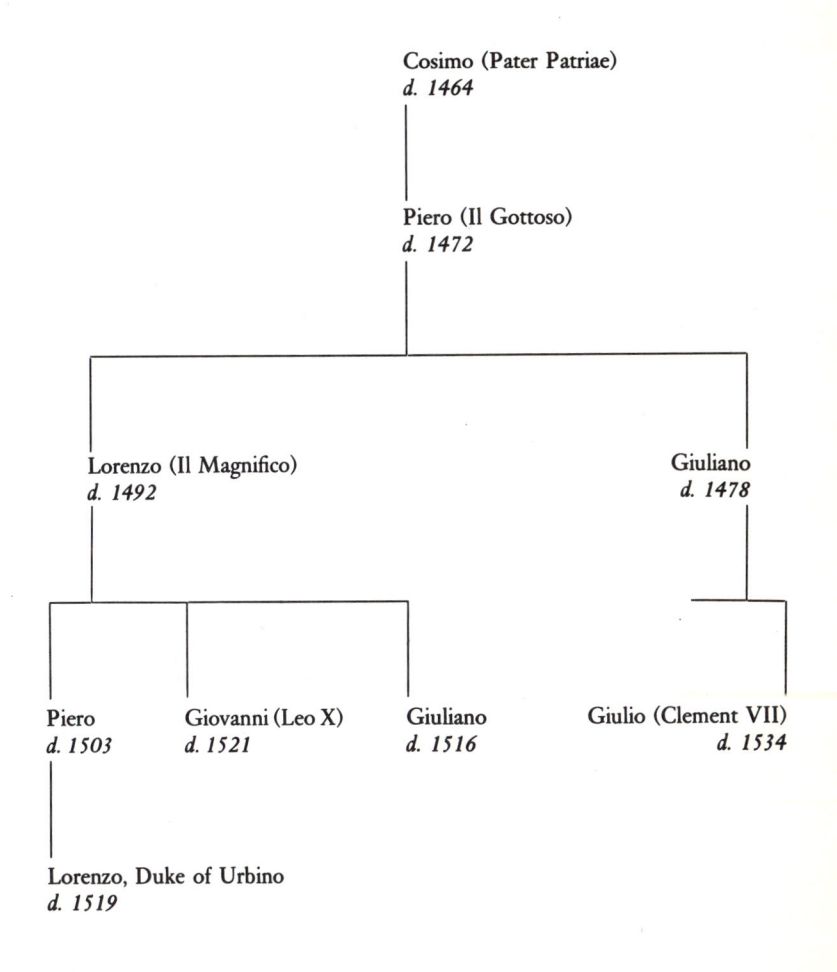

Cosimo (Pater Patriae)
d. 1464

Piero (Il Gottoso)
d. 1472

- Lorenzo (Il Magnifico) *d. 1492*
  - Piero *d. 1503*
    - Lorenzo, Duke of Urbino *d. 1519*
  - Giovanni (Leo X) *d. 1521*
  - Giuliano *d. 1516*
- Giuliano *d. 1478*
  - Giulio (Clement VII) *d. 1534*

A NOTE ABOUT THE PRODUCTION OF THIS BOOK

The typeface for the text of this special edition of *The Man of the Renaissance* is Janson. It was photocomposed at Time Inc. under the direction of Albert J. Dunn and Arthur J. Dunn.

☓

PRODUCTION STAFF FOR TIME INCORPORATED: John L. Hallenbeck (Vice President and Director of Production), Robert E. Foy, Caroline Ferri and Robert E. Fraser.